The**Green**Guide
Rome

Piazza Navona © pidjoe/iStockphoto.com

MICHELIN

THE GREEN GUIDE ROME

Editorial Director	Cynthia Ochterbeck
Editor	Sophie Friedman
Updating, Photo Editing and Layout	Buysschaert&Malerba, Milan Zino Malerba and Raffaella Esposito
Contributing Writers	Judy Edelhoff, Glenn Michael Harper, John Malathronas
Production Manager	Natasha George
Picture Editor	Yoshimi Kanazawa
Cartography	Peter Wrenn
Interior Design	Chris Bell
Cover Design	Chris Bell, Christelle Le Déan
Layout	Natasha George

Contact Us

Michelin Travel and Lifestyle North America
One Parkway South
Greenville, SC 29615
USA
travel.lifestyle@us.michelin.com

Michelin Travel Partner
Hannay House
39 Clarendon Road
Watford, Herts WD17 1JA
UK
✆01923 205240
travelpubsales@uk.michelin.com
www.viamichelin.co.uk

Special Sales

For information regarding bulk sales,
customized editions and premium sales,
please contact us at:
travel.lifestyle@us.michelin.com

HOW TO USE THIS GUIDE

PLANNING YOUR TRIP

The blue-tabbed PLANNING YOUR TRIP section at the front of the guide gives you **ideas for your trip** and **practical information** to help you organise it. You'll find tours, practical information, a host of outdoor activities, a calendar of events, information on shopping, sightseeing, kids' activities and more.

INTRODUCTION

The orange-tabbed INTRODUCTION section explores the **City Today**. The **History** section spans from the legendary origins of Rome, through monarchy, the republic, the Roman empire to the modern day. The **Art and Culture** section covers architecture, art, literature and cinema.

DISCOVERING

The green-tabbed DISCOVERING section features Principal Sights by region, featuring the most interesting local **Sights**, **Walking Tours**, nearby **Excursions**, and detailed **Driving Tours**. Admission prices shown are normally for a single adult.

ADDRESSES

We've selected the best hotels, restaurants, cafés, shops, nightlife and entertainment to fit all budgets. See the Legend on the cover flap for an explanation of the price categories. See the back of the guide for an index of hotels and restaurants.

Sidebars

Throughout the guide you will find blue, peach and green-colored text boxes with lively anecdotes, detailed history and background information.

😊 A Bit of Advice 😊

Green advice boxes found in this guide contain practical tips and handy information relevant to your visit or a sight in the Discovering section.

STAR RATINGS★★★

Michelin has given star ratings for more than 100 years. If you're pressed for time, we recommend you visit the ★★★ or ★★ sights first:

★★★   **Highly recommended**
★★   **Recommended**
★   **Interesting**

MAPS

🔎 Principal Sights maps of Rome and central Rome.
🔎 Local maps of districts.
🔎 Plans of archaeological sites.
🔎 Plans of major museums.

All maps in this guide are oriented north, unless otherwise indicated by a directional arrow. The term "Local Map" refers to a map within the chapter or Tourism Region. A complete list of the maps found in the guide appears at the back of this book.

PLANNING YOUR TRIP

© sborisov/Fotolia.com

INTRODUCTION TO ROME

DISCOVERING ROME

CONTENTS

YOUR STAY IN ROME

Welcome to Rome

Far more than a city, Rome is a series of eras stacked atop one another. Ruins, churches and *palazzi* provide spectacular detail to this modern metropolis that is, despite its fast pace, quite pleasant. Wide pedestrian boulevards, splendid parks and grand piazze – the spaces where residents and tourists converge – give Rome the feeling of an open-air museum. No other city in the world can compare.

Piazza Navona
©belenox /iStockphoto.com

Spagna, Via Veneto), architectural treasures (Fontana di Trevi), medieval relics (Castel Sant'Angelo), the halls of government (Montecitorio, Quirinale, Campidoglio) and enormous cathedrals housing priceless artworks. Beyond the cobbled alleyways of the centre rises EUR, a marble concept city built in the early 20C to recall Rome's past grandeur.

ROME *(pp92–235)*

The majority of Rome's sites are located within the historic centre (Centro Storico), which is traversed by the River Tiber, bounded by the ancient Aurelian walls and laden with some of the most significant landmarks of antiquity (ⓒ *see Ancient Rome, below*). This area also contains bustling, café-lined squares (Campo de' Fiori, Trastevere), chic shopping and strolling districts (Piazza di

ANCIENT ROME *(pp236–321)*

Evidence of Rome's earliest roots is scattered throughout the city. The Colosseo, looming large as a symbol of Rome's past, casts a shadow on many other remains from the empire, among them the Forum, the Fori Imperiali and the Palatino, legendary birthplace of the city's founders Romulus and Remus. Triumphal arches, temples and victory columns abound in almost every neighbourhood, particularly in the Centro Storico and along the Appian Way. Most of the Appia Antica, the "Queen" of Rome's ancient roads, is preserved parkland, thereby providing visitors a glimpse of ruins without the distractions of modern urban life.

VATICAN CITY *(pp322–347)*

For more than 2,000 years, Rome and religion have been synonymous. Yet few sites in the city are as sacred as the Vatican Hill, where St Peter, Christianity's first pope, was buried. Early Christians built a shrine over the saint's tomb, which would become the foundation – both literally and figuratively – of the Christian Church. Basilica di San Pietro, constructed between the 16–17C, is the crown jewel in Rome's unmistakeable skyline and a centrepiece of the Vatican

Pantheon
© S. Greg Panosian/iStockphoto.com

Vatican City

EXCURSIONS FROM ROME
(pp356–379)

Through the ages, Romans have not had to travel far to find relief from the bustle of the city.

Emperor Hadrian built a lavish estate in Tivoli, a hilltop town that today is also famous for the Renaissance-era, fountain-lined Villa D'Este. (Both are UNESCO World Heritage Sites.) Since the early 17C, popes have summered in Castel Gandolfo, one in a set of peaceful, picturesque villages that make up the Castelli Romani. Nestled southeast in the Alban Hills, the Castelli are ideal for wine tourism and on weekends host flower fairs and antique markets. A visit to Italy's famed film studios Cinecittà, producer of many major movies, should add excitement to your tour. Ostia Antica has long been one of the most popular daytrips from Rome. The city's ancient port, which is easily accessible by rail and minutes from the seashore, boasts impressive ruins, including an amphitheatre and forum. To the northwest in the Sabatini Mountains, languid Lake Bracciano is an excursion well-suited for anglers, nature lovers and families.

City, the 44ha/109 acre papal-controlled city-state in existence since 1929. While the Vatican City is an undeniable place of pilgrimage, its artistic heritage – from Bernini's colonnade framing St Peter's Square to Michelangelo's frescoes in the Sistine Chapel and the priceless works in the Musei Vaticani – merits attention from travellers of all faiths.

Fountains at Villa d'Este, Tivoli

© Davide Romanini/Dreamstime.com

© track5/iStockphoto.com

PLANNING YOUR TRIP

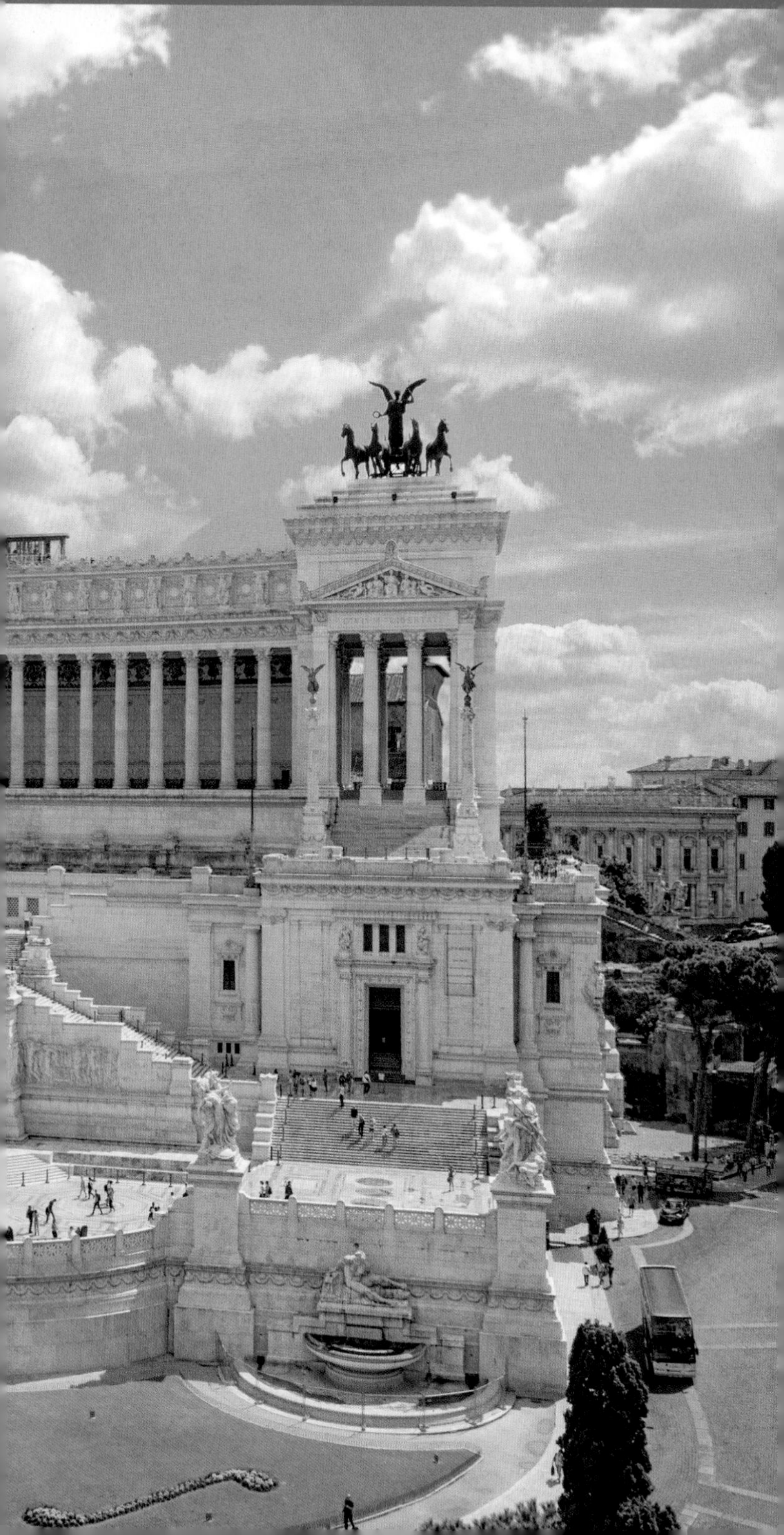

When and Where to Go

WHEN TO GO

CLIMATE

Located 28km/17mi from the coast, Rome enjoys a mild Mediterranean climate: bright and crisp in winter, hot in summer.

The most temperate months are May, September and October, and sometimes June, if the summer heat arrives late. During July and August, the temperature rarely dips below 30°C/86°F and the high humidity makes the heat hard to bear. September and October are splendid, with sunny skies and mild temperatures (although squalls sometimes dampen October). November is the wettest month of the year – often the result of heavy downpours – and the temperature falls, signalling winter. It can be cold in December, January and February, February, months increasingly beset by rain and light snow. The mild weather returns again in March and April, occasionally accompanied by more rainfall.

BEST TIME TO VISIT

April, May, September or October provide the best weather. Unsurprisingly, these months attract the most visitors (especially over Easter). Some hardcore travellers – especially those without children or elderly companions – praise July and August, despite the heat. The city empties, as many Romans head to their second homes on the coast or in the mountains. However, many shops and services close down, and the shell of the city doesn't convey its dynamic character. In winter, the air is fresh, the light sharp and the sky often a clear blue. You may not even need a coat in December, as you wander among the street fairs and elaborate nativity scenes in unheated churches. The epicentre is the Piazza Navona, where stalls sell sweets and toys. Many feature Befana, the witch that brings Italian children toys on Epiphany.

SUGGESTED ITINERARIES

THE MUSTS

Foro Romano: The administrative centre of ancient Rome, once full of buildings, temples and squares; its ruins are an evocative reminder of the Imperial capital.

Colosseo: Let your inner gladiator out at this monumental structure, built by the Emperor Vespasian in AD 72 to house bloody battles for popular entertainment.

Fori Imperiali: Five Emperors each built a forum here. Trajan's Forum is dominated by the elaborate Trajan's Column, covered in reliefs.

Palatino: Legend has it that wolf-raised Romulus climbed the Palatine and founded Rome in 753 BC. Today, the site is covered in gardens and remains, including the House of Augustus, with four recently opened rooms of frescoes.

Campidoglio and Musei Capitolini: The world's two oldest museums sit on either side of Michelangelo's study in architectural perspective, the Piazza del Campidoglio.

Basilica and Piazza di San Pietro: The world centre of Catholicism, the Holy See is a suitably awe-inspiring spectacle of ecclesiastical grandeur.

Musei Vaticani and the Sistine Chapel: Staggering collections of art and sculpture at these museums, plus Michelangelo's masterpiece ceiling. Be prepared for long queues.

Museo Nazionale Romano – Palazzo Massimo alle Terme: One of the most important archaeological museums in the world, with masterpieces from the Republican era to late Antiquity: statues, paintings, mosaics, and an important coin collection.

Spanish Steps and shopping in the Tridente: Sit on these iconic steps, then head to Rome's most exclusive streets to buy Italian designer fashion.

Villa Borghese: Rome's most beautiful park, a spread of green that

Foro Romano

© Hornet83/iStockphoto.com

rises up the hill behind the Spanish Steps. Locals stroll under plane trees, past statuary, and visitors flock to the museums of the Villa Giulia, with its Etruscan works, and the stunning collections at the Galleria Borghese.

Fontana di Trevi: Three coins thrown in this extravagant Baroque fountain, and you'll come back to Rome, according to legend. Sadly, you can't dance in it *La Dolce Vita* style...

Terme di Diocleziano: Once the largest baths in Rome, built in AD 298–306, they were turned into this elegant convent, designed by Michelangelo, in the 16C.

Santa Maria Maggiore: This, the most important church dedicated to the Virgin Mary in Rome, was founded in 402 AD and still holds absolute masterpieces, including a mosaic from the 5C to 13C.

Galleria Doria Pamphili: Superlative private collection of artworks, including Caravaggio and Titian, hung in 16C state apartments.

The Pantheon: Built by the Emperor Hadrian, this amazingly well preserved pagan temple with its distinctive dome and *oculus* (opening) was converted to a church in AD 608.

Piazza Navona: Watch all Rome pass by in this bustling, theatrical square, with Bernini's Four Rivers Fountain at its centre.

Castel Sant'Angelo: A symbol of the reuse of buildings in ancient Rome, it is formed by the remains of an imperial mausoleum, a medieval fortified castle, and papal apartments dating from the Renaissance.

Views from the Gianicolo and Pincian Hill: Enjoy the stunning panoramas of the city from these vantage points – particularly evocative at sunset.

WEEKEND SNAPSHOT
DAY 1

Morning: Start at the **Colosseum**, then continue to the **Roman Forum**. Exit near the Mamertino prison in the direction of **Piazza del Campidoglio,** and wander around the collections in the **Capitoline Museums**.

Afternoon: Head to the **Pantheon** and the Piazza della Rotonda, strolling from here through small streets lined with curio shops, to Piazza Navona. Savour a *gelato* on the way, from **I Tre Scalini** (Piazza Navona 28). Linger over coffee, as buskers croon beside the piazza's uplit fountains and Rome enjoys its evening *passeggiata*.

DAY 2

Morning: Visitors interested in art and religion should spend the morning at **St Peter's** and **the Vatican** (even a brief taste requires at least half a day); those keen on antiquity may prefer to explore the **Fori Imperiai.**

Afternoon: Admire the Spanish Steps at **Piazza di Spagna**, then explore **Via dei Condotti** and Rome's main shopping street, **Via del Corso.** The district of **Trastevere** is perfect for an authentic Roman dinner at one of its many small *trattorie.* Finish, as every trip must, at the **Fontana di Trevi**, romantically lit in the evening.

WEEKEND: ANCIENT ROME
DAY 1
Morning: Start at the grand amphitheatre, the **Colosseo**, then admire the nearby **Arch of Constantine**, still almost completely intact. A stroll through the **Foro Romano** takes you past remains of temples, basilicas and the august Senate House.

Afternoon: When the temperature rises, rest among the shady gardens and excavations on the **Palatine Hill**. Finish at the attractive Piazza della Rotonda, home of the **Pantheon.**

DAY 2
Morning: Visit the **Imperial Fora**, the **Capitoline Museums** and **Trajan's Market**, followed by a stroll round **Caracalla's Baths.**

Afternoon: Conclude with a ramble, or cycle ride, along the **Appian Way** and a peek at one of the many catacombs along the sweep of ancient Rome's most important highway.

FOUR DAYS: EXPLORING ROME
DAY 1
Start in the **Imperial Fora**, then continue to the **Roman Forum** and the **Palatine Hill**, concentrating on the most important monuments *(marked with stars in the main text)* in all sites. Book ahead to visit the **Domus Aurea** (Nerone's Golden House), not far from the Colosseum.

Stop at the **Colosseum**, pausing to admire the **Arch of Constantine**, then make your way to the **Basilica of St John Lateran**. Enroute to the basilica, stop briefly at **San Clemente** to admire its mosaics. Spend the evening in exploring the **Testaccio district**, with its bars and restaurants.

DAY 2
Start at the busy **Piazza Venezia**, dominated by the imposing bulk of the **monument to Vittorio Emanuele II** and continue towards the **Santa Maria d'Aracoeli** steps. After pausing to admire the Renaissance elegance of **Piazza del Campidoglio**, spend some time in the **Capitoline Museums** with a panoramic coffee break on the café terrace (Palazzo dei Conservatori).

Shopping in Via dei Condotti

© piola666/iStockphoto.com

The **Chiesa del Gesù**, with its magnificent interior, is just a short walk away. From here, continue to the **Pantheon**, an exceptional domed structure dating from the 1C BC, and then on to **Piazza Navona**. The nearby church of **San Luigi dei Francesi** houses masterpieces by Caravaggio. Others well worth a visit include **Santa Maria della Pace**, the hidden gem of **Sant'Ivo alla Sapienza** and **Sant'Andrea della Valle**.

DAY 3

Start your day early at the colourful market in **Piazza Campo de' Fiori**, and barter for the fresh produce or flowers, which gave this vibrant square its name. Next door is the quieter **Piazza Farnese** with grandiose fountains of Egyptian granite (adapted from the ancient Baths of Caracalla).A stroll along Via di Monserrato and the elegant **Via Giulia** brings you to **Castel Sant'Angelo**. This papal fortress lies close to the centre of religious Rome: Via della Conciliazione leads directly to **St Peter's**. After admiring the famous square and a short tour inside the basilica, make your way to the magnificent **Vatican Museums** to visit the Sistine Chapel. Expect long queues, unless you've booked a guide (*See VATICANO–SAN PIETRO*). Wind down with a quiet dinner in one of Trastevere's small traditional *trattorie*.

DAY 4

After visiting **Santa Maria Maggiore**, a leisurely ramble takes you to **Piazza di Spagna**. Enroute, stop at **San Carlo alle Quattro Fontane** and **Sant'Andrea al Quirinale**, as well as making a short detour via **Piazza del Quirinale** to the **Trevi Fountain**. Explore the district between **Piazza di Spagna** and **Piazza del Popolo**, wandering along some of the most elegant streets in Rome (**Via del Corso** and **Via dei Condotti** for the latest fashions and gold, **Via Margutta** for arts and crafts and **Via del Babuino** for antiques). At sunset, climb the **Pincian Hill** for a breathtaking city view from the gardens.

THEMED VISITS
FRESCOES IN ROME

Frescoes that should not be missed include those in the **Sistine Chapel** and **Raphael Rooms** in the Vatican Museums. Also by the painter from the Marches, you can see the Sibyls inside Santa Maria della Pace. Turning west of the Tiber, visit **Villa Farnesina**, decorated with 16C frescoes by Raphael, Giulio Romano, Giovanni da Udine, Baldassarre Peruzzi and Sodoma. From here, a walk up the Janiculum Hill takes you to **San Pietro in Montorio**, which houses the fresco of the Flagellation by Sebastiano del Piombo. Below in Trastevere, discover a masterpiece of medieval painting: the Last Judgement by Pietro Cavallini in the church of **Santa Cecilia**. Elsewhere, stop off in the Baroque **Sant'Ignazio** for the fresco on the ceiling with its unusual *trompe l'oeil* effect. Don't miss the magnificent large frescoes on the piano nobile of Palazzo Barberini, where the Triumph of Divine Providence is a milestone in Baroque painting, and of Palazzo Farnese, where the Triumph of Bacchus and Ariadne by Annibale Carracci tends to a more classical naturalism. The Carafa Chapel in the church of **Santa Maria Sopra Minerva** boasts delicate 15C frescoes by Filippino Lippi, while the church of **San Luigi dei Francesi** has 17C frescoes by Il Domenichino, illustrating the legend of St Cecilia. Across Corso Vittorio Emanuele is the 16C **Palazzo della Cancelleria**, where Vasari spent 100 days adorning the Sala dei Cento Giorni. On the other side of the city, the church of **Santa Maria del Popolo** houses the *Adoration of the Child* by Pinturicchio in the Della Rovere chapel.

MOSAICS IN ROME

The Esquiline and Caelian hills are home to the capital's greatest masterpieces of mediaeval mosaic art. Start in **San Giovanni in Laterano**,

13

where the decoration of the 13C apse shows the figure of Christ, who miraculously appeared during the consecration of the church. Then visit the **Lateran Baptistery** where the bowl-shaped apse of the chapel of Santa Rufina decorated in tones of green, blue and gold, dates from the 5C. Continuing, admire the scenes of life framed by acanthus leaves that surround the cross of the mosaic apse of **San Clemente**. Mounting the Esquiline Hill once more, you can admire the **Chapel of San Zeno** in **Santa Prassede**, ordered by Pope Pasquale as a mausoleum for his mother Teodora, and containing the most important example of Byzantine mosaics in Rome, and the apse of **Santa Pudenziana**, one of the oldest in Rome (390 AD), where the saint appears beside St Praxedes in the act of placing the crown on Christ enthroned. To end with, you arrive at **Santa Maria Maggiore** where the mosaics on the facade designed by Filippo Rusuti (14C) are the prelude to the decoration in the 5C nave (scenes from the Old Testament), the triumphal arch (scenes from the Nativity), and in the apse (Coronation of the Virgin by Jacopo Torriti, 1295). Also see the magnificent mosaics on a gold ground in the apses of **Santa Maria in Trastevere** and **Sant'Agnese fuori le Mura**.

MUSEUMS IN ROME

The **Museo Nazionale Romano** collections feature in a number of different locations, the most important of which are the **Palazzo Massimo alle Terme**, the **Aula Ottagona** and **Palazzo Altemps**. Other notable exhibits are in the Sezione Epigrafica e Protostorica (at Diocletian's Baths) and at the Crypta Balbi. The **Capitoline Museums**, dedicated mainly to Roman art, are also of major importance. Unusual for its layout and location is the **Centrale Montemartini**, an old power station slightly outside the historic centre. Etruscan art has pride of place in the **Museo Nazionale di Villa Giulia**; the gold- and iron work – along with the vivid tomb paintings – represent the best of this pre-Roman civilization. The **Galleria Borghese** exhibits both Renaissance masterpieces (Raphael) and works by Baroque masters such as Bernini and Caravaggio. The **Galleria Doria Pamphili** showcases works by Carracci, Caravaggio, Velázquez and Titian; while the **Galleria d'Arte Antica in Palazzo Barberini** displays paintings by Sodoma and Raphael. Explore non-European art in the **Museo Preistorico Etnografico L Pigorini** situated in the EUR district, near the **Museo delle Arti e Tradizioni Popolari Italiane**. Dedicated entirely to modern and contemporary art are the **Galleria Nazionale d'Arte Moderna** and the two 21C museums, the **Maxxi** in the Flaminio district, and the **Macro** not far from Termini station. Lastly, Rome's headliner is the **Vatican Collection**: a group of museums housing a vast collection of paintings, sculptures and other exhibits.

UNUSUAL SIGHTS

Rome's most famous quirk is the view of St Peter's through the **Knights of Malta keyhole** of no 3, Piazza dei Cavalieri di Malta, on the Aventine Hill. Farther south in the city stands the **Cestius Pyramid**, the unusual mausoleum of a Roman magistrate, in the Protestant Cemetery, which also houses remains of English poets John Keats (1795–1821) and Percy Bysshe Shelley (1792–1822). At Palazzo Spada near Campo de' Fiori, you will find one of Italy's most famous trompe-l'oeil, the **Borromini Perspective**. As you descend from Trinità dei Monti to Via Gregoriana, you will come across one of Rome's most curious buildings, the Palazzo Zuccari, called the **Casa dei Mostri** for its main door. This opens to be a gigantic mouth while the nose acts as a keystone in the vault. The **Centrale Montemartini**, where a collection of ancient sculptures from the Capitoline Museums contrasts

Fontana di Trevi

© C. Handl/imageBROKER/age fotostock

with the turbines of the old power station, is also of interest. Architectural buffs adore the sporting complex of the **Foro Italico**, Fascist-built and renovated for the 1960 Olympic Games. Back in the historic centre, the crypt of **Santa Maria della Concezione**, along the *dolce vita* Via Veneto, contains the bones of 4,000 Capuchin monks incorporated into its macabre decoration. According to legend, Salome requested the beheading of St John the Baptist – and the results are on display in the church of **San Silvestro in Capite**. In Via Giulia, the **oratory of Santa Maria della Morte**'s unusual décor includes skulls inserted into the walls which recall that the order that once lived here was responsible for the organisation of Christian funerals for the poor.

FOUNTAINS

Rome's many fountains include grandiose Baroque creations, as well as more modest, traditional sculptures. Only the most famous or most unusual are mentioned below.
For more history, refer to the index, or log onto *www.turismoroma.it*. Without a doubt, the most famous water feature is the **Trevi Fountain**, which dominates the small piazza of the same name. Of almost equal renown are the installations in **Piazza Navona**, in particular the Fountain of the Four Rivers, a magnificent sculpture by Bernini. At the Spanish Steps is the **Fontana della Barcaccia (boat fountain)**. The **Fontana della Botticella**, close to Augustus's Mausoleum, is also of interest.
Between Via Veneto and Via XX Settembre: The **Fontana del Tritone** (Triton Fountain) and the **Fontana delle Api (Bee Fountain)**, the symbol of the Barberini family, both by Bernini; the **four 16C fountains** adorning the crossroads of Via delle Quattro Fontane and Via XX Settembre, constructed by private citizens during the urban renovation promised by Sixtus V; and the **Fontana dell'Acqua Felice**, crowned with a monumental statue of Moses.
Pantheon area: Cool down at the 16C **fountain in Piazza della Rotonda** which, like so many others in Rome, was sculpted by Giacomo della Porta. Nearby is the typical **Fontana del Facchino**, the subject of a local legend (⌚*See PANTHEON*).

Campo de' Fiori: This district is full of fountains: the **fountain in Piazza Sant'Andrea della Valle**, the **fountains in Piazza Farnese**, the **Fontana del Mascherone** on Via Giulia (which spouted wine on ancient festival days) and the **Fontana della Terrina**.

Finally, sample the city's sweet aqueduct waters via the *nasone* (noses): the free-flowing street spigots. Seal the faucet's mouth with a thumb, forcing an arc of liquid through the small hole. *Cin cin!*

BRIDGES AND BANKS OF THE TIBER RIVER

The Tiber, which cuts the city in two, provides some fascinating views of the city (*See Themed Tours – On the Water*). Follow the river either on foot or by bike (short sections of the bank have proper cycle tracks). The most attractive section is the stretch from the Ara Pacis Augustae to Piazza Bocca della Verità. The peaceful **Isola Tiberina** stands besides the ruins of the **Ponte Rotto** (Broken Bridge). The ancients played upon its ship shape, constructing a travertine prow. Its bridges are particularly evocative: **Ponte Cestio** leads to Trastevere and the Janiculum, and **Ponte Fabricio**, the city's oldest functional span which dates back to the IC BC, leads to the synagogue and the old Jewish quarter on the opposite bank. Nearby is **Ponte Sisto**, built in the 15C by Pope Sixtus IV, which crosses the Tiber near Piazza Trilussa. There is a beautiful city view from **Ponte Sant'Angelo**.

BIRD'S-EYE VIEWS

The best time to enjoy a view of the tiled rooftops and marble domes of the capital is at sunset, when the sky is streaked with pale red in winter and blazing scarlet in summer. Don't miss the **city vista from the Janiculum**, along **Passeggiata del Gianicolo**. Equally impressive is the panorama from Piazzale Napoleone I in the **gardens on the Pincian Hill**, the **dome of St Peter's** and the **Piazza del Campidoglio**. For the best views, however, take a seat at the **Caffè Capitolino**, in Palazzo Caffarelli, or pause in the **Galleria del Palazzo Senatorio** during your visit to the Capitoline Museums. For an excellent view of the **Roman Forum**, walk along Via del Campidoglio to behind the

Palazzo Senatorio, or climb the Palatine Hill, where the views from the **Orti Farnesiani** extend from the temples in the forum to the Basilica of Maxentius, the bell-tower of San Francesca Romana and the Colosseum. From the **terrace of Castel Sant'Angelo**, a panorama unfolds from the Borghese Gardens to the Pantheon, the monument to Victor Emmanuel II and the dome of St Peter's. For a scenic outlook, try the **Giardino degli Aranci** (Parco Savello) near Santa Sabina on the Aventine Hill; just be wary on steep footpaths nearby, sometimes the haunt of flashers.

GARDENS

Escape the hustle and noise of the city, spread a picnic blanket alongside locals or stroll in the shade of the stately umbrella pines. Known as *ville* (villas), these gardens once belonged to noble families. Open from dawn to dusk, many contain museums, cafés and other recreational options (*few public toilets here*).

The most famous of Rome's green lungs is the **Villa Borghese**, which bustles on Sundays with locals. In this popular park, decorated with statues and fountains, it is still possible to find quiet areas, such as the Giardino del Lago, an English-style garden with magnolias, aloe and yucca, or the Italianate Parco dei Daini. Home to the Villa Giulia – a national museum of Etruscan art – the park also includes a train trolley and bike rentals. Exhausted after the **Vatican Museums**? Relax in its beautiful **gardens** (*reservation necessary*). The itinerary suggested in the *TRASTEVERE–GIANICOLO* chapter combines gardens, museums, shaded avenues and Renaissance residences: walk from **Villa Farnesina** to the **Orto Botanico**, visit **San Pietro in Montorio**, and finish with the panoramic **Janiculum walk**. Or stroll in the delightful **Villa Celimontana park** (*See COLOSSEO–CELIO*), which has a skating rink in winter and hosts summer jazz concerts, after admiring the magnificent

mosaics in the church of San Clemente. Another green oasis – dotted with old churches – is the Aventine Hill. Enjoy the panoramic **Giardino degli Aranci** (Parco Savello) next to **Santa Sabina**, or combine a visit to Santa Prisca with a walk through the rose gardens, the **Roseto Comunale**, open exclusively during bloom (end of April to end of June). Don't miss the **Casina delle Civette**, in the Villa Torlonia gardens, or Via Nomentana, with its Belle Époque stained-glass windows.

Parco dell'Appia Antica

Closed to cars on Sundays all the way to the Cecilia Metella mausoleum, allowing pedestrians and cyclists rule the *basoli*, or polygonal basalt paving stones. Information, bike rental, guided tours, bus tickets and gadgets available at the Info Point at Via Appia Antica 58/60 ⏱ Mar–Oct 9:30am–1:30pm and 2–6:30pm (Sat, Sun and public holidays 9:30am–7:30pm); and Nov–Feb 9:30–1:30am and 2–5:30pm (Sat, Sun and public holidays 9:30am–5:30pm). *(www.parcoappiaantica.it)*. Highlights include ancient catacombs *(www.catacombe.roma.it)*, the Quo Vadis church and the Fosse Ardeatine, the cave where Nazis massacred 335 Roman men and boys, now a pilgrimage site. Ⓜ Line B (direction Laurentina), San Giovanni station. Take bus 118 (direction Villa Dei Quintili), or Archeobus Ⓜ Line A (direction Anagnina), or bus 714 (direction Palazzo Sport) to Piazza di S. Giovanni in Laterano. Then take bus 218 and get off at Fosse Ardeatine. You can also take the 714, 716, 160, 670, 30 or 130 buses. *(www.atac.roma.it)*.

Orto Botanico

⛵*see TRASTEVERE–GIANICOLO.*
Not far from Trastevere, these gardens burst with cacti, orchids and tropicals. A small garden of flowers and plants with strong scents has been planted for the benefit of the visually impaired.

Riserva Naturale di Monte Mario

Northwest of the city, this nature reserve has Prehistoric, Roman and Renaissance ruins as well as a wide variety of flora.

Riserva Naturale del Litorale Romano

Typical Mediterranean vegetation sprouts here, alongside spacious open areas of dunes and holm oak woods. The oasis also contains Roman ruins from sites such as Ostia Antica, Trajan's Ports, ruins from the ancient Via Severiana and Pliny's villa.

Villa Ada *(Gate Via Salaria 265, 267, 273 and 275.* ⏱*Open 7am–dusk, www.villaada.org)* – 160 hectares between the Aniene and the Tiber make up Rome's second largest park. The lake is the most beautiful and visited area. Reach the park Ⓜ Line B station Libia/Annibaliano and bus 56, 57, 92, 135, 168, 235, 319, 342, 351, 391, N13.

Villa Doria Pamphili

⛵*see TRASTEVERE–GIANICOLO.*
The "lungs" of the western district, this park is very popular late in the evening with athletes and kite-flyers. It houses a number of buildings, greenhouses, an 18C lake and many rare plants.

Villa Glori

⛵*see PARIOLI.*
Shaded by olive trees, this spacious and charming garden has children's pony and donkey rides.

Villa Sciarra *(Gate Via Calandrelli 35, via Dandolo, viale delle Mura Gianicolensi 11)* – In the Monteverde Vecchio district, this park is full of statues, fountains and antiquities, as well as playgrounds.

Villa Torlonia

⛵*see CATACOMBE DI PRISCILLA.*
A rare species, known as the Californian palm, grows in the former residence of the Mussolini family.
The Casina delle Civette contains a fine collection of Liberty-style stained glass and designs.

Know Before You Go

USEFUL WEBSITES

The internet enables visitors to contact tourist offices, consult programmes and brochures and make bookings online. The following sites provide information on Roman history and art as well as practical suggestions.

ART AND CULTURE IN ROME

Rome tourism's cultural portal lists details of events and exhibitions taking place in the city: *www.060608.it* and *www.turismoroma.it*.

TOURIST INFORMATION

The Comune di Roma's website *(www.comune.roma.it)* has general information on the city. Its official tourist website lists regularly updated addresses, plus details on transport, events, shows, sport and a range of other topics: *www.turismoroma.it*.

THE IMPERIAL FORA

This site contains reconstructions of ancient Rome and virtual visits around the via dei Fori Imperiali two webcams. It also provides information on daily life in antiquity and on the excavation work in the fora: *www.capitolium.org*.

FOR TOURISTS AND LOCALS

Cultural events, museums, monuments, guided tours, cinemas and theatres, children's activities, shops, bars and nightclubs etc: *www.romainweb.com* (in Italian only) and *www.wantedinrome.com*. Attention – Many museums are closed on public holidays; on days such as December 24th-25th, and August 14th opening hours are reduced. Be sure to check before organizing your visit. For all information on films, theater shows, concerts and exhibitions in Rome, please visit: www.oggiroma. it or www.trovaroma.com (Website of the supplement of the newspaper La Repubblica, issued every thursday).

CINECITTÀ

This site provides information on the history of the Cinecittà film studios, as well as virtual reconstructions of famous sets, details of cinema events and festivals taking place around the world and an introduction to digital technology and other facilities available at the studios: *www.cinecittastudios.it*.

TOURING CLUB ITALIA

Natives have a soft spot for TCI, purveyors of maps, guides and member discounts. The Milan-based association began in 1894 as the Touring Club Ciclistico Italiano (Cycling Touring Club of Italy). Today it caters to a wide range of travellers. A €39 annual membership includes discounts on car rentals, accommodations, ferries, spas, museums and historic sites *(www.touringcard.it/en)*.

TOURIST OFFICES
INTERNATIONAL

The **Ente Nazionale Italiano per il Turismo** (www.enit.it) has offices abroad and in Italy. *For local tourist information see below.*

UK AND IRELAND

London: 1 Princes Street, W1B 2AY. ℘(020) 7408 1254 (*toll free from UK and Ireland*). london@enit.it. italiantouristboard.co.uk.
Dublin: 17 Old Naas Road, Inchicore, D12 T8P4. dublin@enit.it.

USA

New York: 686 Park Avenue, New York, 3rd Floor, NY 10065. ℘(212) 245 5618. newyork@enit.it. www.enit.it.
Chicago: 401 N. Michigan Avenue, Suite 1720,Chicago IL 60611. ℘(312) 644 0996. chicago@enit.it. www.enit.it
Los Angeles: 10850 Wilshire Blvd. - Suite 575, Los Angeles, CA 90024. ℘(310) 820 1898. losangeles@enit.it. www.enit.it.

CANADA

Toronto: 365 Bay Street, Suite 503 Toronto (Ontario) M5H 2V1. ℰ(416) 925-4882 toronto@enit.it. www.enit.it.

AUSTRALIA AND NEW ZELAND

East Sydney: Level 2, 140 William Street, East Sydney NSW 2011.ℰ(0) 2 9357 2561. sydney@enit.it, www. enit.it.

LOCAL OFFICES
TOURIST INFORMATION POINTS (P.I.T.)

Brochures and maps of the city. A service from Roma Capitale, ℰ06 06 08, www.turismoroma.it, www.060608.it, www.romapass.it, offers a comprehensive source of information for visitors.

Tourist Infopoints

Information kiosks (www.turismo roma.it) open daily (except where stated) at:

- **C.G. Pastine Ciampino:** Baggage Claim Area, International Arrivals (8:30am–6pm).
- **Fiumicino:** Terminal 3, International Arrivals (8am–8:45pm).
- **Stazione Termini:** Via Giolitti 34, Platform 24 (8am–6:45pm).
- **Fori Visitor Centre:** Via dei Fori Imperiali (9:30am–7pm).
- **Navona:** Piazza delle Cinque Lune (9:30am–7pm).
- **San Pietro:** Largo del Colonnato 1 (9am–6pm).
- **Castel Sant'Angelo:** Lungotevere Vaticano (Piazza Pia) (9:30am–7pm).
- **Minghetti:** Via Marco Minghetti, corner Via del Corso (9:30am–7pm).
- **Nazionale:** Via Nazionale, near Palazzo delle Esposizioni (9:30am–7pm).
- **Ostia Lido:** Lungomare Paolo Toscanelli, corner Piazza Anco Marzio (May–Sept only Sat and Sund 4–9:45pm).

- **Sonnino:** Piazza Sidney Sonnino(Trastevere), (10:30am–8pm).

INTERNATIONAL VISITORS
ITALIAN EMBASSIES AND CONSULATES

UK Embassy

14 Three Kings Yard, London W1K 4EH. ℰ(020) 7312 2200. Fax 020 7312 2230. www.amblondra.esteri.it.

USA Embassy

3000 Whitehaven St, NW Washington, DC 20008. ℰ(202) 612 4400. www.ambwashingtondc.esteri.it.

Canada Embassy

275 Slater St, 21st floor Ottawa, Ontario K1P 5H9. ℰ(613) 232 2401. www.ambottawa.esteri.it.

UK Consulates

"Harp House", 83/86 Farringdon St, London EC4A 4BL.ℰ(020) 7936 5900. www.conslondra.esteri.it

32 Melville St, Edinburgh EH3 7HA. ℰ(0131) 226 3631. www.consedimburgo.esteri.it.

USA Consulate

690 Park Avenue, New York NY 10065. ℰ(212) 737 9100. www.consnewyork.esteri.it.

Canada Consulates

3489 Drummond St, Montreal, Quebec H3G 1X6. ℰ(514) 849 8351. www.consmontreal.esteri.it.

136 Beverley Street, Toronto, Ontario, M5T 1Y5, Canada. ℰ(416) 977 1566. www.constoronto.esteri.it.

FOREIGN EMBASSIES IN ROME

Australia – Via Antonio Bosio 5 00161 Rome. ℰ06 85 27 21. www.italy.embassy.gov.au.
Canada – Via Zara 30, 00198 Rome. ℰ06 85 44 42 911. www.canada.it.

Ireland – Villa Spada, Via Giacomo Medici 1, 00153 Rome. ℘06 58 52 381. www.dfa.ie/irish-embassy/italy.
New Zealand – Via Clitunno 44 00198 Rome. ℘06 853 7501. www.nzembassy.com/italy.
South Africa – Via Tanaro 14 00198 Rome. ℘06 852 541. www.sudafrica.it.
UK – Via XX Settembre 80a 00187 Rome. ℘06 42 20 00 01. www.italiantouristboard.co.uk.
USA – Via Vittorio Veneto 121 00187 Rome. ℘06 46 741. italy.usembassy.gov.

DOCUMENTS

Passports – British and US citizens must carry a valid passport. Citizens of other European Union countries only need a national identity card. In case of loss or theft, report to the embassy or consulate and the local police.

Visas – Entry visas are required by Australian, New Zealand, Canadian and US citizens if your stay exceeds three months. Apply to the Italian Consulate (visa issued same day; delay if submitted by mail). US citizens may find the booklet *Your Trip Abroad* useful for visa requirements, customs regulations, medical care etc. – available from the US Government Printing Office (℘866 512 1800; *www.access.gpo.gov*).
Tips for travelling abroad, visa requirements and other travel information can also be found at *www.travel.state.gov*.

HEALTH

As long as the UK is a member of the European Union, British citizens are entitled to reduced cost or free medical treatment when temporarily visiting a EU country. Obtain a **European Health Insurance Card (EHIC)** before leaving home (*www. ehic.org.uk*). Separate travel and medical insurance is recommended.

CUSTOMS

EU member states have generous allowances for travellers arriving from other EU countries, provided the merchandise is for personal use (up to 800 cigarettes and 10 litres of spirits or 90 litres of wine – although excessive quantities may flag up at customs and you may be required to prove it is not for commercial use). Keep receipts for all goods acquired abroad.
For more detailed information look at HM Revenue and Customs website, *www.hmrc.gov.uk*. For non-EU citizens, "**duty-free**" only alleviates taxes at the shopping source: you still must declare articles in excess of your home country's allowance. For example, the US permits $800 of goodies before the taxman cometh (charging a flat rate of duty on the next $1,000), as long as the traveller was abroad at least 48 hours and hasn't made another international trip in the last 30 days. Edible souvenirs can fall foul of officials (who mete out fines of $250 for forbidden foods). The US Customs Service offers a free publication with a full run-down of allowances and duty-free tips, **Know Before You Go**, for US citizens, *www.cbp.gov*.

DRIVING IN ROME

Also see the Getting Around chapter.
Nationals of the European Union require a valid **national driving licence**. Non-EU citizens may wish to carry an **international driving licence**, obtainable in the US from the American Automobile Association (℘1-800-222-4357. www.aaa.com). Other documents required include the vehicle's current **log book** and a **green card** for insurance.

ACCESSIBILITY

Accessible attractions include the Musei Vaticani, Musei capitolini e Centale Montemartini, Museo nazionale Romano, Castel Sant' Angelo, Galleria Doria Pamphili, Palazzo delle Esposizioni, Maxxi, Macro, Ara Pacis, Museo Etrusco di Villa Giulia, Museo

Roman tram

© Judy Edelhoff/Michelin

della Civiltà Romana, Museo delle Navi Romane, Basilica di San Pietro, S Giovanni in Laterano, Palazzo Venezia, Galleria Nazionale d'Arte Moderna, Galleria Borghese and the Bioparco-Zoo. Rome's exceptional effort is the walkway between the Piazza Navona and the Trevi Fountain. Not only does smooth brick designate a pedestrian-friendly path, but Braille plaques explain the landmarks en-route.

Many Roman historic monuments do not have modern lifts or wheelchair facilities. For detailed information prior to departure contact **Disability Rights UK** (*Plexal, 14 East Bay Lane, Here East, Queen Elizabeth Olympic Park Stratford, London E20 3BS. www. disabilityrightsuk.org*).

English-speaking staff man the **Roma per Tutti** advice line for tourism, information and mobility for persons with special needs in Rome (*www.romapertutti.it*).

Explore Rome with **Accessible Journeys** (*www.disabilitytravel.com*) and **Flying Wheels Travel** (*www. stridetravel.com*).

Society for Accessible Travel and Hospitality (*www.sath.org*) offers excellent information as do the **American Foundation for the Blind** (*www.afb.org*).

For further information: ☎060608 and the section titled Accessibilità at *www.turismoroma.it*.

Sights in this guide marked with the symbols ♿or (♿) have full or partial access for wheelchairs.

TRANSPORT

All the stations on Metro line A, B, C are equipped with lifts or stairlift. Many of the city buses now have lower platforms and so are suitable for wheelchair users. Large train stations have an office for the disabled (*ufficio disabili*); Termini's is beside platform one. Request assistance 24 hours before travel.

For more information on access on Rome's public transport contact ATAC on, www.atac.roma.it.

The website has a list of all metro stations with wheelchair access. About 75 percent of buses in Rome are wheelchair-accessible and about 25 lines have voice announcements for the visually impaired.

Getting There

BY PLANE
AIRLINES

Several airline companies fly direct
to Rome. The following is a brief
selection:

Alitalia
- www.alitalia.com.

British Airways
- www.ba.com.

Delta Airlines
- www.delta.com.

For information on low-cost flights
to Italy, *See Basic Information –
Discounts.*

Major **US airlines** that fly to
Rome include:

- **American Airlines** – www.aa.com.
- **Continental Airlines** –
  www.continental.com.
- **Delta Airlines** – www.delta.com.
- **USAirways** – www.usairways.com.

Tour operators offering flight-only
or package holidays include:

- **Citalia** – ☏01 293 762 410.
  www.citalia.com.
- **Tour & Explore** – ☏02 082 341 532.
  www.tourandexplore.co.uk.

AIRPORTS

Rome is served by two airports:
Leonardo da Vinci Airport at
Fiumicino, ☏06 65 951, (26km/16mi
southwest of Rome) and **Ciampino
Airport**, ☏06 65 951, (15km/10mi
southeast of Rome).
For information about both airports:
www.adr.it. Fiumicino handles
domestic and international traffic
(di bandiera e low cost). Ciampino
concentrates on low-cost flights.

Ground Transport

Fiumicino is linked to the centre
by **train**: services to Roma-
Termini (Leonardo Express €14
one-way) depart every 30min,
6:23am–10:23pm, from the airport;
between 5:35am–10:35pm from
Roma-Termini; journey time
32min. FL1 Fiumicino-Fara Sabina-
Montelibretti services run trains
to Trastevere, Ostiense, Tuscolana
and Tiburtina (€11) every 15min
Mon–Sat 5:57am–11:27pm and
every 30min Sun. Going directly
to these neighbourhoods can save
considerable time and hassle, but
be careful: taxis are rare during
rainstorms and late at night without
prior booking.
Four COTRAL night buses loop
between the airport, Termini and
Tiburtina stations from 1:15am to 5am.
Tickets are €5 (€7 on board).
Fiumicino's stop is outside the arrivals
hall (☏800 174 471, Mon–Fri 8:00am–
6:00 pm; www.cotralspa.it).
A **taxi** to city centre takes 35- minutes
from both airports and costs a flat rate
of €48 (Fiumicino) or Ciampino (€50).
Use only the authorized white cabs at
the taxi stand.
Ciampino is linked to city centre
by **bus**. ATRAL buses serve Roma
Termini (€6.90 one-way) departing
every hour 4am–10:50pm from the
airport and 4:50am–midnight from
Roma Termini (*www.atral-lazio.
com*). Buses to Ciampino train station
(€1.20 one-way) run every 50-60min
6:40am–11:30pm from the airport
and 5:50am–10:20pm from Ciampino
station. ATRAL buses link Ciampino
with metro station Anagnina on
Line A (€1.20 one-way) every 40min
6:10am–10:40pm and from Anagnina
6:30am–11:10pm.
A private **bus service** (€5.80 one-way,
€9 return) also connects Termini to
both airports. All information and
schedules can be found on
www.terravision.eu.

Parking

In addition to a multistorey car park,
Fiumicino Airport also has a long-
stay car park with a capacity for
2 000 vehicles. The car park sits east

of the airport, and is directly linked to the Rome–Fiumicino motorway. A free bus shuttles to the domestic and international terminals every 10min during the day (from 7am–midnight) and every 20min at night. The cost of parking starts at €5.50–7.50 per day if you take advantage of discount rates by booking ahead at *www.adr.it*.

BY TRAIN

Italy has an extensive train network. Service is generally reliable and inexpensive – making rail the most pleasant way to explore the country. Whenever possible, purchase tickets from an automated machine at the rail station, which has menus in English. The computer allows you to browse destinations, scrutinize schedules and pay by credit card. Best of all, you avoid the long, panicked queues. Travel agents – with the FS sticker – may charge a slight commission. Tickets are good for two months, but must be stamped before boarding or you may get a fine. Orange validation machines are at the end of platforms. The mainline national and international trains arrive at **Stazione Termini** or **Tiburtina**. Termini is on both Metro lines (**A** – Battistini–Anagnina and **B** – Laurentina–Rebibbia/Conca d'Oro) and the bus station in the forecourt serves almost all the routes in Rome. Several nearby towns – such as Viterbo, Pantano and Ostia – are accessible on routes from the city: the Rome–Viterbo line leaves from Piazzale Flaminio Station; Rome–Pantano from Roma Laziali Station; the Rome–Lido line leaves from Porta San Paolo Station and makes three stops before Ostia Lido, one of which is the ruins at Ostia Antica. Timetables are available at the Italian Tourist Office in London and from newsstands in Italy.

USEFUL NUMBERS

Italian State Railways (Ferrovie dello Stato), *℘89 20 21 (information in Italian, 24hr) from abroad ℘06 68 47 54 75*;

information office at Termini Station, ℘ 199 89 20 21; information for disabled travellers, ℘199 30 30 60, www.rfi.it, www.trenitalia.com.
Italia Rail *(website dedicated to train travel in Italy, run by the official agents for Trenitalia in the UK, US and Canada)* ℘1-877 375 7245 or 06 9763 2451; www.italiarail.com.
Italo, high-speed trains, www.italotreno.it. ℘06 07 08.

BY COACH/BUS

Coach services from Victoria Coach Station in London are operated by Eurolines: *℘08717 818 in the UK (charges of 10 pence per minute apply); for assistance for disabled travellers, choose option 4 when calling the number above. www.eurolines.co.uk*.

BY CAR

The Michelin companion maps and plans for this guide are listed at the back of the guide.
On the outer edge of the city is the **Grande Raccordo Anulare** (GRA), a multi-lane ring road from which all the motorways *(A1 to Florence and Bologna to the north, to Naples in the south; A12 to Fiumicino, Civitavecchia and the west coast; A24 east to Aquila and the Adriatic)* and main roads *(strade statali)* radiate.
The **Tangenziale Est** links the Stadio Olimpico to the Piazza San Giovanni in Laterano via such eastern quarters as Nomentano, Tiburtino and Prenestino.

Arrival from the North

If you are approaching Rome from the north along the A1, and heading north (Cassia, Flaminia or Salaria districts) or west (Aurelia) of the city, leave the motorway at Roma Nord and follow the Grande Raccordo Anulare (GRA).

Eastern and Southern Rome

For the eastern and southern districts of Rome, stay on the motorway, follow signs to Roma Est–Napoli and take the GRA at the Roma Est exit.
From the A16 and A24 motorways, the GRA is clearly signposted.

23

Getting Around

Visitors are best advised to explore Rome on foot and by public transport because traffic in the city is heavy and parking places are difficult to find. For information on hiring a bicycle or moped, *see When and Where to Go.*

BY PUBLIC TRANSPORTATION

Public transport services are organised by **ATAC** *(Azienda Tramvie e Autobus del Comune di Roma 06 0606; www. atac.roma.it; muoversiaroma.it).* City route plans are on sale in bookshops and kiosks as well as on the website, where real-time information can be found.

Tickets should be purchased before the beginning of the journey and punched in the machine in the bus and on the underground. Different types of ticket *(biglietto)* are sold at newspaper kiosks or in tobacconists' shops: those bearing the name **Metrebus** may be used on all means of transport – bus, tram, metro and overground FS *(Ferrovie dello Stato)* trains in second class except on services Roma Termini–Fiumicino Aeroporto and Ponte Galeria–Fiumicino Aeroporto. Individual tickets may also be acquired from machines at metro stations and end-of-line bus stops. Details are available on www.atac.roma.it.

Tickets available include:
- a **BIT** ticket, costing €1,50, is valid for a journey up to 100min on various lines from the time it is stamped;
- a **BIT** ticket, costing €7, is valid until midnight of the day of purchase;
- a **BTI** pass, costing €12,50, is valid for two days;
- a **BTI** pass, costing €18, is valid for three days;
- a **CIS** pass, costing €24, is valid for one week.

A monthly pass is also available for €35. Bus and trams stops are indicated by a sign *fermata*; request stop = *fermata richiesta.*

Buses operate from 5:30am–midnight, but some 20 night bus lines run from 1am–5:30am. The main terminal stations are Piazza dei Cinquecento and Piazza Venezia. Following established routes are amongst the most useful:
- **64** and **40** from Termini Station to the Vatican, stopping at Via Nazionale, Piazza Venezia, near the Gesù Church, Largo di Torre Argentina and Corso Vittorio Emanuele II. However, beware of pickpockets, notably at rush hour;
- **87** Piazza San Giovanni in Laterano south to Via Ardeatina (passing the north end of the Old Appian Way);
- **310** from Termini Station to Piazza Vescovio;
- **117** (not on festive days) run through the historic centre on electric minibuses. The former runs from Piazza San Giovanni in Laterano and from Piazza del Popolo;
- **85** Colosseum, Imperial Fora, Piazza Venezia, Via del Corso.

Trams operate from 5am–9pm. There are six lines; the following routes are amongst the most useful to tourists:
- **3** Trastevere, Colosseum, San Giovanni in Laterano, Piazza Thorwaldsen (Villa Giulia and the Galleria Nazionale d'Arte Moderna);
- **14** from the east side of the city (Togliatti) to Termini Station, Via Piazzale di Porta Maggiore and Piazza Vittorio Emanuele II;
- **19** from Piazza dei Gerani to Risorgimento S. Pietro, stopping at Piazza dei Gerani, Piazzale del Verano, Viale Regina Margherita, Piazza Thorwaldsen, Via Flaminia and Viale Tiziano;
- **8** from Trastevere Station stopping at Viale Trastevere, Via Arenula, Via di Torre Argentina and Piazza Venezia.

Speed limits

© meskolo/Fotolia.com

Metro (underground) trains operate from 5:30am–11:30pm (until 01:30am on Fri and Sat). There are two Metro lines:

♦ **Line A** runs from Battistini to Anagnina. The most useful stops include Flaminio (Piazza del Popolo), Spagna (Piazza di Spagna), Barberini (Piazza Barberini), Termini (Termini Station), San Giovanni (St John Lateran) and Cinecittà.

♦ **Line B** runs from Laurentina to Rebibbia – the **line B1** branches north, (Conca d'Oro). The most useful stops include Termini (Termini Station), Cavour (Piazza Cavour), Colosseo (Colosseum), Circo Massimo (near the Circus Maximus and the Baths of Caracalla), Piramide (Mausoleum of Caius Cestius), San Paolo (Basilica of St Paul Outside the Walls) and EUR Fermi (EUR district).

♦ **Line C** connects the south-east of the city with San Giovanni, although construction is not finished and many stops are yet to be open.

BY TAXI

To call a taxi dial ℘06 35 70, ℘06 49 94, ℘06 88 22, ℘06 66 45, ℘06 06 09. Basic fixed starting charge: €3 (6am–10pm), €6.50 (10pm–6am); rising €1,10 per kilometre. First piece of luggage is free; each piece thereafter costs

€1. Night or call-out service is an additional €6.50. Extra charges also apply Sundays and public holidays (€4.50). For a detailed breakdown of taxi tariffs log on to *www.comune. roma.it.*

BY CAR

Driving in Rome is not advised as access to the city centre is very difficult and parking severely restricted; many streets are reserved for pedestrians, taxis, buses and local residents. The historic centre is delineated as *ZTL* (check on www.romamobilita.it/it/servizi/ztl the hours when traffic is limited in various zones) from which private cars are excluded between 6:30am–7pm Mon–Fri and 2–7pm Sat. The Automobile Club d'Italia's website has a comprehensive section on Driving in Italy:www.aci.it.
For car sharing, check the site *www.romamobilita.it/it/carsharing.*

ROAD REGULATIONS

Traffic drives on the right. The minimum age in Italy to drive a car, or a motorbike over 125cc, is 18 years. **Seat belts** must be worn in the front and back of the vehicle. Drivers must wear shoes, carry spare lights and a **red triangle** and a **yellow vest** to be displayed in case of a breakdown or accident.
A valid **driving licence** must be carried at all times.

Motorways (*autostrade* – subject to tolls) and dual carriageways *(superstrade)* are indicated by green signs; ordinary roads by blue signs; tourist sights by yellow signs.
Italian **motorway tolls** can be paid with money or with the **Viacard**, a magnetic card sold at the entrances and exits of the motorways, in tobacconists and service stations.

The following **speed restrictions** apply:
♦ 50kph in built-up areas;
♦ 90–110kph on open country roads;
♦ 110–130kph on motorways depending on engine capacity.
♦ Low beams must be on at all times when driving on a motorway.

PARKING

Parking spaces are like gold dust in Rome, and their scarcity is another good reason not to drive. If you must drive, however, be aware that metres charge €1.20 per hour in the city centre €1 per hour outside the centre), except on weekends and evenings.
Avoid streets marked "*Sosta Vietata*" – no matter how many cars cluster there. Illegally parked vehicles may be towed (℘*06 6769 2303*). Hotel car parks are the best option.
This website has a list of all car parks in Rome: www.atac.roma.it/index. asp?p=24&i=15. The main car parks are marked on the separate map Michelin Plan of Rome 38.

PETROL/GASOLINE

Fuel is sold as super, *senza piombo* (unleaded 95 octane), super plus or *Euro plus* (unleaded 98 octane) or *gasolio* (diesel).
Petrol stations are usually open between 7am–7pm. Many close at lunchtime (12:30pm–3pm), Sundays and public holidays and some refuse payment by credit card. As well as the service stations on the ring road (Grande Raccordo Anulare), petrol can be bought 24hrs a day from automatic petrol pumps or petrol stations throughout the city.

MAPS AND PLANS

A list of Michelin maps that would be useful for getting to Rome and finding your way around the city is given at the back of the guide (℘*See Maps and Plans*).

RESCUE SERVICE

The Royal Automobile Club and the American Automotive Association both have reciprocal agreements with the Automobile Club d'Italia for breakdown assistance and general information.
In case of breakdown, contact ℘116 (24hrs). This breakdown service (tax levied) is operated by the ACI for foreign motorists. Telephone information in English (and other languages) for road and weather conditions as well as for tourist events: ℘803 116, www.aci.it.

RENTAL CARS

All the main car hire agencies have offices at Fiumicino Airport and Ciampino Airport and at Termini Railway Station. Weekly rentals cost between €300 and €400 for a medium-sized car. Agencies require a credit card, passport, license and a driver over 21 or 23 years of age. Outlets include:

♦ **AutoEuropa**
  www.autoeuropa.it
♦ **Avis**
  www.avis.co.uk
♦ **Hertz**
  www.hertz.co.uk
♦ **Europcar**
  www.europcar.co.uk
♦ **Maggiore**
  www.maggiore.it
♦ **Rhino Cars**
  www.rhinocarhire.com

What to See and Do

ACTIVITIES FOR KIDS

Unless they have studied some Roman history, young children are unlikely to enjoy trailing around ruins, museums and churches. However, Rome does have a number of sights that interest youngsters, especially in its large parks. The most popular of these is **Villa Borghese**, with its charming carousels and pony rides, and a BioPark Zoo. A walk around the **Janiculum** is delightful with puppet shows every afternoon, miniature-horse rides, and the noon cannon blast. Other attractive public gardens include the vast **Villa Doria Pamphili**, whose lake is now home to the gentle coypu, a type of aquatic rodent similar to a small beaver; the **Villa Sciarra** in old Monteverde; and **Villa Celimontana**, not far from the Colosseum. The **Orto Botanico**, behind Palazzo Corsini, is one of Italy's most important botanical gardens and contains many rare plants.

The changing of the palace guard at **Piazza del Quirinale**, near the Trevi Fountain, is colourful and entertaining. The EUR district is also worth exploring as a family: visit the Museo delle Arti e Tradizioni Popolari (Folk Museum), enjoy the rides at the funfair (Luneur, closed for renovation; opening planned for 2015-16, with the city's new aquarium), or walk around the small lake, stopping for an ice cream at the popular Giolitti *gelateria*. Other children's entertainment parks are outside the city: Cinecittà World (Via di Castel Romano 200,t06 64 00 92 93.,www. cinecittaworld.it); Rainbow Magic Land (Via della Pace, Valmontone,t06 95 31 87 00, www.magicland.it). A space entirely devoted to children's entertainment is Explora, Museo dei Bambini, close to Piazza del Popolo.

SIGHTSEEING
GENERAL INFORMATION

For information, free publications and maps, contact the 060608 or stop at one of the city information kiosks (♻See *Know Before You Go*).

PRICES AND HOURS

♻See *Basic Information*.
Information on admission times and charges for museums and monuments is given in the Discovering Rome section of the guide. Because of fluctuations in the cost of living and the constant change in opening times, the details should merely serve as a guideline. Phone ahead to confirm. The prices indicated are for single adults benefiting from no special concession; reductions for children, students, the over-60s and parties should be requested on-site and be backed by ID. Special conditions often exist for groups, but arrangements should be made in advance.

For EU nationals, state-run or city-run museums provide free admission to visitors under 18 and over 65 with proof of identification, and a 50 percent reduction for visitors under 25.

Since 2014, the Franceschini Law has been in force, which has ended free entrance to museums for the over-65s, given reductions to under-25s, and free entrance to under-18s and for every first Sunday of the month. Remember that in the Discovering Rome section, the closing times of museums, monuments and archaeological sites are only given if they shut at an hour different from one hour before the exhibition areas close. Also, early closing times on the 24 and 31 December are not given as they vary from site to site.

Museums

For security reasons, many museums in Rome, especially the major ones, do not allow large purses, knapsacks and backpacks to be carried inside. These items must be temporarily stored for visitors. So plan accordingly to avoid having to check these items.

Churches

The major basilicas *(St. Peter's, St John Lateran, St Paul Outside the Walls, St Mary Major)* are open from 7am–6:30pm, but most churches close at noon and reopen in the afternoon from 4–8pm; exceptions are marked in the *Selected Sights* section, but it is important to check the times as they may be altered for services.

Visitors should be appropriately dressed: long trousers for men; no bare shoulders or very short skirts for women. Churches are closed during services; tourists already inside should avoid disrupting the worshippers. As many of the works of art are positioned high up, it is a good idea to take binoculars. Small change is needed for the lights.

BY BICYCLE

Rome is not an ideal city to explore by bike or moped because of its dense, chaotic traffic, heavy pollution and the uneven road surfaces. However, keen cyclists follow the bike path along the Tiber and explore the city's public parks.

BICYCLE HIRE

Bicycles can be hired in various locations in the city. The best known are **Top Bike** Rental *(daily 9.30/10am–7pm; via Labicana 49; ℘06 488 2893; www.topbikerental.com)*, and **Roma rent bike** *(daily 8:30am–7pm; Via di S. Paolo alla Regola, 33; ℘06 88 922 365, www.romarentbike.com)*.

Roma Bike Tour, outside metro station Manzoni, offers guided bike tours in English daily *(reserve online at www.romabiketour.com or ℘331 743 9944)*. Other rental companies may be found at *www.aboutroma.com/rent-a-bike-in-rome.html.*

BY SCOOTER

Mopeds *(motorini)* are the essential Roman mode of transport and fashion accessory. A credit card and photo identification – or cash deposit – may be required for a rental, costing about €45, €55 per day. Helmets are the law. The smaller vehicles, like the standard 50cc put-puts, aren't approved to transport passengers, but often do. Mopeds can enter the historic centre (the limited traffic area "ZTL") and park free in blue-line areas or just about anywhere else they can wedge out of traffic. Drivers must be 14-plus for models up to 50cc.

Brave souls can rent from **Scooter Hire** *(Via Cavour 80a, Monti; ℘06 481 5669; www.scooterhire.it)*. **Romarent** also offers guided bike and scooter tours in English *(Vicolo dei Bovari 7a, near the Piazza Navona; ℘06 689 6555; web.tiscali.it/romarent/indexie.html)*. Lastly, **EcoMoveRent** supplies scooters as well as bicycles. *(Via Varese 48/50, Esquilino; ℘06 44 704 518; www.ecomoverent.com)*.

The **Paseggiata del Gianicolo** offers atmospheric views of the cityscape, but its switchbacks and one-way streets promote panic and funnel drivers into the Vatican traffic jams. Instead, bump along the back streets of Trastevere or the Aventine Hill, away from the horns and hustle. Coasting past the Circus Maximus – the ancient Roman horse track – can be memorable.

Rome by scooter

BY HORSE-DRAWN CARRIAGE

Horse-drawn carriages (*carrozzella* or *botticella* in Roman dialect) are likely to be near parks such as Borghese Gardens during the week. At weekends you should be able to hail them at key spots such as the Colosseum, the Pantheon, Piazza Venezia and the Spanish Steps. For information contact **Associazione Vetturini Romani** (*Via Monte Testaccio 23*, *℘ 3347 00 05 732*). Rates are very expensive (as much as €150 an hour). Be aware that animal-rights activists oppose the use of horses to pull carriages in Rome and seek a total ban.

BY METRO AND BUS

See Public Transportation above. In a rare display of cooperation, the metro, buses and trams work together under the direction of the company ATAC (*Via Prenestina 45*; *℘06 46 951*; *www.atac.roma.it*).
The city's rich history stunted the extent of the subway *(metropolitana)*. The overlapping ruins run deep, making tunnel excavation difficult. The city managed a simple two-line system, aimed mainly at suburban commuters. The metro is efficient and safe, but stay on guard for pickpockets and groping in the crowds.
There are two hop-on hop-off buses operating for **tourists**:
Line 110 (Open Bus) departs daily every 30 min from Viale Einaudi from 8:30am–8:30pm. Ticket price is €20 for 2h of hop-on, hop-off travel during a 48hr period with the formula Hop-on, Hop-off.
Archeobus departs every 30min from Piazza dei Cinquecento (Termini) daily 9am–4:30pm, for 1h30 of hop-on, hop-off travel. Tickets cost €8, valid for 48hrs (€12 if paired with purchase of a bus ticket departing from Roma Ciampino airport).
For more information, access www.atral-lazio.com.

ON THE WATER

For an unusual view of the city, why not take a **boat trip** on the River Tiber? **Batelli di Roma** (*www.battellidiroma.it*) has hop-on hop-off cruises between Mar–Oct (winter schedules are reduced), between Tiberina Island (Lungotevere degli Anguillara) and Piazza di Ponte Sant'Angelo(*first departure 10am*). There is a pre-recorded commentary on the cruise in English languages (with earphones). **Rome Boat Experience** offers vari types of boat trip: the classical tour, €15, valid for 24 hours with the formula Hop-on, Hop-off; and a trip with live music and a fixed menu dinner. (*www.romeboatexperience.com*).

BY PLANE

For a bird's-eye view of the city in a Cessna 182 or Highlander or other light airplane, contact the dell'Urbe Airport at Via Salaria 825, where 20min flights may be available. Advanced reservations are necessary; cost is €70 per person with a minimum of two people required).
For more information, contact Diamond Aereo (*open daily 9am–7pm; ℘06 886 44 990; www.urbe.aero/it*).

GUIDED TOURS

For independent group visits, contact: SNGT (Centro Guide turitsiche, *Via Esquilino 38 ℘ 06 89 16 69 36; Mon-Fri 8:30am–1:30pm);* CAST (Centro ufficiale Guide e Accompagnatori turistici, *Via Cavour 184, ℘06 48 25 698. www.cast-turismo.it*).
For ideas for self-guided tours, see the suggested itineraries beginning on page 10 of this chapter.

Line 110 (Open Bus) departs daily every 30 min from Viale Einaudi from 8:30am–8:30pm. Ticket price is €20 for 2h of hop-on, hop-off travel during a 48hr period.

Calendar of Events

Obtain calendar details from the Vatican Information Office *(Ufficio Informazioni Pellegrini e Turisti)* **and from Roma Capitale.**

JANUARY

6 JANUARY
Festival of the Befana: the last of the Twelve Days of Christmas; market stalls in Piazza Navona overflow with presents and sweets (or candy coal). Befana, the good witch, brings presents to children.

21 JANUARY
In the Church of Sant'Agnese Fuori le Mura, the **saint's feast day** is celebrated with the benediction of two lambs. They're given to the Benedictines of Santa Ceciliam, who spin the wool into *paliums,* which each new archbishop receives from the Pope.

FEBRUARY

FEBRUARY - START OF MARCH
Carnival: Tasting of local sweets *(frappe)* during the week before Lent. Procession of floats in Via Tiburtina on Carnival Day.

17 FEBRUARY
The Inquisition burned Giordano Bruno alive for heresy in 1600. Honor this freethinker at his poignant statue in Rome's Campo de' Fiori, where maskers caper through the famous piazza.

MARCH

8 MARCH
Women's Festival *(Festa della Donne)*: The day honours women, who are given yellow puffball blossoms *(mimosa)*.

9 MARCH
The **blessing of automobiles** near the Church of Santa Francesca Romana, patron saint of drivers.

19 MARCH
In the Trionfale district on the **Feast of St Joseph** stalls sell typical *bignè*, a sort of doughnut, and *frittelle,* a sort of choux pastry.

SPRING
Explore Italy's private gardens, monasteries, villas and castles for free. Rome opens St Anthony's Abbey. The date falls on the weekend closest to the 21, the first day of spring.

THIRD SAT
Thousands of runners taking part in Rome's **marathon** dash past the ruins on the third Saturday of the month *(www.maratonadiroma.it)*.

APRIL
The steps of Trinità dei Monti are decked with blooming azaleas, a dazzling sight.

GOOD FRIDAY
Stations of the Cross by night between the Colosseum and the Palatine Hill.

EASTER
At noon in St Peter's Square the Pope gives his *Urbi et Orbi* blessing.

21 APRIL
Solemn ceremony on the Capitoline Hill commemorates the anniversary of the 753 BC birth of the Eternal City.

25 APRIL
Liberation Day marks the end of German occupation in 1945.

MAY

1–31 MAY
Antique Fair in Via dei Coronari: Stalls crammed with furniture and antiques line this historic street.

1–31 MAY
Roses in bloom in the municipal rose gardens of the Roseto di Roma (Via di Valle Murcia 6).

1 MAY
Parades and fiery speeches honour the nation's labourers. Businesses are closed on this popular holiday.

JUNE

2 JUNE
Festa della Repubblica Italiana. Republic of Italy holiday.

23–24 JUNE
On the **Feast of St John**, in the district bearing his name, there is great rejoicing: popular games and spectacles; snails in broth and roast pork.

29 JUNE
Service in St Peter's Basilica on the **Feast of St Peter and St Paul**, the most solemn of the religious festivals in Rome.

JUNE–JULY
Lungo il Tevere: Tevere Expo, a real exhibition of Italian and international crafts on the Tiber banks.

15–30 JULY
Festa de Noantri: A week of singing, dancing and feasting in Trastevere to celebrate the eccentric neighbourhood and – to a lesser degree – the Virgin of Carmine. *Noiantri* roughly means "our very own", a fitting motto for this area, famous for outsiders and foreigners.

JUNE–AUGUST
Estate Romana (Roman Summer, www.estateromana.comune.roma.it): Concerts and spectacles held (especially in Caracalla's Baths).

5 AUGUST
Festa della Madonna della Neve: commemoration in the Basilica of Santa Maria Maggiore of the miraculous fall of snow which led to the construction of the church: a shower of white flower petals is released in the Pauline Chapel.

15 AUGUST
Assumption Day (Ferragosto): Celebrates the Virgin Mary's ascent to heaven. The entire nation goes on holiday – often for weeks.

SEPTEMBER
Throughout the month, Romans visit the peaceful Alban Hills, especially Ariccia, to savour *porchetta*, sandwiches of crispy roast pig, and wine.

LATE SEPTEMBER (AND OCTOBER)
European Heritage Day: Private gardens and palaces open their doors on the fourth Sunday. Freebies, discounts and related events in the most important museums.

OCTOBER

1–31 OCTOBER
Wander Fiera d'Arte di Margutta Street and the nearby Via Orso, lined with paintings, handicrafts and exhibitions.

LATE OCTOBER
Festival Internazionale del Film di Roma: Rome's film festival at the Auditorium is now an international event, even it is still relatively new.

NOVEMBER

1 NOVEMBER
On **All Saint's Day** (Ognissanti), Catholics visit graveyards, as business grinds to a halt. Costumed children race in the squares, flinging confetti and shaving cream. Snack on the "bones of the dead" (osso di morto) from a pastry shop.

DECEMBER
The famous Piazza Navona hosts a month-long fair selling sweets, ornaments and toys. A handmade crèche (presepio) or Epiphany witch (Befana) make the best souvenirs. Wander the brightly lit streets – Frattina, Condotti, Sistina and Del Babuino in particular – or the twisting alleys of Trastevere.

8 DECEMBER
Celebration of the doctrine of the Immaculate Conception in Piazza di Spagna in the presence of the Pope.

CHRISTMAS
In Via Giulia every year there is an exhibition of over 50 nativity scenes, with beautiful cribs in the following churches: Santi Cosma e Damiano, Santa Maria in Via, Sant'Alessio, Basilica dei Santi Apostoli, San Marcello, Chiesa del Gesù, Santa Maria d'Aracoeli, Santa Maria del Popolo and Santa Maria Maggiore *(13C crib)*. Midnight mass is celebrated with particular solemnity in Santa Maria Maggiore and in Santa Maria d'Aracoeli. In St Peter's Square the Pope's blessing, *Urbi et Orbi*, is bestowed.

Basic Information

BUSINESS HOURS
MUSEUMS, ARCHAEOLOGICAL SITES AND GARDENS
Many, but not all, museums are closed Mondays (the Colosseum, Foro Romano and the Foro Palatino remain open); on other days ticket offices usually shut 1hr before closing time. Ancient monuments, archaeological sites and public parks (Roman Forum, Colosseum, etc.) close about 1hr before dusk, according to the following timetable:
Many museums require visitors to leave bags and backpacks in a luggage deposit area. Flash photography is usually forbidden.

Attention – Many museums are closed on holidays and reduce their opening hours, such as on December 24th-25th and august 14th. Be sure to check the opening hours in advance.

DISCOUNTS
The **Where to Stay** section details budget options, including B&Bs, *pensioni*, youth hostels, campsites, and convents and monasteries.
If you plan to visit Rome's archeological attractions, the following discount passes are available *(all valid 7 consecutive days, unless otherwise stated)*:
Roma Archeologica card *(€25)* covers the Colosseum, Forum, Palatine and Palatine Museum, Baths of Caracalla, Museo Nazionale Romano, Tomb of Cecilia Metella and the Villa dei Quintili. *(www.060608.it)*
Appia Antica card *(€12)* covers Baths of Caracalla, Tomb of Cecilia Metella and the Villa dei Quintili. *(www.coopculture.it)*
Roma Pass Three-day Roma Pass or Two day Roma Pass *(€38.50 and €28)* provides free access to the first archaeological site or museum (Two day pass one only), reduced entrance on others and free public transport, excluding to and from the airport. *(www.romapass.it)*.
Pratomusei card *(€16)* covers Centro per l'Arte Contemporanea Luigi Pecci, Museo del Tessuto, Museo di Palazzo Pretorio, Musei Diocesani.

S.u.p.e.r tickets… Seven Unique Places to Experience in Rome
The S.U.P.E.R., Seven Unique Places to Experience in Rome, is a new sightseeing experience. The ticket gives access to an itinerary organized by the Parco archeologico del Colosseo, that includes entry to the Colosseum, the Forum, Palatine Hill, the Neronian Cryptoporticus and the Palatine Museum. Visitors will immerse themselves in the Roman world and its art thanks to new technologies and virtual narration.

AIRLINES

Several airlines, such as those below, offer budget fares to Rome and other destinations in Italy, although prices vary according to how far in advance the reservation is made.

- **easyJet**:
  www.easyjet.com
- **German Wings**:
  www.germanwings.com
- **Ryanair**:
  www.ryanair.com

TRAIN

The **Carta Verde** (*€40, valid for a year*) gives travellers age 12–26 a 10 percent discount in both first and second class, including wagon lits and couchettes, on all trains within Italy, and in conjunction with the RAILPLUS scheme, up to 25 percent off when travelling around Europe, including fast Eurocity trains for all participating national train companies as long as the journey spans two countries. For travellers over 60 years of age (free for 75 years and over), the **Carta d'Argento** (*€30, valid for a year*) offers a 15 percent discount in first and second class on the Italian section of all routes (10 percent off wagon lits and couchettes) and, in conjunction with the RAILPLUS scheme, 25 percent off international connections, as per the Carte Verde (www.trenitalia.com, section Special offers).

FOR FAMILIES AND SMALL GROUPS

Train

Families and groups of at least three people and no more than five (of whom at least one is an adult and one a child younger than 14 years) are entitled to a 20 percent discount in both first and second class if they are travelling together. Children aged between four and 14 travel at half-price of the discounted fare and children under four travel free.

ELECTRICITY

The voltage is 220V, 50 cycles per second, with a two-pin plug. Pack an adaptor for hairdryers, shavers, computers, etc. North American visitors may need a transformer for appliances beyond a laptop. Seek out an electrical or hardware store (*ferramenta*).

EMERGENCIES

- **112**: General number for all kind of danger.
- **113**: General emergency services (*soccorso pubblico di emergenza*); to be called in cases of real danger.
- **115**: Fire Brigade (*vigili del fuoco*).
- **118**: Emergency Health Services (*emergenza sanitaria*).
- **06 46 861**: Central police station.
- **1515**: Forest Fire Service. Environmental emergencies.
- **803 116**: Automobile Club d'Italia Emergency Breakdown Service.

EMERGENCY NUMBERS	
Polizia Municipale	06 67 691
ATAC Lost Property	06 67 693214
Ambulance – Red Cross	118
American Hospital	06 22 551
San Camillo Hospital	06 58 701
Children's Hospital/ Bambin Gesù	06 68 591
San Carlo Hospital	06 39 701

INTERNET

Rome has firmly entered the cyber age over the past few years, and surfers can now use free city-subsidised wireless Internet throughout much of the central area and main parks.

MONEY

The unit of currency is the **euro** which is issued in notes (€5, €10, €20, €50, €100 and €200) and in coins (1 cent,

2 cents, 5 cents, 10 cents, 20 cents, 50 cents, €1 and €2).

BANKS

Banks are usually open Monday to Friday, 8:30am–1:30pm and 2:30pm–4pm. Some branches open in the city centre and shopping centres on Saturday mornings, but most are closed on Saturdays, Sundays and public holidays. Most hotels will change travellers' cheques.
Money can be changed in post offices (except travellers' cheques), money-changing bureaux and at railway stations and airports. Commission is always charged.

CREDIT CARDS

Payment by credit card is widespread in shops, hotels and restaurants (although some smaller *trattoria* may not accept plastic – check before ordering) and in petrol stations. Money may also be withdrawn from a bank or from ATM, but may incur interest pending repayment.

NEWSPAPERS

The main Roman newspapers (available throughout Italy) are *la Repubblica*, *Il Messaggero* and *Corriere della Sera.* The *Osservatore Romano* is the official newspaper of the Vatican City. Foreign newspapers are widely available throughout the city.

PHARMACIES

These are identified by a red-and-white or emerald-neon cross. When closed, each advertises the names of the pharmacy on duty and a list of doctors on call. Central 24-hour pharmacies include: Piazza dei Cinquecento 51, Piazza Barberini 49 and Via Nazionale 228. For up-to-the-minute info: farmaturni.federfarmaroma.com.

POST/MAIL

Post offices are open from 8:20am–1:35 or 3:00pm (Sat until 1pm). The main post office is open until 7:05pm; letters sent **poste restante** (*fermo posta*) arrive here.

PUBLIC HOLIDAYS

In addition to the usual Italian public and religious holidays listed below, Rome celebrates 21 April (the birth of Rome) and 29 June, the feast day of St Peter and St Paul, the patron saints of the city.
A working day is *un giorno feriale; giorni festivi* include Sundays and the following public holidays.

January	1 (New Year); 6 (Epiphany)
Easter	Sunday and Monday (lunedì dell'Angelo)
April	25 (St Mark's Day and liberation in 1945)
May	1 (Festa dei Lavoratori, Labour holiday)
June	2 (Republic of Italy holiday); 29 (The Feast of St Peter and St Paul, patron saints of Rome)
August	15 (The Assumption – Ferragosto)
November	1 (All Saints – Tutti i Santi)
December	8 (Immaculate Conception), 25 and 26 (Christmas and St Stephen's Day).

TAXES AND TIPPING

Like every EU country, Italy imposes a sales **tax** on most goods and services. The *Imposta sul Valore Aggiunto* (IVA), currently 22 percent with some reductions to 12 percent, lurks unseen, part and parcel of the bill.
Visitors from non-EU countries can reclaim IVA on merchandise over €50 for one year.
Tipping in Italian restaurants is not expected, as they often charge a *coperto*, or service charge. If you wish, tip about 5 percent in a *pizzeria* or humble *trattoria*, or just round up to the nearest euro. The rate should rise in posher places, but never top 10 percent. For taxi drivers, round up to the nearest euro. For bar service or porters, a €1 will not appear offensive.

TELEPHONES

Since June 2017, all roaming fees have been removed throughout the European Union. A European tourist travelling in another country of the Union is thus not charged additionally for phone calls, SMS and Internet connection.

CELL/MOBILE PHONES

Telecom Italia Mobile (TIM, www.tim.it), Vodafone (www.vodafone.it), Wind (www.wind.it) and 3 (www.tre.it) are the major mobile companies in Italy.

AREA CODES

It is now mandatory to dial the area code (06 for Rome), even when making a local call. For international calls dial 00 plus the following country codes:

- ✆ **61** for Australia
- ✆ **1** for Canada
- ✆ **64** for New Zealand
- ✆ **44** for the UK
- ✆ **1** for the USA

If calling from outside the country, the international code for Italy is +39 For Rome dial +39 (0)6 xx xx…

PUBLIC PHONES

Telephone cards *(sold in post offices and tobacconists)* and telephone credit cards ("Call It", issued free, *www.telecomitalia.it*, section "carte telefoniche") are accepted in call boxes. To make a call: lift the receiver, insert payment, await dial signal, punch in the number and wait for a response.

USEFUL NUMBERS

Telecom Italia's Customer Service:
✆ 187.

TIME

The time in Italy is the same as mainland Europe *(one hour ahead of the United Kingdom)* and changes during the last weekend in March and October between summer time (*ora legale*) and winter time (*ora solare*).

TOBACCONISTS

Tabacchi (sign with a white T on a black background) sell postcards, stamps, phone cards and public transport tickets in addition to cigarettes.

USEFUL WORDS AND NUMBERS

	Translation
si, no	yes, no
Signore	Sir
Signora	Madam
Signorina	Miss
oggi	today
ieri	yesterday
domani mattina	tomorrow morning
mattina	morning
sera	evening
pomeriggio	afternoon
per favore	please
grazie tante	thank you very much
mi scusi	excuse me
basta	enough
buon giorno	good morning
arrivederci	goodbye
quanto?	how much?
dove? quando?	where? when?
dov'è?	where is?
molto, poco	much, little
più, meno	more, less
tutto, tutti	all
grande	large
piccolo	small
caro	dear
la strada per ...?	the road to ...?
si può visitare?	may one visit?
che ora è?	what time is it?
non capisco	I don't understand
desidero	I would like
zero	0
uno	1
due	2
tre	3
quattro	4
cinque	5
sei	6
sette	7
otto	8
nove	9
dieci	10

Castel Sant'Angelo
© sborisov/Fotolia.com

The City Today

Rome has seen widespread and uncontrolled urban expansion since World War II, and increased traffic that has, in turn, threatened its ancient monuments. Preserving the cultural heritage remains a hot topic for city hall problem solvers. However, Rome's mille-feuille of historical layers continues to provide the backdrop to the city's modern bustle, as befits the Eternal City.

THE ETERNAL CITY

Rome had to double in size to fulfil its modern role as capital of a united Italy (since 1870). Architects used concrete, metal and glass to house its population, construct administrative buildings, and improve its traffic flow.

Italy's capital is not a quick study. The metropolis struts and shouts like Napoleon, languidly simmers like Sophia Loren and, then – just as the kaleidoscope shifts towards a coherent pattern – slips into business mode, shrewd-tongued and silk-suited. Rome is ephemeral, enigmatic. Small wonder early residents revered Janus, the two-faced ancient God of new beginnings, who looks forwards, while peering back. The Eternal City, solid on the bedrock of history, reinvents itself daily.

Eleanor Clark best captured the chaos, contradictions and coquetry of this city in her 1950s classic, *Rome and a Villa*. "The ordinary traveller," she observed, "runs off in relief to Florence, to the single statement, the single moment of time, the charming unity of somewhat prison-like architecture, and is aware later of having retained from his tour of Rome some stirring around the heart, those images, huge, often grotesque, were what he had been looking for, only it would have taken so long..."

A VISIBLE PAST

Rome's many famous monuments continue to delight tourists: the Pantheon and Forum, the majestic Colosseum, St Peter's, the Spanish Steps, the Trevi Fountain and the Villa Borghese, to name a few. The **ancient ruins** form the backbone of this stunning landscape; scattered around the city, these are often hemmed in by modern buildings. Their survival is amazing; armies repeatedly sacked Rome during the Middle Ages and in the past, the citizens themselves have torn down structures and even put cows to pasture in the Forum.

Others colonized the old temples and amphitheatres, building onto their tiers. Churches and monuments often have multiple layers, each dating to a different historical period. The best example is the basilica of San Clemente sul Celio, built in the 4C on Republican-era foundations, then reconstructed in the 12C, and modified in the 18C.

Another important characteristic of Rome is its old villas, where noble families once lived far from the plebeian crowds. Now public parks, the gardens of the Villa Borghese, Villa Doria and Villa Ada provide an attractive and essential splash of greenery.

Although Rome still operates under the emblem of the wolf and the old Republican formula SPQR (*Senatus Populusque Romanus*), not much remains of the marble glory of Augustus and the emperors. The Renaissance and Baroque have both left their marks, mainly as a consequence of the architectural ambition of many of the popes. And the modern citizens overlay it all with Vespas, fashion billboards, football flags and minimalist chic constructions.

Still, the Eternal City remains poetic and potent – dangerously so. As the poet Henry Wadsworth Longfellow warned: "Tis the centre to which all gravitates. One finds no rest elsewhere than here. There may be other cities that please us for a while, but Rome alone completely satisfies. It becomes to all a second native land by predilection, and not by accident of birth alone."

GOVERNMENT AND ECONOMY

Industrial growth in the area around Rome grew with post-war vigour, and local industries included textiles, paper

Piazza Navona

and metal products, which survive today. Since the 1930s, cinema has also played its part in the city's economy, with Cinecitta studios, known as the Italian Hollywood, producing most Italian movies and television programmes. The modern Roman economy, however, is now largely dominated by tourism and government operations, as the seat of the Italian Parliament. The city government is currently headed up by Mayor Gianni Alemanno.

Although Papal power has declined, the Holy See remains the focal point for world Catholicism. The fortified Vatican City, lying within the city limits, has been recognized as an independent state by the Italian government since 1929, with a Sovereign Pope. As of January 2009 the Pope divorced the Vatican State from Italian law, and now has supreme authority over which laws it will abide by.

TOURISM

Rome is the third most visited tourist destination in the EU. Visit during August and you may be hard pressed to find a Roman to talk to amid the swathes of tourists pounding the piazzas. As one of Europe's most popular tourist spots since the days of the Grand Tour, Rome is used to welcoming visitors and pilgrims. As such, its tourist infrastructure is good, all the better for a spruce up of some of it's oldest museums over the past few years, and with plenty of hotels and restaurants for all budgets and preferences. Tourists would do well to see Rome on a Roman schedule – mornings and late afternoons are the times for activity, with many shops and trattorias closing for an afternoon nap. A bugbear for visitors and Romans alike though is transport, with a congested road system and limited tram and Metro. Crime against tourists is low, but watch out for pickpockets – especially on the infamous 64 bus route and on the Metro.

PEOPLE AND POPULATION

2016 census; 2,865,945 (estimate).

When in Rome do as the Romans do, as the cliche goes, and that means throwing away your shyness and self-deprecation. Romans are an abundantly confident group of people; small wonder with the weight of 500 years of Caput Mundi on their side. You can sense the sense of implacable local entitlement in the way that cars and pedestrians face off with equal bravado at road crossings and passionate, animated conversations are held at top volume around you. There's no place like Rome for the Romans; it's bigger, better, more beautiful and certainly more stylish than anywhere else – something the marked absence of anything resembling casual sportswear on anyone but a tourist bears out. But most importantly, larger-than-life Romans are notably warm, welcoming and sociable

39

people who will happily pass the time of day, laugh, flirt or try to follow your faltering attempts at Italian with equal good humour.

FOOD AND DRINK

Like the city itself, the flavours of Roman cooking are rich and robust, heavy on sauces, meat and hearty bean stews, in a rustic local cuisine based on peasant food. Carnivores can chomp down with gusto – palma ham (saltimbocca), fried sweatbreads and milk-fed lamb (abbacchio) are local specialities, while sea bass (spigola) and fried cod (baccala) are popular fish alternatives. Gnocci and pasta dishes are garnished with vegetables such as artichokes, and washed down with the area's best-known wines, those of the surrounding Castelli Romani region, commonly known as Frascati. And whether upmarket restaurant or trattoria, food will inevitably be sourced locally, and served with the relaxed respect that befits the birthplace of the Slow Food Movement (borne out of a mid-1980s protest against the opening of a McDonalds by the Spanish Steps). For food on the run, the holy trinity of the Italian diet, wafer light pizza, strong coffee and delicious gelato (ice cream) are found in every corner of the city.

History

According to legend, Aeneas, the heroic founder of Rome, was the son of Venus. Such divine origins helped to give credence to the city's grandiose destiny and its position as the "capital of the world".
The decadence of the Empire led to the rise and fall of Rome, and despite becoming the cornerstone of the Christian world, the city was repeatedly sacked by barbarian tribes during the early Middle Ages. Restored to its former splendour during the era of the Papal States, Rome was finally declared the capital of a united Italy in 1870.

ORIGIN AND GROWTH

Before the Empire, before even the Etruscans, the peninsula was home to elephants, hippopotamuses, rhinoceroses – and the first Italians. *Homo erectus* roamed this landscape from around 200 000 BC.
By 10 000 BC, more advanced humans displaced Neanderthals; most likely Cro-Magnons, who had fire, but no herds or agriculture. They dabbed crude art onto their cavern-homes, including the Grotto Polesini near Tivoli.
In Neolithic times, farmers and herders built clusters of huts, wove fabrics and cast pots. They were recognizably Mediterranean: short and narrow-headed. After 2 000 BC, this stock mixed with round-headed alpine people from central Europe.
Regional cultures emerged between 1 000–800 BC. The southern Villanovans occupied the site of Rome. They hammered bronze armour, fought with iron weapons and lived in round homes. Other tribes – mostly speaking Indo-European dialects – dwelt nearby, including the Oscans, Sabines, Latins and Umbrians.
The Tiber's left bank – eroded lava-flows from the Alban Hills (**Monti Albani**) – provided excellent defensive positions: particularly the Palatine. It rose steeply from the surrounding marsh with a clear view of the Tiber. This site was, moreover, an ideal staging post on the salt road (**Via Salaria**).

ROME'S LEGENDARY ORIGINS

According to Livy in his *Roman History* and the Greek historian Dionysius of Halicarnassus in his *Early Roman History*, Aeneas, son of the goddess Venus and the mortal Anchises, fled from Troy as it fell. He landed at the Tiber's mouth and married Lavinia, the king of Latium's daughter. After his death, his son Ascanius (or Iulus) left to found Alba Longa (see Index). The last king of this Alban dynasty was Amulius, who deposed his brother Numitor and forced the latter's daughter, Rhea Silvia, to become a Vestal Virgin. Raped by the god Mars, she birthed the twins **Romulus** and **Remus,** whom Amulius set adrift on the Tiber. The basket carrying the infants washed up at the foot of the Palatine where they were nursed by a wolf and brought up by shepherds.

As ambitious adults, they decided to found a city. A dispute about sites and bird omens led to fratricide. Romulus alone founded the city on 21 April 753 BC, and populated it with outlaws who settled on the Capitoline (*See CAM-PIDOGLIO – CAPITOLINO*). Females were in short supply. So the first king threw a party, invited the local tribes and stole their daughters; this "Rape of the Sabine Women" later became an overly popular theme in classical art.

A succession of kings followed, alternately Sabine and Latin, until the arrival of the Etruscans.

THE ETRUSCANS

A band of 12 city states flourished from the 8C–3C BC. Brilliant urban planners, they transformed villages into city grids with temples, roads and drained fields. Their rock-cut theatres, tunnels and tombs honeycomb central Italy.

The Etruscans' origin is much disputed; some even suggest this high civilization was Atlantis. Skilful jewellers, they cast metal sculptures (including the **Capitoline Wolf, Rome's symbol**), as well as painting frescoes and black clay pots. The last three rulers were Etruscan and steadied the upstart city, at least initially. **Lucius Tarquinius Priscus** introduced drainpipes and games. **Servius Tullius** reorganized the army, bolstered the middle classes and encouraged a basic political assembly. This peace exploded in 510, when Romans expelled the tyrant **Tarquin Superbus**. The trigger for this was unclear: power struggles or grain shortage, perhaps. Legend points the finger at his son's rape of a pious wife, who then committed suicide (The Rape of Lucretia).

Try as they might, the Etruscans couldn't retake Rome. Unable to reach their southern settlements, the city-states dwindled. A 474 BC defeat at Cumae crushed their naval supremacy. Bullied by Celtic tribes to the north, the Etruscans were conquered by the Romans; Volsinii fell last in 265 BC.

Greek and Latin accounts claim moral superiority over the "debauched" people. Yet politics probably undermined the Etruscan League: internecine strife, cruelty towards peasants, elite snobbery and perhaps just a little ruling-class corruption towards the end.

Many mourn the passing of this quick-silver artistic empire, which once nearly united the Italian peninsula. DH Lawrence, author of the classic 1932 travelogue *Etruscan Places*, rhapsodized about "the long-nosed, sensitive-footed, subtly smiling Etruscans, who made so little noise outside the cypress groves".

"Italy to-day is far more Etruscan in its pulse than Roman: and will always be so. The Etruscan element is like the grass of the field and the sprouting of the corn, in Italy: it will always be so. Why try to revert to the Latin-Roman mechanism and suppression?"

THE MONARCHY (753–509 BC)

753   Legendary foundation of Rome by **Romulus** on the Palatine Hill.

715–616   Reigns of three Sabine kings Numa Pompilius, Tullus Hostilius and Ancus Martius.

616–509   Etruscan hegemony: Tarquin the Elder, who laid out the Forum, Servius Tullius and Tarquin the Proud.

THE REPUBLIC (510–27 BC)

Tradition dates the Republic to 510 BC. Citizens expelled the ruling Tarquins, and granted executive and military power to two consuls, elected annually. The **Senate**, formed by the old patrician families, had a purely advisory role. **Praetors** bore judicial power, while **aediles** and **quaestors carried out**

INTRODUCTION TO ROME

administrative and financial tasks; all these officials served for one year.

The city divided into two ordines: the **patricians** (aristocrats "able to trace their ancestors") and the **plebeians**, who were forbidden to assume political or priestly office, or to marry "up". Inevitably, these groups clashed. The patricians saw their privileges gradually reduced over the years and a new mixed ruling class, known as the *nobilitas*, formed at the end of the 4C. The last prohibitions to fall were those relating to censorship and religious offices.

The patricians controlled many slaves, who formed the most wretched section of society, but who could be freed and become *liberti*. A boss–supplicant system – known as *clientela* – emerged during this period. A patron gave his clients financial or political assistance, and they returned this support during elections and tribunals.

This period saw Roman expansion within the Italian peninsula and across the Mediterranean. As the army grew in importance, so did the power of the men behind it. Its generals struggled for dominance throughout the late Republican period.

Proconsuls administered – and often plundered – the conquered provinces. During the Empire, the consuls' powers were united in one person, an emperor. Many later claimed divinity to reinforce their right to rule.

494   Rome leaves the Latin League. First plebeians' secession. They obtain a magistrature to defend their rights (tribunate of the plebeians).

451–449   The city codifies civil and penal laws in the **Twelve Tables**, described by Cicero as "the very height and pinnacle of the law".

396   Romans capture Etruscan Veia, which controlled the River Tiber, after a 10-year siege.

390   Invasions by the Gauls and Roman defeat on the River Allia. Sacking and burning of Rome (See CAMPIDOGLIO–CAPITOLINO).

367   Plebeians granted access to consulship, reform of magistrature of censorship, and proposal for the distribution of territorial areas to citizens (*ager publicus*).

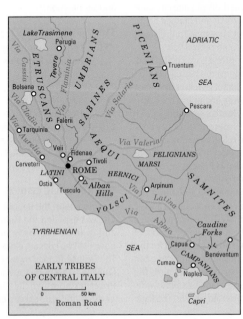

EARLY TRIBES OF CENTRAL ITALY

343–341 Rome forms alliances with Greek cities of the Campania region. This leads to the **First Samnite War**.

326–304 **Second Samnite War**. Rome suffers the famous defeat of the **Claudine Forks**. Tactical reform of the legions (into groups of 60 men) guarantees Rome a partial victory.

312 Appius Claudius Caecus, writer and orator, becomes censor. Construction of the first section of the Appian Way.

298–290 **Third Samnite War**; Rome defeats the combined armies of the Samnites, Etruscans, Gauls and Umbrians at the battle of Sentinum, in the present-day Marche region. The victory brings central Italy under Roman control.

282–272 The capture of Tarentum – the last powerful Greek *polis* on the peninsula – brings the Romans into contact with the Hellenic culture.

264–241 **First Punic War** between Rome and **Carthage**. After fierce fighting on land and at sea, Rome captures Sicily, with its prosperous cities, and the island becomes the first province governed by a *propraetor*. A few years later, Rome conquers Sardinia.

218–201 **Second Punic War** and march by Hannibal from Spain to Italy (elephants over the Alps!). **Hannibal** defeats the Romans in Ticinus, Trebia, Lake Trasimene, and Cannae, not far from Venosa. The Roman counter-offensive chases the Carthaginians out of Spain and prevents supplies from reaching Hannibal's army. **Scipio Africanus** (a young general from the noble Cornelii Scipiones family) settles in Sicily; from here he extends the fighting to Africa. Hannibal, summoned home, is defeated by the army of Scipio Africanus at Naraggara-Zama. The peace treaty gives the Romans control over the western section of the Mediterranean basin. The destructive war has far-reaching consequences in Italy, such as an influx of slaves, the destruction of small peasant farms, and an increase in the urban population, as food funnelled into Rome.

201 The first comedies of Plautus.

197–168 War in the east against the Hellenistic states of Macedonia, the Seleucids in Asia Minor and the Syrian–Mesopotamian region.

179 Construction of a wooden theatre. (Pompey builds the first stone version in 55.)

148–146 **Third Punic War**: capture and destruction of Carthage.

133–121 The brothers **Tiberius** and **Caius Gracchus**, both plebeian tribunes, inspire social and economic reforms. Angered, the Senate orders their assassinations.

111–105 War against Jugurtha of Numidia. The continuous strife and probable corruption of senators weakened the Roman republic. Two famous generals are victorious: **Caius Marius**, consul for the first time in 107, and Lucius **Sulla**.

91–88 War between Rome and its Italian allies, who demanded Roman citizenship. After much violent fighting, the toughest rebels are defeated, although citizenship is awarded to all Italian peoples.

88 **First Civil War** between the Senate (nobility) and people (*populares*). Lucius Sulla, supporter of the Senate and the *nobilitas*, is deprived of supreme command of the war against Mithridates in favour of **Marius**, a supporter of the *populares*. After marching on

Rome to silence the *populares*, Sulla earns the war command.

87 Sulla departs. Caius Marius and Cornelius Cinna establish the rule of the *populares*.

84 Sulla returns and defeats Cinna (Marius was killed in 86). The following year, Sulla assumes dictatorial powers: exiles have no recourse to law, and their killers can claim their property. Fear, loathing and bloodshed ensue.

82–79 Sulla reforms the Republic. The Senate is strengthened and the powers of the plebeian tribunes reduced. Sulla retires from public life and dies the following year. He was described by one of his biographers as a frustrated monarch: unlike Augustus, he did not actually abolish the Republican political system.

73–70 **Licinius Crassus**, a rich businessman, is elected consul in 70 with **Pompey**, after putting down the slave revolt led by Spartacus (6 000 prisoners crucified). Pompey is away fighting Mithridates and pirates until 62.

63 **Catiline Conspiracy**, secretly supported by Caesar. The conspiracy is put down by the consul, Cicero, the champion of the agreement drawn up between senators and *equites* (which included businessmen and speculators). Catiline is killed in battle near Pistoia.

60 **First Triumvirate**, a private agreement between Crassus, Pompey and Caesar is signed at Lucca. The following year Caesar is elected consul.

58–52 Caesar's campaign against the **Gauls**, followed by his conquest of Britain and fighting against Germanic tribes. Troubles in Asia Minor, where in 54 Crassus is defeated and killed by the Parthians near Carrhae in Upper Mesopotamia.

49–45 Civil war between Caesar and Pompey.

49 Caesar becomes dictator.

48 Assassination of Pompey, who had taken refuge at the court of the Ptolemy in Egypt.

44 Assassination of Caesar on the **Ides of March** (15 March).

VENI, VIDI, VICI

Gaius Julius Caesar (100–44 BC)
Soldier and statesman, orator and writer (*The Gallic Wars* and *The Civil War*) – was instrumental in the establishment of the Roman Empire. A supporter of the *popu-*

Augustus and His Achievements

Gaius Julius Caesar Octavianus was the first Roman Emperor, and remains among the most important. Shipwrecked in Hispania, the teen crossed hostile territory to rejoin Julius Caesar. Impressed, the ruler adopted his great-nephew. After the Ides of March – that fateful assassination – Octavius, though just 18, pushed for his inheritance. Seven years later, he had eliminated the competition, right down to the lovers Cleopatra and Mark Antony.

In 27 BC, he offered to return power to the Roman Senate. They named him *princeps* (first leader) and Augustus ("grower"). He grew into a model leader, who inspired reform in politics, religion and the arts. As Historian Paul Zanker says: "Following the long, dark years of civil war, the Romans enjoyed 45 years of peace and security. Monarchy had at last brought orderly government to the vast empire, bread and circuses to the Roman plebs, and a tremendous boost to the economy. The Romans looked out at their empire filled with a powerful sense of mission," he wrote in *The Power of Images in the Age of Augustus*.

Julius Caesar Octavianus

©ROMAOSLO/iStockphoto.com

lares, he proved his outstanding political abilities while he was still very young. In 58 Caesar became Governor of Cisalpine Gaul and of Provincia (now Provence); by 51 he had conquered the whole of Gaul, at the cost of perhaps a million lives. In January 49, he crossed the Rubicon (the boundary across which armies were not supposed to tread) and marched on Rome and its officials; Pompey, who had been sole consul since 52, and the Senate fled. Civil war followed. Pompey's army was defeated at Pharsalus in Thessaly, Pompey himself was murdered in Alexandria and his supporters fell in Africa and Spain.

Early in 44, Caesar appointed himself consul and dictator for life; he gave his name to the month of his birth (July), pardoned his enemies and weakened the power of the senators by reducing their number to 900. On 15 March 44 BC (the Ides of March), while planning a campaign against the Parthians, he was stabbed to death by a group of senators in the Curia Pompeia.

43   **Second Triumvirate** established: the young **Octavian** (Caesar's great-nephew and adopted heir, who took the name Gaius Julius Caesar Octavian – later "Augustus"), **Mark Antony** (Caesar's fellow consul) and **Lepidus**. Antony is assigned the east, Octavian the west and Lepidus Africa. Assassination of Cicero, who had attacked Antony in public debates.

31   **Battle of Actium** (not far from Patras) between the troops of Octavian and those of Mark Antony (aligned politically – and romantically – with Cleopatra, Queen of Egypt). The lovers commit suicide; Octavian annexes Egypt to Rome and proclaims himself successor to the Ptolemy dynasty.

THE ROMAN EMPIRE
JULIO–CLAUDIAN DYNASTY (27 BC–AD 69)

27   The Senate grants Octavian the title **Augustus** (from the Latin "*augere*" – "to grow").

14 BC   Augustus dies at Nola having witnessed the premature death of many family members. He is succeeded by **Tiberius**, the son of his wife Livia, distinguished for his military achievements in Germany and Pannonia. Proud of his family tradition (he belonged to the noble Claudian family), this introvert retired to Capri towards the end of his life (27 AD). The historian Tacitus was one of his most fierce detractors.

45

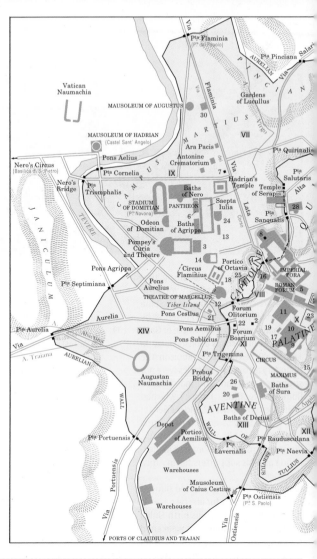

ROME DURING THE EMPIRE

Amphitheatrum Castrense	V
Antonine Crematorium	IX
Ara Pacis	IX
Arch of Constantine	XI 1
Arch of Janus	XI 2
Arx	VIII 4
Augustan Crematorium	IX 30
Augustan Naumachia	XIV
Basilica of Constantine	IV 5
Basilica of Neptune	IX 6
Baths of Agrippa	IX
Baths of Caracalla	XII
Baths of Constantine	VI 28
Baths of Decius	XIII
Baths of Diocletian	VI
Baths of Helena	V
Baths of Nero	IX
Baths of Sura	XIII
Baths of Titus	III 29
Baths of Trajan	III
Circus Flaminius	IX
Circus Maximus	XI
Colosseum	III
Column of Marcus Aurelius	IX 7
Depot	XIII
Domus Augustana	X 9
Domus Aurea	III
Domus Flavia	X 10
Forum Boarium	XI
Forum Olitorium	VIII-IX-XI
Gardens of Lamia and Maia	V
Gardens of Licinius	V
Gardens of Lucullus	VII
Gardens of Maecenas	III
Gardens of Sallust	VI
Hadrian's Temple	IX
Imperial Fora	IV-VI-VIII
Largo Argentina Sacred Precinct	IX 3
Ludus Magnus	II
Mausoleum of Augustus	IX
Mausoleum of Caius Cestius	XIII

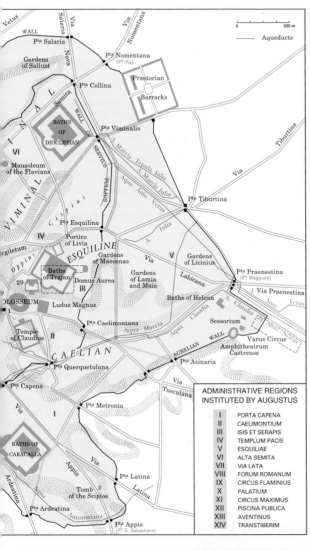

ADMINISTRATIVE REGIONS
INSTITUTED BY AUGUSTUS

I	PORTA CAPENA
II	CAELIMONTIUM
III	ISIS ET SERAPIS
IV	TEMPLUM PACIS
V	ESQUILIAE
VI	ALTA SEMITA
VII	VIA LATA
VIII	FORUM ROMANUM
IX	CIRCUS FLAMINIUS
X	PALATIUM
XI	CIRCUS MAXIMUS
XII	PISCINA PUBLICA
XIII	AVENTINUS
XIV	TRANSTIBERIM

Mausoleum of Flavians	VI	Porta Ardeatina	I-XII	Porta Pinciana	VI-VII
Mausoleum of Hadrian	IX	Porta Asinaria	II-V	Porta Portuensis	XIV
Nero's Bridge	IX-XIV	Porta Aurelia	XIV	Porta Praenestina	V
Nero's Circus	IX	Porta Caelimontana	II-III	Porta Querquetulana	II
Odeon of Domitian	IX	Porta Capena	I-XII	Porta Quirinalis	VI
Pantheon	IX	Porta Collina	VI	Porta Raudusculana	XII-XIII
Pompey's Curia	IX	Porta Cornelia	IX	Porta Salaria	VI
Pons Aelius	IX	Porta Esquilina	III-IV	Porta Salutaris	VI-VII
Pons Aemilius	IX-XIV	Porta Flaminia	VII-IX	Porta Sanqualis	VI-VII
Pons Agrippa	XI-XIV	Porta Latina	I	Porta Septimiana	XIV
Pons Aurelius	IX-XIV	Porta Lavernalis	XIII	Porta Tiburtina	V
Pons Cestius	XIV	Porta Metronia	I-II	Porta Trigemina	XI-XIV
Pons Fabricius	IX-XIV 12	Porta Naevia	XII	Porta Triomphalis	IX
Pons Sublicius	XI-XIV	Porta Nomentana	VI	Porta Viminalis	IV-VI
Porta Appia	I	Porta Ostiensis	XII-XIII	Portico of Aemilius	XIII

47

AD 30 **Jesus of Nazareth**, known as Christ, is condemned to death.

37–41 **Caligula** as *princeps* (head of State). He suffers from bouts of madness, but is determined to wield absolute power as Emperor, moving away from the compromise with Republican ideals achieved by Augustus. He is assassinated.

41–54 **Claudius**, Caligula's uncle and a scholar of the Etruscan civilisation, assumes power. Britain annexed to the Empire. Some of Claudius's freed slaves, very loyal to him, are appointed in official posts. The reaction of the Senate is violent. **Seneca** is one of the victims of repression and is exiled to the island of Corsica.

54–68 **Nero** as Emperor. Declared Emperor after Caligula, Claudius wed Agrippina, then adopted her son **Nero**.

Nero

©Imagestate/Tips Images

Rumour claims she assassinated her husband, making her dotty offspring *princeps*. Nero's tutor Seneca succeeded in controlling the young Emperor's behaviour for the first five years, tempering his more absolute tendencies. The repression of a senatorial conspiracy led to the suicide of Seneca and to violent and authoritarian behaviour by the Emperor. His diplomatic successes (the annexing of Armenia to the Roman Empire) did nothing to dispel the general level of discontent. Violent persecution of the Christians took place in 64, followed by the famous fire. The German legions rebelled and imposed Sulpicius Galba as the new Emperor. Following this, Nero committed suicide.

69 Succession disputed. Galba is followed by the prefect of Lusitania, Otho, who is in turn defeated and forced to commit suicide by Vitellius. Vitellius is challenged by Flavius Vespasian and **civil war** breaks out in the city of Rome. The Campidoglio fire damaged the Temple of Jupiter: a highly sacrilegious act.

FLAVIAN EMPERORS (AD 70–96)

69–79 After much destruction and a year of civil war, **Flavius Vespasian** – head of a troop responsible for putting down the Jewish revolt – is proclaimed Emperor. This skilful administrator restores the finances of the state and promulgates the *Lex de imperio*, which sets out the powers of the *princeps* (head of State) for the first time. He promotes the construction of public works, such as the huge Flavian Amphitheatre, now known as the **Colosseum**.

79–81 **Titus**, Vespasian's eldest son, becomes Emperor. In 79, Vesuvius erupts, destroying Herculaneum, Stabia and Pompeii. **Pliny the Elder** dies while valiantly attempting to rescue the victims.

81–96 Titus's brother, **Domitian**, becomes Emperor. He advocates anti-Senate policies, carries out military offensives in the Germanic regions and in Dacia with little success, and instigates the persecution of the Christians in 93. A conspiracy leads to his assassination.

Statue of Marcus Aurelius in Piazza del Campidoglio

©D. Chapuis/Michelin

ANTONINE EMPERORS AND ADOPTED HEIRS

96–98 **Nerva**, a former senator, becomes Emperor. Nerva is responsible for inaugurating the procedure of emperors to nominate their successor.

98–117 **Marcus Ulpius Trajan** is elected Roman Emperor.

117–38 **Hadrian** becomes Emperor. He promotes peace, abandoning Mesopotamia and fortifying the boundaries *(limes)* of the Empire. A cultured and passionate Hellenist, he travelled widely, spending time in Africa and Asia Minor. His reign was blighted by a serious Jewish revolt in Palestine, Egypt and Cyrene (131–35).

138–61 A long period of peace under the reign of **Antoninus Pius**. During this period Rome had a population of around one million, a figure exceeded only by imperial Peking.

161–80 Reign of **Marcus Aurelius**, a Stoic philosopher and statesman who wrote a philosophical work in Greek, entitled *Meditations*. After a campaign against the

Trajan – The Best of Emperors

Marcus Ulpius Trajan was a Spaniard of Italian descent, and was the first Emperor to come from the provinces. Intelligent and energetic, he was described as the best of Emperors *(optimus princeps)*. He carried out great public works such as building a forum with markets and two libraries (one Greek and one Latin), enlarging the ports of Ostia and Ancona, and constructing a bridge in Alcantara and an aqueduct in Segovia, both in Spain. In Italy, he instituted the *alimenta* for children, the first major example of social spending. His conquests in Dacia brought gold and slaves to Rome and helped to improve the economy of the Empire. He also led campaigns against the Parthians and penetrated as far as the Persian Gulf to enable the Empire to profit from the trade between the Far East and the Mediterranean. Other campaigns included those against the Nabataean kingdom and the capture of the capital Petra, an important commercial centre on the caravan route. In 117 he died of exhaustion while returning to Rome.

49

Parthians, he faced the German tribes (Quadi and Marcomanni) in the Upper Danube region.

180–92 Reign of **Commodus**, son of Marcus Aurelius. Commodus was immature and not very capable; he was killed by a conspiracy of the Senate.

SEVERAN EMPERORS AND MILITARY ANARCHY (3C)

193–211 The African general **Septimius-Severus** becomes Emperor after the civil war between Albino and Nigro. He starts the offensive against the Parthians and the Scots. Government assumes the form of a military autocracy.

211–17 Rule of Aurelius Antoninus, known as **Caracalla**, a fierce and unstable character. In 212 he publishes the *Constitutio Antoniniana de civitate,* which granted citizenship to all free men in the Empire, probably for tax purposes. High inflation

begins and continues until the early 4C.

218–22 Reign of **Elagabalus**, high priest of the sun god, El-Gabal, from the city of Emesa in Syria. His outrageous behaviour leads to his assassination.

222–35 **Severus Alexander** attempts to work with the Senate to prevent German tribes invading. He is killed by Maximinus from Thracia, an uncouth professional soldier. Military **anarchy** follows, along with German and Persian threats.

256–60 Persecution of Christians under **Valerian**. The Emperor and his army are defeated by the Persians and Valerian is held prisoner. He is succeeded by his son Gallienus, protector of the famous philosopher **Plotinus**, who opened a school in Rome.

270–75 **Aurelian**, a skilful general, takes Palmyra, a Syrian capital. Preoccupied by the invasion of Germanic tribes on Italian soil,

Aurelian has a new wall built around Rome, later reinforced by Honorius. The wall had 16 gates and 383 towers.

IMPERIAL AUTOCRACY (4C–5C)

The Empire was reorganised under Diocletian and Constantine. Italy and Rome lost some of their importance, imperial power became autocratic, and administrative and fiscal reforms replaced the old Augustinian laws. Christianity became the religion of the Emperor and his family, and the seat of power shifted east, with the founding of Constantinople in 331.

284–305 Diocletian, a high-ranking official, becomes Emperor. He attempts to harness inflation with fixed prices and devises a system that splits the Empire administratively, at the same time guaranteeing a peaceful succession.

The **tetrarchy**, or rule by four, creates two leaders under the title of Augustus, assisted by two Caesars (who were also heirs). In 286 **Maximian** becomes Augustus in Milan; Galerius is given the title of Caesar and control of the east in Mitrovizza, assisting Diocletian, and **Constantius-Chlorus** assists Maximian as his Caesar and settles in Trier, governing Gaul and Britain. Rome is no longer the capital, but assumes a symbolic value as the original home of the Empire.

303 Systematic persecution of Christians by Diocletian.

311 Galerius grants permits to eastern Christians to worship.

306–37 Chlorus's son, **Constantine**, takes advantage of the dissolution of the tetrarchy and proclaims himself Augustus. He routs enemies, including the pagan, Maxentius, supported by the Senate.

337–60 The Empire is divided among Constantine's three sons who soon begin fighting. **Constantinus II**, supporter of the Arian faith, emerges victorious. He visits Rome.

360–63 **Julian** as Emperor. Cousin of Constantius II, he was a very cultured man. He embraces paganism and attempts to reinstate this ancient religion. Christian teachers are refused work, although there are no real acts of hostility towards the Church. He leads a successful campaign against the Persians, but dies near Ctesiphon, in Mesopotamia.

378 Disastrous Roman defeat at **Adrianopolis** (Thracia). The Emperor Valentian is killed and the **Goths** establish themselves in the Balkans, often acting as mercenaries for the Roman army.

382 **Leo the Great** proclaims the Pope "Head of the Church" and the fount of episcopal authority, reinforcing the supremacy over Constantinople. During this period, Gratian, a pupil

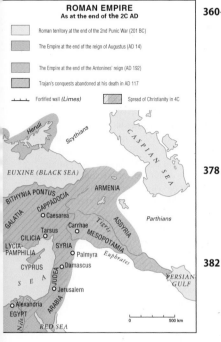

ROMAN EMPIRE
As at the end of the 2C AD

Roman territory at the end of the 2nd Punic War (201 BC)

The Empire at the end of the reign of Augustus (AD 14)

The Empire at the end of the Antonines' reign (AD 192)

Trajan's conquests abandoned at his death in AD 117

Fortified wall *(Limes)*   Spread of Christianity in 4C

Heruli

Scythians

CASPIAN SEA

EUXINE (BLACK SEA)

BITHYNIA PONTUS
GALATIA   CAPPADOCIA   ARMENIA
                    Caesarea
            Carrhae   Parthians
CILICIA   Tarsus   MESOPOTAMIA
LYCIA-   SYRIA   ASSYRIA
PAMPHILIA   Palmyra   Euphrates
CYPRUS   Damascus
   SEA   PERSIAN
         Judea   GULF
          Jerusalem
   Alexandria   ARABIA
EGYPT
   Nile   RED SEA

0   500 km

of Ambrose, renounces the traditional and pagan title of *Pontifex Maximus*, once the prerogative of all Emperors after Augustus.

379–95 **Theodosius I** resolves the problem of the Goths and reigns as sole Emperor (the last in Roman history). In 380 Nicean Christianity is proclaimed the state religion by the Emperor in Thessalonica. In 392, at the suggestion of **Ambrose** of Milan, paganism is outlawed. Following Theodosius' death, the Empire is divided between his sons: **Arcadius** in the east and **Honorius**, whose guardian was the Vandal general Stilicho, in the west.

403 After the invasion of the Po Plain by the Visigoth, **Alaric** (later defeated by Stilicho), Honorius leaves Milan and settles in Ravenna, defended by marshland. A conspiracy murders Stilicho in 407.

410 Alaric sacks Rome for three days. A huge outcry follows. Jerome and Augustine write pages on the desecration of the city. The previous year, various Germanic tribes had invaded Gaul. The west is on the verge of collapse.

430 **Aurelius Augustine**, a Christian writer and philosopher, dies at Ippona (in present-day Algeria), attacked by Vandals.

Constantine and Christian Rome

Constantine ruled as sole Emperor. In 313 he issued an **edict** in Milan, along with Licinius, stating that henceforth all religions would be tolerated, except Manicheism. Christianity was therefore officially recognised for the first time and Constantine himself converted to the religion. In 325 the Emperor headed the **First Ecumenical Council** of Christianity, which was held in Nicaea (Asia Minor), during which the Arian heresy was outlawed. Constantine was responsible for the construction of basilicas in Jerusalem (Holy Sepulchre) and Rome (St Peter's and St John Lateran, which remained the Papal seat for centuries). The conversion of Constantine confirmed the birth of a Christian empire.

The Church of Rome assumed superiority over the other Bishoprics and the other four Patriarchates of Christianity because Peter and Paul were said to have preached and been martyred in Rome. Tertullian states that Paul was beheaded in 67 and in 2C AD the Gaulish writer Irenaeus recorded the *principalitas* of the Church of Rome. Other writers recounted Paul's martyrdom and Peter's crucifixion during the reign of Nero. Eusebius of Caesarea (4C AD) recalls the words of Gaius about the trophies of the Apostles: "I can point out the trophies of the apostles. For if you are willing to go to the Vatican or the Ostian Way, you will find the trophies of those who founded this Church". Gaius's trophy can be identified in the crypt of St Paul Outside the Walls – and archaeological evidence would appear to agree with this interpretation; a more recent tradition suggests that the tomb of the first Pope is located in the catacombs of **St Peter's**. Christian preaching, according to Suetonius and Tacitus, would appear to have taken place near the Jewish community which was established in Trastevere as early as the end of the 1C BC (this community is therefore the oldest in Rome), and was soon to interest the Gentiles. The aristocrat Acilius Glabrio was martyred in 91 and **Flavius Clemens**, Domitian's cousin, was killed because he was Christian. It is believed that it was his wife Domitilla who donated the land for use as a Christian cemetery. A number of churches were built over the martyrs' tombs or near the homes of the rich protectors of the Christian community *(tituli)*.

He wrote the *Confessions* and a
major work on the civilisation
and decadence of Rome,
De Civitate Dei.

455 **Genseric**, king of the Vandals,
sacks Rome from his African
territory with extreme ferocity.
Just four years earlier, the
Roman general Ezio had stopped the Huns in Gaul, and in
452 **Attila** had turned back at
the Po Plain, either as a result
of the intervention of the Pope,
or from fear of an outbreak of
plague in Italy.

476 The barbarian **Odoacer**
deposes the last Emperor of
the west, **Romulus Augustus**.
The Emperor of the east is now
universally recognised as the
legitimate ruler.

PAPAL POWER (6C–15C)

493 The Arian **Ostrogoths** settle
in Italy. Their educated king,
Theodoric, initiates a period of
collaboration.

527–65 **Justinian** becomes
Emperor of Byzantium. In 540,
he orders his general Belisarius
to invade Sicily. This leads to
the disastrous Gothic War,
which devastated parts of Italy
and marks the ancient era's
end. Belisarius captures, then
loses Rome. In 552, the eastern
Empire annexes Italy.

568 Invasion by the **Lombards**, a
Germanic people more unruly
than the Visigoths. Rome,
officially part of the Byzantine
Empire, is, in fact, defended
and sustained by the Pope.
The Byzantine exarch has his
residence in Ravenna. The
disappearance of the Senate
and the destruction of the
city signals the beginning of
Rome's decay.

590–604 Papacy of **Gregory the
Great**, known as *Consul Dei*
because of his political ability.
A writer and theologian,
he was responsible for the

evangelisation of Britain. Under
his Papacy, the Bishop of Rome
becomes a moral and political
force of European importance.
In spite of this, records of
the time (many of which are
pilgrims') show Rome to be a
small city, with a population
of less than 20 000. The influx
of monks from the east and
the Greek language influences
the city for two centuries.

752 Lombards threaten Rome.
Pope Stephen II appeals for help
from the king of the Franks,
Pepin the Short (the Franks
were Catholics, unlike the other
Germanic tribes, who were
Arian), marking the beginning
of the alliance between the
French and the Pope.
The latter had little faith
in Byzantium, involved in
iconoclasm conflicts.

758 Donation of Querzy-sur-Oise.
The Pope acquires Sutri and
other territories, leading to the
birth of the *Patrimonium Petri*,
otherwise known as the
Papal States.

800 **Charlemagne**, who had
conquered the Lombards in 776,
is crowned Emperor by Pope
Leo III, despite the opposition of
Byzantium, reviving the Roman
Empire of the west. Rome
is the seat of this *Republica
Christiana*.

824 Ludovic the Pius, son and
successor to Charlemagne,
passes his *Constitutio* stating
that no Pope could be
elected without first swearing
allegiance to the Emperor.

846 The Moors, landing at Ostia,
sack the Basilica of St Peter's.
As a result, the Leonine Walls
are built around the Vatican
basilica in 852.

9C–10C Unsettled period for the
Papacy. The social-climbing
aristocratic families of Rome
(the Theophylacti, **Crescenzi**
and later the Tuscolani) all push

962 John XII calls **Otho I**, king of Germany, to Rome and crowns him Emperor. Otho imposes major reforms on the Papacy, establishing that a Pope could not be elected without the consent of the Emperor. In 963 Pope John XII is deposed and Leo VIII, a German prelate loyal to the Emperor, elected.

996 **Otho III** resides in Rome, on the Aventine, and dreams of restoring Rome to its ancient grandeur. The Pope is the scholar **Sylvester II**. In 998 the Emperor issues a *Privilegium* attesting the pre-eminence of Rome above all other cities in the Empire. Otho's death cuts short the city's renaissance in 1002.

1057 Stephen IX elected Pope without the Emperor's approval.

1075 **Gregory VII**, a strong advocate of absolute theocracy, confirms the superiority of the Papacy over the Empire and declares that laymen cannot make ecclesiastical appointments (the **Investiture Controversy**). He also denounces the sale and acquisition of Church goods and the marriage of priests. In his *Dictatus Papae* the Pope sets out the holy and political power of the Papacy, which exceeds that of all bishops and other Christians, including the Emperor. The Emperor Henry IV, angered by this statement, captures Rome. He is then expelled by the Norman army of Robert Guiscard, called upon by Gregory VII. Rome is violently sacked and its population massacred; many of those inhabitants not killed are sold as slaves.

1122 **Concordat of Worms**. The Pope and the Emperor reach a compromise to end the Investiture Controversy. At the suggestion of the canonist, Yves (Ivo) of Chartres, the Pope will from now on invest future bishops spiritually with a ring and pastoral staff; the Emperor will concede temporal power with a sceptre.

1130–55 Arnaldo da Brescia, a monk who was a pupil of the philosopher Abelard, attempts to reform the papacy and institute a republic in Rome, divided into *Comune*.

1153 Pope protected by **Frederick Barbarossa** under the Treaty of Constance. Arnaldo da Brescia captured and hanged. New conflict between the Pope and the Emperor. Rome fortified with towers (*Roma turrita*) built by powerful aristocratic families.

1198–1216 Papacy of **Innocent III**. Medieval papal theocracy culminates in this period.

1309–77 **Avignon captivity**. As a result of the influence of the French monarchy, the Popes (most of whom were French) move to Avignon. The Pope returns to Rome following the protests and prayers of Catherine of Siena, Bridget of Sweden and the poet Petrarch.

1347 Rome dominated by **Cola di Rienzo**, a notary of the city and ardent admirer of ancient history, who is eager to return the city to its former glory. His attempt fails miserably because of the hostility of the aristocratic families. After only three years, he exits the city. He returns with the Pope's support, but is soon forced to flee once more and is tragically slaughtered. The anonymous *The Life of Cola di Rienzo* captures his sad tale in the vulgar Roman dialect.

1357 Cardinal Egidio di Albornoz publishes his *Constitutiones Aegidianae*, laws with which the Papal States were ruled until the 19C.

1378–1417 Great Schism of the West. Two Popes reign simultaneously, one in Rome and one in Avignon. A third emerges in Pisa in 1409. Pope **Martin V** brings the seat of the Papacy back to Rome and rules.

1447–55 Nicholas V founds the **Vatican Library**, which today has around 500 000 books and 60 000 manuscripts. Rome becomes a centre of the European Humanist movement.

1453 Turks capture Constantinople, ending the eastern Empire. Humanist Pope Pius II (Enea Silvio Piccolomini) issues a protest over the apathy of western sovereigns.

THE MODERN ERA

1494 The French king, **Charles VIII**, enroute to Naples, enters Rome. This marks the beginning of foreign intervention in central and northern Italy.

1508–12 After a period of fighting to subjugate the aristocratic families to the power of the Church, **Julius II** goes to war to retain Romagna, to weaken the Venetian Republic and to expel the French king, Louis XII.

1517 **Luther**, who had visited Rome and been shocked by the immorality of the Curia, nails his 95 Theses on the church door at Wittenberg. The Medici Pope Leo X underestimates the danger of Luther's gesture.

6 May 1527 The **sack of Rome** by the Protestant Swiss and Spanish troops under Emperor Charles V, who holds the city for seven months. Only 32 000 of the 55 000 inhabitants remain. The later influx of central Italians distanced the Roman dialect from other southern strains. In November Clement VII surrenders to the imperial troops, promising a council to reorganise Catholicism.

1543–63 **Council of Trent** and birth of the Counter-Reformation.

1585–90 Pontificate of **Sixtus V**, during which crime and brigandry are rife. The Church and State are divided into 15 congregations at this time; a cardinal administers each. Sixtus V erected the obelisks of Piazza dell'Esquilino, Piazza del Popolo, Piazza San Pietro and Piazza San Giovanni in Laterano. He constructed the Via Sistina, partially linked the main churches and numerous districts of Rome with wide roads, rebuilt the Lateran and constructed the Scala Santa, replaced the statue of the Emperor on Trajan's Column with that of St Peter and had a chapel built to house his own tomb in the basilica of Santa Maria Maggiore.

1600 The philosopher **Giordano Bruno** is burnt at the stake in Campo de' Fiori.

1631 **Urban VIII** obtains the duchy of Urbino. The Papal States reach their greatest extent.

1791 Renunciation by the Papacy of Avignon and the Comtat-Venaissin, French annexes.

1798 Rome is occupied by the French troops of **Napoleon**; the Jacobin Roman Republic proclaimed. Pius VI dies in exile in Valence.

1800 The new Pope, Pius VII, is elected in Venice and returns to Rome, where the Republic is defeated. The following year the Pope signs a concordat with Napoleon.

1808 Rome occupied by the French. Following political disagreements (Pius VII refused to blockade Britain), the Papal States are invaded by Napoleonic troops and the Pope banished to Savona, then Fontainebleau. Pius VII returns to Rome in 1814.

1820–61 Struggle for the unification of the Italian States.

1848 **Pius IX** sends troops to fight the Austrians, during the First War of Independence. The Pope's conservative stance leads to the proclamation of the Roman Republic, defended by **Garibaldi** against the French troops, who ensure the return of the Pope.

CAPITAL OF ITALY

1870 Rome captured by the Italian army, ending the Pope's temporal authority. Pius IX retires to the Vatican. The State proposes the Law of Guarantees, to safeguard the Pope's liberty, which is refused by the Pope. Rome becomes the Italian capital.

1915 Italy enters World War I on side of Allies.

28–29 October 1922 Fascist march on Rome. **Mussolini** named Prime Minister.

1929 Mussolini and Cardinal Gasparri sign the **Lateran Treaty** (re-newed in 1984). Foundation of the Vatican City State.

1936 Mussolini forms an axis with Nazi Germany.

1937 Creation of Cinecittà film studio and the Istituto Luce.

1940 Italy enters World War II on the German side.

1943 San Lorenzo bombardment. King Victor Emmanuel III imprisons Mussolini. Armistice with Allies. Italy declares war on Germany.

1944 British and American forces liberate Rome.

1946 **Republic Proclaimed**. Rome becomes the administrative centre of the Lazio region.

1948 New constitution. Christian Democrats win elections.

1957 Treaty of Rome sets up the Common Market (now the European Union). Rome also becomes the headquarters of the Food and Agriculture Organisation (FAO), a United Nations organisation.

1960 Olympic Games held in Rome.

1963 Italian Socialist Party joins Christian Democrat-led coalition under Prime Minister Aldo Moro.

1963–65 **Second Vatican Council**, called by John XXIII (1958–63) and completed by Paul VI (1963–78). The Church tries to enter the modern world. Liturgical reform abolishes Latin in services.

1968 Clashes between students and police near Villa Giulia.

1960s–70s Right- and left-wing terrorists jostle. Citizens cower inside during the "Years of Lead".

1972 Giulio Andreotti becomes prime minister, a post he will hold seven times.

1975 Holy Year celebrated.

1978 Former PM Aldo Moro kidnapped and killed by the Red Brigades. Paul VI dies and is succeeded by John Paul I, pope for just 33 days. The Archbishop of Cracow, Karol Wojtila, is elected and takes the name **John Paul II**. Abortion is legalised.

1984 Renewal of the Lateran Pact between the Holy See and the Italian Government. Roman Catholicism loses status as state religion.

1990 Football World Cup held in the Eternal City.

1992 Mafia probes spark several years of arrests and investigations. Top anti-crime prosecutor, Giovanni Falcone, his wife and three bodyguards killed in car bomb attack.

2000 Celebration of the **Jubilee**.

2001 Silvio Berlusconi wins the general election, backed by a centre-right coalition. First constitutional referendum since 1946 creates greater autonomy to the country's 20 regions in tax, education and environment policies.

2002 Inauguration of the Rome Auditorium by Renzo Piano. Euro replaces the lira.

2003 PM Berlusconi appears in court on corruption charges.

2005 Death of **John Paul II**; election of the new pope **Benedict XIII**. Parliament ratifies EU constitution. Berlusconi resigns, then reforms government.

2006 Prodi becomes PM. Giorgio Napolitano, a former communist, is elected as president.

2007 Romano Prodi resigns as PM in January after losing a vote of confidence in the Senate. Elections result in a victory for Berlusconi's Freedom People coalition.

2011 European Commission announces that Italy surpassed France in wine production. Berlusconi forced from office. Mario Monti becomes Interim Prime Minister, serving also as Minster of Economy and Finance.

2012 A new train company, Italo, opened limited lines from Rome to other major cities.

2013 Cardinal Jorge Mario Bergoglio elected Pope, choosing the name Francesco. Ignazio Marino(Democratic Party) is elected Mayor of Rome.

2014 Matteo Renzi, member of the Democratic Party and Mayor of Florence, becomes Prime Minister.

2016 Astronaut Samantha Cristoforetti, the first Italian woman to join a European Space Agency crew, partaking in the Futura mission, during which she set European and women's records for time spent in space during a single flight (199 days).

2015 Giorgio Napolitano, President of the Italian Republic handed in his resignation on 14 January 2015, at the end of the term for an Italian presidency of the European Union. On 3 February Sergio Mattarella was nominated President of the Italian Republic in his stead.

2016 Pope Francis proclaims the Extraordinary Jubilee of Mercy through the papal bull *Misericordiae Vultus*.

2016 In June Virginia Raggi, a candidate for Italy's 5 Stelle (5 Star) movement, is elected Mayor of Rome, becoming the first female mayor in the history of Rome.

INFLUENTIAL FAMILIES

Many of Rome's powerful families funded monumental works, commissioned artistic treasures and occupied high levels of government.

BARBERINI

This Roman family, originally from Tuscany, produced Pope **Urban VIII** (1623–44). He funded the Barberini Palace on the Quirinal, upon which both the young **Bernini** and Borromini worked: it contains a magnificent picture gallery. He commissioned the Triton Fountain and the Fountain of the Bees in Piazza Barberini. A friend of Galileo, he was the first to employ Bernini – for a bust of himself and the baldaquin above the high altar in St Peter's Basilica.

MICHELIN

BORGHESE

This noble family from Siena settled in Rome when one of its members was elected Pope **Paul V** (1605–21). The family has left its mark in the Palazzo

Borghese, in the city centre, and in the Villa Borghese to the north of Rome. During his Papacy, the Villa became a museum and houses many important art works collected over the years by generations of the family. Paul V also commissioned the Pauline Fountain (Fontana Paolina) on the Janiculum. He is buried in the Pauline Chapel in the church of Santa Maria Maggiore.

the Villa Farnesina. The Chigi Palace, official residence of the president of the Council of Ministers, owes its name to Alexander VII (1655–67), a member of the illustrious family who acquired it in the 17C. The Pope commissioned Bernini to build the colonnades of St Peter's. The Chigi coat of arms also appears on the fountain in Piazza d'Aracoeli.

BORGIA

This Spanish family produced two Popes: **Calixtus III** (1455–58) and **Alexander VI** (1492–1503). During the latter's reign, America was discovered. He used Peruvian gold to decorate the ceiling of Santa Maria Maggiore; his coat of arms is shown there. Alexander VI also decorated the Vatican's Borgia Apartments. His son, **Cesare**, inspired Machiavelli to write *The Prince*; his daughter, **Lucrezia**, was the victim of family political intrigue.

COLONNA

This ancient noble family was very powerful from the 13C to the 17C. The election of one of its members, **Martin V** (1417–31), as Pope during the Council of Constance ended the Great Schism of the West. When the papacy returned to Rome, Martin concentrated totally on reinstating the primacy of the Vatican.

CHIGI

Originally came from Siena, these bankers became more important from the 15C through Agostino Chigi, who commissioned the young Raphael to decorate

DELLA ROVERE

Two great Popes were born into this family from Savona: **Sixtus IV** and Julius II. **Sixtus IV** (1471–84), whose secular name was Francesco della Rovere, was a scholarly and industrious man. He wrote a thesis on the blood of Christ and a study on the Immaculate Conception. He also rebuilt Sante Maria del Popolo and constructed the Santa Maria della Pace and the Sistine Chapel. Sixtus IV called upon some of the greatest artists of the day – including Botticelli, Ghirlandaio and Perugino – to decorate the chapel. Having appointed his nephews Gerolamo and Pietro Riario as Bishop and Archbishop of Imola, he came into conflict with Lorenzo de' Medici and was involved in the Pazzi conspiracy, which led to the assassination of Giuliano de' Medici (Lorenzo's brother) in Florence Cathedral, and to the massacre of the conspirators by the mob. Like his nephew Giuliano della Rovere (the future Pope Julius II), Sixtus IV was a warrior Pope; he fought against other Italian states and was victorious against Muhammad II, who had landed at Otranto and massacred many of the local inhabitants.

Julius II (1503–13) was blessed with great gifts both as a politician and as a generous patron: the implementation of Bramante's design for St Peter's, the painting of the Vatican Rooms by Raphael, the designing of his mausoleum, which remained unfinished, by Michelangelo *(in the church of San Pietro in Vincoli)*, and the collection of antique sculptures in the Vatican. He was also responsible for the building of Via Giulia, a long, straight thoroughfare between the bend in the Tiber and the island downstream.

FARNESE

This aristocratic family from Umbria, already famous by the 12C, came to Rome through **Paul III** (1534–49), the Pope who convened the **Council of**

Trent (1545–63). He was the driving force behind major projects. While still a cardinal, he commissioned Sangallo to build the Farnese Palace, finished by Michelangelo. When he became Pope, he turned again to the Florentine master for the *Last Judgement* in the Sistine Chapel and put him in charge of work on St Peter's Basilica.

MEDICI

This Florentine merchant and banking family ruled Florence and the whole of Tuscany from the 15C to the 18C. It produced several Popes: **Leo X** (1513–21), son of Lorenzo the Magnificent, a man of letters and patron of the arts, who put Raphael and Giulio Romano in charge of the Loggias in the Vatican: **Clement VII** (1523–34), an ally of François I, who was not able to prevent the sack of Rome or the Lutheran reforms which erupted during his Papacy; **Pius IV** (1559–65) who presided over the closure of the Council of Trent (1545–63); and **Leo XI**, who died a few days after he was elected in 1605, but who, while still a cardinal, had acquired the Villa Medici, which later became the French Academy in Rome.

59

PAMPHILI

Originally from Umbria, the family settled in Rome during the 15C. In 1461 its members were honoured with the title of Counts of the Holy Roman Empire. In the 16C Giovanni Battista became Pope **Innocent X** (1644–55). He was responsible for many changes in Piazza Navona: the rebuilding of the Pamphili Palace, the transformation into a family chapel of the church of Sant'Agnese in Agone and the building of the Fountain of the Four Rivers (Fontana dei Quattro Fiumi) which he commissioned from Bernini. He turned, however, to Borromini, a rival of Bernini, for the Palace for the Propagation of the Faith and the rebuilding of St John Lateran. The Villa Doria Pamphili was built for the Pope's nephew, whose wife inherited the palace known as Palazzo Doria Pamphili.

MICHELIN

Art and Culture

During the Republican period, art was valued for its practical and social significance, rather than for its aesthetic value. The priorities changed under the Roman Empire, when art celebrated power and demonstrated the prestige of the capital. The decadence of the Empire and the recognition of Christianity as the state religion saw the development of large basilicas; since then, these have often been restored or rebuilt. Many still welcome pilgrims today.

ART OF ANCIENT ROME
ARCHITECTURE

The remains of only a few public works have survived from the period of the kings and the early Republic, such as the channel of the **Cloaca Maxima** (the Forum's vast drainage system, dug in the 6C BC), the **town wall** built by **Servius Tullius** (578–534 BC), the **Appian Way** and the **Aqua Appia**, both the work of **Appius Claudius Caecus**, censor in 312 BC.

The major artistic influences came from the Etruscans, whose works they pillaged, and from the East. Victorious generals returned from there, dazzled by the splendours and accompanied by artists engaged in cities such as Athens or Alexandria.

Materials and techniques – Early Rome was built of very simple materials: **tufa**, a soft brownish stone, volcanic or calcareous in origin; and **peperine**, also of volcanic origin, which owes its name to its greyish hue and its granular texture, suggestive of grains of pepper (*pepe* in Italian). **Travertine**, a whitish limestone, mostly quarried near Tivoli, is a superior material to the earlier ones employed sparingly in the early centuries. **Marble** made rare appearances as a decorative material from the 2C BC, but became very popular under the Empire. **Brick** was first used in the 1C BC; it is usually seen today stripped of its marble facing.

The principles of classical Roman architecture were undoubtedly modelled upon those of ancient Greece. The mastery of three distinctive feats of civil engineering, however, heralded new building practices here. Firstly the Romans discovered concrete, allowing them to build more quickly and therefore more prolifically. Secondly they learnt how to apply marble (and any other finely finished stone like granite, porphyry and alabaster) as surface decoration, rather than using large (and expensive) quantities as blocks. Today, many ruins are reduced to reddish or greying husks, long stripped of their marble facing and friezes.

Thirdly the Romans learnt from their campaigns in the eastern Mediterranean (modern-day Turkey and Syria) the use of the arch, vaulting, squinches and, consequently, the art of constructing domes. At last they were able to break the linearity of the Hellenistic style with round arcs.

They poured concrete between simple brick parapets to make solid walls or over brick layers to anchor the voussoirs of an archway, vault or dome. Indeed, the Romans seemingly avoided wooden coffering because of its expense. One particular feature of their concrete is its ability to harden through the centuries: the honeycomb appearance of ruins is largely due to brick erosion.

In their constructions the Romans used the **semi-circular arch**. The one built over the Cloaca Maxima in about the 2C BC is a true masterpiece. There are some impressive examples of vaulting in the Domus Augustana, in the Pantheon, in Hadrian's Villa at Tivoli, in the Baths of Caracalla and in the Colosseum.

The Romans were masters of building theatres on level ground, rather than set into a hillside, as was the Greek practice. This involved the construction of vaults to support the terraces, as in the Theatre of Marcellus.

Classical orders – Greek architectural orders were employed, but with modifications: in the Tuscan or Roman Doric order, the column rests on a base rather than directly on the ground. The Ionic order was seldom used here; the Corinthian, however, was very popular – the Romans sometimes replaced the curling acanthus leaves on the capital with smooth overhanging leaves and substituted animals, gods and human figures for the central flower. To the three Classical orders, they added a fourth, called Composite: a capital on which the four scrolls of the Ionic order surmounted the acanthus leaves. The entablature (comprising the architrave, frieze and cornice) was very ornate, richly decorated with pearls, ovoli and foliage.

The names of two architects have survived: Rabirius, active under Domitian (AD 81–95), and Apollodorus of **Damascus** who worked for Trajan (AD 98–117) and Hadrian (AD 117–138).

Buildings and Monuments

Theatres – Pompey built the first permanent theatre *(Teatro di Pompeo)*, which he passed off as a temple with semi-circular steps, to avoid a ban. Unlike the Greeks, the Romans built on flat sites, using vaults to support the rows of seats which often ended in a colonnade. The space in front of the stage

Colosseum

© Piotr Rzeszutek/Dreamstime.com

(the orchestra) was reserved for actors and later people of rank, who came to watch the play. Thespians came on to the stage, which was raised above the orchestra, through three doors in the wall at the back of the stage. Animals and chariots entered from the sides.

The rear wall, the most beautiful part of the theatre, was decorated with many columns, statues set in recesses and marble and mosaic facings. Behind the rear wall of the stage were the dressing rooms, storerooms and a portico overlooking a garden.

The stage hands were responsible for special effects: smoke, lights, thunder, apparitions and grand finales, gods and heroes who descended from heaven or disappeared into the clouds. The male actors wore masks to differentiate characters. The acoustics were influenced by the canvas awning slanting down over the stage, which concentrated the sound so it penetrated to the top row of the terraces and also, perhaps, by resonant vessels strategically placed to act as loudspeakers. It has been suggested that when the actors sang, they stood in front of the rear wall of the stage so the doors acted as sounding boards.

Amphitheatres – The Romans invented venues, such as the Colosseum, for displays of gymnastics and horse-drawn chariot races. Their main use, however, was for combats between gladiators, who were mostly slaves or prisoners. Wild beasts also battled. Romans considered these bloody events so important that candidates for public office incorporated them into their campaigns. During the spectacle, slaves burned or sprayed perfume to neutralise the smell of the animals, covered the sand in the arena with red dust to hide the bloodstains and used lead-weighted whips to coerce human contestants or animals into the fray. Loud music played throughout the spectacle.

Amphitheatres were more or less oval in shape. The outer wall consisted of three storeys of arcades, surmounted by a wall with poles that supported the huge awnings. The most important spectators sat on a podium, protected by a balustrade; it was raised above the arena and positioned in the centre of one of the longer sides at the foot of the terraced area *(cavea)* that surrounded the arena on all sides.

Baths – Bathing occupied an important place in the Roman day, particularly during the Empire. Free public clubs provided thermal pools, gymnasia and places to stroll, read or converse. Built on a large scale, the pleasure palaces

Mosè di Michelangelo in San Pietro in Vincoli

© Violetastock/iStockphoto.com

contained columns, capitals, mosaics, coloured marbles, statues and frescoes.

Basilicas – Originally, basilicas accommodated law courts and stallholders, where people might congregate out of the sun or rain. The term, which means "royal portico", referred to it being a covered area. Rows of free-standing columns upheld the roof and divided the internal rectangular space into a "nave" flanked by two side aisles. Rome's first was the Basilica Porcia at the foot of the Capitolino in 185 BC. Unfortunately nothing remains. The use of basilicas for religious functions was assumed with the rise of the early Christian Church.

Triumphal arches – These monuments commemorate the triumph of a victorious general or raised a statue into prominent view. Some had only one opening *(Arch of Titus)*; others had three *(Arch of Septimus Severus, Arch of Constantine)*. Perhaps the original designs linked to the belief that a defeated army lost its powers of destruction on passing under the arch.

Circuses – The huge oblong arenas hosted popular chariot races; these include the Circus Maximus and Maxentius's Circus off the Old Appian Way.

Stadiums – These, too, were oblong in shape, but showcased athletic competitions. The site of Domitian's Stadium (Stadio di Domiziano) is now occupied by Piazza Navona.

Aqueducts – The impressive engineering of these great constructions has probably contributed more than anything else to the Roman reputation for building. The Aqua Appia, the oldest aqueduct, originally stretched more than 16km/10mi in length and was built in 312 BC by Appius Claudius the Blind. Approximately 100m/328ft of the aqueduct is still standing.

Roads – In some places, considerable stretches of the old paving are intact. The word *civus* alludes to a street going up or down hill; a *vicus* is a side street.

TEMPLES AND WORSHIP

Temples celebrated the gods or an emperor, who, since the time of Caesar, rose to divine status. Inspired by Etruscan and Greek models, their design varied from the elemental simplicity of the Temple of Fortuna Virilis to the more complex design of the Temple of Venus and Rome. Each temple had a place **(cella)** reserved for the statue of its divinity. Before this was a **pronaos,** set behind a colonnade. The whole structure stood on a podium.

As far as religion was concerned, Rome drew on all mythological sources for her deities; the 12 main gods and goddesses were the same in number, if not always in name, as their Greek counterparts on Mount Olympus. Public worship was held in the temples, but people also worshipped various household gods *(lares et penates)*. Many houses had a sort of shrine **(lararium),** where offerings were made to the souls of ancestors.

Cult of the Dead

Tombs often lined the roads outside the city. Romans practised both burial and cremation. During the Republic, tombs with several chambers enclosed sarcophagi. The most common and elementary marker was a **tablet** *(cippus)*, a simple block of stone bearing an inscription. More elaborately worked memorials, made of stone or marble, were called **steles** *(steli)*.

Much later, large underground communal chambers **(colombarium)** became the popular form of burial for the poor and for slaves. Much like a dovecote, small niches in walls housed urns. The dead person was often "accompanied" on his journey to the other world with clothing, weapons, tools, jewellery (for a woman) and playthings (for a child).

HOUSING

Depending on their social and financial status, the ancient Romans lived in a multistorey building **(insula)** containing several dwellings (☞*see OSTIA ANTICA in the Excursions from Rome section)*, a small middle-class house, or a large-scale patrician house **(domus)**. Though luxurious, the latter seem modest by modern standards, with their simple walls and lack of windows.

Mosaics, San Paolo Fuori le Mura

These early houses contained a large rectangular room *(atrium)* with an open roof in the centre, which allowed rainwater *(pluvial)* to collect in a basin *(impluvium)*. This atrium contained the room where the head of the family worked and received visitors, as well as other smaller rooms. Top-ranking officials, wealthy farmers and prosperous merchants had a second house, built in a more elegant Greek style, which was reserved for the family. Used only at certain times of the year, it consisted of rooms built around various atria and a colonnaded courtyard *(peristylium)*, with a garden or sometimes a fishpond in the centre. In the dining room *(triclinium)*, guests semi-reclined on couches.

SCULPTURE

In this discipline, the Romans most imitated Greek art. They erected mass-produced sculptures all over town: pre-fab bodies in togas took custom heads. The Romans liked white and coloured marble, dark red spotted porphyry and alabaster. They also worked in bronze (notably Marcus Aurelius' statue).

Their originality sparked with **portraits**, fostered by the aristocratic practice of wax death masks. Caesar's portraits always show a calm, reflective and energetic character, whereas Augustus, with his prominent ears, displays serenity and coldness. Malice unfurls in Vespasian's face and thick neck. Trajan must have had a very broad face and his hairstyle curiously accentuates this peculiarity. The equestrian statue of Marcus Aurelius is the sole survivor of a tradition established by Julius Caesar: the Emperor as an all-powerful conqueror.

The Romans also excelled in **historical low-relief sculptures**. The scenes on a sarcophagus or on Trajan's column are models of composition and precision.

Decorative sculpture, exceptionally rare in the Republican era as the sarcophagus of Scipio Barbatus shows, reached its apogee in the Augustan era with the **Ara Pacis**. One type of sculpture gave expression to **popular taste**, depicting various crafts and scenes from everyday life on the tombstones of working people.

Decadence in sculpture became apparent in the 3C AD: the folds of garments were scored too deep, making the figures rigid, the expressions became fixed because of excessive hollowing out of the pupil of the eye and the hair was carelessly treated.

PAINTING

A study of the frescoes in Pompeii has identified **four periods** in Roman painting. The "first style" consists of simple panels imitating marble facing. The "second style" is marked by architectural features in *trompe l'oeil,* to which small illustrated panels were added in the "third style". With the "fourth style" the *trompe l'oeil* became excessive and the decoration overloaded.

Examples of Roman painting can be seen in Livia's House and the Griffin House on the Palatine and in the National Roman Museum *(housed in the Palazzo Massimo alle Terme).*

MOSAIC

This technique developed from an attempt to strengthen the floor surface, which was made of a mixture of broken tiles and chalk, by inserting pebbles and then small pieces of marble, which could be cut to a uniform size and arranged to form a design.

Roman workshops also copied the **opus sectile** technique, which originated in the East. A stencil of a decorative motif was applied to a marble base. The outline was traced onto the marble, then hollowed out and filled with small pieces of coloured marble. Examples are on display at the Picture Gallery in the Conservators' Palace and in the Ostia Museum *(⚓See OSTIA ANTICA in the Excursions from Rome section).*

CHRISTIAN ART

The pagan cult of idols and the commandment in the Bible against "graven images" inhibited the spontaneous development of a new style of art among the early communities.

At first Christian art borrowed from the pagan repertoire those subjects that could be used as symbols: the vine, the dove, the anchor, etc. **Paintings** appeared on catacomb walls, following the earlier tradition; the oldest date from the 2C AD. The chief Christian building was the **basilica** (not to be confused with the secular pagan basilicas). Constantine erected the first of these over the tombs of Peter and Paul the Apostles *(St Peter's in the Vatican; St Paul Outside the Walls)* and next to the Imperial Palace *(St John Lateran).*

ARCHITECTURAL GLOSSARY

Some of the terms given below are further explained by the illustrations on the previous pages.

Words in italics are Italian

Altarpiece (or **ancona**): a large painting or sculpture adorning an altar.

Ambulatory: extension of aisles around the chancel for processionals.

Antependium: a covering over the front of an altar.

Apse: semi-circular or polygonal end of a church behind the altar; the outer section is known as the chevet.

Apsidal chapel: small chapel off the ambulatory of a Romanesque or Gothic church.

Archivolt: arch moulding over an arcade or upper section of a doorway.

Atlantes (or **Telamones**): male figures used as supporting columns.

Atrium (or **four-sided portico**): a court enclosed by colonnades in front of the entrance to a paleo-Christian or Romanesque church.

Avant-corps: part of a building that projects out from the main façade.

Bastion: in military architecture, a polygonal defensive structure projecting from the ramparts.

Bay: the area between two supporting columns or pillars.

Buttress: external support of a wall, which counterbalances the thrust of the vaults and arches.

Caisson (or **lacunar**): decorative square panel sunk into a flat roof or vaulted stonework.

Caryatid: female figure used as a supporting column.

Cathedra: high-backed throne in Gothic style.

Chancel: the part of the church behind the altar, with carved wooden stalls for the choir.

Ancient Art

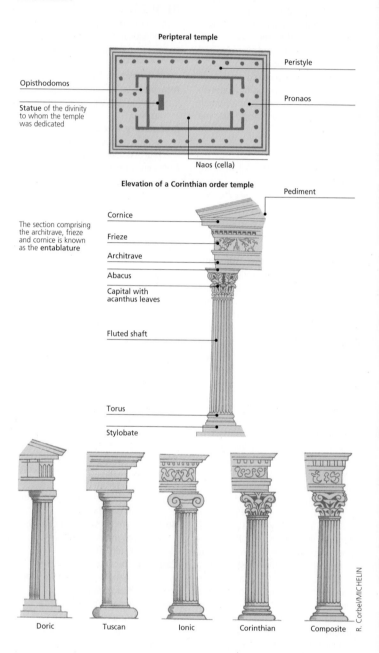

Peripteral temple

Peristyle

Opisthodomos

Pronaos

Statue of the divinity to whom the temple was dedicated

Naos (cella)

Elevation of a Corinthian order temple

Pediment

Cornice

The section comprising the architrave, frieze and cornice is known as the entablature

Frieze

Architrave

Abacus

Capital with acanthus leaves

Fluted shaft

Torus

Stylobate

Doric   Tuscan   Ionic   Corinthian   Composite

R. Corbel/MICHELIN

Baths of Caracalla (3C AD)

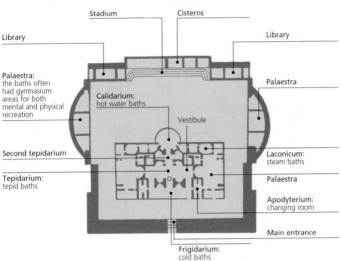

Stadium

Cisterns

Library

Library

Palaestra:
the baths often
had gymnasium
areas for both
mental and physical
recreation

Palaestra

Calidarium:
hot water baths

Vestibule

Second tepidarium

Laconicum:
steam baths

Tepidarium:
tepid baths

Palaestra

Apodyterium:
changing room

Main entrance

Frigidarium:
cold baths

Colosseum (1C AD)

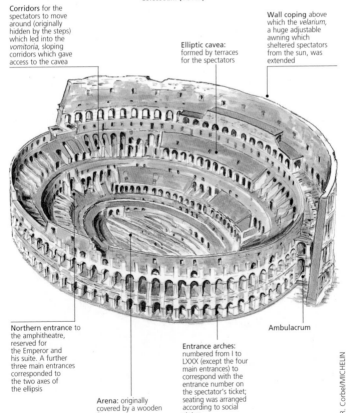

Corridors for the
spectators to move
around (originally
hidden by the steps)
which led into the
vomitoria, sloping
corridors which gave
access to the cavea

Wall coping above
which the velarium,
a huge adjustable
awning which
sheltered spectators
from the sun, was
extended

Elliptic cavea:
formed by terraces
for the spectators

Northern entrance to
the amphitheatre,
reserved for
the Emperor and
his suite. A further
three main entrances
corresponded to
the two axes
of the ellipsis

Ambulacrum

Arena: originally
covered by a wooden
floor

Entrance arches:
numbered from I to
LXXX (except the four
main entrances) to
correspond with the
entrance number on
the spectator's ticket;
seating was arranged
according to social
status

R. Corbel/MICHELIN

Arch of Constantine (4C AD)

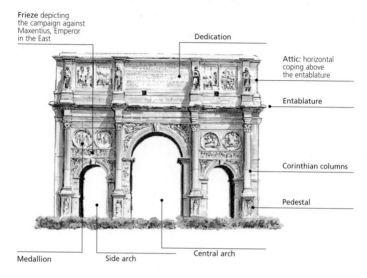

Frieze depicting the campaign against Maxentius, Emperor in the East

Dedication

Attic: horizontal coping above the entablature

Entablature

Corinthian columns

Pedestal

Medallion

Side arch

Central arch

Castel Sant'Angelo: from mausoleum to fortress

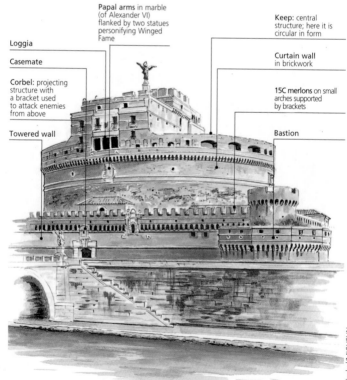

Papal arms in marble (of Alexander VI) flanked by two statues personifying Winged Fame

Keep: central structure; here it is circular in form

Loggia

Curtain wall in brickwork

Casemate

Corbel: projecting structure with a bracket used to attack enemies from above

15C merlons on small arches supported by brackets

Towered wall

Bastion

Religious architecture

Sant'Andrea della Valle (1591-1623)

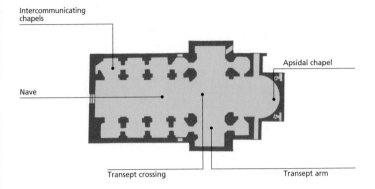

Intercommunicating chapels

Apsidal chapel

Nave

Transept crossing

Transept arm

Gesù Church, façade (1575)

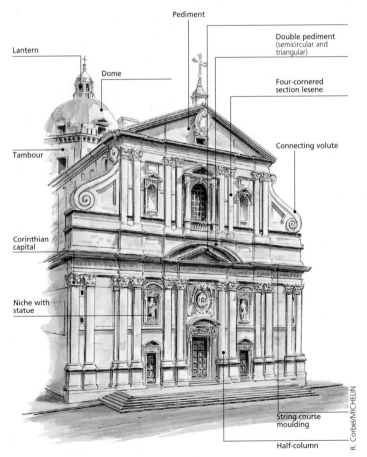

Pediment

Double pediment (semicircular and triangular)

Lantern

Dome

Four-cornered section lesene

Connecting volute

Tambour

Corinthian capital

Niche with statue

String course moulding

Half-column

R. Corbel/MICHELIN

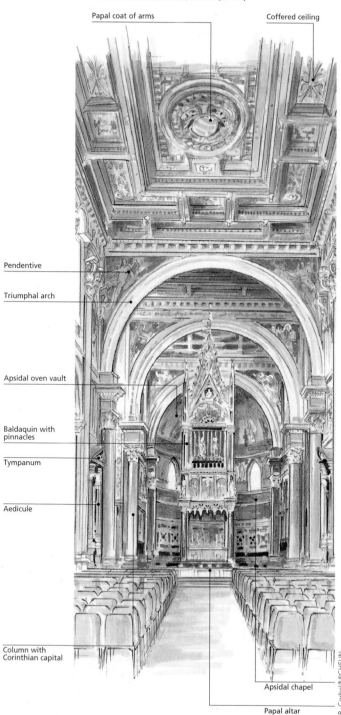

San Giovanni in Laterano, interior (4C-17C)

Papal coat of arms

Coffered ceiling

Pendentive

Triumphal arch

Apsidal oven vault

Baldaquin with pinnacles

Tympanum

Aedicule

Column with Corinthian capital

Apsidal chapel

Papal altar

R. Corbel/MICHELIN

Civil architecture

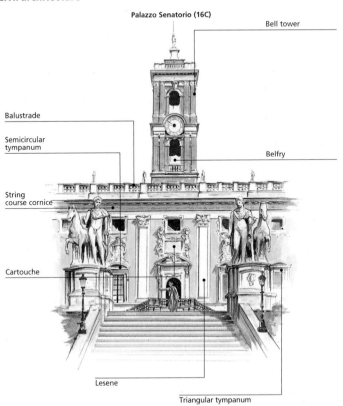

Palazzo Senatorio (16C)

Bell tower

Balustrade

Semicircular tympanum

Belfry

String course cornice

Cartouche

Lesene

Triangular tympanum

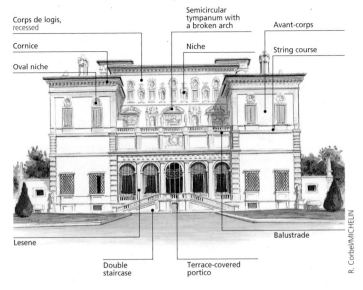

Villa Borghese (17C)

Corps de logis, recessed

Semicircular tympanum with a broken arch

Avant-corps

Cornice

Niche

String course

Oval niche

Lesene

Double staircase

Terrace-covered portico

Balustrade

R. Corbel/MICHELIN

Ciborium: a canopy (baldaquin) over an altar.

Coffer (or **panel**): small square ornamental panel, painted or sculpted in various materials.

Console: projecting stone or wooden bracket that supports cornices or beams.

Corbel (or **truss**): triangular bracket, usually made of wood, supporting a roof.

Counter-façade: internal wall of a church façade.

Cross (**church plan**): churches are usually built either in the plan of a Greek cross, with four arms of equal length, or a Latin cross, with one arm longer than the other three.

Exedra: section in the back of a Roman basilica containing seats; by extension, curved niche or semi-circular recess outside.

Ghimberga: a triangular Gothic pediment adorning a portal.

Grotesque: a decorative style popular during the Renaissance in which parts of human, animal and plant forms are distorted and mixed. The term comes from the old Italian word *grotte*, the name given in the Renaissance period to the Roman ruins of the Domus Aurea.

High relief: sculpture or carved work projecting more than one half of its true proportions from the background (halfway between low relief and in-the-round figures).

Intrados: inner surface of an arch or vault.

Jamb (or **pier**): pillar flanking a doorway or window and supporting the arch above.

Keystone: topmost stone in an arch or vault.

Lantern: turret with windows on top of a dome.

Lesene (or **Lombard strips**): decorative band of pilasters joined at the top by an arched frieze.

Matroneo: the gallery reserved for women in paleo-Christian and Romanesque churches.

Modillion: small bracket supporting a cornice.

Moulding: an ornamental shaped band that projects from the wall.

Narthex: interior vestibule of a church.

Overhang: overhanging or corbelled upper storey.

Ovolo: egg-shaped decoration.

Pala d'altare: Italian term for altarpiece.

Pediment: ornament in Classical architecture (usually triangular or semicircular) above a door or window.

Pendentive: connecting piece positioned at a corner of a square space to support an octagonal or circular dome.

Pilaster strip: structural column partially set into a wall.

Pluteus: decorated balustrade made from various materials, separating the chancel from the church.

Polyptych: a painting or relief consisting of several folding leaves or panels.

Portico: an open gallery facing the nave in paleo-Christian churches; it later became a decorative feature of the external part of the church.

Predella: base of an altarpiece, divided into small panels.

Presbiterio: the chancel or sanctuary of a church, reserved for the clergy.

Pronaos: the space in front of the *cella* or *naos* in Greek temples; later the columned portico in front of the entrance to a church or palace.

Protiro: small porch on columns in front of the portal in Romanesque churches.

Pulpit: an elevated dais from which sermons were preached.

Pyx: a cylindrical box made of ivory or glazed copper for jewels or the Eucharistic host.

Retable: large and ornate altarpiece divided into several painted or carved panels, especially common in Spain after the 14C.

Rib: a projecting moulding or band on the underside of a dome or vault,

Mosaics on the façade of Santa Maria in Trastevere

©Judy Edelhoff/Michelin

which may be structural or ornamental.

Rustication: deliberately rough texture of dressed and uniformly cut stone that projects from the outer wall of a building and has deeply chiselled markings. In fashion during the Renaissance.

Splay: a surface of a wall that forms an oblique angle to the main surface of a doorway or window opening.

String course: projecting ornamental band or continuous moulding that separates one floor from another.

Tambour: a circular or polygonal structure supporting a dome.

Triforium: an open gallery above the arcade of the nave, comprised mainly of three-light windows.

Vault: arched structure forming a roof or ceiling; **barrel vault**: produced by a continuous rounded arch; **cross vault**: formed by the intersection of two barrel vaults; **oven vault**: semicircular in shape, usually over apsidal chapels, the termination of a barrel-vaulted nave.

Vaulting cell: one of the four segments of a cross vault.

Volute: architectural ornament in the form of a spiral scroll.

Window cross: a stone or wooden post that divides the opening of a window or door. The vertical posts are known as **mullions**.

MEDIEVAL PERIOD

Only a few rare, but splendid, examples survive from the Middle Ages in Rome. Supplanted by Constantinople as the capital of the Empire and invaded by barbarians, by the 6C Rome was a ruined city with barely 20 000 inhabitants. In the 10C it became the battleground in the struggle between the Pope and the German Emperor. Until the 15C only simple constructions appeared.

ARCHITECTURE

Civil architecture consisted mainly of fortresses for noble families on strategic sites (*Crescenzi House, Militia Tower*). Builders quarried ancient sites for **church decoration**: capitals, friezes and columns like those in Santa Maria Maggiore, Santa Sabina, etc. As such material grew scarcer, items from different sources blended into one church (*columns in San Giorgio in Velabro, Santa Maria in Cosmedin, etc*).

The **basilical plan** of the early churches was retained during the medieval era. It consisted of a rectangular building divided down its length into a nave flanked by two or four aisles separated by rows of columns; one of the shorter sides contained the entrance, the other the apse (with quarter-sphere vault). Between the apse and the nave and at right angles to them ran the transept. The nave extended above the side aisles and was lit by clerestories. It was covered by a pitched roof, left open or masked by a flat ceiling in the interior. The façade was often flanked by a bell-tower (campanile). In Rome these towers are decorated with horizontal cornices dividing them into several storeys, with white miniature columns standing out against the brickwork and ceramic insets in brilliant colours.

By the 6C a rail had been introduced separating the congregation from the clergy and creating the chancel **(presbyterium)** on either side of the bishop's throne **(cathedra)**, which stood in the apse. In front were the choristers in the **schola cantorum**. Churches also often housed a **martyrium** with the relics of the saint. The high altar was covered by a baldaquin or canopy **(ciborium)**.

SCULPTURE, PAINTING AND MOSAIC

The architect and sculptor **Arnolfo di Cambio** (c. 1235–c. 1302) moved to Rome from Florence around 1276. He created the baldaquins in St Paul Outside the Walls and in Santa Cecilia, and the statue of Charles of Anjou in the Museo del Palazzo dei Conservatori.

Frescoes and mosaics were the chief forms of medieval decoration. The Romans had a taste for anecdotes and bright colours.

The period from the 12C to the 14C is dominated by the **Cosmati**, all descended from one Cosma, who formed a guild of marble workers. Their workshops used fragments of ancient materials to create beautiful floors with decorative motifs of multicoloured marble and the furniture of a medieval church: episcopal throne, *ambones* (lecterns), paschal candlesticks. The early works, composed entirely of white marble, are very simple. Later they added porphyry and serpentine marble (green) cut in geometric shapes (roundels, lozenges etc). They produced lively effects with incrustations of enamels – blue, red and gold – on the friezes and wreathed columns of cloisters.

In the latter half of the 5C, Byzantine mosaics influenced Rome's style: figures with enigmatic expressions, often richly dressed, in conventional poses, which express the mysticism of the Eastern Church through symbolism.

Carolingian art brought a less rigid fashion, for example, works dating from the reign of Paschal I (817–24) *(Santa Prassede; Santa Maria in Domnica)*. From the 11C to 13C the Roman workshops produced sumptuous masterpieces *(the apse in San Clemente)*. **Pietro Cavallini**, the greatest artist in this period, must have worked in Rome at the end of the 13C and early in the 14C. He was both painter and mosaicist – a master of the different influences. His pure art is best expressed through the mosaic of the life of the Virgin in Santa Maria in Trastevere and by the fresco of the Last Judgement in Santa Cecilia. **Jacopo Torriti** and **Rusuti** were disciples of his.

RENAISSANCE ART

After almost 10 centuries of invasions and plundering, the Popes brought new life and renewed prosperity to the capital of the Roman Catholic Church, thanks to the contribution of talented artists such as Michelangelo, Bramante and Raphael. This new explosion of art attracted wealthy patrons to the city, and the period saw the construction of a number of fine Renaissance *palazzi*. After the Council of Trent, the canons of religious architecture were influenced mainly by the religious orders, which created an austere, yet grandiose style. In painting, the first hints of the bold new style could be seen. The Renaissance made less impact on Rome than on Florence.

At the beginning of the 15C Rome was exhausted by the struggles of the Middle Ages and had nothing to show of artistic merit. By the end of the century, the city was an important archaeological centre and famous for its abundant artistic activity commissioned by popes and prelates. It was **Martin V** (1417–31), the first pope after the Great Schism, who inaugurated this brilliant period. It all ended in 1527 when the troops of Charles V sacked Rome.

ARCHITECTURE

The inspiration for Roman Renaissance buildings springs from classical monuments. The Colosseum's superimposed orders and engaged columns are imitated in the court of the Farnese Palace. The vaulting of Maxentius' Basilica led to the dome of St Peter's in the Vatican. And the Pantheon's curved and triangular interior pediments have been reproduced many times.

The churches are austere in appearance. The nave is covered by rib vaulting and flanked by apsidal side chapels; the arms of the transept end in rounded chapels. The first domes began to appear (*Santa Maria del Popolo, Sant'Agostino*). The screenlike façade has two stages: one above the other linked by scrolls. Broad flat surfaces predominate; shallow pilasters are preferred to columns. The first hints of the Counter-Reformation and the Baroque can be seen through broken lines, recesses and columns progressively more accentuated.

Sixtus IV (1471–84) was responsible for the majority of the Renaissance churches: Sant'Agostino, Santa Maria del Popolo and San Pietro in Montorio were built in his reign. He founded Santa Maria della Pace and made great alterations to the Church of the Holy Apostles. The *palazzi* were large private houses between Via del Corso and the Tiber. Pilgrims crowded these streets, alongside the feast-day papal processions from the Vatican to the Lateran: Via del Governo Vecchio, Via dei Banchi Nuovi, Via dei Banchi Vecchi, Via di Monserrato, Via Giulia, etc.

They supplanted the medieval fortresses; the Palazzo Venezia, begun in 1452, has retained its crenellations. From the outside the *palazzi* are gaunt and austere (*barred windows on the ground floor*). The inside was designed for a cultivated lifestyle, associated with sculptures and paintings.

SCULPTURE AND PAINTING

After working in Rome from 1496–1501 **Michelangelo** returned in 1505 to design a tomb for Julius II. Despite the magnificent monument, the Pope, preoccupied with the construction of St Peter's, suddenly lost interest. In 1508 the Pope summoned Michelangelo back and commissioned the Sistine Chapel. The painter revolutionised the concept of religious decor and produced a huge architectural structure, dominated by powerful figures (the Prophets, Sybils and *Ignudi*, or naked figures) and panels illustrating episodes from Genesis. In both his painting and sculptures, Michelangelo emphasises the human body and radically changed the way man was represented. He portrays people as grandiose and dramatically aware of their own existence: physically powerful, muscular and tormented figures.

The other artist of major importance in the Renaissance period was **Raphael**. He, too, attempted to portray pure beauty, firstly in his gentle and balanced portraits, then by using the *sfumato* technique perfected by **Leonardo da Vinci**, and finally by acquiring the anatomical mastery of Michelangelo.

In **decorative sculpture,** delicate ornamental foliage and floral motifs often appear in gold (door-frames, balustrades, etc). Funeral art flourished under **Andrea Bregno** and **Andrea Sansovino**, who combined a taste for decoration with ancient architecture.

AN ARTISTIC MELTING-POT

The Renaissance style reached Rome after being developed elsewhere and all the artists came from outside the city: the Umbrians were known for their gentle touch, the Tuscans for their elegant and intellectual art and the Lombards for their rich decoration.

♦ **Gentile da Fabriano** and **Pisanello** were summoned to Rome in 1427 by Martin V and Eugenius IV to decorate the nave of St John Lateran (destroyed 17C–18C).

- **Masolino da Panicale**, who came from Florence, painted St Catherine's Chapel in St Clement's Basilica between 1428 and 1430.
- From 1447–1451 **Fra Angelico**, also from Florence, decorated Nicholas V's Chapel in the Vatican.
- For the painting of the Sistine Chapel walls Sixtus IV called on **Pinturicchio**, **Perugino** and **Signorelli** from Umbria and on **Botticelli**, **Ghirlandaio**, **Cosimo Rosselli** and his son **Piero di Cosimo** from Florence. He also commissioned **Melozzo da Forli** to paint the Ascension in the apse of the Church of the Holy Apostles (*fine fragments in the Vatican Picture Gallery and in the Quirinal Palace*).
- In about 1485 **Pinturicchio** painted the life of St Bernard in Santa d'Aracoeli and a Nativity in Santa Maria del Popolo. Between 1492 and 1494 he decorated the Borgia Apartment in the Vatican for Alexander VI.
- From 1489–1493 **Fra' Filippino Lippi** was at work on the Carafa Chapel in Santa Maria Sopra Minerva.
- **Bramante**, who arrived in 1499, designed the tempietto beside San Pietro in Montorio (1502), built the cloisters at Santa Maria della Pace (1504) and extended the choir of Santa Maria del Popolo (1505–09).
- From 1508–12 **Michelangelo** was at work painting the ceiling of the Sistine Chapel for Julius II. In 1513 he began the Pope's tomb. The *Last Judgement* was painted between 1535 and 1541 and he worked on the dome of St Peter's from 1547 until his death in 1564. His last work was the Porta Pia (1561–64).
- From 1508–11 **Baldassarre Peruzzi** constructed the Villa Farnesina for Agostino Chigi.
- In 1508 **Raphael** began to paint the *Stanze* in the Vatican. In 1510 he designed the plan for the Chigi

Chapel in Santa Maria del Popolo. From 1511 he worked on the decoration of the Villa Farnesina for Agostino Chigi. In 1512 he painted *Isaiah* in Sant'Agostino and the *Sibyls* in Santa Maria della Pace in 1514.

- **Sodoma** arrived in Rome from Milan in 1508 to paint the ceiling of the Signature Room in the Vatican for Julius II. He worked on the Farnesina in about 1509.
- Early in the 16C **Jacopo Sansovino** built San Giovanni dei Fiorentini for Leo X.
- In 1515 **Antonio da Sangallo the Younger** began to build the Farnese Palace; Michelangelo took over in 1546.

COUNTER-REFORMATION

The Counter-Reformation, which covered the period from the reign of Paul III (1534–49) to the reign of Urban VIII (1623–44), was marked by the sack of Rome in 1527 and by the rise of Protestantism. The movement sought to put down the heretics, restore the primacy of Rome and to rally the faithful to the Church. The Society of Jesus, formed in 1540, proved to be a most efficacious instrument in the struggle. Henceforward the influential power of art was put at the service of the Faith.

Several successes ensued – the Battle of Lepanto (1571), the conversion of Henri IV of France (1593) and the Jubilee (1600) – all expressed in an artistic style which presaged the Baroque.

ARCHITECTURE

The **church style** is sometimes called "Jesuit" because of the comprehensive contribution made by the Society of Jesus. The architecture combines an austere solemnity with a rich marble decor: churches appeared majestic and powerful. Designed to assemble the faithful together, these structures are vast. The Gesù Church is a typical example. The nave is broad and uncluttered, so that every member of the congregation could see the altar and hear the preaching. On the façade, the plain surfaces of the Renaissance are replaced with recesses and projections, and engaged columns are gradually substituted for the flat pilasters.

The most prolific period for **civil architecture** was in the early Counter-Reformation, during the reigns of Paul III, Julius III, Paul IV and Pius IV, who lived like Renaissance princes. The family illustrates the Church triumphant: Paul V acquired the Borghese Palace and built the Pauline Fountain; his nephew, Cardinal Scipione Borghese, led a cultivated life, evident from the ornate splendours of the Palazzo Pallavicini and the "Palazzina" or Villa Borghese, which now houses the Borghese Gallery.

SCULPTURE AND PAINTING

In the spirit of the Counter-Reformation, painting had to exalt the themes rejected by the Protestants: the Virgin, the primacy of St Peter, the doctrine of the Eucharist, the cult of the saints and their intercession for the souls in purgatory.

MANNERIST

Wild emotion and wit burst onto the European art scene between 1520 and 1600. This movement – perhaps best personified by Michelangelo Buonarroti – rejected the serene balance of the High Renaissance.

Figures bend, bounce and bulge muscles in paintings. Colours fly off canvases. References and dirty jokes lace through virtuoso compositions. Fountains play music or wheeze animal cries. Branches weave into bowers. Hydraulics mischievously squirt visitors. Mannerism (from the Italian *maniera*, "style") is all about self-conscious grandstanding.

The pranks and preening reflected the new status of artists: no longer craftsmen, they were admired as intellectuals beside scholars, poets and humanists. Some experts connect the trippy hues, illogical compression of space and convoluted poses to the upheaval of the plague, Reformation and sack of Rome in 1527.

Lazio – the area around the capital – is the epicentre of Mannerist gardens with Vignola's **Villa Lante** in Bagnaia and **Palazzo Farnese** in Caprarola and Ligorio's **Villa d'Este** in Tivoli and **Monster Park** in Bomarzo. Examples in Rome include Raphael's **Villa Madama** and the tatty remains of the Farnese Garden on the Palatine Hill.

In sculpture there is the work of two of Michelangelo's close followers: **Ammanati** (1511–92) and **Guglielmo della Porta** (1500–77). The end of the period is marked by the presence in Rome of **Pietro Bernini** (1562–1629), the father of Gian Lorenzo Bernini.

Among the painters are **Daniele da Volterra**, who worked with Michelangelo, and **Giovanni da Udine**, **Sermoneta**, **Francesco Penni** and **Giulio Romano**, who formed part of the "Roman School" around Raphael. The style of the next generation – **Federico** and **Taddeo Zuccari**, **Pomarancio**, **Cesare Nebbia**, **Cavaliere d'Arpino** etc – is a direct development of Raphael's art. **Barocci**, whose soft and emotional style never lapsed into affectation, deserves a special place.

In their attempts to imitate, the Mannerist painters were often guilty of excess. Their colours are pallid, as if faded by the light; fresco paintings are framed with stucco and gilding or elaborate combinations of marble; large areas are often divided into smaller panels, which are easier to paint.

REACTION

Reaction to Mannerism began with the earthy and often offensive **Caravaggio**, who heralded the first signs of the Baroque, and the **Bologna Group**, led by the **Carracci** who ran an academy in Bologna from 1585–95: Ludovico (1555–1619), founder of the academy, and his cousins Agostino (1557–1602) and **Annibale** (1560–1609), who were brothers. **Guido Reni** (1575–1642), **Domenichino** (1581–1641) and **Guercino** (1591–1666) tried to achieve more verity of expression without abandoning idealism.

Michelangelo Merisi (1573–1610), known as **Caravaggio** after the name of his home village near Bergamo, began to work in Rome with Cavaliere d'Arpino

Caravaggio in San Luigi dei Francesi

©isogood/iStockphoto.com

in 1588. But he was quarrelsome and had to flee from the city in 1606 after murdering a man over a tennis match. Never a dull moment then, as Caravaggio swashbuckles through history beating acquaintances, murdering and fleeing the authorities. Biographer Peter Robb explains: "He is portrayed as a violent, psychotic man, but he was much more wronged than wronging. His actions were entirely defensive.

"Caravaggio was hounded from the moment he became famous. He lived in an ugly, repressive society." Robb explains that the emotion-choked paintings exploded on the "decadent, stilted world of Roman art. His vigorous, clean realism was absolutely stunning."

He claims the bad boy was harassed – and ultimately killed – for love. The traditional view holds that Caravaggio set off for Rome and a papal pardon. Arrested by mistake, he missed the boat – which contained paintings he hoped would influence his case. Enraged, he followed on foot up the coast, where he caught fever and died in the wilds.

"He was murdered. It was revenge," Robb insists. "Many mysterious and sinister things happened in the last years of his life. He slept with a sword under his bed – that is the behaviour of a hunted man... He suffered some overnight reversal of fortune in Malta, where he was celebrated. I think it was a sexual crime and that's why it has been dropped from the records."

ROMAN BAROQUE
THE STYLE

The Baroque style is characterised by its theatrical architecture, comprising a riot of concave and convex curves and twisted columns, sculptures that capture a moment of action, and are embellished by *putti* statues, golden rays, and *trompe l'oeil* ceilings suggesting non-existent domes. The dominant feature is movement, pulling the eye from façade to fountain to piazza, each sight as superb as the last. This rich, dramatic style found the perfect home in the Italian capital, evolving over the years to create its own specific quirks, now known as "Roman Baroque".

The Baroque style evolved in the 17C and 18C. Several theories expound the origin of the term: in Portugus"). In both cases, however, the attributed meaning tends to be pejorative, deriding the conscious deviation from established rules, and canons of harmony and beauty. It was a long time before the style was re-evaluated and appreciated.

Baroque, meanwhile, enjoyed a great vogue in the papal city during the reign of Urban VIII (1623–44), becoming synonymous with the triumph of Catholicism over heresy. The Church, with its newly acquired strength and spiritual power, and the popes, with their desire to glorify God through new works of art, attracted illustrious talent to the city.

LEADING ARTISTS

The two most important artists in the world of Roman Baroque art were **Gian Lorenzo Bernini** and **Francesco Borromini**. **Gian Lorenzo Bernini** (1598–1680) was born in Naples. Early on, Cardinal Scipione Borghese recognised Bernini's genius and commissioned sculptures for his villa *(now in the Borghese Gallery)*. At the age of 17, he produced his first work, *Jupiter and the Goat Amalthea*, followed by the magnificent sculptural groups of the *Rape of Proserpina*, *Apollo and Daphne*, and *David*. On the election of Urban VIII, he was appointed official artist to the papal court and to the Barberini family. After Maderno's death in 1629, the Pope put him in charge of the rebuilding of St Peter's Basilica.

During the reign of Innocent X (1644–55), Bernini sculpted his extraordinary *Ecstasy of St Theresa* and the *Fountain of the Four Rivers* (📖 *See PIAZZA NAVONA*). Under Alexander VII (1655–67), he built the church of St Andrew on the Quirinal, the colonnade enclosing St Peter's Square, redesigned St Peter's Chair and built the Royal Stair (Scala Regia) in the Vatican Palace. Eventually he was summoned to Paris by Louis XIV and his minister, Colbert, to mastermind the façade of the Cour Carrée in the Louvre, but as the King turned his attention to Versailles, Bernini's design was never carried out. Not only an architect and sculptor, Bernini probably painted a hundred pictures, of which only a few have survived. He produced a great deal of work, rose rapidly and was very successful.

His genius was recognised in his lifetime and he received many decorations; his contemporaries saw in him another Michelangelo. He was welcome in the most brilliant circles; he put on plays for his friends, designing the stage sets, writing the words and playing a role. He was fleetingly eclipsed by Borromini when Innocent X succeeded Urban VIII, but soon returned to favour with his *Fountain of the Four Rivers*.

Francesco Borromini (1599–1667) was the son of Giovanni Domenico Castelli, an architect to the Visconti family in

The Sleeping Hermaphroditus, marble copy of a Greek original in Palazzo Massimo

©R. Mattes/mauritius images/age fotostock

Milan. He trained as a stonemason and acquired great technical experience. The artist worked as Carlo Maderno's assistant on St Peter's, Sant'Andrea della Valle and the Barberini Palace. In 1625, he received the title of *maestro* and in 1628 took his mother's name: Borromini. He based his art on rigour and sobriety, excluding marble decorations and paintings. In Borromini's art, the Baroque style is expressed by architectural lines that he cut and curved with a sure hand. As an architect, he was critical of Bernini's over-dramatic and excessive style. Unsurprisingly, the two artists were supported by different patrons: the papal court favoured Bernini; Borromini's style agreed mainly with the religious orders, such as the Trinitarians and the followers of St Philip Neri.

San Carlo alle Quattro Fontane, Borromini's first full-scale work, probably shows his genius at its best *(1638, although he envisioned the façade much later, in the year when he died)*. At the same period, he designed the Oratory of St Philip Neri, typical of his original and balanced style. Around 1643 he built the small church of Sant'Ivo alla Sapienza, with its convex and concave curves culminating in a multi-lobed cupola. These projects earned him the protection of Fra Spada, who became Innocent X's adviser. The Pope raised him to the first rank and appointed him to renovate St John Lateran for the Jubilee of 1650.

Borromini, an introvert who shunned the world, lived in constant anxiety and never knew the fame enjoyed by his rival. One night, in a fit of anguish and anger against his servant, he took his own life.

Other architects worked in Rome at that period. **Carlo Maderno**, responsible for the façades of St Peter's and Santa Susanna, and **Giacomo della Porta**, probably the most active architect around 1580, were both great admirers of Michelangelo and are often included among the Mannerists. **Flaminio Ponzio** worked for the Borghese *(front of their palace, Pauline Fountain)*. **Giovanni Battista Soria** designed the façades of Santa Maria della Vittoria and St Gregory the Great. The well-proportioned architecture of **Pietro da Cortona** is most attractive *(St Luke and St Martina, the façade of Santa Maria in Via Lata, the dome of San Carlo al Corso)*. In contrast with the dramatic architecture of Bernini and Borromini, this artist took his inspiration from the 16C models of Bramante and Palladio. He paid particular attention to the position of his work in an urban context *(the façade of Santa Maria della Pace)*. The name of **Carlo Rainaldi** deserves to be remembered for his work in Santa Maria in Campitelli (1655–65) and for his arrangement of the "twin" churches in the Piazza del Popolo, which frame the entrance to Via del Corso.

BAROQUE ART

An inherent quality of Baroque art is restlessness – movement and contrast. Water, with its undulations and reflection, was an essential element. Effects dazzled from expensive materials, such as marble and precious stones. Cesare Ripa's dictionary, which appeared in 1594, explained how to express an abstract idea – even in stone.

In **architecture**, building plans hoped to express movement *(San Carlo alle Quattro Fontane, Sant'Andrea al Quirinale)*. Façades were embellished with disengaged columns, bold projections, curved contours and recesses.

Flowing garments and figures expressing abstract qualities dominated **sculpture**. The altarpieces are decorated with pictures of marble and wreathed columns; the latter, a feature of ancient Roman art, were very popular with Bernini *(baldaquin in St Peter's)*. Church interiors are full of cherubs perched on pediments and cornices.

In addition to the sculptors associated with Bernini (Antonio Raggi, Ercole Ferrata, Francesco Mochi, etc), mention must be made of **Alessandro Algardi** (1592–1654), inspired by classical art; he produced remarkable portraits and marble pictures, including the funerary monument of Leo XI in St Peter's.

Baroque **painters** sought to achieve effects of perspective and *trompe l'oeil* with spiralling or diagonal compositions. They included **Pietro da Cortona**, an architect as well as an interior designer, whose masterpiece is the fresco depicting the triumph of the Barberini family in the palace of the same name. Also worthy of note is Giovanni Battista Gaulli. Known as **Baciccia**, he was a Bernini protégé who frescoed the Chiesa del Gesù ceiling. The artist **Giovanni Lanfranco** (1582–1647), from Parma, painted the dome of Sant'Andrea della Valle with great technical skill. **Andrea Pozzo**, a Jesuit, who was a painter, studied the theory of architecture and had a passion for *trompe l'oeil*. The best expression of which is without a doubt his fresco on the ceiling of the church of Sant'Ignazio: it is hard to believe that the cupola figured here is only an illusion. His book *Prospettiva de' pittori e architetti* appeared in 1693 and circulated throughout Europe.

Rome attracted artists of all nationalities. Rubens made several visits; he admired Michelangelo, the Carracci and Caravaggio and completed the apse paintings of the New Church. During his long stay, Velazquez painted a fine portrait of Innocent X *(now in the Galleria Doria Pamphili)*.

CLASSICISM

The 18C etchings of Piranesi don't always resonate now. After 1870, in an attempt to fulfil its role as the new-minted capital, the city spewed forth vast new residential districts. During the Fascist period, the layout transformed further. Buildings such as the Law Courts *(palazzaccio)*, the monument to Victor Emmanuel II (the "wedding cake" or "typewriter"), and the Palazzo delle Civiltà del Lavoro ("square colosseum") may initially have been unpopular, but they now form a familiar backdrop.

NEOCLASSICISM

This trend developed from the middle of the 18C until the early 19C and was marked by a return to Greek and Roman architecture, recently rediscovered during the excavations of Herculaneum, Pompeii and Paestum. Following Baroque exuberance, Neoclassicism was characterised by simplicity and symmetry, even a touch of frigidity. This was the period when Winckelmann, who was Librarian at the Vatican and in charge of Roman antiquities, published his works on art. Francesco Milizia launched his criticism of the Baroque and superfluous decoration, while praising the simplicity and nobility of ancient monuments.

Fresco on the ceiling of Sant'Ignazio by Andrea Pozzo

©Judy Edelhoff/Michelin

Piranesi (1720–78), engraver and architect, took up permanent residence in Rome in 1754. He produced some 2 000 engravings, including the series "Views of Rome", published in 1750: an incomparable collection full of charm and melancholy. He also designed the attractive Piazza dei Cavalieri di Malta.

Antonio Canova (1757–1821) was the showy talent at this time and Napoleon's favourite sculptor. His works' calm regularity enchanted his contemporaries.

In architecture, mention should be made of **Giuseppe Valadier**, who laid out Piazza del Popolo (1816–20). Non-Italians, such as the German Mengs and the French at the Villa Medici, stand out in painting (&See PIAZZA DI SPAGNA).

The end of the 19C saw artists – such as Cesare Maccari (frescoes in the Palazzo Madama) and Guilio Aristide Sartorio (frieze in the chamber of the Parliament building) – working in Rome.

MODERN ART

An exponent of Roman Futurism, **Giacomo Balla** (1861–1958) moved to Rome in 1895. With Fortunato Depero, he signed the 1915 manifesto of the "Futurist Reconstruction of the Universe"; after 1930 his painting reverted to pre-Futurist themes. Other important artists were **Mario Mafai** (1902–65) and **Gino Bonichi** (also known as Scipione) (1904–33), members of the Roman School, which Renato Guttuso joined in 1931. The major developments in both painting and sculpture can be seen in the National Gallery of Modern Art.

ARCHITECTURE AND TOWN PLANNING

For its first 20 years as the capital of Italy, Rome was a building site.

The town plans of 1871 and 1883 provided for the construction of housing for the new civil servants around Piazza Vittorio Emanuele, Piazza dell'Independenza, at Castro Pretorio and in the Prati; for the demolition of the slum districts of the inner city; for the construction of administrative buildings; for the establishment of banks and newspapers; and for the provision of arterial roads. Via del Corso and Via Nazionale, which were opened soon after the inclusion of Rome in the kingdom of Italy, were followed by Corso Vittorio Emanuele II and Via XX Settembre.

First Quarter of the 20C

The government undertook more public works. In 1902, the Humbert I tunnel linked the Quirinal and the business centre. Extensive parks, formerly the private property of the great families, were opened or, like the Villa Ludovisi, sold as building lots for residential development. Romans constructed the Tiber embankment and cut away the Campidoglio to make room for the monument to Victor Emmanuel II. The International Exhibition in 1911 developed the district around Piazza Mazzini, while a benefactor contributed a huge museum of modern art in a leafy setting. The year 1920 heralded the onset of the garden suburbs: near to Monte Sacro in the north and at Garbatella in the south.

Mussolini's Rome

The arrival of Mussolini in 1922 ushered in a policy of grandiose town planning linked to the Fascist ideology which favoured a return to ancient grandeur. Three new streets – Corso del Rinascimento, Via della Botteghe Oscure and Via del Teatro di Marcello – were opened up to allow traffic to penetrate the Campus Martius. Via dei Fori Imperiali was opened in 1932 to give a clear view of the Colosseum from Piazza Venezia.

The reconciliation of the Church and State, sealed in the Lateran Treaty in 1929, was marked by the opening of Via della Conciliazione (1936) to the detriment of the medieval district of the Borgo. As it had been decided that Rome should expand towards the sea, construction began on the new district known as EUR.

From the Second World War to the Present Day

The Holy Year in 1950, when masses of pilgrims were expected, saw the completion of both Via Cristoforo Colombo and the railway station (Stazione Termini). The Flaminia Stadium, the small Sports Palace in Via Flaminia and the Sports Palace in EUR were built for the 1960 Olympic Games. The Olympic Village in Via Flaminia was built on a site cleared of old run-down housing. Corso di Francia, a wide elevated highway, is also a daring piece of architectural design. In the west, Via Olimpica connects the Foro Italico to EUR. In 1961 the international airport at Fiumicino (Leonardo da Vinci) was built to complement the existing one at Ciampino. In 1970 the main orbital road around the city *(Grande Raccordo Anulare – 70km/44mi)* was finished.

Among Rome's modern buildings, mention should be made of the RAI block *(☞ See MONTE MARIO–FLAMINIO)*, the British Embassy *(☞ See PORTA PIA)*, buildings in EUR, the Chamber for Papal Audiences built by Pier Luigi Nervi in 1971 and the Gregorian Profane and Christian Museums *(both in the Vatican)*, and the more recent structures by American architect Richard Meier *(the Ara Pacis museum and the Church of Tor tre Teste)* and Italian Renzo Piano *(Rome Auditorium)*.

LITERATURE

Rome has long been a popular subject for foreign writers, detailed by travellers such as Mark Twain, Stendhal and Goethe. However, perhaps the best portraits of this fascinating and contrasting city appear in the satire of the Roman author Bellini, or more recently in the complex novels of Alberto Moravia.

Rome's contribution to Italian literature is an important one. Over a period spanning at least seven centuries *(from the 3C BC to the famous sack of Rome in AD 410)*, Latin literature flourished. The different literary genres included epics, by writers such as **Ennius** (239–169 BC), **Virgil** (70–19 BC), **Lucan** (39–65) and **Statius** (40–96); comic dramas by **Plautus** (?250–184 BC) and **Terence** (?184–?159 BC; satirical works by **Lucilius** (?168–102 BC), **Horace** (65–8 BC) and **Juvenal** (2C AD); didactic poetry by **Lucretius** (?98–?55 BC); love poetry by **Catullus**

(87–?55 BC), **Propertius** (97–16 BC), **Tibullus** (55–19 BC) and **Ovid** (43 BC–AD 17); rhetorical and philosophical prose by **Cicero** (106–43 BC) and **Seneca** (?4 BC–AD 65); and romances by **Petronius** (2C AD) and **Apuleius** (AD 125–180).

Historians have left fascinating accounts. **Caesar** (100–44 BC) wrote about his own military campaigns in *The Gallic Wars* and *The Civil War*. Two monographs by **Sallust** (86–35 BC) have survived, the *Bellum Lugurthinum* (an account of the war in Numidia from 105–11 BC) and the *Bellum Catilinae*, on the Catiline conspiracy of 63 BC, which was also the subject of four famous orations by **Cicero** (known as the *Catilinarie*). These works, along with others by the same author (such as the *Pro Murena* and *Pro Milone*), paint an illuminating picture of the political climate during this period of the Republic.

Other annalistic works include the *Libri Ab Urbe Condita* by **Livy** (59 BC–AD 17), containing vivid descriptions of events that took place between the founding of the city and the 9C BC (of which about 30 books have survived intact), and the *Annales* (a history of the period from the death of Augustus to that of Nero) and *Historiae* (the period from Galba to Domitian) by **Tacitus** (55–117).

These official histories are complemented by the *Lives of the Caesars* (from Julius Caesar to Domitian) by **Suetonius** (?70–?125) – a kind of biography – and the 10 books of the *Epistulae* by **Pliny the Younger** (61–113), letters on a range of themes written to characters of the time, including the Emperor Trajan, which are fascinating for their portrait of high society during the Imperial era. In contrast, **Petronius** paints a grotesque and parodistic portrait of this society in his *Satiricon* (brilliantly adapted for cinema by the director Fellini).

From the Middle Ages Rome gradually lost her supremacy in the literary arts to other cities in Italy (especially Florence). Not until the founding of the Roman Academy by **Pomponio Leto** (1428–97) did the city regain literary eminence. This role was consolidated by the **Arcadia Society**, founded in 1690 by **Giam-**

The Grand Tour

A continental tour of one or two years, culminating in a visit to Rome, was a peculiarly British custom which lasted 300 years, reaching its height in the 18C when the Grand Tour formed part of a gentleman's education. A young man would set out with a tutor, known as a "bear leader", who would superintend his studies, protect him from bad company and show him the sights. On arriving in Rome, preferably at Easter time, these early tourists would set out "equipped with all things needful to measure the dimensions of the antiquities they would be shown". It was important to engage a good guide such as Winckelmann, a German archaeologist, who was superintendent of antiquities in Rome, or Gavin Hamilton, who became well known as a dealer and antiquary. The tour had great influence at home on manners, architectural style and the formation of art collections. Lord Burlington, the arbiter of good taste in the early 18C, made two tours, which led to his patronage of William Kent and the introduction of the Palladian style into England.

Many English artists studied in Rome: Richard Wilson (1752–56); Sir Joshua Reynolds (1750–52); and Sir George Romney (1773–75), whose portraits show the influence of the Classical style in their backgrounds and draperies; John Flaxman, the sculptor (1787–94), nicknamed the "English Michelangelo", who encouraged John Gibson to become a pupil of Canova. Benjamin West (1760–63) and John Copley (1774) from America visited Rome before settling in London.

In the 19C, instead of the established tour of the most famous cities, works of art and monuments, with its accent on antiquities, visitors preferred to settle in less well-known towns, taking an interest in Italian life and customs and even in the nationalist movement. Charles Dickens visited Rome in 1845 while writing a travel book, *Pictures of Italy*.

Rome provided poetic inspiration: in May 1817 **Byron** toured the ruins gathering material for the *Fourth Canto of Childe Harold*; **Shelley** composed *Prometheus Unbound* and *The Cenci* while lodging in the Corso in 1819; in 1860 Robert and Elizabeth Barrett Browning made a visit to Rome which inspired his greatest work, *The Ring and the Book*, a poem based on a 17C Roman murder trial.

Rome still attracted many artists: Eastlake made invaluable purchases of early Italian art for the National Gallery in London; Turner visited Rome twice (1819, 1828) and used quotations from Childe Harold as titles for his paintings. From America came William Page (1849–60), who painted portraits of Robert and Elizabeth Browning; he had trained under Samuel Morse, an artist who studied in Europe in 1832 and invented the electric telegraph.

Many American writers visited Rome: Washington Irving (1804–06), Fenimore Cooper (1820–27), Longfellow (1828), Herman Melville (1856–57), Nathaniel Hawthorne (1858–59) and Mark Twain (1867), while collecting material for *Innocents Abroad*. Most famous of all was Henry James, who first visited Italy in 1869; his first important novel was set in Rome.

battista Felice Zappi (1667–1719) and his wife Faustina Maratti (1680–1745). This society, situated at the time on the Janiculum Hill, championed a style reminiscent of the *Canzoniere* by Petrarch, as opposed to the Baroque "bad taste" of the 17C. Among the main exponents of this style were **Paolo Rolli** (1687–1785) and **Pietro Metastasio** (1698–1782). The latter was appointed official poet at the Imperial court in Vienna and his melodramas, such as *Catone in Utica* and *Dido Abandoned*, met with notable success both in Italy and abroad.

The city played a marginal role in cultural debate during the Enlightenment, a movement that greatly influenced Milan and Naples. Writers who visited Rome seemed to appreciate its unique nature, which gave rise to extremes of high praise or fierce condemnation. Although **Goethe** hurled abuse at the noise in Via del Corso during the Carnival, he confessed that he felt reborn the day he arrived in Rome *(Italianische Reise – Italian Journey)*. **Mark Twain** did not look favourably on the papacy or its superstitious trappings. He claimed that walking through the streets of Rome it was difficult to believe in the city's magnificent past *(The Innocents Abroad)*.

Leopardi had a deeply disturbing impression of the city at the beginning of the 19C; he saw it as somehow shut in, lacking in imagination, and full of "quite repulsive" women.

Giuseppe Gioacchino Belli (1791–1863) wrote in dialect, using popular themes similar to those of the Romantic movement. Belli wrote over 2 000 sonnets *(sonetti)*, which portray the life of the common people, using the language and vocabulary of the lower social classes. He succeeds in painting a clear picture of Roman society, divided between the aristocracy and clerics on the one hand, and the "plebs" on the other, interspersed with occasional references to folklore. Another author who wrote in the Roman dialect was Carlo Alberto Salustri, better known as **Trilussa** (1873–1950), whose colourful and witty works describe popular dissatisfaction with the Fascist regime of the time.

A superb evocation of Rome is found in *Il Piacere* (1889) by **Gabriele D'Annunzio**. The author describes 16C courts and sumptuously decorated Baroque palaces in great detail, providing the backdrop for the elegant receptions and grand banquets held by high society. Places appear as symbols of the various characters, so that the city almost becomes a protagonist in the novel.

Two other leading lights of the city were **Vincenzo Cardarelli** (1887–1959) and **Antonio Baldini** (1889–1962) who produced the magazine *La Ronda* between 1919 and 1923.

Among contemporary writers, **Alberto Moravia** (1907–90) described the apathy and inadequacy of Rome's bourgeoisie in *Gli Indifferenti* and *La Noia*, and put forward a clear portrayal of the lower echelons of Italian society in *La Romana*, *Raconti Romani* and *La Ciociara* (successfully adapted for the cinema by De Sica). During WWII, author **Elsa Morante** hid in villages south of Rome with Moravia. Thirty years later, in 1974, she based a sweeping novel on this fugitive existence. The story revolves around Ida Mancuso: widowed, raped and abandoned, yet resilient. As *Esquire* reviewer Alfred Kazan observed, *History* is "one of the few novels in any language that renders the full horror of Hitler's war, the war that never gets into the books".

Born and educated in Milan, **Carlo Emilio Gadda** (1893–1973) owed some of his fame to a novel based in Rome, entitled *Quer pasticciaccio brutto de via Merulana* (1946). The title translates literally as "That Awful Mess on Via Merulana". The novel effectively portrays Rome during the Fascist period, set around events taking place in 1927 and depicting all strata of society, from the bourgeoisie to the working class. Much of the novel's success lies in its use of the Roman dialect, for which Gadda consulted with friends who were experts on the subject, resulting in a new, bold and original mix of language.

An important figure in the cultural world of the 1960s and 1970s was **Pier Paolo Pasolini** (1922–75), also not originally from Rome. This widely debated figure was a poet, novelist, critic, film director and dramatist. He portrayed a sadly realistic picture of the Roman underclass in *Ragazzi di vita* and *Una vita violenta*.

For a wide array of writing about the city, turn to *Smiles of Rome*. Editor Susan Cahill compiled this literary companion. Sample Freud on Michelangelo, Edith Wharton on the Villa Borghese and **Eleanor Clark**, author of the classic travelogue *Rome and a Villa*, on the Pyramid of Cestius in the Protestant Cemetery (in which the remains of both Keats and Shelley lie).

BOOKS

Rome has long been a favourite subject with writers of all nationalities. The selection below includes recommendations of guide books, fiction and historical works on the city.

ART AND ARCHITECTURE

Roman Building Jean Pierre Adam (Routledge 1999)

Roman Art and Architecture Sir Mortimer Wheeler (Thames & Hudson 1964)

A Handbook of Roman Art: A Survey of the Visual Arts of the Roman World Martin Henig (Phaidon 1995)

Roman Imperial Architecture JB Ward-Perkins (1981, Yale University Press 1992)

Lives of the Artists G Vasari (1965, Oxford Paperbacks 2008 [2 vols])

The Italian Painters of the Renaissance B Berenson (Ursus Press 1999)

COMMENTARIES AND FICTION

Italian Journey Wolfgang Goethe (1788, Penguin Classics 2004)

Pictures from Italy Charles Dickens (1846, Penguin Books 2006)

Daisy Miller Henry James (1878, Penguin Popular Classics 2007)

The Child of Pleasure Gabriele d'Annunzio (1889, Biblobazaar 2009)

Quo Vadis Henryk Sienkiewicz (1896, Norilana Books 2006)

Italian Hours Henry James (1909, Penguin Classics 1995)

I, Claudius Robert Graves (1934, Penguin Classics 2006)

The Woman of Rome Albterto Moravia (1949, Zoland Books 1999)

Death in Rome Wolfgang Koeppen (1954, Granta Books 2004)

Leaving Winter Kathleen A Quinn (Silver Lake Publishing, 2003)

Romanitas Sophia McDougall (Orion Books 2005)

Imperium Robert Harris (Simon & Schuster 2006)

HISTORY

A History of Italy Stuart Woolf (1979, Routledge 1991)

A Traveller's History of Italy Valerio Lintner (1989, Chastleton Travel 2007)

Roman Society D Dudley (Penguin History 1991)

The Romans: An Introduction to their History and Civilization K Christ (University of Chicago Press 1985 [translated from German])

Sound of the Cinema

"Mussolini didn't want to hear any foreign languages, so we started dubbing," Francesco Vairano – one of the nation's top dubbing directors – told *The Walrus Magazine*. Indeed, today *versioni originali* are scarce: Italians, quite rightly, fell in love with the sound of their own voices. The mouthpieces of the stars often become celebrities in their own right, like Giuseppe Rinaldi, the rugged voice of Marlon Brando, Robert Redford and Paul Newman. Emilio Cigoli gritted out lines for both John Wayne and Clark Gable. Oreste Lionello capered as Woody Allen. Greta Garbo even wrote a fan letter to her Italian songbird, actress Tina Latenzi.

Laurel and Hardy rode dubbing to new heights of success in this country. Originally mouthed by Italian-American actors, the soundtrack produced much hilarity in the olde worlde. So the pair remained in dialect, while the supporting cast purred fluently. A nationwide contest appointed Alberto Sordi the bumpkin-emigrant voice of Ollie. By the time this comic actor died in 2003, he'd starred in almost 200 films, including Fellini's *I Vitelloni*. Soldi was so popular, Rome appointed him mayor for a day on his 80th birthday – and 250,000 locals mourned at his funeral.

Cinecittà

© nito100/iStockphoto.com

Rome: Its People, Life and Customs
UE Paoli (Bristol Classical Press
1996 [translated from Italian])

Renaissance Rome: 1500–59 P Partner
(1980, University of California
Press 1992)

*The Risorgimento and the Unification
of Italy* D Beales (1982, Longman
2002)

The Pope and the Duce PC Kent
(Macmillan Press Ltd 1981)

JUBILEE

The Holy Year in Rome: Past and Present
EM Jung-Inglessis (International
Scholars Publications 1998)

PEOPLE

Stories of Rome Livy, translated by
R Nicholls (Cambridge University
Press 1982)

The Italians Luigi Barzini (1964, Simon
& Schuster 1996)

Romans, their Lives and Times
Michael Sheridan (Phoenix
Paperbacks 1995)

Rome, the Biography of a City
Christopher Hibbert
(1995, Penguin 2001)

The New Italians Charles Richards
(Penguin 1995)

USEFUL GUIDES

*Guide to the Vatican Museums;
Guide to the Vatican City*
(Monumenti, Musei e Gallerie
Pontificie)

The Companion Guide to Rome
Georgina Masson (1998,
Companion Guides 2007)

CINEMA

Rome has always provided the perfect
backdrop for the big screen and for a few
decades it was also home to the most
important film studios in Europe, **Cinecittà**. (The name, pronounced chee-
nay chee-TAH, means "cinema city").
The Fascist dictator Benito Mussolini
founded the lot in 1937, aping Hitler's
and Stalin's propaganda machines. Set
on the Via Tuscolano (*See CASTELLI
ROMANI*), the studios covered an area
of 600 000m²/6 456 000sq ft and housed
16 film sets, offices, restaurants, a huge
pool for shooting water scenes and all
the latest technology and gadgetry.
These state-of-the-art facilities contributed to an increase in domestic film
production, which was now completely
autonomous. In the first six years, some
300 films were produced here – and not
all were Fascist boosterism. "Black" films
championed the cause, while middle-
class melodramas – called "white telephone" after that ubiquitous prop –
peddled escapism.

Cinecittà is also the cradle of neo-realism (the Italian School of *cinéma vérité*). Although films of this type are usually shot outside, giants like **Vittorio de Sica** and **Roberto Rossellini** did make some of their earliest works in the studios. The main theme of the neo-realists was the war and all its tragic consequences. In *Roma Città Aperta* (1945), *Paisà* (1946) and *Germania Anno Zero* (1948), Rossellini portrayed Nazi–Fascist oppression. De Sica, in *Sciuscià* (1946) and *Ladri di Biciclette* (1948), drew a searing portrait of postwar unemployment and misery. In *Riso amaro* (1949) and *Pasqua di Sangue* (1950), **De Santis** described a working class divided between a submission to the dominant ideology and its revolutionary aspirations.

The government began discouraging left-leaning productions in the 1950s. Gritty truths gave way to gloss, earning Cinecittà the nickname "Hollywood on the Tiber". Cheap and cheerful, the studio fostered American feature films like *Roman Holiday, The Quiet American, Ben Hur, Quo Vadis?* and *The Pink Panther*. Elizabeth Taylor first met her great love, Richard Burton, while filming *Cleopatra* here. And the world learned what to call the photographers pursuing the pair – *paparazzi* – thanks to **Federico Fellini**'s *La Dolce Vita*. The director captured many of the Eternal City's most enduring cinematic images, including Anita Ekberg and Marcello Mastroianni in the Trevi Fountain, and the bubble-headed fabulousness of the Via Veneto. He shunned locations and constructed lavish foam copies of monuments, including St Peter's cupola, on the lot (Soundstage Five, Europe's largest, was his preferred workspace for four decades). He considered the studio a temple of dreams: "For me, every journey starts and ends at the studios of Cinecittà... It's my ideal world, the cosmic space before the Big Bang."

For Italian cinema, the 1960s were a golden age. Supported by a powerful industrial infrastructure, the studios produced more than 200 films a year – and of the best quality. **Luchino Visconti** was a key player during this era. His early work focused mainly on themes relating to social injustice. Later films examined the decadence and disenchantment of the middle classes. Among his masterpieces were *Ossessione* (1943), *Notti Bianche* (1957) and *Ludwig* (1972).

The 1960s also brought a new generation of directors keen to record their political and social commitment, such as **Pasolini**, **Rosi** and **Bertolucci**. During the same period, the work of **Sergio Leone**, who produced a vast quantity of "spaghetti westerns", also kept the studios at Cinecittà in the limelight. From the 1970s into the 90s, Italian cinema suffered a crisis, both in terms of production and creativity, which only a few *films d'auteur* managed to resist. Among the most recent are *La Famiglia* (1987) by **Ettore Scola**, *Caro Diario* (1994) and *La Stanza del Figlio* (2001) by **Nanni Moretti**, none of which were produced at Cinecittà. In 1997, the government sold the ailing studio to private companies, captained by Diego Della Valle, who runs JP Tod's, the Italian shoe company. A $25m infusion attracted Martin Scorsese's *Gangs of New York* (2002) and Mel Gibson's *The Passion of the Christ* (2004), among other high-profile projects, but the studio still struggles. And computers threaten its strong suits: superb artisans and space for replica worlds. Cinecittà celebrated its 70th birthday in 2007. In 2011 Cinecittà opened its doors to visitors with an exhibit, made it permanent and added tours to some of its lots and sets.

FILMS IN ROME

Rome was a favourite venue for directors of Italian neo-realist films during the late 1940s and the city continues to be a popular backdrop for Italian cinema today. Below is a list of well-known movies that were shot in the capital.

Roma, Città Aperta by R Rossellini, 1945. A portrayal of the Italian Resistance in Nazi-occupied Rome. This film represents a landmark in Italian cinema, with a memorable performance by Anna Magnani.

Ladri di Biciclette by V de Sica, 1948. This masterpiece of neo-realism depicts the working-class districts of Rome, postwar, when a bicycle represented survival.

Domenica d'Agosto by L Emmer, 1949. Episodes from daily life taking place at the same time on a Sunday in August on the road leading from Rome to the beach in Ostia.

La Dolce Vita by F Fellini, 1960. Evocative shots of Rome serve as a backdrop to the portrayal of an empty-headed generation with little interest in anything other than forgetting the past and enjoying themselves.

C'eravamo Tanto Amati by E Scola, 1974. Three friends who were in the Resistance together meet up in Rome years later and compare their loss of hope and illusions.

Una Giornata Particolare by E Scola, 1977. The story of an intense relationship between a resigned housewife and a homosexual anti-fascist on the day in May 1938 when Hitler visited Rome.

Un Sacco Bello by C Verdone, 1979. The three episodes of this film portray an average man from Rome, with all his faults and qualities.

Caro Diario by N Moretti, 1994. One of the three episodes that make up this film is a wonderful autobiographical trip through Rome by scooter.

La Parola Amore Esiste by M Calopresti, 1998. A touching story of loneliness, love and psychological hardship.

The Talented Mr Ripley by A Minghella, 1999. Matt Damon as Tom Ripley, a loner who takes over the life of playboy Dickie Greenleaf (Jude Law).

The Passion of the Christ by M Gibson, 2004. A depiction of the last 12 hours in the life of Jesus Christ, filmed in ancient Aramaic.

Rome 2005. This HBO mini-series chronicles the fortunes of two noble families and two Roman soldiers during the reign of Julius Caesar. Filmed entirely in Rome and Cinecittà.

Angels & Demons 2009. Taken from the infamous novel by Dan brown, the scenes in St Peters were shot in California as the troupe was denied access to Catholic churches.

When in Rome by M Steven Johnson 2009. New Yorker Beth attends her sister's wedding in Rome and finds herself embroiled in a romantic comedy of multiple suitors after taking coins from a "fountain of love"

To Rome with Love by Woody Allen 2012. Allen directs and stars in this romantic comedy focusing on the lives of four people in Rome.

La grande Bellezza by P Sorrentino, 2013. The film won Best Foreign Language Film at the 86th Academy Awards (2014). Journalist Jep Gambardella (T Servillo) has charmed and seduced his way through the lavish nightlife of Rome for decades.

Sacro GRA by G Rosi, 2013. Eschewing external comments or interviews, this film documents real life scenes shot near the Grande Raccordo Anulare (hence „GRA" in the title), the ring road that circles Rome.

Spectre by S Mendes, 2015. The 24th film starring Agent 007 has Bond battling the shadow organization Spectre, and includes scenes shot in the Italian capital.

Zoolander 2 by B Stiller. As in the original, this sequel includes plenty of cameos by famous people playing themselves. Note the participation of P P Piccioni (Valentino's artistic director), who plays a paparazzo.

Lo chiamavano Jeeg Robot by G Mainetti, 2016. This homage to Gō Nagai's manga series "Jeeg robot d'acciaio" (Jeeg, Steel robot) echoes themes introduced in the original.

ROME

The Emperor Augustus *"found a city of clay and left it marble."* His legacy was more than a millenia of beautification that leaves Rome today with elegant architecture piled high – ancient frescoes flaking in basements, and amphitheatres topped with minimalist penthouses. Bathed in the gold of sunset, the mélange ensures that Rome numbers among the world's most striking cities. The Italian capital is home to many of Europe's greatest wonders, such as the Pantheon and Foro Romano, the Colosseo, the Basilica di San Pietro, Piazza Navona, the Spanish Steps, the Fontana di Trevi and the Villa Borghese. Like any beauty, she can be mercurial: cars and people jostle the narrow alleyways. The mix of sounds and styles often leaves visitors exhausted. Best to schedule *soste* (breaks) to balance the intensity of the Eternal City.

Highlights

1. Eat gelato and people watch in the bustling **Campo de' Fiori** (*p94*)
2. Throw three coins in the iconic **Trevi Fountain** (*p115*)
3. Retreat to the shade of the elegant **Borghese Gardens** (*p223*)
4. Imagine yourself as a victorious gladiator in **The Colosseum** (*p270*)
5. Ascend to the dome of **St Peter's Basilica** for stunning views over Rome (*p329*)

Location

Rome lies about halfway down the shin of "the boot", on Italy's west side, 24km/15mi inland from the Tyrrhenian Sea. The **Tiber River** (*Tevere*), known to the ancients as the *flavus Tiber* (the fair or blond Tiber), bisects the city.

The Seven Hills

Historians emphasise the strategic location of Rome's seven hills, especially the **Palatino**, which was a staging post on the Salt Road (*Via Salaria*) and was first inhabited in the 10C BC. Its twin peaks gave a clear view of the Tiber River. Today the Palatine and the **Capitoline** hills rise west of the Colosseo, the **Caelian** to the south and the **Aventine** to the southwest. The **Esquiline** rises east of the Colosseum, the **Quirinal** and **Viminal** hills sit farther to the northeast.

The **Gianicolo**, south of the Vatican across the river, didn't make the original cut, though it remains a key landmark, as does **Monte Testaccio**. Made from discarded ancient *amphorae* (terra-cotta shipping jars), the man-made hill rears 54m/177ft near the Piramide Metro and Ostia Railway Station.

The Streetscape

No other city combines so successfully such a diverse heritage of Classical antiquities, medieval buildings, Renaissance palaces and Baroque churches. Far from being discordant, they constitute a logical continuity where revivals, influences and contrasts display the ingenuity of Roman architects and builders. Today Rome is still impressive as a lively urban core.

The main thoroughfares bustle with traffic, vehicular and pedestrian. Yet quiet alleys wind among ochre façades to small market squares, or stairs descending to fountains. Rome rewards a wanderer endlessly.

Climb high for views of the city's splendour. From the belvedere on **Gianicolo**, a view east above the rooftops reveals countless domes, such as the elegant **Sant'Ivo alla Sapienza**, the **Pantheon** and the majestic orb of **St Peter's**. The **Pincian Hill**, above the Piazza di Popolo, facing west, is a favourite sunset perch. Rome is the city of churches: some 300 in all, a fitting number for the home of Roman Catholicism. Since the 7C pilgrims have visited the tombs of **St Peter** and St Paul and the catacombs, and, more recently, the **Vatican State**. Rome is famed for water features: liquid dances from street nozzles, the

Garden in Villa Borghese

Baroque splendour of the **Fontana di Trevi** and the Renaissance tracery of the **Turtle Fountain**. Obelisks – Egyptian, Imperial and Papal – seem to grow like trees: perched on an elephant's back, boldly mounted on the **Fountain of the Four Rivers,** and once the pointer for a gigantic sundial, now in **Piazza Montecitorio.**

Neighbourhoods

For density of sights, it's worth starting in the **Centro Storico**, Rome's ever-palpitating heart, bordered by the Tiber River to the west and **Via del Corso** to the east. Largely rebuilt during the Renaissance, this area is a patchwork of fine palaces (some now museums) and churches, endowed with the material wealth of rich family patrons – a Raphael here, a Caravaggio there, behind unassuming façades. **Piazza Navona** and **Campo de' Fiori** provide convenient crossroads for pedestrian traffic; they are natural theatres for the daily *passeggiata* (stroll). At the heart of the area, the **Pantheon** rises in dignified harmony above tourists paying exorbitant prices for coffee on the **Piazza della Rotonda**. To the east, the Capitoline and Palatine hills cradle the largest visible concentration of Ancient Roman remains; don't expect shops, restaurants or nightlife here.

On **Capitoline Hill**, tucked beside the vast Monumento a Vittorio Emmanuele II, is the **Campidoglio**, designed by Michelangelo.

Beyond, tourists throw coins in the **Fontana di Trevi**, set in the labyrinth below the **Quirinale**, an area of atmospheric alleys, small shops and trattorias that leads into the **Esquilino**, which is centred on Santa Maria Maggiore.

The backdrop to the forbidding **Castel Sant'Angelo** across the Tiber to the west is **Vatican City**, gazing down on a city of sinners; around it lies the well-to-do Prati district.

For more secular pleasures, the **Tridente**, northeast of the Centro Storico, is pure retail therapy. From the Spanish Steps and the Piazza di Spagna along **Via dei Condotti**, Via del Babuino and Via del Corso, Italian fashion boutiques and shops selling luxury goods sit side-by-side with lively local restaurants. Behind this ever-restless scene lies the city's peaceful green lung, the vast and beautiful **Villa Borghese**, where Romans stroll under majestic umbrella pine trees. Closer to the Tiber, visitors buy prints at the Piazza Fontanella 's Borghese market.

For the flip side to the city's grace and imperial grandeur, the once-grittier working class districts of **Testaccio**, **Aventino**, and **Trastevere** are now full of authentic Roman restaurants tucked into cobbled alleys, as well as some of the city's liveliest night spots, from jazz clubs to hole-in-the-wall cocktail bars.

Campo de' Fiori★★

The area around Campo de' Fiori is one of the liveliest districts in Rome, with narrow streets full of boutiques, cafés, restaurants and artisans' workshops. The early morning bustle of the market gives way to diners, strollers and kids playing football on the cobblestones. In small squares, graceful **palazzos** stand alongside older, shabbier properties. Set between the Piazza Navona and Trastevere, this neighbourhood is a marvelous one to wander – just remain alert for *motorini* (mopeds), cars and pickpockets in the crowds.

A BIT OF HISTORY

In antiquity, the district was just to the south of the Campus Martius. **Pompey** set several important buildings here: a huge theatre, the first in Rome to be built of stone; a temple to Venus and a *curia* to house occasional meetings of the Senate. A decisive event in Roman history occurred in the latter: on the Ides of March, 44 BC, Brutus and other conspirators assassinated **Julius Caesar** at the foot of Pompey's statue. Almost nothing remains of this building.

The first Christian sanctuary here was San Lorenzo in Damaso, founded in 380. In the Middle Ages, palaces and houses of worship grew in number. The churches were quite simple buildings, serving tradesmen. The various guilds gave a certain character to the

- **Michelin Map:** 38 L 10–11, M 10–11.
- **Location:** The walk follows the narrow streets of the district lying between the Tiber, Corso Vittorio Emanuele II and the Campidoglio.
- **Timing:** Allow 2hrs.
- **Don't Miss:** Morning and night bustle in the Campo de' Fiori, S. Andrea della Valle, Piazza Farnese at night, with uplit fountains and palazzi.
- **Also See:** *CASTEL SANT'ANGELO; TRASTEVERE–GIANICOLO; ISOLA TIBERINA–GHETTO–LARGO ARGENTINA; PIAZZA NAVONA; PANTHEON.*

GETTING THERE

BY BUS: Bus C3, 30, 70, 81, 87, 130, 492 and 628.

Campo de' Fiori

© J. C. Muñoz/age fotostock

district: many leather curriers *(vaccinari)*, boiler-makers *(calderari)*, and rope-makers *(funari)* prospered along the streets, crowded by pilgrims heading to St Peter's.

After Charles V's troops sacked Rome in 1527, civil architecture revived. Cardinal Riario spent his gambling profits on the Palazzo della Cancelleria, countering the scruples of his relative, Sixtus IV. Cardinal Farnese, later Pope Paul III, built the prestigious palace that bears his family name.

WALKING TOUR

Piazza Campo de' Fiori★★

The square's name ("Field of Flowers") probably goes back to the Middle Ages, when the area was one vast meadow, dominated by the fortress of the powerful Orsini family.

By the 16C, the area was Rome's centre, a meeting place for people of all ranks, crowded with inns. The **"Hostaria della Vacca"** belonged to **Vannozza Cattanei** (1442–1518), famous for her liaison with Rodrigo **Borgia**, who became Pope **Alexander VI**. She bore him several children, including the notorious Cesare and Lucrezia. The façade of her hostelry still bears her heraldic arms, in which Vannozza brazenly inserted the Borgia bull. Historically, the Campo hosted all sorts of festivals, as well as executions. At the centre stands a statue of Giordano Bruno, a monk burned for heresy on 17 February 1600, during the Counter-Reformation.

Every morning except Sunday, the modern square bustles with an extensive food market that sells everything from luscious vegetables to bouquets of beautiful flowers (✆see below).

Palazzo della Cancelleria★★

Piazza della Cancelleria 1. ⏱*Visits to the Sala Riaria and the Salone dei Cento Giorni: Tue afternoon and Sat morning. Booking required (one month in advance)* ✆€9. *Separate courtyard entrance for Leonardo da Vinci's exhibit (www.mostradileonardo.com, where machines' interactivity plays the key role) and sepulcher* ✆€9 *Sun–Sat 9:30am–7:30pm.* ☎*06 69 88 76 16.*

The **Chancery Palace** was built by an unidentified architect between 1483 and 1513 for Cardinal Raffaele Riario, upon whom "honours and riches were heaped" by his great-uncle Pope Sixtus IV. The palazzo housed the law courts, during the Napoleonic occupation (1809–14). Now it's occupied by the Papal Chancery, which houses the Supreme Court of the Vatican and drafts pontifical acts.

Façade and Courtyard

This palazzo is one of the most elegant products of Rome's Renaissance. The broad smooth surfaces, straight lines and shallow pilasters of the façade give it a majestic quality. The granite columns of the courtyard arcade – a harmonious composition attributed to Bramante – come from San Lorenzo in Damaso.

Interior

On the main floor of the palace are the Aula Magna (the Great Hall) and the so-called Sala dei *"Cento Giorni"* (Room of the Hundred Days – perhaps how

Campo de' Fiori Market

In the centre of this busy food market stands a statue of the scientific martyr Giordano Bruno, amid cheese and cream, cured meats, fruit and vegetables, meat and poultry, colourful flowers, and accented voices trading local gossip and exchanging ills for miraculous cures. With his pedal-powered grindstone, the knife-sharpener is a periodic visitor. The market is active from about 6:30am–2pm Mon–Sat. On Sunday various vendors occupy the square at times. Avoid mid-afternoon each day when street cleaning vehicles are active. The bars and cafes of Campo de' Fiori remain lively until 2am.

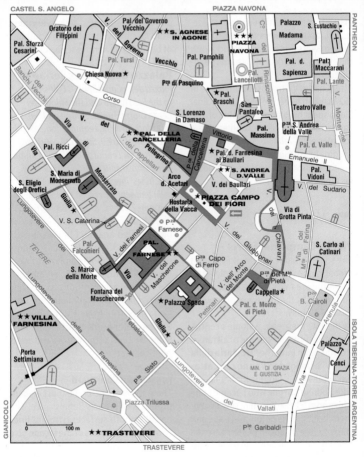

CASTEL S. ANGELO   PIAZZA NAVONA   PANTHEON

★★ TRASTEVERE

TRASTEVERE

long its painting took). The latter contains frescoes by Giorgio Vasari and his assistants, which depict the meeting of Paul III, Charles V and François I in 1538 in Nice. The influence of Michelangelo's Laurentian Library figures is evident.

San Lorenzo in Damaso

Piazza della Cancelleria 1. ⏾*Open 7:30am–noon and 4:30– 7:30pm.*
The church, founded by Pope Damasus in the 4C, was later rebuilt as part of the Cancelleria palace. It was restored during the 19C. The ceiling, damaged by fire in 1939, has been entirely restored. The church consists of a nave and side aisles preceded by a vestibule. The first chapel on the right contains a 14C

wooden crucifix; the last chapel on the left in the nave contains a 12C Virgin inspired by Byzantine icons.

▶ Turn right into Corso Vittorio Emanuele II.

Palazzo della Farnesina ai Baullari★ (Museo di Scultura Antica Giovanni Barracco)

This little Renaissance building was begun in 1523 for Thomas le Roy, a French diplomat accredited to the Holy See. Raised to the peerage by François I of France, he added the lily of France to the ermine of Brittany, his country of origin. The lily was mistaken for the iris of the Farnese and the building was called the "Piccola Farnesina". As the palazzo overlooks **Via dei Baullari** (luggage-makers), it acquired the name of Farnesina ai Baullari. The Corso Vittorio Emanuele II façade dates from 1898–1904; the original Renaissance style can be seen by walking around the building. Le Roy never actually lived in the building however, and it was soon sold on to others, including the Silvestri, an Abruzzo family who added frescoes to the first floor loggia.

The interior, radically restored in the 19C, was used as offices for institutions up until 1948, when it was turned into a museum space, now the **Barracco Museum of Ancient Sculpture**, a prestigious collection left by Baron Giovanni Barracco (◷ *open Oct/May Tue–Sun 10am–4pm, Jun/Sep Tue–Sun 1–7pm. ✆06 06 08. www.museobarracco.it).*

The collections range over Egyptian, Assyrian, Greek and Roman sculpture to the end of antiquity. The museum also houses many original Greek statues. The elegant internal courtyard stairs lead to the first floor, where the arch bears admirable 17C frescoes. The **Egyptian sculptures** date from the third millennium and include a head hewn in black granite of the young Pharaoh Ramses II, and two low-relief sculptures dating from the Old Kingdom, IV Dynasty *(Room I)*. Among the **Assyrian exhibits** *(Room II)*, note the low relief showing a group of women in a palm grove (late 8C BC); on display in the same room are a beautiful woman's funeral mask in gilded pasteboard from the period of Ptolemy, an interesting head in painted stucco of a mummy from Ermopoli, and Egyptian art from the Roman period (2C). **Rooms III and IV** house a group of **Etruscan and Cypriot works**: Etruscan *antefixae* and memorial stones; a woman's head (2C BC) found near Bolsena; a little statute of the god Bes, a minor Egyptian deity also venerated by other races; and interesting Cypriot statues such as the *quadriga* (6C BC). On the second floor are **Greek, Roman and medieval** works of art.

Michelangelo's "Fake" Cupid

Cardinal Riario's (architect of the Palazzo della Cancelleria) well-known taste for antiquities gave Michelangelo the idea of sculpting a magnificent Cupid, skilfully applying an artificial patina of age and selling it to the cardinal for 200 ducats as a genuine antique. The collector got wind of the deceit and decided to recover his money and return the statue to the artist, but Michelangelo never saw his Cupid again. It was transferred to France and disappeared.

▷ Continue along Corso Vittorio Emanuele II.

Sant'Andrea della Valle★★

Corso Vittorio Emanuele II 115-121. ◷*Open 7:45am–7:30pm.* Often referred to as the "Tosca church" because Act I of Puccini's opera is set here, **Piazza Sant'Andrea della Valle** is graced with a fountain attributed to Carlo Maderno: it bears the eagle and dragon of the Borghese family and was probably put up for Pope Paul V.

Construction of the **church** began in 1591 under the direction of **Giacomo della Porta**: it was completed between 1608 and 1623 by **Carlo Maderno**. The **façade**★★(1661–67), one of the most elegant of the Baroque style, was built by **Carlo Rainaldi**. The two-storey elevation ripples with columns and projections; the original scrolls intended to unite the two levels have been replaced by angels with spread wings – although only the left-hand statue was executed.

Interior

The Latin-cross plan with a single nave flanked by intercommunicating side chapels, as in the Gesù Church, is typical of the Counter-Reformation. The severity of the art of this period is exemplified in the extremely sober architecture of the second chapel on the right and the altar in the right transept. Conversely, the nave vaulting and left transept were decorated early in the 20C.

The dome★★, built by Carlo Maderno, is one of the loveliest in the city and second only to St Peter's in size. It was painted between 1624 and 1627 by **Lanfranco**, who expertly handled its curved surface. The *Glory of Paradise*, with its rich colouring, is an imitation of Correggio's dome for Parma Cathedral. The Evangelists on the pendentives were painted by Domenichino. The vigour and expressiveness are reminiscent of Michelangelo's art.

The upper section of the **apse★**, which was frescoed by **Domenichino** (1624–28), is in late Renaissance style: *St Andrew is led to his death (right); the Calling of St Andrew and St Peter (centre); the Flagellation of St Andrew (left); St Andrew being received into Heaven (above); St Peter and St Andrew are shown the Saviour by St John the Baptist (arcade centre).* The **Piccolomini Popes' tombs** lie above the last bay in the nave before the transept. The monuments to Pius II (*left*) and Pius III (*right*) are typical of late 15C funeral art.

▷ Take Via dei Chiavari beside the church.

Cinema Farnese

Originally a theatre dating to the 1930s, this cinema has been run by the same family since 1968. Its partnership with Persol (sunglasses) brings quality films often in their original language, as well as foreign film festivals with top directors and actors. Scenes from *Cinema Paradiso* (1988) and Woody Allen's *To Rome with Love* (2012) were filmed here. Restored with rose velvet seats, it's one of the few cinemas left with balcony seating. Piazza Campo de' Fiori 56. ℘06 68 64 395. *www.cinemafarnese.it.*

Via dei Giubbonari runs very close to the site of Pompey's great theatre (*Teatro di Pompeo*), of which little remains visible except the semi-circular line followed by the houses in Via di Grotta Pinta. By tradition, it is the street where doublet-makers (*giubbone* = doublet), silk merchants and garment repairers worked. It remains very commercial. Behind the stage, the great crowned portico of Pompey's Curia is where Julius Caesar was fatally stabbed in 44 BC. The remains of the Curia can be seen in the Largo Argentina Sacred Precinct (℘*See Area Sacra del Largo di Torre Argentina,* p127).

▷ Turn right into Via dei Giubbonari and left into a side street leading into Piazza del Monte di Pietà.

Cappella del Monte di Pietà★

Piazza di Monte di Pietà 33. ⏱*Visitable only on special occasions.* ℘*060608.*
This small oval **chapel** within the Monte di Pietà Palace is a gem of Baroque art. Originally the work of Maderno, it was redesigned by architects Giovanni Antonio de'Rossi (who worked with Bernini) and Carlo Bizzaccheri (a pupil of Carlo Fontana). He took over after the maestro's death in 1695, and was responsible for the entrance hall and dome. The chapel was consecrated in 1641, although decoration was not completed until 1725. The interior retains works whose themes reinforce the aim of the institution: to put down usury.

▷ Take Via dell'Arco del Monte; turn right into Piazza Capo di Ferro.

Palazzo Spada★

Piazza Capo di Ferro 13. ⏱*Piano Nobile is open only first, second and third Sat month, in the morning, booking required.* ℘*06 68 32 40 93.*
During the 16C, cardinals went to great lengths to "keep up with the neighbours". Gerolamo Capo di Ferro built this lavish white stucco edifice, later acquired by Cardinal Bernardino Spada and finally by the Council of State. On the **façade** are statues of Roman patrons

Sant'Andrea della Valle

© F. M. Frei/Look/Photononstop

– such as Romulus, Numa and Augustus – and faithful dogs. One inscription reads: "The dictator Julius Caesar: He filled the whole world with his enemy's gore, and at the end he drenched the senate with his own blood."

The delicate execution of the friezes in the **courtyard★★** is noteworthy.

Galleria Spada★

🕑*Open Tue–Sun 8:30am–7:30pm.*
🕑*Closed 1 Jan and 25 Dec.* 🎫*€5.*
📞*06 68 32 40 93.*

The Caesar motif reoccurs within this gallery, which presents Cardinal Spada's collection in its original setting, typical of a wealthy Roman in the 17C. It includes a statue of Pompey, which may have witnessed the famous assassination in 44BC.

The cardinal, Bernardino, was a major 17C art dealer and the patron of Guercino and Guido Reni, whose noble manner pleased him. At the same time, he was interested in *bambocciate*, realistic paintings that appeared in Rome in about 1630 in the circle of the painter Pieter Van Laer, a Dutchman nicknamed *Il Bamboccio* (the puppet) because of a physical deformity.

The gallery is of interest both for its collection and for the building in which it is housed. In Room I, crowned by an 18C ceiling, note two canvases by **Guido Reni** (1575–1642): *Portrait of Cardinal Bernardino Spada*, a good example of the artist's use of pure delicate line, and the *Slave of Ripa Grande*. Guercino's *Death of Dido* is quite lavish.

The frieze along the top of the walls in **Room II** (tempera on canvas) echoes the original frieze on the wall opposite the window and was produced by Perin del Vaga, possibly as a model for a tapestry to be placed under the *Last Judgement* in the Sistine Chapel, which was never completed. Room III, created in the 17C, was the cardinal's original gallery. On the ceiling, a series of panels dating from the end of the 17C portrays allegories of the four continents of the world (the first two panels), the four elements and the four seasons. The decoration of the fascia around the top of the walls is echoed by the *trompe-l'œil* low reliefs in the two middle panels. The console tables in gilded wood are by late 17C Roman craftsmen. Paintings on display include a delightful and masterly *Landscape with Windmills* by Bruegel the Elder (1607) and the allegory of the *Massacre of the Innocents*, a masterpiece by Pietro Testa (first half of the 17C); note how the violent contrast between light and dark accentuates the dramatic aspect of this work. Jesus (escaping in the boat) is depicted embracing the cross, symbol of the Passion.

The two globes in the centre of the room (one of the earth, the second of the heavens) are by the Dutch cartographer and printer, Bleau (Caesius) and date from 1616 and 1622.

Room IV contains works influenced by Caravaggio. Particularly noteworthy is the portrait of an enraptured Saint Cecilia (149) by Artemisia Gentileschi. A fetching Cleopatra wearing a helmet was painted by Lavinia Fontana.

Borromini "Perspective"★★

On the ground floor, behind the library and visible from the courtyard. Enquire about access.

The colonnade stretches into the distance, or at least appears to, thanks to clever a *trompe-l'œil* effect. In fact, the tunnel is a mere 9m/29ft with a petite 60cm/2ft statue. For a modest tip, the guard will sometimes escort sceptics behind the glass partition.

▶ Continue to Piazza Farnese.

Palazzo Farnese★★

English guided tours only Wed afternoon, booked 1 week in advance: visite-farnese@inventerrome.com. www.ambafrance-it.org or directly at www.inventerrome.com/index.php/en.

At either end of this quiet and elegant piazza are two huge granite basins found in the Baths of Caracalla and converted into fountains in 1626. On the far

side stands one of the most beautiful Roman palaces, which bears the name of the family for whom it was built. The fame of the Farnese began when Cardinal Alessandro was elected Pope in 1534, taking the name of **Paul III**. As the first Pope of the Counter-Reformation, he set up the Council of Trent, yet conducted his reign like a Renaissance monarch: he had four children whose mother has not been identified, and made three of them legitimate, loading them with riches.

He was a patron of the arts, continuing the work on St Peter's and the Sistine Chapel and building the Farnese Palace. He and his descendants amassed a magnificent collection of works of art. One of his grandchildren, Ranuccio (1530–65), commissioned Salviati to celebrate the glory of the Farnese in a series of frescoes. Another, Odoardo (1573–1626), invited the Carracci to paint the gallery on the first floor. The last of the Farnese was Elizabeth (1692–1766), who married Philip V of Spain. Their son, Don Carlos of Bourbon, who became king of Naples in 1735, inherited the Farnese family riches; almost all the works of art from the Farnese Palace are now in the Naples Archaeological Museum or in the Royal Palace at Capodimonte.

The palace was purchased by the French Government in 1911 and bought back by the Italian Government in 1936. It

Façade of Palazzo Farnese

© Urbano Lulli/Dreamstime.com

was then leased to France for 99 years in exchange for the La Rochefoucauld-Doudeauville Palace, the building occupied by the Italian Embassy in Paris.

Façade
The absence of pilasters and the clear horizontal lines contribute to a masterpiece of balance and proportion. Construction began in 1515 on Cardinal Alessandro Farnese's orders, to the designs of his favourite architect, Antonio da Sangallo the Younger. When Sangallo died in 1546, Michelangelo took over. He retained the first-floor windows, framed by columns with alternate pediments, curved or triangular like the recesses in the Pantheon. He added the impressive upper cornice and over the central balcony he carved the irises of the Farnese coat of arms (not to be confused with the French lily). Recent restoration work has brought to light a delicate decorative design in subtle pinkish tones.
The **courtyard** was designed by three great architects: Sangallo, Vignola and Michelangelo. The rear **façade** – overlooking Via Giulia – is the best example of the building's elegance.
Its treasures include remarkable **frescoes** (1595–1603) by Annibale Carracci (in the Farnese Gallery) with the assistance of his brother Agostino and his pupils Domenichino and Lanfranco.

▶ To admire the rear façade of the palace through an opening in the gate, take Via del Mascherone and turn right into Via Giulia (*for a description of Via Giulia, ⓘSee CASTEL S. ANGELO*).

At the intersection of Via del Mascherone and Via Giulia stands the 1626 **Fontana del Mascherone**. Carlo Rainaldi combined two ancient sculptures at the old ferry landing: a vast marble basin and a grotesque face with a vacuous expression. The mask dribbles water from the Acqua Paola, though for festivals, it would spout red wine. Sadly, this tradition has fallen by the wayside. Via Giulia then runs past the Farnese Palace's **rear façade**, designed by Vignola who took over from Michelangelo as

architect. In 1573 he was succeeded by Giacomo della Porta, who built the loggia. In 1603 the "*Passetto Farnese*", the bridge over Via Giulia, linked the palace to the convent of Santa Maria della Morte and to several rooms where the Farnese kept their collection of antiquities. Legend claims Alessandro Farnese, one of the most rapacious rulers in papal Rome, disliked crossing the Tiber on public bridges with the riffraff. He envisioned a private walkway connecting the Palazzo with the Villa Farnesina: a mighty status symbol, the 16C equivalent of, say, an executive helipad. Michelangelo designed the archway, now trailing with ivy, but its span stopped well short of the river. Farnese vanity contrasts markedly with the area's hospices and confraternities, such as Santissima Trinità dei Pelligrini and **Santa Maria dell'Orazione e della Morte**. Dedicated to burial of unclaimed bodies, it contained a spacious morgue-hall and easy river access to net floating bodies each morning.
The 1737 façade by Fernando Fuga depicts gaping skulls flanking the door. Two plaques, which invite alms, don't pull punches either. One image, black-etched in ghostly white marble, shows a winged skeleton with a banner reading "*hodie mihi, cras tibi*" ("today for me, tomorrow for you"). The other begs on behalf of country plague victims, showing a skeleton gloating over a body.

▶ Farther on, turn right into Via di S. Caterina and left into Via de Monserrato.

Under the eyes of its beautiful madonnas, **Via di Monserrato** is lined by craft and antique shops, by palaces where the many Spanish prelates, who came to Rome in the suite of the Borgia Popes (Calixtus III and Alexander VI), used to live. Many of the courtyards are worth a glance: the beauties of the Renaissance have not all disappeared. **Santa Maria di Monserrato** is the Spanish national church (*first chapel on the right*).

▶ Turn left into Via della Barchetta.

Sant'Eligio degli Orefici

Via di S. Eligio 8. ⊙ *Open Mon–Fri 9:30am–1pm by request. To visit, press the intercom at Via S. Eligio 7 (office).* ✆*06 68 68 260.*

Raphael began this church of the goldsmiths, often considered one of the purest expressions of the Renaissance (1516). It is dedicated to St Eligus, their patron.

A **cupola** crowns this small gem, laid out in an austere Greek cross plan. The *chiesa* can be damp, but lighting has been improved recently. It remains outstanding in its beauty.

▶ Return to Via di Monserrato.

The elegant **Palazzo Ricci**, tucked in at the back of its attractive little Renaissance square, has great charm; the façade bears traces of frescoes painted by Polidoro da Caravaggio and Maturino da Firenze.

Via del Pellegrino, created by Sixtus IV in 1483 to provide pilgrims with easier access to St Peter's, was once home to printing houses, and still has bookshops, as well as restaurants and boutiques. The façade of Palazzo della Cancelleria facing Via del Pellegrino is decorated with fine corner balconies.

Small, picturesque **Via Arco degli Acetari**, a popular photo spot, lies off Via del Pellegrino between nos. 19 and 44.

ADDRESSES

SHOPPING

Chez Dede – *Via di Monserrato 35.* ✆*06 8377 2934 - www.chezdede.com.* An atelier with a unique and much curated atmosphere for the Italian-French brand for manswear, womenswear as well as houseware.

Lela – *Via dei Pettinari 37.* ✆*06 8777 5792. www.lelacasa.* Simple and funny things from houseware to little everyday objects in a well decorated shop full of treasures.

Society Limonta – *Piazza di Pasquino 6.* ✆ *06 683 2480. www.societylimonta.com.* Very beautiful linens: sheets, towels and tablecloths in tasteful original colors and virgin fibers (linen and cotton).

CAFÉS

Corona Gelateria Artigianale – *Largo Arenula 27.* ✆*06 68 80 80 54.* This *gelateria* is genuinely artisanal, makes superb *granita* (pistacchio) and excellent ice cream using inventive and top quality ingredients.

VyTA Caffé Farnese – *Via dei Baullari 106.* ✆*06 87737552.* Far more upscale than the Campo, this cafe offers outdoor seating with views of the namesake palace. Chic Romans come here to conduct business and gossip.

TAKING A BREAK

Forno di Campo de' Fiori – *Piazza Campo de' Fiori 22 (Vicolo del Gallo 14). Closed Sun.* ✆*06 68 80 66 62. www.fornocampodefiori.com.* This bakery, visible from the street, is besieged by locals for its excellent pizza, bread (*pane alle olive*, *pane alle noci…*), cokies and cakes.

Roscioli – *Via dei Chiavari 34.* ✆*06 68 64 045. www.anticofornoroscioli.it.* Three generations have sold perfectly topped pizzas here at all hours. A modern oven that produces pizzas typical of the past.

BARS AND WINE BARS

Open Baladin – *Via degli Specchi 5–6.* ✆*06 68 38 989. www.openbaladinroma.it.* A lively, inviting microbrewery that offers a vast selection of Italian beers on tap.

Il Nolano – *Piazza Campo dei Fiori 11.* ✆*06 68 79 344.* Facing the *piazza*, this delightful bar is perfect to taste a good artisanal beer. Nice dehors.

Il Vinaietto – *Via Monte della Farina 38.* ✆*06 68 80 69 89.* Wine shop with a family atmosphere. A couple of steps from Campo de' Fiori, one of the wine bars in the city center frequented by Romans.

Castel Sant'Angelo★★★

This itinerary focuses on the River Tiber, the fortress-like building of Castel Sant'Angelo, and one of the most famous and romantic districts of Rome, dominated by the old fortress of the popes. The dome of St Peter's presides over this landscape. The other river bank is home to antique shops, art galleries and restaurants in streets such as Via Giulia and Via dei Coronari, where Madonna icons smile on the alleys, recalling the old pilgrimage route.

A BIT OF HISTORY

This district, densely populated in the Middle Ages, was gradually cleared and redeveloped as a centre for commerce. **Sixtus IV** (1471–84) initiated the transformation. Magnificent mansions were built on the route of religious processions between the Vatican and the basilica of St John Lateran, lining Via Banco di Santo Spirito, Via dei Banchi Nuovi and Via del Governo Vecchio. In 1599 Beatrice Cenci was beheaded at the base (*See Palazzo Cenci, p126*).

- **Michelin Map:** 38 K 9–10, L 9–10.
- **Location:** Castel Sant'Angelo is in the northwest section of Rome's historic centre, on a sharp loop of the Tiber. From here, Via della Conciliazione runs straight up to the Vatican City. The walk starts at the castle and then crosses the Tiber via the magnificent Ponte Sant'Angelo.
- **Don't Miss:** the Castel S. Angelo terrace views, Via Giulia, Via dei Coronari.
- **Timing:** Allow 2hrs 30min.
- **Also See:** *CAMPO DE' FIORI; PIAZZA NAVONA; VATICANO–SAN PIETRO.*

GETTING THERE
BY METRO AND BUS: Lepanto, Ottaviano-San Pietro (A). Bus 23, 34, 40, 46, 49, 64, 87, 62, 271, 280, 926, 982 and 990.

Castel Sant'Angelo

© F. Guiziou/hemis.fr

The Angel's Castle

In 590, Pope Gregory the Great led a procession against the plague and floods decimating the city. Suddenly, atop the mausoleum, appeared an angel sheathing his sword. The gesture was interpreted as a sign that the plague would abate. In gratitude, the pope built a chapel on the mausoleum.

VISIT

Lungotevere Castello 50. Open Mon–Sun 9am–7:30pm. Closed 1 Jan and 25 Dec. €14. 06 32 810. www.castelsantangelo.com.

The Castel Sant'Angelo squats upon ancient chunks of peperine and travertine stone. The angel statue crowns the complex. Entry is through the old mausoleum entrance, raised 3m/10ft higher than its original position.

Mausoleo di Adriano

This fortress-like building was intended as a sepulchre for **Hadrian** and his family. Begun by the emperor in AD 135, it was finished four years later by his adopted son and successor Antoninus Pius. The base (84m/276ft square) is surmounted by a drum (20m/66ft high), on which was heaped a small mound of earth *(tumulus)*. It was crowned by a statue of the emperor and a bronze *quadriga* (four-horse chariot). The mausoleum contained the urns of all the rulers from Hadrian to Septimius Severus (AD 211). When Aurelian walled the city in 270, he turned it into a fortress.

Fortress

During the medieval struggle between the papacy and the noble families, the structure became a fortified stronghold. Nicholas V (1447–55) built a brick storey atop and added turrets at the corners. The octagonal bastions were the work of Alexander VI (1492–1503). In 1527 Clement VII took refuge there from the troops of Charles V and made several rooms

habitable. These were later improved by Paul III, who already knew the castle, as he was imprisoned there by Innocent VIII when he was only Cardinal Alexander Farnese.

In his 16C autobiography, sculptor and metalworker **Benvenuto Cellini** details his imprisonment there. Cagliostro was an inmate in 1789. After the unification of Italy, the Castel Sant'Angelo became a barracks and military prison. Today, surrounded by a public garden, its only assaults are of hoards of tourists.

A high defensive wall – the **Passetto**, built by Leo IV (847-855) with a corridor added by Nicolas III c.1277 – links the castle to the Vatican Palace. Alexander VI fled along the passage in 1494, as did Clement VII during the 1527 Sack of Rome.

Spiral Ramp

The entrance to the spiral ramp is below on the right, next to the entrance to the Tiber embankment.

When the castle was a mausoleum, the ramp (125m/410ft) led up to the chamber where the funeral urns were kept. The walls were originally covered in marble, the floor was paved with mosaic, and the vault was decorated with stucco.

Main Courtyard

This courtyard is also known as the Angel Courtyard from the 16C statue that graced the castle's crown until the 18C. On the right are medieval rooms, now the lower armoury.

The end of the courtyard is closed by a shrine designed by Michelangelo. It forms the side wall of the chapel built for Leo X and probably stands on the site of Gregory the Great's cell (See above).

On the left are the Papal rooms.

Sala dell'Apollo

Access from Sala della Giustizia or from the main courtyard.

Over the doorways and fireplace is the name of Pope Paul III and the date 1547. The room takes its name from its paintings, attributed to Perin del Vaga. The fine panels and ceiling illustrate mythological figures and grotesques. One of the two openings is the door to the lift (♿See above).

The other leads to a 9m/29ft-deep shaft into a small room. Castel Sant'Angelo has many such trapdoors and secret passageways, which have given rise to a number of gruesome legends.

Sala di Clemente VII

The wooden ceilings bear the name of Pope Clement VII, and 15C and 16C paintings.

▷ From Sala dell'Apollo take the tiny hall to the semi-circular courtyard.

Bagno di Clemente VII★

Access from the corridor separating Cortile di Alessandro VI from Cortile Leone X and the stairs up on the left.

The beautiful décor by Giovanni da Udine, a pupil of Raphael, is evidence of the civilised lifestyle of the pope in the 16C.

Prigioni

Access by steps down from Alexander VI's Court.

Many people were incarcerated in these prisons, including sculptor Benvenuto Cellini, and Giordano Bruno, the heretic monk who was imprisoned here for six years.

Oil and Grain Store

The jars could hold 22 000 litres/4 839gal of oil and the capacity of the five large silos was about 100kg/3 700cwt of grain. It was Alexander VI who made these provisions in case of siege.

▷ Return to Alexander VI's Court and take the steps up from the centre of the semi-circle, which lead to the loggias. of Pius IV, Paul III and Julius II (walking anticlockwise).

Loggia di Pio IV

The rooms that open onto the loggia were living quarters for the staff. The loggia was rebuilt in the 19C to house political prisoners. For many years here, the gun was fired to announce noon.

▷ Bear left.

Loggia di Paolo III

The Pope commissioned Antonio da Sangallo (the Younger) to design the loggia *(which faces north)* in 1543, and had it decorated with stucco work and grotesques.

▷ Continue beyond the restaurant-bar.

On the left is the upper armoury *(armeria superiore)*, containing arms and uniforms of the Italian and papal armies.

Loggia di Giulio II

It faces south with a fine view of St Angelo Bridge *(Ponte Sant'Angelo)* and the city of Rome. Giuliano da Sangallo probably built this loggia for Julius II.

▷ Steps lead to the papal apartment.

Appartamento Papale★

After the siege of 1527, when Clement VII sought refuge in Castel Sant'Angelo, Paul III had a suite of rooms constructed on top of the castle. These apartments are protected by the succession of ramps and steps.

The Sala del Consiglio *(Sala Paolina)* was a waiting room for visitors to the pope. Its floor is marble and the frescoes are by a group of artists instructed by Perin del Vaga, a Florentine artist who followed Raphael.

The name of the **Camera del Perseo** (Perseus's Room) is derived from the frieze by del Vaga himself. In the **Camera di Amore e Psiche** (Cupid and Psyche's Room), the frieze illustrates the story of the beautiful girl beloved by Venus' son.

▷ Return to the Sala del Consiglio and, after the steps, turn into the corridor decorated with frescoes.

Two sets of steps – linked by a passage – lead up to the **library** and two series of rooms *(one above the other),* named after their decorations: **Hadrian's Mausoleum Room** and the **Festoon Room**, which opens into a smaller apartment

▶ Beside the Sala del Tesoro.

Scala Romana

The Roman staircase, part of Hadrian's Mausoleum, leads to the Hall of Flags and Columns (Sala Rotonda) and the terrace.

Terrace

The bronze statue of Archangel Michael (by P A von Vershaffelt) presides over a **panorama**★★★, one of Rome's most famous. From west to east: the Prati district and the green patch of the Villa Borghese; close to the castle, the great white mass of the Law Courts, then the Quirinal Palace, the Militia Tower and the shallow dome of the Pantheon; farther right, the monument to Victor Emmanuel II and the domes and turrets of the city: the Gesù Church, St Ivo's corkscrew tower, the belfry of Santa Maria dell'Anima with its ceramic tiles, Sant'Andrea delle Valle, San Carlo ai Catinari and the Synagogue. On the extreme right is the Janiculum Hill, San Giovanni dei Fiorentini, Via della Conciliazione, St Peter's and the Vatican Palace linked to Castel Sant'Angelo by the "Passetto" and Monte Mario, scene of Act III of Puccini's opera *Tosca*.

It is also possible to walk along the parapets to the four bastions: St John's, St Matthew's, St Mark's (which gives access to the "Passetto") and St Luke's.

👣WALKING TOUR

Ponte Sant'Angelo★

Supremely elegant, this bridge dates to Hadrian's era – the three central arches, at least. The 17C others were altered when the Tiber embankments were built 1892–94. The statues of St Peter and St Paul (south bank) were erected by Clement VII in 1530; the ten Baroque angels, supervised by **Bernini**, were commissioned by Clement IX (1667–69).

▶ Cross the Ponte Sant'Angelo and bear right into Via Paola.

San Giovanni dei Fiorentini

Piazza dell'Oro 1. 🕐*Open 7:30am–12am and 5pm–7pm.*

Pope Leo X, a Medici from Florence, decided to build a "national" church for his fellow countrymen in Rome. Famous Renaissance artists competed for the commission, including Peruzzi, Michelangelo and Raphael: Jacopo Sansovino won. Work began early in the 16C; it was continued by Antonio da Sangallo and Giacomo della Porta and completed in 1614 by Carlo Maderno. The 18C façade is late Counter-Reformation style. The chancel is Baroque.

Ironically, the architect **Borromini** was buried here; a plaque reflects the shame of suicide (the architect had a long, messy death, allowing time to repent, pass away in the "grace of God" and receive a Christian burial). Carlo Maderno is also buried here.

The basilica's modern notoriety comes from an earlier parish priest who allowed pets to attend its masses.

Via Giulia★

The Via Giulia slices through the historic district. Part of the pilgrimage route, this wide, straight avenue once led the faithful to St Peter's. In fact, the road replaced a cluster of alleys, where brigands and pickpockets lurked. The 16C urban renewal produced one of the city's best addresses. For elegance and unity, Bramante was supposed to design all the buildings. The plan failed.

At Via Giulia's debut, it was much in demand. The irreverent goldsmith Benvenuto **Cellini** lived here, as did Sangallo the Younger (his home, number 79, was the Tuscan Embassy before unification). **Raphael** died before his design at Via Giulia 85 was completed. Today a hodge-podge of palaces line the street, now flanked by shops and fancy restaurants.

Palazzo Sacchetti

Via Giulia 66. The left balcony inscription notes that this was the home of Antonio Sangallo the Younger, architect of Farnese Palace

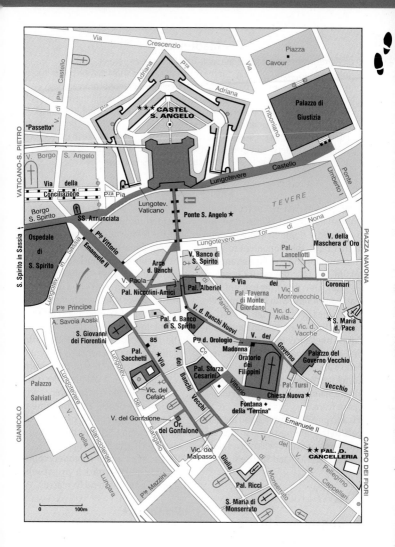

where Cagliostro was imprisoned, now comprising the **Dolphin Room** and the **Salamander Room**.

▶ Return to the library.

The **Sala del Tesoro** (Treasure Room), at the centre of the fortress, is a circular chamber. Its walnut presses contain the papal records, transferred here from the Vatican in 1870.

▶ Beside the Sala del Tesoro.

Scala Romana

The Roman staircase, part of Hadrian's Mausoleum, leads to the Hall of Flags and Columns *(Sala Rotonda)* **and the terrace.**

Terrace

The bronze statue of Archangel Michael (by P A von Vershaffelt) presides over a **panorama★★★**, one of Rome's most famous. From west to east: the Prati district and the green patch of the Villa Borghese; close to the castle, the great

Madonnas

In Rome images of the Madonna smile from almost every street – at intersections, along alleyways, at the corner of a piazza. They may be painted, frescoed or in terra-cotta bas-relief, brightly coloured or monochrome. They seem to keep a watchful eye over passers-by and many still retain the little lanterns, which for many years often provided the only illumination after sunset. In January 1854, Rome introduced street lighting by gas – in Via del Corso. James Shepherd, an Englishman, was instrumental; he's now buried in the Testaccio Cemetery. Bagpipers come from Abruzzi and Molise to play their instruments in the streets, and in the shops and bars.

white mass of the Law Courts, then the Quirinal Palace, the Militia Tower and the shallow dome of the Pantheon; farther right, the monument to Victor Emmanuel II and the domes and turrets of the city: the Gesù Church, St Ivo's corkscrew tower, the belfry of Santa Maria dell'Anima with its ceramic tiles, Sant'Andrea delle Valle, San Carlo ai Catinari and the Synagogue. On the extreme right is the Janiculum Hill, San Giovanni dei Fiorentini, Via della Conciliazione, St Peter's and the Vatican Palace linked to Castel Sant'Angelo by the "Passetto" and Monte Mario, scene of Act III of Puccini's opera Tosca.

It is also possible to walk along the parapets to the four bastions: St John's, St Matthew's, St Mark's (which gives access to the "Passetto") and St Luke's.

◣◣WALKING TOUR

Ponte Sant'Angelo★

Supremely elegant, this bridge dates to Hadrian's era – the three central arches, at least. The 17C others were altered when the Tiber embankments were built 1892–94. The statues of St Peter and St Paul (south bank) were erected by Clement VII in 1530; the ten Baroque angels, supervised by **Bernini**, were commissioned by Clement IX (1667–69).

▶ Cross the Ponte Sant'Angelo and bear right into Via Paola.

San Giovanni dei Fiorentini

Piazza dell'Oro 1. ◷Open 7:30am–12am and 5pm–7pm.

Pope Leo X, a Medici from Florence, decided to build a "national" church for his fellow countrymen in Rome. Famous Renaissance artists competed for the commission, including Peruzzi, Michelangelo and Raphael: Jacopo Sansovino won. Work began early in the 16C; it was continued by Antonio da Sangallo and Giacomo della Porta and completed in 1614 by Carlo Maderno. The 18C façade is late Counter-Reformation style. The chancel is Baroque. Ironically, the architect **Borromini** was buried here; a plaque reflects the shame of suicide (the architect had a long, messy death, allowing time to repent, pass away in the "grace of God" and receive a Christian burial). Carlo Maderno is also buried here.

The basilica's modern notoriety comes from an earlier parish priest who allowed pets to attend its masses.

Via Giulia★

The Via Giulia slices through the historic district. Part of the pilgrimage route, this wide, straight avenue once led the faithful to St Peter's. In fact, the road replaced a cluster of alleys, where brigands and pickpockets lurked. The 16C urban renewal produced one of the city's best addresses. For elegance and unity, Bramante was supposed to design all the buildings. The plan failed. At Via Giulia's debut, it was much in demand. The irreverent goldsmith Benvenuto **Cellini** lived here, as did Sangallo the Younger (his home, number 79, was the Tuscan Embassy before unification). **Raphael** died before his design at Via Giulia 85 was completed.

Today a hodge-podge of palaces line the street, now flanked by shops and fancy restaurants.

Palazzo Sacchetti
Via Giulia 66.
The left balcony inscription notes that this was the home of Antonio Sangallo the Younger, architect of Farnese Palace upon whose death (1546), it was sold to Cardinal Ricci di Montepulciano.

Between the next two side turnings on the right, Vicolo del Cefalo and Via del Gonfalone, are huge blocks of masonry. Bramante designed law courts for Julius II, which never progressed beyond these foundations. The Romans christened them "the Via Giulia sofas".

Pope Innocent X built the model prison at no 52 "for a safer and more humane imprisonment of the guilty", as the inscription explains.

Now Valadier's structure houses the **Museum of Criminology,** full of antique papal torture instruments and interesting documents *(entrance on Via del Gonfalone 29; ☞ Temporarily closed for restoration at the moment writing; www.museocriminologico.it).* ☎ 06 68 89 94 41.

Oratorio del Gonfalone
Via del Gonfalone 32a.
🕐*Open Mon–Fri 10am–2pm or by appointment at ☎ 06 68 75 952. www.oratoriogonfalone.eu.*
A magnificent cycle of frescoes dedicated to the Passion of Christ, a work by the leading masters of Roman Mannerism. Concerts and season of the Coro Polifonico Romano.

▶ Turn left into Vicolo del Malpasso and left again into Via dei Banchi Vecchi.

It was in **Via dei Banchi Vecchi**, the street of bankers in the 15C, that the **Palazzo Sforza Cesarini** was built by Pope Alexander VI, then only a cardinal.

▶ Turn right into Via Sforza Cesarini and cross Corso Vittorio Emanuele II to reach Piazza della Chiesa Nuova.

Chiesa Nuova★
🕐*Open 7:30am–noon, 4:30pm–7:30pm.*
The **New Church** was founded in the 12C as Santa Maria in Vallicella; the name probably alludes to a little valley nearby.

The history of the church is linked to **St Philip Neri**, the Florentine founder of the Oratorians. In 1605, they rebuilt Santa Maria into the New Church.

The **façade** is decorated with the shallow pilasters and recessed columns typical of the Counter-Reformation. Neri wanted the **interior** to be plain, but during the Counter-Reformation, it was given a more elaborate Baroque format inspired by **Pietro da Cortona**. On the coffered stucco ceiling, he painted *St Philip's Vision* (1664–65). During construction, Neri had a vision of the Virgin supporting the ceiling, which threatened to collapse onto the altar.

Cortona enjoyed equal celebrity in Rome with Bernini. Between 1648 and 1651, he had already painted the dome, which depicts Christ abolishing punishment for mankind. In the pendentives, he placed the Prophets Isaiah, Jeremiah, Ezekiel and Daniel (1659–60). Meanwhile, he began an Assumption on the vault of the apse.

The chapel *(left of the chancel)* contains the remains of St Philip Neri and is decorated in grandiose style with gold, bronze and marble encrusted with mother-of-pearl.

A number of Mannerist and Baroque paintings star here, including three early works by **Rubens** (1608) in the chancel and the *Presentation in the Temple* by Cavalier d'Arpino *(first chapel on the left.)* The chapel *(left transept)* contains a picture by Barocci, in a style typical of the late 16C. A beautiful Visitation *(fourth chapel on the left)* is by the same painter.

On the altar in the sacristy *(entrance via the chapel in the left transept)* stands a beautiful marble sculpture of St Philip with an angel, executed in 1640 by Alessandro Algardi.

Oratorio dei Filippini

🕐 *Visits by reservation only;*
📞 *06 68 93 868.*

Adjoining the New Church *(to the left),* the Oratorio was built between 1637 and 1662 to house the assemblies of the Congregation of the Oratory, where laity and clergy met under St Philip Neri.

It includes **Borromini Hall**, occupied by the Capitoline Archives. In addition to the Oratorian priests, the vast palace also houses the Vallicelliana Library, the Roman Library, the archives of the city of Rome, which include a collection of Roman newspapers dating back to the 18C, and various cultural institutes. The **façade★** overlooking Piazza della Chiesa Nuova is, in fact, the side elevation, designed by **Borromini** to form a unit with the church. Monumental, yet subtle, it is an interaction of calm and frenzied movement characteristic of this great Baroque architect.

Fontana della "Terrina"

Romans moved the **fountain** here in 1925; it had stood in the Campo de' Fiori until 1899. The basin was carved in 1590, but a few years later was covered with a travertine lid bearing the inscription: "Love God, do good and let others talk".

▷ Take Via della Chiesa Nuova beside the church and turn right into Via del Governo Vecchio.

Via del Governo Vecchio

One of the district's main streets, it continued the Papal Way, and is now lined with artisans' workshops, restaurants and antique dealers. Some of the Renaissance palaces still bear noble coats of arms. By Piazza di Pasquino sits the **Pasquino**, a fragment of a Hellenistic statuary group. This "talking statue" bears witness to the frustrations of citizens, who have posted rants – usually against war or the government – on it since the 16C.

Palazzo del Governo Vecchio

The building at no 39 was completed in 1478. In 1624 it became the residence of the Governor of Rome. When the Government was transferred to the Palazzo Madama under Benedict XIV (1740–58), it became known as the Old Government Palace. The attractive doorway has friezes and diaper-work.

▷ Take Piazza dell'Orologio.

Piazza dell'Orologio

The plain Oratory ends unexpectedly in a graceful clock tower. The wrought-iron scrollwork on the bell cage is Borromini's work (1647–49). Beneath the clock is a mosaic of the Virgin of Vallicella. On the corner is a beautiful street **Madonna**, surrounded by a "glory" of cherubs.

▷ Take Via dei Banchi Nuovi.

Via dei Banchi Nuovi and Via Banco di Santo Spirito

By the 15C, bankers from Florence, Siena and Genoa had set up shop. Their fortunes were immense and intricately linked to the Holy See. The Papal State also granted them concessions on mining and customs dues. The bankers controlled the finances of the pope and the great noble families.

Together with money-changing, conducted in the streets, there was gambling. People bet on the election of the pope and the sex of unborn babies.

Until 1541, a working mint inhabited the **Palazzo del Banco di Santo Spirito**. From the end of Via Banco di Santo Spirito, stretches a pleasant view of Castel Sant'Angelo and its bridge.

Via dei Coronari★

One of the city's most attractive streets, this *via* boasts antique shops and palaces glowing in ochre and stone. During festivals, it rolls out a red carpet, framed at the sides with open-flame braziers. Overall it has retained the form acquired under Sixtus IV (1471–84). Dei Coronari is named for the vendors of rosaries (corone), who targeted pilgrims.

Arco dei Banchi

The Bankers' Arch leads to the Chigi bank. On the left is a Latin inscription, which comes from the nearby church of St Celsus and St Julian: it marks the Tiber's high-water mark in 1277.

▶ Turn left under Arco dei Banchi.

Ponte Vittorio Emanuele II

Nero built a bridge here in AD 60, which collapsed in the 4C. The present construction, decorated with allegorical groups and winged Victories, was begun soon after the unification and completed in 1911, linking Rome and the Vatican.

▶ Cross the bridge to the right (north) bank and turn right.

On the left is the imposing **Santo Spirito Hospital** (Ospedale di Santo Spirito), founded by Innocent III and rebuilt in the 15C by Sixtus IV. The **Church of the Santissima Annunciata** (Most Holy Annunciation), although small, is graced by an attractive façade full of perceived movement (18C).

Santo Spirito in Sassia

Via dei Penitenzieri 12. ◷Open 7:15am–noon, 2:50pm–7:30pm (Sun open at 9am). ☎06 68 79 310. The church was built in the 8C for Anglo-Saxon pilgrims and rebuilt in the 16C, after being sacked. The architect was **Sangallo the Younger,** who died before its completion. The façade – which bears the arms of Sixtus V (1585–90), in whose reign the building was finished – is in the Renaissance style. The interior, beneath a beautiful coffered ceiling, is richly decorated with paintings in the Mannerist style. There is a fine 16C organ.

▶ Take Lungotevere Castello.

Palazzo di Giustizia

Piazza Cavour.
The **Law Courts**, nicknamed the "Palaz-zaccio", were built from 1889–1911 by Guglielmo Calderini. They rank among the most conspicuous modern buildings in Rome. With a bronze quadriga by Ximenes (1855–1926) and colossal statuary, the Law Courts can claim both Classical and Baroque inspiration.

ADDRESSES

SHOPPING

Gran Tour Collection – Via dei Coronari 32. ☎06 68 68 72 026. www.grandtourcollection.net. This jewelry shop belonging to the Borrazzi family, Roman antique dealers and craftsmen for three generations, boasts a collection called the Grand Tour, inspired by classical and neoclassical art. There is also an online shop.

TAKING A BREAK

Casa delle Letterature – Piazza dell'Orologio 3. www.casadelleletterature.it. Set in the prestigious Borromini complex of the former Filippini oratory, this centre of 19C and contemporary literature from Italy and abroad offers an agreeable pause to enjoy a moment of relaxation and culture.

Prati Urbani – Via Giovanni Pierluigi Da Palestrina 41. www.pratiurbani.it. Open 11am-2pm - Sun 6pm-2am. Bar, restaurant and tea room to enjoy a tasty meal every moment of the day. International cuisine.

EUR★

Loved and loathed, this Fascist-built neighbourhood stands south of Rome. EUR stands for "Esposizione Universale di Roma", a boastful movement that inspired all this monumental white marble and grand avenues. According to art historian Sylvia Pressouyre, in "a certain light, the district resembles the imaginary cities painted by Giorgio de Chirico." Leisure options here include pedal boats on the lake, a fair ground, and a new aquarium, slated to open.

A BIT OF HISTORY

In 1937, the government conceived a grandiose project for a 1942 universal exhibition. The idea was to develop along the motorway linking Rome and Ostia. The contract was given to the architect Marcello Piacentini. Building began in 1939; on 10 June 1940, Italy entered the war allied to Germany and work stopped the next year. Following Rome's bombing and the fall of the Fascists, the scheme was abandoned.

Two events – Holy Year in 1950 and the 1960 Olympic Games – brought EUR to the fore again. The new Via Cristoforo Colombo and metro stimulated an administrative and cultural centre, a business forum and residences. The **Sports Palace**, by Piacentini and Pier Luigi Nervi, and the cycle racetrack were built for the Olympics.

Today, EUR's colossal white buildings look much like the scheme proposed by the Fascists.

SIGHTS

👥 Museo della Civiltà Romana★★

Piazza Giovanni Agnelli 10. &
☞ *Temporarily closed for restoration at the moment writing.* ☎ *06 06 08.*
www.museociviltaromana.it.

This huge **Museum of Roman Culture** sprawls over two buildings linked by a portico. It illustrates the city's history from foundation through to the Empire. Exhibits, grouped chronologically, tell

- 👤 **Michelin Map:** 38 T2, T3, U2, U3, U4, V2 and V 3.
- ▷ **Location:** EUR lies between the Via del Mare leading to Ostia to the west and Via Laurentina out to the east. The neighbourhood is intersected by Via Cristoforo Colombo.
- 👁 **Don't Miss:** Roman Civilisation Museum and the Palazzo della Civiltà del Lavoro.
- 🕐 **Timing:** 4hrs if you wish to include a museum.
- 👥 **Kids:** The various museums, the model of ancient Rome in the Museum of Roman Civilisation, the *gelateria* Giolitti on the lakeside.
- 👤 **Also See:** The itinerary can be combined with *OSTIA ANTICA*. Catch a train from Magliana Station (Metro B: EUR–Magliana) or Ostiense Station (Metro B: Piramide).

GETTING THERE

BY METRO AND BUS: Line B: EUR Palasport or EUR Fermi. Bus 708, 709, 777 and 778.

the story of conquest and influence for more than 1 000 years.

The highlight is a large **model★★ of ancient Rome** (5C BC), called the "*plastico*". Other replicas bring to life the Colosseum, Domitian's Stadium (*Stadio di Domiziano*), and Hadrian's Villa. Of particular interest are the plaster casts taken directly from the spiral of low-relief panels on **Trajan's Column** (*Room LI*).

👥 Museo delle Arti e Tradizioni Popolari★★

Piazza Guglielmo Marconi 8. 🕐 *Open Tue–Sun 8am–19pm.* 🕐 *Closed 1 Jan, 25 Dec.* ☎€10. ☎*06 54 95 21.*
www.museocivilta.beniculturali.it.

Palazzo della Civiltà del Lavoro

This **Folk Museum** focuses on Italian folklore and traditions. Exhibits include a Sicilian carriages and a grape-cart. Left of the stairs, slightly out of view, is a Venetian **gondola**. Other displays explore peasant life. Children enjoy the puppets.

👥 Museo Preistorico Etnografico L. Pigorini★
Piazza Guglielmo Marconi 14.
♿🕐*Open Tue–Sun 8am–19pm.*
🕐*Closed 1 Jan and 25 Dec.* 🚫€10.
☎*06 54 95 21. www.museocivilta.beniculturali.it.*

One of the world's largest ethnographical collections is housed here.

The Prehistory section has a wooden pirogue dating from 5 500 BC found on Lake Bracciano. The rich **African Section** assembles more than 60 000 objects, including weapons and costumes. The **Oceanic Section** displays aceremonial canoe from the Trobriand Islands.

The American section hosts objects from Central America and the region of the Andes in Latin America. A must see is the masterpiece of Caribbean art: **zemi taino★** which represents a deity worshipped by the indigenous people tainos.

The second floor is dedicated to palaeontology. The last room focuses on the increasing Eastern influence, during the early Etruscan era (late 8C to mid-6C BC). The **Praenestina fibul★**bears one of the oldest inscriptions in Latin.

Since 2017 the museum also houses the Museo Nazionale d'Arte Orientale Giuseppe Tucci.

Museo Nazionale dell'Alto Medioevo
Viale Lincoln 3. ♿🕐*Open Tue– Sat 8am–7pm.* 🕐*Closed 1 Jan and 25 Dec.* 🚫€8. ☎*06 54 22 81 99.*

The **Medieval Museum** contains exhibits from the 5C to the 11C, and plans of Classical and Christian Rome.

👥 Planetario e Museo Astronomico
Via dello Scalo San Lorenzo 10.
🕐*Open 9am–7pm.* ⚠*Temporarily closed for restoration at the moment writing. Shows and activities continue at the Ex-Dogana Planetario (www. exdogana.com).* ☎*06 06 08.*
www.planetarioroma.it.

The planetarium's 14m tall dome has a model of the night sky. The museum offers visitors an illustrated journey through the Universe.

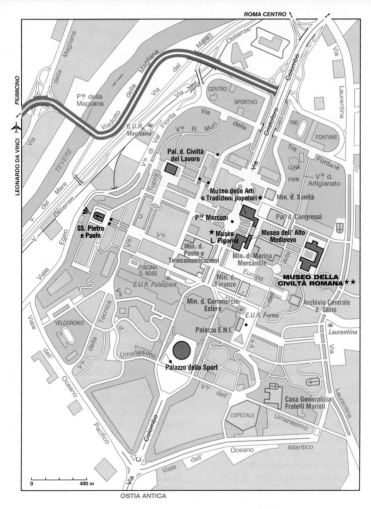

ROMA CENTRO

FIUMICINO

LEONARDO DA VINCI

OSTIA ANTICA

0   400 m

Piazza Guglielmo Marconi

Also known as Piazza Imperiale, it is made of a perfect series of monumental constructions that will delight 1930s architecture lovers.

A marble obelisk (1950) has been raised here to the glory of the Italian physicist Guglielmo Marconi (1874–1937), inventor of wireless telegraphy.

Palazzo della Civiltà del Lavoro★★

Quadrato della Concordia

Between 1938 and 1943, three architects – Guerrini, La Padula and Romano – designed and built EUR's most iconic building. The stark mass of the palazzo is

The square Colosseum

As such, the palazzo is also sometimes referred to as the *"Colosseo Quadrato"* (square Colosseum). Fellini exploited this monumental oddity in his 1962 film *Le Tentazioni del Dottor Antonio*, when giantess Anita Ekberg chased a tiny professor outside the square Colosseum. The building now houses the Fendi fashion company's offices, as well as temporary exhibitions..

covered in travertine marble and accentuated by only by arches, that give it a sort of Swiss-cheese effect. Mussolini intended the structure to celebrate the Colosseum, and all that the older Roman landmark represented.

Santi Pietro e Paolo
Piazzale Santi Pietro e Paolo
This spectacular travertine church, dedicated to **St Peter and St Paul**, was built between 1937 and 1941 on the highest point in the EUR. Set among shrubs and flowers, its white mass dominates the district. Atop the steps stand two

large statues of St Peter and St Paul. The Greek-cross plan is stressed by the clean angles and sober lines. The dome, covered in little tiles overlapping like fish scales, rests on a drum pierced by *oculi*.

ADDRESSES

SHOPPING

Craft market – *Quadrato Civiltà Italiana della Concordia. Sun Sept-Jun.* This craft market is held every Sunday in front of the Palazzo della Civiltà del Lavoro.

Fontana di Trevi–Quirinale★★★

The Trevi Fountain, one of the most famous sights in Rome, has been immortalised in films such as the American-produced Three Coins in the Fountain and Federico Fellini's *La Dolce Vita*. Nowadays the square is crowded with souvenir sellers and tourists, yet it's still breathtaking, especially when the white marble monument glows at night. From the fountain, a short walk leads up to Quirinal Hill, Rome's highest. Its piazza has one of the city's best views and is home to the President's palace, as well as fine palazzi and churches.

A BIT OF HISTORY
This district is situated to the west of the Quirinal Hill, the most northerly of Rome's hills, and is bordered by Via del Corso to the west and Via del Tritone to the north. The name Quirinale is now synonymous with power, since the Quirinal Palace is now the official residence of the President of the Republic. The hill was the traditional home of the Sabines and took its name from one of their lesser-known gods, **Quirinus**, who, with Mars and Jupiter, formed the basis of Roman religion. It is thought that the god's name may have derived from the Sabine word *curi*, which meant spear. Although uncertainty surrounds

- **Michelin Map:** 38 k 12–13, l 12–13.
- **Location:** This district is southwest of the Quirinale, the most northerly hill, and bordered by Via del Corso (west) and Via del Tritone (north).
- **Don't Miss:** The Trevi Fountain at night, the duelling architectures of Bernini and Borromini in S. Andrea al Quirinale and S. Carlo alle Quattro Fontane, Carracci's *Mangiafagioli* in the Galleria di Palazzo Colonna.
- **Timing:** Allow two and a half hours and note that the Quirinae is open on Sundays.
- **Kids:** Changing of Quirinale palace guard.
- **Also See:** *PIAZZA DI SPAGNA, VIA VENETO, MONTECITORIO AND PANTHEON.*

GETTING THERE
BY METRO AND BUS: Line A: Barberini (500m/ 550 yd from the Fontana di Trevi). Bus C3, 60, 62, 63, 64, 70, 80, 83, 85, 160, 170.

Fontana di Trevi

© S. Greg Panosian/iStockphoto.com

his exact role and attributes, Quirinus is believed to have been a warrior god who, unlike Mars, was responsible for maintaining peace and order in the city. A legend identifies this god with the founder of Rome: during a solar eclipse, Romulus is said to have disappeared and been captured by the gods, who then transformed him into Quirinus. Until the end of the 19C only the fringes of the city reached the Quirinal; the Flavian Mausoleum (Mausoleo dei Flavi) was built there by Domitian (AD 81–96); Caracalla built a temple to Serapis (the ruins survived until the Middle Ages); Constantine built a bathhouse that disappeared in the 17C.

✦●WALKING TOUR

Fontana di Trevi★★★
This late Baroque fountain, one of Rome's most famous monuments, is an impressive sight, made all the more striking by its position in a tiny piazza. The key to the work is given in two high-relief carvings: in 19 BC Agrippa decided to build a long canal (20km/13mi) to bring water to Rome *(left)*. He named it "Aqua Virgo" after a young virgin who revealed the spring to the Roman soldiers *(right)*. Repairs were made under Pope Nicholas V and Urban VIII. Clement XII commissioned Nicolà Salvi (1732) to adorn the end of the canal with a fountain. It fills

the whole width of the façade, which gives the impression of a commemorative arch. Salubrity and Abundance flank the central figure, Oceanus, who rides in a chariot drawn by sea horses and two tritons, and provides a photogenic spectacle for faithful tourists. Tradition claims one coin (cast backwards over the left shoulder) ensures a return to Rome, two bring love and three a wedding in the Eternal City. Romantic notions aside, be wary of pickpockets and excessive rose sellers.

Santi Vincenzo e Anastasio
In front of the fountain stands the church dedicated to St Vincent and St Anastasius. Built in 1650 by Martino Longhi the Younger for Cardinal Mazarin, it is now famous for the embalmed hearts of 25 popes. Detached columns, pediments, projections and recesses create a light and shade interplay typical of Baroque art.

▶ South of the church, turn left into Via della Dataria, which leads to Piazza del Quirinale.

Piazza del Quirinale★★
Changing of the palace guard daily 4pm (6pm in summer). Lined by handsome palaces, adorned with an obelisk and ancient statues and refreshed by a fountain, the square typifies Roman elegance.

Sixtus V (1585–90) transferred statues of the **Dioscuri** from Constantine's Baths nearby; they are fine Roman copies of original Greek works. Some two centuries later, Pius VI moved them slightly apart to fit an obelisk, which formerly stood at the entrance to Augustus' mausoleum. Finally Pius VII (1800–23) completed the group with an antique basin from the time when the Forum was "Campo Vaccino".

Palazzo del Quirinale★★

♿⏱*Open Tue–Wed and Fry–Sun 9:30am–2pm.* ⏱*For annual closures, consult the website www.quirinale.it. Two itineraries.*⌛*€1.50 (itinerary 1) or €10 (itinerary 2). Visits by reservation only.* ☎*06 39 96 75 57.*

The **Quirinal Palace** is the work of some of the finest architects of the Counter-Reformation and the Baroque period. It was commissioned in 1573 by Gregory XIII from Martino Longhi the Elder as a summer residence for the popes. Sixtus V commissioned Ottaviano Mascherino, Domenico Fontana and Flaminio Ponzio. Under Paul V Carlo, **Maderno** added the monumental door with its two half-reclining statues of St Peter and St Paul. **Bernini** was brought in by Alexander VII. The palace was completed by Ferdinando Fuga for Clement XII. The courtyard of the presidential palace – guarded by sentries who must be 1.82m/6ft 3in – leads to the grand staircase.

Napoleonic Storm

In 1808, Napoleon was declared king of Italy and his brother Joseph king of Naples. Pius VII, as head of the Papal States, refused to apply an economic blockade or to recognise any king other than Ferdinand IV of Naples.

On 2 February, General Miollis was ordered to enter Rome with 8 000 French soldiers to bring His Holiness to reason. Pius VII shut himself in the **Quirinal Palace** (⚀*See entry in this section*).

In Vienna, on the evening of 17 May 1809, Napoleon wiped the Papal States off the map of Europe. Pius VII issued a Bull of Excommunication: "Let sovereigns learn once and for all that they are subject by the law of Christ to our throne and our commands." At dawn several French soldiers were found dead in the streets of Rome. On 7 July 1809, French troops broke down the door of the palace. The pope, in cape and stole, awaited them. Despite their great respect for Pius VII, the soldiers spirited him away to spend the rest of the Napoleonic era at Fontainebleau. Thus Napoleon rendered "unto Caesar the things that are Caesar's and unto God the things that are God's."

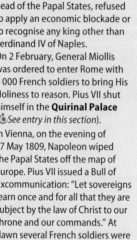

Piazza del Quirinale

© Andrea Izzotti/Fotolia.com

The fresco of Christ *(above the arch)* by **Melozzo da Forlì** (1438–94) was originally part of the Ascension in the church of the Holy Apostles. The tour includes a succession of rooms, all sumptuously decorated, the chapel painted by **Guido Reni** *(Annunciation* on the altarpiece), and the Pauline Chapel.

Scuderie del Quirinale

Entrance at Via XXIV Maggio 16.
♿ 🕐*Open Sun-Thu 10am–8pm, Fri and Sat 10am–10:30pm.* 👓€15. 📞06 81 10 02 56. www.scuderie quirinale.it.
An 18C building which, with the Palazzo del Quirinale and Palazzo della Consulta, lines the attractive urban space housing the Fountain of the Dioscuri and an obelisk that used to adorn the mausoleum of Augustus, contains 1500 meters of galleries designed by architect Gae Aulenti that offer a superb view over the city and important temporary exhibitions.

Palazzo della Consulta

The **façade★** is by **Ferdinando Fuga** (18C), who favoured Baroque motifs. The three doorways – their pediments crowded with statues and sculptures, and the coat of arms of Clement XII, supported by a swarm of cherubs – make a lively contrast with the bare façade of the Quirinal Palace. This is now the seat of the Constitutional Court.

▷ Take Via del Quirinale.

The east wing of the palace, overlooking Via del Quirinale, was built in the 17C and 18C.

Sant'Andrea al Quirinale★★

Via del Quirinale 30. 🕐*Open Tue–Sun 9am–noon and 3–6pm.* 📞064819399. santandrea.gesuiti.it.
St Andrew on the Quirinal by **Bernini** and *St Charles by the Four Fountains (San Carlo alle Quattro Fontane)* by **Bor-**

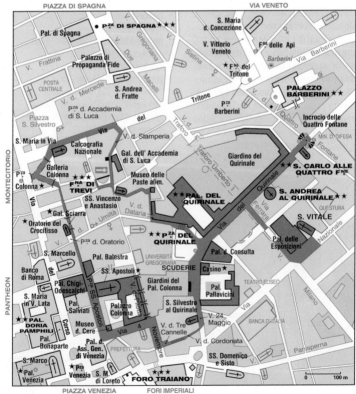

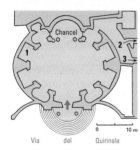

Sant'Andrea al Quirinale

romini express with unusual clarity the genius of two artists whose styles were diametrically opposed. Its façade opens into a semi-circular atrium, and bears a crown showing the arms of Cardinal Camillo Pamphili, Innocent X's nephew, who commissioned the church in 1658.

Interior★★
The interior is elliptical, oriented on the shorter axis and defined by the entrance and magnificent choir stalls. The deep rectangular side chapels and false portico in front of the high altar give a feeling of spaciousness, which helps disguise the proportions of the church. **Bernini**'s skilful use of coloured marble, gilding and stucco figures has created a rich décor. The second chapel on the right contains three paintings by Baciccia (1639–1709); the *Crucifixion of St Andrew* by Jacques Courtois (1621–76), known as the Burgundian, can be admired in the apse. The gilt *Glory* by Raggi over the high altar, lit from above, is a reminder that Bernini had a great liking for theatricality. In a chapel to the left **(1)** note the painting by Carlo Maratta (1625–1713) showing the Virgin appearing to St Stanislas. **St Stanislas' Rooms** *(Camere di San Stanislao)* **(2)** contain a recumbent statue of the saint in marble by Pierre Legros *(entered from the fourth chapel on the right; apply to the sacristan)*.
In the **sacristy (3)** there is a beautiful vault in *trompe-l'œil*.

▶ Continue along Via del Quirinale.

San Carlo alle Quattro Fontane★★
Via del Quirinale 23. ◷ *Open Mon–Sat 10am–1pm, Sun noon–1pm.* ✆ *06 48 83 261. www.sancarlino.eu.*
The **Church of St Charles at the Four Fountains**, also known as San Carlino, is probably the best expression of **Borromini**'s creative genius. Commissioned in 1638, it was his first known work. The façade, added some 30 years later, was his last; it was unfinished when he committed suicide in 1667. It reveals the torment of a man whose art was full of contradictory statements: every curve is followed by a counter curve (in particular the façade and the cornices). A convex shrine (below the medallion) is set against the central concave section of the upper storey.

Interior★★
The form is that of an ellipse oriented on the longer axis. The movement is supplied by the alternating concave and convex surfaces of the walls themselves. The confined space – no larger, it is said, than one of the pillars supporting the dome of St Peter's – is perfectly suited to the architect's distinctive style. It is affected and austere, bizarre and elegant and quite out of sympathy with the Baroque taste for sheer size. The intricately designed coffering in the dome is surmounted by a lantern harbouring the Holy Ghost.

Cloisters★
Borromini's cloisters – two orders of Doric columns and slightly convex canted corners – are perfectly proportioned.

▶ Continue to the crossroads with Via delle Quattro Fontane.

Incrocio delle Quattro Fontane
The **Four Fountains crossroads** feature the Tiber, Arno, Diana and Juno. It was created by Sixtus V (1585–90), who introduced more alterations than the city had known since the empire's end. His aim was to link the main basilicas with broad straight roads. These four straight streets opened up **views★** of the obelisks in

front of the Trinità dei Monti *(west)*, the Porta Pia *(north)*, the west end of Santa Maria Maggiore in Piazza dell'Esquilino *(east)* and in Piazza del Quirinale *(south)*. The crossroads' corners are canted to allow four 16C fountains.

▶ Return to Via del Quirinale and turn left onto Via Ferrara.

Palazzo delle Esposizioni

Via Nazionale 194. ◷*Open Sun, Tue, Wed and Thu 10m-8pm, Fri and Sat 10am-10:30pm.* ✆*06 39 96 75 00; Colonna: restaurant at Via Milano 9/A.* ✆*06 47 82 26 41.* *www.palazzoesposizioni.it.*
Rome's biggest **Exhibition Hall**, opened in 1883, was designed by the architect Pio Piancentini, with a Neoclassical main prospect and two side entrances reminiscent of a commemorative arch. Exensively renovated, this swanky space has been updated inside with a chic rooftop restaurant, café, large arts bookshop, gallery and cinema.

▶ Turn left.

San Vitale

Via Nazionale 194/B. ◷*Open 7:45am –7pm.* ✆*06 48 23 338.*
Built at the start of the 5C, the two aisles of the Church of Santi Vitale e Compagni Martiri in Fovea were removed to create a large nave during restoration work in 1475. Frescoed during the 16C by Cavalier d'Arpino, Andrea Pozzo and Gaspare Poussin, the church sank below street level following construction of Via Nazionale. The original portico was reconstructed during the Fascist period with 5 arches on antique pulvino columns repeated in the facade that contains the beautiful 14C portal with the coat of arms of Pope Sixtus IV and 17C carved panels.

▶ Return to Piazza del Quirinale and take Via XXIV Maggio.

Casino dell'Aurora e Galleria Pallavicini Rospigliosi

Via XXIV Maggio 43. ◷*Open 1st day of the month 10am–noon and 3–5pm or visits by reservation (maximum 15 days in advance),* ✆*06 83 46 70 00.* *www.casinoaurorapallavicini.it.*
The courtyard has palm trees, laurels, pines and holm oaks. On two sides loom the 1603 palace built by Cardinal Scipio Borghese, more or less atop Constantine's Baths.
Just inside the main gates stands the **Casino★** opening onto a terrace. This 17C pavilion is famous for the **Aurora fresco** on the ceiling by Guido Reni, a pupil of the Carracci.
The goddess is shown opening the gates of heaven to the sun's chariot. On the right *(Via XXIV Maggio)*, the impressive doorway is the entrance to the **garden of the Palazzo Colonna**.

San Silvestro al Quirinale

Entrance left of the façade; bell at Via Ventiquattro Maggio 10. ◷*Open daily 9:30–12:30am, 3–6pm.* ✆*06 67 90 240 .*
The façade of the church of **St Sylvester on the Quirinal** is purely decorative; a 19C construction to disguise the difference in level between the church and the street. The latter had been widened and lowered; the church truncated.
The interior decor is surprisingly rich. The 16C coffered ceiling was restored in the 19C. Among the Mannerist decorations are some paintings in the **first chapel** on the left by Polidoro da Caravaggio and Maturino da Firenze (◐*See PIAZZA NAVONA: Via della Maschera d'Oro, p157*).
The floor has been paved with fragments of ceramic tiles, recycled from the Raphael Loggia in the Vatican.
In the left arm of the transept is a beautiful octagonal domed **chapel★**: Domenichino painted the medallions in the pendentives (1628); the stucco statues of Mary Magdalene *(left of the entrance)* and St John *(left of the chancel)* were sculpted at the same time by Alessandro Algardi. The **chancel** vault is decorated with a late 16C fresco on a beautiful grey base. To the left of the chancel is a door opening onto a quiet terrace. Here Vittoria

Colonna, who had composed poems to the glory of her dead husband, spent many hours in the company of scholars and holy men. Sometimes Michelangelo joined them. He developed a great affection for this noble and cultivated lady and was present at her death.

▷ Turn right into Via della Cordonata and right again into Via IV Novembre.

Palazzo Colonna
Entrance at Via della Pilotta 17. ⏱*Open Sat 9am–1:15pm (*🗪*Guided tours available in english at 12; other days by appointment).* 🎫€12. 📞06 67 84 350. *www.galleriacolonna.it.*
The palace dates from the 15C, but was rebuilt in 1730. It is linked to its gardens by four arches spanning the Via Pilotta. **Pope Martin V** (1417–31), a member of the Colonna family, took up residence here when he returned to Rome after the Great Schism of the West. The **picture gallery**, a suite of richly furnished rooms, contains many 15C–18C paintings.

Galleria di Palazzo Colonna★
In the Sala della Colonna Bellica (Column Room), note Narcissus at the fountain by **Tintoretto** (1518–94) and a portrait, which may be of Vittoria Colonna. The name of the room is a reference to the red column: the family emblem. A cannon ball is lodged in the steps down to the salon. It was fired by the French troops who besieged Rome in 1849 in an attempt to re-establish Pius IX.
The Salone★★ (Salon) offers a very handsome perspective, resplendent with gilt, mirrors, crystal chandeliers, yellow marble and paintings.
The **Sala degli Scrigni** (Casket Room) contains two **caskets★**, small 17C chests: one in ebony decorated with ivory low-relief carvings; the other in sandalwood. In the **Sala dell'apoteosi di Martino V**, note the fine portrait of a gentleman (197) by Paolo Veronese (1528–88) and the famous *Peasant Eating Beans★* (43), attributed to Annibale Carracci (1560–1609). Continuing past the **Sala Gialla**, you come to a new wing in the palazzo that contains the **Salone della Cappella**

and the tapestries of the Stories of Artemisia (17C). (🕯*See Address*).

▷ Take Via IV Novembre west; turn left into Piazza Santi Apostoli.

👥 In the square at no. 68A is the **Museo delle Cere** (Waxworks Museum). ♿⏱*Open daily 9am–9pm.* 🎫€9. 📞06 67 96 482. *www.museodellecere.com.*

Basilica dei Santi Dodici Apostoli★
⏱*Open Mon–Sun 7am–noon and 4pm–7pm.* 📞06 69 95 71.
The Basilica of the Twelve Holy Apostles dates back to the 6C, when a basilica on the site was dedicated by Popes Pelagius I and John III to the Apostles Philip and James the Less.
The greatest alterations were carried out by Sixtus IV (1471–84), of which only the lower part of the porch remains. The loggia above was closed with rectangular windows in the Baroque era and topped with a balustrade and statues. The upper section is 19C Neoclassical.
In the porch, guarding the entrance, are three lions from the medieval building. The chancel contains the Renaissance tombs of the two Riario cardinals, Pietro and Raffaele, who helped their uncle, Sixtus IV, to reconstruct the church: **Cardinal Pietro Riario's tomb★** (*left*) is the result of three masters of funerary art working in collaboration: Andrea Bregno, Mino da Fiesole and Giovanni Dalmata.
The **monument to Clement XIV** – at the top of the left aisle – is the first work executed in Rome by the Neoclassical sculptor Antonio Canova (1787).

Palazzo Chigi-Odescalchi
The palace (n. 80) was redesigned by **Bernini** when the Chigi family acquired it in 1661. The master's involvement in the project laid down rules that greatly influenced the architecture of central and northern Europe.

Palazzo Balestra
At the end of the square stands a Baroque palace. Here the **Stuarts**, the royal family of Scotland and England, lived in exile.

Originally known as Palazzo Muti, it was given to James Stuart, the Old Pretender, in 1719, when he married Maria Clementina Sobieska of Poland. His two sons, Charles Edward, the Young Pretender, and Henry, Cardinal of York, were born in the palace. "Bonnie Prince Charlie" returned to die there in 1788.

Oratorio del Crocifisso★

The construction of the Oratory of the Crucifix was entrusted to Tommaso dei Cavalieri, a young Roman noble, who inspired a warm affection in Michelangelo. Nonetheless he chose as his adviser one of the master's bitterest enemies, Nanni di Baccio Bigio. The façade was designed by Giacomo della Porta in 1561. It marked the beginning of a brilliant career, which led to work on the Capitol and on St Peter's (1573). The façade, which harmonises so well with the square, bears traces of Michelangelo's teaching. The interior is decorated with frescoes by Mannerist artists.

▷ Take the alley on the right of the oratory.

The **Galleria Sciarra★**, with its metal framework, glass canopy and fine Art Nouveau paintings in the courtyard, is a highly original late-19C arcade.

▷ Continue north along Via di Santa Maria in Via.

Galleria Colonna

This arcade was built in 1923 linking Via di Santa Maria in Via with Via del Corso and Piazza Colonna.

Santa Maria in Via

St Mary's Church (Largo Chigi) has miraculous origins: an image of the Virgin, painted on a tile, fell into a well. It overflowed and the icon reappeared. Pilgrims still come to drink the water and to venerate the "Madonna of the Well" (Madonna del Pozzo). The late 17C Baroque façade is by Francesco da Volterra and Carlo Rainaldi.

▷ Turn right into Via del Tritone.

Via del Tritone

This busy street links the city centre with the northeastern suburbs.

The Istituto Nazionale per la Grafica - **Calcografia** (Via della Stamperia 6) houses more than 23 000 engravings, including some by Giovan Battista Piranesi (1720–78), who produced some remarkable views of Rome. The upstairs windows directly overlook Trevi Fountain.

▷ From Piazza dell'Accademia di S. Luca, take Via della Stamperia.

Galleria dell'Accademia di San Luca

⏱Open Mon–Sat 10am–7pm. ✆06 67 98 850. www.accademiasanluca.eu.
St Luke's Academy Gallery, housed in **Palazzo Carpegna** – a building that owes its fame to interventions by Francesco Borromini, including portico and ground floor – displays works by members of the academy, founded in 1577. Note the Portrait of Clement IX by Baciccia (1639–1709), a fresco fragment by Raphael, Judith and Holophernes by the Venetian Piazzetta (1682–1754) and a Virgin and Angels by Sir Anthony van Dyck.

ADDRESSES

TAKING A BREAK

Bistrot Quirino – Via delle Vergini 7. ✆0698878090. bistrotquirino.com.
Located alongside Teatro Quirino (see "Evening"), this bistro boasts a literary flair (bookshelves, posters, photographs) and is a comfortable spot for a simple meal.

Open Colonna – Scalinata di Via Milano 9a. ✆06 478 22641. antonellocolonna.it.
Set atop the Palazzo delle Esposizioni, this restaurant sports glass walls and atrium skylights that infuse the interior with Roman light. Enjoy drinks at the stylish bar or have the reasonably priced buffet lunch. The cost of the upscale gourmet dinner will undoubtedly flatten your wallet.

Isola Tiberina–Ghetto–Largo Argentina★★

The peace of *Isola Tiberina* (Tiber Island) provides a striking contrast to the hustle and bustle of the "Ghetto" (old Jewish district), which extends along Via del Portico d'Ottavia. Although besieged in WWII, this district is still home to many traditional shops, such as haberdasheries, fabric shops and groceries specialising in kosher food, as well as to the impressive synagogue. Amid the ancient ruins and medieval alleys is a good choice of bars, restaurants and trattorias.

 WALKING TOUR

Isola Tiberina★

Romans drove Tarquin the Proud, last king of his line, from the city in the 6C BC. They piled his crops into the Tiber; legend claims this seeded the island. The ancients also believed its shape echoes that of the boat that brought Aesculapius, the god of medicine, from Epidauros in Greece.

To stress the resemblance, the southern point was paved with slabs of travertine round an obelisk, set up like a mast. Aesculapius is said to have arrived in Rome in 293 BC in the form of a serpent. The boat had scarcely come alongside, when the serpent disembarked and hid on the island; the Romans obligingly built a temple on the spot. The sanctuary site is now occupied by St Bartholomew's Church. A Catholic hospital (*Fatebenefratelli* – literally "do-good-brothers") and a Jewish hospital continue the island's medical tradition.

San Bartolomeo

Piazza di San Bartolomeo all'Isola 22. ⏰*Open 9:30am–1:30pm and 3:30pm–5:30pm (Sun 9:30am–1pm).* ☏*06 68 77 973. www.sanbartolomeo.org.*
Baroque façade and the Romanesque bell-tower (12C) rise from the centre of the island. Inside the building, at

- 🕭 **Michelin Map:** 38 L11, M11, N11.
- ▶ **Location:** This walk runs from Isola Tiberina to the old Jewish district (Ghetto) on the east bank of the Tiber. From the Jewish district, the walk continues on to Largo di Torre Argentina, where the incessant noise of cars, buses and trams provides an anachronistic soundtrack to one of the city's oldest archaeological sites.
- 👁 **Don't Miss:** The Porticus of Octavia near the Theatre of Marcellus. The lively ghetto neighbourhood. Fried Roman–Jewish artichokes *(carciofi alla giudia)* at *restaurants* Piperno or Al Pompiere, or torta di ricotta at bakery Boccione (Via Portico d'Ottavia 1).
- 🕐 **Timing:** Allow 1hr 30min.
- 👥 **Kids:** A gelato on ship-shaped Tiber Island; outdoor evening cinema on banks in summer.
- 🕭 **Also See:** *CAMPO DE' FIORI; TRASTEVERE–GIANICOLO; BOCCA DELLA VERITÀ; CAMPIDOGLIO; PANTHEON.*

the centre of the great staircase, is a cylindrical well-head (c. 12m/39ft deep) surmounted by an ancient column carved with 12C saintly figures. One of the cannon balls fired during the French siege in 1849 is lodged in the wall *(left)* of the Lady Chapel at the back.

👥 South of *Ponte Fabricio*, near the church, are the remains of the travertine, which faced the bow of the **"ship"** of Aesculapius.

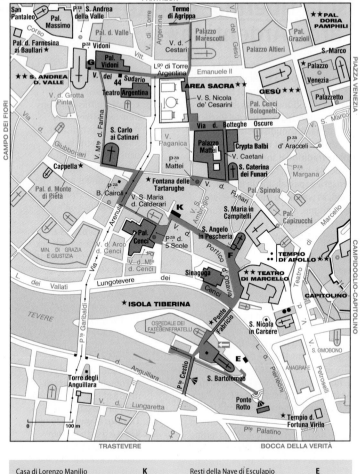

| Casa di Lorenzo Manilio | K | Resti della Nave di Esculapio | E |
| Portico di Ottavia | F | Statua dell'Abate Luigi | G |

Tradition says that Rahere, courtier to Henry I of England, recovered from an attack of malaria, usually fatal then, in a hospice attached to this church. In gratitude, he founded, legend says, this hospital, a priory and another hospital in London's Smithfield, which still stand (&See Michelin Green Guide London).

▶ Return to the square and take the steps opposite the church, which lead to the bank of the Tiber. Downstream of the island, in the middle of the river, are the remains of Ponte Rotto.

Ponte Rotto

In origin "the Broken Bridge" goes back to the **Pons Aemilius**, built here in the mid-2C BC. It had already collapsed twice when Pope Gregory XII rebuilt it in about 1575. It collapsed again in 1598 and only one arch now remains. The channel of the **Cloaca Maxima**, the Forum's great sewer, dug in the 6C BC, is still in use today.

Ponte Cestio

This bridge links the Tiber Island to the popular, bustling Trastevere district. Its origins go back to the 1C BC; it was partially rebuilt in the 19C.

An "Angelic Parricide"

The scandal broke on 9 September 1598. Francesco Cenci, whose father had been Pius V's treasurer, was a violent and perverted man. He was murdered at the instigation of his family, including his daughter Beatrice, her brothers and his wife. Pope Clement VIII sentenced them to death despite public opinion, which supported the plea of self-defence. The scandal (incest and crime were involved) inflamed Rome. On 11 September 1599 the females were beheaded, and a brother drawn and quartered near Piazza di Ponte Sant'Angelo (the youngest brother was spared). Each year on 11 September, a mass is celebrated in St Thomas' Church in *Piazzetta Monte dei Cenci* for the soul of Beatrice Cenci.

◐ Cross to the north side of the island.

Ponte Fabricio★

The only intact classical span in Rome, it is sometimes also known as the "Bridge of Four Heads", because of the multi-faced Hermes set at the east end. Built in 62 BC by the consul Fabricius, it links the east bank with Tiber Island.

◐ Cross the bridge.

Ghetto

Jews have lived in Rome since ancient times, but their numbers increased after Pompey captured Jerusalem (1C BC), and again after the destruction of the Temple of Jerusalem and the campaigns of Vespasian and Titus in Palestine (1C AD). Immigrants also arrived after the expulsion of Jews from Spain in 1492. This ethnic group, which once lived in Trastevere, moved to the east bank of the Tiber in the 13C.

In 1556, Pope Paul IV had the area enclosed within a wall, which ran from Ponte Fabricio, along Via del Portico di Ottavia and around Piazza delle Cinque Scole. This crowded, disease-ridden ghetto was home to some 4 000 people and its gates were opened at dawn and closed at dusk. Jews were prohibited from any commercial activities, with the exception of money-lending and selling fabrics, which explains the large number of haberdasheries and fabric shops here. In 1848, the walls were taken down, in 1870 the new Italian State abolished all restrictions, and in 1885 this insalubrious district was largely demolished, with the exception of the houses on Via della Reginella.

In 1943, during the German occupation, more than 2 000 ghetto residents were deported; few returned. Since WWII, the district has gradually repopulated. Today it has a lively atmosphere.

Museo Ebraico di Roma

Via Catalana (Largo 16 Ottobre 1943) - Lungotevere De' Cenci. ◷*Open 1 Apr–30 Sept Sun–Thu 10am–6pm, Fri 10am–4pm. Rest of the year Sun–Thu 10am–5pm, Fri 9am–2pm.* ◷*Closed 1 Jan, 15 Aug and Jewish holidays.* ◀*Guided tours available in English (1hr, the visit includes the Synagogue).* ◉€11. ℘06 68 40 06 61. www.museoebraico.roma.it.

The Hebrew Museum, inside the synagogue, is a display of souvenirs of the Jewish community in Rome, together with liturgical articles.

Sinagoga

Lungotevere De' Cenci. The visit is included in the ticket to the Museo Ebraico di Roma. (*See above*).

The synagogue, inaugurated in 1904, occupies part of the old ghetto. It was designed by Costa and Armanni and is distinguished by its large, square dome, visible from all over Rome.

◐ Take Via Portico di Ottavia.

Portico di Ottavia★

Once the vast dimensions of this monument, one of Rome's richest, stretched as far as the present Piazza di Campitelli and the Church of Santa Caterina

125

dei Funari. All that remains is part of the entrance porch *(propylaea)*, facing the Tiber. Septimius Severus (193–211) funded the remaining Corinthian columns and entablature.

The original portico had been built in the 2C BC as an enclosure for two temples dedicated to Juno and Jupiter, respectively. Augustus rebuilt the portico, which he dedicated to his sister Octavia *(Ottavia)*, and included two public libraries, one Latin and one Greek, as well as an assembly hall where the Senate sometimes met.

The lower archaeological area is now accessible via a pedestrian ramp (*Open 9am–dusk*).

Sant'Angelo in Pescheria

Via della Tribuna di Campitelli 6. *Open Wed–Sat 4pm–8:30pm.* *06 68 80 18 19.*
Nowadays the *propylaea* of the Portico of Octavia serves only as a monumental entrance to the little Church of Sant'Angelo in Pescheria (founded in the 8C). The name, like those of the neighbouring streets, recalls the **fish market** that occupied the antique ruins in the 12C. The stalls and activity on the huge paving stones made this one of the most picturesque corners of Rome.

▶ Turn left into Piazza delle Cinque Scole.

The piazza's name, Square of the Five Schools, refers to the fact that the synagogues serving the Ghetto once stood here. The arch and two columns on the left are the remains of a 1C building.

Palazzo Cenci-Bolognetto

Vicolo dei Cenci. *Closed to public.*
The narrow streets that surround the palace (nos 7-29) repeat like variations on a theme: the name of the great family involved in a sensational 1598-99 murder trial (*see box p125*).

The palace now hosts a restaurant on the first (noble) floor, which still has some of the frescos and decoration. It extends to a slight rise *(Monte de' Cenci)* formed by the rubble from ancient buildings (perhaps the *Circus Flaminius*), where the Cenci church, San Tommaso, is situated as well as a traditional restaurant (no 9) that dates to 1856.

▶ Follow Via S. Maria de' Calderari. Turn right into Via Arenula and then left into Via dei Giubbonari.

Santi Biago e Carlo ai Catinari

Piazza Benedetto Cairoli 117. *Closed for renovations at time of writing.*
The grandiose, but rather heavy church, with its Counter-Reformation façade, was erected between 1635 and 1638 and dedicated to St Blaise and St Charles.

Horatius Cocles and the Pons Sublicius

Downstream from *Ponte Rotto* and its modern neighbour, the Palatine Bridge, was the *Pons Sublicius*. This was the first to span the Tiber, built to foster relations between the Latins on the Palatine and the Etruscans on the west bank.

Each year on 14 May, the ancients offered human figures made of willow to appease the river. The bridge was made of wood and the law forbade any iron in its repair: it had to be easily dismantled if diplomacy failed. This happened when the last Etruscan king, Tarquin the Proud, was driven out of Rome in the 6C BC. While his men crowbarred the *Pons Sublicius* apart, the Roman Horatius Cocles alone held back the enemy: "withering the Etruscan leaders with his look, he challenged them one by one or taunted them". Finally the bridge was breached. Horatius jumped into the Tiber and rejoined his men. He was treated as a hero: he was granted land, and statue of him was put up in the Comitium.

Area Sacra del Largo di Torre Argentina, Teatro Argentina in the background

© Bjanka Kadic /age fotostock

The **interior★**, which is shaped like a Greek cross, is dominated by a handsome coffered dome. The artists who painted *Sant'Andrea della Valle* are found here too: **Domenichino** painted the Cardinal Virtues on the pendentives of the dome; in the apse **Lanfranco** accomplished his last work (1647), the *Apotheosis of St Charles Borromeo*; above the high altar is St Charles Borromeo leading a procession in Milan to ward off the plague by **Pietro da Cortona** (1650); the 17C St Cecilia's Chapel *(right of the chancel)* is verging on the Rococo, with its strained perspective, its broken lines and animated stucco figures.

▷ Take Via Monte della Farina to where it ends as Piazza Vidoni.

Statua dell'Abate Luigi
In a corner, Piazza Vidoni, along east side of Sant'Andrea della Valle.
This statue of a Roman in a toga is one of the "talking" statues, which dispensed comments with Pasquino, Madame Lucrezia and Marforio.

▷ Turn right into Via del Sudario.

Palazzo Vidoni
Corso Vittorio Emanuele II 116.
The Caffarelli, a rich Roman family, asked Raphael to design a palace here in 1500. Its robust elegance was altered in the 18C and 19C, when the façade was enlarged and re-sited to face the Corso Vittorio Emanuele II, and the top storey added.

▷ Continue on Via del Sudario as far as Largo di Torre Argentina.

Teatro Argentina
Largo di Torre Argentina 52. ℘06 68 40 00 311/14. www.teatrodiroma.net. Guided visits available (3,50 €) by reservation 06 68 40 00 363.
Rossini's *Barber of Seville* was first performed in this theatre in 1816; it was initially one of the most resounding failures in the annals of opera.

Area Sacra del Largo di Torre Argentina★
The site can only be visited externally. Discover the best view of the ruins from Via San Nicola de' Cesarini (east of the site).
This name is given to Roman Republican ruins (sacred precincts) in this square excavated between 1926 and 1929. The remains are among the oldest found in Rome. The marshy ground on the banks

AREA SACRA DEL LARGO DI TORRE ARGENTINA

0 — 30 m

Remains of St Nicholas' Church

Extant parts | Non-extant parts

of the Tiber near the *Campus Martius* often flooded. Traces of five levels from the 5C BC to the beginning of the empire have been revealed by archaeologists. In antiquity, this large precinct was at the heart of a busy district: to the southeast stood the theatre built by Balbus in Augustus's reign, to the west Pompey's Theatre and Curia (*Teatro e Curia di Pompeo*), to the north the rear façade of Agrippa's Baths (*Terme di Agrippa*) and the Saepta. Archaeologists remain unsure which deities were honoured here, so the temples are known, north to south, as A, B, C and D. The tower and portico were part of a group of medieval houses. These temples were very likely the last buildings that Julius Caesar saw before he was assassinated.

Temple A

Probably dedicated to Juturna, this site dates from the 3C BC. The present remains are from the 2C or 1C BC. Temple A was converted into a church to St Nicholas.

Temple B

This circular structure dates to 2C BC. The tufa podium was covered by one of peperine, smothered in turn by stucco.

Temple C

The oldest dates back to the 4C or 3C BC and follows the Etruscan model: a triple *cella* (containing three shrines) and a podium without columns.

Temple D

The greater part of this, the largest, temple lies beneath the road (*Via Florida*). The north and east sides of the precinct were bounded by a portico (1). The high wall (2) on the northwest side behind Temple A belonged to a public lavatory. The drainage trough is still visible. On the west wall, between B and C, large blocks (3) have been identified as the remains of Pompey's Curia, where, in 44 BC, Julius Caesar was assassinated during the Ides of March.

Torre Argentina Cat Sanctuary

Corner of Via di Torre Argentina and Via Arenula. ℘*06 68 80 56 11. www.gattidiroma.net.*
Strays are epidemic in Rome. Women known as *gattare* (cat ladies) cared for abandoned animals here since the 1929 excavations began, and now seek homes for them.

▷ Take Via de' Cestari and turn left into Via Arco della Ciambella.

Wedged between no 9 and no 15 Via Arco della Ciambella, a small fragment of wall remains from the **Terme di Agrippa**, the oldest baths in Rome. Built in 19 BC, these were supplied by purpose-built aqueduct Aqua Virgo. Part of the channel still runs under Via dei Condotti and fills a number of fountains, including the Fontana di Trevi.

▷ Return to Largo Argentina and continue to Via delle Botteghe Oscure.

Via delle Botteghe Oscure was famous in the Middle Ages for its dimly lit basement shops (*"oscura"* means "dark" in Italian), which had been set up in the ruins of **Balbus' Theatre** (1C BC).

Crypta Balbi

 ⏱Open Tue–Sun 9am–7:45pm. ⏱Closed 1 Jan and 25 Dec. ∞€10, €12 combined ticket valid for 3 days. This ticke is also valid for other sites of Museo Nazionale Romano: Terme di Diocleziano, Palazzo Massimo alle Terme (&See PORTA PIA – TERMINI) and Palazzo Altemps (&See MONTECITORIO). www. museonazionaleromano.beniculturali. it. Booking at ☏06 39 96 77 00. www.coopculture.it.

Part of the Museo Nazionale Romano, the Crypta Balbi is housed in medieval buildings above a portico that was added to the theatre by Lucius Cornelius Balbus in 13 BC. The various levels, which include the basement crypt, hold displays that explain the history of the site through archaeological finds, reconstructions, ceramics and excavations.

▷ Turn right into Via Caetani.

A commemorative bronze plaque marks the spot where the body of statesman **Aldo Moro** was found in 1978, 54 days after he had been kidnapped by Red Brigade terrorists.

Aqueducts

As early as 312 BC, the Romans began constructing conduits for channelling water by gravitational force great distances into the city for use in public baths, fountains and gardens, and households (the Tiber's water was unsafe for drinking). The aqueducts were built both underground as well as above ground and made of stone, concrete or brick. Some of them remain to this day.

Santa Caterina ai Funari

Via dei Funari. ⏱Open Mon, Wed and Fry noon–5pm. ⏱Closed 25 Nov. ☏06 67 85 883.

This church has a graceful façade, built between 1500 and 1564; the shallow pilasters are typical of the Renaissance, but garlands attempt decorative effects typical of the Mannerist period. Note the bell-tower.

Palazzo Mattei

Via dei Funari 31 or Via Caetani 32. Enter the courtyard to better appreciate the decorations.

Five palaces were built by the Mattei in the 16C and 17C. Carlo Maderno (1598–1611) was the architect of the palace with two entrances (as shown above).

▷ Follow Via dei Funari as far as Piazza Mattei.

Fontana delle Tartarughe★

This late Renaissance work (1584) by Taddeo Landini is probably from a design by **Giacomo della Porta**.

Local legend tells how Duke Mattei, the owner of the neighbouring palace and an inveterate gambler, lost his fortune in one night. His prospective father-in-law advised him to look for another fiancée. To prove that a Mattei, even when ruined, could achieve wonders, he had the **Turtle Fountain** (*Fontana delle Tartarughe*) built in one night.

Montecitorio★★

The best way to discover the district is on foot, heading out from bustling Piazza di Montecitorio, fronted by banks, newspaper offices, department stores, restaurants and cafés. Also home to the Italian Chamber of Deputies, the piazza is surrounded by narrow Renaissance-style streets lined with luxury shops. Farther from the square the quiet streets of the quarter beyond Via della Scrofa are dotted with 16C buildings and arts and crafts workshops.

A BIT OF HISTORY

This district corresponds to the northern part of the **Campus Martius**, which was mostly reserved for the colossal tombs that belonged to the Imperial families and the funeral pyres *(ustrina)*.

Like the other districts of the city through which the pilgrims passed on their way to the Vatican, this one was elevated out of its medieval misery under Sixtus IV (1471–84). In his 13 years on the Papal throne he changed the face of Rome, using the money from the sale of indulgences to pay for his projects. In the early 16C, Leo X cleared the way for Via Leonina (now Via di Ripetta) to run from Porta del Popolo, through which visitors from the north entered the city, to the Mausoleum of Augustus.

◉◉WALKING TOUR

Piazza di Montecitorio

In the square stands a 6C BC **Egyptian obelisk**, re-erected in 1792 by Pius VI. Brought back from Heliopolis by Augustus in the 10C BC, it served as the gnomon (pointer) for a gigantic sundial, more or less on the site of *San Lorenzo in Lucina*.

Palazzo di Montecitorio

♿◉*Guided tour (30min) of the Chamber of Deputies first Sun of each month. Times may change as a result of*

- **Michelin Map:** 38 K 10–11.
- **Location:** This district lies between the Tiber and Via del Corso, which marks the boundary with the Fontana di Trevi and Quirinale quarter. Piazza Navona and the Pantheon lie a few hundred metres to the south.
- **Don't Miss:** Caravaggio's *La Madonna dei Pellegrini* in S. Agostino, the Palazzo Altemps.
- **Also See:** *CASTEL SANT'ANGELO; FONTANA DI TREVI–QUIRINALE; PIAZZA NAVONA AND DI SPAGNA; PANTHEON.*

GETTING THERE

BY METRO: Line A: Spagna (Approximately 700m/770 yd from Piazza di Montecitorio).

political events taking place. ◐*Closed Jul–half Sept.* ☎*06 67 601.*
The parliament meets where the Antonine family cremated its dead. **Bernini** began this *palazzo* in 1650, completed 47 years later by Carlo Fontana. Little remains of Bernini's Baroque fantasies: rough-hewn stones frame some windows and the effect is rustic, despite the clock tower. Since 1870, it has housed the Chamber of Deputies, thus demonstrations often add to the piazza's bustle.

Piazza Colonna★

This square is one of the most crowded in Rome, sitting at the junction of the two main shopping streets (Via del Corso and Via del Tritone). The **column★** at the centre of the square was probably erected between 176 and 193 in honour of **Marcus Aurelius** (161–80), who preferred philosophy to war but was forced to campaign on the banks of the Danube. He died at the front, not in battle, but of the plague. His victories

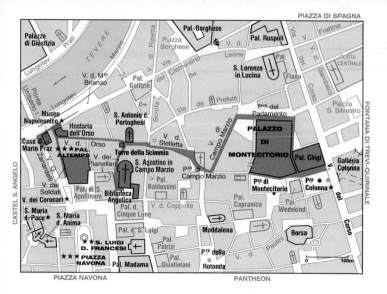

were short-lived and did not contain the barbarian thrust. Just as Trajan's Column illustrated that emperor's exploits against the Dacians, so Marcus Aurelius' Column depicts the significant episodes in his wars, with low-relief carvings arranged in a spiral. The carving was done by a group of sculptors and the designs were likely the work of several artists. To make the work more visible, the scenes are larger and in higher relief than those on Trajan's Column, but the quality of the craftsmanship has suffered. In 1589, Pope Sixtus V had the crowning statue of the emperor replaced with one of St Paul.

Palazzo Chigi

Piazza Colonna 370. Guided tours (1h, free), Sept–Jul 2 Sats every month 9am–noon only. Booking at visite@ palazzochigi.it.
The building was begun in 1562 to designs by **Giacomo della Porta**. Carlo Maderno continued it, according to the severe concepts of the Counter-Reformation. The palace was completed in 1630 in the Baroque era. Two decades later, Pope Alexander VII purchased it for his family, after whom it is named. Since 1917, Palazzo Chigi has housed the Ministry of Foreign Affairs (post WWI),

and the Head of the Government (Fascist period). It now belongs to the Council of Ministers, whose president is the Italian Prime Minister.

▶ Take the street between Palazzo di Montecitorio and Palazzo Chigi; turn left into Piazza del Parlamento and left again into Via di Campo Marzio.

In the reign of Octavius Augustus, a vast area of the Campus Martius was occupied by a **solar clock** (160m/525ft by 60m/197ft). Some pieces of travertine paving, marked with bronze insets representing the signs of the zodiac, lie beneath Via di Campo Marzio.

▶ Bear right into Via di Stelletta, right into Via della Scrofa and immediately left into Via dei Portoghesi.

Torre della Scimmia

The building on the corner of Via dei Portoghesi and Via dei Pianellari incorporates a 15C tower. It has been immortalised by the American novelist, Nathaniel Hawthorne (1804–64): The family living here owned a monkey (*scimmia*) which climbed the tower holding a newborn child. The father was terrified

131

and prayed to the Virgin; the baby was returned safe and sound. Since then, at the top, a light burns continuously before an image of the Virgin.

Sant'Antonio dei Portoghesi

Via dei Portoghesi 2. ◷*Open Mon-Fri 8:30am–1pm and 3pm–6pm, Sat 8:30am–noon and 3pm–6pm, Sun 9am–noon. ☎06 68 80 24 96. The church is also open periodically for classical music concerts and recitals.*
The 17 C Portuguese national church has a Rococo façade; the interior is gorgeous with gold, stucco, marble and paintings. The first right hand chapel contains a monument by Canova.

▶ Take Via dei Panellari.

Sant'Agostino in Campo Marzio★

Piazza Sant'Agostino 80. ◷*Open Mon–Sun 7:30am–noon and 4pm–7:30pm. ☎06 68 80 19 62.*
The church, dedicated to St Augustine of Hippo, was built between 1479–1483. The broad travertine façade, with its rose windows, was one of the city's first Renaissance efforts. The two orders are linked by large loose scrolls; the powerful moulding adds character.
The interior, decorated by Luigi Vanvitelli in 1760, has been cluttered by 19C additions, which rob it of its soaring elegance, now only faintly perceptible in the nave.
The church contains several fine works of art: near the main door is the *Madonna del Parto★* (1521) by **Jacopo Sansovino**. The third pillar on the left in the nave bears a fresco by **Raphael** (1512) of the *Prophet Isaiah★*, which owes much to the Sistine Chapel.
The first chapel on the left contains the *Madonna of the Pilgrims★★★* (1605) by Caravaggio. His contemporaries slammed this work for its rugged pilgrims, inspired by ordinary people, and for the ugliness of the man's feet. Even the Virgin nurses her bonny baby in a very realistic manner.

▶ Continue into Via dei Panellari.

Biblioteca Angelica

Piazza Sant'Agostino 8. ☎06 68 40 801. www.bibliotecaangelica.beniculturali.it.
Founded in 1614 by Angelo Rocca, an Augustinian bishop, this was the first European library open to the public. The library became state property in 1871, and boasts over 170,000 volumes, 2,668 manuscripts and 1,112 incunabula, including an impressive, 14th-century illuminated manuscript of the *Divina Commedia,* and the famous 13th-century *De Balneis Puteolanis,* with miniatures by the Sicilian school. Incunabula include Cicero's *De oratore* and Saint Augustine's *De Civitate Dei,* printed in Subiaco in 1465, and reveals important autographs including those of Cola di Rienzo, Pope Sixtus V and Torquato Tasso.

▶ Return to San Antonio dei Portoghesi and continue west along Via dell'Orso.

Hostaria dell'Orso (Bear Inn)

From the Middle Ages to the Renaissance, this district consisted almost entirely of inns, which provided lodgings for pilgrims making their way to St Peter's. The hostelry at the sign of the bear was set up in a fine 15C building. Montaigne stayed here for a few days during his visit to Rome in 1580; more recently Hollywood royalty has dined and nightclubbed here.
Inside there is an elegant restaurant-piano bar (*Via dei Soldati 25c. ☎06 68 30 11 92. www.hdo.it*).

PALAZZO ALTEMPS★★★ (MUSEO NAZIONALE ROMANO)

Via di Sant'Apollinare 46 (no Wheelchair entrance). ♿◷*Open Tue–Sun 9am–7:45pm (last admission 6:45pm). ◷Closed 1 Jan, 1 May and 25 Dec. ⊜€10, €12 combined ticket. This ticket is also valid for other sites of Museo Nazionale Romano: Terme di Diocleziano and Palazzo Massimo alle Terme (◉See PORTA PIA–TERMINI), Crypta Balbi (◉See ISOLA TIBERINA– GHETTO–TORRE ARGENTINA).*

Loggia decorated with frescoes, Palazzo Altemps

© DEA/G DAGLI ORTI/De Agostini Editore/age fotostock

ww.museonazionaleromano.
beniculturali.it. ☞English guided
tours (1hr 30min) by request at ✆06 39
96 77 00. www.coopculture.it.
The palace was begun in about 1480 by
Girolamo Riario, Sixtus IV's nephew. In
1568 it was acquired by Cardinal Marco
Sittico Altemps who had it rebuilt by
Martino Longhi the Elder. In 1725 it
became the residence of Cardinal de
Polignac, the French Ambassador.

The museum, which underwent a
15-year restoration in the late 20C,
houses the Ludovisi–Boncompagni
collection. In the first half of the 17C
Cardinal Ludovico decided to decorate
his villa with a substantial number of
ancient statues, some of which had
been found during construction of the
villa itself (in the area known in Antiquity
as the Sallustian Gardens), and others
which had been purchased by the Cardinal (some probably from the Altemps
family).

The statues were restored very much
according to the ideas and criteria of the
17C. Some of the greatest artists of the
time, including Algardi and Bernini, were
called upon to work on the statues; they
not only restored them but replaced any
missing parts. One of the more unusual
aspects of this collection is the strange
(and nowadays unthinkable) combination of the Ancient original and the
Baroque restoration.
Of equal interest is the palace itself, with
its frescoed drawing rooms, old 15C and
16C structures and beautiful ceilings.

Visit

A harmonious 16C courtyard – designed
by Antonio da Sangallo the Elder, Baldassarre Peruzzi and Martino Longhi
the Elder – greets visitors. Four Roman
statues can be seen under the northern portico (copies of Greek originals),
arranged in their original location. The
loggia above bears a beautiful fresco.
Cross the Atrium of Antoninus Pius *(Atrio
di Antonino il Pio)*, who is depicted wearing only a cloak, and enter the room
dedicated to the Ludovico marble statues.

Two heavily restored statues of Apollo
with his lyre *(Apollo Citaredo)* can be
seen in the *Sala delle Erme*. The Athena
Algardi is a good example of 17C restoration work; perhaps it originally
portrayed Hygeia. In the next room
is the *Athena Parthenos*, a 1C Greek
copy thought to have been inspired by
the imposing statue (12m/39ft high)
sculpted by Phidias for the Parthenon.
On the first floor, the *Sala delle Prospettive Dipinte* contains late 16C frescoes
with a false colonnade. The 15C **fresco★**

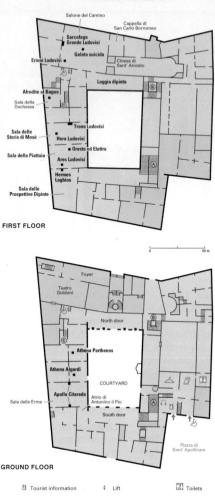

PALAZZO ALTEMPS

Salone del Camino

Cappella di
San Carlo Borromeo

Sarcofago
Grande Ludovisi

Galata suicida

Erinni Ludovisi

Chiesa di
Sant' Aniceto

Loggia dipinta

Afrodite al Bagno

Sala della
Duchessa

Trono Ludovisi

Sala delle
Storie di Mosè

Hera Ludovisi

Oreste ed Elettra

Sala della Piattaia

Ares Ludovisi

Hermes
Loghios

Sala delle
Prospettive Dipinte

FIRST FLOOR

0   50 m

Foyer

Teatro
Goldoni

North door

Athena Parthenos

Athena Algardi

COURTYARD

Apollo Citaredo

Atrio di
Antonino il Pio

Sala delle Erme

South door

Piazza di
Sant' Apollinare

GROUND FLOOR

	Tourist information		Lift		Toilets
	Audio guide	Ⓐ	Stairs		Bookshop
	Wheelchair access		Cloakroom		Telephone

in the **Sala della Piattaia** is of outstanding beauty. This room takes its name from the kitchenware painted on the walls. *Orestes and Electra★ (Oreste ed Elettra)* is the work of the Greek sculptor Menelaos and dates from the 1C AD. The Ares Ludovisi★★, identified as Apollo, is a Roman copy of a statue from the Hellenistic period.

The **Sala delle Storie di Mosè** (Room of the Stories of Moses) contains the most famous exhibit of the collection, the **Ludovisi Throne★★★** *(Trono Ludovisi).*

This strange monument suggests a throne for a cult statue (probably part of a ritual ornament from a place of worship) and was found in the Villa Ludovisi in 1887. This Greek masterpiece dates from the early classical period (5C BC). The main panel shows a young woman being assisted by two attendants, who shield her body with a veil. Archaeologists have interpreted this scene as the birth of Aphrodite (Venus), goddess of love, who emerged from the sea foam, accompanied by the Seasons, whose

Courtyard, Palazzo Altemps
© Zsolt Biczó/Fotolia.com

feet brush the pebbles of the shore. The artist has endowed the face of Aphrodite with joyful serenity. In the side panels, a naked woman plays the flute, while another, fully clothed, burns incense – these figures are often regarded as embodiments of sensuality (the courtesan) and modesty (the wife). In the same room is the monumental head known as the *Hera Ludovisi*, which is, in fact, a portrait of Antonia, wife of the Emperor Drusus and mother of Claudius.

Decoration of the **Loggia dipinta**★★ was commissioned at the end of the 16C by Marco Sittico Altemps. The fresco mimics an arboured garden, intertwining vegetal, animal and cupid motifs. The portraits of the Caesars from the Ludovisi collection are displayed here. Three of the most interesting exhibits are in the *Salone del Camino*. The **Gaul taking his own life**★★★ (*Galata suicida*), a Roman copy of an original Greek bronze, dominates the centre of the room. Note the strength and movement of the barbarian, with the dramatic twist of the bust, and the forlorn stance of the wife, supported only by her husband's hand. This is a magnificent example of Hellenistic art, copied for Julius Caesar after his Gallic victory. The *Dying Gaul (Galata morente)* in the Capitoline Museum is part of the same group.

The **Grande Ludovisi sarcophagus**★★ (*sarcofago Grande Ludovisi*), dating to 3C, depicts battles between the Romans and the barbarians. The victorious

Romans can be seen in the top level; in the middle, the soldiers attack the barbarians, depicted on the bottom.
Note the different characteristics: the Romans appear proud and courageous; the barbarians wince in pain. The delicate face of the **Ludovisi Erinyes**★ (*Erinni Ludovisi*) is emphasised by its dark base.

Museo Napoleonico★

Piazza di Ponte Umberto I 1. ⏱*Open Tue–Sun 10am–6pm; 24 and 31 Dec 10am–2pm.* ⏱*Closed 1 Jan, 1 May and 25 Dec.* Free. ☏*06 68 74 240. www.museonapoleonico.it.*
The museum was founded in 1927 by Giuseppe Primoli, a descendant of Lucien Bonaparte, and contains souvenirs of the Napoleonic presence here. Two rooms are devoted to the emperor's son, declared king of Rome at his birth in 1811. Room VI, devoted to Pauline, Napoleon's sister, contains a couch similar to that in her sculpture by Canova.

Casa di Mario Praz

Via Zanardelli 1. ⏱*Guided tour. Open Thu , Fri and Sat 9am–1pm, 2:30pm–6:30pm.* Free. ⏱*Closed 1 Jan, 1 May and 25 Dec.* ☏*06 68 61 089. www.museopraz.beniculturali.it.*
This house is was the residence of Mario Praz (d. 1982), a renowned Anglicist and essayist and scholar of English 19C literature. A passionate collector, he accumulated a huge number of knick-

knacks, pictures, sculpture, Neoclassical furniture and *objets d'art*. Of particular note is the rare collection of 17C–19C wax models.

ADDRESSES

TAKING A BREAK

Antica Gelateria Giolitti– *Via Uffici del Vicario 40. Open daily 7:30am–1:30am ℘06 69 91 243. www.giolitti.it.* The story of this ice cream shop began in 1900 when the Giolitti couple, who used to sell milk from the Roman countryside, created what has today become an institution, a synonym for ice cream.

I Dolci di Nonna Vincenza – *Via Arco del Monte 98a/98b. Open Mon–Sat 7:30am–8:30pm, Sun 8am–8:30pm. ℘06 92 59 43 22. www.dolcinonnavincenza.it.* Almonds, pistachios, mandarins and ricotta are all typical Sicilian flavours found in this elegant pastry shop in the heart of Rome where you can enjoy excellent *cannoli* and pastries filled with water ice.

SHOPPING

Galleria Alberto Sordi – *Piazza Colonna. ℘06 69 19 07 69. www. galleriaalbertosordi.it. Open Mon–Sat 8:30am–9pm, Sun 9:30am–9pm).* 19C civil architecture dedicated to the commerce of the new millennium. A multifunctional building that has been transformed from a temple of finance to a temple of shopping.

Monte Mario–Flaminio

The green slopes of Monte Mario form an attractive backdrop to this district, once the city's sporting hub, now also a crossroads of Roman culture. Today, like the past, it is a center for architectural experimentation. National and international events are held here, either in the austere, but impressive, Stadio dei Marmi, so typical of the Fascist period, or in the more modern Palazzetto dello Sport, Shows, exhibitions and more wide-ranging events are held in the rooms of the large new cultural institutions represented by the Auditorium and the Maxxi. Football fans should experience the excitement of a Roma–Lazio match at the Olimpico.

SIGHTS
Monte Mario

Popular with Romans looking for a stroll with a lovely **view★** (at the bottom of *Viale del Parco Mellini*), or a walk in the park (Riserva naturale di Monte Mario) that extends across the crest of the highest of the Farnesina hills (139 metres),

- ⛪ **Michelin Map:** 38 C8–12, D7–12, E7–8, F7–10, G9–10.
- ▶ **Location:** The district is bordered to the north by Viale del Foro Italico and to the south by the Prati quarter.

GETTING THERE

BY METRO AND BUS: Flaminio for the left bank of the Tiber. Tram 2. Bus C3, 53, 280, 628 and 910.

overlooking Tevere valley and hosting elegant residential villas.

Villa Madama★
Walk up Via di Villa Madama.
This 16C Renaissance villa, with an enchanting **position★** on the Monte Mario slopes, was built in 1515 by Cardinal Giulio de' Medici to to plans by **Raphael**. It was passed to Madam Margaret of Austria and named for her.

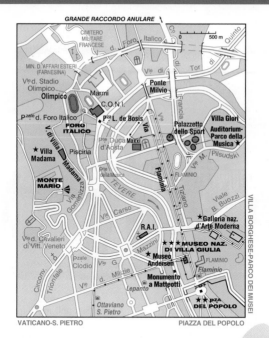

VATICANO–S. PIETRO   PIAZZA DEL POPOLO

Villa Mazzanti

Entrance in Via del Parco Mellini and in Via Gomenizza 81.

On the eastern slope of Monte Mario park, an elegant villa built in the mid-19C with decorations inspired by Villa Madama, offering a wonderful view over the city.

Villa Mellini

Viale del Parco Mellini.

Originally a suburban residence, owned first by the Chancellor of Rome, Marco Mellini (15C), then by the Falconieri family (18C), since 1935 Villa Mellini has housed the twin-domed astronomical observatory with space telescopes and a sun tower with coelostat for following the orbit of the sun during the day.

RAI (Palazzo della Radio e della Televisione)

Viale G. Mazzini 14.

The Radio and TV Centre is one of the many modern constructions in Rome. It is distinguished by a bronze statue of a rearing horse by Francesco Messina and is situated in the district that has grown up around the **Piazza Mazzini.**

WALKING TOUR

PONTE MILVIO TO FORO ITALICO

Ponte Milvio (Milvian Bridge)

A bridge has spanned the Tiber here since the 2C BC; frequently restored and rebuilt, particularly in the 15C and 19C. Nearby, the famous battle between **Constantine** and **Maxentius**, rivals for the imperial throne, took place in 312.

▷ Take Viale Tiziano till Piazza Apollodoro.

Palazzetto dello Sport

Piazza Apollodoro 10.

This concave concrete structure was designed by Annibale Vitellozzi and Pier Luigi Nervi for the 1960 Olympics.

▷ Continue into Viale Tiziano.

Stadio Flaminio

Along the modern road that follows the ancient Flaminian Way (220 BC) from the city center to Rimini on the Adriatic (314km/195mi), stands the **Stadio Flaminio** designed.

137

MAXXI, designed by Zaha Hadid

© Sime/Photononstop

▶ Turn into Via Pietro de Coubertin.

Auditorium–
Parco della Musica★

Viale Pietro de Coubertin 15/30.
🕐*For opening hours see the website.*
📞*06 80 24 12 81.*
www.auditorium.com.
This auditorium by **Renzo Piano** is the headquarters of the **Accademia di Santa Cecilia**. This large multifunctional complex includes a *cavea* for exhibitions, the ruins of a Republican villa and three main rooms (Santa Cecilia, Sinopoli and Petrassi) designed as sound boxes, gigantic musical instruments surrounded by a hanging garden. Besides being a well-known place, it has become a setting for music and the arts, including theatre, dance, cinema and literature.

▶ Return on your steps and continue on Via Guido Reni.

MAXXI – Museo Nazionale delle Arti del XXI secolo★★

Via G. Reni 4A. 🕐*Open Tue–Sun 11am–7pm (Sat –10pm). €12 .* 🕐*Closed 1 May and 25 Dec.* 📞*06 32 01 954.*
www.fondazionemaxxi.it.
Since 2010 the Capital of Antiquity has also been able to boast a museum dedicated entirely to contemporary art and cultural events of all kinds. Its program of temporary exhibitions turns it into a multidisciplinary place for artistic and architectural experimentation. The beautiful structure of the museum designed by **Zaha Hadid** was not founded on the classical concept of an exhibition space, but conceived as a promenade, a single, uninterruptedly communicating space featuring galleries, stairways and corridors. Do not miss the projecting and glazed Suite 5, with a sloping floor.

© P. Raftery/age fotostock

Inside MAXXI

Outside, the great courtyard full of trees hosts giant sculptures and installations, while the second building is called BASE, which is the Italian acronym for "library, archive, studio and edition", and hosts a modern bistro.

▷ Continue along Via Guido Reni as far as Piazza Gentile da Fabriano.

Teatro Olimpico
Piazza Gentile da Fabriano 17. ✆06 32 65 991. www.teatroolimpico.it.
Opened in 1931 as an Olympic cinema–theater, after WW2 it became the principal setting for concerts by the Accademia Filarmonica Romana. Since the 1980s its programme has included more theatrical performances and variety shows. In 1965 the first Italian performance of Stravinsky's *Abraham and Isaac* was given there.

Ponte della Musica
The bridge connects the Flaminio district, with its contemporary architecture, to the district of Le Vittorie and the Foro Italico, built by Mussolini. Pedestrians only.

▷ Cross the street and turn right into Viale and turn right into Viale delle Olimpiadi.

Foro Italico–Stadio Olimpico
Piazzale del Foro Italico.
The Fascist Government started construction of this sports centre in 1928, with the Stadio dei Cipressi (today Stadio Olimpico), the Stadio dei Marmi, the Centrale del Tennis, the Stadio del Nuoto and the Accademia dello Schermo (today Casa delle Armi). The road, from the Piazza L. de Bosis to the Piazzale del Foro Italico, is paved with mosaics of "Il Duce". It is now home to the National Olympic Committee.

OUTSKIRTS
Villa di Livia
Villa di Livia 10km/6mi from Ponte Milvio taking Corso Francia. Via della Villa di Livia 126. ◷Open Apr–Oct Thu–Fri 9:30am–1:30pm; first, third and fifth

Sat of the month, from 9:30am–1:30pm; first, third and fifth Sun of the month, from 9:30am–6:30pm. ⟶ Free. Guided visit on payment ⊚€7 + €2 booking fee. ✆06 33 62 68 26. www.coopculture.it.
Once more open to visitors, the Villa of Livia Drusilla, the wife of Emperor Augustus, boasts an Antiquarium and areas reserved for otium (leisure). The villa was the original site of the statue of Augustus now in the Vatican Museums, and of the paintings with a view of the garden now in the Museo Nazionale Romano.

ADDRESSES

TAKING A BREAK
Bar Due Fontane – *Piazza Perin del Vaga 13. ✆06 324 0786. Open 7am-7pm. Closed Sun*. On a charming little piazza, this secret oasis is right next to MAXXI. The kitchen prepares delicious plates full of fruits and vegetables accompanied by smoothies really high in vitamins.

Caffetteria and Bookshop – TYPO – *Via Guido Reni 4. ✆06 44 70 28 84. www.lineaetypo.it. Open 11am-7pm (10pm Sam) Closed Mon*. The design café of the museum MAXXI. Perfect for a quick meal or an ice cream (delicious) before or after your visit to the museum.

Dolce Forno – *Piazza Antonio Mancini 9–7:30. Closed Sun. ✆06 32 20 191*. Sweets, cakes, small pizzas and an absolute must: pizza by the slice, low and extremely crunchy.

Lo Zodiaco – *Viale Parco Mellini 90. ✆06 3549 6744. Open 9am-2am, Mon. 18pm-2am*. A little detour, but absolutely worthy to enjoy the great view of this terrace and veranda facing the city. It is possibile to eat anytime or just enjoy a delicious ice cream.

Neve di latte – *Via Luigi Poletti 6. ✆06 32 27 125*. Unusual ingredients like biodynamic German milk and the eggs of hens fed on a diet of fresh goats' milk make the products of this ice cream shop very special.

Piazza del Popolo★★

In the days of the Grand Tour, travellers approaching from the north would arrive through the Porta del Popolo. The surrounding "piazza" is one of the city's largest and most grandiose squares. A famous trio of streets run south from here; the quiet Via di Ripetta, popular for its boutiques; the bustling Via del Corso, the main commercial artery; and the elegant Via del Babuino, with antique and designer shops.

PIAZZA DEL POPOLO★★

The square was laid out by **Giuseppe Valadier** (1762–1839), the favourite architect and town planner of Pius VI and Pius VII. In an effort to open up Rome, he made Piazza del Popolo one of the largest squares in the city. He retained the Porta del Popolo, the central obelisk and the twin churches flanking Via del Corso, and opened out the space into two semi-circles adorned with fountains and Neoclassical statues. The east side of the square was linked to the Pincio Gardens by a series of monumental terraces with trees and shrubs. On 18 December 1813, the Government erected a guillotine to deter the local gangs.

Porta del Popolo★

This gateway in the 3C **Aurelian Wall** stands more or less on the site of the ancient *Porta Flaminia*.

The exterior façade was built between 1562 and 1565 by Pius IV, who wanted to impress visitors arriving from the north with an entrance worthy of his splendid capital. The Medici arms are the dominant feature. On 24 May 1814, Pius VII – liberated by Napoleon – was given a delirious welcome here.

Obelisk

The pillar was brought from Heliopolis in Lower Egypt in the Augustan era and set up in the *Circus Maximus*. It was

- **Michelin Map:** 38 H 11–12, J 11–12.
- **Location:** The area extends between the Tiber and the Pincian Hill, backed by the magnificent Villa Borghese gardens. Three main streets run south towards Augustus's Mausoleum and Piazza di Spagna from Piazza del Popolo, which is dominated by its twin churches and by the Porta del Popolo, a gate in the Aurelian walls.
- **Don't Miss:** Caravaggio's masterpiece in Santa Maria del Popolo, a stroll through the Tridente, the view from the Pincian Hill.
- **Kids:** The water clock on the Pincio, The Children's Museum of Rome (Explora).
- **Also See:** *PIAZZA DI SPAGNA; VILLA BORGHESE– VILLA GIULIA; MONTE MARIO–FLAMINIO.*

GETTING THERE

BY METRO: Line A: Flaminio or Spagna.

Sixtus V and his architect, **Domenico Fontana**, who raised it in the centre of Piazza del Popolo in 1589. The basins and marble lions at the base were added by Valadier at Leo XII's request in 1823.

Chiese gemelle

From the obelisk, you can appreciate the impact of good town planning on the south side of the square. **Carlo Rainaldi** designed the Twin Churches to provide a background to the obelisk and a theatrical entrance to *Via del Corso*. Their apparent similarity is false: only the drums facing the square have the same dimensions. In fact, the church on the left is elliptical beneath a 12-sided dome and the right-hand

Obelisk in Piazza del Popolo, framed by the twin churches of Santa Maria di Montesanto (left) and Santa Maria dei Miracoli (right)

one is circular, with an octagonal dome, and occupies a broader site. The domes were covered with slates by Leo XII in 1825. **Santa Maria di Montesanto** was the first of the twins: built from 1662–67 by Carlo Rainaldi and from 1671–75 by Bernini. **Santa Maria dei Miracoli** was begun by Rainaldi and completed (1677–79) by Carlo Fontana.

SANTA MARIA DEL POPOLO★★

Open Mon–Fry 7am–noon and 4pm–7pm; Sat 7:30am–7pm; Sun and public holidays 7:30am–1:30pm and 4:30–7pm. 392 36 12 243. *www.smariadelpopolo.com.*
Despite its simple exterior, the church contains **art treasures★** worthy of a museum. The building, which was commissioned by Sixtus IV in 1472 and finished in 1477, is one of the first examples of the Renaissance style in Rome. Its façade rises, almost devoid of ornament, to a triangular pediment. The plainness is relieved by shallow pilasters and simple scrolls linking the lower and upper stages of the façade (the elaborate curves are Baroque additions).

The **interior** abounds in Renaissance features. The Latin-cross plan is used in preference to a basilical one. The nave, which has groined vaulting, is flanked by two aisles lined by side chapels. The usual columns and walls of a basilical church have been replaced with massive square pillars. During the Baroque period, Bernini added stucco statues above the nave.

Chapels

The chapel rail in the **Cappella della Rovere (1)** shows the coat of arms of the Della Rovere family to which Pope Sixtus IV belonged.
Above the altar is the **fresco★** depicting the *Adoration of the Child* by the Umbrian painter **Pinturicchio** (1454–1513). The scene is animated with incidental detail: a grazing goat, a lamb suckling its mother and a watchful ox. **The Cappella Cybo (2)** is a Baroque chapel designed by Carlo Fontana (1682–87) on a Greek-cross plan beneath a dome.
On the right-hand wall of the **Cappella Basso della Rovere (3)** lies the tomb of Giovanni Basso della Rovere (15C) by a pupil of Andrea Bregno; the frescoes

141

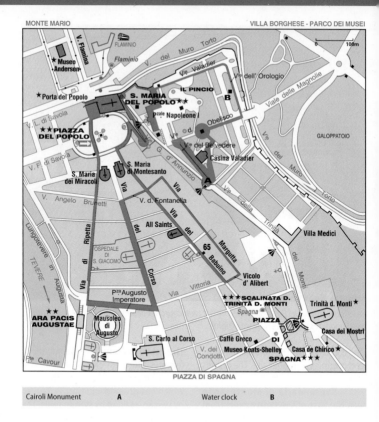

MONTE MARIO

VILLA BORGHESE - PARCO DEI MUSEI

PIAZZA DI SPAGNA

Cairoli Monument	A		Water clock	B

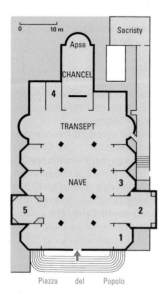

Piazza del Popolo

above the altar and on the left-hand wall are by the Pinturicchio School.

Transept

The chapels opening off the east side of the transept and the apses at either end are characteristic of the Renaissance. The Baroque style is represented by the cherubs supporting the picture frames above the transept altars.

The dome above the crossing was probably the first of its kind in Renaissance Rome: the technology had been lost since ancient times.

The chancel arch is decorated with gilded stucco low reliefs, one (right) showing Pope Paschal II (1099–1118) chopping down a walnut tree. According to legend, the church was built on the site of the tomb of the terrible Nero, which was marked by said tree. Demons lived within the trunk and took the form of black crows. The population, fearing Nero's ghost, appealed to Paschal II. He felled the tree, threw the emperor's remains in the Tiber and erected a chapel, which became *Santa Maria del Popolo* under Sixtus IV.

Apse and Chancel

Go round behind the high altar.

The apse was extended by **Bramante** for Julius II (1503–13). The ceiling fresco is by Pinturicchio. The stained glass – in predominantly neutral tones picked out with flashes of brilliant colour – is the work of Guillaume de Marcillat (16C). Look out for the two elegant **tombs★**, carved around 1505 by **Andrea Sansovino**.

Caravaggio's Paintings★★★

The **Cerasi Chapel (4)** houses two magnificent pictures painted in 1601, which illustrate scripture scenes. In the *Conversion of St Paul (right)*, as in all **Caravaggio**'s works, light is the dominant feature. Here, the divine rays fall first on the horse, which is out of proportion, before touching the foreshortened saint.

The *Crucifixion of St Peter (left)* illustrates Caravaggio's taste for creating a diagonal axis. Above the altar is *The Assumption of the Virgin* by **Annibale Carracci**.

Cappella Chigi★ (5)

The design of this chapel was entrusted to **Raphael** in 1513 by his champion, Agostino Chigi, banker, patron and consort of princes and popes. The dome mosaic, from a drawing by Raphael, dates from the Renaissance, as do the figures of Jonah (after Raphael) and the Prophet Elijah, and the altarpiece, a muted *Nativity* by Sebastiano del Piombo.

In the Baroque period, **Bernini** faced the base of the pyramid-shaped tomb of Agostino and Sigismondo Chigi with green marble, carved the figures of Daniel, the lion, Habakkuk and the angel, and inserted in the floor a winged skeleton with the Chigi coat of arms.

IL TRIDENTE

To Romans this name – The Trident – indicates the trio of streets that diverge from Piazza del Popolo like three prongs: Via di Ripetta, Via del Corso and Via del Babuino.

Via di Ripetta

This street follows the course of an ancient Roman one beside the Tiber. Originally called Via Leonina, it was remodelled in 1515 by Leo X and perhaps financed by a brothel tax. Via di Ripetta contains a multitude of shops and boutiques.

Via del Corso

Following the route of the ancient Via Flaminia, the modern street runs in a straight line (1 500m/1 640yd) from Piazza del Popolo to Piazza Venezia. Its medieval name was Via Lata, but now it is named after the famous horse races organised by Pope Paul II in the 15C. Handsome Renaissance palaces

---

At the Heart of the Festivities

In earlier years, fashionable Romans always made an appearance on the Corso. In the 18C, it was good form for a lady to be seen there with her *sigisbeo*, a faithful admirer. Even the Church tolerated this custom, and clauses permitting a wife to have one or more admirers were included in marriage contracts. During **Carnevale** (February), masquerades proceeded along the Corso. The horse race was the high point of the celebrations. Each evening in the week before Ash Wednesday, grooms led the horses round the course. On the last, the *moccoli* (wax tapers) appeared; everyone carried a lighted candle and tried to put out their neighbours' flames. Only in 1809 did the Romans boycott the Carnival to protest the French Government.

line this busy thoroughfare. Nowadays "the Corso" is a shopping street.

This area is where people from overseas traditionally gathered. Indeed, before the railways extended to Rome, most travellers arrived southwards down the Via Cassia, crossing the Tiber over the Ponte Molle (now called the Ponte Milvio) to enter through the Porta del Popolo.

Via del Babuino

The street was opened by Clement VII for Jubilee Year in 1525. Its present name came from popular usage; the statue of Silenus was discovered in such a hideous state that the Romans compared it to a baboon. The statue is now next to the fountain by St Athanasius' Church *(San Atanasio, opposite no 65)*. Today the street is known for antique shops, often located in the 17C and 18C *palazzi*.

Chiesa Anglicana (All Saints Anglican Church) – Now a protected building, it was designed by **GE Street** in the early 1880s, shortly before his death. He built in the English Gothic style of specially made bricks, with a distinctive white travertine spire erected in 1937. The spacious interior is enriched by a variety of coloured marble from different parts of Italy: white and green Carrara, red Perugia, black Verona, yellow Siena and white Como. The pulpit designed in 1891 by AE Street, the architect's son, is reminiscent of the early Christian basilicas. Above the high altar hang seven lamps bought in Venice by a former Honourable Assistant Chaplain from money given him by the congregation "to be spent on himself".

The stained glass, depicting various saints and commemorating people connected with the church, is English. So too is the organ, a large and complex instrument, originally made in Huddersfield and in demand by famous musicians for recitals and masterclasses.

Via Margutta

This street in the artistic heart of Rome is named after a famous little 15C theatre. Here parodies of chivalrous epic poems – such as Luigi Pulci's comedy *Morgante* with its two heroes, Morgante and Margutta – were performed. Via Margutta leads into **Vicolo d'Alibert**, which in the 18C contained the Teatro delle Dame, where women first sang on stage in the Papal States. Formerly *castrati* played female roles in opera.

Fontana delle Arti in Via Margutta

©ROMAOSLO/iStockphoto.com

IL PINCIO (PINCIAN HILL)

Take the flight of steps behind the Fontana della Dea di Roma leading to the Pincio.

The Pinci family, which had a garden here in the 4C, has left its name to this little hill, still covered by one of the most pleasant gardens in Rome. The Pincio was laid out in its present style during the Napoleonic occupation (1809–14), according to designs by **Giuseppe Valadier**. Magnificent umbrella pines, palm trees and evergreen oaks shade the avenues. Giuseppe Mazzini (1805–72) added the statues of patriots.

From the terrace of Piazzale Napoleone I, there is a magnificent **view★★★**, particularly at dusk. Below the terrace is Piazza del Popolo with the domes of the twin churches marking the beginning of the Corso. Opposite are the buildings of the Vatican grouped round the dome of St Peter's next to the slopes of the Janiculum; in front stand Castel Sant'Angelo and the white bulk of the Law Courts.

The **water clock** ♟♗ in Viale dell'Orologio was built in 1867 by a Dominican monk, Giovan Battista Embriago, and presented to the Universal Exhibition in Paris (1889). Halfway along Viale dell'Obelisco, which leads to the gardens of the Villa Borghese, stands an obelisk. Pius VII set it here in 1822. Found near the Porta Maggiore in the 16C, it was originally erected by Emperor Hadrian in memory of his young friend Antinoüs.

The **Cairoli Monument** commemorates Enrico and Giovanni, Italian patriots who fought beside Garibaldi and died in 1867. From here an extensive view of the city stretches out.

MUSEUMS AND MONUMENTS
Explora – Il Museo dei Bambini di Roma★
Via Flaminia 80/82. ♟♗ ⏰*Open Tue–Sun timed-ticketing system (1h45). Shifts at 10am–noon and 3pm–5pm. Booking necessary Sat and public holidays.* ✆€8. ✆06 36 13 776. *www.mdbr.it.*

The first Italian museum devoted to children is a child-size playtown where everything can be touched and experimented with, to help them learn about the environment, communication, the economy and everyday life.

Monumento a Matteotti
Lungotevere Arnaldo da Brescia.
This bronze gilt monument was erected in 1974. Its symbol – a shoot bursting from the earth – commemorates Socialist MP Giacomo Matteotti, assassinated in 1924 for denouncing the Fascists.

Museo di Hendrik Christian Andersen★
Via P. Stanislao Mancini 20. ♿ ⏰*Open Tue–Sun 9am–7:30pm.* ✆06 32 19 089.

Villa Helene was built by the Norwegian sculptor and painter Hendrik Christian Andersen at the beginning of the 20C as his residence and art studio. Now a museum, it houses 700 works, including sculptures, paintings and graphic art.

Palazzo della Marina
Lungotevere delle Navi 17.
A work of eclectic architecture, the building was designed by Giulio Magni, the nephew of Giuseppe Valadier, and inaugurated in 1928. It is the home of the Stato Maggiore della Marina.

ADDRESSES

TAKING A BREAK
Rosati and Canova– *Both on Piazza del Popolo.* These traditional bars with outside tables are a great place for a drink and people-watching (*www.barrosati.com*).

Canova Tadolini Museo Atelier Bar – *Via del Babuino 150A.* ✆06 32 11 07 02. *www.canovatadolini.com. Bar 8am–noon, rest. noon-11pm.* Enjoy at least a stop in the bar at this lovely atelier filled with sculptures by Antonio Canova amid its tables.

Zuma – *Via della Fontanella di Borghese 48.* ✆06 99 26 66 22.*www.zumarestaurant.com. Open 12am-3pm, 7pm-11:30pm.* After New York, London and Dubai, Zuma came all the way to Rome. Situated on the fourth floor of Palazzo Fendi, this Japanese restaurant reaches a really high level; from the lounge bar at the fifth floor you can enjoy a beautiful view of the roofs of the city.

Gelateria Venchi – *Via della Croce 25/26.* ✆06 6979 7790. *www.venchi.com. Open 10:30am-10pm.* Chocolate and ice cream lovers found the right spot. This infamous chocolatier makes unrivalled ice creams in many variations of chocolate.

SHOPPING
Piazza del Popolo lies in the heart of one of Rome's busiest shopping districts. **Via del Corso** has boutiques on its side streets, while upscale shops, antiques and art galleries line **Via del Babuino** and **Via Margutta**.

Piazza di Spagna★★★

This district was once popular with artists and writers such as Goethe, Keats, De Chirico and Stendhal, and later became a favourite meeting place for actors and film stars. Now it's one of the main tourist sights; crowds mill around Piazza di Spagna day and night, stopping to sit and chat on the famous Spanish Steps, or wandering the narrow streets leading off the square. Despite the invasion of fast-food outlets in the area, these elegant alleys are still home to some of the most prestigious names in the worlds of fashion, jewellery and design.

PIAZZA DI SPAGNA★★★

This square is famous throughout the world and its iconic steps are a popular rendezvous point, as well as a scenic backdrop for fashion shoots and publicity events.

Shaped like a bow tie, the *piazza* got its name in the 17C when the Spanish ambassador to the Holy See took up residence in the **Palazzo di Spagna**. After that, the area bounded by Via dei Condotti, Via del Corso and Via della Mercede became Spanish territory and any non-national crossing the boundaries at night might be press-ganged into the Spanish army. The French, however

- 🕭 **Michelin Map:** 38 J 11–12, K 11–12.
- ▷ **Location:** The walk illustrated in this section covers the district south of the Piazza del Popolo, between Villa Borghese and the Tiber. The area falls within the "*Tridente*", the streets leading south from Piazza del Popolo: Via del Babuino, which emerges into Piazza di Spagna; Via del Corso, which cuts the district in two; and Via di Ripetta, near the River Tiber.
- 😊 **Don't Miss:** The stairs of Trinità dei Monti at night, a treat at Caffè Greco, Richard Meier's the Ara Pacis, window-shopping in Via dei Condotti.
- 🕭 **Also See:** *FONTANA DI TREVI–QUIRINALE; MONTECITORIO; PIAZZA DEL POPOLO; VILLA BORGHESE– VILLA GIULIA.*

GETTING THERE

BY METRO: Line A: Bus 117.

Scalinata della Trinità dei Monti

© phant/Fotolia.com

– who owned the land around the convent of the *Trinità dei Monti* – claimed the right to pass through.

They named part of it "French Square" and set out to rival the Spanish by giving sumptuous entertainments. In 1681, the Spanish celebrated the birthday of their queen, Marie-Louise, by transforming the square with a variety of paste-board decorations.

In 1685, the French celebrated the Revocation of the Edict of Nantes; they covered the whole hillside with candelabra and decorated the church to look like a wayside altar; from here they set off fireworks that lit up the whole town. In the 18C, the area became popular among the English on the Grand Tour. In 1820 Henry Matthews set down his first impressions in his diary:

"We were soon in the Piazza di Spagna, the focus of fashion and the general resort of the English... little more than an irregular open space, a little less nasty than the other piazzas in Rome because the habits of the people are in some measure restrained by the presence of the English..."

In 1803 the French made Villa Medici their art academy in Rome.

The Keats–Shelley Memorial House (no. 26) and the Casa–Museo di Giorgio de Chirico are here.

Fontana della Barcaccia★

At the foot of the steps.

It was designed by Bernini's father, Pietro (1627–29) for Pope Urban VIII. The boat (*barcaccia*), decorated at either end with the suns and bees of the Barberini coat of arms, seems to be letting in water. Allegedly, the sculptor was inspired by a boat stranded in Piazza di Spagna by flood waters.

Scalinata della Trinità dei Monti★★★

Built between 1723 and 1726, the steps show the Baroque taste for perspective and *trompe-l'œil*. At certain times of the year, they are smothered in flowers – azaleas in April – as well as idlers.

The idea of a stairway linking Piazza di Spagna with the church of the Trinità dei Monti began in the 17C. Cardinal Mazarin proposed to make the steps a symbol of the greatness of the French monarchy in Rome. A grandiose design was prepared, dominated by an equestrian statue of Louis XIV. The idea of a king's statue in the papal city! Alexander VII objected. Neither the cardinal's death in 1661 nor the Pope's in 1669 ended the quarrel. It was not finally settled until Innocent XIII (1721–24) agreed to the French architect and the French abandoned the statue of Louis XIV. De Sanctis, in accordance with designs by De Specchi (a pupil of Carlo Fontana), built three successive flights of steps, some broader, some narrower, some divided, exaggerating the effect of height and creating a graceful and majestic effect. From the upper terrace there is an excellent view of the city. In front of the church of the Trinità dei Monti stands an imitation Egyptian obelisk transported from the Gardens of Sallust (*Giardini di Sallusto*).

Trinità dei Monti★

Open Tue–Sun 6:30am–8pm (Thu–midnight). 06 67 94 179.

The church of Holy Trinity on the Hill was founded in 1495 by Charles VIII. Damaged by French revolutionaries, it was completely rebuilt in 1816. Now French property, the convent is occupied by the Monastic Fraternity of Jerusalem, which runs a school.

An elegant stairway, built in 1587 by Domenico Fontana, leads up to the **façade,** surmounted by two belfries, erected in 1588 and modelled on those designed by Giacomo della Porta for St Athanasius in Via del Babuino.

The single nave flanked by intercommunicating chapels is reminiscent of the Gothic churches in the south of France. The side chapels are decorated with Mannerist paintings. The third on the right contains a fresco of the *Assumption* by Daniele da Volterra. The figure in red on the right of the picture is a portrait of Michelangelo, which was much admired

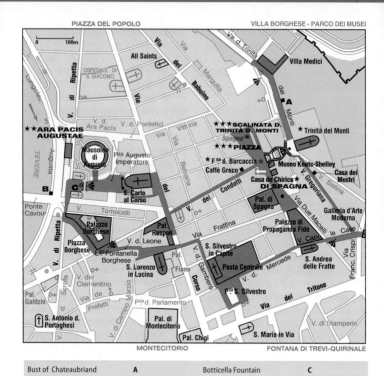

PIAZZA DEL POPOLO   VILLA BORGHESE - PARCO DEI MUSEI

MONTECITORIO   FONTANA DI TREVI-QUIRINALE

Bust of Chateaubriand	A	Botticella Fountain	C
kiosk	B		

by the artist. The much-restored **Deposition from the Cross★** (1541) in the second chapel on the left is a masterpiece by **Daniele da Volterra**. See how skilfully he has arranged his composition around the pale body of Jesus.

🐾 WALKING TOUR

▶ From the Spanish Steps, turn left into Viale della Trinità dei Monti.

On the right is a **bust of Chateaubriand**; better known as a writer, he was the French ambassador from 1828 to 1829.

Villa Medici
Viale della Trinità dei Monti 1. The Villa Medici now houses the French Academy (Accademia di Francia) which hosts temporary exhibits, lectures and concerts.
⊙Guided tours of apartments and gardens (1h30) given in English Tue–Sun
11am, 15:30pm and 17:30 with purchase of a ticket at least 30min in advance.
⊙Closed 1 Jan, 1 May and 25 Dec. ⊛€12. ℘06 67 61 311. www.villamedici.it.

The villa was built c. 1570 for Cardinal Ricci di Montepulciano and passed to Cardinal Ferdinando de' Medici in 1576. In the 1C BC, the site was covered by the Gardens of Lucullus (Giardini di Luculio). There is a fine view from the terrace opposite the entrance.

The famous fountain, installed in 1587 by Cardinal Ferdinando de' Medici, is the subject of several 19C paintings and engravings, including *The Fountain at the Villa Medici* by Corot. Legend has it that the basin's cannon ball was fired at the Villa from Castel Sant'Angelo by Queen Christina of Sweden, who adored practical jokes. She wanted to wake up the master of the house to join a hunting party.

The main façade contrasts sharply with the richly decorated **inner façade★**; the latter faces the luxuriant gardens and was decorated by Bartolomeo Ammannati in the late 16C with statues, reliefs and garlands from the Ara Pacis.

▶ Return to Trinità dei Monti and continue along Via Gregoriana.

In the 17C and 18C, **Via Gregoriana** provided lodgings for the wealthier visitors to Rome. ✆ Al No 30, the **Casa dei Mostri**, built by Federico Zuccari, has a door and windows framed by carved monsters with gaping mouths.

▶ Continue on Via Gregoriana; left at the end on Via F. Crispi.

Galleria d'Arte Moderna

Via Francesco Crispi 24. ✆*Open Tue– Sun 10am–6:30pm (24 and 31 Dec 10am–2pm) .*✆*Closed 1 Jan, 1 May and 2 Dec.* ✆*€7.50.* ✆*06 06 08. www.galleriaartemodernaroma.it.*
The gallery contains a collection of paintings and sculptures executed between 1880 and 1945. Outstanding sculptures are Rodin's bust of a woman, and, among the paintings, **Balla**'s beautiful portrait of his wife titled *The Doubt*, and Amadeo Bocchi's large *In the Park*, with its vivid, almost violent colors. The collection includes works by artists Sartorio… Trombadori, Casorati, Morandi, Guttuso.

▶ Take Via Capo le Case and cross Via Due Macelli.

Palazzo di Propaganda Fide

⚠ *Temporarily closed for restoration at the moment writing. www. museopropagandafide.va/.*
This imposing building, the property of the Holy See, houses the Congregation for the Evangelisation of Peoples. **Urban VIII** (1623–44) began construction by inviting his protégé, **Bernini**, to design the façade overlooking Piazza di Spagna. The result is unexpectedly sober for this brilliant Baroque architect. On Innocent X's accession, Bernini fell into disgrace. The new pope wished to give his reign a new look and he turned to **Borromini** for the façade overlooking Via di Propaganda. A touch of fantasy was introduced, in the cornices and in the elaborate pediments over the windows.Within the *palazzo (left of the door in Via di Propaganda 1/c)* is another building (1666) by Borromini, the tiny **Church of the Re Magi** (Three Wise Men). Inside, the **Museo Missionario** (✆*Open Mon–Sat 9am–6pm; last admission 4pm. Last Sun/month 9am–2pm.* ✆*€16.* ✆*06 69 88 46 76)* boasts works by Ezzelino Romano and some of the extraordinary gifts the Pope has received over the years.

Sant'Andrea delle Fratte

✆*Open Tue–Sun 6:15am–1pm and 4pm–7pm.* ✆*06 69 88 46 76. www.madonnadelmiracolo.it.*
St Andrew's Church, which originated in the 12C, stands in Via di Capo Le Case (end of the houses), which in the Middle Ages was the northeastern limit of the city. Its name recalls the thickets *(fratte)* that once abounded here.
Early in the 17C, the rebuilding of the church was begun; the work was completed by **Borromini.** Higher up the street is a view of the **campanile★** and the **dome★**.
Inside, at the entrance to the chancel, are two statues of **angels★** presenting the Instruments of the Passion. When **Bernini** sculpted them in 1669, his art was very close to the extreme delicacy characteristic of the Rococo period.

▶ Take Via della Mercede.

At numbers 11 and 12a you'll find one of 4 Roman residences of **Gian Lorenzo Bernini**, and the home where the sculptor died. Number 11 was also home to Scottish novelist **Walter Scott** (1771– 1832).

Piazza San Silvestro is dominated by the façade of the Central Post Office, which was established in the 19C in the monastery of the church of *San Silvestro in Capite*. Its church and post office, café and newspaper stall make this a good people-watching spot.

Ara Pacis Augustae

© Iamio/Fotolia.com

▶ Turn right into Via del Gambero and left into Via Frattina to reach Piazza S. Lorenzo in Lucina.

San Lorenzo in Lucina

Via In Lucina, 16/A. ◷*Open 8am–8pm.*
The **Church of St Lawrence** was built in the 12C on the site of a 4C *titulus*, the house of a woman called Lucina. The bell-tower, porch and two lions flanking the door date from the medieval period. The fourth chapel on the right contains a bust of Dr Gabriele Fonseca by **Bernini**, a late and rather theatrical work (1668).

▶ Take Via del Leone, which leads into Largo Fontanella Borghese.

Ara Pacis Museum

Pieced together and rebuilt from fragments in the early 20C, this monumental altar – the Altar of Peace – is now singularly housed in its own museum, the first major work of modern architecture in the historic centre of Rome since the 1930s. Designed by American architect Richard Meier (2006), it initially caused mixed reaction among Romans, including comparison to a petrol station to high praise. The furor has subsided.

From the piazza, there is an interesting view of the church of Trinità dei Monti.

Palazzo Fontanella Borghese

The late 16C Borghese Fontanella Palace overlooks the Piazza Borghese and demonstrates the dignity and austerity of the Counter-Reformation. The palace was acquired by Cardinal Camillo Borghese, who became Pope Paul V in 1605. The courtyard *(entrance in Largo della Fontanella di Borghese)* – with its loggias, statues, fountains and rockeries – is a beautiful evocation of the luxurious life of Rome's noble families.

▶ Take Via di Ripetta north as far as Piazza Augusto Imperatore.

Botticella Fountain

It was built in 1774 at the expense of the Ripetta watermen's association. There is a fine **view** of the apse and dome of San Carlo al Corso.

Mausoleo di Augusto

⊶ *Temporarily closed for restoration at the moment writing; the site can only be visited externally.*
The ruins of the **Mausoleum of Augustus** are now surrounded by the modern buildings of Piazza Augusto Imperatore, which was laid out in 1940. This mausoleum was one of the most sacred monuments in antiquity. Built between 28–23 BC, it has a cylindrical

base surmounted by a conical hillock of earth *(tumulus)* planted with cypress trees. A bronze statue of the emperor stood in the middle of the monument, at its highest point. On the south side, flanking the entrance, stood two obelisks, Roman imitations of Egyptian models, which now stand in Piazza dell' Esquilino and Piazza del Quirinale.

In the Middle Ages, the mausoleum was converted into a fortress by the Colonna family; Gregory IX (1227–41) dismantled it and stripped it of its blocks of travertine. In 1936, its concert hall was closed and the remains were restored.

▷ The Ara Pacis is housed in a modern building between the Mausoleum of Augustus and Lungotevere in Augusta. Follow Via dell'Ara Pacis and Via dei Pontefici; right on Via del Corso.

Santi Ambrogio e Carlo al Corso

Via del Corso 437. ⏰*Open 7am–7pm.*
In 1471, the Lombard community in Rome was given a small church in the Corso by Sixtus IV. They rebuilt it and dedicated it to **St Ambrose**. In 1612, they enlarged the building in honour of Charles Borromeo, Archbishop of Milan, who had just been canonised. The full name of the church is therefore Sant'Ambrogio e San Carlo al Corso. The majestic interior is in the shape of a Latin cross with an ambulatory, a rarity in Rome and more usually found in northern churches.

The heart of St Charles Borromeo now rests in the chapel behind the high altar. The **dome★** is the work of **Pietro da Cortona** (1668). The *Apotheosis of St Ambrose and St Charles* on the high altar is one of the finest works by Carlo Maratta (1685–90), and was restored in the 19C.

Palazzo Ruspoli

Via della Fontanella di Borghese 56. The first floor is only open to the public during temporary exhibits.
This 16C palace is now a mixed-use space (residence-office-exhibits). After

the downfall of Napoleon in 1825, it became the refuge of Hortense de Beauharnais, ex-Queen of Holland, under the name of the Duchess of St Leu. Her salon was the centre of attraction for pleasure-loving members of society. Her son, Prince Charles Louis Napoleon, the future Napoleon III, brought this sumptuous life to an end. He was implicated in a scheme to declare a republic in Rome and was subsequently expelled, along with his mother.

▷ Go back to Via dei Condotti.

Via dei Condotti

The street is named after the conduits *(condotti)* that brought water to Agrippa's Baths *(Terme di Agrippa)* in 19 BC. One of the most famous streets in Rome, it is lined with smart boutiques and elegant *palazzi* housing prestigious names in fashion. **Caffè Greco**, the famous literary hangout, can be seen at no 86 (⌖*see Addresses*).

SIGHTS
Ara Pacis Augustae★★

Lungotevere in Augusta (corner Via Tomacelli). ⏰*Open Mon–Sun 9:30am–7:30pm.* ⏰*Closed 1 Jan, 1 May and 25 Dec.* ✐€13 *(during exhibitions, the ticket may be subject to variations).* ℘*06 06 08. www.arapacis.it.*
The monumental altar was inaugurated in 9 BC in honour of the peace that Augustus established throughout the Roman world and in the capital, where he ended 20 years of civil war. The Ara Pacis originally stood in the Campus Martius, beside the Via Flaminia (now Via del Corso), where the Palazzo Fiano stands today. The altar was the major work of the Augustan "golden age" and marks the apogee of Roman art.

Casa-Museo di Giorgio de Chirico★

Piazza di Spagna 31. ⏰*Tue–Sat and first Sun/month 10am–1pm. Visits by appointment.* ✐€7. ℘*06 67 96 546. www.fondazionedechirico.it.*
The house in which this artist lived from 1947 to 1978 (the year he died) occupies

the top three floors of a 16C *palazzo*. The visit starts in an entrance hall, which houses two oval works, inspired by the great masters, and the *Thinker*. Self-portraits are exhibited in the drawing room along with portraits of the artist's wife. De Chirico's armchair can be seen in his favourite corner, where he used to watch the television with the sound turned down. The second drawing room, added around 1970, is very different from the rest of the house, both in its furnishings and in the works on display here. These are known as the "neo-metaphysical works", produced towards the end of the artist's life, and include Piazza d'Italia and **Hector and Andromache★**.

De Chirico's tiny bedroom and his wife's room can be visited on the top floor. The artist's studio, lit by a skylight, houses the paintings he was working on at the time of his death.

Keats Shelley House

Piazza di Spagna 26. ◑*Open Mon–Sat 10am–1pm, 2pm–6pm.* ◑*Closed 8, 23–31 Dec and 1 Jan* ⊛*€5.* ℘*06 67 84 235. www.keats-shelley-house.org.*

The "Young English Poet" passed away here of tuberculosis on 23 February 1821. The painter Joseph Severn nursed him to the end. Keats, the author of the romantic *Odes* and *Endymion*, requested his tomb bear no name, only the bitter epitaph: "here lies one whose name was writ on water". He died believing he'd failed his talent's early promise.

Shelley wrote *Adonais* about this tragic fate. On 8 July 1822, Shelley drowned off Livorno. His goldbricking friend Edward Trelawney snatched the author's heart from the beachside pyre. It's also buried in the Protestant Cemetery, not far from Keats (*See PIRAMIDE CESTIA–TESTACCIO*).

The poet's rooms on the first floor contain manuscripts and letters on the lives not only of Keats but also of Shelley, Byron and Leigh Hunt, together with a library of 10 000 volumes.

ADDRESSES

TAKING A BREAK

Caffè Greco – *Via dei Condotti 86.* ℘*06 67 91 700. www.anticocaffegreco.eu.* One of the oldest literary cafés in Rome, it has a rich history. Famous patrons include Goethe, Wagner, Baudelaire and Shelley. Splurge and sit in the back for the old ambience.

Ciampini – *Piazza San Lorenzo in Lucina 29.* ℘*06 68 76 606. www.ciampini.com.* Situated in a beautiful piazza since 1990, this place, open year-round, has some of Rome's best gelato. Next door, Vanni has excellent pastries.

Babingtons Tea Rooms – *Piazza di Spagna 23-25.* ℘*06 67 80 846. www. babingtons.com. Open 10 am–9:15pm.* This marvellous tea room, founded in the late 1800s by the Cargill sisters, is currently managed by the 4th generation of the same family and is considered a must-see locale for anyone who wants to enjoy a cup of tea in an elegant, refined atmosphere. The shop at the entrance sells unique tea blends and an excellent selection of teas from all over the world.

Museo Atelier Canova Tadolini – *Via del Babuino 150/A.* ℘*06 32 11 07 02.* This café-restaurant is a paean to lovers of the unusual. Housed in the former workshop of famous sculptor Antonio Canova, today a museum, you can enjoy chocolate, gnocchi and more while admiring the artist's handiwork. Budget €4 for an espresso, and double that for tea.

SHOPPING

Whether you're window shopping or exploring with an intent to buy, the area around the Piazza di Spagna is dense with Italian designer shops, including familiar upscale retailers **Versace** (*Via Bocca di Leone 26–27*), **Dolce e Gabbana** (*Via dei Condotti 49/51*), while off the Via del Corso is **Fendi** (*Largo Carlo Goldoni 419–421*), and in Piazza San Lorenzo Lucina you'll find the **Bottega Veneta** (*Via del Tritone 62*), joined by **Louis Vuitton's** new flagship store.

Piazza Navona★★★

Domitian's ancient stadium now
bears the fantasy of Bernini's genius:
the fountains of the Piazza Navona.
Smack in the Centro Storico – Rome's
heart – this square teems with
tourists, vendors, mime artists,
musicians and portrait painters, and
seasonal festivals. Medieval streets
emanate from this hub, lined with
pizzerias, gelaterias, restaurants and
shops: a secular reminder of when
the district serviced pilgrims enroute
to St Peters.

A BIT OF HISTORY

Except for the outline of Domitian's Stadium, which is preserved in the shape
of the Piazza Navona (↺See below), few
traces of ancient Rome have survived
here. The square is now adorned with
fine Renaissance and Baroque buildings
designed by the most famous architects
of the 16C and 17C.

The popes attempted to smarten up
the narrow medieval streets around the
piazza. Cardinals, ambassadors, papal
officials, wealthy bankers and distinguished courtesans took up residence
here. Around them intellectual life flourished: booksellers, engravers and min-
iaturists settled in the vicinity of Piazza
Navona and Piazza Pasquino. To this day,
numerous craftsmen still work here.

PIAZZA NAVONA★★★

This square perhaps characterises the
true spirit of the Eternal City most
effectively. Set apart from the thrum
of traffic, Piazza Navona seems permanently on holiday: the balloon
seller has his pitch beside a caricatur-
ist who sketches his customer with a
few deft strokes of charcoal; an old
woman lovingly feeds the pigeons
next to a trade unionist exhorting his
comrades; tourists and locals come to
savour a *tartufo* gelato at Tre Scalini.
The long and narrow shape of the square
is due to **Domitian**: in AD 86, he had
a **stadium** built on this site *(Stadio di*

- **Michelin Map:** 38 K 10,
  L 10–11.
- **Location:** On a loop in
  the Tiber, this area is bordered
  by Corso Vittorio Emanuele II,
  Corso Rinascimento and Via
  Zanardelli and was once part
  of the Campus Martius. The
  piazza is a few minutes' walk
  from both the Campo de' Fiori
  and the Pantheon.
- **Timing:** Allow at least 2 hrs.
- **Don't Miss:** The piazza of
  Santa Maria della Pace and its
  famous café, Pasquino "the
  talking statue", Sant'Ivo alla
  Sapienza, and Caravaggio's
  masterwork in San Luigi dei
  Francesi.
- **Also See:** *CAMPO DE' FIORI;
  CASTEL SANT'ANGELO;
  MONTECITORIO; PANTHEON.*

GETTING THERE
BY BUS: Bus C3, 30, 70, 81, 87, 130, 492
and 628.

Domiziano) and immediately instituted a
series of games in the Greek style.

Unlike the games in the amphitheatre, where the gladiators confronted
one another with violence, these were
contests of wit and physical fitness. The
speaking, poetry and musical competitions were held in the Odeon, situated
roughly where Palazzo Massimo and
Piazza S. Pantaleo now stand, with running, wrestling, discus and javelin in the
stadium.

Stripped of its marble by Constantinus
II, the stadium was in ruins by the 5C. It
was revived in the Renaissance into one
of the most beautiful sights in Rome.

In 1477, the Capitoline market was
moved here and other attractions added,
such as the *cuccagna*, a greased climbing pole, and puppet shows. In the mid-
17C, the square was partially flooded to
accommodate summer weekend water
games. Since 1869, market stalls appear
only at Christmas and Epiphany.

Piazza Navona

© belenov/iStockphoto.com

Fontana dei Quattro Fiumi★★★

The **Fountain of Four Rivers**, which occupies the centre, was created by **Bernini** for Innocent X. The pope wanted to provide worthy surroundings for his residence, the Palazzo Pamphili, which stood on the piazza. The Baroque architect contrived a pile of rockwork, hollowed into grottoes and crowned by an obelisk. The rigidity and symmetry of the latter contrasts strikingly with the fluid lines of the base. The wind seems to tear at the trees, as the marble statues gesticulate. They represent four rivers, symbolising the quarters of the world: the Danube for Europe, the Nile for Africa (the veiled head indicated that the source was unknown), the Ganges for Asia and the Plata for America.

Artistic Rivalry

A number of stories illustrate the alleged rivalry between **Bernini** and **Borromini**, who designed the façade of St Agnes' Church. One Roman legend explains that the statue of the Plata, his arms raised in a defensive gesture, is trying to protect himself from the façade, which is about to collapse. In fact, the façade was built several years after the fountain.

The obelisk, a Roman work dating from Domitian's reign, was recovered by Innocent X from the Via Appia. The fountain was completed in 1651.

Fontana del Moro

The **Fountain of the Moor** was built at the end of the 16C. **Bernini** later designed the central figure of the Moor; one of his pupils was responsible for the vigorous interpretation. The statues on the tritons and the edge of the basin date from the 19C.

Fontana del Nettuno

The **Fountain of Neptune** was moved to Piazza Navona at the end of the 16C. The water god's central statue and those around it date from the 19C.

Sant'Agnese in Agone★★

🕐 *Open Tue–Sun 9am–1pm and 3:30pm–7pm.* ℘*06 68 19 21 34. www.santagneseinagone.org.*

According to tradition, a small oratory was built in the 8C on the site where St Agnes might have been martyred. In 1652, Pope Innocent X commissioned Girolamo Rainaldi and his son Carlo to rebuild the church as a family chapel attached to his palace. From 1653–57, **Borromini** took charge of the work. The church was completed at the end of the century by a group of architects. Borromini was responsible for part of the

Pasquino, the "Talking Statue"

The statue of **Pasquino**, identified as Menelaus in a 3C BC group, was found in Piazza Navona in the 15C. Placed by Cardinal Carafa in 1501 on a corner (which the Palazzo Braschi later graced), there it stayed. People called it "Pasquino", probably after a local barber, teacher or tailor with a very caustic tongue. Soon the sculpture became their mouthpiece. During the night, satirical or even libellous comments – sometimes in Roman dialect – were secretly hung here. The following day the "Pasquinades" spread through Rome, as far as the doors of the papal officials; some were carried to the ears of foreign sovereigns and started more than one diplomatic incident. Laws sentencing the perpetrators of these libels to death were rarely applied; or if they were, the prisoner was pardoned. Pasquino was the most famous and loquacious of the Roman "talking statues", which included Madama Lucrezia, Marforio and the Abate Luigi. He continues his ways today, protesting war or the state of the economy.

dome and for the façade, which demonstrates his taste for contrasting convex and concave lines.

The **interior★** is captivating: the deep recesses in the pillars supporting the dome transform the Greek-cross plan into an octagon. The altars are adorned with beautiful "marble pictures" by Bernini's pupils. The decorations in stucco, gilt and painting are far from the spirit of Borromini's sober interiors and were added at the end of the 17C.

Palazzo Pamphili

The Pamphili residence was enlarged between 1644 and 1650 by Girolamo Rainaldi when Giovanni Battista Pamphili became Pope Innocent X.

 WALKING TOUR

▷ At the north end of the Piazza, take Via Agonale.

Area Archeologica dello Stadio di Domiziano

Via di Tor Sanguigna 3. ○*Open 10am–7pm (Sat 8pm).* ⊜€8. ℘*06 68 80 53 11. www.stadiodomiziano.com.*
The **Domitian's Stadium**, built between 85-86 A.D., is the first example of brick masonry stadium ever built in ancient Rome. The remains can be seen below Via di Tor Sanguigna, adjacent to the piazza.

Santa Maria dell'Anima

Via Santa Maria dell'Anima 66. ○*Open daily 9am–12:45pm and 3pm–7pm (6pm pre-holiday and public holidays).* ℘*06 68 28 181.*
This edifice is the church of German-speaking Roman Catholics. There had been a pilgrim hostel on the site since 1386, when the present building was begun in 1500. It was restored in the 19C. The **façade** in Via dell'Anima was designed by Giuliano da Sangallo and built in 1511. Its flatness, which gives it the appearance of a screen, belongs to the Renaissance period. The pediment above the central door contains a sculpture of the Virgin between two figures, each representing a soul (*"anima"* in Italian), which is a copy of the painting that gave the church its name. The original is kept locked away *(apply to the sacristan).* To the right of the façade is a view of the bell-tower, capped by a slim cone faced with multicoloured ceramics.

Interior

Designed as a "hall church", where the nave and aisles are all of the same height, the plan is rather unusual for Rome, which has almost no Gothic architecture. The decoration dates from the 19C. Above the high altar is a *Holy Family with Saints* by Giulio Romano, one of Raphael's assistants. Inside it hosts a beautiful funereal monument, designed by Baldassarre Peruzzi, dedicated to Pope

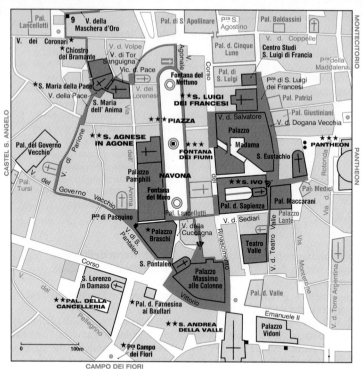

CAMPO DEI FIORI

Hadrian VI (the only Dutchman ever to be pope).

 Turn left into Vicolo della Pace and left again beneath the arch.

Santa Maria della Pace★

🕐*Open 9:30am–6:30pm.* 🕐*Closed public holidays.* ✆*06 68 61 156.*

There was already a small church on this site in the 12C. Sixtus IV had it rebuilt in 1480. In the Baroque era, Alexander VII (1655–67) invited **Pietro da Cortona** to design a new **façade**. He created a pleasing combination: a semi-circular porch flanked by two concave wings. The architect also sketched a charming square with elegant *palazzi*.

Interior

The 15C plan is very unusual; it comprises a short rectangular nave and an octagonal domed section. The first chapel's arch on the nave's right was decorated by **Raphael** in 1514. He painted the four **Sibyls★**– possibly inspired after seeing

Michelangelo's versions in the Sistine Chapel. His skill at turning an awkward surface to good account is to be admired. The first chapel on the left is decorated with frescoes by **Baldassarre Peruzzi** (1481–1536), who also worked on the Farnesina. In the octagonal section over the high altar is an image of the Virgin, which is supposed to have bled when struck by a stone in 1480. Sixtus IV had the church rebuilt to house the miraculous image.

Chiostro del Bramante★

Entrance at Via Arco della Pace 5 on left of facade of the church. 🕐*Open Mon–Fri 10am–8pm, Sat–Sun –9pm.* ⊙*15.50.* ✆*06 91 65 08 451.* *www.chiostrodelbramante.it.*

Built in 1504, these were one of **Bramante**'s earliest Roman works. The handsome proportions lend an air of great simplicity. The columns on the ground floor are complemented by those on the first, which alternate with smaller columns placed centrally over the lower arches. Once the church cloister, today it hosts major temporary exhibits and an atmospheric café.

From the window in the bar you can admire the Sybille frescoes (1514) by Raphael.

▶ Between the churches turn into Via Arco della Pace, which leads into Via della Pace. Follow this street to Via dei Coronari; tu rn left into Piazza Lancellotti to find Via della Maschera d'Oro.

Via della Maschera d'Oro

No 9, on the corner of Vicolo di San Simeone, is a small palace that shows how secular architecture developed in the 16C, as a result of Sixtus IV's essays in town planning. During this period, the streets of Rome were lined by charming façades engraved and painted with monochrome frescoes. **Polidoro da Caravaggio** and **Maturino da Firenze** were the masters of this technique. The wall was first given a rough rendering blackened with smoke and then covered with a coat of plaster. The artist then engraved mythological scenes or motifs taken from antique art to reveal the dark undercoat. These decorations were extremely fragile and almost all have now disappeared.

▶ Return to Via della Pace and continue south along Via di Parione; turn left into Via del Governo Vecchio to reach Piazza di Pasquino.

Palazzo Braschi★

Pope Pius VI built this in the late 18C for his nephews; the last papal family palace erected in Rome. The Neoclassical style produced the ponderous façades that dominate the surrounding streets. It now houses the Museum of Rome.

Museo di Roma★

Palazzo Braschi, Piazza San Pantaleo 10 or Piazza Navona 2. ♿🕐*Open Tue–Sun 10am–7pm (24 and 31 Dec–2pm).* 🕐*Closed 1 Jan, 1 May and 25 Dec.* ☞€11. 📞06 06 08. *http://en.museodiroma.it.*

The paintings and frescoes exhibited trace the history of the city from the Middle Ages to the present day. The colossal staircase leading to the first floor is by Cosimo Morelli, who designed the palace. A number of anonymous paintings depict the jousts held in the 16C and 17C in the Belvedere courtyard in the Vatican, Piazza Navona and on the Testaccio. These are followed by **frescoes★** taken from demolished buildings. Anonymous paintings illustrate the bustle of the old Capitoline market in the 17C and the pageantry of the Corpus Christi processions in St Peter's Square. One room displays 18C Gobelins tapestries.

In the first room on the second floor, three canvases portray the Greek myths of Helen and Paris by **Gavin Hamilton**, a Scottish painter who settled in Rome in 1755 and spent most of his working life in Italy.

Some of the famous **watercolours★** in the series "Lost Rome" *(Roma sparita)* and fragments of mosaic from the old St Peter's Basilica (late 12C–early 13C) are also on exhibit.

On the ground floor *(entrance in northeast corner of the courtyard)* is the papal train built for Pius IX in 1858. One of the coaches is fitted out as a small chapel. Facing Piazza Navona on the ground floor is Caffè Braschi. *(see Addresses).*

Palazzo Massimo alle Colonne

Corso Vittorio Emanuele II 141. 🕐*Open only 16 Mar 7am–1pm for viewing first courtyard and chapel.*

The palace – which belongs to the Massimo, one of the oldest families in Rome – comprises three separate buildings. The one on the right of the **Church of San Pantaleo** (designed by Valadier in 1806) is known as the Pyrrhus Palace, because of a statue that was kept there. The Palazzo Massimo is screened by a fine curved portico of Doric columns, designed (1532–36) by **Baldassarre Peruzzi**. The original windows of the upper storeys of the façade herald the Mannerist style. The oldest part of the *palazzo* is on the north side *(access from Corso Vittorio Emanuele II via a narrow lane into Piazza de' Massimi)* and is known as the "illustrated palace" because of the grisailles painted on the façade c. 1523 by some of Daniele da Volterra's pupils. The column standing in Piazza de' Massimi may have been part of the **Odeon** of Domitian. From the north end of the piazza there is a view of the Fountain of Four Rivers in Piazza Navona.

▶ Turn right and then left into Corso del Rinascimento.

Palazzo della Sapienza

Until 1935, this *palazzo* was occupied by Rome University. Now it houses the national archives, including those of the **Papal States** from the 9C to the 19C. The simple façade, begun in 1575 to a design by Giacomo della Porta, and coloured burnt umber, gives little hint of the gentle elegance of the inner courtyard.

Sant'Ivo alla Sapienza★★

Corso del Rinascimento 40. ○*Open Sun 9am–noon (except Jul and Aug).* *Donations welcome.* ℘*06 68 64 987.*
Equally unexpected is the audacity of Borromini's façade for St Ivo's Church, which closes the fourth side of the courtyard. Just as **Bernini** aimed at extensiveness, so Borromini tried to confine his ideas within a restricted space. His exaggerated curved lines were termed perverse and contrary at the time. An amazing variety appear here: in the multi-faceted drums, in the convex lines of the dome and the concave buttresses; in the spiral surmounting the lantern. The interior, very high and light, is a constant interplay of concave and convex surfaces, a foretaste of the Rococo style; it incorporates the bee from the Barberini coat of arms.

▶ Exit left into Corso del Rinascimento, left into Via dei Sediari, right into Via del Teatro Valle.

In this street, where basket-makers still work, stands the 1727 **Teatro Valle**.

▶ Return up the street to Piazza Sant'Eustachio.

From the piazza unfurls a splendid **view★★** of the spiral dome of St Ivo's Church. On the south side stands the **Palazzo Maccarani Stati** (1521), an austere building in the Renaissance style by Giulio Romano; it incorporates one of the most popular cafés in Rome, the Caffè Sant'Eustachio (*see Addresses, p317).*
The early 18C façade of the **Church of Sant'Eustachio** is screened by a portico. The head of a deer bearing a cross between its antlers recalls the vision that St Eustace experienced in the hunting field while he was still a Roman general – which led to his conversion.

▶ Take Via della Dogana Vecchia to Piazza S. Luigi dei Francesi.

San Luigi dei Francesi★★

○*Open 10am –12:30pm–3–7pm.* ○*Closed Thu afternoons.* *Donations welcome.* ℘*06 68 82 71.*
The first stone of this building was laid in 1518 by Cardinal Giulio de' Medici, the future Pope **Clement VII**. The church was completed in 1589, partly with subsidies from Henri II, Henri III and Catherine de' Medici. It was consecrated as the national church of the French in Rome, dedicated to St Louis.
The façade was probably designed by Giacomo della Porta between 1580 and 1584. Its elegant lines accord well with Piazza di San Luigi dei Francesi. The prominent columns hint at the flamboyance of the Baroque style.
The interior, consisting of a nave, side aisles and lateral chapels, was embellished in the Baroque period and in the 18C with marble, paintings, gilding and stucco work. The church houses tombs of famous Frenchmen, the beautiful chapel of St Cecilia and the chapel of St Matthew with its magnificent frescoes by **Caravaggio**.

Frescoes by Domenichino★

In the chapel of St Cecilia (second chapel in the north aisle).
The frescoes, which were executed in 1614, tell the story of St Cecilia. Domenichino, who had arrived in Rome in 1602,

resisted the exuberance of the Baroque and strove instead after balance and clarity of texture.

Caravaggio's Paintings★★★

In St Matthew's Chapel *(fifth on the south aisle)* are three works depicting the saint's life, painted between 1599 and 1600. The vault is by **Cavaliere d'Arpino**, in whose studio Caravaggio worked. Above the altar, the painting *St Matthew and the Angel* expresses the artist's delight in contradiction with the unusual posture of the old man, who has one knee balanced on a footstool and his face turned towards the angel, who is absorbed in the act of dictation.

On the left – *The Calling of St Matthew*: in a dark room five men, seated at a table, are distracted from their occupation by the entrance of Christ accompanied by St Peter. His pointing finger singles out Matthew, seated beside an old man counting out money. The light striking the wall and illuminating the faces is typical of Caravaggio and here symbolises the calling of the future disciple. The young man with a feather in his cap is a familiar figure.

On the right – *The Martyrdom of St Matthew*: in the middle lies the saint, wearing only a band of cloth around his hips, towered over by his persecutor, a soldier sent by the Ethiopian king. To the right, an altar boy runs away in terror. The most innovative element of the painting is the angel who emerges from a cloud to offer the saint the palm of martyrdom, thus immediately drawing the visitor into the action, which is both violent and dramatic in tone. To the left a face can be seen in the dark background: this is a self-portrait of the artist, who observes the scene with a contrite expression.

▶ Take Via Salvatore; turn left into Corso del Rinascimento.

Palazzo Madama

🕐*Open first Sat/month 10am–6pm.*
🕐*Closed Aug.* 📞*06 67 06 21 77. www.senato.it/visitareilsenato/privati.*
The palazzo was built by the Medici in the 16C. In the days of Cardinal Giovanni de' Medici, the future Leo X, banquets and literary gatherings were held here. Later Pope **Clement VII** made it the residence of his great-niece, Catherine de' Medici. When she became the queen of France, the palace passed to Alessandro de' Medici, whose wife, Madama Margherita d'Austria (1522–86), gave the palace its name. Since 1870, when Rome became the capital of Italy, the Senate of the Italian Republic has occupied the building. The Baroque façade in the Corso del Rinascimento was built c 1642.

The façade of Sant'Andrea delle Valle rises at the southern end of the street (👉*see CAMPO DE' FIORI*).

ADDRESSES

TAKING A BREAK

Tre Scalini – *Piazza Navona 28.* 📞*06 68 80 19 96. www.trescalini.com.* This café is renowned for its chocolate truffle gelato. The sit-down prices are high, but it does boast ringside views of Bernini's fountain.

Bar del Fico – *Piazza del Fico 26/27.* 📞*06 68 80 84 13. www.bardelfico.com.* This bar, one the of busiest nighspots in the district, has tables set out in the shade of the namesake fig. It has expanded to include a full restaurant serving Roman specialties.

Fratelli Paladini– *Via del Governo Vecchio 29. Closed 5pm.* This joint serves excellent freshly baked *pizza bianca* (pizza without a tomato base), topped with artichokes, cheese, different types of ham or Nutella.

Vivi Bistrot – *Piazza Navona 2. Open Tue–Sun 10am–midnight* 📞*06 68 33 779. www.vivibistrot.it.* The refreshments bar in the Museo di Roma is a sheltered corner in the lobby of Palazzo Braschi facing onto Piazza Navona, where you can enjoy something hot to eat or a drink on your way out of an exhibition.

CHRISTMAS MARKET

Piazza Navona is particularly atmospheric around Christmas time and the New Year, when the square is decorated with brightly coloured market stalls. Look for the historic carousel, figurines for Nativity scenes and those of Befana, the witch who arrives with presents on Epiphany.

Piazza Venezia★

Piazza Venezia was transformed at the end of the 19C and is dominated by the overwhelming and controversial monument to Victor Emmanuel II, which obscures the view of Capitoline Hill from Via del Corso. Not far from the *piazza*, close to one of the centres of political power in the city, stands the magnificent Baroque Chiesa del Gesù. Because of its position and its imposing 19C monuments, Piazza Venezia is a convenient reference point for those new to the city. Today Rome's principal thoroughfares all converge on the square, resulting in all-too-frequent gridlock.

◔ **Michelin Map:**
38 L11–12, M12.
◔ **Also See:** *GHETTO – LARGO ARGENTINA – FORI IMPERIALI – FONTANA DI TREVI– QUIRINALE; CAMPIDOGLIO.*

WALKING TOUR

Piazza Venezia★

Formerly this grand square was much more compact. The south side – towards the Victor Emmanuel II monument *(Monumento a Vittorio Emanuele II, below)* – was closed by the smaller Palazzetto Venezia, a building in harmony with the tower of the more

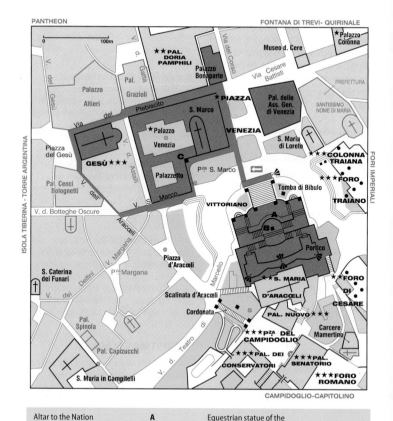

| Altar to the Nation | A | Equestrian statue of the | |
| Statue of Madama Lucrezia | C | Vittorio Emanuele II | B |

Vittoriano

famous Palazzo Venezia. In 1911, however, the *palazzetto* was "moved" to its present position at the far end of Piazza San Marco. Although this change allows a better view of the monument, it has undoubtedly spoiled the subtle balance of a Renaissance square. Behind the Palazzo Venezia stands the beautiful Gesù Church, the main Jesuit church in Rome.

Monumento a Vittorio Emanuele II (Vittoriano)

Begun in 1885, this huge monument by **Giuseppe Sacconi** was completed in 1935. It honours King **Victor Emmanuel II**, who achieved the unification of Italy in 1870, with Rome as the capital city. The dazzling white marble clashes with the warm tones of the cityscape and the grandiloquent style strikes a jarring note. The monument has many insulting nicknames, including "the wedding cake" and "typewriter".

A broad flight of steps, flanked by two allegorical groups in bronze gilt representing *Thought* and *Action*, leads up to the **Altar to the Nation** (*Altare della patria*). An eternal flame burns before the tomb of the unknown soldier, guarded by branches of the military. Victor Emmanuel II inaugurated the enormous bronze equestrian statue in 1911, which hosted a dinner party in its belly upon completion.

Ascensori panoramici e terrazza del Complesso del Vittoriano

Open Mon–Sun 9:30am–7:30pm. Closed 25 Dec and 1 Jan. ≈€7. ℘06 67 83 587. www.060608.it.

The top of the monument provides the finest **view★★** of the city – namely the only one that omits the *Vittoriano*. The Complesso hosts three historical museums (Museo Centrale del Risorgimento, Museo Nazionale Emigrazione Italiana and the Museo Sacrario delle Bandiere delle Forze Armate) and has a space – **Ala Brasini** – where they hold temporary exhibitions (*℘06 87 15 111*).

Palazzo Venezia★

With this building, which extends from Piazza Venezia to Via del Plebiscito and Via degli Astalli, the Renaissance made a timid debut into civil architecture. Construction of the palace was started in 1455 by Pietro Barbo, who required a palace worthy of his rank as cardinal; when he became Pope in 1464 as **Paul II,** he continued his project on a larger scale.

The Pope died In 1471, the palace was completed by his nephew. It was later altered several times: under Sixtus IV (1471–84) a smaller palace (*palazzetto*) was added opening onto a garden surrounded by a portico.

It was Pius IV, in 1564, who gave the palace its present name, when he allowed ambassadors of the Republic of Venice to lodge in part of the building.

Following the Treaty of Campo Formio between Austria and Napoleon in 1797, the Republic of Venice ceased to exist and almost all of its property (including Palazzo Venezia) reverted to Austria. By order of Napoleon in 1806 the palace became the seat of the French administration. It was at the forefront of Roman history again in 1910 when the Italian Government decided to lay out a huge square in front of the monument to King Victor Emmanuel II; the *palazzetto* that stood at the foot of the tower in the southeast angle was pulled down and put up again where it stands today on the corner of Piazza di San Marco and Via degli Astalli. The **Palazzo delle Assicurazioni Generali** was built on the other side of the square, in imitation of Palazzo Venezia.

During the Fascist era, Mussolini set up the Grand Council of Fascism and his office in the palace; he addressed the crowds in the piazza from the palace balcony. Now Palazzo Venezia is one of the city's most prestigious buildings, housing a museum and the library of the Institute of Art and Archaeology.

Exterior – The crenellations on the façade overlooking Piazza Venezia and the tower in the southeast corner show how the severe style of the fortified houses of the Middle Ages persisted. The mullion windows, the doors onto the square and in Via del Plebiscito, and above all, the façade of St Mark's Basilica, are pleasing manifestations of the Renaissance.

Statue of Madama Lucrezia – The statue stands in Piazza di San Marco in the angle where Palazzo Venezia and the *palazzetto* join. It was one of the four "talking statues" of Rome.

Interior – *Access from Piazza di San Marco; entrance beside the statue of Madama Lucrezia.* The unsophisticated outward appearance of Roman Renaissance palaces gives no hint of the elegant décor often to be found within. The **courtyard**'s garden is partially flanked by an elegant, but incomplete, portico by Giuliano da Maiano (1432–90). The

east side is formed by St Mark's Basilica, which stands within the palace, beneath its medieval belfry. The fountain dates from the 18C: Venice, the lion of St Mark at its feet, is throwing a ring into the waves, a symbol of the marriage between La Serenissima and the sea.

Museo Nazionale del Palazzo di Venezia

Via del Plebiscito 118. &. ©*Open Tue–Sun 8:30am–7:30pm.* ©*Closed 1 Jan, 1 May and 25 Dec.* ⊚€10. ℘06 69 99 43 88. www.museopalazzovenezia. beniculturali.it.

The first few rooms, devoted to medieval art, contain some particularly interesting antique ceramics, which include several 14C pieces from Orvieto. In the subsequent rooms, note the fine Byzantine enamel **Christ Pantocrator★★** from the second half of the 13C, a very finely carved ivory **Byzantine Triptych★★** from the 10C and a small bronze head sculpted by Nicola Pisano in 1248. The museum also contains paintings on wood by primitive artists from Florence and Siena belonging to the **Sterbini Collection★★**, as well as the 14C "Orsini" cross, made of embossed silver. In the last room, note the painted ceiling taken from Palazzo Altoviti (1533) with its central figure, Ceres, framed by medallions of the agricultural labours of the year.

Paul II's suite of rooms *(overlooking Piazza Venezia and Via del Plebiscito)* comprises the Royal Room, where ambassadors waited to be received by the pope; the Battle Room (from the battles of the First World War); and the Map Room (thanks to a 15C map), which was the balcony where Mussolini addressed the crowds.

Basilica di San Marco

Piazza di San Marco 48. ©*Open Tue–Fri 10am–1pm, 4–6pm. Sun and public holidays 10am–1pm, 4–8pm.*
Founded in 336 and dedicated to St Mark the Evangelist, this basilica was rebuilt by Gregory IV in the 9C. Excavations have uncovered traces of an earlier building and of the 9C crypt

Horse drawn carriages, Piazza Venezia

©Tupungato/iStockphoto.com

where Gregory IV had the relics of Abdon and Sennen, Persian martyrs, deposited. A belfry was added in the 12C, and in 1455 the church was rebuilt and incorporated into the Palazzo Venezia by Cardinal Pietro Barbo. Further restoration and alterations took place in the 17C and 18C.

The **façade**★ overlooking Piazza San Marco is attributed to Giuliano da Maiano or Leon-Battista Alberti: the double row of arches, in which the upper ones are carried on slimmer supports, lends elegance to this charming Renaissance composition.

The sumptuous **interior**★ is a typical Roman example of the overlapping of styles down the centuries. The medieval basilica plan of a nave and two aisles remains. In the 15C, the elegant coffered ceiling was added.

▶ Head to the beginning of Via del Corso.

Palazzo Bonaparte (Misciatelli)
Via del Corso.

This 17C *palazzo* of modest appearance was once the property of Napoleon's mother, who lived here from 1818 until her death in 1836. She supposedly spent much of her time sitting in the first-floor loggia, watching the busy street from behind shutters.

▶ Via del Plebiscito to Piazza del Gesù.

Chiesa del Gesù★★★
Piazza del Gesù. ◷*Open daily 7am–12:30pm and 4pm–7:45pm.* ℘*06 69 70 01.*

The **Gesù Church** is the main **Jesuit** church in Rome. The Society of Jesus was founded in 1540 by Ignatius of Loyola (1491–1556), a Spaniard. After the Council of Trent, the society became the prime mover in the Counter-Reformation, which sought to rebut the ideas of **Martin Luther** and Calvin. In 1568, the decision was taken to build a church in the centre of Rome. Cardinal Alexander Farnese undertook to provide the funds and insisted on his choice of architect: **Vignola**.

The design chosen for the façade in 1575 was by **Giacomo della Porta**. Solemn and severe, it became a model for a transitional style, halfway between Renaissance and Baroque art, known as the "Jesuit style", often copied by Italian and foreign architects.

In the interior, a distinction must be made between the architecture, a fairly plain product of the Counter-Reformation, and the ornate decoration, added a century later in the Baroque period. The majestic Latin-cross **plan** was ideal for the Society's main purpose:

Frescoes in Cappella di Sant'Ignazio di Loyola

© benedek/iStockphoto.com

preaching. In the single broad nave, unobstructed and well lit, the worshippers could concentrate on the celebrant and read the prayers with him. Special attention was paid to the acoustics to give resonance to the canticles.

The **decoration** was intended to celebrate the victory of the Roman Catholic Church and reinforce the conclusions of the Council of Trent. For example, the third chapel on the right shows angels and the Virgin interceding for the souls in Purgatory, and illustrates the ideas that were contested by the Reformers.

Baciccia Frescoes★★

In 1672, through the good offices of Bernini, Giovanni Battista Gaulli, (known as "*Il Baciccia*") was commissioned to fresco the Gesù Church. *The Triumph of the Name of Jesus*, which he painted on the nave ceiling, was certainly his masterpiece. The work was completed in 1679, and combines the technique of composition with the exuberance of *trompe-l'œil*; the eye moves without check from the painted surface to the sculptures by Antonio Raggi. He also painted the *Adoration of the Lamb* in the apse and the *Assumption* on the dome.

Cappella di Sant'Ignazio di Loyola★★★

Open Mon–Sat 4pm–6pm, Sun and public holidays 10am–noon. ℘06 69 70 01.

This chapel (left of the transept), where the remains of St Ignatius rest in a beautiful urn, was built by Andrea Pozzo, a Jesuit, between 1696 and 1700. Behind a bronze rail embellished with cherubs stands the altar, bearing a statue of the saint in marble and silver. The solid silver original, the work of Pierre Legros, a Frenchman, was melted down by Pius VI for taxes imposed by Napoleon under the Treaty of Tolentino.

On the sides of the altar, two groups of allegorical statues illustrate the work carried on by the Jesuits. On the left Faith Triumphing over Idolatry by Giovanni Théodon and on the right Religion Vanquishing Heresy by Pierre Legros, a pupil of Pozzo.

In the building to the right of the church are the rooms where St Ignatius lived and died (access from Piazza del Gesù 45). The ceiling and walls of the flanking passage are decorated all over in Pozzo's *trompe-l'œil* frescoes (17C).

Porta Pia–Termini★

Rome's main train station, Stazione Termini, is often the first introduction visitors have to Rome. Sadly, most flee the crowds and hustlers – and miss the gentrifed elegance and worthy sights, such as the Baths of Diocletian and ancient collections of the Museo Nazionale Romano. The area is typical of many station districts: large urban spaces, noisy traffic, fast-food outlets, small hotels and travel agencies. But it is also characterised by wide avenues and grand ministerial palazzi.

- **Michelin Map:** 38 H 15–16, J 14–15, K 14–15.
- **Location:** Northwest of the station stands the Porta Pia in the old Aurelian walls, as well as the Nomentana district.
- **Don't Miss:** The Palazzo Massimo alle Terme, the meridian at Santa Maria degli Angeli, and opera at Teatro dell'Opera.
- **Timing:** Allow 1 hr, excluding museum visits.
- **Also See:** *Fontana di Trevi; Quirinale; SAN LORENZO FUORI LE MURA; SANTA MARIA MAGGIORE–MONTI– ESQUILINO; VIA VENETO.*

MUSEO NAZIONALE ROMANO – TERME DI DIOCLEZIANO

Viale Enrico de Nicola 76. Audioguides recommended. &Open Tue–Sun 9am–7:45pm (last admission 7pm). Closed 1 Jan and 25 Dec. €10, €12 combined ticket valid for 3 days. This ticket is also valid for other sites of Museo Nazionale Romano: Palazzo Massimo alle Terme, Palazzo Altemps and Crypta Balbi. *06 39 96 77 00. www.coopculture.it.*

The few extant rooms and the bold vaulting are evidence of the original splendour of the building, part of which now houses the church of St Mary of the Angels (&*See below*). Some rooms are devoted to works from the National Roman Museum.

In the 4C, there were some 900 bath-houses in Rome, but the largest (13ha/ 32 acres) and most beautiful were the baths of **Diocletian** (&*See p46*). Construction took 10 years (295–305) under the direction of Maximian (the emperor lived in Asia Minor until he moved to Split – in modern-day Croatia – after his abdication in 305; he never visited Rome). The bathhouse could accommodate up to 3 000. The complex also included libraries, concert halls, gardens, galleries and gyms.

In 538 the baths were abandoned, when the aqueducts were destroyed by the Ostrogoths under Witigis. Michelangelo was commissioned by Pius IV

GETTING THERE

BY METRO AND BUS: Line A: Termini or Repubblica. Bus: C2, H, 36, 38, 40, 64, 86, 90, 92,105, 170, 175, 217, 310, 360, 714 and 910.

(1559–65) to convert the ruins into a church and Sixtus V (1585–90) removed a great deal of material for his many buildings.

To celebrate the bimillenary of Augustus, from 24 September 2014 the facade of the restored monumental *Natatio* will be exhibited. In the adjacent Aula VIII, architectural fragments of the baths themselves will be displayed. And the Renaissance structures of the Certosa di Santa Maria degli Angeli (built over the ancient remains) and the Small Cloister are once again open to the public.

Santa Maria degli Angeli★

Piazza della Repubblica. Open Mon–Sat 7am–7:30pm, Sun 7:30am– 7:30pm. *06 48 80 812. www.santa mariadegliangeliroma.it.*

165

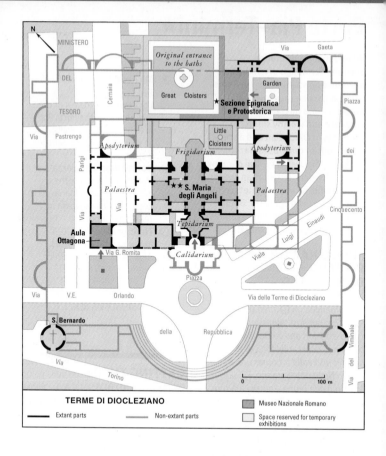

TERME DI DIOCLEZIANO

— Extant parts
— Non-extant parts

▨ Museo Nazionale Romano
□ Space reserved for temporary exhibitions

According to tradition, the Baths of Diocletian were built by 40 000 Christians condemned to forced labour; in 1561 Pius IV decided to convert the ruined baths into a church and a charterhouse. **Michelangelo**, by then 86 years old, was put in charge. His design, which closely followed the architecture of the original baths, was continually altered after he and the pope died within a year of one another (1564 and 1565 respectively). By 1749, the church was a jumble of dissociated features and **Vanvitelli**, the Neapolitan, was commissioned to reintroduce a degree of uniformity.

The outer façade he designed was demolished in the early 20C, revealing the unusual unadorned curved wall of the *calidarium* of the original baths. The interior, which is designed to the Greek-cross plan, was remodelled by Vanvitelli.

Vestibule

This was the *tepidarium* of the baths. On the left is the tomb **(1)** of the Neapolitan poet and painter **Salvatore Rosa**, who died in 1673. To the right, the tomb **(2)** of **Carlo Maratta** (1625–1713), who designed it himself. Between the vestibule and the transept stands the statue of **St Bruno** (**3** – *right*), founder of the Carthusian order, by the French sculptor Houdon (1741–1828). On either side of the entrance to the transept are two **stoops**; the one on the right is 18C Baroque **(4)**, the other modern **(5)**.

Transept★

This part of the church gives the best idea of the solemn majesty of the ancient building. It occupies the central bath hall, with its eight monolithic granite columns. To create a uniform

S. MARIA DEGLI ANGELI

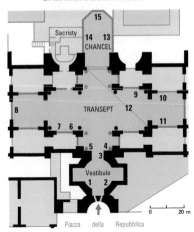

effect, Vanvitelli copied the columns in painted masonry, adding four more. The transept is a virtual picture gallery, particularly of 18C works. The majority come from St Peter's, where they were replaced by mosaics.

Here in St Mary's, Vanvitelli arranged them to cover the wall spaces between the pillars.

Of particular significance is the painting depicting *St Basil Celebrating Mass before Emperor Valens* **(6)** by the French painter Subleyras (1699–1749), who settled in Rome in 1728; the Emperor, overwhelmed by the dignity of the ceremony, has fainted; his uniform and background are treated in the classical manner. *The Fall of Simon Magus* **(7)** by **Pompeo Batoni** (1708–86) is typical of this artist's work, with its fine colours and subtle effects of contrasting light and shade. *The Virgin with St Bruno and other saints* **(8)** is a gentle and luminous work by Giovanni Odazzi (1663–1731), a pupil of Baciccia; he worked in the Baroque Mannerist style.

Frescoes, Santa Maria degli Angeli

© sedmak/istockphoto.com

The south transept contains the **tombs** of three First World War heroes: Marshal Armando Diaz **(9)**, who won the Battle of Vittorio Veneto in 1918; Admiral Paolo Thaon di Revel **(10)**, commander-in-chief of the Allied forces in the Adriatic 1917–18; Vittorio Emanuele Orlando **(11)**, Minister of State.

Running across the floor from the south transept to the chancel is a 1702 meridian **(12), still operational today**. Between 1702 and 1846, Rome's clocks were regulated by it.

Presbytery – Like the transept, the presbytery is generously decorated with paintings, the most notable being *The Martyrdom of St Sebastian* **(13)** by **Domenichino** (1581–1641), and *The Baptism of Jesus* **(14)** by Carlo Maratta. Behind the high altar is a much-venerated picture **(15)** showing the Virgin surrounded by adoring angels. It was commissioned from a Venetian artist in 1543 by Antonio del Duca, a Sicilian priest, who had a vision in which he saw a cloud of angels rising from the Baths of Diocletian. From that day forward he never stopped demanding the construction of a church on the site of the baths; eventually Pius IV acceded to his request.

Aula Ottagona (or Baths of Diocletian Planetarium)
Via Giuseppe Romita 8. ©*Open Mon–Fri 9am–1pm, 2–5pm, Sat 9am–2pm. Visits by reservation. The visit is included in the ticket for Museo delle Terme di Diocleziano.* ℘*06 39 96 77 00. www.coopculture.it.*
Until 1928 a planetarium, this domed octagonal room houses bronze and marble sculptures taken from Roman baths (2–4C BC). Set into the central part of the floor is a glass panel, revealing the foundations.

Museo Epigrafico and Museo Protostorico★
Garden – Facing Piazza dei Cinquecento, this 16C garden – the entrance to the museum – houses a collection of archaeological fragments. The huge central vase once adorned the villa of a wealthy Roman citizen.

Museum – This 1920s building houses the rich epigraphical collection of the Museo Nazionale Romano. The ground floor covers the archaic era to the late republican period (8C–1C BC). The two upper levels are dedicated to inscriptions (1C BC–4C AD), which inform about the emperor and his entourage, social structure, political and economic activity, and religion.

The raised floor around Michelangelo's cloisters *(access from the second floor of the Epigraphical Museum)* houses a section dedicated to the prehistory of the Latins between the 9C and 7C BC.

Chiostro Michelangiolesco – The Great Cloisters of Santa Maria degli Angeli are sometimes attributed to Michelangelo, although he died in 1564, aged 89, and the cloisters were probably completed in 1565. The sec-

The Calendar

The first recorded Roman calendar is attributed to Romulus and consisted of 304 days divided into 10 months (March was the first). Numa Pompilius then added January and February, bringing the total number of days to 355. An extra day (23 February) was inserted every three years, so that the course of the sun and moon would coincide. Julius Caesar radically reformed the calendar: he increased the days to 365 and added an extra one in February every four years. The names of the months were taken either from gods and goddesses (March from Mars, May from Maia, June from Juno), from emperors (August from Augustus and July from Julius Caesar) or from their position in the calendar (September was the seventh month and October the eighth). The name February is an exception; it derived from the verb *februare*, meaning to purify, as this was the time of cleansing ceremonies.

ond floor now houses the **Protohistoric Museum**, with ancient finds from Latium 11-10C BC-4C BC, and recent finds from digs around Rome.

MUSEO NAZIONALE ROMANO – PALAZZO MASSIMO ALLE TERME★★★

Largo di Villa Peretti 1. ♿🕐*Open Tue–Sun 9am–7:45pm.* 🕐*Closed 1 Jan and 25 Dec.* ♒10, €12 combined ticket valid for 3 days. This ticket is also valid for other sites of Museo Nazionale Romano: Terme di Diocleziano (🕯See above), Palazzo Altemps and Crypta Balbi. 📞06 39 96 77 00. www.coopculture.it.

The largest part of the **National Roman Museum's** collection is now permanently housed in the former *Collegio Massimo*. The collections are displayed on four floors in a few rooms arranged around the inner courtyard and divided into bays. Greek and Roman statues are exhibited on the ground and first floors, frescoes and mosaics on the second, and gold and numismatics in the basement.

Ground Floor

The entrance to the museum is dominated by a statue of **Minerva** (seated) **(1)**, which dates from the 1C BC and is made of pink alabaster, basalt and Luni marble; the face is a plaster cast of another statue of the goddess.

Gallery I houses a series of portraits from the Republican era.

Room I: The two fragments on display in this room **(2)** represent a typical calendar and a list of consuls and censors who held office between 173 and 67 BC. The **Tivoli General (3)** is an excellent example of the union of the ideal of Greek idealism and Italian portraiture. The classical beauty of the body contrasts with the realistic features of the face, which clearly shows signs of age. A **floor mosaic (4)** (late 2C–early 1C BC) is seen at the end of Gallery I; the emblem panel in the centre shows the abduction of Hylas (depicted with his cloak billowing in the wind) by water nymphs. Rooms II-IV host temporary exhibits: look for a **young girl**, similar to Artemis, depicted wearing a richly draped chiton. Attention to detail is shown in the footwear, carved with panthers' heads.

Room with three arches – Room V is devoted to power. It encloses the **Statue of Augustus** as Pontifex Maximus★★★ *(Statua di Augusto)*. The emperor is shown at about the age of 50, dressed in the High Priest's toga, with his head covered, as was the custom for priests about to offer a sacrifice. The face is treated with simple realism, and perhaps flattery. The Palestria Calendar is also here. On the back of the **Altar to Mars and Venus (6)** can be seen the *Lupercale*, which tells the legend of Romulus and Remus, suckled by a she-wolf. The personification of the Palatine can be seen at the top to the left, with, beneath it, the eagle, symbol of Jupiter, and to the side the two shepherds, Faustulus and Numitor, the former the adoptive father of the twins. The personification of the Tiber can be seen at the bottom.

The theme of Rome's founding is also taken up in the **frescoes from a Columbarium on the Esquiline (7)**. A colourful and realistic **mosaic (8) of a cat and ducks** can be admired in **Gallery III**.

Gli Horti Sallustiani (Gardens of Sallust) – The exhibits in Room VII include some original Greek statues from this residential district of the city, including the noteworthy **Wounded Niobe★★★** *(Niobide Ferita)*, dating from 440 BC (*see also Palazzo Altemps and Centrale Montemartini*). The statue represents an episode in Greek mythology: **Niobe** was mother of 14 children, and was scornful of Leto, who had borne only two. The angry goddess asked her children, Artemis and Apollo, to avenge her by killing all of Niobe's offspring. This statue was one of the first representations of the naked female figure in Greek art after the Cycladic statues from the third millennium BC. **The Pugilist★★★**, a superb figure cast in bronze, is an original from the Hellenistic period. This fighter is no longer the ideally handsome hero represented by the classical artists, but a man overwhelmed with fatigue. The figure was found in 1884, at the same time as the **Hellenistic Prince ★★★**,

169

PALAZZO MASSIMO ALLE TERME

SECOND FLOOR

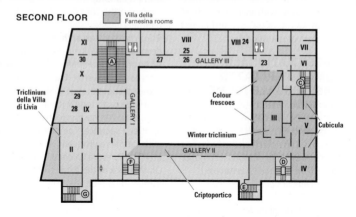

Villa della Farnesina rooms

Triclinium della Villa di Livia

Colour frescoes

Winter triclinium

Cubicula

Criptoportico

FIRST FLOOR

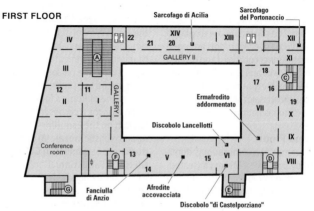

Sarcofago di Acilia

Sarcofago del Portonaccio

Ermafrodito addormentato

Discobolo Lancellotti

Conference room

Fanciulla di Anzio

Afrodite accovacciata

Discobolo "di Castelporziano"

GROUND FLOOR

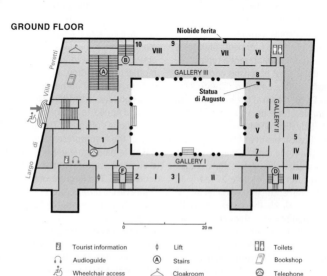

Niobide ferita

Statua di Augusto

Tourist information	Lift	Toilets
Audioguide	Stairs	Bookshop
Wheelchair access	Cloakroom	Telephone

0   20 m

the young man leaning against the post beside him.

Neo-Attic period – *Room VIII*. Note the statue of the **Melpomene Muse (9)**, dating from the 1C BC, and the various ornamental garden pieces, including a base of dancing maenads **(10)**.

First Floor

These imperial works reveal the propagandist use of portraits.

Portraits – Among the portraits from the Flavian dynasty *(Room I)*, that of **Vespasian (11), builder of the Colosseum,** is particularly worthy of note. This realistic work depicts an old man with a wide and solid face, small eyes and a furrowed brow. The portrait of **Sabina (12)** *(Room II)*, Trajan's wife, shows a woman of quite advanced years, but is fairly idealised in tone.

Villas and gymnasia – *Rooms V–VI*. This large double room, once the theatre of the college, houses sculptures from three of the large imperial villas: Nero's at Subiaco and Anzio, and Hadrian's at Tivoli (🕭 *See Tivoli*).

The **Ephebe of Subiaco (13)** is thought to represent one of Niobe's children, hit by Apollo's arrow *(see Room VII)*. Admire the beautiful drapery of the chiton of the **Young Girl from Anzio★★** *(Fanciulla di Anzio)*, shown with the upper half of her body twisting slightly. The statue of **Apollo (14)** is also from the villa at Anzio and is a Roman copy (1C AD); typical features from the Hellenistic period (4C BC) include the gentle, swaying pose, the shoulders at different heights and the slightly bowed head. These features contrast with those of the **Apollo of the Tiber (15)**, which is typical of the classical period in its statuary pose, with its level shoulders, strong body and idealised beauty – perhaps a replica of a Phidias masterpiece. The **Aphrodite Crouching★★★** (*Afrodite Accovacciata*) is one of the most beautiful copies of an original Greek work of the 3C BC; the goddess is shown bathing, a theme often reproduced by the Romans.

Lancellotti Discobolus★★★ *(Discobolo Lancellotti)*, named after its former owner, is considered to be an excellent copy. The athlete has already grasped the discus in his right hand and is flexing the muscles of his whole body prior to the throw. The impassive expression, devoid of any sign of physical effort, is characteristic of Greek works from the classical period. The hair and the veins in the arms are highly detailed.

The other replica is the **Castelporziano Discobolus★** *(Discobolo "di Castelporziano")*, named after the estate where it was found in 1906.

Detail of mosaics depicting a Satyr's head (2C BC)

© R. Mattes/hemis.fr

Portraits of gods – *Rooms VII-IX*. The **Sleeping Hermaphroditus**★★ *(Ermafrodito Addormentato)* is a beautiful copy of a Greek original thought to date from the 4C BC. The graceful, pure lines and the gently twisting body emphasise the ambiguity (the sexual organs are not visible from one side of the statue). Myths claim *Hermaphroditus* (son of Hermes and Aphrodite, hence the name) was sitting by a lake, when he was spotted by Salmacis, a water nymph. She fell in love with him. Rejected by the youth, the nymph requested to be joined to Hermaphroditus for ever. Her wish was granted and a new being of both genders emerged from the lake. The headless statue of **Apollo with his lyre (16)** is wearing a full chiton, which emphasises the movement of the body. Also exhibited in this room are two very different statues of Dionysus. The first, in bronze, shows **Young Dionysus (17)** with his traditional attributes: the thyrsus and the *taenia* (headband) with vine leaves in his hair; note the copper inserts (nipples and lips) and the glass paste eyes. The second – a marble copy of an original, probably by Praxiteles – portrays an older **Dionysus (18)**, with a long beard and dressed in a long chiton covered with a himation thrown over the left shoulder. It presents a different representation of the god, and is known as **Sardanapalo**, from the name carved by one owner on the back of the statue. **Room X** houses a collection of **bronzes** from the ships found in Lake Nemi. Note the balustrade decorated with herms **(19)**.

Historical events – *Room XII*. The large **Portonaccio Sarcophagus**★ *(Sarcofago del Portonaccio)* is decorated with a powerful battle scene between the Romans and barbarians.

The figures are crowded together and overlap to highlight the fighting. Two defeated figures to one side show their unbound hands to symbolise *Roman Pietàs*. The commander, who can be seen in the middle, is faceless, probably because he would have been among the last figures completed.

Iconography and celebrations from Severus to Constantine – *Room VII*. The 3C AD oval-shaped **Acilia Sarcophagus**★★ *(Sarcofago di Acilia)* is finely and elegantly decorated with high-relief carvings, illustrating a consular procession. The youngest figure wears the consular ring and is possibly the consul's son (on his shoulders to the right). The character wearing the toga and diadem is the personification of the Roman Senate. From a later period are the **Sarcophagus with Muses (20)**, fitted with internal recesses, and the **Annona Sarcophagus (21)**, with a wedding scene shown in the middle of the sarcophagus. The **Sarcophagus of Marcus Claudianus (22)** was made after the edict of Constantine and is carved with scenes from the Old and New Testaments. The commander in the centre is portrayed as Christ praying.

Second Floor

This floor features mosaics and frescoes. Most of the floor is in Galleries I and III.

Il giardino della Villa di Livia★★★ – *Room II*. This is the reconstruction of a semi-underground room, probably a summer *triclinium* (dining room) from a villa where Livia, wife of Augustus, lived at Prima Porta (north of Rome). The fine decoration, dating from 20–10 BC, runs along the four walls and depicts a garden in full bloom. An incredible variety of plants (firs, cypresses, oaks, pines, pomegranates, oleanders and palm trees) and birds can be seen. Perspective is heightened by the skilful use of *chiaroscuro* and the varying heights of the plants. Muted fresco colours suggest depth and relief, making this cycle of frescoes a masterpiece of Roman painting.

Villa della Farnesina★★★ – The stuccoes, mosaics and paintings in this part of the museum come from a suburban villa dating from the Augustan era. Built on the banks of the Tiber, it had a large semi-circular porch facing the river. The stuccoes that decorated the ceilings are marvellously delicate. The paintings are typical of the second and third styles and were probably executed for the marriage of Giulia, the daughter of Augustus and Agrippa. The frescoes that decorated the cryptoporticus *(criptoportico)*, an underground corridor lit by narrow slits, can be admired in Gallery II. The decoration shows a fine colonnade with panels of Bacchic and Dionysiac scenes painted on a white background between the columns. At the end of the corridor is a reconstruction of the **winter triclinium** *(triclinium invernale, Room III)*. Slender columns hung with vegetal festoons are painted on a black background. The panels have an Egyptian theme and contain illustrations of sphinxes and trial scenes. Panels showing scenes from everyday life and tragic and comic masks can be admired on the other side of the corridor. The magnificent frescoes from the three *cubicola* (bedrooms) of the villa are very well preserved. The ceilings still retain some beautifully executed stuccoes.

Gallery III – The mosaic of a Nike *(centre)* surrounded by Dionysiac masks **(23)** dates from the end of the 1C BC. Small openings run off the gallery *(Room VIII)* which house the **Water Nymph from Anzio (24)** with, in the middle recess, a portrait of Hercules resting (the hero is easily recognisable by his club) and **frescoes (25)** of underwater fauna (2C AD) found near a river port on the Tiber. At the end of the gallery is a beautiful **mosaic with a Satyr's head and Pan (26)** and a large **mosaic of Nile landscape (27)** from the 2C AD, characterised by the presence of crocodiles and hippopotami, similar to the fresco on display at the Museo di Palestrina.

Villa di Baccano – *Room IX*. This room houses floor mosaics from *Villa di Baccano (on Via Cassia)*, which date from the 3C AD. The large **marine mosaic (28)** – centred around the personification of Neptune, god of the sea – would have decorated the bathing area. The four panels depicting the charioteers **(29)** (the colours of their tunics correspond with the four factions competing) would have decorated a bedroom.

Megalographs – *Room X*. Dedicated to a collection of *megalographs*, this room contains a fresco **(30)** portraying a goddess understood in the 17C to be Roma, but since identified as Venus.

Basement

Room I: Numismatic Collection★★ – This large room displays coins from the 4C BC onwards, including models for the euro, and measures and weights used for minting coins.

Room II: Jewels and Mummy of Grottarossa – The 2C AD mummy of an eight-year old girl was found in 1964 north of the centre along Via Cassia. Inside the sarcophagus with her are a hinged wooden doll and other objects.

Room III: Prices and wealth in Rome – In AD 301, Diocletian promulgated an edict to fix prices and measures. In the first display case is a collection of calculus equipment, including an abacus. The second contains an unusual statuette. The "convivial skeleton" was placed in the middle of the table during banquets as a *memento mori* (eat, but remember that you must die). Other cases exhibit collections of Roman goldwork.

 WALKING TOUR

Piazza dei Cinquecento

This vast, open space is the terminus for some public transport services in the city and home to the main **railway station, Stazione Termini**. The present building was begun before the WWII to replace the old station (1846–78). Interrupted during the war; work began again in 1947 and was completed to mark the Holy Year in 1950. The roof, with its undulating lines, is considered to be one of the most significant examples of architecture of this period. In the station forecourt are imposing remains of a wall that girdled the city after the Gauls invaded in the 4C BC.

On the south side of Viale Luigi Einaudi stands a monument to 500 Italians *(see the piazza's name)* who died at Dogali in Eritrea in 1887. This was an incident in the wars of Italy's colonial expansion. The crowning obelisk comes from the Temple of Isis in Campus Martius.

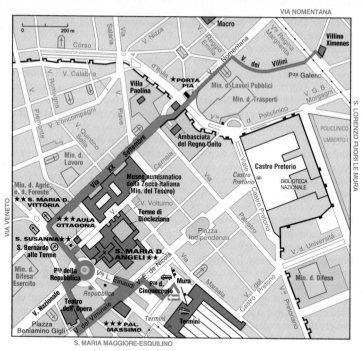

S. MARIA MAGGIORE-ESQUILINO

In Piazza Beniamino Gigli, south of Piazza della Repubblica, is the **Teatro dell'Opera**, a theatre begun by A Sfondrini and completed in 1880. The façade is the work of M Piacentini, who restored and enlarged part of the building in 1926.

▶ Follow Via Torino alongside the theatre, then turn right into Via Nazionale.

Via Nazionale – This long, busy street links Piazza della Repubblica with Piazza Venezia. It is one of the city's most important commercial centres, and is lined with shops that attract both tourists and Romans. Halfway down is the **Palazzo delle Esposizioni** (⚲ *see p120*), which houses art exhibitions of international reputation. Near the south is the reputable **Teatro Eliseo**.

Piazza della Repubblica

Despite the heavy traffic, the roundabout is one of the better post-1870 examples of town planning. Formerly called Piazza dell'Esedra, because of the semi-circle formed by the ancient baths, it is now crowned by two palaces that flank the southwest side. They were designed in 1896 by Gaetano Koch to trace the line of the exedra in the southwest wall of the Baths of Diocletian. The Naiad Fountain at the centre is adorned with bronze water nymphs and sea monsters, sculpted by the Sicilian artist Mario Rutelli (1901).

▶ Via Vittorio Emanuele Orlando to Via XX Settembre.

Via XX Settembre

The street is named after the date – 20 September 1870 – when Italian troops entered the papal capital. It replaced the old Strada Pia and was the first street developed in the post-1870 boom. Designed to link the ministries and reflect the grandeur of the city's new status, it was lined with pompous buildings in imitation of the Renaissance and Baroque styles. The Ministry of Finance, to the right, is home to the Museo Numismatico della Zecca Italiana. At the end of the street (80a) is a modern building by Sir Basil Spence, which houses the **British Embassy** (Ambasciata Britannica).

Villa Paolina-Bonaparte

Via Piave 23. ◔Open by appointment to groups only. www.inventerrome. com. ◉10.

The villa is named after Napoleon's sister Pauline, who in 1803 married Prince Camillo Borghese. She took up residence here after the fall of the empire, since her husband, whom she had abandoned earlier, banished her from the family property. She spent long periods in the house until her death in 1825.

Porta Pia

The **inner façade★** of the gate, facing Via XX Settembre, is the last architectural design by **Michelangelo**. It was erected between 1561 and 1564 at the request of Pope Pius IV. At the centre are six balls, the crest of the Medici family. The curious white motif is said to be a barber's basin wrapped in a fringed towel, a reminder to Pius IV that one of his ancestors was a tradesman. The outside façade, facing down Via Nomentana, is the work of Benedetto Vespignani (1808–82), who was very active during the 19C.

⊙ Continue along Via Nomentana and turn right into Via dei Villini.

Via dei Villini – This road is an excellent example of early 20C urban planning. Observe *palazzini*, four- or five-storey flat blocks for rentals, and the *villini*, smart little houses with gardens.

SIGHTS
MACRO★

Via Nizza 138. ◔Open Tue–Sun 10am–8pm. Sat –22pm. ◉Closed 1 Jan, 1 May and 25 Dec. ℘06 69 6271. www.museomacro.it.

In 2010 the former Peroni brewery designed in the early 20C was renovated by **Odile Decq**, in a project of industrial archaeology with architecture as the main constituent. The MACRO offers glimpses, realizations, discoveries, but never offers an overall view. The large foyer is crossed by balconies and ramps, and an angular red volume at the centre, suggestive of the keel of a ship, is in fact an auditorium. Temporary shows are given in the exhibition space.

ADDRESSES

TAKING A BREAK

Eataly – *Piazza della Repubblica 41. ℘06 06 90 27 92 01. www.eataly.* Walking among the stalls of Eataly is such a pleasure: all the best Italian products under the same roof. Really tempting!

La Cucina di Oliver Glowig – *Via Giovanni Giolitti 36. ℘06 4620 2989. www.lacucinadioliver.* At the first floor of Mercato Centrale, the starred chef Oliver Glowig proposes an elaborated cuisine: *escargot* with mint and coffee sauce, grilled octopus with lentils and et burrata.

Quelli di Via Nizza – *Via Nizza 16.* This pizzeria stays open until 3am or 4am and serves croissants too. Specialities include original toppings such as turkey, porcini mushrooms and rocket salad, prawns or apple purée and nutella.

San Giovanni in Laterano★★★

As in so many parts of the capital, pagan ruins sit beside important Christian churches: the basilica of St John Lateran – the Pope's seat as Bishop of Rome – and Santa Croce in Gerusalemme, one of the seven pilgrimage churches. Today, the noisy junction Piazza di Porta San Giovanni contrasts with the calm solemnity of the east front of the basilica.

A BIT OF HISTORY

The name is taken from the wealthy Laterani family who owned a property confiscated by Nero and restored by Septimius Severus. Excavations in Via dell'Amba Aradam *(beneath the INPS building)* have revealed traces of a house identified as belonging to the **Laterani**. It was combined with a neighbouring property in the 4C and may have been the residence of Fausta, who was Maxentius' sister and Constantine's wife. In 313, she lent her house to Pope Melchiades so that he could hold a council of bishops, one of the first official manifestations of Christianity.

Beneath the St John Lateran Hospital (Ospedale di San Giovanni in Laterano) are traces of a building that has been identified as the house of the Annii, Marcus Aurelius' family.

The remains of the base of a statue were found in a peristyle; it may have carried the statue of the Emperor that now stands in the Capitoline Museum. **St John's Gate** (Porta San Giovanni) was erected in the 16C in the **Aurelian Wall** (Mura Aureliane), which was built around Rome in the 3C and remains very well preserved.

The **monument to St Francis of Assisi** is a reminder that the saint and his companions came to the Lateran in 1210 hoping to have their rule approved by Innocent III.

◔ **Michelin Map:** 38 P 15–16, N 16–17, M 16.

▷ **Location:** This district stretches from the city's southeast to the Caelian Hill and is almost wedged inside the Aurelian walls. The Tangenziale provides a fast road link with the districts of San Lorenzo and Nomentano.

◔ **Timing:** Allow 3hrs.

◔ **Don't Miss:** The clothing market that runs along Via Sannio, on the other side of Porta San Giovanni.

🚹 **Kids:** Museo degli Strumeni Muscali.

◔ **Also See:** *COLOSSEO– CELIO; SAN LORENZO FUORI LE MURA; SANTA MARIA MAGGIORE–MONTI– ESQUILINO.*

GETTING THERE

BY METRO AND BUS: Line A: San Giovanni or Manzoni. Bus 16, 51, 81, 85, 87, 117, 218, 650, 665, 714 and 792.

BASILICA DI SAN GIOVANNI IN LATERANO★★★

◔*Open Mon-Fri 7am–6:30pm; cloisters and museum (◔see p180) 9am–6pm. Audioguides to left of the entrance.* ✆*06 69 88 64 33.*

This Basilica St John Lateran was the first church to the Holy Redeemer; it symbolised the triumph of Christianity over paganism and thus deserved its title of "Mother and Head of all the churches in the city and the world". It is the cathedral of Rome. The dedication to St John came later.

Constantine's Basilica – On 28 October 312, after defeating Maxentius in battle, Constantine made a triumphal entry into Rome and immediately forbade the persecution of the Christians. In 314, Pope Sylvester I took up residence in the Lateran (a group of buildings comprising a palace, a basilica and a basilica and a baptistry). The *palazzo* became the official papal residence from the 5C until the papacy departed to Avignon. Before starting St Peter's in the Vatican, Constantine built the Lateran basilica on the site of Maxentius' bodyguards' barracks. He thus asserted his victory by destroying one of the signs of his enemy's greatness and by stressing his intention of giving the Christians his approval.

After being sacked by barbarians in the 5C, damaged by an earth tremor in 896 and destroyed by fire in 1308, the basilica was rebuilt in the Baroque era and in the 18C. Over 20 popes contributed to its structure, from Leo the Great (440–61) to Leo XIII (1878–1903).

Lateran Councils – Some of the most decisive meetings in church history took place in the Lateran. In **1123,** the Diet of Worms was confirmed, putting an end to the Investiture Controversy. The council of 1139 condemned **Arnold of Brescia**, a canon, who challenged episcopal authority and preached in favour of a return to the poverty of the early Church. He founded a free commune in Rome and drove out Eugenius III.

In **1179,** Alexander III called for a crusade against the Albigensian (Cathar) heresy. Following the Council in **1215** – attended by 400 bishops and 800 abbots and at which every court in Europe was represented – it was laid down that the faithful must confess once a year and take Communion at Easter. Innocent III decided to put an end to the Albigensian heresy and launched a crusade in the Languedoc. In **1512,** Julius II opened the fifth Lateran Council by asserting the supremacy of the Church of Rome.

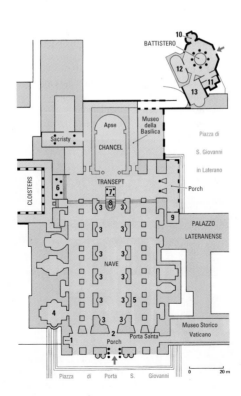

A Strange Trial

The trial took place in 896 in the Lateran. The accused was the corpse of Pope Formosus, dressed in his papal vestments.

His enemies had not forgiven him for bestowing the emperor's crown on the "barbarian" Arnoul, last of the Carolingians.

He was set opposite his judge, Pope Stephen VI, declared unworthy and a perjuror, and thrown into the Tiber.

Stephen VI was, in his turn, punished and strangled in prison.

Exterior

The well-balanced 18C **façade** is the major work of Alessandro Galilei (1691–1736), a Baroque architect. He had a masterly touch in contrasting the clear lines of the columns with the dark cavities behind them. On the roof, the gigantic figures of the saints surrounding Christ, St John the Baptist and St John the Evangelist preach to the heavens.

The **huge statue of Constantine**, the first Christian emperor **(1)**, in the porch comes from the Imperial Baths on the Quirinal. Since 1656, the **cen-** tral entrance **(2)** has been fitted with bronze doors from the Curia in the Forum.

Interior

It is hard to envisage the basilical plan of Constantine's building. Today's central nave and four aisles are those of a Baroque church, sometimes considered cold and severe because of its grandiose dimensions and pale stuccoes. In fact, it is a very old building dressed in 17C taste.

Nave and aisles – This part of the church was designed by the great Baroque architect **Borromini**; his plan included a dome. Just as Urban VIII had commissioned Bernini to complete St Peter's, so his successor **Innocent X**, desired to mark his reign in a prestigious manner. He invited Borromini in about 1650 to refurbish St John Lateran. Where Bernini knew how to adapt Baroque art to earlier constructions, Borromini was unable to give free rein to his genius, as Innocent III asked him to retain the existing ceiling. It seems to crush the pillars in the nave, which replace the ancient columns and were designed to support a dome. The prominent niches faced with dark marble spoil the effect of the low-relief sculptures and the oval medallions.

San Giovanni in Laterano

© salvo77_na/ iStockphoto.com

Ceiling★★ – Pius IV began this in 1562; his arms are in the centre. It was completed in 1567 by Pius V, whose arms are near the chancel. In the 18C, it was restored by Pius VI, who added his arms near the main door. The original design was by a group of Michelangelo's pupils.

Statues of the Apostles★ **(3)** – They are in the late Baroque style by some of Bernini's followers. Borromini created 12 huge recesses in the pillars of the nave to receive them. The columns of green flecked marble, which Borromini shortened and re-employed, originally separated the nave and aisles in the ancient basilica. Above each recess, he placed the dove from the arms of Innocent X.

The low-relief sculptures *(above)*, executed under the direction of Algardi, depict stories from the Old and New Testaments. The prophets in the oval medallions *(top)* were painted in the 18C. This decoration replaced the 15C frescoes painted by Pisanello and Gentile da Fabriano for **Martin V** and Eugenius IV.

Corsini Chapel★ **(4)** – Alessandro Galilei, who designed the east front, was also responsible for this chapel, which is built on the Greek-cross plan beneath a dome. The red porphyry coffer *(left)* beneath Clement XII's tomb came from the Pantheon. The allegorical statues are fine 18C work. The fragment of heavily restored **fresco (5)**, attributed to **Giotto**, shows Boniface VIII announcing the Jubilee Year in 1300.

Transept – The nave is as bare of ornamentation as the transept is adorned with frescoes, marble and gilding. It was renovated in about 1595 by Clement VIII, with **Giacomo della Porta** as architect. Mannerist decoration includes the great wall frescoes that resemble theatrical décor. These were painted principally by Cesare Nebbia, Pomarancio and Cavaliere d'Arpino who, in the *Ascension (end of left transept)*, imitated the *Transfiguration* by Raphael *(Vatican Gallery)*.

The elaborate marble decoration includes high-relief angels, placed in small niches, which do not show the liberty of movement that charac-terises Baroque art. The ostentatious **ceiling**★★, bearing the arms of Clement VIII, is rich in colour and gilding and was designed by Taddeo Landini (late 16C).

The pediment in the **chapel of the Holy Sacrament (6)** is supported by four beautiful Antique **columns**★ in gilded bronze, the only ones of this kind in Rome. Legend recounts that in the 1C BC they belonged to the Temple of Jupiter.

The 14C **baldaquin (7)** was repainted during the Renaissance. At the top, some relics of the heads of St Peter and St Paul – placed in silver reliquaries – are kept, partly paid for by Charles V of France (repaired in the 18C). In the 19C, Pius IX had the high altar faced in marble. During this work it became apparent that the wooden altar contained some much older planks, one of which very probably belonged to the altar at which Pope Sylvester I officiated (314–35).

The 9C confessio **(8)** contains the tomb of Martin V, the first pope to reign after the Great Schism. His tomb is the work of Donatello's brother.

Apse – The apse of Constantine's Basilica was rebuilt in the 5C and again in the 13C, but was not substantially altered until the 19C, when Leo XIII moved it back in order to extend the chancel. The ogival windows and particularly the **mosaic** in the top of the apse were retained. This mosaic had already been restored in the 13C by **Jacopo Torriti**, who took several features from the original model: the representation of the Cross, celestial Jerusalem with the palm and the phoenix, symbols of the Resurrection *(beneath the cross)* and the Jordan full of fishes, birds and boats, which forms the base of his composition. To these he added the Virgin and Nicholas IV kneeling, St Peter and St Paul *(left)*, St Andrew and the two St Johns, the Baptist and the Evangelist *(right)*. He also included two smaller figures: St Francis of Assisi *(left)* – Torriti was a Franciscan monk – and St Anthony of Padua *(right)*. The first representation of Christ in the apse dates from the 4C. Not long before, paganism was still the state religion, so when Pope Sylvester consecrated the basilica, the appearance of such an image was considered miraculous by the faithful. In his desire to perpetuate the "miracle", Jacopo Torriti managed to transfer the ancient figure to his own composition. During the 19C alterations this original figure was broken and replaced by a copy.

Museo della Basilica – *Right of the chancel.* ©*Open daily 10am–5:30pm.* ⊜€10 ℘06 69 88 64 09. The Basilica Museum displays the treasures of the basilica – gold chalices and reliquaries. The **station cross** *(Cabinet V)* is in silver gilt (12C).

Chiostro★ – ©*Open daily 9am–6pm.* ⊜€2. These charming 13C cloisters are one of the most remarkable by the Vassalletti (father and son). Their art, like that of the Cosmati, consisted of cutting and assembling fragments of antique marble. The twisted columns with varied capitals, the mosaic frieze and the delicate carving of the cornice make this a poetic place to linger.

▷ Leave the basilica by the right transept.

In the **porch** is a bronze statue of Henri IV of France **(9)** by Nicolas Cordier (1567–1612) in recognition of the king's gift to the Lateran Chapter of the Abbey of Clairac in Agsenais. The **façade of the north transept** is so majestic it could be the main front: by Domenico Fontana in 1586.

BATTISTERO★

Entrance in Piazza S. Giovanni in Laterano ©*Open daily 7am–12:30pm, 4pm–7pm* ℘06 69 88 64 52.

The **baptistery** was built by Constantine. In the 4C, every Christian was baptised there; nowadays it is used for the ceremonies of Holy Saturday. It was rebuilt in the 5C by Sixtus III, who set up the eight porphyry columns in the centre. The upper colonnade and the lantern are 16C additions. Various popes sponsored the adjoining chapels and Urban VIII added the 17C frescoes.

Chapels

Entrance in Piazza S. Giovanni in Laterano. Ask the keeper to open the doors.

The **chapels of St John the Baptist (10)** and **St John the Evangelist (11)** were built by Pope Hilary (461–68). The chapel of St John the Baptist has kept its original door, which is made of an alloy of silver, bronze and gold and is very heavy. The Evangelist chapel was given a new bronze door in the 12C. The ceiling is covered with a beautiful 5C mosaic (delicate colours on a gold ground).

Cappella di Santa Rufina e di Santa Secunda (12)

In the 12C, the original narthex, which was the entrance to the baptistery, was converted into a chapel. The Chapel of St Rufina and St Secunda is rectangular in shape with an apse at either end, one of which is decorated with a fine 5C mosaic.

Cappella di San Venanzio (13)

Built in the 7C by John IV, the Chapel of St Venantius is decorated with mosaics in the Byzantine style (slim, slightly stiff figures) and has a fine cedar ceiling.

PIAZZA DI SAN GIOVANNI IN LATERANO

In the piazza stands a fine **Egyptian obelisk** made of granite, the tallest in Rome. It dates from the 15C BC and was brought to Rome in the 4C by Constantinus II to adorn the Circus Maximus at the foot of the Palatine, where it was found in 1587. It was repaired and re-erected in its present position by Domenico Fontana, at Sixtus V's behest.

Palazzo Lateranense

Piazza San Giovanni in Laterano 6.

When Gregory XI returned to Rome in 1377 after the Avignon era, the palace had been gutted by fire. He installed his household in the Vatican.

The present building was constructed in 1586 by **Domenico Fontana**, during the reign of Sixtus V. The **Lateran Treaty** *(©See VATICANO–SAN PIETRO)* was signed here. The palace is now the headquarters of the Diocese of Rome (Vicariate), with the pope at its head, in his capacity as Bishop of Rome, and of the Vatican Historical Museum.

Traces of the medieval palace

In the Middle Ages, the papal palace extended from its present site as far as Via Domenico Fontana. Two features from this building, the banquet hall of Leo III and the Sacred Steps, have been reconstructed on the east side of the square.

Triclinium di Leo III

This pope (795–816) built two rooms in the palace. All that remains of the triclinium (dining room) is an apse decorated with a mosaic, repaired in the 18C. It celebrates the alliance of Leo III with Charlemagne: the emperor reinstated the pope on his throne and the pope crowned the emperor in St Peter's in the Vatican.

Santuario della Scala Santa

⏰Open 6am–2pm and 3pm–7pm; Sun and hols 7am-2pm and 3pm–7pm; Sancta Sanctorum open Mon–Sat 9:30am–12:40pm and 3pm–5:10pm. ⊚€3.50. Guided visits available (30min). ☏06 77 26 641.

Sixtus V (1585–90) demolished what remained of the medieval palace with two exceptions: the stairs, which according to tradition came from Pontius Pilate's palace and had been used by Christ, and the private chapel of the popes. This was relocated to a building specially designed by Domenico Fontana to incorporate the famous steps, climbed by the faithful on their knees. An alterante on the other side permits foot-traffic.

At the top is the popes' chapel, known as the **Holy of Holies★★** (Sancta Sanctorum), by analogy with the temple in Jerusalem, because of its precious relics. The interior is decorated with fine Cosmati work. The paintings in the chapel, damaged by rainwater over the centuries, were carefully restored in 1995. Now it's possible to see the 11C frescoes, considered by medieval experts to be one of the most important discoveries of the 20C. Above the altar is the famous icon of Christ called the Acheiropoeton, which means it was not made by human hand. Begun by St Luke, it was completed by an angel, then arrived in Rome miraculously from Constantinople in the 8C. The ancient bronze door – which gives access to the popes' chapel – can be seen from St Lawrence's Chapel (right).

☙WALKING TOUR

PORTA MAGGIORE DISTRICT

▷ Piazza S. Croce in Gerusalemme.

In antiquity, the district to the east of the Esquiline was a suburb of Rome, well wooded and covered with tombs that stretched for miles along the Praenestina Way and the Labicana Way (now Via Casilina). From Augustus' reign (31 BC to AD 14) onwards, the cemeteries gradually gave way to huge gardens laid out by rich Romans. Under the empire, these sumptuous properties, designed by skilful landscape gardeners, with temples and avenues lined with works of art, were absorbed into the imperial estates either by confiscation or by legacy (members of the patrician class often willed their property to the emperor). This practice restricted development to the east and aggravated the problem of lack of space in the city centre, which was becoming overcrowded with huge, prestigious buildings. In the 3C, the district was enclosed by the **Aurelian Wall** (Mura Aureliane). Untouched by the popes, it was not developed until the 19C, when Rome had become the capital of Italy.

Santa Croce in Gerusalemme★

Piazza di Santa Croce in Gerusalemme 12. ⏰Open Mon–Sat 7am–12:45pm and 3:30pm–7:30pm, Sun and public hols 7:30am–12:45 and 3:30–7:30pm. The garden is not open to visitors. ☏06 70 61 30 53. www.santacroceroma.it.

In this church, originally known simply as "Jerusalem", the legend of the Holy Cross is closely linked with history. Here stood the **Sessorium** where Constantine's mother, Helen, lived; built in the 3C, it remained an imperial palace until the 6C. In the 4C, Helen went on a pilgrimage to Jerusalem, as was customary. She returned in 329 bearing a fragment of the True Cross, which she kept in the palace. She died later that year. A legend developed that she had found the True Cross. The cult of the Holy Cross was not introduced to Rome until the 7C.

History of the church – In memory of his mother, the Emperor Constantine (or perhaps his sons) converted part of the Sessorian Palace into a church to house the precious relic. It consisted of one large chamber with an apse, where the services were held, and a smaller room (the present St Helen's Chapel), which housed the relic. In the 12C, Pope Lucius II (1144–45) divided the larger chamber into three and built a campanile without altering the outside walls. He raised the level of the church, but not the chapel, perhaps because its floor was composed of soil brought back from Calvary. The church acquired its present appearance in the 18C.

Visit

The 12C campanile is flanked by a lively façade and oval vestibule in the 18C style, consistent with the principles dear to Borromini. The nave vault was refashioned in the 18C; the impressive baldaquin over the altar is of the same period. The apse has conserved the mark of the Renaissance; it is decorated with an attractive fresco by Antoniazzo Romano (late 15C), illustrating the legend of the *Discovery of the Cross by St Helen*.

Cappella di Sant'Elena (Chapel of St Helen) – *Access by one of the sets of steps beside the chancel.* The chapel is decorated with beautiful **mosaics★**, designed by Baldassarre Peruzzi and, perhaps, by Melozzo da Forlì. The statue above the altar is a Roman work originally representing Juno, but converted into St Helen.

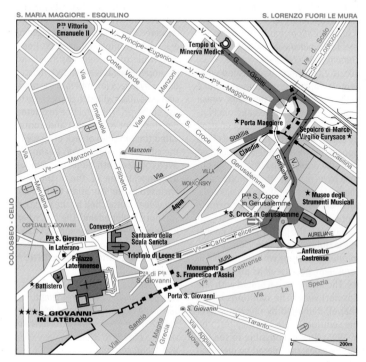

Santa Croce in Gerusalemme

Cappelle della Croce e delle Reliquie
(Chapel of the Holy Cross and Relics
Chapel) – *Access by steps to the right of
the left aisle.* The relics of the Passion
kept in the chapel of the Holy Cross
attract large numbers of pilgrims. In the
first chapel, they venerate the arm of
the cross of the robber crucified beside
Christ *(at the beginning of the flight of
steps opposite the entrance).* In the Relics Chapel, a glass case behind the altar
displays fragments of the True Cross; the
"heading" on the Cross (the inscription
it bore); two thorns from the Crown; St
Thomas' finger; some fragments from
the Flagellation stake, from the grotto
in Bethlehem and the Holy Sepulchre;
a nail from the Cross.

▷ On leaving the church, bear left
through the opening in the Aurelian
Wall.

Anfiteatro Castrense
*Piazza di Santa Croce in
Gerusalemme 3.* Open 1 and 3 Sats.
Booking required 06 39 96 77 00.
Its name comes from the Latin word
"*castrum*", which in the 4C meant an
imperial residence. This amphitheatre,
like the Sessorian Palace *(see above)*, was
probably part of the Imperial properties
in this district. The Aurelian Wall detours
to enclose it, suggesting great importance. Built entirely of red brick, this 3C

structure originally had three storeys, of
which only the first is well preserved.

▷ Take Via Eleniana to Porta Maggiore.

Porta Maggiore★
The gate was built in the 1C AD to
carry the Claudian Aqueduct across
the Praenestina Way and the Labicana
Way where it entered the city. The use of
huge, roughly hewn blocks of travertine
(even for the supports) is an innovation
typical of the Claudian era.
In the 3C, the gate was incorporated
into the Aurelian Wall. When Honorius
(395–423) restored the fortifications,
a bastion was added on the outside;
its demolition in the 19C revealed the
tomb of Marcus Vergilius Eurysaces.

Sepolcro di Marco Virgilio
Eurysace★
Marcus Vergilius Eurysaces was a baker
who lived in Rome at the end of the
Republic. As supplier to the army, he
probably grew rich during the civil wars.
His enormous travertine tomb (dating
from c. 30 BC), commemorates this
trade.
The cylindrical motifs, some vertical and
some horizontal, recall the receptacles
that held flour. The low-relief frieze
around the top illustrates the different
steps in bread-making.

©alessandro0770/iStockphoto.com

Porta Maggiore

▶ Go west along Via Statilia.

On the left among the trees are the elegant arches of the Claudian Aqueduct.

Aqua Claudia

Aqueducts are without doubt the most remarkable public works in Roman architecture. This one, begun by Caligula in AD 38 and completed by Claudius in AD 52, is the most impressive. Starting in the mountains near Subiaco, it reached Rome after 68km/42mi, of which 15km/9mi were above ground. From Porta Maggiore, Nero (AD 54–68) built a branch channel, traces of which remain in the gardens of Villa Wolkonsky, in Piazza della Navicella and in the Arch of Dolabella, at the eastern end of Via di San Paolo della Croce. This aqueduct was extended by Domitian as far as the Palatine, to supply his palace.

▶ Turn left into Via G. Giolitti.

Tempio di Minerva Medica

Via Giovanni Giolitti 100. ⚒ *Closed to public.*
The circular temple (4C) was originally covered by a dome and was probably a *nymphaeum* (nymphs garden).

ADDITIONAL SIGHT

👥 Museo Nazionale degli Strumenti Musicali★

Piazza Santa Croce in Gerusalemme 9/a. ⏱*Open Tue–Sun 9am–7pm.* ⏱*Closed 1 Jan, 1 May and 25 Dec.* ⊚€5. Free entrance 1st Sun of the month. ℘06 70 14 796. www.museostrumentimusicali. beniculturali.it.

The charming **Museum of Musical Instruments** sweeps from antiquity to the 19C. Antique whistles, horns and handbells are succeeded by exotic instruments, such as inlaid mandolins, tambourines and ocarinas.

The sumptuous exhibits include the 17C **Barberini harp**, decorated with magnificent gilt carvings that belonged to the prestigious family, and a rare example of a vertical harpsichord (17C) with a pretty painted lid.

ADDRESSES

TAKING A BREAK

Il Sorì – *Via dei Volsci 51. San Lorenzo.* ⏱*Open Mon–Sat 6pm–2am.* ℘393 43 18 681 (mobile). www.ilsori.it. A real wine and food shop where you can taste selected wines (not just Italian) and chat directly with winemakers in one of the many events organised here.

Palazzo del Freddo Fassi – *Via Principe Eugenio 65.* ⏱*Open Mon–Thu 12am–midnight, Fri-Sat 12–half past midnight, Sun 10am- midnight.* ℘06 44 64 740. www.gelateriafassi.com. Closed Mon. Sitting right by the tram tracks, this 1880 ice shop, transformed later to a *gelateria*, is considered to be one of the best in Rome. It has kept its old-fashioned ambience and maintained its quality.

🍴 EAT

🍴 Santa Maria Maggiore is a better area to find a place to eat.

Ristorante Crab – *Via Capo d'Africa 2.* ℘06 7720 3636. This classic resturant specialises in fresh fish dishes, prawn, clams and some of the most original specialty.

San Lorenzo Fuori le Mura★

The major point of interest is the Basilica of San Lorenzo Fuori le Mura, situated in the heart of the university district. Don't expect ivory towers here, but the area remains lively with its crowds of students, the consstant noise of mopeds and trams, and many specialised bookshops and other small outlets. This vibrant atmosphere is intensified since some of the departments have moved off-campus and are now dotted around the quarter.

SAN LORENZO FUORI LE MURA★★

Piazzale del Verano 3. ○*Open daily 7am–12pm and 4pm–7pm (winter 7:30am–12:30pm and 3:30pm–7:30pm).* ℘*06 49 15 11.*

The basilica is also known as San Lorenzo al Verano since it is built on land that belonged to a certain Lucius Verus in antiquity.

To the north ran the Via Tiburtina, lined with pagan tombs and then with Christian catacombs. One contains the grave of St Lawrence, highly venerated in the Middle Ages, who was martyred in 258 under the Emperor Valerian, soon after Pope Sixtus II was put to death.

According to legend, Lawrence was roasted on a grill.

As pilgrims to the tomb of St Lawrence became more and more numerous, the Emperor Constantine had a sanctuary built (330). By the 6C, it was in such a poor state of repair that Pope **Pelagius II** (579–90) had it redone.

Enlarged in the 8C, it underwent major alterations in the 13C under Pope **Honorius III** (1216–27). The apse of Pelagius's church was demolished, the church was extended westwards and its orientation reversed. The original nave was raised and became the chancel.

Later Baroque additions were removed by Pius IX in 1855; he also revealed the original nave but retained Honorius'

> 🚲 **Michelin Map:** 38 K 17–18.
> ▷ **Location:** This district lies to the east of the city and is bordered by the inner bypass (the *tangenziale*) that leads to San Giovanni. From here, the suburbs of Rome stretch as far as the eye can see.
> ○ **Timing:** Allow 1 hr.
> 🚲 **Also See:** *CATACOMBE DI PRISCILLA; PORTA PIA– TERMINI; SAN GIOVANNI IN LATERANO; Santa Maria Maggiore– Monti–Esquilino*

GETTING THERE

BY METRO and BUS: Line B: Policlinico (500m/550yd from the university campus). Bus: C3, 71, 163, 492 and 545.

chancel. On 19 July 1943, a bomb fell on the church; the roof, the upper part of the walls and the porch were demolished. Repair work aimed for the church's 13C appearance.

Façade

The Romanesque bell tower dates to the 12C. The elegant porch, which dates to the time of Honorius III, was reconstructed after bomb damage in 1943. Above the architrave is a beautiful mosaic frieze in vivid colours. Higher still is a cornice delicately carved with flowers, fruit and acanthus leaves punctuated with lion-head gargoyles. This fine example of medieval decorative sculpture is attributed to the Vassalletto (c 1220), a family who worked in marble with the Cosmati from the early 12C.

Under the portico there is a rare example of a sarcophagus **(1)** with a sloping canopy. The work is probably 11C. Next to it is a 4C sarcophagus **(2)** with the likeness of the occupant in a medallion. The **"grape harvest" sarcophagus★** *(3, left)* is remarkable. It was carved in the 5C or 6C; the clear-cut relief and the

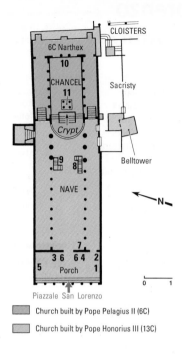

CLOISTERS

6C Narthex

10

CHANCEL
11

Sacristy

Crypt

Belltower

9

8

NAVE

N

7

3 6   6 4   2

5   1

Porch

Piazzale San Lorenzo

Church built by Pope Pelagius II (6C)

Church built by Pope Honorius III (13C)

0   1

large smooth surfaces are characteristic of the Middle Ages. Two modern works honour Pope Pius XII **(4)** and Alcide de Gasperi **(5)**, President of the Council from 1945–1953, in recognition of their assistance in the work of restoration following the bomb damage. The two lions **(6)** on either side of the main door are Romanesque.

Interior

The two distinct parts of the church are immediately apparent, divided by the triumphal arch and built on two different axes: one by Honorius III (13C) and the other by Pelagius II (6C).

Church built by Honorius III

The funerary monument (**7** – *right of entrance)* of Guglielmo Fischi (1256), nephew of Pope Innocent IV, was reconstructed in 1943. Beneath a small temple resembling a 13C baldaquin is a 3C sarcophagus decorated with a marriage scene.Honorius' church comprises a nave and two aisles separated by 22

antique granite columns of varying diameters. The Ionic capitals, like those in the porch, date from the Middle Ages and are attributed to the Vassalletto. They show the success that the medieval marble workers had in adapting their technique to ancient columns.

The lighting of the nave has hardly changed since the 13C. After 1943 the ceiling was rebuilt exactly as it had been in the 19C when Vespignani, who was working for Pius IX, had inserted a wooden coffered ceiling beneath the open roof frame.

The floor, damaged by the bomb, is bright with 13C **Cosmati** work.

The two **ambones★** are not identical. They are Cosmati work: a combination of white marble, porphyry and serpentine, encrusted with multicoloured insets gleaming with touches of gold.

Church built by Pelagius II

The central section containing the high altar has been raised and is approached by two sets of steps. Its original orientation with the apse projecting west of the present chancel arch was reversed so that it could serve as the chancel of Honorius' church, as it does today. Pelagius' church comprised a nave and two aisles. From the raised nave only the tops of the Ancient fluted columns are visible, supporting a magnificent sculpted architrave composed of disparate fragments that once belonged to a frieze or a door lintel.

Over the aisles are galleries (matrones) for the women; the arcades rest on fine slim columns, their capitals decorated with leaves (6C).

The bishop's **throne**★ at the east end of the chancel is by the Cosmati (1254). The whiteness of the marble contrasts with the vivid colours and the gold inlays to create a fine effect.

In the **crypt** are the remains of St Lawrence, St Stephen and St Justin.

Cloisters

Entrance through the sacristy in the south aisle or from the outside on the right of the bell-tower.

The 12C cloisters with their archaic charm formed part of the fortified convent, like a citadel in the Middle Ages. St Lawrence's Basilica, outside Rome's walls, was easy prey for thieves and looters. The cloister walk contains inscriptions from neighbouring catacombs.

CITTÀ UNIVERSITARIA

In 1935, the University of Rome was transferred from laSapienza at Sant' Ivo to the new campus near the Municipal Clinic (Policlinico Umberto I) built in 1890. The design was awarded to **Marcello Piacentini**, who was a major exponent of large-scale building projects (*See EUR*). He applied the rules so dear to the "Twenties", seen in the Rectorate and entrance area. The overall impression is one of balance and shows no grandeur for its own sake. The final effect was the work of various architects. One of the most important of the Rationalists was Giuseppe Pagano, whose style can clearly be seen in the Institute of Physics. The architects who collaborated on the project were: Pietro Aschieri –

Institute of Chemistry; Giò Ponti – Mathematics; Giovanni Michelucci – Mineralogy and Physiology; Giuseppe Capponi – Botany.

ADDRESSES

Being near the university, this area has many restaurants, cafés and bars for patrons to choose.

TAKING A BREAK

Panificio Faloci – *Via dei Reti 59.* ℘*06 49 57 717.* This bakery attracts locals, with its well-priced *pizza bianca* and biscuits.

Said Antica Fabbrica del Cioccolato – *Via Tiburtina 135.* ℘*06 44 69 204. www.said.it* This 1923 chocolate factory in San Lorenzo has been converted to a cosy bar. Here, chocolate is served in various forms, as well as drinks and light fare. Popular with locals and students.

EAT

La Mucca Bischera – *Via Degli Equi 56.* ℘*06 44 69 349. Lunch Sat–Sun only. Booking recommended.* This atmospheric and popular pizzeria has a lovely summer terrace and a large rustic interior. The homemade soups are tasty.

Pommidoro – *Piazza dei Sanniti 44.* ℘*06 44 52 692. Booking recommended.* Run by the same family since 1892, this classic Roman trattoria specialises in antipasti, classic home-style *cucina*, fish and grilled meats. Popular with locals, and a favourite hangout for politicians, journalists, film-makers and artists. Small terrace.

Pastificio San Lorenzo – *Via Tiburtina 196.* ℘*06 97 27 35 19. www.pastificiocerere.it.* This gourmet restaurant is concealed in the Pastificio Cerere, a former factory converted into a contemporary art centre. An elegant way to combine modernity and tradition. One of the many noteworthy dishes is amatriciana with smoked jowl bacon.

BARS

Locanda Atlantide – *Via dei Lucani 22b.* ℘*06 96 04 58 75. www.locandatlantide.com.* Daily program of musical and theatrical events in one of the theaters best known to the public and professionals alike.

San Paolo Fuori le Mura★★

This area contains two sites outside the Aurelian Wall, which are linked by the history of St Paul: the basilica of St Paul Outside the Walls, built over the saint's tomb, and the Demesne of Tre Fontane, a few kilometres away, the site of his martyrdom. The Abbazia delle Tre Fontane is situated on Via Laurentina farther to the south.

A BIT OF HISTORY

Saint Paul – Paul was a Jew called Saul, born early in the 1C AD at Tarsus in Cilicia in Asia Minor (southeast Turkey). At first he persecuted Christ's disciples; then on his way from Jerusalem to Damascus, he was blinded by a light, fell from his horse and heard Jesus' voice saying, "Saul, Saul, why persecutest thou me?" This event precipitated his conversion: he changed his name from Saul to Paul and became the chief agent in preaching Christianity to the gentiles. Accused by the Jewish community of Caesarea in Palestine, he demanded to be brought before the Emperor Nero (Paul was a Roman citizen). He set out in AD 60. Two years later, the imperial court acquitted him.

- **Michelin Map:** 38 W 11, T 5.
- **Location:** This region lies to the south of the capital on Via Ostiense, which joins with the Via del Mare to link Rome to Ostia.
- **Timing:** Allow 1hr for San Paolo Fuori le Mura and 45min for the Abbazia delle Tre Fontane, excluding travelling time.
- **Also See:** *PORTA PIA–TERMINI; S. GIOVANNI IN LATERANO; SAN LORENZO FUORI LE MURA.*

GETTING THERE

BY METRO AND BUS: Line B: Basilica S. Paolo (Metro station 300m/330yd from the basilica) and Laurentina (1.5km/1mi from the Abbazia delle Tre Fontane). Bus: 23 and 271.

The date of Paul's martyrdom is not known for certain. Like Peter, he may have been a victim of the persecution of the Christians organised by Nero after the terrible fire in AD 64, which destroyed the greater part of Rome. As a citizen, St Paul was sentenced to beheading.

Interior of Basilica di San Paolo Fuori le Mura

© silviacrisman/iStockphoto.com

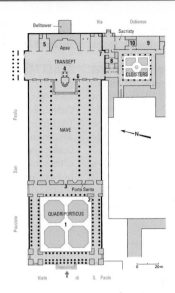

BASILICA DI SAN PAOLO FUORI LE MURA★★

Piazzale di San Paolo 1. ⏲*Open daily 7am–6:30pm. Cloisters and Picture Gallery open 9am–6pm. Cloisters* ⊗€4. ☎*06 69 88 08 00. www.basilicasanpaolo.org.*

St Paul Outside the Walls is one of the major basilicas in Rome. Its historical significance attracts visitors and pilgrims from all over the world. The saint's body was buried beside the Via Ostiensis, which was lined with tombs, as were all the major roads leading out of Rome. A small shrine *(memoria)* was erected over his grave. In the 4C, the Emperor Constantine built a basilica over the tomb, as he had done for St Peter's.

This first basilica was consecrated by Pope Sylvester I in 324. It was smaller than St Peter's Basilica and faced the Via Ostiensis. By 386, it had become such a popular place of pilgrimage that three Emperors – Valentinian II, Theodosius I and his son Arcadius – decided to enlarge the building. It could not be extended across the road (because of the rising ground), and since the Apostle's tomb could not be moved, the orientation was reversed, with the apse on the *Via Ostiensis* and the façade facing the Tiber.

The new structure was magnificent; it was larger than the contemporary basilica of St Peter in the Vatican. The huge project was not completed until 395, in the reign of the Emperor Honorius. For the next 14 centuries, it was maintained with great care and attention.

When the building was sacked by the Lombards in the 8C and by the Saracens in the 9C, the damage was immediately repaired. John VIII (872–82) walled the basilica and the community around it; this came to be known as "Johannipolis", after the Pope.

The greatest artists were employed to embellish the basilica: from Pietro Cavallini and Arnolfo di Cambio to Carlo Maderno.

Rebuilt after a 19C fire, St Paul's Basilica is now adorned with gleaming marble and vivid colours.

Interior★★ – No visitor can fail to be impressed by the multitude of columns – 80 granite monoliths that divide the nave and four aisles.

The gold and white coffered ceiling bears the arms of Pope Pius IX (1846–78), who consecrated the new basilica.

The Ciborium★★★ is a Gothic work by **Arnolfo di Cambio** (1285). Detail and proportion are delicately blended: the many decorative figures are executed with great skill, from the pairs of angels

189

supporting the pierced rose-window on each of the four pediments to the animals on the vault.

To the left of the apse is the **Chapel of the Holy Sacrament★**, the work of Carlo Maderno (1629), which contains a 14C wooden crucifix, a statue of St Bridget kneeling by Stefano Maderno (c. 1576–1636) and a wooden statue of St Paul dating from the 14C.

The Paschal **candlestick★★** by Nicolà di Angelo and Pietro Vassalletto (12C) is a remarkable piece of Romanesque art. The base is decorated with monsters and on the shaft are decorative motifs, scenes from the life of Jesus (note the expressions of the squat figures), tendrils and more monsters supporting the candle socket.

Cloisters★★ – These probably formed part of the work done by a member of the Vassalletto family (13C) who, like the Cosmati, was skilled in marble encrustation work. The north gallery (backing onto the church) is particularly fine. The great variety among the columns, their marble encrustation picked out in gold and the exquisite workmanship of the mosaic frieze above the arcades make the cloisters a charming composition.

ADDITIONAL SIGHTS
ABBAZIA DELLE TRE FONTANE★ (THREE FOUNTAINS ABBEY)

▶ From Via Laurentina a drive leads to Three Fountains Abbey, in Via Acque Salvie 1.

The place known in antiquity as *Ad Aquas Salvias* is where St Paul was beheaded. Legend has added an epilogue: the apostle's head bounced three times and three fountains sprouted from the ground.

Pilgrims have been coming here since the Middle Ages. Many oratories were built; one of them, still decorated with traces of 9C painting, is now the entrance gateway. Surrounded by green hillsides and the scent of eucalyptus trees is a group of buildings: a Trappist monastery, a convent of the Little Sisters of Jesus and three churches.

Santa Maria Scala Coeli
🕐*Open daily 8am–1pm and 3pm–6pm.*

Cistercian monks settled here in 1140. The history of the church is connected with one of St Bernard's ecstatic visions. During mass in the crypt, he had a vision of the souls in purgatory ascending into heaven, released by his intercession. The present church (restored 1925), was built in 1583 by **Giacomo della Porta** to an octagonal plan beneath a dome. Behind the altar in the crypt is a room which is supposed to be where St Paul waited before his execution.

Santi Vincenzo e Anastasio alle T2wre Fontane
🕐*Open daily 6:30am–12:30pm and 3pm–8:45pm.*

The church, dedicated to **St Vincent** and **St Anastasius**, is the abbey church of the Trappist monks who have occupied the neighbouring monastery since 1868. The church's origins date to the 7C, when Pope Honorius I (625–38) built a convent to house some Oriental monks. Rebuilt in the 13C, the church is austere in appearance and still retains traces of paintings of the apostles by some of Raphael's pupils.

San Paolo al Martirio
🕐*Open daily 8:30am–12:30pm and 3pm–7pm.*

The church of **St Paul at the Three Fountains**, dedicated to St Paul the Apostle, was designed in the 16C by Giacomo della Porta to replace two chapels.

Here, according to legend, three fountains had spouted miraculously from the earth on the exact spots where the saint's severed head bounced (although somewhat inconveniently, the springs themselves were actually known about in pre-Christian times, when they were called the Aquae Salviae).

However, a small building commemorating St Paul's martyrdom has stood here since as early as the 5C.

The statues of St Peter and St Paul on the façade are by Nicolas Cordier. The ancient mosaics in the nave come from Ostia. The sites of the three fountains are marked by three shrines with symbolic, monumental covers, each set at different levels.

ADDRESSES

TAKING A BREAK

Doppiozeroo – *Via Ostiense 68.* ℘*06 57 30 19 61. www.doppiozeroo.it.* Sleek and chic; specially for morning coffee and pastries as well as the lunch buffet. Evenings get busy, especially at the bar.

Cafe du Parc – *Viale della Piramide Cestia 67.* ℘*06 57 43 363.* Set in the small park to the left of Porta San Paolo, this small café is known for its speciality called *cremolatte,* a rich milkshake in a variety of flavours. Or, if you are not that hungry, just opt for a straight-up scoop of its rainbow selection of ice cream.

Santa Maria Maggiore–Monti–Esquilino★★★

Augustus transformed this sprawling slum into a desirable district, where the mad emperor Nero later built part of his Golden House (Domus Aurea). Now this bustling quarter – with its myriad shops, offices and crowded streets – has a distinct ethnic flavour.

The piazza's market sells mainly low-end clothes and shoes. Oriental shops and supermarkets line the streets around the square. Anchored by the major basilica of Santa Maria Maggiore, this area warrants a deeper exploration than most tourists (fleeing Termini train station crowds and disarray) manage.

A BIT OF HISTORY

Esquiline Hill has been inhabited since the 8C BC. The uneven plateau has three peaks, which the Romans named the **Oppius**, now covered by the *Parco Oppio,* the **Fagutalis**, which overlooks the Imperial Fora, and the **Cispius**, now crowned by *Santa Maria Maggiore.* Long a burial ground for impoverished people, the Esquiline was one of the most sinister parts of Rome. Augustus gave it a new face. He divided the city into 14 districts, one of which was the

- ♿ **Michelin Map:** 38 L 14, M 14–16.
- ▶ **Location:** The neighbourhood is largely concentrated around Piazza Vittorio, which extends from the northern slopes of the Esquiline Hill (the Domus Aurea once stood on the southern side, overlooking the Colosseum) and Termini Railway Station. The Via Cavour separates it from the Viminal Hill.
- 👁 **Don't Miss:** The mosaics in Santa Maria Maggiore and the chapel of San Zenone in Santa Prassede.
- 👪 **Kids:** The Magic Gate in Piazza Vittorio Emanuele II.
- ♿ **Also See:** *COLOSSEO–CELIO; FORI IMPERIALI; PORTA PIA; SAN GIOVANNI IN LATERANO; SAN LORENZO*

GETTING THERE

BY METRO AND BUS: Line A: Vittorio Emanuele.

Esquiline; he arranged for part of it to be given to his friend Maecenas, who built a magnificent villa surrounded by gardens. In a classic example of gentrification, the district came to be coveted by the emperors, and it was confiscated into the imperial domain. After a fire in AD 64 cleared the ground, Nero built his Golden House partly on the Oppius.

PIAZZA DI SANTA MARIA MAGGIORE

The fluted column at the centre is the sole survivor of the eight columns that graced the Basilica of Maxentius in the Forum. Brought here in 1614 by Pope Paul V, it was erected by Carlo Maderno and crowned with the Virgin.

SANTA MARIA MAGGIORE★★★

Piazza di Santa Maria Maggiore.
🕐 *Open daily 7am–6:45pm.*
✆ *06 69 88 68 00.*
This Basilica is one of the four Roman basilicas that bear the title "major" (the others are St John Lateran, St Paul Outside the Walls and St Peter's in the Vatican) and enjoys the privilege of extraterritoriality conferred by the Lateran Treaty in 1929.

St Mary Major was built by Sixtus III (432–40) in honour of Mary a year after the Council of Ephesus, at which Nestorius, the Patriarch of Constantinople, had claimed that Mary was not the Mother of God.

Subsequent popes have left their mark; in their desire to contribute to the glory of the Virgin, they made numerous alterations. The campanile, the highest in Rome, was added in 1377 by Gregory XI. In the 17C and 18C, the apse was remodelled. The main façade was given its present appearance in the 18C under Benedict XIV by Ferdinando Fuga (1743–50).

Façade

The porch and loggia are sandwiched between two identical wings, although more than a century elapsed between the construction of the one on the right (1605) and the one on the left (1721–43). Like the majority of architects in the first half of the 18C, **Ferdinando Fuga** had a taste for classical forms, but also adopted certain elements from the Baroque art of Borromini. The façade is enlivened by sculptures, the broken lines of the pediments and the interplay of the openings in the porch and the arcade of the loggia.

Santa Maria Maggiore

© Leonid Andronov/iStockphoto.com

Central nave, Santa Maria Maggiore

©Judy Edelhoff/Michelin

In the porch stands a statue of Philip IV of Spain **(1)**, a benefactor of the basilica; it is by a pupil of Algardi (1692). The loggia from which the Pope used to give his blessing *Urbi et Orbi* was added to the original façade. It still retains its early 14C mosaic decoration, restored in the 19C.

Loggia Mosaic★

Access by the steps on the left of the porch. The upper part – Christ, angels, the evangelistic symbols, the Virgin and the saints – is the work of **Filippo Rusuti** (late 13C), who took over from Pietro Cavallini.

Below are four scenes illustrating the **legend of the basilica★**, which was built here late in the 4C by Pope Liberius. The Virgin appeared in a dream to a Giovanni Patrizio, a rich man, and to Pope Liberius, inviting them to build a church in her honour; the site for the sanctuary was to be marked by a fall of snow on the morrow. When the pope and Patrizio consulted one another, they were astonished to find that, in spite of the time of year (5 August 356), there had been a snowfall on the Esquiline. The pope drew up a plan of the church; Patrizio financed the construction. The graceful lines, richly apparelled figures and fine, deep perspectives link these scenes with the Florentine style of Cimabue and Giotto.

👥 The basilica rains white rose petals onto the congregation each 5 August to celebrate the portentous snowstorm.

Interior★★★

The interior has also undergone many alterations: at the end of the 13C Nicholas IV (1288–92) extended the chancel and, in the middle of the 15C, Cardinal Guillaume d'Estouteville, archpriest of the basilica, covered the aisles with vaulting in keeping with Renaissance taste. Despite that, the interior, with its almost perfect proportions and two rows of Ionic columns, is a remarkable early Christian architecture; brilliant with colour, it is most spectacular on Sundays and feast days.

Mosaics★★★

Those in the nave, on the chancel arch and in the apse are beyond compare.

Nave – Dating from the 5C, they consist of a series of panels above the entablature. They are some of the oldest Christian mosaics in Rome, together with those in Santa Pudenziana, Santa Costanza and the Lateran Baptistry. This art redeveloped vivid narrative, after accepting the rigidity of the late empire. The scenes are taken from the Bible's Old Testament with Abraham, Jacob, Moses and Joshua in the leading roles. On the left-hand side of the nave, beginning at

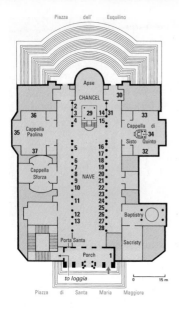

Next between two painted panels:

(11) The meeting of the two brothers, Jacob and Esau.

(12) Hamor and his son Shechem ask Jacob for the hand of his daughter Dinah, whose brothers are angry.

(13) Dinah's brothers insist that the men among Hamor's people be circumcised. Hamor and Shechem explain to their tribes.

The last three panels on this side are painted. On the right-hand side of the nave, starting at the chancel end, there is first a painted panel and then:

(14) Pharaoh's daughter receives Moses. He speaks with the Egyptian doctors.

(15) Moses marries Zipporah. God appears in the burning bush.

the chancel end, are incidents from the book of Genesis:

(2) Melchizedek comes to meet Abraham.

(3) Abraham's dream near the oak.

(4) The separation of Abraham and Lot.

Next comes the arch opened up in the 17C during the construction of the Pauline Chapel, which entailed the destruction of the mosaics at this point. Then:

(5) Isaac blesses Jacob. Esau returns from hunting.

THE NEXT PANEL IS A PAINTING.

(6) Rachel tells Laban of the arrival of Jacob, his nephew. Laban and Jacob embrace.

(7) Jacob agrees to serve Laban for seven years and to receive Rachel as his wife.

(8) Jacob reproaches Laban for giving him Leah, his elder daughter, in marriage. Jacob marries Rachel.

(9) Jacob asks Laban for the speckled and spotted sheep. The division of the flock.

(10) God tells Jacob to leave. Jacob announces his departure to the women.

Then comes the arch opened up during the construction of Sixtus V's Chapel, which takes the place of the mosaics (1741–50).

(16) The passage of the Red Sea.

(17) Moses and the people of Israel. The miracle of quails.

(18) The salt sea of Mara. The people of Israel reproach Moses who, after praying to God, touches the water with a rod sent by God and makes it fresh. The meeting of Moses and Amalek.

(19) The battle against the people of Amalek, and Moses praying.

(20) The return of the chiefs of the tribes who had gone to explore the Promised Land. The stoning of Moses, Joshua and Caleb.

(21) The tablets of Law are handed down. The death of Moses. The transport of the Ark.

(22) The passage of the Jordan. Joshua sends spies to Jericho.

(23) The angel of God (the captain of the Lord's host) appears to Joshua. The harlot Rahab helps the spies to scale the walls of Jericho. The return of the spies.

(24) The besieging of Jericho. The procession of the Ark to the sound of trumpets.

(25) The taking of Ai. Joshua before God and among the soldiers.

(26) Joshua fights the Amorites. Hail of stones on Israel's enemies.

(27) The sun and moon stand still upon Gibeon.

(28) Joshua punishes the rebel kings. The last three panels are paintings.

Chancel Arch – The arch dates from the 5C and has the liveliness of the first Christian mosaics. It is divided into four horizontal bands. Probably later than the mosaics in the nave, it shows Byzantine influence:

♦ In the *Annunciation* scene *(top row left)*, where Mary is dressed like an Oriental empress;

♦ In the Epiphany scene *(second row left)*, presented as a sumptuous court reception, where the Child Jesus is sitting on a throne decorated with precious stones. Jerusalem and Bethlehem, with sheep representing the Apostles, can be seen in the two lower rows.

Apse – This dazzling composition comprises elements taken from a 5C mosaic, which was transformed at the end of the 13C by **Jacopo Torriti** when Nicolas IV rebuilt the apse.

All the figures are the work of Torriti, since the earlier mosaic consisted only of birds, foliage and scrolls. The main subject of the composition is the *Crowning of the Virgin*, surrounded by groups of angels and a procession of saints. Kneeling before them are Nicolas IV and Cardinal Colonna.

Baldaquin (29)

Designed by Fuga, it's supported on porphyry columns wreathed in fronds of bronze. Unfortunately, it hides some of the mosaic.

Beneath is the **Confessio**, where Pope Pius IX (1846–78) is resplendent in bronze gilt, marble and frescoes (19C). Fragments thought to belong to Jesus's crib rest in the silver urn.

Ceiling★

The coffers were decorated with the first gold to come from Peru, which was offered to Pope **Alexander VI** (1492–1503), a Borgia and a Spaniard, by Ferdinand and Isabella of Spain. The pope continued the work begun by Calixtus III (1455–58) in constructing this ceiling. The roses at the centre of the coffers are 1m/3.75ft in diameter. Vasari, a 16C art historian and author of *Lives of the Artists*, attributes this work to Giuliano da Sangallo (1445–1516).

Floor

The 12C Cosmati work was radically restored by Ferdinando Fuga in the 18C.

Right Aisle

The tomb of Cardinal Consalvo Rodriguez **(30)** (late 13C) is typically Gothic (a recumbent figure, flanked by angels beneath the Virgin). In the floor is the tombstone **(31)** of the family of Bernini.

Cappella di Sisto Quinto

The chapel is named after Sixtus V, who, during his five-year reign (1585–90), turned Rome into a huge building site with his restorations, conversions and new constructions. His favourite architect was **Domenico Fontana**, to whom he entrusted the design of this chapel. It is almost a church in itself. Designed on the Greek-cross plan beneath a dome painted with frescoes, it is resplendent with gilding, stucco and marble. In the right and left arms of the cross are the monumental tombs of Popes Sixtus V **(32)** and Pius V **(33)**, decorated with low-relief sculptures.

Beneath the high altar **(34)** in 1590 Domenico Fontana set up the Oratory of the Crib, which had held the relics of the grotto in Bethlehem since the 7C.

Baptistry

The baptistry is the work of the Baroque architect Flaminio Ponzio.

The beautiful porphyry font was decorated in the 19C by Giuseppe Valadier. The high relief of the *Assumption* on the altar is by Pietro Bernini, father of Gian Lorenzo.

Left aisle

It contains, in particular, two beautiful chapels.

Cappella Sforza (Sforza Chapel) – Its highly original architectural style is by Giacomo della Porta, probably from designs by Michelangelo.

Cappella Paolina (Pauline Chapel) – It is also called the **Borghese Chapel**, after the family name of Pope Paul V, who commissioned it in 1611 from Flaminio Ponzio. It is identical in plan to Sixtus V's Chapel but with even more sumptuous decoration. In 1612, Cigoli painted the dome without first subdividing it with ribs; he was the first to follow this course and the result was not perfect. When, some 10 years later, Lanfranco (who also worked on the Pauline Chapel), painted the dome of *Sant'Andrea della Valle* using the same process, he achieved a masterpiece. The main altar **(35)** is incomparably rich, like a jewel, set with jasper, lapis lazuli, agate and amethyst.

The 12C altarpiece is of a *Virgin and Child* in the Byzantine style. She is greatly venerated among the faithful and has even been attributed to St Luke.

Above is a sculpted panel by Stefano Maderno illustrating the legend of the tracing of the basilica's plan (*see above*). As in Sixtus V's Chapel, the right and left arms of the cross contain Papal tombs: Clement VIII **(36)** and Paul V **(37)**.

▷ Leave the church by the door at the end of the aisle to the right of the choir.

👣 WALKING TOUR

Piazza dell' Esquilino

From here there is a fine **view**★★of the apse of Santa Maria Maggiore. When the Pauline and Sistine Chapels were added beneath their domes, they looked like two separate buildings. Clement IX (1667–69) therefore commissioned Bernini to integrate them with the basilica by altering the apsidal end of the church. **Bernini** conceived a grandiose design, but the excessive cost prevented its execution. The following pope, Clement X, therefore gave the work to Carlo Rainaldi.

The **Egyptian obelisk** at the centre of the square comes from the Mausoleum of Augustus. Sixtus V ordered it to be moved and set up by Domenico Fontana, a specialist in such matters.

▷ Turn left into Via Urbana.

Santa Pudenziana al Viminale

Via Urbana 160.
🕐*Open Mon-Sat 8am–noon and 3pm–6pm.* 📞*06 48 14 622.*

The church, dedicated to St Pudens or the Roman virgin St Potentiana, is one of the oldest in Rome and is now very popular with the local Filippino community, who have their own chaplain here. Legend tells how Senator Pudens, who lived in a house on this site, welcomed Peter under his roof.

A bathhouse stood on the site in the 2C. Late in the 4C, a church (*Ecclesia Pudentiana*) was established in the baths. The word resembles the name of the senator's daughter. Pudentiana and her sister Praxedes, are shown with the martyrs, whose bodies they prepared for burial.

The façade was repaired in the 19C.

The bell-tower dates from the 12C, as does the elegant doorway, with its fluted columns and its sculpted frieze inset with five medallions. The interior shows the signs of many changes: in 1589 the dome was built and the chancel altered so that several figures in the fine 4C **mosaic**★ were lost. It is one of the oldest examples of a Christian mosaic in Rome.

Excavations– *Area may be closed if excavations are scheduled. For information about hours* 📞*06 48 14 622.* On display are the remains of Pudens' house, mosaics and the baths, as well as the Roman road built in the 3C.

▷ Return to Piazza di Santa Maria Maggiore and, beyond the church, bear right into Via Santa Prassede.

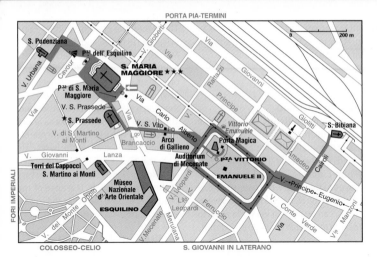

Santa Prassede★

🕐 *Open daily 7am–noon and 4pm–6:30pm (Sun open at 7:30am). Via di Santa Prassede, 9/a.*

The brick façade with the main doors leading to a small courtyard can be seen through the entrance arch *(often closed)*, which opens out into Via di San Martino ai Monti beneath a loggia supported on two columns. The church is an old *titulus* – a private house where Christian services were held in antiquity. The present building was put up by Paschal I in 822.

Chancel Mosaics★ – They date from the 9C and show the influence of both Byzantine traditionalism and Carolingian art. Colour is paramount and no longer used in half-tones. Against a background of sky quite lacking in depth, the figure of Christ is flanked by St Peter and St Paul presenting Praxedes and Pudentiana. The other two figures are St Zenon and Pope Paschal I offering his church (his square halo an indication that he was alive at the time). The two palms represent the Old and New Testaments and the phoenix on the one on the left symbolises the Resurrection.

Cappella di San Zenone★★

Right aisle.

St Zenon's Chapel was built between 817 and 824 by Pope Paschal I. The doorway is made up of various ele-ments taken from earlier buildings. Above this are several portrait medallions arranged in two arcs, one centred on Christ surrounded by the apostles and the other on the Virgin and Child surrounded by various saints. The interior is covered in mosaics with a gold background: on the central vault Christ, in strict Byzantine style, is supported by four angels; above the opening to the left of the altar, the Virgin is accompanied by two saints and the mother of Paschal I with a blue halo; the mosaic above the opening to the right of the

Mosaics, Santa Prassede

©sedmak/iStockphoto.com

altar was spoiled in the 13C when an oratory was built to house a fragment of the scourging column.

▶ Take Via S. Vito.

Arco di Gallieno

The **Arch of Gallienus** was erected in 262 to Emperor Gallienus (253–68), who was assassinated by Illyrian officers. It stands on the site of the Esquiline Gate *(Porta Esquilina)* in the Servian Wall. Traces of this wall, which was probably started in the 6C BC and repaired several times, can be seen in Via Carlo Alberto *(next to the church of St Vito e Modesto)*.

Piazza Vittorio Emanuele II

The square once hosted a daily market, now moved to the nearby *Via Turati*. Today the piazza is a park. It was laid out in 1870 by Gaetano Koch and other architects, with arcades at street level, as in Turin.

In the north corner of the square are the ruins of a huge 3C fountain, which was adorned with the "Trophies of Marius". The adjacent **Magic Gate** (Porta Magica) continues to excite speculation; the signs inscribed round the doorway (bricked up) have never been deciphered.

▶ Take Via Principe Eugenio, then turn left into Via Cairoli.

Santa Bibiana

Via Giovanni Giolitti 154. �🕐*Open daily 8am–7pm.*

The church was rebuilt in the 17C and was one of Bernini's first architectural projects. His **statue★** of St Bibiana (or Viviana) *(inside above the altar)* is also one of his early works; note her left hand gathering up the folds of the garment.

ADDITIONAL SIGHTS
Santi Silvestro e Martino ai Monti

Viale Monte Oppio 28.
🕐*Open Mon–Sat 7:30am–noon and 4pm–7pm (before holidays 6pm).*
℘06 47 84 701.

This venerable church, built by Pope Sylvester I in the 4C and dedicated to St Martin, was founded in the 5C next to a titulus existing in the 3C in the house of Equitius *(the underground remains can be visited: ask in the sacristy)*. In the 17C the church was completely transformed. The interior was divided into a nave and two aisles by two rows of ancient marble columns with 5C capitals (the bases date from the 17C). The aisles are frescoed with Roman landscapes and the story of the Prophet Elijah. The apse of the church dates from the 9C. In the square are two **Cappocci towers**.

Auditorium di Mecenate

🕐*Closed 1 Jan, 1 May, 25 Dec. ⬤€5. Pre-booking necessary at ℘06 06 08.*
The **Auditorium of Maecenas**, part of the luxurious Villa of Maecenas (early 1C) was discovered in 1874. The underground sstructure, with its drainage system and frescoes, was probably a nymphaeum originally, but Maecenas used it as an auditorium, where he entertained his learned friends.

ADDRESSES

BARS

Ai Tre Scalini – *Via Panisperna 251. ℘06 48 90 74 95.* Ai tre Scalini is one of the oldest bistro bars in the upcoming Monti district. An institution. You will recognize it by the building facade entirely covered by ivy.

TAKING A BREAK

Grezzo Raw Chocolate – *Via Urbana 130. ℘06 483443. grezzorawchocolate.com. Open 1pm- 11pm (midnight Fri and Sat).* The first «raw» bakery in the world: cooking temperatures never exceed 42 °C. Everything is organic, lactose-free and refined sugar-free. No one will be disappointed by its deliciousness!

Pasticceria Cipriani – *Via Carlo Botta 21/23. ℘06 7045 4229 - www. pasticceriacipriani.com - summer: daily except sun and bank holidays*. One of the most famous bakeries in Esquilino, specialized in cookies. You will also find delicious little donuts and fresh pastries.

Terme di Caracalla★★★

This pleasant district of abundant greenery is home to ancient ruins and small medieval churches. From the impressive FAO building, follow Viale delle Terme di Caracalla, parallel to the original Appia Antica, and step back in history at the Baths of Caracalla. Once frequented by senators and guttersnipes alike – up to 1 600 people at a time – the complex included soaking tubs, gyms, lecture halls and gardens, where ancients could strive for "healthy mind in a healthy body".

A BIT OF HISTORY

Four sets of urban baths had already been built – by Agrippa, by Nero on the Campus Martius, by Titus near the Golden House and by Trajan on the Aventine – when the Emperor **Antoninus Caracalla** began the largest baths Rome had ever seen (11ha/25 acres); only Diocletian's Baths would be more extensive. Work started on them in AD 212, and in AD 216 they were opened. They were finished by **Elagabalus** (AD 218–22) and **Alexander Severus** (AD

- **Michelin Map:** 38 R 13–14, S 14–15.
- **Location:** The area surrounding the Baths of Caracalla is inside the Aurelian Walls, to the south of the Colosseum. The district of San Giovanni lies to the northeast, beyond the Caelian Hill. Those visitors travelling here by Metro should refer to the Walking Tour.
- **Timing:** Allow 3hrs including the baths (1hr) for the Walking tour (Tour: 2.5km/1.5mi).
- **Also See:** *APPIA ANTICA; AVENTINO; COLOSSEO–CELIO.*

GETTING THERE

BY METRO: Line B: Circo Massimo.

222–35), the last two Emperors of the Severan dynasty.

The sober exterior concealed a contrastingly rich interior: floors paved with marble and mosaic, walls covered

Terme di Caracalla

© lamio/Fotolia.com

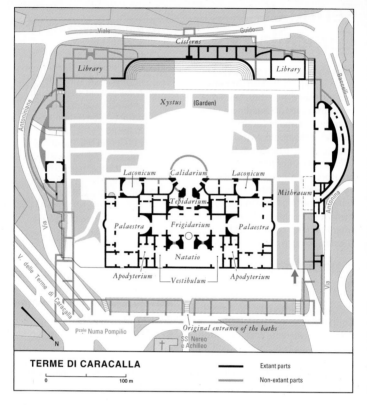

Viale — Guido

Cisterns

Library — Library

Antonniana

Xystus (Garden)

Baccelli

Antonina

Laconicum — Calidarium — Laconicum

Mithraeum

Tepidarium

V. delle Terme di Caracalla

Palaestra — Frigidarium — Palaestra

Natatio

Apodyterium — Vestibulum — Apodyterium

Original entrance of the baths

N

P.zale Numa Pompilio

SS Nereo e Achilleo

TERME DI CARACALLA

0 — 100 m

——— Extant parts

——— Non-extant parts

with mosaic and gilded stucco work; the white marble capitals and cornices contrasting with the multicoloured marble, porphyry and granite of the columns. The huge building, with its massive walls and bold vaulting (30m/98ft high), was much admired; it offered facilities for 1 600 bathers at one time and was able to cater for 6 000 people a day. The Romans used the baths daily, around noon at the end of a hard day's work. The poorest people were not excluded, although they had fewer slaves than the rich to assist.

Baths were an important element in Roman life; they offered facilities for keeping fit through bathing and physical exercise, as well as libraries for the cultivation of the mind. Yet they were also places of assignation, and by Caracalla's time, the Romans were already denouncing notorious episodes.

The Baths of Caracalla were in use until 537, when the Goths under Witigis damaged the aqueducts that supplied Rome. **Shelley's** poem *Prometheus Unbound* "was chiefly written upon the mountainous ruins of the Baths of Caracalla".

A typical day at the baths – The Romans followed the routine prescribed by their doctors. From the changing rooms (traces of fine floor mosaics) they went into the gymnasia for various forms of exercise; it is such a setting that Petronius described in his *Satyricon*, when Encolpius and his friends meet the rich Trimalchio, a "bald old man... who played ball with his long-haired slaves ...".

Already sweating, the bather went on into an oval room heated to a very high temperature *(laconicum)*, which induced greater perspiration. The heating system was quite efficient; hot air from huge stoves in the basement circulated beneath the floors, which were supported on sturdy brick pillars, and spread into ducts in the walls.

Next the bather passed into the *caldarium* for a good soak, after which he scraped his skin to remove all impurities. The *caldarium* was a huge circular room (34m/112ft in diameter), covered by a dome; some of the supporting pillars can still be seen. From here, they went into the *tepidarium* for a lukewarm dip, before plunging into the bracing water of the cold bath *(frigidarium)*. They could then take a swim in the open-air swimming pool *(natatio)*. Some then caroused. Less wealthy or more serious Romans stayed to talk to friends, walk in the gardens or read in the libraries. Excavations were carried out in the 16C (by Cardinal Farnese for the construction of his magnificent *palazzo* in the square of the same name), and later in the 19C and 20C. These digs uncovered statues, vases and mosaics, in addition to a **mithraeum** (temple of Mithras), and a network of underground tunnels. Here horse-drawn carts transported wood to the 50 ovens that heated the baths.

EXPLORING THE BATHS

Viale delle Terme di Caracalla 52.
♿🕐*16 Feb–15 Mar 9am–5pm, 16 Mar last Sat Mar 9am–5:30pm, last Sun Mar–31Aug 9am–7:15pm, Sep 9am–7pm, 1Oct last Sat Oct 9am–6:30pm, last Sun Oct–15Feb 9am–4:30pm.* 🕐*Closed 1 Jan, 1 May and 25 Dec.* ✆*€8.* ✆*06 39 96 77 00. www.coopculture.it.*

Caracalla Fourth Dimension

A time travel through fourth dimension: the Terme di Caracalla is the first great archological site to experience in 3D.

Virtual reality will show you the Terme as they are today, as well as the original site as it was in 216 a.D., when it was inaugurated. A strongly recommended experience. 9 € (booking required on the website www.coopculture.it).

For more info on the extraordinary summer shows hosted in the Caracalla baths by the Opera di Roma theatre (opera, classical music, dance and a variety of concerts), please visit www.operaroma.it

After passing the chambers (right), which were perhaps used for meetings, one enters (left) the central block. Immediately on the right is an oval room (*laconicum*), where the temperature was kept constantly high for a Turkish bath. This space leads to the gymnasium *(palaestra)*, where coloured mosaic fragments can still be seen. In the changing room *(apodyterium)*, a

Terme di Caracalla

© Iarnio/Fotolia.com

fair amount of the mosaic floor is still intact. Next comes the swimming pool (natatio); the fresco (right) has a religious theme and was probably added in the 17C, when the baths housed the oratory of St Philip Neri.

The tour returns to the starting point symmetrically via the second changing room and the second gymnasium, which has fine mosaics.

👣 WALKING TOUR

Begin this tour from the Circo Massimo Metro station or directly from the Baths of Caracalla. If the latter, see the church of Santi Nereo e Achilleo below.

Porta Capena is a gate in the defensive wall built by Servius Tullius in the 6C BC. Here Livy recounts that in the reign of Tullus Hostilius (672–640 BC), the last of the Horatii, who had defeated the Curi-

atii of Alba, Tullus slew his sister with his sword because she had dared to weep for her fiancé, one of the Curiatii; "Let that be the fate of any Roman who mourns the enemy."

▷ Take Viale delle Terme di Caracalla and bear right into Via Guido Baccelli.

On the right stands the building of the **Food and Agriculture Organisation (FAO)**, an agency of the United Nations, which employs more than 3 000 people of all nationalities. Its mandate is to raise nutrition levels, improve agricultural productivity, better the lives of rural populations and contribute to the growth of the world economy.

Santa Balbina all'Aventino
Piazza di Santa Balbina 8. Santa Margherita Rest Home (Casa di Riposo), to the right of the church, has

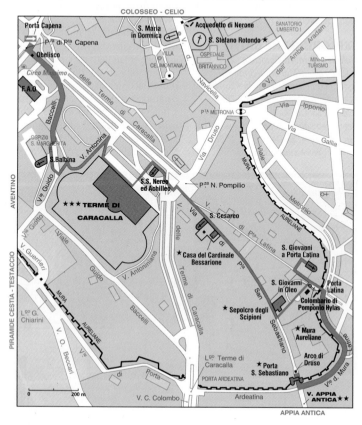

remains of Hadrian's wall. ⏰*Open Sun 10:30am–11:30am.* ☎*06 57 80 207.*
A 1927 restoration returned the church to its medieval simplicity. It was erected in the 4C over a Roman consul's house. A pitched roof covers a single nave punctuated by recessed chapels and lit by high barred windows.

On the right of the entrance, Cardinal Surdi's **tomb★** is decorated with multi-coloured marble inlay (1295) and bears a recumbent Gothic figure. Behind the high altar, the **episcopal chair★** is a fine piece of Cosmati work (13C). The frescoes in the apse are 17C.

▶ Beyond the church turn left into Via Antonina and then sharp right. Turn left in front of the Baths of Caracalla.

Santi Nereo e Achilleo

Via delle Terme di Caracalla 28. ⏰*Open Thu–Mon 10am–12pm and 4pm–6pm.* ☎*335 40 17 89.*
A little church stood here in the 4C called Titulus Fasciolae. Its presence is explained by the legend of the bandage *(fasciola)* that bound St Peter's leg, covering sores from the Mamertine Prison chains. When Peter fled Rome, the dressing fell from his leg on this spot, which was venerated as a place of worship. Further along the Appian Way came St Peter's meeting with Christ and his question *"Domine, quo vadis?"* (▶*See APPIA ANTICA*).
Completely rebuilt by Leo III (795–816), the church was later restored by Sixtus IV (1471–84). In 1596, the incumbent appointed to the church was Clement VIII's confessor, Cardinal Baronius, who had a great devotion to St Nereus and St Achilleus. He had their relics transferred here from Domitilla's Catacombs.

▶ From Piazzale Numa Pompilio take Via di Porta San Sebastiano.

Via di Porta San Sebastiano is edged by buildings of historical and architectural interest in rural surroundings.

San Cesareo in Palatio

Via di Porta San Sebastiano. ⏰*Open by request. Reservation requested* ☎*338 49 16 838.*
Originally constructed over a 2C Roman building, the church was likely rebuilt by Giacomo della Porto in the late 16C. Clement VIII entrusted its restoration to Cardinal Baronius. The latter followed contemporary taste in the coffered ceiling bearing the arms of Clement VIII and the paintings by **Cavaliere d'Arpino**. Elsewhere he tried to reproduce medieval decoration.

Some Renaissance work survives: the two angels drawing back the curtains before the *confessio (below the altar)* and the pretty little fresco of the Madonna and Child *(above the throne)*.

▶ Continue along Via S.Sebastiano to the Casa del Cardinale Bessarione and the Sepolcro degli Scipioni (▶*See below*).

Casina del Cardinal Bessarione★

Via di Porta San Sebastiano 8. ⏰*Open Sat and Sun only for groups max 15 people.* ☎*06 06 08.*
This handsome house belonged to **Cardinal John Bessarion**, the Humanist scholar (c. 1402–72). Note the two large, Guelph cross windows on the façade, and the loggia. Restoration work has retuned the two large, decorated and frescoed halls, as well as the elegant Italian gardens, back to their original splendour.

Sepolcro degli Scipioni

Via di Porta S. Sebastiano 9. ⏰ *Open by appointment only for groups max 12 people.* ☎*06 06 08.*
The **Scipio family tomb** was discovered in 1614 and restored in 1926. The funeral inscriptions constitute a remarkable document of the republican period and of the infancy of Latin literature. Their concentration on the dead man's public spiritedness and his moral rectitude reveal the mentality of those days, when Roman civilisation was being forged.

▷ Turn left immediately after the Sepolcro degli Scipioni to reach the temple of San Giovanni in Oleo.

San Giovanni in Oleo

To visit, inquire at San Giovanni a Porta Latina. ℘06 77 40 00 32.

This small octagonal temple was built in the Renaissance style in 1509 by Benoit Adam, a Frenchman and member of the *Rota* (Roman Catholic ecclesiastical court). Over the door, he placed his arms and his motto *"Au plaisir de Dieu"* (at God's pleasure).

Columbarium of Pomponius Hylas

Via di Porta Latina. ◷*Open by appointment only for groups max 7 people;* ⬭€4. ℘06 06 08.

Decorated with stucco work and fine paintings, this cremation urn repository probably dates from the Julio–Claudian period (AD 31–68).

▷ Turn left into Via di Porta Latina, then right to Via di San G. a Porta Latina.

San Giovanni a Porta Latina

◷*Open 7:30am–12:30pm and 3pm–6pm.* ℘06 70 47 59 38.

The church of **St John at the Latin Gate** occupies a charming **site★**; the peaceful forecourt, flanked by the campanile, is decorated by a medieval well and shaded by a cedar tree.

The beautifully simple interior is decorated with 12C frescoes; although damaged, they are a fine example of Romanesque painting.

▷ Return to Via di Porta Latina.

Porta Latina

This gate in the Aurelian Wall (Mura Aureliane) was restored by Honorius (5C) and again by Belisarius (6C). The keystone bears a Greek cross on the town side and the *chi-rho* on the outside.

▷ Turn right outside the gate into Viale delle Mura Latine.

Mura Aureliane★

Work on the wall was initiated under the Emperor Aurelian in the 3C, as the existing walls could no longer contain the expanding city. Punctuated by towers, this is a compelling piece of Roman civil engineering, notably between the Porta Latina and Porta San Sebastiano (*the opposite that goes on to Porta Metronia, also very interesting, is visibile from the bus n. 218*).

Access up onto the wall itself is from Porta San Sebastiano (◔*See below*).

Porta San Sebastiano★

The gate is without doubt the most spectacular in Rome, with its base of tall marble blocks supporting crenellated towers. Known as the Porta Appia in ancient times, it was constructed by Aurelian (AD 271–75) when he built his defensive wall.

Housed withIn the gate, the **Museo delle Mura** (*Via di Porta S. Sebastiano 18.* ◷*Open Tue–Sun 9am–2pm. Free.* ℘06 06 08; www.museodellemuraroma.it) chronicles the evolution of the Aurelian Walls. It is possible to walk along an expanse of the wall and continue westwards as far as Via C. Colombo.

Arco di Druso

The arch dates from the 2C AD and was not therefore raised in honour of Drusus (39–38 BC), the younger brother of the Emperor Tiberius. It was used by Caracalla (AD 211–17) to support the aqueduct that supplied water to his baths.

ADDRESSES

TAKING A BREAK

Ristorante Orazio – *Via di Porta Latina 5.* ℘06 7049 2401. www.ristoranteorazio.it. Open 12am–3:30pm, 7-11pm. In the heart of Porta Capena park, this restaurant is a delightful venue to enjoy a little break after a promenade.

Trastevere–Gianicolo★★

Trastevere, on the west bank of the Tiber, was for centuries inhabited by artisans and small traders, known for their proud, independent nature. Today, that rogue energy continues – and is celebrated each July during the traditional "Festa de Noantri". However, the neighbourhood is now "molto chic", attracting wealthy Italians and expats, all drawn by the vibrant atmosphere with its picturesque, narrow streets and small piazzas, excellent bakeries and trattorias. The pace here tends to dawdle during the day, but the quarter stirs at dusk, especially in its northern section, where most of the nightclubs, bars and restaurants lie. Climbing back up the slopes to the west, you reach the Gianicolo, a leafy hill between the Vatican and Villa Pamphilj where locals stroll and savour the fine views of their city. In summertime the park containing the Fontana Paola – the grand fountain at the belvedere – transforms into a sprawling open-air theatre complex with an outdoor bar, as do many nooks in this neighbourhood.

- **Michelin Map:** 38 M 10, N 10–11 (Trastevere) and 38 L 9, N9.
- **Location:** This district, divided into two by Viale Trastevere, sits across the Tiber from the historic centre, facing Isola Tiberina. Another axis (that runs parallel to the river) crosses the area along Via della Lungara and its hypothetical continuation in Via della Lungaretta. The Janiculum Hill and the vast green area of Villa Pamphilj lie to the west.
- **Timing:** Allow at least 3hrs.
- **Kids:** The puppet show (Sat–Sun), carousel and pony rides near the Piazzale G. Garibaldi.
- **Don't Miss:** The animation of Piazza Santa Maria della Trastevere, *Giudizio Universale* by Cavallini in S. Agnese. The noon cannon, il Tempietto at San Pietro in Montorio, views from the Fontana Paola. Gardeners enjoy the Villa Farnesina
- **Also See:** *BOCCA DELLA VERITÀ; CAMPO DE' FIORI– ISOLA TIBERINA –GHETTO– TORRE ARGENTINA– VATICANO.*

Terrace of a bar, Trastevere

© L. Vaccarella/Sime Photononstop

GETTING THERE

BY METRO AND BUS: Tram 3B and 8. Bus: 23, 115, 125, 780 and 871.

A BIT OF HISTORY

Trastevere (from *trans-Tiberim* meaning "over the Tiber") was not originally part of Rome; it was the beginning of Etruscan territory.

From the republic, it was inhabited mainly by Jews and Syrians and was incorporated into Rome by Augustus as the 14th administrative district. Not far from the present San Cosimato Hospital,

Augustus created a *naumachia*, a vast pool where naval warfare spectacles were mounted. Close to the Mediterranean harbour of Ostia and the river port of Ripa Grande, trade flourished, especially in food produce.

This continues in the number of small groceries and trattorias here – contrasted with the artisanal trades on the opposite bank. Few public buildings are here; rather utilitarian services, such as a 2C fire station near Via dei Genovesi, of which traces were discovered in the 19C. Among the religious buildings is a Syrian sanctuary, traces surfaced under the Villa Sciarra near Via Emilio Dandolo. In the 3C, the whole of Trastevere was enclosed by the **Aurelian Wall** (Mura Aureliane) pierced by three gateways: the Porta Settimiana to the north, the Porta Aurelia (now Porta S. Pancrazio) (☞*See p215*) to the west and to the south the Porta Portuensis (further south than the present Porta Portese).

Though some powerful Roman families had palaces in Trastevere, the area never lost its popular character. Throughout the centuries the inhabitants have kept their reputation of stout fellows ready to lend strength and courage to a revolutionary cause. Stendhal thought it superb and "full of energy".

Poets who celebrated Rome in the local dialect have always found a response there. The exploits of the Trasteverians, who defied the inhabitants of the *Santa Maria Maggiore* district with catapults, have been the subject of several sonnets in Roman folklore.

☙WALKING TOUR

Torre degli Anguillara
Piazza Sidney Sonnino.
The 12C tower, attached to a small palace of the same name, recalls one of the most powerful Roman families. Whether as warriors, magistrates, outlaws, forgers or clerics, the Anguillara were at the forefront of events from the Middle Ages to the Renaissance.
The palace, built in the 15C, underwent major restoration in the 19C and now

houses the Institute for Dante Studies (*www.casadidanteinroma.it*).

San Crisogono
Piazza Sidney Sonnino 44. ◷*Open daily 7am–11:30pm (Sun and holidays 8am–1pm) and 4pm–7:30pm.* ℘*06 58 10 076 or 06 58 18 225.*
The church of **St Chrysogonus,** which dates from the 5C, evolved over the centuries. The **belfry,** erected in the 12C when the church was almost entirely rebuilt, was altered in the 16C by the addition of a spire.
The **façade** is the work of **Giovanni Battista Soria**, who was put in charge of the refurbishment of the building in the 17C by Cardinal Scipione Borghese, a nephew of the Pope and incumbent of the church at the time.
Interior★ – Only the basilical plan of a nave and two aisles has survived from the 12C; the floor is 13C work by Roman marble masons. The overall effect – half-Mannerist, half-Baroque – was created in the 17C by GB Soria, who retained the ancient granite columns, refashioned their capitals in stucco, opened up great windows in the nave to let in more light and installed a fine coffered ceiling of complex design, showing the arms of Cardinal Borghese. Two monolithic porphyry columns support the chancel arch. The baldaquin is also the work of Soria. The fine wood carving in the chancel dates from 1863. The mosaic in the apse, showing the Virgin and Child with St James and St Chrysogonus, comes from the Cavallini School (late 13C).
Palaeo-Christian church *Access from the sacristy by an awkward iron stair.* ◷*Same opening times as the church* ◷*Closed for visits during church services.* ⊛€*3.* ℘*06 58 10 076.* At a depth of 6m/20ft below floor level archaeologists have discovered traces of the 5C building, which was altered in the 8C and abandoned in the 12C, when the present church was built. Here is the lower part of the apse (probably partially 5C) below which Gregory III hollowed out a *confessio* in the 8C; it follows the curve of the apse before drawing in on each side into a horseshoe shape,

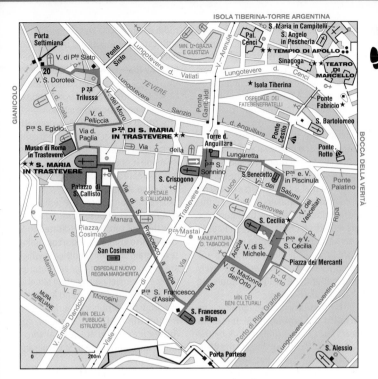

thus creating a semi-circular corridor. Also it's bifurcated at the end: towards the nave is a relic chamber. This passage and the apse still bear traces of 8C painting. There are 10C paintings on the walls of the semi-circular corridor.

The baptistry (left), now divided into two by a wall, was used for the baptism of early Christians.

▶ From Piazza Sonnino take Via della Lungaretta to reach Piazza in Piscinula.

San Benedetto in Piscinula

Piazza In Piscinula 40. 🕐*Open Tue–Sun 9:45am–11:45am and 4:30pm–7:30pm.* ✆*06 58 33 16 09.*

Tradition has it that in this church, which has the smallest bell-tower in Rome, was visited by St Benedict of the Anicii family, founder of Western monasticism. Note the beautiful Cosmatesque floor.

▶ From Piazza in Piscinula take Via dei Salumi and Via dei Vascellari to reach Piazza Santa Cecilia.

Santa Cecilia★

Piazza di Santa Cecilia 22. 🕐*Open daily 10am–1pm and 4pm –7pm.* ✆*Crypt: €2.50.* ✆*06 58 99 289.*

A sanctuary dedicated to St Cecilia existed in a private house on this site in

Santa Cecilia

© Paco Romero Photography/iStockphoto.com

the 5C. Pope Paschal I (817–24) replaced it with a church, which was much altered in the 16C, 18C and 19C.

The church is preceded by a courtyard planted with flowerbeds around a large antique vase. A fine 12C campanile was remodelled in the 18C, but its coeval porch, with its ancient columns and mosaic frieze, was preserved.

Interior – The medieval appearance is generally lost, although it still retains the **mosaic** from Paschal I in the 9C. The influence that Byzantine art exerted on Roman mosaic workers in earlier centuries is evident in the way the figures are presented: on Christ's right – St Paul, St Agatha and Pascal I, with a square halo since he was still alive; on the left – St Peter, St Valerian and St Cecilia; the lively postures and the beautiful colours are also typically Roman.

The **baldaquin** over the high altar is by **Arnolfo di Cambio** (1293); it is eight years later than a similar work by the same artist for St Paul Outside the Walls and shows a growing heaviness of style and the influence of Classical works; in the left back corner is an equestrian statue of a saint, reminiscent of the statue of Marcus Aurelius, now in the Capitoline Museum.

The statue of **St Cecilia**★ *(below the altar)*, a fine sculpture by Stefano Maderno (1599), recalls her history and legend. Paschal I (817–24) who was desperately searching all the Christian cemeteries for the remains of St Cecilia, was guided by a dream. He found the saint's corpse lying beside her husband, St Valerian, in a catacomb on the Old Appian Way. He had them transferred immediately to a place beneath the altar. Seven centuries later, during the reign of Clement VIII, Cardinal Sfondrati undertook alterations to the chancel. During the work the sarcophagi came to light and St Cecilia's body was discovered showing the posture in which Maderno has represented it.

The cardinal also wanted to restore the little room venerated as the site of St Cecilia's martyrdom. This work disclosed several pipes against the wall, thought to have raised the temperature in the room where Cecilia was condemned to suffocate. She was saved by a miraculous dew, only to be beheaded so inefficiently that she lingered in agony for three days. The cardinal commissioned Guido Reni to paint the *Decapitation of the Saint,* now above the altar.

The tomb of Rampolla is a dramatic exercise in perspective (1929) and commemorates the cardinal whose generosity made it possible to open the crypt. It was created from 1899–1901 in the Byzantine style.

Excavations uncovered the remains of several ancient houses, among which was the first sanctuary dedicated to St Cecilia. Also visible is a room containing seven grain silos and another in which are exhibited *sarcophagi* and inscriptions: a low-relief representing Minerva (2C BC) in a little recess and a column also from the Republican period.

Behind the grating in the *confessio (beneath the apse)* are several *sarcophagi,* including those of St Cecilia and St Valerian.

The Last Judgement by Pietro Cavallini★★★ – (*In the convent.* ◯*Open daily (except festivity) 10am–12:30pm; ⊜€2.50*) This masterpiece of Roman medieval painting by Pietro Cavallini (c. 1293) was formerly on the inside wall of the façade of the church and is now kept in the monks' chancel. A magnificent work of art, the painting was badly damaged in the 16C. All that remains is the figure of *Christ in Judgement* surrounded by angels with magnificent outspread wings, flanked by Mary and John the Baptist, hands raised beseechingly; below are the apostles, and angels blowing trumpets.

Note the perfect distribution of light and shade, the individual expression on each face and the subtle harmony of the colours.

Piazza dei Mercanti

An ancient meeting place for merchants and seafaring captains arriving from Ripa Grande port, today it hosts restaurants where visitors can enjoy typical dishes served in a picturesque, medieval context.

▷ Take Via di San Michele.

Leaving the San Michele a Ripa Grande monumental complex on your left, an apostolic hostel and prison from the 17th century, after turning into *Via Madonna dell'Orto,* note the impressive 19C tobacco factory behind the church.

▷ Turn left into Via Anicia.

San Francesco d'Assisi a Ripa

Piazza San Francesco d'Assisi 88.
🕐*Open daily 7am–1pm and 3pm–7:30pm.* 📞*06 58 19 020 or 06 58 03 509. www.sanfrancescoaripa.com.*
St Francis stayed here in 1219. Modified in 1231, the church was rebuilt in 1862. It remains in the Franciscan order.
The fourth chapel in the left-hand aisle contains a **statue of Blessed Ludovica Albertoni★★** by **Bernini;** she was a member of the Franciscan Tertiaries (1474–1533) and is buried beneath the altar. Bernini shows her suffering and in this, one of his later works (1674), the marble perfectly expresses the final agony of a saintly life.

▷ Take Via di S. Francesco a Ripa and turn left into Via Natale del Grande.

San Cosimato

Piazza di San Cosimato. Nonspecific hours. Entrance from the hospital next door.
Behind the small, picturesque portico, a garden leads to a double cloister – one Romanesque, the other Renaissance – while the church, founded in the 10th century, displays 14th-century architecture. Inside, in the presbytery, there is a beautiful fresco by Antonio Massaro da Viterbo, known as "il Pastura", portraying the Madonna with child between Saints Francis and Chiara.

▷ Return to Via di S. Francesco a Ripa to reach Piazza Santa Maria in Trastevere.

Piazza Santa Maria in Trastevere★★
the heart of the district, is probably the most charming corner of Trastevere, full of local colour. The fountain at the centre was restored by **Bernini** in 1659 and modified in 1692 to designs by Carlo Fontana. On the left is the fine 17C façade of the **Palazzo di San Callisto.**

Santa Maria in Trastevere★★
Piazza di Santa Maria in Trastevere.
🕐*Open daily 7:30am–9pm (Aug 8am–noon and 4pm–9pm).* 📞*06 58 14 802.*
On this spot in 38 BC, a fountain of oil *(fons olei)* flowed for a whole day.

Piazza Santa Maria in Trastevere

© Francesco Cantone /iStockphoto.com

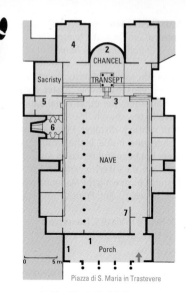

Piazza di S. Maria in Trastevere

Basilica di Santa Maria in Trastevere

The statues of the saints on the balustrade over the porch were erected from the 17C to the 18C. The porch, which was restored early in the 18C, shelters several fragments, some from the buildings which preceded the present one. Two 15C frescoes (1), (one rather damaged), depict the *Annunciation*. The door frames are made of friezes dating from the time of the empire.

Interior

The basilical plan of Pope Innocent II's 12C church is still visible. The 22 granite columns dividing the nave from the aisles were taken from the ancient Baths of Caracalla; all are crowned with their classical capitals in either the Ionic or the Corinthian orders. The figures of some Egyptian divinities were removed in the 19C by Pope Pius IX.

The cornice is composed of an assortment of ancient fragments.

Chancel mosaics★★★ – The mosaics on the chancel arch (the Prophets Isaiah and Jeremiah and the symbols of the Evangelists) date from the 12C; so do those in the half-dome of the apse. To the right of Christ and the Virgin are St Callixtus, St Lawrence and Pope Innocent II offering his church to Mary; on the left are St Peter, St Cornelius, St Julius and St Calepodius. During the Romanesque period, mosaic art was still influenced by the Byzantine style: the Virgin is adorned with gold like an empress, the group of figures betrays a certain oriental rigidity and loses some of its expressive force in the multitude of detail (the Virgin's dress). At the top is paradise, with the hand of God placing a crown on Christ's head; at the bottom are lambs, symbols of the apostles, coming from the cities of Jerusalem and Bethlehem and facing the Lamb of God. The mosaics between the windows and at the base of the chancel arch are a masterpiece by **Pietro Cavallini** (late 13C), representing scenes from the life of the Virgin. The medallion above the throne shows the Virgin and Child between St Peter and St Paul, with Cardinal Stefaneschi, who commissioned the work, on a smaller scale.

Christians interpreted this as a sign of the grace that would spread worldwide. Pope Calixtus (217–22) is said to have built the first Christian sanctuary in Rome, but it was the energetic Pope Julius I (337–52), a keen builder, who constructed a proper basilica. The building was altered in the 9C by Gregory V, to provide a crypt in which he laid the saintly remains of Callixtus, Pope Cornelius and Calepodius.

The present basilica dates from the 12C; it was built about 1140 during a brief period of calm in the troubled reign of Innocent II, who was beset by the anti-Popes, Anacletus II and Victor IV. Despite St Bernard's assistance, when Innocent II died, Rome was in the hands of revolutionaries, who proclaimed a Republic. His successors restored and embellished the church on many occasions right up to the 19C.

Façade

The belfry is 12C; a small recess at the top is decorated with a mosaic of the Virgin and Child, to whom the basilica is dedicated. The *Virgin and Child* are also celebrated in the mosaic on the façade (12–13C), which shows a procession of women approaching from both sides.

The bishop's throne **(2)** standing in the apse is made of marble (12C).

An inscription **(3)** before the chancel marks the site of the oil fountain.

Altemps Chapel (4) – The stucco and frescoes of this chapel are in the style of the Counter-Reformation, which developed after the Council of Trent (late 16C).

Transept – The fine coffered ceiling is late 16C work. The central low relief in gilded and painted wood illustrates the Assumption.

The **Sacristy** lobby contains two very fine old mosaics **(5)**.

The **Avila Chapel (6)** and its dome are the exuberant creation of Antonio Gherardi (late 17C); the *trompe-l'œil* has been used to create a Baroque effect.

Among the treasures of this church is the charming tabernacle **(7)** by Mino da Fiesole (late 15C).

A warren of narrow, shady, picturesque streets lead to the square, making this an ideal spot for a leisurely stroll.

▶ Take Via della Paglia, then turn right into Piazza S. Egidio, home to the Museo di Roma in Trastevere.

Museo di Roma in Trastevere

Piazza di Sant'Egidio 1/b.
&⊙*Open Tue–Sun 10am–8pm; 24 and 31 Dec 10am–2pm.* ⊙*Closed 1 Jan, 1 May and 25 Dec.* ⊛€8.50. ℘*06 06 08. www.museodiromaintrastevere.it.*

The museum occupies what was once the Convent of St Egidius in Trastevere. Many artefacts (watercolours, prints and ceramics) tell the story of life and popular dress in 18C and 19C Rome. As well as various display cases showing scenes from everyday life, there is a reconstruction of the room in which the poet Trilussa worked.

▶ Take Via Pelliccia and Vicolo di Moro to reach Piazza Trilussa.

The Piazza Trilussa commemorates Carlo Alberto Salustri, who wrote poetry in the Roman dialect under the pseudonym **Trilussa** (1871–1950). In his racy and mildly satirical style, he highlights the spirit of the Roman people, describing their lives in a long and colourful story. A monument was set up in his honour in 1954.

Nearby is a colossal fountain installed by Paul V in 1612 at the beginning of Via Giulia and moved here in the 19C, when the Tiber embankments were built.

Opposite is the **Sistine Bridge** (Ponte Sisto), named after Sixtus IV (1471–84), who had it built (modernised in the 19C).

▶ Take Via di Ponte Sisto and then Via di Santa Dorotea.

According to local tradition, the house before the corner (no 20), with the charmingly decorated window on the second floor, was the home of **La Fornarina,** Raphael's mistress, whom he immortalised in his famous painting now in the National Museum of Antique Art in Palazzo Barberini.

GIANICOLO
A BIT OF HISTORY

Legend claims that the two-faced god Janus founded a city on the **Janiculum** Hill (*Monte Gianicolo*). One of his children, Tiber, gave his name to the river. The *Gianicolo* was a country district until the 17C, when Urban VIII constructed a defensive wall with bastions along the present-day Viale delle Mura Aurelie and Viale delle Mura Gianicolensi.

From Mucius Scaevola to Garibaldi

Myth and truth entwine in this area, so crucial to Rome's development.

The oldest tale goes back to the 6C BC, when the town had broken free of the Etruscan kings and was besieged by **Lars Porsenna**. This young Roman noble infiltrated the enemy camp on the Gianicolo to assassinate their chief. He mistakenly killed one of the aides instead and was arrested. To prove to Lars Porsenna that life was of little account to a Roman defending his country, Mucius burned away his right hand on a brazier. Porsenna was so struck by this bravery that he let him go. Mucius was nicknamed "*Scaevola*", left-handed.

French Interlude

On 31 August 1797, the Ambassador of the Directory, **Joseph Bonaparte**, accompanied by the young General Léonard Duphot, settled in the Palazzo Corsini (👁 *See Walking Tour*). On 28 December, a few revolutionaries led a riot in front of the palace. They called for the intervention of the French against the papal government. Shots were fired and General Duphot was killed. On 10 February 1798, General Berthier besieged Rome and drove out Pius VI, who died in exile in Valence in France. Until 29 September 1799, Rome took its cue from the French Republic.

In his footsteps came Cloelia. According to Livy, she showed courage "without precedent among women". Held hostage in Porsenna's camp, she escaped with her companions and made them swim the Tiber to reach Rome.

While banqueting on the hill in 1611, the scientist Galileo Galilei tested a new telescope. In daylight, he managed to read the inscription on Saint John Lateran several miles away.

In 1849, one of the battles in the struggle for Italian unity raged here. **Garibaldi** defended the Gianicolo valiantly in the name of the Roman Republic against the French troops commanded by Marshal Oudinot. Tales claim he would take his morning coffee within view of the enemies, taunting them. On 4 July, the Papal Government was re-established after a month of bloody combat, particularly in the Villa Pamphilj.

Later, in 1862, the great general uttered famous war cry – "*Roma o morte*" (Rome or death) – now memorialized on a Mussolini-built marble monument on the Via Garibaldi.

VILLA FARNESINA★★

Via della Lungara 230. ♿ 🕐*Open Mon–Sat 9am–2pm and second Sunday of every month.* 🕐*Closed public holidays.* 👓€6. *English Guided tour Sat at 10am.* ✆*06 68 02 72 68. www.villafarnesina.it.*

Background

The villa was set in this garden in 1508–11 for Agostino Chigi, the great banker. Known as "the Magnificent", he entertained his guests, including Pope Leo X, in sumptuous style. Designed as a suburban house, it has two projecting wings.

For the construction and the decor, Chigi commissioned the best Renaissance artists: **Baldassarre Peruzzi**, architect and painter, and Raphael with his usual following of Giulio Romano, Francesco Penni, Giovanni da Udine, Sebastiano del Piombo and Sodoma. The friendship linking these men is enshrined in villa: Agostino Chigi was Raphael's most ardent patron and Leo X had a sincere affection for him. None of them saw the sack of the city, which ended the Roman Renaissance. Raphael died, aged 37, in 1520; Chigi died a few days later; the following year Leo X succumbed to a "slight fever". Later, in the 16C, the villa was sold to Cardinal Alessandro Farnese and assumed the name of its new owner.

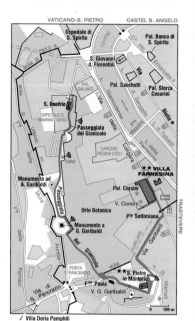

Fresco in the vault of Galleria della Villa Farnesina depicting Council of the Gods

©Judy Edelhoff/Michelin

Interior

On the ceiling of the **gallery,** along the garden front, a fresco depicts the legend of Cupid and Psyche (in the centre *The Council of the Gods* and *The Marriage of Cupid and Psyche*), painted by Raphael, assisted by Giulio Romano, Francesco Penni and Giovanni da Udine. Finished in 1520, the paintings contain elements that became characteristic of the Mannerist style (a series of scenes, as in a tapestry, framed by garlands).

At the gallery's east is the **Galatea Room** (1511) where Nereus' sea maiden was painted by **Raphael** riding in a shell drawn by dolphins. The monstrous Polyphemus, as well as the scenes from Ovid's *Metamorphoses (in the lunettes),* are by **Sebastiano del Piombo**. The Constellations on the ceiling are the work of **Baldassarre Peruzzi.** The young man's head painted in grisaille *(left of the entrance)* is probably by Sebastiano del Piombo, but tradition attributes it to Michelangelo, who wanted to show Raphael that his figures were too small.

On the **first floor,** the **salon** is decorated with landscapes in *trompe l'oeil* by Peruzzi and assistants; views of Rome are revealed between the painted columns. In the next room is the *Marriage of Roxana and Alexander* by Sodoma (1477–1549). Dismissed by Julius II in favour of Raphael, Sodoma was commissioned by Agostino Chigi to decorate the room, probably in 1509. In a Renaissance setting, Alexander extends the crown to Roxana against a cloud of cherubs.

To the left of the entrance are Alexander and Bucephalus (late 16C).

●●●WALKING TOUR

Palazzo Corsini
Via della Lungara 10.

This handsome palace was built in the 15C by the Riario, nephews of Sixtus IV, and passed in the 18C to Cardinal Corsini, nephew of Clement XII, who had it rebuilt by Ferdinando Fuga.

At one time it was residence to the Queen of Sweden. It now houses the **Galleria Corsini** (⊙*Open Wen–Mon 8:30am–7pm;* ⊙*Closed Tue, 1 May, 25 Dec and 1 Jan;* ⊚*€12;* ℘*06 68 80 23 23; www.galleriacorsini.beniculturali.it or www.galleriaborghese.it)* with works by Caravaggio, Rubens and Van Dyck, and the **Accademia dei Lincei,** a learned society of scholars and men of letters.

The palace is also home to part of the collection of the **National Gallery of Ancient Art**; the rest is housed in Palazzo Barberini (*⛳See VIA VENETO).*

This gallery houses a collection of mainly 17C and 18C paintings, with special

View of Rome

From the square in front of the *Ospedale del Bambino Gesù* (Hospital of the Infant Jesus *See local tour map in this section*), there is a spectacular **view★★★** of Rome. To the left is the drum of Castel Sant'Angelo surmounted by its angel and the white mass of the Law Courts; just below the Janiculum, across the river, is the dome of San Giovanni dei Fiorentini; in the background on the edge of the park is the Villa Medici with its two towers and the dome of San Carlo al Corso; slightly to the right are the two belfries of the Trinità dei Monti; then the Quirinal Palace behind the shallow dome of the Pantheon; next, nearer the river, is the high dome of Sant'Andrea delle Valle with the lower dome of the Gesù Church behind it; in the background is the Militia Tower; before it rises the monument to Victor Emmanuel II and the flat façade of Santa Maria d'Aracoeli.

emphasis on the Venetian, Emilian and Neapolitan Schools.

Particularly noteworthy are the *Portrait of Philip II* by Titian, in which its stiff posture and death-like complexion are striking; *St John the Baptist* by Caravaggio; and, in the room devoted to Tuscan primitives, the *Triptych* by **Beato Angelico** showing the *Last Judgement*, the *Ascension* and *Pentecost*. This painter, who experienced the silence of the cloister, expressed his deep faith by painting serene and saintly faces (central panel of the *Last Judgement*) and a Christ who inspires adoration (right panel of the *Ascension*).

▶ As you exit Galleria Corsini, turn right on Via della Lungara, then right again on Via Corsini, which leads to Largo Cristina di Svezia, and the entrance to Orto Botanico, the Botanic Garden.

Orto Botanico

Note: If you climb the hill, you will not find entry. Be sure to enter via Largo Cristina di Svezia 24, off Via Corsini. ◟*Open 4 Jan–26 Mar and 31 Oct–31 Dec 9am–5:30pm. 29 Mar–29 Oct 9am–6:30pm. Greenhouses close 1:30pm. Closed public holidays.* €8. 06 49 91 71 08 or 06 49 91 71 07. *web.uniroma1.it/ortobotanico.*
Rome's University – "La Sapienza" – runs this beautiful hillside garden, which contains some 3 500 species of plants and eight glasshouses. Relax among the

luxuriant vegetation and curiously wild upper slopes, dotted with crumbling fountains and staircases.

Porta Settimiana

One of the gates in the Aurelian Wall (*Mura Aureliane*), this gate spans Villa della Lungara just north of Via Garibaldi. Alexander VI (1492–1503) reinforced it with merlons.

▶ Turn right into Via Garibaldi; beyond the junction with Via G. Mameli, take the second flight of steep steps on the right uphill.

San Pietro in Montorio★

Piazza S. Pietro at Montorio 2. ◟*Open daily 8:30am–noon and 3pm–4pm.* 06 58 13 940.
Legend claims that St Peter was crucified here, though the church is best known for **Bramante**'s *tempietto* (*See below*). It was built in Sixtus IV's reign at the end of the 15C by Ferdinand II of Spain. From the piazza in front of the church, commanding **views★★** extend from Monte Mario (*left*) and Castel Sant'Angelo to the gaudy "wedding cake" monument to Victor Emmanuel II. You can also see the arches of the Basilica of Maxentius in the Forum; farther right again, beyond the green Palatine, is the façade of St John Lateran spiked with statues. The simple façade is typical of the Renaissance, as is the interior, which consists of a nave flanked by apsidal chapels. The chancel was damaged in the siege

of 1849 and has been restored. Several Renaissance works have survived, particularly the *Flagellation*★ *(first chapel on the right)* oil painting by Sebastiano del Piombo, clearly influenced by the monumental art of Michelangelo.

The ceiling in the next chapel was painted by **Baldassarre Peruzzi** (1481–1536). The pale fresco of the Virgin, by Pomarancio (1552–1626), and the two transept chapels were added at the Counter-Reformation. In the right-hand chapel, the allegorical figures on the tombs and the cherubs on the balustrade are by Bartolomeo Ammanati, a pupil of Michelangelo. Beatrice Cenci is buried (unmarked) beneath the high altar.

Bernini designed the second chapel on the left in the Baroque period.

Il Tempietto★★

Via Garibaldi 33. Request access from adjacent Reale Accademia di Spagna ⏱*Open Tue–Sun 10am–6pm.* ☎*06 58 12 806.*

This charming miniature temple was one of Bramante's first works on his arrival in Rome in 1499. Despite its small scale, the construction has all the grandeur and rigorous conformity of a classical building. Perfectly proportioned, it is surrounded by a portico, supported on Doric columns and surmounted by a dome. Behind the building in a little chapel is a small cavity said to have held St Peter's cross.

▷ Return to Via Garibaldi, walking uphill.

On the left rises a **monument** erected in 1941 for soldiers who died fighting for Garibaldi and Rome's inclusion in Italy.

Fontana Paola

This fountain was commissioned by Pope **Paul V**; its shape – a commemorative arch – shows the nascent taste for Baroque pomp. In summertime, outdoor stages colonize the area and an impromptu cafe sprawls by the road.

▷ Either detour uphill to Porta San Pancrazio by Via di San Pancrazio – a narrow road, packed with high-speed traffic – which leads to Villa Doria Pamphilj (1km/0.5mi – 45minutes on foot return) or turn right into Passeggiata del Gianicolo.

Villa Doria Pamphilj

A vast public park surrounds the 17C country house *(casino)*, which is decorated with statues and low-relief sculptures and set among terraces.

Under the arch *(to the right)*, Casa dei Teatri houses theatre-related exhibits.

👥 A popular place for picnics, the park features majestic umbrella pines, grotto-fountains and playgrounds that appeal to families. Restrictions about playing on the grass, however bizarre, are often enforced.

Villa Doria Pamphilj

©ROMAOSLO/iStockphoto.com

▷ Return to Passeggiata del Gianicolo and turn left onto it.

PASSEGGIATA DEL GIANICOLO

This road winds along the crest of Janiculum Hill beneath umbrella pines; it is lined by busts of Garibaldi's men and offers some of the finest **views★★★** of Rome.

👪 A carousel, pony rides and balloon vendors hold sway here. A puppet show runs weekends periodically between 10am and 3pm; the content is often smackdown Punch and Judy skits, which may alarm toddlers.

Monumento a Giuseppe Garibaldi (Garibaldi Monument)

In Piazzale Garibaldi. Cannon fired daily at noon (from below the parapet).
Historian A.J.P. Taylor claims "Garibaldi is the only wholly admirable figure in modern history." The dashing and charismatic patriot led many of the battles that unified Italy (the *Risorgimento*).
In Emilio Gallori's grandiose work (1895), the hero is shown on horseback. Garibaldi struggled to reduce the temporal power of the papacy. In 1929, the Vatican requested the statue be turned, so it no longer gazed at St Peter's. Wags now point out that the horse's bot-tom faces the heart of Catholicism. From here unfurls a **view★★★** of Rome from Villa Medici to St John Lateran; on a clear day, the Alban Hills (southeast) and Abruzzo mountains (east) can be seen in the distance.

Monumento ad Anita Garibaldi (Anita Garibaldi Monument)

Garibaldi's Brazilian wife, who often fought beside him, scored a much better monument. Astride a rearing horse, she carries a baby and a pistol. Anita died – ill, pregnant and in Giuseppe's arms – after the 1849 retreat. Eleven years later, when Garibaldi rode to hail Victor Emanuel II as king of Italy, he wore Anita's striped scarf over his grey poncho.
Farther on, near the lighthouse, there is a fine **view★★★** over the whole of the city of Rome.

▷ Farther on, go down the steps on the right that cut off the hairpin bend of the Passeggiata.

The old tree stump is all that remains of the oak tree beneath which Tasso sat and reflected on all his misfortunes (inscription). 👪 Take an ice-cream break at the outdoor bar at the overlook in front of Bambino Gesù children's hospital.

Sant'Onofrio

Piazza di Sant'Onofrio 2. ⏱*Open Mon–Fri and Sun 9am–1pm and 3pm–6pm.* ⏱*Closed Sat and Aug.* ✆*06 68 64 498.*
This church has retained the appearance and atmosphere of a hermitage, which it received from its founder, a monk of the order of the Hermits of St Jerome, in 1434. Here **Tasso** (1544–95) came to die, pursued to the end, even to madness, by his religious doubts. His poem, *The Liberation of Jerusalem*, is a masterpiece of Italian Renaissance epic poetry. Chateaubriand, too, would have liked to finish his days here; on the outside wall of the church overlooking the river is a long quotation from his *Memories from Beyond the Grave*. On the right of the main door beneath the arcade are fres-

---

Giuseppe Garibaldi

This famous military leader (1807-82) is one of the giants of the country's history. He is credited with the unification of modern Italy. A sailor in his early years, he lived in Latin America. In Uruguay, he and his Italian Legion of red-shirted volunteers fought guerilla-style wars for Uruguayan freedom. Revolutionary fervor in Italy in 1848 drew him home. In 1849 his Republican army, though outnumbered, defeated the French. He fought many subsequent battles in Italy and served in the Italian parliament.

---

coes by **Domenichino,** illustrating the life of St Jerome (1605). The attractive frescoes in the **apse★** were probably painted by Baldassarre Peruzzi assisted by Pinturicchio.

ADDRESSES

TAKING A BREAK

Antica Caciara – *Via San Francesco a Ripa 140a/b. 7am–2pm and 4–8pm. Closed Sun, Aug. ℰ06 58 12 815. www.anticacaciara.it.* The smell of Roman pecorino cheese wafts into the street from Roberto's speciality cheese and wine shop run by the same family since 1900.

La Gourmandise – *Via Felice Cavallotti 36b. Monteverde district. ℰ06 96 03 90 81. www.lagourmandise.it.* Lying outside the tourist districts, this family run gelateria offers gourmet ice cream. To be enjoyed pure (without a cone!).

Panificio Renella (Arnese) – *Via del Moro 15. Daily 7am–midnight (Sat and Sun till 3am). ℰ06 58 17 265.* This forno is famous for its traditional pane casareccia, the crusty spongy home-style Roman bread, baked in a wood-burning oven. Also biscotti and pizza by the slice.

Sora Mirella – La Grattachecca *Lungotevere degli Anguillara. Closed Oct–Feb.* Enjoy traditional Roman *grattachecce* (shaved ice with syrup), while those in the know look for classics made with seasonal fresh fruit like *cocco* (coconut) and *limone* (lemon).

CAFÉS

Bar Calisto – *Piazza San Calisto 3. 6am–2am. Closed Sun, end of Aug. ℰ06 58 35 869.* Packed with people each night, Calisto serves cheap coffee, beer and ice cream. It's a true slice of old Trastevere. Try the granita di caffè or a slushy vodka with granita (*sorbetto al limone*).

Caffè di Marzio – *Piazza di Santa Maria in Trastevere 15. 7am–1am. ℰ06 58 16 095.* The tables are costly (justifiably so, given the view), but counter service remains affordable. A good spot for a Prosecco, artisanal Italian or Belgian beer, cocktails or hot drinks.

Trastevere in festa

The first Sat after Jul 16, the district celebrates Festa de Noantri ("Festival of We Others").

Since 1927, the "Festival of We Others" is held every year (from mid-July) to honor Madonna del Carmine, patront saint of Trastevere. The statue of the virgin Mary is carried by a jubilant crowd from the church of Sant'Agata to San Crisogono, where after eight hours of popular veneration, it is brought back to its original site. Street shows and stalls full of artisanals products and food accompany this holiday. *www.festadenoantri.it.*

BARS

Freni e Frizioni – *Via del Politeama 4/6. ℰ06 45 49 74 99. www.freniefrizioni.com.* A must in the district, the Freni e Frizioni is an ideal spot to sip a drink on the terrace in the midst of the Trastevere movida. Excellent cocktails and a very trendy clientele.

♈/EAT

Trattoria da Augusto – *Piazza de' Renzi 15. ℰ06 58 03 798.* Simple food, typical roman cuisine, family run, tables face the square.

Bir&Fud – *Via Benedetta 23. Thu–Mon 12pm–2am. www.birandfud.it.* Plenty of real ales on tap, pizza, fries and Roman dishes that you can eat inside or out. The tris di *supplì* is an absolute speciality.

Via Veneto★

This famous street once defined glamour, as international film stars and the local glitterati mingled here. "La Dolce Vita" – the sweet life – soured in the 1970s–1980s, when terrorism scared wealthy Italians inside. Although it has lost some of its former romance, the Via Veneto is still lined with some of the smartest hotels and restaurants in the city. This wide avenue attracts locals and visitors for a stroll past famous cafés like Café de Paris and Doney.

WALKING TOUR

Porta Pinciana

The gateway in the 3C Aurelian Walls was fortified in the 6C by Belisarius, the Emperor Justinian's great general, who strove to regain the western territories. He captured Rome in 537 and expelled the Ostrogoths and Pope Silverius.

Via Vittorio Veneto

This street, created after 1879, bears the name of the commune of the Veneto, which, in 1866, adopted the name of King **Victor Emmanuel II** (Vittorio Emanuele) and in 1918 was the scene of the battle in which the Austro-Hungarian army was beaten by Italian troops.

The Via Veneto, as it is often called, runs through the heart of the beautiful **Ludovisi district**, which was divided into building lots in 1883 when Prince Ludovisi sold up his magnificent 17C property. Federico Fellini's classic 1960s film La Dolce Vita was centred around this area, cementing its iconic status as a glamorous hangout. Today, it is mainly known for its luxury hotels, boutiques and elegant cafés still frequented by a smart set, albeit a little less decadent in nature than the black and white melodrama of Anita Ekberg and Marcello Mastroianni.

Palazzo Margherita

It was designed by Gaetano Koch in 1886 and was the residence of Margaret of

Michelin Map: 38 J 13, K 13.

Location: Near the Villa Borghese gardens, the Via Veneto winds downhill from Porta Pinciana in the Aurelian Walls (now the Muro Torto), through the Ludovisi quarter to Piazza Barberini. Via Veneto is easily reached from the Barberini Metro station.

Don't Miss: *The Ecstasy of Saint Teresa of Avila* by Bernini in Santa Maria della Vittoria, the Triton Fountain in Piazza Barberini, the Palazzo Barberini masterpieces, the bone crypt in Santa Maria della Concezione.

Timing: 1 hour 30 minutes.

Also See: *FONTANA DI TREVI–QUIRINALE; PIAZZA DI SPAGNA; PORTA PIA–TERMINI; VILLA BORGHESE–VILLA GIULIA.*

GETTING THERE

BY METRO: Line A: Barberini or Spagna.

Savoy, King Humbert I's wife; it is now part of the United States Embassy.

Santa Maria della Concezione

Via Vittorio Veneto 27. ◐*Open Mon–Sat 7am–1pm and 3pm–6pm, Sun and public holidays 9:30am–noon and 3:30pm–6pm. Museum and crypt 9am–7pm.* ◐*Closed Eastern, 1 Jan, 25 Dec.* ◐€8.50. ☎06 88 80 36 95. *www.cappucciniviaveneto.it.*

The 1624 church has an austere Counter-Reformation style. At the chapel's entrance lies the tombstone of Cardinal Antonio Barberini, the church's founder, which bears the Latin inscription: "Here lie dust, ashes and nothing."

Below the church *(access on the right of the front steps),* friars prayed before bed

VILLA BORGHESE - PARCO DEI MUSEI

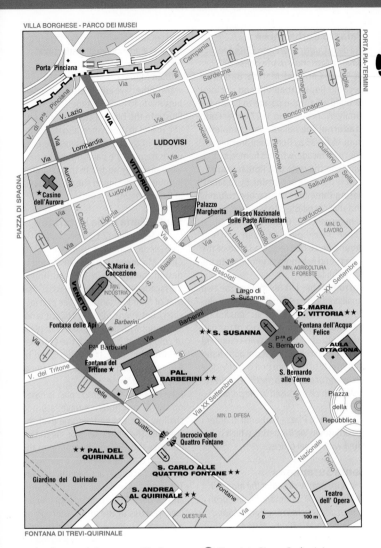

FONTANA DI TREVI-QUIRINALE

in the **Cappuccini crypt** ★★. The bones and skulls of 4 000 Cappuccino monks decorate this galley, woven into Baroque artworks: a rosette of shoulder blades, a chandelier and wall sconces made of bone, and a baldacchino made of pelvises with a vertebrae. The *memento mori* message is simple: "death closes the gates of time, and opens those of eternity."

Fontana delle Api

The fountain, which incorporates the **bees** (*api*) from the Barberini coat of arms, is the work of **Bernini** (1644).

▷ Turn into Piazza Barberini.

Fontana del Tritone★

Bernini's **Triton Fountain** (c 1642) is a happy example of Roman Baroque. The composition – four dolphins supporting an open scallop shell, where a triton sits blowing into a conch shell – demonstrates the powerful and lively qualities of his art. The Barberini bees on the coat of arms recall that a Barberini, Urban VIII, was then pope.

Palazzo Barberini★★

Via delle Quattro Fontane 13 (See Galleria Nazionale d'Arte antica p221).

In 1623 Cardinal Maffeo Barberini became Pope Urban VIII and decided to build a Baroque palace to house his family. Work began in 1627 under Carlo **Maderno**; the palace was completed from 1629–33 by Borromini and Bernini. The main façade, which is framed by two wings, in the style of a Roman country villa, is the work of **Bernini**. By superimposing three tiers of attached columns and shallow pilasters to frame two floors of huge windows *(slightly splayed on the upper storey)* over an open porch at ground level, he created a sense of the dignity and solemnity appropriate to the Barberini family.

Borromini has left his mark in the two small curiously pedimented upper windows in the intermediate sections linking the wings to the central block of the palace; he also designed the twin-columned **oval spiral staircase★** at the right-hand *(south)* end of the front porch *(also visible at the end of the visit to the Galleria di Arte Antica, which is housed in the palazzo).*

 Return to Piazza Barberini in order to turn down Via Barberini, which is lined with travel offices.

Santa Susanna★★

 Temporarily closed at the moment writing. Via XX Settembre 15. American church. Mass held in English, Sat 5pm, Sun 9am and 10:30am. 06 42 01 45 54. www.santasusanna.org.

A Christian sanctuary was probably established here in the 4C in the house of Pope Caius, where St Susanna was thought to have been martyred. Rebuilt by Leo III in the 9C and restored at the end of the 15C by Sixtus IV, the church was completed by **Carlo Maderno** in 1603.

Façade★★ – This beautifully proportioned masterpiece was designed by Carlo Maderno. It is derived from the Counter-Reformation style typified by the façade of the Gesù Church, but the use of semi-engaged columns and the effect of perspective, created by recesses

and pediments which relieve the austerity, give it an individual distinction.

Interior – The decoration is typical of the Roman Mannerist style (late 15C): the walls of the nave are covered with paintings made to look like tapestries, which illustrate the biblical story of Susanna. The scenes in the chancel also depict the history of this saint. The wreathed columns framing the paintings in the nave were probably added in the 17C, after Bernini had designed the baldaquin in St Peter's (1624).

Santa Maria della Vittoria★★

Via XX Settembre 17. Open daily 7am–noon, 3:30pm–7.15pm.

Carlo Maderno was commissioned to design the church in 1608. Although the façade was built some 20 years after that of Santa Susanna (*See previous entry)*, between 1624 and 1626, it is not as daring; with its flat pilasters in place of columns, it is closer to the Counter-Reformation style. It was designed by **Giovanni Battista Soria** for Cardinal Scipione Borghese.

Interior★★★ – Maderno's plan is based on the Gesù Church: a nave, a broad shallow transept and a dome over the crossing. The simple lines of the design enhance the elegant decoration of the cornice. During the 17C, a very rich Baroque décor was applied throughout. The vault, originally white and coffered, and the dome, were painted with *trompel'œil* frescoes of the Virgin triumphing against heresy and entering into Heaven. The walls were faced with multicoloured marble, their tones mingling with the gilded stucco and the white cherubs.

The Baroque decoration culminates in the **Cornaro Chapel** *(left transept)*, which was designed by **Bernini** in 1652: eight members of the Cornaro family, as if in boxes at the theatre, gaze at the **Ecstasy of St Theresa of Avila★★★**. The finish in marble is a stunning rendition of texture; including that of rough cloth (the Carmelite habit), the angel's light veiling and the delicacy of the flesh.

The paintings in the chapels include the *Life of St Francis* by Domenichino *(second chapel on the right).*

Detail, Pietro da Cortona Salon

©Judy Edelhoff/Michelin

Fontana del Mosè (also Fontana dell'Acqua Felice)

This huge fountain was designed in 1587 by Domenico Fontana. It is supplied by an aqueduct built by Sixtus V, which bears his Christian name: Felice Peretti. A colossal statue of Moses reigns here, sculpted by Prospero Bresciano, who was, no doubt, inspired by Michelangelo's *Moses*. He died from disappointment when he saw the finished work.

San Bernardo alle Terme

Via Torino 94. ⏰*Open daily 6:30am–noon and 4pm–7pm.* ℘*06 48 82 122.*
St Bernard's Church was created late in the 16C in a rotunda in a former tower in the southwest corner of the Baths of Diocletian (⏰*See PORTA PIA–TERMINI*). The handsome coffered dome, similar to the Pantheon's, lends a certain dignity to the interior.

GALLERIA NAZIONALE D'ARTE ANTICA★

Palazzo Barberini. Via delle Quattro Fontane 13. ⏰*Open Tue–Sun 8:30am–7pm.* ⏰*Closed 1 Jan and 25 Dec.* ⊘€12. ℘06 48 14 591. www.barberinicorsini.org. Works may be temporarily not on view or displayed elsewhere than described below. Guided tours first Sun of the month.* ℘06 42 01 00 66.*

Ground Floor

12C–16C Paintings – *The visit starts in the first room to the left of the entrance.* The *Virgin and Child* by the **master of the Palazzo Venezia** is an elegant drawing where the influence of Simone Martini can be seen. The *Virgin and Child* and the *Annunciation* are by **Filippo Lippi** (1406–1469). Note the attention paid to perspective via architectural elements (the windows and columns): a novelty in early Italian art. Also interesting are a fine *Mary Magdalene* by **Piero di Cosimo** and *San Nicolò da Tolentino* by **Perugino**. Three works by **Antoniazzo Romano**, chief exponent of the firm style being used in Latium at the end of the 15C, are also exhibited, among them the *Nativity with St Lawrence and St Andrew*.

First and Second Floors

16C Paintings – Worthy 16C works include *The Holy Family* by **Andrea del Sarto** and a fine *Virgin and Child with St John* by Domenico Beccafumi, which plays with contrasting light and uses the *sfumato* technique perfected by Leonardo da Vinci. Works by **Sodoma** (1477–1549) – a great admirer of Raphael's flowing lines and his friend and collaborator in Rome – include *The Mystical Marriage of St Catherine* and *The Rape of the Sabine Women*.

The collection also boasts a masterpiece by **Raphael**, **La Fornarina★★★**, painted by the artist during the year he died. The portrait is of Raphael's beautiful

221

mistress, Margherita, known as *La Fornarina* because she was the daughter of a baker ("*fornaio*" in Italian). *La Fornarina* often features in Raphael's work and is depicted here with an unusual sensuality and a hint of cunning in her expression. The *Portrait of Stefano Colonna* (1546) is by **Bronzino** and is typical of this refined artist and portrait painter. He endeavoured to present subjects in a suitably noble pose, rather than bring out their more ordinary characteristics. The gallery also houses works by **Titian** and **Tintoretto**, as well as the beautiful *Holy Conversation* by Lorenzo Lotto, a magnificent painting notable for the detail of clothes and jewels.

Pietro da Cortona Salon★★★ – The ceiling is the best work ever produced by **Pietro da Cortona**, who showed the true measure of his talent here. It was painted between 1633 and 1639 to celebrate the glory of the Barberini family, whose coat of arms (bees in a crown of laurel) is carried by allegorical figures representing the Virtues. On the left, Divine Providence, holding a sceptre, reigns from the clouds. Note how skilfully the painter has used grisaille to separate the scenes.

17C–18C Paintings – Works by **Guido Reni** (1575–1642) include the delicate **Portrait of Beatrice Cenci★** and a foreshortened fresco, the **Sleeping Putto★★**. The *Portrait of Bernini★* by **Baciccia** (1639–1709) is a rare portrait by this artist, who was famous mainly for his decorative skill. Two other Baroque masters are **Pietro da Cortona** with his *Guardian Angel* and **Bernini** with his two paintings *David with the Head of Goliath* and the *Portrait of Urban VIII*.

Two famous paintings can be seen among the works by non-Italian artists. The **Portrait of Henry VIII★★★** (1540) is by **Hans Holbein the Younger**, who became the official painter at the English court and produced portraits with impartiality and keen insight. The very expressive **Portrait of Erasmus★★★** (1517), by **Quentin Metsys**, also shows deep analysis. The **Narcissus★★** illustrates the novel style of **Caravaggio** (1573–1610), who was a contemporary of Guido Reni and Guercino. Dispensing with background, he portrays Narcissus bending over the water, lost in admiration for his own reflection. As always, light plays a primordial role, highlighting the rapt face, immaculate corset and knee and hiding Narcissus' expression with shadow. **Judith and Holofernes★** contrasts sharply with this painting. The cruelty here is conveyed in dramatic detail – made even more striking by the troubled figure of the old woman.

ADDITIONAL SIGHT

Casino dell'Aurora Ludovisi★

Via Lombardia 46. Open by appointment to groups only, min 15 people. €20. ℘06 48 39 42.
The Aurora Casino is the loggia built by Cardinal Scipione Borghese in 1612-13. The central section featured Aurora in her chariot painted in 1613-1614 by Guido Reni and other artists. The side rooms were painted primarily by Giovanni Baglioni and Domenico Cresti.

▲▲ Museo Nazionale delle Paste Alimentari

☞ *Temporarily closed for restoration at the moment of writing. Via Lucullo 9. www.museodellapasta.it.*
Housed in Palazzo Scanderberg, the **National Pasta Museum** charts the history of this culinary icon.

ADDRESSES

TAKING A BREAK

Bistrot c/o Hotel Majestic – *Via V. Veneto 50.* ℘06 42 14 41. *www.hotelmajestic.com.* The expert hand of chef Massimo Riccioli makes the culinary offerings always modern. You can't go wrong with the seafood.

Mirabelle c/o Hotel Splendide Royal – *Via di Porta Pinciana 14.* ℘06 42 16 89. *www.splendideroyal.com.* An incredible view from the exclusive 7th-floor roof. The perfect welcome is orchestrated by Bruno Borghesi and the cuisine rich in flavours.

Lotti Caffè Pasticceria– *Via Sardegna 19/21.* ℘ 06 48 21 902. Homemade gelato and pastries are specialties here. The interior is a bit gloomy, but the sidewalk seating makes for a pleasant break.

Villa Borghese– Villa Giulia★★

Home to three of Rome's most important museums, this district is also graced by one of the largest areas of greenery (5.5km/3.5mi in circumference). The 17C pleasure garden is now a park, dotted with small lakes, temples and majestic umbrella pines. Major international equestrian events are held here.

A BIT OF HISTORY

In the early 17C, Paul V became pope – and lavished gifts upon his family. His nephew even inherited his name: Scipione Borghese. When this newly made man became a cardinal, he built a little palace (palazzina) in his vineyards. The section of the **Aurelian Wall** from the Porta del Popolo to the Porta Pinciana follows such an irregular line that the Romans call it the crooked wall (**Muro Torto**) and tell many legends about it. When the Goths besieged the city in the 6C, they failed to take advantage of a fortifications breach here. Locals concluded that the area had St Peter's protection. In the Middle Ages, this was a cemetery for people denied Christian burial.

GIARDINI DI VILLA BORGHESE★★

This walk wanders through a romantic landscape of lakes, trees and flower gardens set with imitation antique sculpture.

▶ Take Viale di Valle Giulia and then the first path on the right which leads to Viale Pietro Canonica; turn left.

The little **castle** (castello medievale) was the house and studio of the sculptor Pietro Canonica (1869–1959). The **Temple of Antoninus and Faustina** was built in the late 18C.

▶ Continue along the path as far as Viale dell'Uccelliera; turn right.

- ◔ **Michelin Map:** 38 G–H 11–13.
- ▷ **Location:** This walk explores Rome's largest public park, which borders on the elegant Parioli district and contains two museums, an art gallery and various national academies of art in a setting of lakes, lawns and groves of trees.
- ◷ **Timing:** Allow 1 day, including the museums.
- ♟ **Kids:** The bikes, rowboats and the static-line balloon in the leafy green Villa Borghese. The carousel is beside the *Teatro dei Burattini*, which shows cartoons and movies for *bambini* (www.sancarlino.it). Pack a picnic to avoid overpriced snacks from vendors. The Bioparco (Rome's zoo) .
- ◔ **Also See:** *PIAZZA DEL POPOLO; PIAZZA DI SPAGNA; VIA VENETO.*

GETTING THERE

BY METRO AND BUS: Line A: Flaminio. Bus 53, 61, 86, 89, 160, 490, 495 and 910.

The building topped by a wrought-iron cage is a 17C aviary. The Viale dell'Uccelliera (Aviary Avenue) leads to the Villa Borghese.

Villa Borghese★★★

This little palace (palazzina) was designed in 1613 by Flaminio Ponzio for Cardinal Scipione Borghese and is a delightful example of a rich prelate's house. Construction was continued after Ponzio's death by a Dutchman, Jan van Santen (called "Vasanzio" in Italian). During a late 18C restoration, the southwest façade (the present front entrance) was considered too ornate; builders stripped some decoration and

Villa Borghese garden

© fotoVoyager/iStockphoto.com

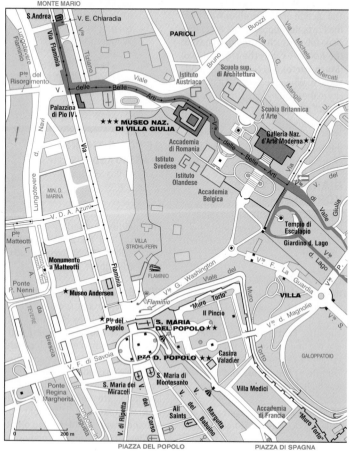

altered the steps. Early in the 20C, the balustrade bounding the forecourt (but not the statues, which were classed as works of art) was acquired by Lord Astor and removed to Cliveden.

Between 1801 and 1809, the Borghese horde was greatly depleted; Prince Camillo, Pauline Bonaparte's husband, sold over 200 sculptures to the Louvre. In 1891, the Borghese Palace paintings were moved to the *palazzina*. Its sylvan setting, its elegant late 18C décor and its outstanding collections make this gallery one of Rome's best.

The massive square villa is embellished by two avant-corps topped with towers and framed by a portico. Statues peer from the façade.

▷ Take Viale dei Pupazzi.

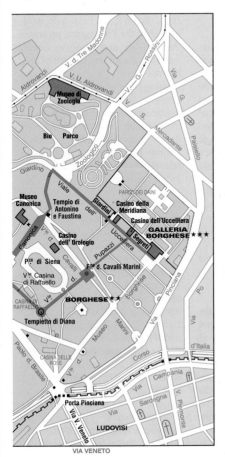

The **Seahorse Fountain** was commissioned in 1791 by Prince Marcantonio Borghese, who renovated the gardens. The **Piazza di Siena** further on is named after the native town of the Borghese. Set among umbrella pines, it hosts international equestrian events. On the northeast side stands the late 18C **Casina dell' Orologio**. Viale dei Pupazzi leads to the **Temple of Diana**, modelled on an ancient building. From there, an avenue runs north to the **Lake Garden** (Giardino del Lago), one of the most popular corners of the park. The architect Asprucci created it; he helped enlarge the Borghese Gardens at the end of 18C. The lake reflects the columns of the little **Temple of Aesculapius**, another imitation. Taking Viale Giardino Zoologico on the other side of the lake, you come to the **Bioparco** (&⏱Open daily 9:30am–dusk. ⊜€16 adults, €13 children under 10. ℘06 36 08 211 www.bioparco.it).

▷ Return to Viale di Villa Giulia and turn left into Viale delle Belle Arti.

Various academies stand on both sides of this avenue, between the Galleria Nazionale d'Arte Moderna and the Museo Nazionale di Villa Giulia. One of these is the **British School**, which brings artists, architects and scholars to the Eternal City. (⏱Lectures are held weekly. Exhibition dates vary. Via Antonio Gramsci 61. ℘06 32 64 939. www.bsr.ac.uk.

▷ Follow Via delle Belle Arti to the intersection with Via Flaminia.

Palazzina di Pio IV

The little palace was built by Pius IV (1559–65), who offered it to his nephew Cardinal Charles Borromeo.

The slightly concave façade exhibits the mannered style

typical of late Renaissance works. Since 1929, the building has housed the Italian Embassy to the Holy See.

▶ Turn right into Via Flaminia.

Sant'Andrea del Vignola
Via Luigi Canina.
St Andrew's Church was built in the 16C by Vignola for Julius III. It is an unusual little building, with a clear-cut silhouette, stressed by heavy dentilated cornices, an elliptical dome resting on a solid base and plain brick walls.

GALLERIA BORGHESE★★★
Piazzale del Museo Borghese 5.
♿🕐*Open Tue–Sun 9am–7pm.*
🕐*Closed 1 Jan and 25 Dec. Visits are scheduled for 2hrs.* ⊜€13. *Tickets must be reserved (*⊜€2*) and collected at least 15min before entry.* ☎06 32 810. *www.galleriaborghese.it.*

The collection – Cardinal Scipione Borghese, nephew of Pope Paul V, was an avid collector of ancient, Renaissance and Neoclassical art, although he showed little interest in the medieval period. He accumulated a substantial art collection and also commissioned some of the best-known sculptors of his time, such as Bernini and Cordier. Unfortunately, Camillo Borghese sold part of the collection to his brother-in-law Napoleon. These works are now exhibited in the Louvre. The cardinal also bought and commissioned paintings from Caravaggio, Rubens, Reni, Guercino and other great artists.
Works may not always be displayed in the locations described below.

Ground Floor
Cross the portico to enter the **main hall**, which is decorated with antique statues (originals and copies), paintings and reliefs, and provides a good idea of **Neoclassical** taste. The 4C mosaic fragments were discovered near Tusculum and depict hunting and wrestling. On the ceiling, a fresco by Mariano Rossi illustrates the deification of Romulus, who is welcomed to Olympus by Jupiter *(centre)*. Also exhibited in the main hall

is an unfinished sculpture by **Bernini**, *Truth Being Unveiled by Time* (the figure of Time is missing).

Canova – *Room I*. The **statue of Pauline Bonaparte★★★** as Venus was immediately accepted as a masterpiece, despite its scandalous nature. The polished, translucent goddess lounges half naked, holding the "apple of discord". The model – Napoleon's sister – was the "idol of high society"; appearing without drapery was a risqué move. Yet her celebrity, combined with the wattage of Canova, proved irresistible.
The ceiling fresco by Domenico de Angelis repeats this theme. The small hooded marble statues in the corners are the Roman precursors of gnomes, said to bring fortune or disaster.

Opere del Bernini★★★ (Bernini Rooms) – The artist was 25 when he sculpted *David* (Room II). Michelangelo, working during the Renaissance, presented the hero calm and victorious. Bernini instead captured the moment of most intense effort, emphasised by the twisting body and the lips pursed in concentration, making this statue a masterpiece of Baroque sculpture.
In his *Apollo and Daphne* (Room III), Bernini shows the metamorphosis of Daphne from nymph to laurel bush. Note the movement of the hair, almost indistinguishable from the branches. Behind this sculpture, a painting by **Dosso Dossi** (c. 1489–1542) treats the same theme quite differently. Apollo mourns his lost love, a tiny figure to the left. Metamorphosis is also the theme of a second masterpiece by this artist from Ferrara: *Circe the Sorceress*.
The *Rape of Proserpina* (Room IV) is one of **Bernini**'s early commissions of Scipione and was given as a gift to Cardinal Ludovisi. Although the statue of Pluto, god of the Underworld, shows traces of the academic style, the supple modelling of Proserpina foreshadows Bernini's works of genius. The subtle tears streaking her face and the fingermarks in her thigh show the artist's attention to detail and texture.
Aeneas carrying Anchises (Room VI) – rather stiff figures with set expressions

– is now considered a collaboration between Bernini and his father.

Room V – The **Sleeping Hermaphroditus★** is a beautiful Roman copy of an original 2C BC Greek statue. Note the feminine shape of the back of the body and the way the head rests, turned to one side, on the arm.

Caravaggio Room★★★ – (*Room VIII*). This room houses masterpieces by **Caravaggio** (1573–1610). The artist led an adventurous and occasionally unlawful life. Yet he revolutionized painting, drawing his inspiration from nature. His figures sprang from the canvas with dazzling effects of light and were extremely realistic. Angry patrons often refused works they had commissioned. This was the case with the altarpiece of the *Madonna dei Palafrenieri*, intended for an altar in St Peter's Basilica. It remained there only two days, before being banished to the Chiesa di Santa Maria dei Palafrenieri. The traditional iconography of the characters is distorted: St Anne – here an old woman – stands to one side, her hands clasped on her stomach. The Virgin supports Jesus, who helps crush the serpent's head. The scene may refer to a theological debate, in which the Protestants denied the Immaculate Conception (and therefore the Virgin's power to overcome evil). The Rosario Bull of Pius V (1569) could well be reflected in the painting: the Virgin can triumph with her son's assistance.

The *Boy with a Basket of Fruit* is an admirable still life. For the *Ailing Bacchus*, Caravaggio gave the god his own features. He appears frail and wan (possibly following a leg injury that required hospitalisation). Death infuses this work, suggested not only by the colour palette, but also by the yellowed leaves and the bare grey slab that evokes a tombstone. These early works were most likely painted for the open market, without a specific patron in mind. The same sorrowful atmosphere can be sensed in *David Showing Goliath's Head*. The boy is hardly a triumphant victor. He wears an expression of sadness, compassion and horror; the expression of one who has carried out a just act, but is aware of the grave consequences.

An event in the artist's life may shed some light. Caravaggio was in exile in Naples when he painted this work, having killed a companion in a brawl. Anyone who came across his path had the right to behead him. It is not surprising that he has represented himself as Goliath, and perhaps also as David, who vaguely resembles the ailing Bac-

Galleria Borghese

© fabiomax/Fotolia.com

FIRST FLOOR

0   10 m

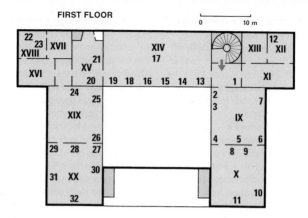

chus. He sent the painting to Cardinal Scipione, asking him to plead his cause. *St Jerome* was painted by Caravaggio for the cardinal. The saint is portrayed as a thin and muscular figure, absorbed in his task of translating the holy texts. The last work by the artist is a sorrowful *St John the Baptist*.

First Floor

Two superb mosaics by Marcello Provenzale **(1)** (1577–1639) portray Orpheus, with references to Scipione Borghese (the eagle and the dragon on the left), and Paul V Borghese.

Room IX – The *Crucifixion with St Jerome and St Christopher* **(2)** by **Pinturicchio** (1454–1513) reflects the artist's liking for miniatures, which characterised the art of the 15C Primitives. In the *Virgin and Child with St John the Baptist* **(3)** by **Lorenzo di Credi** (1459–1537) and the *Adoration of the Child* **(4)** by **Fra Bartolomeo** (1475–1527), the influence of **Leonardo da Vinci** and the Renaissance is clearly evident. The room also houses three remarkable **works★★★** by **Raphael** (1483–1520). The *Deposition* **(5)** was commissioned by Atalanta Baglioni.

The Etruscans

This people's origin is lost in prehistory. Around the year 1000 BC, Indo-Europeans from the north settled in central Italy. These new arrivals were skilled in the use of iron and they also cremated their dead. This civilisation, which seems to have spread northwards from central Italy, is known as the **Villanovan** culture. The sophisticated Etruscans may have blossomed from these roots. More advanced than their neighbours, the Etruscans governed Rome from the end of the 7C BC. Their domain stretched from Corsica to the shores of the Adriatic and from Capua to Bologna, but centred in modern Lazio, Umbria and Tuscany (which bears their name). Decline set in at the end of the 6C BC. Rome rebelled, expanded and attacked their cities; in the 1C BC the Etruscans became Roman citizens.

Traces of their civilisation have mostly disappeared. Their tombs still reveal much: richly decorated and full of funeral goods, these cluster together into *necropoli,* cities of the dead. Until the 18C, Etruscan art was thought to be a derivative of the Greek tradition, without any aesthetic value. Now its elegance and rogue spirit are very much in vogue – and scholars honour this people for style, as well as substance (their elegant engineering, urban planning and liberal social structure).

The patron had just lost his son (the character on the right) in the struggle for the Signoria of Perugia, hence the importance of the Virgin, grieving her child.

The portrait of a *Lady with a Unicorn* **(6)** – spoiled by being changed into a St Catherine but restored in 1935 – is a fine example of the nobility of Raphael's art. Note the delicacy of the necklace and pendant. The *Portrait of a Man* **(7)**, a work of admirable vigour, still shows signs of 15C art with a full-face presentation and an indistinguishable background.

Room X – *Venus* **(8)** by **Lucas Cranach** (1472–1553) is one of the rare works by a northern artist in Cardinal Borghese's collection; the more sensual *Venus* **(9)** is by **Brescianino**. In his painting of the *Virgin and Child with St John the Baptist* **(10)**, **Andrea del Sarto** (1486–1531) was influenced by Michelangelo's drawing and by Leonardo da Vinci's *sfumato* technique. The outstanding painting in the back of the room is *Danaë*★★★ **(11)** by **Correggio** (c 1489–1534), which illustrates the myth of Zeus as a shower of gold. The use of oils has produced very subtle colour tones.

Room XII – Highlights of the Lombardy–Veneto and Sienese regions (Sodoma) include The *Portrait of a Man* **(12)** by the Venetian **Lorenzo Lotto** (c. 1480–1556), thought to represent the widower Mercurio Bua.

Room XIV – The three **Bernini** paintings depict a young man **(14)**, possibly the artist's cousin, and two self-portraits, one as a youth **(16)** and another as an old man **(15)**. Of the two fine busts of Cardinal Scipione Borghese, the second **(13)** was executed because there was a vein in the marble in the first one **(18)** on the cardinal's forehead. *Young Jupiter with the Goat Amalthea* **(19)** was probably the artist's first work (c. 1615). A small bronze statue, *Sleep* **(17)** by Algardi is also on display.

Room XV – Works by Dosso Dossi and **Jacopo Bassano** (1516–1592) are on exhibit. Bassano was a Venetian who used exceptional colour effects. He enjoyed painting country scenes and interiors, which he used even in his religious works, as demonstrated in his *Last Supper* **(20)**. This lively colourful scene represents a gathering of ordinary people, such as peasants and fishermen, crowded around a table. Some are deep in discussion, others gesture wildly, others still are lost in their thoughts and appear to be on the point of falling asleep. Only the figure of Christ in the centre of the picture remains calm and composed.

Tobias and the Angel **(21)** by **Girolamo Savoldo** (1480–1548) presages Baroque painting in the powerful figures and the bold effects of light.

Room XVIII – The *Mourning the Death of Christ* **(22)** by **Rubens** was painted early in the 17C during the artist's visit to Rome. The *Portrait of Monsignor Merlini* **(23)** by **Andrea Sacchi** (1559–1661) shows a restraint unusual in the Baroque era.

Room XIX – After the insipid Mannerist style, two currents brought about the transition to Baroque painting. In Bologna, a style based on tradition developed around the Carracci, which **Domenichino** (1581–1641) helped to propagate; his painting of **Diana the huntress**★★★ **(24)** demonstrates the Bologna expertise very well (the detail of the trees and the bird hit by arrows). The beautifully coloured **Sibyl**★ **(25)** is by the same painter. Annibale Carracci succeeds in capturing expression in just a few strokes in his *Laughing Boy* **(26)**.

Room XX – The **Portrait of a man**★★★ **(27)** by **Antonello de Messina** (1430–79), with its powerfully expressive look, its precision (garment folds) and the delicate modelling of the face, is a masterpiece. The *Holy Conversation* **(28)** by **Palma the Elder** (1480–1528) is remarkable for its colours and for the keenly observed portrait of the pious woman *(left side of the painting)*. In the *Virgin and Child* **(29)** by the Venetian **Giovanni Bellini** (c. 1429–1516) the firm line of the figures is bathed in a beautiful luminosity.

Sacred and Profane Love★★★ **(30)** by **Titian** (c. 1490–1576) shows the young artist's search for an ideal of beauty.

When he painted *Venus tending Love* **(31)** at 75, his art had been utterly renewed. As well as Titian in 16C Venice there was **Veronese**; *St John the Baptist Preaching* **(32)** demonstrates Veronese's attraction to the narrative picture.

MUSEO NAZIONALE ETRUSCO DI VILLA GIULIA★★★

Piazzale di Villa Giulia 9. ♿ 🕐*Open Tue –Sun 9am–8pm* 🕐*Closed 1 Jan and 25 Dec.* ⊛€8. 𝒫*06 32 26 571.* *www.villagiulia.beniculturali.it.*
The exceptional interest of the collection is enhanced by its charming situation in Julius III's country villa.
The museum is devoted to **Etruscan civilisation**. In his classic 1932 book, *Etruscan Places*, DH Lawrence mourned the passing of this mysterious people "who occupied the middle of Italy in early Roman days and whom the Romans, in their usual neighbourly fashion, wiped out entirely in order to make room for Rome with a very big R."

Etruscan Art

(👉See also VATICANO–SAN PIETRO).
Pottery – The impasto technique used for rudimentary clay pots was succeeded in the 7C BC by **bucchero** (black terracotta). At first the vases were simply decorated with a stippled design, but the shapes grew ever more ornate up to the 5C, when they were fashioned in the form of humans or fantastic animals. **Ornamentation** – The work is exquisitely rich: engraved on bronze, in gold filigree or granulation, in finely carved ivory.
Sculpture – The Etruscans never used marble; they worked in bronze and clay. Their statues are distinguished by an enigmatic smile and large staring eyes.
Frescoes – Art historians praise the painters' fluidity, but struggle to categorize the style, usually falling back on a lame "mixture of Greek, indigenous and eastern influences". Only a handful, 6C–2C BC tomb decorations, survived. The Villa Giulia displays replicas; the originals are in Tarquinia, 90km/56mi northwest.

Architecture – An Etruscan temple was approached by a flight of steps that led up to a columned portico. The sanctuary itself was a rectangular building, standing on a high podium and containing three shrines *(cellae)* at the rear.

Villa Giulia★

Although Julius III's reign (1550–55) was contemporary with the Council of Trent, the pope did not lose his taste for the cultivated life of a Renaissance prince. In 1551, he invited Vignola to design a summer villa. The plain and sober façade is typical of this artist, who also studied and wrote about architectural theory. The first courtyard is framed by a semicircular portico with **frescoed vaulting★**, decorated with trellises of vines, climbing roses and jasmine.
In the main courtyard beyond is a charming Mannerist construction by Bartolomeo Ammanati, who collaborated on the Villa Giulia from 1552. The little loggia, perfectly proportioned, opens onto horseshoe steps descending to a nymphaeum adorned with caryatids, rockeries and false grottoes. Several pieces of Roman sculpture are on display. In the past, the public was permitted to enjoy the tranquillity of this villa and to gather the fruit and flowers. When the poet Joachim du Bellay visited, he disapproved severely of the pope for leading a life of pleasure to the detriment of affairs of State. When Julius III raised a young man of 17, who led a troop of performing monkeys, to be a cardinal, Du Bellay did not omit to poke fun at the new Jupiter and his Ganymede.
The courtyard is laid out in pleasant gardens bordered by the wings built at the beginning of the 20C to house the museum. To the right of the nymphaeum the Etruscan temple of Alatri has been reconstructed.

Ground Floor

Vulci – *Rooms 1–46.* This major centre of Etruscan civilisation occupied the area corresponding to the present-day Maremma and excelled in bronzework. Particularly worthy of note is the lami-

The Evolution of Ceramic Techniques

From the beginning of the 5C to about 480 BC, the red-figure technique made Athens the capital of Attic vase painting. Articles produced during this period show the heads in profile, but the eye is drawn full-face. The quality is remarkable; the detail within the outline of the body and garments is done with a fine brush.

Artefacts from the 4C BC demonstrate a clear change in style. Hellenistic artists started to experiment with other techniques, not only in Athens, but in *Magna Graecia* (southern Italy) and Apulia. Flowers, fronds and elaborate decorations appeared in white, yellow and dark red against a background of black varnish. The ceramics from Egnatia in Apulia belong to this period.

The raised decoration on some pieces cheaply imitated metal vessels.

nated bronze cinerary urn shaped like a hut.

Maroie Tomb – This is a reconstruction of a tomb dating from the 6C BC, with two funeral chambers, found in the Banditaccia necropolis at Cerveteri to the northwest of Rome.

Bisenzio Tombs – Among the objects found in the tombs in this city are two remarkable **pieces of bronze★**, typical examples of early Etruscan art (late 8C to early 7C BC): a **miniature chariot** adorned with figures in the round depicting various aspects of everyday life (such as ploughing, hunting, and a duel), and a covered **vessel** decorated with warriors (also in the round), who are taking part in a ritual dance around an animal, on top of the vessel.

Veii (Veio) Sculptures★★★ – The statue of **Apollo and Heracles** represents a dispute between the god and the hero over possession of the Ceryneian Hind, which lies at Heracles' feet; the sculpture dates from the end of the 6C BC, when Etruscan art was at its zenith. The display echoes the original configuration on the temple's roof ridge: the statues once were silhouetted against the sky. They are made of terracotta and are strikingly realistic and animated.

The other sculptures include a goddess with a child, which probably represents Apollo and his mother Leto, a fine head of Hermes and several *antefixae* in the shape of Gorgon, Maenad, Silenus and Achelous heads, which masked the ends of the roof beams and the painted pedi-

ments. These sculptures all come from the same temple and may be the work of **Vulca**, the only Etruscan sculptor known by name. The king of Rome sent for him in 509 BC to ornament the Temple of Jupiter on the Capitoline (*See CAMPIDOGLIO*).

Terracotta sarcophagus★★★ – One of the masterpieces of Etruscan terracotta sculpture, it dates from the end of the 6C and comes from Cerveteri. The husband and wife, reclining as if at a banquet, seem to be pursuing their life in the beyond. In contrast to the stylised lower bodies, the torsos are realistic in tone, emphasising the couple's bond. Note the husband's loving stance, his head slightly turned towards his wife and his arm across her shoulders.

First Floor

The **Antiquarium** of the museum is chiefly devoted to small **bronze objects★**, both useful and decorative. Bronze was one of the main Etruscan exports, which contributed largely to their wealth. They fashioned it with great creative skill: rudimentary **clasps** dating from the 8C to the 6C BC, **mirrors** finely etched with elegant scenes from family life or mythology, statuettes with astonishingly modern forms. The Etruscans' liking for bronze is explained by the rich copper deposits in Etruria and the island of Elba, which belonged to them. The tin may have been imported from Great Britain or the neighbouring islands.

The **Chigi wine pitcher★★** is one of the most famous items in the collection. Found at Veii *(Veio)*, it is one of the most beautiful examples of Greek art from the middle of the 7C BC. This is the proto-Corinthian period when the ceramics produced in Corinth, an important port on the sea routes to the East, were decorated with subjects treated in miniature in bands of delicate silhouettes. On the upper part, two groups of warriors march into battle. The incision work shows each detail clearly. The lower part is covered with figures and hunting scenes.

Two *bucchero* **vases★** date from the 6C BC (*bucchero* is a sort of clay); the technique for producing this particular type of Etruscan ceramic, which is black, is not well understood. One of the vases bears the Etruscan alphabet, the other a long inscription. Their alphabet has been deciphered, but the meaning is still unknown.

Biga di Castro – Of particular interest is the reconstruction of this chariot, with the skeletons of two horses sacrificed in the burial place.

Castellani Collection★ – *Semi-circular corridor*. The collection traces the evolution of Greek and Etruscan ceramics from the 8C BC to the Roman era. The Etruscans imported a considerable amount of Greek pottery.

The following exhibits are particulary worthy of note:

♦ The elongated **vases**, which date from the 7C and 6C BC and come from eastern Greece. These are imitations of Egyptian alabaster vessels and were used by athletes for the perfumed oil with which they massaged their bodies; hence the flat lip. There are several *bucchero* vases dating from the 7C and 6C BC.

♦ The beautiful **wine bowl** made in Sparta in about 570 *(stile laconico)* and decorated with lotus flowers, an Eastern motif.

♦ The two **water pitchers**, dating from between 530 and 520. These Caere *hydriae* are a type of water pot found in a necropolis in Cerveteri (ancient *Caere*). The decoration of picturesque mythological scenes includes the abduction of Europa by Zeus on one and on the other Hercules in his lion-skin leading Cerberus against Eurystheus, who is hiding in a large jar in terror.

♦ The **red-figure Attic vases**. From 540–530 BC, Attic ceramic art was transformed by the change from black- to red-figure technique. Henceforth artists signed their work, as can be seen on the two *amphorae* signed by Nicosthenes. Note the two vases by Cleophrades; one is decorated with a very realistic painting of Hercules and the Nemean lion.

Castellani Collection of Jewellery★ – This stunning collection of over 2 500 pieces was assembled by the Castellani family of jewellers. The antique ornaments date from the 8C BC to the Roman and medieval periods. Also on display are 19C copies and arrangements of antique jewels.

Pyrgi Antiquities – The old port of Cerveteri, where excavation work has uncovered the foundations of two temples, was mostly famous as a religious centre. The pediment of temple A (460 BC) can be admired in these rooms. The decoration on the back pediment (470–460 BC) recounts two of the most dramatic episodes of the legend of the Seven against Thebes. In the first, Zeus faces Capaneus, one of the seven rebels, and in the second, Tydeus lies mortally wounded on the ground, about to devour Melanippus's brain.

Tombs from Capena and the Faliscan Region – The Capenans and Faliscans occupied neighbouring areas to the north of Rome, bordered to the east by the River Tiber. The two regions became known at the beginning of the 7C BC for their production of *impasto* ceramics. The black-varnished ceramic **plate** is a more recent (3C BC) example of their art. It was found at Capena and is decorated with an elephant accompanied by its calf and guided by an Indian; archers perch on the animal's back. The decoration is thought to refer to a parade that took place after the Roman victory over Pyrrhus (275 BC) in Benevento. There the enemy lost eight elephants, four of which were brought to Rome. The beautiful gold trousseau (necklace with granulated decoration) comes from the *Tomba degli Ori*, in Narce, a Faliscan centre in southern Italy.

Among the exhibits from Falerii Veteres, the capital of the Faliscans, now occupied by Città Castellana, note the beautiful **Aurora wine bowl**. This mid-4C BC piece shows Aurora and Cephalus in their chariot and Peleus abducting Thetis; around the neck a deer and a bull are being attacked by griffins.

Ground Floor

Temples of Falerii Veteres★ – The architecture of these buildings is known to us from plans left by Vitruvius, a Roman architect and theorist (1C BC). The room contains interesting partial reconstructions of pediments, examples of *antefixae* and *acroteria* (decorative elements, often in terracotta, which were placed on the peak and at either end of the pediments, from the 4C).

The **Bust of Apollo★** shows late Greek classical influence.

Praeneste: "Barberini" and "Bernardini" Tombs – These rich tombs, situated near Palestrina (*Ancient Praeneste*. *See Excursions Outside Rome*) contained mid-7C BC articles, including carved **ivory pieces** – the result of trading relations between the Etruscans and Phoenicians.

The Etruscans were expert goldsmiths and worked in this metal from the 7C BC using the filigree technique. They also perfected granulation: splitting the gold into beads only a few tenths of a millimetre in diameter. The **jewellery★** on display includes some beautiful brooches and **rectangular plates★★**, adorned with animal figures, such as chimera, lions, mermaids and horses, and embellished with granulations; these were used as ornaments worn over the chest.

Ficoroni Cists★★★ – The cists were marriage coffers; they were also sometimes used for toilet or religious articles. Some magnificent examples were produced by the Etruscans between the 4C and 2C BC. Their manufacture was a speciality of *Praeneste (See Palestrina in Excursions Outside Rome)*, where the largest known example – called the Ficoroni cist after its owner – was found in the 18C. Its feline feet are attached to the body by carved plaques; it is decorated with fine engravings of the Argonauts arriving among the Bebryces, with Pollux tying King Amycos to a tree. On the lid are hunting scenes and three statues in the round – the central figure is Dionysius.

GALLERIA NAZIONALE D'ARTE MODERNA★★

Viale delle Belle Arti 131 (wheelchair access at 71 Via Gramsci). &◐ *Open Tue–Sun 8:30am–7:30pm (exibitions open at 10:30am).* ◐ *Closed 1 Jan and 25 Dec* ⊕ *€10.* ✆ *06 32 29 82 21. www.gnam.beniculturali.it.*

Housed in a lovely building built in 1911 by Cesare Bazzani for the World's Fair, the gallery is primarily dedicated to 19C and 20C Italian painting and sculpture. It also accommodates importants temporary exhibitions and a good library.

Art of the 19C to 1883

Ground floor, to the left of the ticket counter.

This section presents Italian art from the 19C arranged according to school. In the first three rooms, Roman Neoclassicism is followed by the Tuscan School **Macchiaioli**, who rejected academic art in the name of more immediate and realistic works.

The next room, dedicated to the **Piedmont and Lombard schools**, displays works by F. Hayez *(The Sicilian Vespers)*, T. Cremona and A. Fontanesi, whose landscapes vibrate with suffused light. The large central room is dominated by the powerful **Hercules and Lichas** (Antonio Canova) "escorted" by 12 statues of the gods of Olympus, which were moved here prior to the demolition of the Palazzo Torlonia at Piazza Venezia in 1910.

The three rooms on the other side of the great hall are dedicated to the **Southern Schools**. The Neopolitan **D. Morelli**, student of the Tuscan

Galleria Nazionale d'Arte Moderna

Macchiaioli, reintroduced a historical painting style in which colour took precedence over design. The other two rooms feature artists from around Naples. In the Cleopatra Room, Verist works from M. Cammarano, G. Toma and A. Mancini; in the Palizzi Room, the landscape paintings by Giacinto Gigante from the school of Posillipo and the naturalistic colourful paintings from the Palizzi brothers.

Art of the 19C after 1883

Ground floor, to the right of the ticket counter.

This section features works of mostly Italian artists active at the end of the 19C. The first room displays Verist landscapes, imbued with great symbolism, while the second room displays works from Tuscany, including the Ghetto di Firenze from Macchiaiolo T. Signorini. Historical theme works by various artists are on exhibit in the big central hall, while on the opposite side of the hall, the Stanga Room features works from Piedmont in addition to Divisionist painting by G. Segantini of Trento. The adjacent Gardener's Room (to the left, facing away from the central hall) contains a collection of works from France and Italian artists active

in France: Cézanne (**Les Cabanon de Jourdan**, unfinished due to the artist's death), Degas, Monet, Van Gogh (**L'Arlesien** and *The Gardener*) and, among the Italian works, an intense **portrait of Verdi** by G. Boldini.

Crossing again through the Stanga Room you get to the Previati Room, dedicated to the **Divisionist works** of G. Previati, G. Segantini and G. Pellizza da Volpedo, who "divided" the colours in their paintings by using thin brushstrokes.

The room also displays soft wax sculptures by **M. Rosso**. This part of the collection ends in the Veranda Sartorio, an enclosed former veranda displaying works from Sartorio and others inspired by the Symbolist and Pre-Raphaelite movements.

Art of the 20C to 1950

The visit continues on the ground floor, at the back of the building in the Bazzari Wing (1933).

This section begins with the Expo of 1911, which opened in Rome on the occasion of the 50th anniversary of the unification of Italy. Dominated by the symbolism of the secessionists, this section reflects the taste of the times. In a small hall to the right is the celebrated **Three Stages of Woman** by G. Klimt, one of the founders of the Viennese Secessionist movement. The work was acquired by the State on the occasion of the unification anniversary. The adjacent veranda is dedicated to the youthful works of the Divisionist period of Balla, follower of Segantini and Pelizza da Volpedo, a major figure in the emergence of Futurism; Boccioni, the most rigourous adherent of the movement, even frequented his studio. Boccioni is represented later among other **Futurists** who, faithful to the manifesto of Marinetti, tried to create a feeling of movement and speed on their canvases.

At the base of the veranda, the last hall has portraits from the Belle Epoque, such as that of Marquesses Casati, a work by Boldini.

The next room houses Dadaist and Surrealist works which were donated to the museum in 1998 from the collector Arturo Schwarz. It includes many of Marcel Duchamp's ready-made compositions, in which found objects were elevated to the status of art. Following is a grand central room dedicated to the "historic" avant-garde (Modigliani, Van Dongen, Braque), but also Futurists such as Boccioni, Balla and Carrà. Noteworthy examples of **metaphysical paintings** (de Chirico, Carrà and Morandi) create a mysterious and dreamlike atmosphere by including some items in an unlikely and irrational way. A painting by Mondrian, done in black, red, grey, yellow and blue, dominates the centre of the room. The next room features diverse Italian works from 1920–1940: Constructivism, Neoplasticism, but also a return to traditional values and a rediscovery of popular traditions. One room is dedicated to works in which we see a rebirth of true Classicism, characterised by a particular primitivism, and a return to the archaic values of the Italian village, in direct opposition to the avant-garde Futurists. Another room groups artists who lived in Paris: de Chirico, Savinio, de Pisis.

The large central hall is dedicated to the period between the two World Wars: the "second" Futurism, the art of the regime and the experience of the 19C with a return to order and tradition.

The "metaphysical" works by Carrà and Morandi and the compositions from the Roman School (School of Via Cavour) highlight the position of these Expressionist artists against official art. Of note is *La Solitudine* (Solitude) by Mario Sironi.

The final three rooms contain a collection of postwar works, from the Neorealism of Renato Guttuso and Leoncillo to abstract art.

Art of the 20C after 1950

On the west side of the building.

The first rooms are dedicated to the three components of **informal art**: matter, sign and gesture, all interpreted in a personal way by each artist (A. Burri, A. Tàpies, G. Capogrossi and E. Colla). This exhibition in the main hall looks at the development and surpassing of informal art with works by L. Fontana, E. Vedova, G. and A. Pomodoro and P. Consagra. The final two rooms of the museum recall works of Italian pop art and creations by J. Kounellis.

ADDRESSES

TAKING A BREAK

The museum cafés are open to passers-by, as well as ticket-holders.

You can enter the **restaurant-bar** at the Villa Giuila from inside or from the gardens. The **Caffé delle Arti** at the Galleria Nazionale d'Arte Moderna is a pleasant place for tasty sandwiches and snacks, especially on its nice terrace at Via Gramsci 73. The Galleria Borghese's eatery is best avoided.

Opt instead for **Caffè del Lago** within the Villa Borghese, near Museo Bilotti. This spot is especially enjoyable for lunch or a break.

Also **Cinecaffè Casina delle Rose** at the Casa del Cinema has snacks, sandwiches or a lunch buffet.

Roman Forum and the Triumphal Arch of Septimius Severus
© Sylvain Sonnet/hemis.fr

All roads lead to Rome, so the Romans have been saying since 753 BC, and today a visit to the former (and still, if you listen to the locals) *Caput Mundi* is as awe-inspiring an experience as it would have been for a visitor entering the capital two millennia ago. With a little imagination, it's possible to time travel in Rome; ancient history is all around you, rearing up between Renaissance palaces, green hills, bustling roads and honking cars, happy to be out facing the elements as it has done since antiquity, rather than shut away in museums (although there are plenty of superlative examples in museums to explore as well). Its ancient remains are a monumental bookmark of a city that underpinned an empire – we were here first, they seem to sigh, stubbornly refusing to fade into modernity. Stand underneath the vast columns of the Temple of Saturn in the Forum or in the shadow of the Colosseum, and there's no doubt that the Eternal City truly lives up to its name.

Most of the key sights – the Colosseum, Roman Forum, Pantheon, Circus Maximus, Domus Aurea and Foro Imperiali are concentrated in the city centre, between the Palatine, Esquiline, Capitoline and Quirinal hills. Even with the wealth of riches that remain from Rome's ancient past – weathered, upended and sometimes, startlingly intact – it's still only a hint of what this magnificent capital would have looked like in its heyday. Initiatives such as Google Earth have mapped Ancient Rome in cyber detail (http://earth.google.com/rome/) to give an idea of the scale and grandeur. But still, to walk beneath a giant travertine arch or column is to feel the scale and weight of history in a visceral sense. A visit to the Roman Forum in high season, overflowing with its volume of visitors,

Stadio of Domitian
© titoslack/iStockphoto.com

offers an empathic experience of the chaos and bustle that is at the core of Ancient Rome.

The best time to visit the Forum – and other outdoor sites – is early morning or late afternoon, when the heat and crowds have lessened (shade and facilities such as cafés and toilets are sparse in archeological zones). As the sun sets, Rome's ruins take on a theatrical air; view the Forum backlit by pink-purple sunsets from the Campogolio for maximum effect. If you're planning to dig deep into Rome's ancient past, it's worth investing in a Roma Archeologica card, or the three-day Roma Pass (◎see DISCOUNTS p32).

If you want to see a good number of the ancient sites, there's a substantial area to cover. Take comfortable shoes, as foot power is the main way to travel around most sights, although you can hop on the open-top 110 tourist bus to take in all the major attractions on a whistlestop tour.

And when wandering ruins has left you in need of a break, a bike, foot or bus journey along the cobbled Appian Way, the "Queen of Roads", offers shade from majestic umbrella pine trees, as well as ancient catacombs and the Baths of Caracalla.

Or else, do as the Romans did and take to the hills, where ancient nobles built glorious villas on the Palatine, legendary birthplace of the city, or out to the coast for sea breezes at Ostia Antica, only a 45-minute Metro and train ride from Rome, and the best preserved Roman town ruins outside Pompeii.

Appia Antica★★

The Old Appian Way is a narrow road, flanked by rows of graceful umbrella pine trees, ruins and ancient tombs. It runs through a semi-rural oasis, spared the prolific construction seen elsewhere around Rome. With its catacombs and the Quo Vadis Church, the "Queen of Roads" is an important part of Christian history.

A BIT OF HISTORY

The first-century poet Publius Papinius Statius dubbed this the *Regina Viarum* (Queen of Roads). The route once stretched from the city's core to Brindisi on the Adriatic coast, where ships sailed east, forming the umbilicus of the Empire. All its citizens – living and dead – mingled here. Tombs and monuments to notable citizens line the ramrod-straight "highway of antiquity". The Via Appia is familiar from the saga of Spartacus. The charismatic ex-gladiator led a slave revolt, known as the Third Servile War, and defeated many Roman legions. After his defeat, some 6 000 crucified slaves lined the Via Appia all the way to Capua.

GETTING THERE

BY METRO: Line A: San Giovanni.
BY BUS: The **110** loops from the Viale Aventino out to the Porta Domine Quo Vadis and Catacombe di San Calisto, among other stops. The **218** runs a similar route from Porta San Giovanni, stopping at the Fosse Ardeatine. The **660** circuits between the Metro at Largo Colli Albani and the Tomba di Cecilia Metella. The small **Archeobus** makes hourly stops at 15 sites, running from Termini Station to the Baths of Caracalla, along the Via Appia Antica to the Villa dei Quintili and the Parco degli Aquedotti; the full journey takes 1hr 30min (reserve ahead, as the shuttle fills quickly).

- **Michelin Map:** 38 U 15 to W 15–16.
- **Info:** Via Appia Antica 42. ℰ06 51 26 314. www.parcoappiaantica.it.
- **Location:** Mon–Sat the Old Appian Way is accessible by car only as far as the tomb of Cecilia Metella; beyond that, visitors must walk or cycle.
- **Parking:** Various car parks include the Largo Martiri Fosse Ardeatine for the catacombs, the Via Arco di Travertino for the Via Latina tombs and Via Lemonia for the Parco degli Acquedotti. Sundays are car-free. However, police allow access to Le Catacombe di San Callisto.
- **Don't Miss:** The most interesting part of Via Appia Antica passes the catacombs and the nearby ancient monuments (Romulus's Tomb, Maxentius' Circus and the tomb of Cecilia Metella). The catacombs of St Callistus, St Sebastian and Domitilla are particularly noteworthy.
- **Timing:** Allow half a day for the catacombs of St Callistus, St Sebastian and Domitilla. Best days to visit are Thu–Sat, when all the monuments and catacombs are open. Guides lead speedy tours.
- **Kids:** Bike rides along the ancient highway. Rentals cluster around Via Appia Antica 58/60.
- **Also See:** *CASTELLI ROMANI* (☺*see Excursions*) can be easily visited after Appia Antica by turning left into Via Casal Rotondo and taking Appia Nuova towards Albano; TERME DI CARACALLA.

Decorative Motifs

Originally, Christians decorated their tombs with motifs found on pagan tombs (garlands of flowers, birds and cherubs). Then other motifs began to appear, illustrating the metaphors of the Holy Scriptures, depicting scenes from the Bible and symbolising manifestations of spiritual life. The meaning of the paintings and symbols found in the catacombs is still a subject of much controversy.

The **dove** holding a twig in its beak is a symbol of reconciliation between God and man. The **anchor** signifies hope; sometimes the horizontal bar is stressed to form a cross. The **fish** is a symbol for Christ: the Greek word for fish is composed of the initial letter of each word in the Greek phrase meaning "Jesus Christ, God's son, Saviour."

The **dolphin**, which comes to the rescue of shipwrecked sailors, indicates Jesus the Saviour. The **fisherman** means a preacher because of Jesus's words to his disciples, "I will make you to become fishers of men."

Jonah and the whale foretells the Resurrection.

The **Good Shepherd** or Jesus searching for the lost sheep was one of the most popular ways of representing Christ among early Christians.

Other favourite scenes were the miracle of the feeding of the 5 000, the healing of the man suffering with the palsy and the baptism of Jesus, or the institution of baptism.

In the Middle Ages members of the Caetani family converted the tomb of Cecilia Metella to a fortress and plundered travellers on the Appian Way. This danger led to the opening of the New Appian Way. Late in the 17C the Old and New Appian Ways were linked by the Via Appia Pignatelli.

THE CATACOMBS

In medieval Rome the Latin expression *"ad catacumbas"* referred to St Sebastian's Cemetery, which lay in a hollow beside the Appian Way. When other similar cemeteries emerged in the 16C, they borrowed the name. "**Catacomb**" now means an underground Christian cemetery composed of several storeys that generally extend downwards.

HV Morton observed in his 1957 classic *A Traveller in Rome*: "About fifty catacombs are grouped in circle around Rome and new ones continue to be discovered... Father Marchi estimated that six million Christians must have been buried in the catacombs and that is all the galleries were placed end to end, they would stretch for 600 miles."

Christians in the Catacombs

Until the middle of the 2C Christians had no formal cemeteries. Often a sympathetic family would volunteer a private burial ground. The situation changed early in the 3C, when Pope Zephyrinus put Callistus in charge of the cemetery on the Appian Way.

For a long time the catacombs were simply graveyards where Christians came to pray at the tomb of loved ones. Visits became more frequent in the 3C when the persecutions (by Septimius Severus in 202, Decius in 250, Valerian in 257 and Diocletian in 295) created many martyrs. The catacombs, however, were never a place of refuge. The imperial authorities closed them at the height of the persecution. Only rarely, when they had broken the closure rule, were Christians killed in the catacombs.

After a period of great popularity in the 4C, the catacombs were abandoned (except for St Sebastian's: always a place of pilgrimage). In the 5C and 6C, barbarians ravaged the Roman countryside. Gradually the martyrs' relics were transferred to the city and churches built to house them.

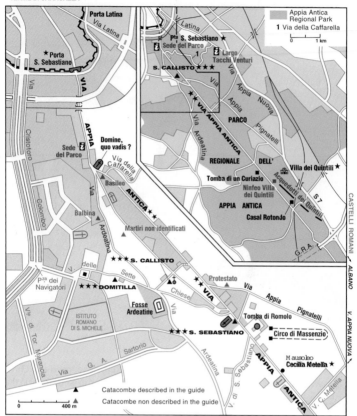

In the 16C, Archaeologist Antonio Bosio rediscovered an ancient cemetery in Via Salaria. Their systematic investigation is primarily due to archaeologist Giovanni Battista de Rossi (1822–94).

Modern Memorial

During WWII, a partisan bomb killed 32 Wehrmacht soldiers on the Via Rassella. The next evening, the SS took 335 Roman men and boys outside Rome to the **Fosse Ardeatine** (*see p 245*), a quarry connected to early Christian catacombs. Eleanor Clark evoked the site's horror in *Rome and Villa*: [They were] "taken out to this bleak country place… shot in the nape of the neck, and dumped into a pit". She concluded: "It is considered by many people the most moving war memorial in Europe." Seventy-seven were Jews, the rest were political prisoners. German troops

Domine, Quo Vadis?

While fleeing persecution in Rome, **Peter** supposedly met Christ on the Via Appia and asked **"Domine, quo vadis?"** ("Lord, whither goest thou?"). "To Rome, to be crucified a second time," he replied and disappeared, leaving his footprints in the road. Ashamed of his weakness, Peter returned to Rome and met his death. The Santa Maria in Palmas church marks the spot of the legendary encounter.

exploded the tunnel to hide the death chamber. In March 1998, former SS officers Erich Priebke and Karl Hass were

Appia Antica

© jannswerner/iStockphoto.com

condemned to life imprisonment for the massacre.

SIGHTS
Catacombe di San Callisto★★★

Via Appia Antica 110/126. *Guided tours (35min).* *Open daily (except Wed) 9am–noon and 2pm–5pm. Lucina's precinct open to specialists only.* *Closed 1 Jan, Feb, Easter and 25 Dec.* €8. *06 51 30 151. www.catacombe.roma.it.*

More than 20km/12mi of tunnels connect half a million tombs in Rome's first official Christian cemetery. The catacombs sprawl between the Appian Way, Via Ardeatina and Via delle Sette Chiese. This cemetery, resting place of almost all the 3C popes, is also famous for its paintings. The Christian cemetery could have grown from the tomb of the patrician Caecilii. By the 2C, the Church owned the site and developed a huge burial ground, probably thanks to **Calixtus**. A Trastevere native, this slave oversaw money for his Christian master. Financial failure prompted him to flee.

He was caught, denounced as a Christian and sentenced to hard labour in the Sardinian quarries. Released under an amnesty, he was excluded from Rome by the Pope, Victor I, who regarded him as an adventurer.

Calixtus returned to favour under Zephyrinus, Victor's successor. He was made a deacon and appointed administrator of the cemetery that bears his name. In 217, he succeeded as pope: five years later he died. He was buried in Calepodius' Cemetery on the Aurelian Way, near the Janiculum, where his tomb is.

Cripta dei Papi (Papal Crypt)

Calixtus decided this should be the popes' official burial place and interred his 3C colleagues in this chamber's walls. Among them was Sixtus II, killed on 6 August 258, together with four of his deacons, while holding a forbidden meeting in the cemetery.

The marble plaques sealing the *loculi* bear the names and titles of the dead Popes. The Greek letters "M T P" – an allusion to "martyr," meaning witness

– underscore the names of Pontianus and Fabian; the former was deported to Sardinia where he died in 235; the latter was a victim of the Emperor Decius, who organised one of the worst persecutions ever suffered by the Christians.

Cripta di Santa Cecilia (St Cecilia's Crypt)

Pilgrims already venerated this chamber as St Cecilia's tomb in the 7C. Two centuries later, Paschal I found her sarcophagus in the *loculus*, which now contains a copy of Maderno's statue of the saint (❧ *See TRASTEVERE–GIANICOLO: Santa Cecilia*).

Sala dei Sacramenti (Sacraments' Crypt)

This group of chambers boasts paintings from the late 2C or early 3C. All the familiar catacomb themes appear here, but no purely decorative motifs. Calixtus's cemetery also contains the crypt of Pope Eusebius (309–10; he was deported to Sicily, but his successor recovered the body); the crypt where Pope Caius (283–96) is buried; and the crypt where, Pope Melchiades (also Miltiades) (311–14) may lie.

Lucina's Precinct, named after a noble Roman lady, and the Papal Crypt form the oldest part of the cemetery. One chamber shows two faint illustrations of the Eucharist.

Catacombe di Domitilla★★★

Entrance at Via delle Sette Chiese 282. ➤ *Guided tours only in various languages (35min) Wed–Mon 9am–noon and 2pm–5pm.* ◷ *Closed 1 Jan, Easter and 25 Dec.* ⬤⬤€8. ✆ *06 51 10 342. www.catacombedomitilla.it.*

This extensive network of galleries began in the private cemetery of Domitilla, whose uncle, the Emperor Domitian (81–96), belonged to the rich Flavian family. In 95 Domitilla's husband, **Flavius Clemens**, was denounced as a Christian and executed on Domitian's orders. Domitilla was exiled to the Isle of Pandataria.

Basilica dei Santi Nereo e Achilleo

Domitilla's Catacombs became famous in the 4C, when a basilica marked the graves of St Nereus and St Achilleus. According to legend, they were her servants, who also converted to Christianity. In fact they were two soldiers martyred under Diocletian (284–305). The **basilica** consisted of a nave and two side aisles preceded by a narthex, was built between 390 and 395 to the detriment of the upper galleries. The saints' sarcophagi probably lay in the apse near St Petronilla's (transferred to the Vatican in the 8C). Pieces of the original structure – in particular of the *schola cantorum* – have been reinstated. Here, in the late 6C, Gregory the Great preached one of his homilies deploring the misery suffered under the barbarian menace. Two centuries later, the basilica was deserted; in future the saints were venerated within the city walls in the new church dedicated to Nereus and Achilleus (❧ *See TERME DI CARACALLA: Santi Nereo e Achilleo, p203*), built by Leo III.

Cubicolo di Veneranda

This chamber behind the apse testifies to the popular enthusiasm for the cemetery in the 4C. The faithful were keen to be buried near the tomb of a saint, hence Veneranda next to St Petronilla. A fresco on the *arcosolium* (boxed tomb) shows them both entering paradise.

Vestibolo dei Flavi

One of the oldest parts of the cemetery, the Flavian Vestibule, is 2C: a long, wide gallery decorated with vine tendrils, birds and cupids. Late in the 3C, Christians created a room for the funeral meal on the entrance's right. Linked is a *cubiculum* named after Love and Psyche.

Ipogeo dei Flavi Aureli

To the left of the basilica is another 2C *hypogeum* (underground noble tomb) with the names of the freed men employed by the Flavians and the Aurelians. Here are simple Christian symbols, such as the anchor or a monogram.

Domitilla's Catacombs contain a multitude of galleries and sarcophagus rooms, like the *cubiculum* of Diogenes and the *cubiculum* of Ampliatus.

Catacombe di San Sebastiano★★★

Via Appia Antica 136. Guided tours only in various languages (35min) Mon–Sat 10am–5pm. Closed 1 Jan, Easter and Dec. €8. 06 78 50 350. www.catacombe.org.

Near the catacombs, the Appian Way passes through a valley. On its slopes stood houses and *columbarii* (dovecote-like chambers for ashes). Below three mausoleums were erected, which probably marked the cemetery's founding. In the 4C, a basilica with a nave and two aisles was built above the earlier structures and surrounded by mausoleums (those round the apse and on the south side remain). Here, close to places sacred to the apostles Peter and Paul, St Sebastian was buried. He was a soldier martyred during the persecution in Diocletian's reign (284–305). His cult became so popular that in the 5C a crypt was excavated around his tomb. The basilica was altered in the 13C and then rebuilt in the 17C for Cardinal Scipio Borghese; the new church rose above the nave of the previous building.

The tour of St Sebastian's Catacombs includes a *colombarium*. Other graves, similar to the one on display, also exist.

Mausoleums

These three structures – with their brick façades, pediments and travertine door frames – probably date from the early 1C. Two mausoleums contain beautiful stucco decorations. Pagan and Christian dead intermingled here, it seems; the central mausoleum contains the Greek symbol for "the Son of God." The right-hand one is decorated with paintings and bears the name of its owner, Clodius Hermes.

Triclia

This section of the catacombs has proven the most controversial. The graffiti on the walls – invoking the Apostles Peter and Paul – suggests that from 258 onwards Christians met here to celebrate their memory. Possibly the saints' relics had been lodged here temporarily while the basilicas of St Peter in the Vatican and St Paul Outside the Walls were being built. Participants sat on the stone benches for the meal.

Catacombe e Cripta di San Sebastiano

In the Middle Ages, a ceaseless procession of pilgrims came to invoke the martyr's name against the plague. The searing pain of bubonic boils was thought to equal the agony of his multiple arrow wounds. Sadly, they damaged the network of galleries, which had developed from the 4C round St Sebastian's tomb.

Mausoleo di Quirino e Domus Petri

One chamber contains the graffiti *Domus Petri* (Peter's House). The other, built in the 5C, was the **Mausoleum of St Quirinus,** who was martyred in Pannonia (western Hungary).

Present Basilica

The atmosphere in the single nave – with its white walls and beautiful 17C painted, wooden ceiling – is fairly solemn and chill. In the relics chapel *(right)* is exhibited the stone that supposedly bears Christs' footprints. It may be an old votive offering. St Sebastian's Chapel *(left)*, built in the 17C over his tomb, contains a statue of the saint by a Bernini pupil (17C). In the sacristy is a beautiful 14C wooden crucifix.

Circo, Villa di Massenzio e Mausoleo di Romolo

Via Appia Antica 153. Open Tue–Sun 10am–4pm, 24 and 31 Dec 10am–2pm. Closed 1 Jan, 1 May and 25 Dec. Free. 06 06 08. www.villadimassenzio.it.

Emperor Maxentius (306–312) built his Imperial residence beside the Appian Way. He erected a handsome tomb nearby when his young son died in 309, and also a hippodrome for chariot races. The oblong shape of the circus is well preserved, as are the stables.

Mausoleo di Romolo

The **Mausoleum of Romulus**, surrounded by a wall punctuated by a quadriporticus, is a domed rotunda preceded by a pronaos in a style reminiscent of the Pantheon. It is partly hidden by a barnacle-like house encrusting the front.

Fosse Ardeatine

Via Ardeatina 174. ♿🕐*Open daily 8:15am–3:30pm (Sat–Sun till 4:30pm). 🕐Closed 1 Jan, Easter, 1 May, 15 Aug and 25 Dec. 𝒸06 67 83 114.*

These tombs commemorate a particularly painful episode during World War II. Here on 24 March 1944 the Nazis killed 335 Italians as a reprisal for an attack by the Resistance in Rome in Via Rasella, in which 32 German soldiers were killed. The tombs *(fosse)* of the victims are sheltered by a sanctuary; a museum provides information about the period.

FROM MAUSOLEO DI CECILIA METELLA TO CASAL ROTONDO

5km/3mi. Some 800m/875yd beyond Cecilia Metella's tomb the Old Appian Way becomes a one-way road.

Mausoleo di Cecilia Metella★

Via Appia Antica 161. 🕐*Open daily 9am–1hr before dusk. 🕐Closed 1 Jan and 25 Dec.* ▱*€10 (combined ticket – Appia Card – valid 1 year from printing date for Villa dei Quintili and Santa Maria Nova).* 𝒸*06 39 96 77 00. www.coopculture.it.*

The iconic grave honours the wife of Crassus, one of Caesar's generals. Her sepulchre was transformed into a defensive tower in 1303. It was incorporated into the adjacent 11C fortress, which extended across the road. Its bulky silhouette is one of the best known in the Roman countryside. On the entrance's left is the way into the tomb's conical funeral chamber.

Although the road surface is poor, this stretch of the Old Appian Way provides pleasant countryside views. The reddish tones of the tombs and the ruined aqueducts blend with the dark green of the cypresses and umbrella pines. These memorials – shaped like pyramids or *tumuli* – were some of the finest in Rome. Now topped by mounded dirt and undergrowth, only inscriptions or a few carvings may remain. The tomb on the right after the junction with Via Erode Attico was long thought to honour one of the **Curiatii**, the Alba Longa triplets who battled their local counterparts, the Horatii, to end a war. Only one Roman survived – and then killed his sister, who grieved her Curiatius fiancee.

Villa dei Quintili

Via Appia Nuova 1092. ♿🕐*Open Tue-Sun 9am–1hr before dusk. 🕐Closed 1 Jan and 25 Dec.* ☜*Tours with archaeologist available by prior appointment.* ▱*€10 (combined ticket – Appia Card – valid 1 year from printing date for Santa Maria Nova and Mausoleum of Cecilia Metella).* 𝒸*06 39 96 77 00. www.coopculture.it*

This villa was once the huge property of Emperor Commodus part of it was made a fortress in the 15C.

Casal Rotondo

Via Appia Antica.

This cylindrical mausoleum dates from the Republican era; it is now topped by a farmhouse. From this point, there is a fine view *(left)* of aqueduct ruins.

ADDRESSES

TAKING A BREAK

Appia Antica Caffè – *Via Appia Antica 175.* 𝒸*06 8987 9575 - www. appiaanticacaff e.it. Open Mar–Oct 8am-8pm, reste de l'année : 8am-5pm.* Available for picnics. Perfect for a delightful break after a bike promenade in this Roman route which on Sunday is closed to traffic.

Aventino★

From ancient Roman times through to the Fascist era, the Aventine has played an important role. Today, the pleasant residential district is dotted with magnificent villas, embassies and opulent religious houses. The area is also home to a number of palaeo-Christian churches; well worth a visit. A superb view of Rome can be enjoyed from the attractive Giardino degli Aranci (the Parco Savello).

A BIT OF HISTORY

Throughout the Roman Republic, this popular district was mainly populated by merchants who traded on the Tiber banks. They built many religious shrines; among the oldest are the Temples to Diana, Ceres and Minerva, between Via di S. Melania and Via di S. Domenico.

During the Empire, the Aventine became a residential area.

Trajan lived there before becoming emperor and his friend Licinius Sura constructed private baths nearby *(northwest of the church of Santa Prisca)*; Decius also built a bathhouse there in 242. Such luxury aroused the envy of the Visigoths. In 410, under their leader Alaric, they sacked Rome for three days, leaving the Aventine devastated.

Plebeian Stronghold

After the expulsion of the last king (509 BC), the Republic was marked by a struggle between the patricians and the plebeians. In the 5C BC, the weary plebeians withdrew to the Aventine as a protest. Menenius Agrippa, who was sent to reason with them. As a result of the crisis, two tribunes were elected from among the plebeians to protect them against the consuls.

Death of a Tribune

The plebeian tribune Caius Gracchus and his brother Tiberius (the **Gracchi**) greatly influenced the Republic. Continuing the work begun by Tiberius

◔ **Michelin Map:** 38 P 11–12.

▷ **Location:** The Aventine is the southernmost of the seven hills of Rome (about 40m/131ft high); it has two peaks separated by a gully down which runs Viale Aventino. The tour described below winds its way over the westernmost side of the hill, overlooking the Tiber, which is separated from the Palatine Hill by the wide oblong Circus Maximus.

☻ **Don't Miss:** Santa Sabina, the view from the Giardino degli Aranci and Knights of Malta.

♙ **Kids:** The keyhole in the Piazza Cavalieri di Malta.

◔ **Also See:** *BOCCA DELLA VERITÀ; ISOLA TIBERINA–GHETTO–LARGO ARGENTINA; PIRAMIDE CESTIA–TESTACCIO; TRASTEVERE.*

GETTING THERE

BY METRO: Line B: Circo Massimo.

(assassinated in 133 BC), Caius proposed reforms in the ownership of land. He took refuge from the consul's mercenaries on the Aventine, until forced to flee over the Sublician Bridge to the foot of the Janiculum, where he was murdered in 121 BC.

☙WALKING TOUR

From the **Piazzale Ugo la Malfa** a fine **view★** unfolds of the ruins of the semicircular façade belonging to the Domus Augustana on the Palatine Hill.

In the square stands a **Monument to Giuseppe Mazzini** (1805–72), a writer and politician. In 1849, he proclaimed the Republic of Rome, but papal power was restored by the French under General Oudinot.

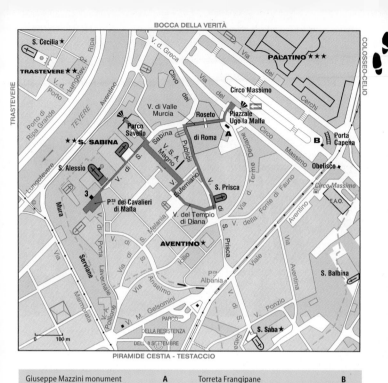

| Giuseppe Mazzini monument | **A** | Torreta Frangipane | **B** |

Circo Massimo

The great circus – in the Murcia Valley between the Palatine and the Aventine, now transformed into a long esplanade – was the largest in Rome. It was used exclusively for two-, three- and four-horse chariot races, which drew larger crowds than any other spectacle.

The track (over 500m/550yd long) was bordered by banks of seats; the stand at the northwest end was reserved for the magistrates in charge of the spectacle. Beneath it were the stalls; at the southeast end stood an archway.

From the 4C BC, the arena was divided by a central reservation, called the *spina*, which linked the two conical turning-posts *(metae)*.

In the Augustan era, the Circus Maximus became truly grandiose. An obelisk *(now in the Piazza del Popolo)* more than 23m/75ft high was erected on the *spina* and a splendid stand was built below Flavian's Palace for the emperor and

his family. The Circus Maximus could accommodate 150 000 spectators.

The emperors continued to make improvements. Claudius (41–54) replaced the wooden turning-posts with new ones in gilded bronze and marbled the stables. After the fire in 64, his successor Nero extended the circus to 600m/656yd long and 200m/219yd wide. Domitian (81–96) and Trajan (98–117) increased the number of stands and the capacity of the circus grew to 300 000 places.

The major events took place during the September games, which originated in the 6C BC. They became pure entertainment, an imperial gift to the people. A passion for racing often led the emperors to foul excesses: Vitellius (68–69) had his favourite charioteer's rivals put to death; Caracalla (211–17) dealt out the same fate to another team.

The few remains near the Porta Capena belong to Trajan's period. The little

Santa Sabina all' Aventino

©Judy Edelhoff/Michelin

An Unexpected View

The door to the Grand Priory of the **Knights of Malta** (Villa del Priorato di Malta, Piazza dei Cavalieri di Malta 3) is famous for a view through the keyhole, which reveals the dome of St Peter's at the end of a well-clipped avenue of trees.

tower at this end dates from the Middle Ages; it was part of a fortress built by the noble Frangipani family.

◗ Take Via di Valle Murcia on the right of the Mazzini monument.

The road is bordered by the **Rome Rose Garden** (Roseto Comunale, Via di Valle Murcia 6. ◷Open Apr–Jun Mon-Fri 9am-7:30pm (Mon and Tue also 2pm-4:30pm). ℘06 57 46 810) blooms are best mid-May.

◗ Turn left into Clivo dei Publicii.

Santa Prisca

Via di Santa Prisca 11. ◷Open daily 7am–noon; 5pm-6:30pm. ℘06 57 43 798. www.santaprisca.it.

The church is one of the first places of Christian worship in Rome. Though reconstructed in the 17C and 18C, its origin stretches back to the 2C.

Various legends connect to the name of the holy woman venerated here. Prisca may have be the first woman martyred in the city. Another tale claims Prisca was the wife of Aquila, mentioned by St Paul in his Epistle to the Romans: "Greet Prisca and Aquila, my helpers in Christ Jesus, who have for my life laid down their own necks..."

Excavations uncovered a late 2C **mithraeum**, a cave-like shrine of the mystery cult Mithras (access from the south aisle of the church). Nearby is a twin-nave building, which may have been an earlier Christian structure (◷open 2nd and 4th Sat/month 10am; guided tours only and by reservation only; ◆ tours in italian, 1hr; ⊜€5.50, €2 for booking. ℘06 39 96 77 00. www.coopculture.it).

Traces of even older buildings, dating from the late 1C and early 2C have also been found nearby; they may belong to Trajan's residence (98–117) or to the house of his friend, Licinius Sura, next to the baths he built (Terme di Sura).

▶ Take Via del Tempio di Diana, Via Eufemiano and then Via Sant'Alberto Magno.

Parco Savello
Entrance from Piazza Pietro d'Illiria.
🕐*Open daily 8am–dusk.*
Better known as the **Giardino degli Aranci**, this park hugs the apse of Santa Sabina. In the 10C, fortifications were built to defend the hill; in the 13C they became the stronghold of the Savelli family. The northwest side, high above the river, offers a pleasant **view★**.

Santa Sabina all'Aventino★★
Piazza Pietro d'Illiria 1. 🕐*Open daily 7:15am–8pm. Access not available during mass. Guided tours by appointment only.* ☏*06 57 94 01.*
Bishop Peter of Illyria built this church in the 5C. In the 16C, Sixtus V (1585–90) and his architect Domenico Fontana transformed the interior into typical Counter-Reformation style. Together with subsequent Baroque additions, this effaced the medieval character. Extensive restoration has revived its glory.
Exterior – Opening into the nave is a beautiful **door★★** of cypress wood; it belonged to the original church and dates from 5C. The two leaves are divided into panels; 18 bear the original low-relief carvings: scenes from the Old and New Testaments. High on the left is a Crucifixion, the oldest representation of this scene in a public place.
Interior★★ – The interior with light streaming through the clerestory windows reflects the vigorous expansion of the early Christian Church.
The basilical plan consists of a nave and two aisles separated by two rows of columns with Corinthian capitals directly supporting a very light arcade. The mosaic above the entrance shows female figures – allegories of the church

of the Jews *("Ecclesia ex circumcisione")* converted by St Peter and the church of the Gentiles *("Ecclesia ex gentibus")* converted by St Paul.
Nave: the frieze of tessellated marble above and between the arches dates from the 5C.
Chancel: the rich marble decor *(schola cantorum, presbyterium, ambones)* dating from the 9C and destroyed by Sixtus V has been reconstructed from fragments of the original; the *ambones* (Early Christian pulpits) and the Paschal candlestick are also replicas. The Mannerist mosaic in the apse by Taddeo Zuccari (retouched in the 19C and 20C) replaced the original 16C mosaic.
North Aisle: the 17C Baroque chapel dedicated to St Catherine of Siena remains; its multicoloured marbles, frescoes and painted dome clash with the serenity of the rest of the church.
In the monks' garden, perfumed by roses and geraniums and shaded by clementine and lemon trees, is a sculpture of the Last Supper (1974) by Gismondi. *(*🕐*For access, apply to the sacristan.)*

Santi Bonifacio e Alessio
Piazza di Sant'Alessio 23.
Legends abound here. The son of a patrician family, Alessio set out for the Holy Land as a mendicant, returning to Rome to die. His family did not recognise him and he spent his last days beneath the staircase of his father's house. The legend of the "beggar beneath the stairs" was a subject of 15C mystery plays.

▶ Continue along the road to Piazza dei Cavalieri di Malta, an 18C square.

Piazza dei Cavalieri di Malta
Designed by Piranesi in the 18C, the piazza is a charming architectural amalgam. 🔍 *A real surprise is in store for the curious who peek through the keyhole of the green doorway at no.3.*

Bocca della Verità★★

This piazza takes its name from the carved face in the portico of the church of Santa Maria in Cosmedin. Legend claims that the "mouth of truth" consumes the hands of liars. In the classic 1953 film *Roman Holiday*, **Gregory Peck's** improvisation and co-star **Audrey Hepburn's** ensuing screech sealed the modern celebrity of this sculpture, which is probably an ancient drain cover. The piazza lies in a pleasant district between the Circus Maximus and the Tiber River, close to ancient temples and paleo-Christian and Renaissance churches.

A BIT OF HISTORY

As early as 6C BC, crowds thronged the vegetable and cattle markets here. The area was also a religious centre, containing several temples. Caesar began construction of the Theatre of Marcellus. Nearby was the Circus Flaminius, a vast oblong arena, where chariot races, hunting events and processions took place. In the Middle Ages, the area was heavily populated, particularly by artisans. Small businesses abounded, owned in particular by Jews.

The removal of the Ghetto in 1888, the clearances undertaken in 1926 to reveal the ancient monuments and the opening of new roads all destroyed a large portion of the narrow lanes and old houses.

Forum Holitorium and Forum Boarium

Not far from the Roman Forum, the administrative and political centre, lay other trade *fora*. One of them, the vegetable market **(Forum Holitorium)**, extended from the Porticus of Octavia along the riverbank to Vicus Jugarius. Another, the cattle market **(Forum Boarium)**, extended further south to the foot of the Aventine and reached as far east as the Arch of Janus (Arco di Giano) and the Arch of the Moneychangers (Arco degli Argentari). These two markets were next to the Port of Rome.

- **Michelin Map:** 38 N 11–12.
- **Location:** The piazza lies on an area of flat land alongside the Tiber, wedged between the Capitoline and Palatine Hills, with the Aventine Hill to the south. The marshy Velabro Valley occupied this area in ancient times.
- **Kids**: Doing a "Gregory Peck" at the Mouth of Truth.
- **Timing:** Allow 1hr 30min.
- **Also See:** *AVENTINO; CAMPIDOGLIO; ISOLA TIBERINA–GHETTO–TORRE ARGENTINA; TRASTEVERE–GIANICOLO.*

GETTING THERE

BY METRO: Line B: Circo Massimio (800m/880 yd from Piazza della Bocca della Verità).

Boats sailed up the Tiber, then navigable, and moored by the left bank level with the Pons Aemilius (Ponte Rotto). This district also contained altars. Hercules, thought to have driven Geryon's cattle through the Forum Boarium, was honoured for his victory over Cacus (*See Scala di Caco, p308*), the blind cow thief. Parallel to the Temple of Apollo, traces have been found of another, attributed to the Roman goddess of war, Bellona. Three temples stood side by side on the site of the church of San Nicola in Carcere. Not far from the church of St Omobono, beside the Vicus Jugarius, a group of sanctuaries has been uncovered; further south stands the Temple of Fortune which Servius Tullius, the slave who became king, dedicated to the god who changes man's destiny. Naturally Portumnus, the protector of harbours, had a place of worship too; this has sometimes been identified as the very old sanctuary known as the Temple of Fortuna Virilis.

Upstream from the Forum Boarium and its quays must have been the military port, known as *Navalia inferiora*.

In 338 BC, when Rome embarked on the conquest of the Mediterranean, her citizens came to admire the ships captured at Antium. They displayed the prows on the Rostra in the Forum. It was here, too, that Cato of Utica disembarked in 58 BC laden with treasures from King Ptolemy Auletes, after an expedition to Cyprus.

👣 WALKING TOUR

Piazza della Bocca della Verità

This open space more or less covers the site of the Forum Boarium. The combination of ancient, medieval and Baroque buildings, framed by umbrella pines and pink and white oleanders, makes a typical Roman scene. Opposite the medieval façade of Santa Maria in Cosmedin stands an 18C fountain supported by two tritons.

Basilica di Santa Maria in Cosmedin★★

Piazza della Bocca della Verità 18.
🕐*Open daily 9:30am–6pm (5pm in winter).* 📞*06 67 87 759.*
The church's soaring **bell-tower★** with its bold arcading was built early in the 12C and is one of the most elegant in Rome.

Bocca Della Verità

In the porch is the marble disc known as the **Bocca della Verità** (Mouth of Truth). According to popular legend, the mouth would snap shut on the hand of anyone with a guilty conscience. The name was also attributed to the fact that the mouth had never spoken. The face is that of a marine divinity, perhaps the Ocean, with two bulls' horns symbolising the surging power of the sea. The plaque is, in fact, a drain cover, possibly from the nearby Temple of Hercules.

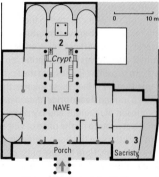

Piazza della Bocca della Verità
● Columns of the "Statio Annonae"

Carved face, Santa Maria in Cosmedin

©Judy Edelhoff/Michelin

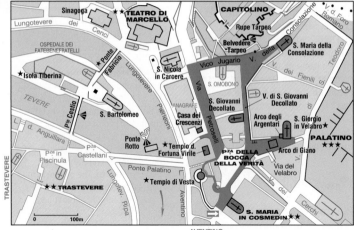

AVENTINO

Foundation

In the 6C, the district between the Aventine and the Tiber was inhabited by Greeks, who like other foreign enclaves, formed themselves into a fighting force (schola) to protect Rome from the Lombards. In order to feed these soldiers, the Church formed **deaconries** (diaconiae), composed of religious and lay people. Their duty was to fix the price of wheat and to distribute the grain, sometimes free of charge. Here lay one of its deaconries, with an oratory in a storerooms. It was enlarged in the 8C by Pope Hadrian I and became the Greek church, called Santa Maria in Schola Greca. It later became Santa Maria in Cosmedin, named for a district of Constantinople. Early in the 12C, the church was restored; the porch and campanile were added by Pope Gelasius II and Pope Callistus II. The church was restored to its medieval appearance in the 19C.

Interior

In the north aisle, on either side of the entrance door and in the sacristy, are huge Corinthian columns, once part of the deaconry. The beautiful floor and marble furnishings (ambones, Paschal candlesticks, canopy above the high altar and the episcopal throne) are all Cosmati work. The schola cantorum (1) for the choristers and the presbytery (2) for

the priests are 19C reconstructions. The presbytery has been screened off by a pergula, a colonnade hung with curtains. The 8C crypt is original for this period. The beautiful 8C mosaic (3) in the sacristy comes from St Peter's Basilica.

▶ From Piazza Bocca della Verità go east into Via del Velabro.

The valley of the **Velabro** (Velabrum), between the Palatine and Capitoline Hills, was once marshy and malarial.

Arco di Giano

This massive 4C construction has four faces, each pierced by an arch, and spanned a busy crossroads. It marked the northern edge of the Forum Boarium. The name reflects the power of the god Janus, who had two faces, to protect junctions.

Arco degli Argentari

This construction is more like a monumental gate against the west wall of San Giorgio in Velabro. The Guild of Moneychangers (argentari) built it to honour the Emperor Septimius Severus and his wife, Giulia Domna, who both appear on the arch (inside right panel). The sharp relief and the abundance of decoration are characteristic of 3C art.

San Giorgio in Velabro★

Via del Velabro 19. ⏱*Open Tue, Fri and Sat 10am–12:30pm and 4pm–6:15pm.*
Founded originally as a deaconry in the 7C, the church was rebuilt and enlarged by Pope Gregory IV (827–44). Since its 1926 restoration, San Giorgio in Velabro has recaptured the charm of the Roman churches of the Middle Ages. The façade, the porch and the bell-tower are 12C. The interior has a monumental simplicity. In the Middle Ages, Rome was poor: builders used existing foundations resulting in asymmetrical designs. The apsidal fresco of Christ flanked by the Virgin and St George, St Peter and St Sebastian is by **Pietro Cavallini** (1295).

▷ At west end of Via del Velabro turn right into Via di S Giovanni Decollato.

Oratorio di San Giovanni Battista Decollato

Via di San Giovanni Decollato 22. ⏱*Open only 24 Jun (patron saint), 9am–12pm.*
The Oratory of the Confraternity of St John the Beheaded was built at the end of the 15C to assist people who had been condemned to death. Those who died in a state of grace were buried beneath the cloisters.
The decoration is by a group of Mannerist artists drawing inspiration from Michelangelo and Raphael. Starting from the right-hand wall, near the altar, are:
The Angel Gabriel appears to Zacharias (Jacopino del Conte); on the left of the painting is a portrait of Michelangelo, who was himself a member of the brotherhood; *The Visitation* (Salviati); *Birth of St John the Baptist* (Salviati); above the entrance: *St John the Baptist preaching* (Jacopino del Conte); *Baptism of Christ* (Jacopino del Conte).
On the left-hand wall, near the entrance: *Arrest of St John the Baptist* (Battista Franco); *Dance of Salome* (Pirro Ligorio); *Beheading of St John the Baptist.* On either side of the altar: *St Andrew and St Bartholomew* (Salviati); above the altar: *Deposition* (Jacopino del Conte).

▷ Continue north and east into Via della Consolazione.

Santa Maria della Consolazione al Foro Romano

Piazza della Consolazione 94. ⏱*Open Mon–Sat 6:30am–6:30pm, Sun 10am–6:30pm.* ☎*06 67 84 654.*
Pause before the broad white façade of the church, at the top of the steps. A 14C chronicler recounts how a prisoner condemned to death asked for an image of the Virgin near the place of execution on the Capitol. As she brought comfort to poor wretches about to die, she was called the **Virgin of Consolation**.
The first church was built in 1470. In the 16C, a hospital was added, according to plans by Martino Longhi the Elder. He also began the façade of the church, which was eventually completed in the 19C in a style inspired by the Counter-Reformation.

▷ Take Vico Jugario and Via Petroselli, direction to Piazza Bocca della Verità.

Casa dei Crescenzi

Via Luigi Petroselli, 54.
This curious building is one of the rare remains of *"Roma Turrita"* when the city bristled with fortresses. This 12C structure defended a toll bridge (Ponte Rotto), controlled by the Crescenzi family.

Tempio della Fortuna Virile (Tempio di Portunio)★

Via di Ponte Rotto. ⏱*Open first and third Sun month; guided tours only and by reservation only;* ☎*06 39 96 77 00. www.coopculture.it.*
The attribution of this 2C BC temple to human fortune is without foundation. Some archaeologists think it is a sanctuary to Portumnus, the god of rivers and harbours. One of the best preserved temples in Rome, it has an austere air typical of the Republican era.

Tempio di "Vesta"★

(♿see Tempio della Fortuna Virile)
Incorrectly attributed to Vesta due to its round shape (only one temple hon-

oured Vesta, the Roman Forum), this site was sacred to Hercules. A bronze statue of the god was found nearby. With its well-proportioned fluted columns and Corinthian capitals, it is an elegant building, which dates from the reign of Augustus. A church was established in the *cella* in the Middle Ages. In the 16C, it was dedicated to St Mary of the Sun, after an image of the Virgin found in the Tiber, which shone.

ADDRESSES

TAKING A BREAK
Anima Mundi – *Via del Velabro 1-2.* ✆*06 96 03 00 61.* This bar with outside tables are a great place for a drink. A view over the whole of the Velabro valley as far as the temples of Vesta and Fortuna.

SHOPPING
Mercato Campagna Amica – *Via di San Teodoro 74.* ✆*06 48 99 31. Sat–Sun 9am–3pm.* This farmers' market has only products that are fresh, local and in season. And its the producers who sell them to you.

BARS
0,75 – *Via dei Cerchi 65 (Circo Massimo).* ✆*06 68 75 706.* Wine bar, live music, draught beer, restaurant. The unusual setting of Circus Maximus and the tunnel con dance nights make it all very enjoyable. Thursday is the big night.

Campidoglio★★★

Once known as the "head of the world", Rome's smallest hill is also her most famous one: the Capitoline ("Campidoglio" in Italian). Today it remains the seat of the local authority that administers the capital. A stepped ramp – the Cordonata – leads to the magnificent square designed by Michelangelo and to the oldest public museums in the world, the Musei Capitolini. From the recently restored Tabularium unfolds a breathtaking view of the Roman Forum.

A BIT OF HISTORY
In 1764, Edward Gibbon observed, *"in the gloom of the evening, as I sat musing on the Capitol, while the barefoot fryars were chanting their litanies in the temple of Jupiter, that I conceived the first thought of my history... the decline and fall of the Roman Empire".* In antiquity, this area was both the city's religious and political centre, providing access to the Forum and dominated by the Temple of **Jupiter Capitolinus** on

- ⊙ **Michelin Map:** 38 M 11–12.
- ▷ **Location:** The hill has two summits: the **Capitolino** and the **Arx** (the Citadel), upon which the church of Santa Maria d'Aracoeli is situated. The dip between them is now occupied by the Piazza del Campidoglio. The tour starts at the monumental Aracoeli staircase.
- ⊙ **Timing:** Allow 1hr 30min. Musei Capitolini allow at least 3hrs.
- ⧖ **Kids:** Capitolino Caffè and Caffarelli terrace is perfect for a gelato snack or lunch break.
- ⊙ **Also See:** *BOCCA DELLA VERITÀ; FORO ROMANO– PALATINO; ISOLA TIBERINA– GHETTO–TORRE ARGENTINA; PIAZZA VENEZIA.*

the Capitoline and that of **Juno Moneta** (Counsellor) perched on the citadel. The impressive Tabularium, the depository

Scalinata d'Aracoeli

© D. Donadoni/Marka/age fotostock

of the Roman state archives, was built in the late Republican period; the Palazzo Senatorio subsequently layered atop this structure. On the southwest edge of the Capitoline Hill, above Via della Consolazione, is the bluff where the legendary **Tarpeian Rock** stood. From here, traitors were hurled to their death during the republic.

Jupiter Capitolinus

By the 6C BC, the Etruscan king, Tarquin the Proud, had already built a temple on the Capitol to Jupiter, the Best and Greatest. This temple was considered second only to the heavens as the god's abode. During triumphs, the generals, dressed in gold and purple, rode here bearing an ivory sceptre surmounted by an eagle, the symbol of Jupiter.

The temple was built on the Etruscan plan and divided into three sanctuaries, the central one to Jupiter and those on either side to Juno and Minerva: the Capitoline Triad. The city treasure was kept beneath Jupiter's statue. In the sanctuary dedicated to Juno, the Romans placed a silver statue in memory of the **"geese of the Capitol"**, (their cries alerted the Romans, when the Gauls attacked). Destroyed by fire, the temple was rebuilt twice, by Augustus and Domitian.

WALKING TOUR

Scalinata d'Aracoeli

In 1348 the plague ravaged Italy. Rome miraculously was spared and built the steps as an offering of thanks. The first person to climb them was **Cola di Rienzo**. At this time, the pope was in Avignon; Rome was in a state of anarchy at the hands of the noble families. Cola decided to revive the city's grandeur. He stood atop the steps dressed like an emperor and roused the people with his speeches. **Petrarch** had begged the pope to restore the capital. In 1354, he set out to lend support to Cola di Rienzo, but learned that the "tribune of Rome" had been killed in a riot by a servant of the Colonna family. Atop the steps, there is a fine **view★** of the dome of St Peter's, the Synagogue *(left)* and Sant'Andrea della Valle and the Gesù Church.

The Root of "Money"

The word "money" comes from the Italian *"moneta"*, the name of the goddess Juno, whose temple once stood here. This derivation is explained by the fact that the building was also used as the Roman mint.

Santa Maria in Aracoeli★★

Scala dell'Arce Capitolina 12 - Piazza del Campidoglio. ⏱*Open May-Sep 9am–6:30pm (Oct-Apr–5:30pm).*

The **citadel** *(arx)* long defended the northern flank of the Palatine, which was naturally protected to the west by the Tiber. During the republic, a temple was built here to *Juno Moneta* (Counsellor). Legend claims the Virgin and Child appeared to the Emperor **Augustus** here after he had asked the Tiburtine Sibyl whether there would one day be a greater man than himself.

Following the arrival in 552 of General Narses from Greece, several Greek monasteries were established in Rome. One occupied an oratory, later turned into the church of Santa Maria d'Aracoeli in 1250 by Franciscan monks. The name comes from an altar *(ara)* dedicated to the goddess of the sky or from the Citadel *(arx)*.

Interior

The interior is built on the basilical plan and contains several works of art. The side chapels and the aisle ceilings were added in the 16C and 17C. The **wood-coffered ceiling** was an ex-voto offering by **Marcantonio Colonna**, who fought with the troops of the Holy League at Lepanto in Greece on 7 October 1571, when the Christians won against the Turks. The **floor** is one of the best preserved examples of the work of the Cosmati, Romans who worked in marble between the 12C and the 14C. **Cardinal d'Albret's tomb (1)** is one of **Andrea Bregno**'s best works. The fine working of motifs, particularly on the sarcophagus, and the use of architectural elements *(pilasters, arcades)* are characteristic of his style. Next to it, **Giovanni Crivelli's tombstone (2)** is attributed to **Donatello**, whose signature used to be legible, it is said, but was worn away when the stone lay on the ground.

The decorative **frescoes★** in the **Cappella di San Bernardino da Siena (3)** were painted by **Pinturicchio** in about 1485 and illustrate the life and death of Bernardino. The funeral scene *(left wall)* shows some portraits against a landscape. The huge statue of Gregory XIII **(4)** complements that of Paul III **(5)**; both are Counter-Reformation works. In the passage leading to the side door there is a tomb **(6)** designed by Michelangelo of a young man, Cecchino Bracci.

👁 Step outside to admire the doorway.

A **mosaic of the Virgin and Child (7)** stands over the side door on the exterior. It comes from the Cosmati workshop and reveals the influence of **Pietro Cavallini**, the greatest Roman artist in the Middle Ages. His style blends balanced composition, Byzantine influence and knowledge of classical art.

👁 *Although Piazza del Campidoglio can be reached from the side door of the church (down the steps), it is best approached up the "Cordonata" from the bottom of the hill. Sometimes in springtime a side passage is open.*

◗ Go back into the church.

The **Tomb of Luca Cavelli (8)** contains an ancient sarcophagus reused for the burial of Luca Savelli. The mosaic decoration and the tiny *Virgin and Child* are the work of Arnolfo di Cambio (14C). Like the floor, the **ambones (9)** are Cosmati work. They belong to the elaborate compositions typical of the late 12C.

The **Cappella di Sant'Elena (10)** is an elegant 17C domed construction. Beneath the porphyry urn is a 12C altar decorated with Romanesque sculptures and mosaic insets commemorating the appearance of the Virgin to Augustus.

Cardinal Matteo d'Acquasparta's Monument (11) is a typical Italian Gothic tomb (vertical composition with angels drawing curtains round the deathbed). The painting of the Virgin and Child is related to the art of Pietro Cavallini. Cardinal d'Acquasparta, Vicar General of the Franciscans, who died in 1302, is mentioned by Dante in his *Divine Comedy* as a man who relaxed his rule's severity. In the left transept is a statue **(12)** of Leo X (16C).

The **Cappella del Santo Bambino** (the Chapel of the Holy Child) **(13)** took its name from a statuette, which, according to legend, had miraculous curative powers; many letters were addressed to it from all over the world. It was stolen on 1 February 1994.

The **third side chapel in the north aisle (14)** was decorated in the 15C with frescoes by Benozzo Gozzoli, Fra Angelico's assistant; only St Antony of Padua remains above the altar. In the pre-Christmas period young children gather in the adjoining **chapel (15)** to recite verses before Santo Bambino.

▶ Down Aracoeli Steps; then left.

La "Cordonata"

Michelangelo's design for this ramp was not faithfully executed. The two lions guarding the entrance are Egyptian (restored in 1955).

Found on the Campus Martius, they were placed here in 1582. In 1588 **Giacomo della Porta** converted them into fountains, which once flowed with red and white wine on feast days.

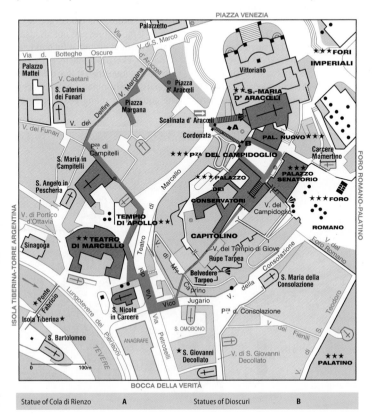

Statue of Cola di Rienzo	A	Statues of Dioscuri	B

The Rape of the Sabines and Tarpeia

With his brother dead and the new city established, Romulus was anxious to increase the population. Since the Campidoglio was declared a safe haven, the area soon became crowded with outlaws. To counter this imbalance, Romulus decided to lure the young Sabine women from a neighbouring tribe with a series of games. The rapacious Romans carried off the ladies. Outraged, Titus Tatius, king of the Sabines, set out to rescue his womenfolk. A bloody confrontation could have ensued, except the Sabine women threw themselves between their fathers and husbands. Thus a new alliance was formed between Romulus and Titus Tatius.

A **statue** of Cola di Rienzo was erected in the 19C on the spot where he was killed.

Piazza del Campidoglio★★★

Every visitor should pause a moment in **Capitol Square**, a haven in which charm and majesty mingle in harmony. In the Middle Ages the piazza was known as "*Monte Caprino*" (Goat Hill); animals grazed among the ruins. Change came in the 16C.

On the occasion of Charles V's visit in 1536, Pope Paul III decided that Rome, which had been sacked nine years earlier by the same Charles V, should be restored to its former elegance. He commissioned **Michelangelo** to draw plans for the Capitoline. The design was executed over the next 100 years or so and altered in certain respects. The square is lined by three buildings (Palazzo Senatorio, Palazzo dei Conservatori and Palazzo Nuovo) and is shaped like a trapezium to accommodate the position of the Palazzo dei Conservatori (Conservators' Palace), which had already been built. Michelangelo turned the square around to face the modern city, rather than the Forum. The balustrade with its over-large statues was not his idea. At the centre of his beautiful geometric design, executed only recently, is a copy of the equestrian statue of Marcus Aurelius. The original – which graced the square for many years and has

Marcus Aurelius statue on Piazza del Campidoglio

© boggy22/iStockphoto.com

undergone extensive restoration – is on display in the Palazzo dei Conservatori. On Saturdays, the square is particularly busy; after the wedding ceremonies in the register office of the Palazzo dei Conservatori, newlyweds pose for photos by the statue of the Tiber and the wolf's head or on the Cordonata Steps.

Statue dei Dioscuri★

The two knights are shown standing beside their horses (*&See Tempio di Castore e Polluce, p297*). The statues are Roman and date from the late Empire; they were found in the 16C on the Campus Martius and restored (one head is modern).

Trofei di Mario

Marius's Trophies is the name given to the sculptures (1C BC) that commemorate Domitian's conquest of the German people. Until the 16C, they adorned a fountain in Piazza Vittorio Emanuele II.

Milestones

Next to the statues of Constantine and Constantine II.
Here stand the first and seventh markers from the Appians Way.

Palazzo Senatorio★★★

☞*The Senate House is closed to the public; occupied by offices of the mayor and local authority. The Tabularium is described as part of the Musei Capitolini (&See p262).*
In 1143, under the influence of **Arnold of Brescia**, the Roman people deprived the pope of his temporal power and set up the Roman Commune. Senators were created to lead the government; their meeting palace was constructed like a castle on the ruins of the Tabularium (the 1C BC storage building for the bronze *tabulae* that recorded legal business).
Michelangelo kept the walls of this old building, but designed a new façade. His plans were carried out from 1582–1605 by Giacomo della Porta and then by Girolamo Rainaldi.
Martino Longhi the Elder built the municipal tower from 1578–82.

The double staircase is the only part completed during Michelangelo's life. The fountain – added in 1588 on Sixtus V's initiative – was not part of the original design. The goddess of Rome, in porphyry and marble, seems lost in her recess, perched on a disproportionately high pedestal. The flanking statues come from Constantine's baths on the Quirinal and represent the Nile and the Tiber. The right-hand one was originally the Tigris: a replacement wolf's head revised the theme.
Some blocks of stone from the old **Arx Capitolina** (Citadel) can be seen in a little garden on the left of the Senate House.

Palazzo dei Conservatori and Palazzo Nuovo★★★

The **Conservators' Palace** was built in the 15C to house the meetings of the Conservators, magistrates who governed the town with the Senators. It was altered in 1568 by Giacomo della Porta according to Michelangelo's designs. Although not built until 1654, the New Palace, the work of Girolamo and Carlo Rainaldi, was identical to the Conservators' Palace. At this time, the Via delle Tre Pile was opened and the development of the Capitol was complete.
The two palaces house the collections of the **Musei Capitolini** (*&See p262*); with their porticos at ground level and decorated façades, they form an elegant ensemble.

▶ From Piazza del Campidoglio take Via del Campidoglio on the right of Palazzo Senatorio.

From the corner of the palace, catch a beautiful **view★★** – ranging from the Palatino and Colosseum (in the background) to the Roman Forum, and in particular the Tabularium, the Portico of the Dei Consentes, the Temple of Vespasian and the Temple of Concord.

▶ Return to Piazza del Campidoglio and take the steps on the left of the Palazzo dei Conservatori and then Via del Tempio di Giove.

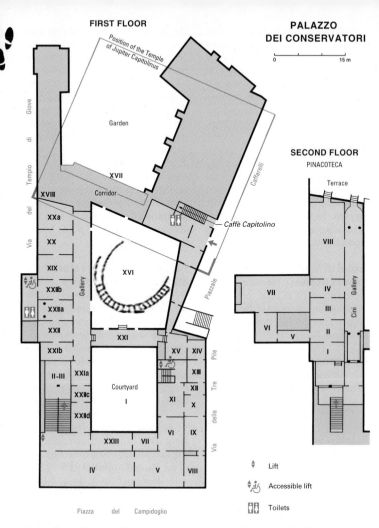

FIRST FLOOR

Position of the Temple of Jupiter Capitolinus

Garden

Tempio di Giove

XVII

Via del

Corridor

XVIII

XXa

XX

XIX

XXIIb

XXIIa

XXII

XXIb

II-III   XXIa

XXIIc

XXIId

Gallery

XVI

XXI

XV   XIV

XIII

XII

XI   X

VI   IX

Courtyard
I

XXIII   VII

IV   V   VIII

Piazza   del   Campidoglio

PALAZZO DEI CONSERVATORI

0   15 m

Caffarelli

Caffè Capitolino

Piazzale

Pile

Tre   delle   Via

SECOND FLOOR

PINACOTECA

Terrace

VIII

VII   IV

III

VI   V   II

I

Cini Gallery

Lift

Accessible lift

Toilets

Below Via del Tempio di Giove are several stone blocks, a corner of the Temple of Jupiter. Beyond, a pleasant garden overlooking the so-called Tarpeian Rock (⚓ *See below*) provides a good **view** of the Roman Forum, the Palatine and other hills.

▶ Take Via di Monte Caprino and go down to the left to Piazza della Consolazione.

Rupe Tarpea
Via della Consolazione, an extension of Vico Jugario, is dominated on the left by the southern slope of the Capitol,

where, after considerable hesitation, scholars have sited the **Tarpeian Rock**. In ancient times, the *Vicus Jugarius* (now called Vico Jugario) was lined with the shops of craftsmen making yokes. It wound under the Capitol and connected the *Forum Holitorium* to the Roman Forum.

🕊 *The ruins here have had a somewhat unsavoury reputation. Families and solo travellers should exercise caution in the evening.*

▶ Cross Via del Teatro di Marcello.

San Nicola in Carcere

Via del Teatro Marcello 46. ○Open daily 10am–5pm. ○Closed Aug and 25 Dec. ☏06 68 89 27 81; 347 38 11 874 (for visits to the crypt and underground ruins).

The 11C little church stands on the ruins of three Republican temples that overlooked the **Forum Holitorium** (See BOCCA DELLA VERITÀ). The church has been restored several times: Giacomo della Porta designed the façade in 1599. The nave stands on the site of the *cella* and *pronaos* of the middle temple. The tower, originally defensive, dates from the 12C when the district belonged to the Perleoni family. The words *"in carcere"* refer to a Byzantine prison that occupied the left-hand temple in the 7C and 8C.

The crypt contains the foundations of ancient temples; fragments of a frieze are visible from the roof of the church.

▷ Continue along the Via del Teatro di Marcello, turn left into Via del Foro Piscario, corner Via Montanara.

Teatro di Marcello★★

Via del Portico d'Ottavia 29. ○Open daily 9am–7pm (6pm autumn and winter). ○Closed 1 May.

The **Theatre of Marcellus** was begun by Caesar and completed between 13–11 BC by Augustus, who dedicated it to Marcellus, his sister Octavia's son. The two tiers of arches that remain were probably topped by a third row of Corinthian pilasters. They form the semi-circular part of the building, which contained the tiers of seats; the stage backed onto the river.

Holding 15 000 spectators, it was the second largest theatre in Rome after Pompey's in the Campus Martius. Its severe and sober style, with the three architectural orders – Doric, Ionic and Corinthian – served as a model for the Colosseum, which was built of the same stone: travertine from the Tivoli quarry. On the day of the inauguration, Augustus suffered a slight mishap that Suetonius recorded: "the official chair *(sella curulis)* gave way beneath him and he fell backwards".

The theatre was damaged in the fire in AD 64 and was finally abandoned early in the 4C. Workmen swiftly quarried it; some stone repaired the Ponte Cesti soon after. Houses were built against the walls and in 1150 it was transformed into a fortress and saved from further depredations.

In the 16C, the noble family of Savelli turned it into a palace. The remains of this house, which was built by Baldassarre Peruzzi, are visible today above the old arches. The palace later passed to the Orsini. The ancient theatre was excavated from 1926–29.

Tempio di Apollo Sosiano★★

Romans venerated the Greek god Apollo chiefly for his power to ward off disease. The first temple dedicated to him was raised on this site in the 5C BC. In 34 BC, Caius Sosius, governor of Cilicia and Syria, rebuilt the sanctuary in marble and it became known as the **Temple of Apollo Sosianus**. The three elegant fluted **columns★★** with Corinthian capitals belonged to the temple's porch *(pronaos)* and were re-erected in 1940.

▷ Return in Via Montanara and turn left into Piazza di Campitelli.

Santa Maria in Portico in Campitelli

Piazza di Campitelli 9. ○Open daily 7am–7pm. ☏06 68 80 39 78.

When the plague struck in 1656, the citizens prayed ceaselessly before the Virgin in the church of Santa Maria in Portico. Now demolished, this church stood on the riverside site of the present Anagrafe. After the epidemic, they built a new sanctuary to house the holy image. The first stone of Santa Maria in Campitelli was laid in September 1661. The building was entrusted to **Carlo Rainaldi** (1611–91), who drew up his own design and oversaw the construction. The exterior, like the interior, is a forest of columns. Variety and movement are provided by the broken and curved pediments, the jutting cornices and multiple recessing.

The **interior**★ space is defined by the columns. The variation on the Greek cross plan (extended and constricted towards the apse), the grandiose elevation of the vault and the dome and the alternating projections and recesses create a bold effect of perspective.

The church contains a few fine 17C paintings including a canvas of *St Anne, St Joachim and Mary (second chapel on the right)* by Luca Giordano (1632–1705), whose picture frame is supported by two kneeling angels. Another Baroque painting *(left of the choir)* is by Giovanni Battista Gaulli (**Baciccia**, 1639–1709).

▷ Turn right into Via dei Delfini which leads to Piazza Margana.

Piazza Margana is a charming and peaceful small square among narrow medieval streets and seemingly far removed from the noise and chaos of modern Rome. The **Margana Tower** *(part of Via Margana 40)* rises from the remains of a Roman portico; a column with an Ionic capital is still extant.

▷ Continue into Via Margana and turn right.

Fountain in Piazza Aracoeli
This fountain is by Giacomo della Porta (1589), the great aquatic designer. In the 17C, the Chigi family added its arms and 100 years later the base was replaced by the present circular basin.

MUSEI CAPITOLINI★★★
Piazza del Campidoglio 1. Allow at least 3hrs. ⏱*Open daily 9:30am–7:30pm; 24 and 31 Dec 9:30am–2pm.* ⏱*Closed 1 Jan, 1 May and 25 Dec.* ⊜*€11,50 (€16 joint ticket with Centrale Montemartini).* ✆*06 06 08. www.museicapitolini.org.*
The collections of classical art in the Capitoline Museums were started by Sixtus IV in 1471, enlarged by Pius V in 1566 and opened to the public in 1734 by Clement XII. This excellent 18C assembly has changed little since, and ranks as one of the most important in Rome.

Palazzo dei Conservatori
In the internal courtyard **(I)**: are the Gothic arches of the 15C palace *(right)* and a few pieces of a colossal statue of **Constantine** (4C).

▷ Take the stairs to the upper floor.

On the first landing are some **high-relief sculptures (II/III)**: these depict a sacrifice, the triumph and clemency of Marcus Aurelius and Hadrian's entry into the city.

The rooms of the *Appartamento dei Conservatori*, decorated from the 16C onwards, recall the grandeur and magnificence of ancient Rome. The frescoes in these rooms depict episodes from the Republican era.

Sala degli Orazi e dei Curiazi (Horatii and Curatii Room) (IV)
The marble statue of **Urban VIII** was sculpted by **Bernini** and his pupils; that of **Innocent X**, in bronze, is a masterly piece by Algardi dating from the mid-17C. Other works on temporary display in the room include parts of the bronze statue of Constantine.
Cavaliere d'Arpino painted the frescoes at the end of the 16C. Treated like tapestries and framed by fake drapes and marble friezes, they depict episodes from the foundation of Rome.

Sala dei Capitani (V)
The Captains' Room is named after the 16C–17C statues of papal generals Marcantonio Colonna and Alessandro Farnese, which are displayed there. The **coffered ceiling**★ with historical scenes painted in the panels comes from a 16C palace, now demolished.

Sala di Annibale (Hannibal's Room) (VI)
The museum's only original 16C frescoes depict episodes from the Punic Wars. The 16C **chapel (VII)** to the right is dedicated to the Virgin, St Peter and St Paul.

▷ Return to the Sala dei Capitani, and continue to reach the Sala dei Trionfi.

Sala dei Capitani (V)

The Captains' Room is named after the 16C–17C statues of papal generals Marcantonio Colonna and Alessandro Farnese, which are displayed there.

The **coffered ceiling★** with historical scenes painted in the panels comes from a 16C palace, now demolished.

Sala dei Trionfi (Triumph Room) (VIII)

The painted frieze on the walls dates from the 16C and illustrates the triumph of Emilius Paulus over Perseus, king of Macedon in 168 BC. This room houses the famous **Spinario★★**, an original Greek work or a very good 1C BC copy. The charming pose of this boy – removing a thorn from his foot – and the studied treatment of his hair and face make this an admirable work.

The bust of **Junius Brutus★★** is a magnificent bronze portrait (3C BC) of the first consul, whose legendary severity and integrity found expression in this head.

Sala della Lupa (IX)

The bronze of the **She-Wolf★★★**, the "mother of Rome" and city icon, is here. In antiquity, the wolf stood on the Capitol and was struck by lightning in 65 BC, as the marks on the rear paws seem to testify. The statue dates from the 6C or 5C BC and could be the work of a Greek or Etruscan artist. The twins were added during the Renaissance. Note the **Fasti Capitolini** on the walls of the sala. These are inscriptions from the Augustan age (27BC–14AD) found in the Roman Forum in 1547. They bear the names of the consuls from 483BC to 19AD and of the victors from Romulus, the founder of Rome, till 19AD.

Sala delle Oche (X)

Two small bronze geese give this room its name. Mounted in a beautiful stucco frame, they recall a famous incident in Roman history, when a gaggle saved the city from Gauls. Also on display here are the head of Medusa by Bernini and a bust of Michelangelo.

Sala degli Arazzi (Tapestry Room) (XI)

The huge tapestries were woven in a Roman workshop in the 18C; they depict works exhibited in the museum.

Sala delle Aquile (Eagles Room) (XII)

The Eagles Room, so called because the two marble eagles sculptures exhibited, has below the fine wooden coffered ceiling (16th century) a remarkable frieze with views of Rome and minor episodes from the history of Republican Rome.

This is the start of the **Museo del Palazzo dei Conservatori** inside the rooms of the Palazzo Clementino-Caffarelli. Reconstruction of this area, completed in 2005, altered the appearance of the museum, remodelling the space to merge it in a large glazed hall designed by architect Carlo Aymonino over a part of the Giardino Romano of the Palazzo dei Conservatori.

Sale Castellani (XIII–XV)

The display cases hold the 19C Castellani collection of exhibits from Etruria and Lazio across a timespan from the 8C to 4C BC. The **Crater of Aristonothos** (7C BC) shows the blinding of Polyphemos and the naval battle between the Greeks and the Etruscans.

Esedra del Marco Aurelio (XVI)

Inside the large glazed hall stands the famous **equestrian statue of Marcus Aurelius★★**, which was transferred from the square outside St John Lateran to Piazza del Campidoglio in 1538 by Michelangelo, who restored it. Cast in bronze and once gilded, it is a fine example of late 2C Roman realism. The bronze Hercules from the round temple in the Boario is among the other sculptures.

The history of this sculpture is particularly interesting: it was mistaken for the sculpture of the Christian emperor Constantine and thereby avoided being melted down.

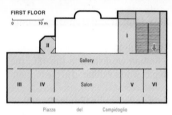

FIRST FLOOR

0   10 m

Gallery

Salon

Piazza   del   Campidoglio

Also beneath the glazed ceiling of the esedra are exhibited some of the large bronzes from the original Capitoline collections of antiquity: a statue of **Hercules in gilded bronze** from the Foro Boario, made in the 2C BC but in a style similar to Lysippos, and the remains of the **bronze colossus of Constantine** from the 4C AD. The **Lion Attacking a Horse**, a Hellenistic sculptural group with the head, legs and tail of the horse added by a pupil of Michelangelo, was returned to display in 2012.

The most important temple in ancient Rome was dedicated to the Capitoline Triad, the gods Jupiter, Juno and Minerva. Begun by the first Etruscan king Tarquinius Priscus, and continued by Tarquinius Superbus, it was inaugurated in 509 BC, during the early years of the Republic. All that remains of it today are the foundations **(XVII)**, however, their enormous size indicates the dimensions (approx. 53x64 m) of what was the largest Tuscan order temple ever built (see the model). The terracotta **(XVII)** exhibited hail from the area of S. Omobono, at the foot of the Capitoline hill.

▷ Take the steps of the Galleria to the Sale degli Horti Romani.

Horti romani

Among the great residential gardens on the Esquiline Hill during antiquity, the Horti di Mecenate **(XIX-XX-XXa)** (Gardens of Maecenas), Augustus's political advisor, featured many decorative features, including the **Marsia**, an important Roman reproduction (2-1C BC) of a Greek original.

Artworks regarding the Horti Lamiani **(XXI-XXII)** (Lamian Gardens) include the 2C sculpture **Commodus as Hercules**, in which Emperor Commodus is shown wearing a lion skin and holding a cudgel

and the Apples of the Hesperides as a reminder of the labours of the Greek hero. At the end of the corridor are the two **Sale dei Fasti moderni** (**XXIIc-XXIId**), containing the inscriptions of the Roman magistrates from 1640, and two beautiful statues of athletes, reproductions of 4C BC originals. Also the **Sala del Medioevo (XXIII)**, with the Honorary Monument to Charles I of Anjou, a sculpture by Arnolfo di Cambio (1277).

▷ Take the stairs to the second floor.

Pinacoteca

On the entrance landing are two fine panels of marble *intarsia* work depicting tigresses attacking cattle. These 4C Roman works use the *opus sectile* technique, developed mainly in Egypt.

Central Italy from the Middle Ages to the 16C (XXIV)

Most of the paintings on display in this room are religious in nature.

The 16C in Ferrara (XXV)

These paintings combine the bold colouring so typical of the Venetian School with the spatial solidity that is characteristic of the Central Italian School.

The 16C in Venice (XXVI)

Venice, with Florence and Rome, was one of the most important centres of Italian painting during the Renaissance period. A characteristic feature was the attention paid to colour, rather than form. Here, note the *Baptism of Christ*, an early work by Titian, which balances colour and composition exquisitely, and Veronese's *Rape of Europa*.

▷ Return to Room XXV and turn right.

The 16C in Emilia (XXVIa)

In addition to paintings from the Emilian School, this room contains two works by Cavalier d'Arpino.

Painting in Bologna from the Carracci to Guido Reni (XXVII)

These 16C and 17C works demonstrate the new religious sensitivity characterised by the Carracci, and the elegant Classicism of Guido Reni (*St Sebastian*).

Sala di Santa Petronilla (XXVIII-XX)

Dominant is the large **painting★** by Guercino in honour of St Petronella. It's particularly noteworthy for the harmony of blue and brown hues, and the tortuous vertical lines, presaging the Baroque style. Also on display are a number of masterpieces from the early 17C Roman School.

The **Gypsy Fortune-teller★★** is an early work by **Caravaggio**. In **St John the Baptist★★**, the same artist pays tribute to Michelangelo's Sistine nudes and portrays the saint as a young boy, contrasting sharply with traditional religious iconography. Finally, spare a moment for *Romulus and Remus* by Rubens.

The 17C in Rome (XXXI)

This room houses paintings by both Italian and foreign artists.

Sala di Pietro da Cortona (XXXII)

Pietro da Cortona was the first major Baroque painter; his work is characterised by the fluid, asymmetrical lines of his **Rape of the Sabine Women★★**.

Galleria Cini (XXXIII-XXXIV)

This room contains 18C porcelain from Meissen, Capodimonte and Cin; several tapestries; a series of views of Rome by Vanvitelli; portraits from the 15C–17C (including a self-portrait by Velázquez and two double portraits by Van Dyck); and examples of 18C painting.

▷ Return to the ground floor and continue to the Tabularium (basement).

Palazzo Senatorio–Tabularium

Excavated in 1930, an underground passage links the Palazzo Nuovo to the Palazzo dei Conservatori. It leads to the rooms of the Tabularium, which housed the Roman archives in the 1C BC, and later became a storehouse and prison (see FORO ROMANO–PALATINO). The gallery overlooks the Roman Forum and offers a magnificent **view★★**.

▷ Return to the connecting gallery and take the stairs back to the ground floor of the Palazzo Nuovo.

Palazzo Nuovo

The fountain in the courtyard is dominated by the recumbent statue of a god christened **"Marforio"**. The large peaceful figure seems a little bored watching the water in the basin. Life once was more exciting, granted. In the Middle Ages, he was one of the "talking statues" papered in satirical notes directed against the people in power. Marforio originally lived next to the church of St Luke and St Martina. The cost of moving him (1595) was so great that the government raised the price of wine. Thus he "wrote" to Pasquino, another talking statue, that the Romans were having to do without wine, so that he could preside over a fountain. Before taking the stairs, the **Egyptian Room** exhibits the sphinx of pharaoh Amasis II (6C BC) next to two 4C BC Cinocephali.

▷ Take the stairs to the first floor.

Gallery

The rooms in the museum are connected by a gallery. The collection is not arranged according to any particular historical or artistic criteria.

Sala delle Colombe (I)

The Dove Room takes its name from the finely crafted **mosaic★★** that decorated Hadrian's villa at Tivoli. It is probably a 2C AD copy of a 2C BC Greek mosaic from Pergamum. The interesting **mosaic of the masks** (2C AD) is also on display. The statue of a young girl holding a dove in her arms and warding off a serpent is a Roman copy of a 2C BC Hellenistic sculpture. During restoration, the serpent was substituted for the original animal (a dog or a cat).

Gabinetto della Venere (II)

This charming room was built at the beginning of the 19C to house the famous **Capitoline Venus★★★**. The Greek original, which inspired this statue (1C BC), depicted the goddess leaving her bath, with a double gesture of modesty.

Sala degli Imperatori (III)
This room houses some 70 portraits of famous people. In the male depictions, note the evolution from short to long beards, favoured by philosophers; in women's fashion, hairstyles morphed from tall layers of curls to the later penchant for ringlets. Every emperor is represented here. Noteworthy are two portraits of **Octavian Augustus**: one at the time of the Battle of Actium *(upper row)*, the other *(facing the window)* as an older man, crowned with myrtle.

Sala dei Filosofi (IV)
The Philosopher's Room contains over 80 busts of poets, philosophers and rhetoricians. Homer's blindness makes him easily identifiable.

Salone
This room is the most typical of the museum. Note the two contrasting statues of **centaurs★★**: the young buck happy and laughing, the older one sad and tired. Other works in the room include the elegant **Apollo with Chitara** – a 4C BC copy of an original by Skopas – and the **Wounded Amazon★**, a fine Roman copy of a statue sculpted by Polyclitus (5C BC).

Sala del Fauno (V)
Made from precious red marble and dating from Hadrian's reign, the famous **Drunken Faun★★** stands here. Also noteworthy is the statue of a child wringing a goose's neck, a 2C Roman sculpture, inspired by a bronze by the Greek Boethos.

Sala del Gladiatore (VI)
The magnificent sculpture in the middle, the **Dying Gladiator★★★**, was previously called the Dying Gaul (*Galata Morente*); it is a Roman imitation of a work in bronze or perhaps even an original work from the Pergamum School (late 3C, early 2C BC). All the nobility and suffering of agony are sensitively expressed in this work, which ranks among antiquity's finest. Another marble masterpiece can be seen in front of the window, a copy in the late period of Hadrian's reign from a 2C BC Greek sculpture. It is **Love and Psyche**, wrapped in a tight embrace as they kiss.

Catacombe di Priscilla★★

The fascinating district around Via Nomentana stands outside the old walls northeast of the city. It is wedged between the River Aniene to the north, and the intersection of Via Nomentana and Viale Regina Margherita to the south. Sights include the paleo-Christian churches of Sant'Agnese and Santa Costanza, the catacombs of Priscilla and the mosque, one of the most interesting recent buildings. Pleasant residential streets are lined with elegant *palazzi* and dotted with the attractive gardens of patrician villas.

🍂 **Michelin Map:** 38 B 14–15, D 16–G 15–16, F 17.
🍂 **Also See:** *PORTA PIA– TERMINI; SAN LORENZO FUORI LE MURA.*

A BIT OF HISTORY
Developed during the Fascist era, many streets bear names of countries that made up the Italian Empire. The large blocks of comfortable 1930s flats and ochre-coloured *palazzi* give way in the **Piazza Mincio** to extravagantly decorated buildings. Here – **district Coppedè★** – reigns a mixture of Renaissance, Baroque and Egyptian styles, designed between 1922 and 1926 by the architect Gino Coppedè.

The vast **Villa Ada di Savoia park** contains the *Monte Antenne*. Livy told of a city here that retaliated after the rape of the Sabine women; Romulus conquered it.

SIGHTS
Catacombe di Priscilla★★

Via Salaria 430. Open Tue–Sun 9am–noon and 2–5pm. Guided tours (40min) available in English. Temperature inside the catacombs is roughly 13 °C. Closed 1 Jan, Easter, Aug and 25 Dec. €8. 06 86 20 62 72.

The catacombs developed out of a private underground chamber (*hypogeum*) beneath the house of the Acilii, a noble family to which Priscilla belonged. Converts, they allowed the Christian community to bury its dead here. During the 3C, two storeys of galleries developed around the *hypogeum*. In the 4C, St Sylvester's Basilica, where several popes lie, was built by Pope Sylvester (314–35) over the Christian graves. The **Chapel of the Taking of the Veil** (*Cappella della Velata*) is named after the fresco, thought to represent three episodes in the dead woman's life: marriage, worship, motherhood. The **Chapel of the Virgin and Child★** (*Cappella della Vergine col Bambino*) contains the earliest representation of the Virgin (*on the ceiling*). The **Greek Chapel★** (*Cappella Greca*) consists of two chambers. Over the arch in the inner room is a painting, possibly a 2C interpretation of the Eucharist.

Moschea

Viale Della Moschea 85. Open Wed and Sat 9am–12am. Closed Aug, during Ramadan, Muslim and Italian holidays. 06 80 82 258.

The **mosque**, set in Parioli in Mount Antenne, is part of the Islamic Centre: a library, an auditorium for 300 people, and several rooms for meetings and lectures. Typical Roman materials, such as brick and travertine stone, underline its connection to the city. The **interior★** is the real masterpiece; the prayer hall is surmounted by a large stepped dome

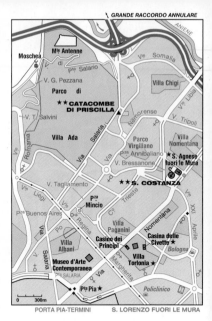

and 16 side domes, supported on 32 sunken pillars. This allows light to run around the base (170m/555ft). Utterly sublime.

Museo Numismatico della Zecca

Via Salaria 712.
Free. Visits by reservation only. 06 85 08 21 25.
www.museozecca.ipzs.it.

The treasury building dates from 1877. The **Currency Museum** displays the currencies of every country in the world, including coins issued by the popes from the 15C. There is also a fine collection of wax impressions by Benedetto Pistrucci (1784–1855), chief engraver to the Bank of England for 40 years: George IV, Victoria, Duke of Wellington, Napoleon, Pauline Borghese

Musei di Villa Torlonia★ - Casina delle Civette★

Via Nomentana 70. Open Tue–Sun 9am–7pm, 24 and 31 Dec 9am–2pm. Closed 1 Jan, 1 May and 25 Dec. €7,50; €11 combined ticket with Casino Nobile. Guided tours available only for groups. 06 06 08. www.museivillatorlonia.it.

Casina delle Civette

Translated as House of the Owls (thanks to a recurring decorative theme), the quirky 19C building is composed of a mixture of art nouveau and neo-Medieval architectural elements and embellished with mosaics, wrought ironwork, sculpted marble and stucco; it is hidden amid the green surroundings of **Villa Torlonia**. The house is best known for its small museum, which exhibits beautiful Roman Liberty-style **stained-glass windows★**. Created between 1908 and 1930, the collection of Liberty glass is one of the best of its kind in the world.

Casino Nobile

The Casino Nobile owes its appearance to the interventions of Giuseppe Valadier and G. Battista Caretti, who, in the mid-19C, added the majestic pronaos to the facade. From 1925 to 1943 the Villa was rented by Benito Mussolini, who had an underground gas and air shelter built (temporarily closed to the public). The building was restored to house the Villa's museum on the two main floors, with period sculptures and furnishings, and on the second floor the Museo della Scuola Romana, with paintings, sculptures and drawings by artists of the Roman School.

CHIESA DI SANT'AGNESE FUORI LE MURA AND MAUSOLEO DI SANTA COSTANZA★

The buildings' history begins with the death of Agnes, a 12-year-old who was martyred under Diocletian (284–305).

Legend of St Agnes – Both St Ambrose and Damasus, writing soon after the Diocletian persecution, mention this child-saint, grounding the 6C legend in truth. Agnes refused to marry the son of the Praetor, declaring that she had vowed her soul to God. She was condemned to stand naked in a place of ill repute – and was miraculously covered. She then escaped the stake unscathed, the flames turning on her executioners. Finally she was beheaded and buried in the Via Nomentana cemetery.

Legend of St Constantia – The saint's name is derived from that of Constantia, the Emperor Constantine's daughter or granddaughter. Suffering from leprosy, she spent a night by the saint's tomb. The young martyr appeared in a dream, urging her to convert to Christianity; she woke cured.

Early Church – After 337 **Constantia** erected a huge basilica near St Agnes's tomb. The structure fell into ruin, but a small chapel survived on the site. Rebuilt and enlarged by Pope Honorius (625–

38), it is now known as St Agnes' Church and has been much restored.

Sant'Agnese Fuori le Mura★

Via Nomentana 349. ○Open daily 9am–noon and 3pm–7pm. ℘06 86 20 54 56. www.santagnese.com.

The **church of St Agnes Outside the Walls** can be reached from below *(Via Sant'Agnese)* or above *(Via Nomentana 349 through the convent courtyard and down a flight of steps into the narthex).* The ceiling and baldaquin are from the 17C. During the 1605–1621 restoration, the bones of St Agnes were discovered. Paul V enshrined her beneath the altar. Note the 7C **mosaic★**, which is typical of Roman art that has Byzantine influences.

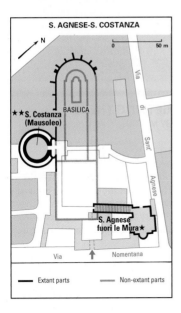

Catacombs

○*Open daily (except Sun and public holiday mornings, Christmas and Easter), 9am–noon and 3pm–5pm. ﹒﹒Guided tours only. ⊛€8. ℘06 86 20 54 56.*

The oldest part dates back to the 2C. After St Agnes's burial, the graves spread behind the apse and down between the church and the mausoleum.

Mausoleo di Santa Costanza★★

○*Open daily (except Sun and public holiday mornings), 9am–noon and 3pm–5pm. ℘06 86 20 54 56.*

The Emperor Constantine's daughters, Helen and Constantia, were buried in this circular 4C mausoleum. It was probably converted into a church in the 13C. The outline of an oval vestibule can still be traced in front of the entrance. The rotunda is covered by a dome resting on a drum. The surrounding barrel-vaulted gallery is still adorned with its original 4C **mosaic★**. The vault has a variety of motifs: floral and geometric details, portraits in medallions, vine tendrils entwined with harvest scenes. The mosaics in the side recesses display Christian themes.

ADDRESSES

CAFÉS

La Limonaia – *Viale Spallanzani 1/a. ℘06 95 06 52 50.* Anchored right on the grounds of Villa Torlonia, this place is good for pizza, grilled meat, hot and cold drinks. It's an ideal spot to sit outside and let the kids run around in the garden (inside can be noisy). Very popular with Romans.

TAKING A BREAK

La Mora – *Piazza Crati 13. ℘06 86 20 66 13. Closed Mon and Tue for lunch.* Crunchy pizzas cooked in the wood-oven and dishes typical of Tuscany in a friendly, family atmosphere. Alternatively, an inviting focaccia with provola cheese and cured pork, or, for the really hungry, a tasty Fiorentino steak.

Paolina Borghese Ristorante and Bar – *Via Frescobaldi 5. ℘06 85 4 4 21.* During the summer months, this upscale restaurant offers light lunches and snacks outside in the garden at the northern edge of Villa Borghese. Have drinks here late in the afternoon and hear the lions roar in the nearby zoo at feeding time.

Pasticceria Cavalletti – *Via Nemorense, 179/181. ℘06 86 32 48 14. www. pasticceriacavalletti.it. Closed Tue.* This small pasticceria is famous throughout the city for its ultra-light millefoglie and excellent Neapolitan pastries.

Colosseo–Celio★★★

This walk spans several centuries, focusing on the Colosseum and the Arch of Constantine, built in the time of the Emperors and now crowded with souvenir stalls, horse-drawn carriages and tourist groups; it then heads to the Caelian Hill, one of the greenest of the seven hills of Rome, to explore the many medieval treasures of this tranquil district.

COLOSSEO★★★

Ticket combined with the Foro Romano and Palatino, valid for 2 days. Tickets are also available in the offices in Via di San Gregorio (Palatino), and Largo della Salara Vecchia (Foro Romano) - formerly Largo Romolo e Remo. Or, with a P2 supplement, in the ticket offices of Palazzo Altemps and the Museo delle Terme di Diocleziano. ○*Open daily 16Feb–15Mar 8:30am–5pm, last Sat Mar 8:30-5:30, last Sun Mar–31Aug 8:30am–7.15pm, Sept. 8:30am–7pm, Oct–last Sat Oct 8:30–6:30, last Sun Oct–31 Dec 8:30am–4.30pm.* ○*Closed 1 Jan and 25 Dec.* ◉€*12. Summer (only Fri) night visits.* ℘*06 39 96 77 00. www.coopculture.it.*

Properly known as the **Flavian Amphitheatre**, the Colosseum is the heart of ancient Rome, dominating the flat southeast end of the Forum. Though quarried and eroded, it remains one of the most enduring symbols of the city – if not Western Civilization.

The stone blocks were brought from the quarries at Albulae, near Tivoli, along specially built roads, 6m/20ft wide. Doric, Ionic and Corinthian columns support three tiers of arcades.

A Bit of History

Vespasian, the first of the Flavian emperors, devoted part of the huge area occupied by Nero's Domus Aurea (Golden House) to public entertainment. He transformed a lake-bed into the world's largest Roman amphitheatre. The Colosseum, begun in AD 72, took that name either because it stood near the huge **statue of Nero** or because of its own

- **Michelin Map:** 38 M 13–14, N 13–14, P 13–14.
- **Location:** The Colosseum stands in the heart of Rome, southeast of the Forum.
- **Don't Miss**: The Colosseum, of course, Michelangelo's *Moses* in S. Pietro in Vincoli, the mosaics of S. Clemente, the tranquil Villa Celimontana park.
- **Timing:** 3 hrs.
- **Kids:** The Colosseum, with its tales of gladiators, naval battles and ferocious beasts, always fascinates.
- **Also See:** *FORO ROMANO–PALATINO; SAN GIOVANNI IN LATERANO; SANTA MARIA MAGGIORE–MONTI–ESQUILINO; TERME DI CARACALLA.*

GETTING THERE

BY METRO: Line B: Colosseo.

massive dimensions (527m/1 728ft in circumference and 57m/187ft high).

The circuses it hosted were originally rites to maintain good relations between the city and the gods. For many years, spectators attended bare-headed, as at a sacrifice.

The Colosseum, though still incomplete, was inaugurated in AD 80 by Titus, Vespasian's son. The spectacle lasted 100 days. The racing and the duels between gladiators were followed by bloody bouts between men and furious wild animals: 5 000 beasts died. Even naval engagements were re-enacted in the flooded arena. In 249, to celebrate the millennium of the founding of Rome, 1 000 pairs of gladiators met in combat; 32 elephants, a dozen tigers and over 50 lions, brought from the provinces, were killed.

The spectacle usually lasted from dawn to dusk. Some were very cruel and spat-

Colosseum

tered much blood. Others, such as the presentation of wild animals, were akin to modern circus acts. Contrary to popular belief, Christians were never martyred in the Colosseum.

Gladiatorial duels were banned in 404 by the Emperor Honorius. Wild animal fights disappeared in the 6C. In the 13C, the Frangipani family turned the Colosseum into a fortress, which then passed to the Annibaldi. In the 15C, it became a quarry: builders hauled away huge blocks of travertine for the Palazzo Venezia, Palazzo della Cancelleria and St Peter's Basilica. Benedict XIV stopped this in the 18C, by consecrating the building to the Christian martyrs thought to have perished there.

Although it is now one of the most thoroughly excavated sites in Rome, the area continues to throw up surprises. In 2008 fragments of an ancient equestrian statue and a marble male head were unearthed in front of the Colosseum, corresponding in size to a monument probably fashioned for an emperor. According to archaeologists, the piece most likely adorned the arch over the Imperial entrance.

According to custom, one should stand before the Colosseum, and quote the 8C prophecy made by the Venerable Bede, an English monk and historian:

"While stands the Colosseum, Rome shall stand; When falls the Colosseum, Rome shall fall; And when Rome falls, also the world."

Visit

In Domitian's time, sailors would extend a linen awning to protect the spectators from sun and rain. Prime spots were reserved for the emperor and his suite, and for the Prefect of Rome and the magistrates. The *cavea*, the **terraces**, began 4m/13ft above the arena. First came the *podium*, protected by a balustrade and with marble seats for VIPs. Then came three tiers, separated by passages and divided by sloping corridors. Places were allotted according to social station. The women sat at the top under a colonnade; the slaves stood on the terrace above. The Colosseum probably had 45 000 seats and standing space for some 5 000 spectators.

The gladiators, dressed in purple and gold, entered through doors at either end of the longer axis. Marching in ranks, they toured the arena and then halted before the emperor. Right arms raised, they solemnly pronounced the formula: *Ave, Imperator, morituri te salutant* ("Hail, Emperor, those who are

271

Arco di Trionfo di Costantino

© powerofforever/iStockphoto.com

about to die salute thee"). During excavations, the arena floor disappeared, revealing the underground warren where animals waited before being brought to the surface by a series of ramps and lifts.

ARCO DI TRIONFO DI CONSTANTINO★★★

Via di San Gregorio.
This magnificent construction, with its three arches, was built in 315 by the Senate and the Roman people three years after Constantine's victory over his rival Maxentius at the Milvian Bridge (◐ *See MONTE MARIO–FLAMINIO*). The abundant decoration was not all 4C work. Many sculptures were taken from 2C monuments (by Trajan, Hadrian and Marcus Aurelius). Like the Colosseum, the arch eventually merged into medieval fortifications.

North Face

The statues of four Dacian prisoners on the upper storey belonged to a monument erected in honour of Trajan (98–117). The four low reliefs between the statues date from the 2C (another three are part of the collection of the Musei Capitolini); they belonged to monuments set up in honour of the Emperor Marcus Aurelius. The four medallions come from a monument to Hadrian (117–138). The subjects are hunting and sacrifices. The other 4C sculptures illustrate the reign of Constantine.

South Face

The design is identical to that on the north face. At the top are four low reliefs belonging to the same series as those in the Musei Capitolini and on the other side of the arch; on the left, two incidents in the wars of Marcus Aurelius; on the right, the Emperor addresses his army beside a sacrificial ceremony (below are the animals being led to the sacrifice).

The Sad End of an Etruscan King

The modern flight of steps leading up to Piazza San Francesco di Paola covers a site linked with legends of early Rome. Etruscan King Servius Tullius's daughter – Tullia – was married to Tarquin. Devoured by ambition, she incited her husband to unseat her father. Wounded by his son-in-law, the old king died in the street linking the Suburra to the Esquiline. Seven centuries later, Livy recounted how Tullia, led astray by her husband's fury, "drove her chariot over her father's body" – the street was then called *Vicus Scelaratus* (Crime Street).

Meta Sudans

Built by Titus and repaired by Constantine, this fountain was a cone of porous stone that oozed water. Named for the *meta* – the pivot pole in a chariot race – this unusual waterwork marked the turning point in a Roman triumphal procession, when a general entered the Via Sacra and the Forum. Mussolini demolished the remains to create a roundabout. Now excavated, its foundations are displayed in the pedestrian area.

👣 WALKING TOUR

SAN PIETRO IN VINCOLI TO SANTI QUATTRO CORONATI

▷ Head to Via di S. Giovanni on the east side of the Colosseum.

The ruins on the street's north side may have belonged to the **Ludus Magnus**, a gymnasium for training gladiators.

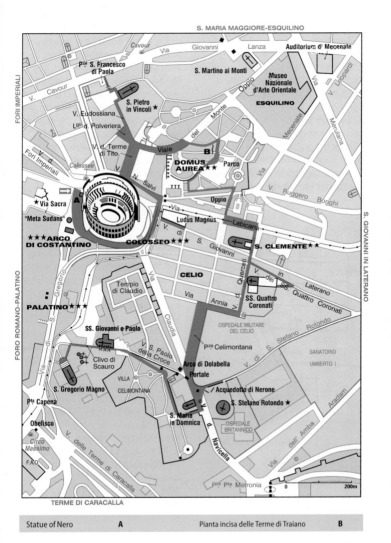

| Statue of Nero | A | Pianta incisa delle Terme di Traiano | B |

Monte Celio (Caelian Hill)

The Caelian is the greenest and most pleasant of the seven hills of Rome. When Alba broke its peace treaty with Rome – following the combat between the Horatii and Curiatii – King Tullus Hostilius captured the rebellious city and transferred its population to the Caelian Hill. It was continuously inhabited until the 11C, when the Investiture Controversy brought war to Rome. In 1084, the army of Robert Guiscard "liberated" the papal capital from the German troops, but caused terrible devastation. Since then, there has been little rebuilding on the Caelian Hill. Both Basilica di Santi Giovanni e Paolo and Santo Stefano Rotondo are sited on the Caelian Hill.

Proceed north up Via N. Salvi and Via di Terme di Tito. Turn left into Via Eudossiana to reach Piazza San Pietro in Vincoli.

San Pietro in Vincoli★

Piazza di San Pietro in Vincoli 4/A.
Open daily 8am–12:30pm and 3pm–7pm (Oct–Mar –6pm).

The church St Peter in Chains was consecrated in the 5C by Sixtus III (432–40), although it probably stands on a much older construction. One of the chief tourist attractions in Rome, it contains the famous *Moses* by **Michelangelo★**. It

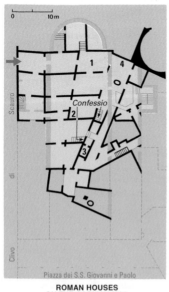

ROMAN HOUSES
ON THE CAELIAN HILL

━━━ Roman wall   ▨ Excavations
▥▥▥ Substructure of the basilica

also attracts pilgrims who venerate the chains that bound St Peter. In 1475 Cardinal **Giuliano della Rovere** added the porch, which would be quite elegant if an awkward upper storey had not been added in the 16C.

The broad interior is divided into a nave and two aisles by two rows of Doric marble columns. The medieval decor was altered in the 17C and 18C: the nave was vaulted and painted with frescoes.

On the left of the main door is the tomb of Florentine Renaissance artists, Antonio and Piero Pollaiuolo.

Mausoleo di Giulio II
(Julius II's Mausoleum)

This monument occasioned the meeting of two of the most powerful personalities of the Renaissance: **Julius II** and **Michelangelo**. The pope, with his unquenchable appetite for grandeur, wanted a tomb of such splendour that it would reflect his glory forever. In 1505, he summoned Michelangelo from Florence to assist. The tomb would dominate the centre of St Peter's Basilica, three storeys high, with 40 huge statues and bronze low reliefs: all surmounted by the sarcophagus. Michelangelo spent eight months in Carrara choosing marble. While there, he dreamed of sculpting a single gigantic figure out of the mountain of marble. He returned to Rome and a pope who had a new pet: **Bramante**. Hurt, Michelangelo retreated to Florence.

After Julius II's death in 1513, the project declined steadily. Michelangelo sculpted only the *Slaves* (in Florence and Paris) and *Moses*; he began the statues of the daughters of Laban, Leah and Rachel, but left the mausoleum to his pupils.

Moses★★★
Pope Paul III grew tired of **Michelangelo** working on the tomb of Julius II. Anxious for him to start on the *Last Judgement* in the Sistine Chapel, the pope visited the sculptor at work. There one of his cardinals remarked with great diplomacy that *Moses* was so beautiful that it alone would suffice to honour the grave. The authoritative attitude of the huge seated figure is enhanced by the steady gaze of the eyes.

St Peter's Chains
The chains lie in the *confessio* beneath the chancel. Originally one bound the apostle in Jerusalem, the other in Rome.

Crypt
⊶ *Closed to public.*
The crypt is visible through the grill in the *confessio (beneath the high altar).* A fine 4C sarcophagus conserves the relics of the Maccabees, seven brothers whose martyrdom is recounted in the Old Testament.

▶ On leaving the church take the covered passage (right), which leads to Piazza San Francesco di Paola.

The steps are dominated by the former Borgia Palace (attractive 16C loggia); it was the residence of Vannozza Caetani, mother of Caesar and Lucrezia Borgia, the children of Pope Alexander VI.

▶ Return via Piazza San Pietro in Vincoli to Via Eudossiana which leads into Viale del Monte Oppio.

The **Parco del Colle Oppio** contains the relics of **Trajan's Baths** (Terme di Traiano). The immense palace built by Nero, known as the **Domus Aurea** (Golden House), once stood here (⚜*See below*).

▶ Walk south along Via Labicana and then turn right towards San Clemente.

Basilica di San Clemente★★

Via Labicana 95.
🕐*Open daily 9am–12:30pm and 3pm–6pm (Sun and public holidays 12:15pm–6pm).* ℘*06 77 40 021. www.basilicasanclemente.com.*
The church was founded in the 4C in a private house belonging to a Christian *(titulus)* and was immediately dedicated to St Clement, the fourth Pope. It is, therefore, one of the oldest Roman basilicas. Ruined in 1084, it was rebuilt on the same site by Paschal II in 1108.

Upper Basilica
The main entrance through an atrium shows the simple austerity of medieval buildings *(usual entrance into south aisle from Via di S. Giovanni in Laterano).* The interior has preserved its 12C basilica plan with a nave and two aisles divided by recycled ancient columns. The unity of style, however, has been broken by the addition of Baroque stucco decorations and 18C alterations *(ceiling and wall frescoes).* The marble furnishings are particularly remarkable: in the *schola cantorum* **(1)** where the choristers sang. The **Cosmati** floor (12C) is one of the best preserved in Rome.

Apse Mosaic★★★
This 12C composition has dazzling colours, symbolism and beauty. Atop the apse is an illustration of the Crucifixion: on the cross are 12 doves, symbolising the Apostles, flanked by the Virgin and St John. Above is Paradise, shown in irridescent colours *(fan-shaped)* with the hand of god holding out the crown to his son. Below the cross are stags coming to quench their thirst *(symbolising candidates for baptism).*

Cappella di Santa Caterina (St Catherine's Chapel) (2)
The decorative **frescoes★** by **Masolino da Panicale** (1383–1447) combine a taste for the attitudes, thin faces and subtle colours of the Primitives with the early Renaissance search for well-defined space: consider the architectural décor in the Annunciation scene above the entrance arcade.

The scene to the left of the arcade shows St Christopher carrying Jesus; in the chapel are scenes from the life of St Catherine of Alexandria *(left wall)*, the Crucifixion *(end wall)* and scenes from the life of St Ambrose *(right wall – damaged)*.

Lower Basilica

🕐*Open daily 9am–12:30pm and 3pm–6pm; Sun and public holidays 12:15pm–6pm.* 🕐*Closed 25 Dec.* ⊛€10 *(ticket for the archeological area,* *inferior basilica, mithraeum and Roman domus.* 📞*06 77 40 021.* *www.basilicasanclemente.com.*

◗ From the north aisle steps lead down to the lower basilica (4C).

This basilica consists of a narthex, a nave and two aisles and an apse. The upper basilica is built over the nave and south aisle of the lower one; a wall supporting the upper construction **(3)** divides the lower church into four.

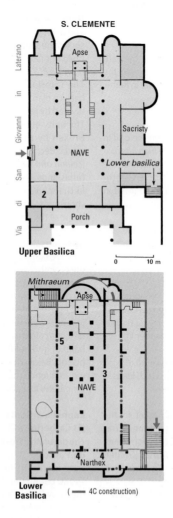

Basilica di San Clemente

Frescoes★

Some of these **(4)** date from the 11C and 12C; others are older (9C). Those in the nave **(5)** – notable for their good state of preservation and their lively scenes – illustrate the legend of Sisinius, Prefect of Rome. He went to arrest his wife, who was attending a clandestine Mass celebrated by Pope Clement, but was struck blind in the presence of the holy man. The figures are accompanied by sentences – ancient cartoon captions. The language is often quite colourful and an extremely rare example of the transition from classical to vulgar Latin.

Mithraeum

Beneath the 4C basilica are the remains of two houses built in Republican times. The one beneath the apse was converted in the 3C into a *mithraeum*, a small temple for the cult of the god **Mithras**. Initiates sat on parallel stone benches. A statue of the god stood at the far end; the central altar shows the god cutting the throat of the bull. Symbols of evil try to prevent the sacrifice that releases life-giving forces.

▶ Take Via dei SS. Quattro Coronati.

Santi Quattro Coronati

Via dei Santi Quattro 20.
🕒*Open daily 10am–11:45am, 4pm–5:45pm, Sun only afternoon (times valid for visiting the basilica, cloister and oratorium of San Silvestro). ☏06 70 47 54 27.*
In the Middle Ages, the church of the **Four Crowned Saints** was part of a fortress that protected the Lateran Palace against attack. The Early Christian Church (4C) – erected by Leo IV (847–55) – lasted until 1084, when it was sacked and left in ruins by Robert Guiscard's troops. Paschal II (1099–1118) built a much smaller church, shorter and without side aisles. From the 12C to the 15C it belonged to Benedictine monks, but in the 16C the whole building passed to a community of Augustinian nuns. Neither archaeologists nor historians can identify the saints honoured.

The story of four martyred soldiers is mixed up with the story of five sculptors martyred in Pannonia (western Hungary). According to a list of martyrs, their remains all rest in this crypt.

Visit

The door beneath the tower, which served as a belfry in the 9C, leads into an outer courtyard. The wall opposite the entrance was the eastern façade of the early church. The **interior** of the church is as Paschal II left it. The wooden ceiling and the women's galleries *(matronea)* date from the 16C. In the apse are 17C paintings and stuccoes depicting two groups of saints venerated in the church with a glory of saints in the vault. The crypt goes back to Leo IV's era. The sarcophagi of four martyrs were found in it, together with the silver reliquary containing St Sebastian's head.

Chiostro★

The Benedictines added these delightful **cloisters★** in the 13C. The Augustinian nuns replaced the simple roof with vaulting. The ornamental basin dates from the time of Paschal II. The charming simplicity of the small columns is offset by the capitals, which are decorated with waterlily leaves.
In the eastern walk is St Barbara's Chapel, with three small apses, added by Leo IV (9C).

Cappella di San Silvestro★

Entrance beneath the portico in the inner courtyard. Key available in the convent entrance on the north side of the inner court.
The 13C **chapel of St Sylvester** contains curious frescoes, very naive in execution. Beneath the figure of Christ – flanked by Mary, John the Baptist and the Apostles – is an illustration of the legend of Pope Sylvester (314–35) curing the Emperor Constantine's leprosy.

FROM ARCO DI DOLABELLA TO SAN GREGORIO MAGNO

▶ From Via dei SS. Quattro Coronati, walk south to Piazza Celimontana.

Arco di Dolabella

The 1C **Arch of Dolabella** – at the narrow entrance to Via S. Paolo della Croce – carries the remains of **Nero's Aqueduct**, which supplied water to the Palatine Hill from the Porta Maggiore. Nearby is an attractive **doorway**; it was decorated by Roman marble workers in the 13C with a mosaic showing Christ flanked by two figures, one black and one white, representing the Trinitarians, who ransomed captives. This sect had a hospice next to the church of San Tomaso in Formis.

Santo Stefano Rotondo al Celio★

Via di Santo Stefano Rotondo 7.
◔*Open Tue–Sun 10am–1pm, 3:30pm–6:30pm; winter 10am–1pm, 2pm–5pm.* ℘*06 42 11 99.*
www.santo-stefano-rotondo.it
The unusual round plan was inspired by the church of the Holy Sepulchre in Jerusalem. Built on the Caelian Hill in the late 4C to early 5C, it was dedicated to St Stephen *(Stefano)* by the Pope at the end of the 5C. The church was originally one of the most opulent in Rome. By 1450, it lost its roof and, for conservation purposes, the outer aisle was demolished and walls built along the line of columns of the second circle. The diameter of the basilica was thus reduced from 65m/213ft to 40m/131ft. In the 16C, Pomarancio (1530–92) painted the walls with 34 frescoes of martyrdom.
A charming 2C **mithraeum** is still visible beneath the church. The cult of the god Mithras, who was usually depicted in the act of killing a bull, was widespread among soldiers from the East and was particularly common during the reign of the Antonine emperors.

▶ Cross Via della Navicella.

Santa Maria in Domnica alla Navicella

Via della Navicella 10.
◔*Open daily 8:30am–12:30, 4:30pm–7:30pm.* ℘*06 77 20 26 85.*
www.santamariaindomnica.it
The **Navicella Fountain**, in front of the church porch, was created in 1931 out of a 16C sculpture, in imitation of an ancient boat. This church, a favourite for weddings, has retained a rural charm. Founded in the 7C, it was greatly altered during the Renaissance. The façade and elegant, round-arched porch were restored at the request of Pope Leo X (1513–21) by Andrea **Sansovino**; the Pope's name is echoed by the lions on the keystones. The interior has retained certain 9C features: the basilica plan with a nave and two aisles, the columns with antique capitals and the beautiful apsidal **mosaic★**, an example of the artistic renewal that took place in the reign of Paschal I (817–24). The artist has abandoned the Byzantine rigidity for a more lifelike representation: a current of air seems to stir the raiment of the angels, grouped around the Virgin.

👥 At the end of the church is an entrance to the **Villa Celimontana** park. In its centre is the intimate piazza dei SS. Giovanni e Paolo.

▶ Walk through the Villa Celimontana Park (entrance next to the church) to Piazza dei Santi Giovanni e Paolo.

Basilica dei Santi Giovanni e Paolo

Piazza dei Santi Giovanni e Paolo 13.
◔*Open daily 8:30am–noon (Sun 12:45) and 3:30pm–6pm. Closed during liturgical celebrations (working days 10:45am–11am)* ℘*06 70 05 745.*
The quiet square is dominated by the porch and the bold campanile, both dating from the 12C.
The tower rests on the foundations of the **Temple of Claudius** (Tempio di Claudio), visible beneath the porch of the convent of the Passionist Fathers. Its history is similar to that of other buildings on the Caelian Hill: in the 4C, a cer-

tain Pammachius established a church in a private house; it was sacked by Robert Guiscard's Normans in 1084, but rebuilt in the 12C.

The five arches above the porch and the gallery, which comprise the upper stage of the façade, belong to the original building. Two handsome medieval marble lions guard the entrance. The **interior** dates from the 18C. The main interest lies underground in the rooms of the **ancient house★** where excavations have revealed traces of beautiful paintings (*Case Romane, Clivio di Scauro;* ⏱ *Open Thu–Mon 10am–1pm and 3pm–6pm;* ✎ *English guided tours by request;* ✆€8; ☎06 70 45 45 44. www. caseromane.it).

At the foot of the stairs is a *nymphaeum* decorated with a marine fresco, **(1)** dating from the 2C; its fine state of preservation is due to a coat of whitewash applied to cover up the pagan décor when the house became a Christian place of worship. There follows a suite of parallel rooms beneath the nave and the south aisle; one **(2)** contains traces of sophisticated paintings of adolescents and spirits among garlands of flowers, vine tendrils and birds. The introduction of Christianity is evoked in a vaulted room; one wall **(3)** shows a woman at prayer, her arms extended as if on the cross.

▷ Take Clivo di Scauro on the left.

This tranquil, picturesque little street, built in the 2C BC by the Roman magistrate Scauro, passes under the medieval buttresses of the church. From here the apse of the basilica, the only one of its kind in Rome, can be admired. With its small columns it is reminiscent of Romanesque churches in Lombardy.

▷ At the end of Clivo di Scauro, the road turns to the left and the church of San Gregorio al Celio comes into view.

San Gregorio al Celio
Piazza di San Gregorio 1.
⏱*Open daily 9am–1pm, 3:30pm–7pm.*
☎*06 70 08 227.*

Its imposing 17C façade rises atop a steep flight of steps, framed by cypresses and umbrella pines. It was begun in 1633 by **GB Soria** for Cardinal Scipione Borghese (the eagle and dragon of his arms appear above the lower arches).

Legend tells how, in the 6C, Gregory converted his house into a church and convent. From here, he sent a group of monks to evangelise England; among them were **St Augustine**, the first Archbishop of Canterbury, St Lawrence, St Melitas, St Justus and St Honorius. All succeeded him to the See of Canterbury. Beyond the façade is a four-sided portico.

In the chapel at the head of the south aisle stands Gregory's Altar (15C), decorated with low reliefs of his legend. At the head of the north aisle is a chapel decorated with 17C paintings; it contains a curious Virgin on the wall (13C) and, opposite, a 15C tabernacle.

▷ At the top of the steps, enter the small square to the left of the church.

In the small square, there are three **chapels**, linked by a portico of antique columns. In St Sylvia's chapel (*right*), dedicated to St Gregory's mother, the apse is painted with a concert of angels (1608) by Guido **Reni**. St Andrew's Chapel (*centre*) has the *Flagellation of St Andrew* (1608) by **Domenichino** and the saint going to his martyrdom by Guido Reni. The altarpiece is by Pomarancio and portrays the Virgin with St Andrew and St Gregory. St Barbara's Chapel (*left*) was first restored in the 17C.

DOMUS AUREA★★
Viale Domus Aurea 1, behind the Colle Oppio gardens. ⏱*Open Sat and Sun guided tours only, 8:30am–4:15pm (6:15pm in Summer). Booking required.* ✆€12 + reservation fee; ☎06 39 96 77 00. For information on the works progress, consult www. coopculture.com.

The **Golden House** is the palace built by **Nero** after the fire in AD 64. The vestibule was on the Velia (where the Arch of

Domus Aurea

©Salajean/iStockphoto.com

Titus stands) and contained the famous statue of Nero; the rooms were on the Oppian Hill. In the hollow between, now occupied by the Colosseum, was a vast lake, and all around were gardens and vineyards.

Inside, Suetonius reported "the dining-room ceilings were composed of movable ivory tiles pierced with holes so that flowers or perfume could be sprinkled on the guests below; the main dining room was circular and turned continually on its axis, day and night, like the world".

Nero committed suicide in AD 68, after the Senate condemned him. The lake was drained and the Colosseum erected here. Then the upper part of the house was razed and the remainder lumped into foundations for the Baths of Titus and Trajan.

The Golden House was not discovered until the Renaissance. Raphael and some of his fellow artists were very enthusiastic about the paintings: geometric designs, foliated scrolls and decorations with faces and animals. These underground grottoes gave these motifs the name "**grotesques**".

Visit

This residence, whose beautiful brick façade belonged to Trajan's Baths, was divided into two wings. The imperial

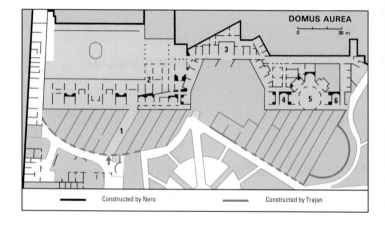

DOMUS AUREA

0   30 m

3

2

1

4 5 6

——— Constructed by Nero   ——— Constructed by Trajan

The Roman Gods

Jupiter (*Zeus* in Greek), senior god and ruler of the heavens, the elements and light, is often shown with an eagle, holding a thunderbolt and wearing a crown.

Juno (*Hera*), his wife, protectress of womanhood and marriage, is shown with a peacock and a pomegranate.

Minerva (*Athena*), goddess of wisdom, is represented by an owl. She is the third member of the Capitoline Triad together with Juno and Jupiter, her father, from whose head she sprang fully armed, and is often shown with a shield and a helmet.

Apollo, god of beauty, the sun and the arts, sings to a lyre accompaniment and carries a bow like his sister **Diana** (*Artemis*), goddess of hunting, chastity and the moon (she wears a crescent moon on her head). The animal representing Diana is the doe.

Mercury (*Hermes*), protector of commerce and travel, wears winged sandals and carries a staff (*caduceus*) in his hand.

Vulcan (*Hephaistos*), god of fire, works in a forge with an anvil and hammer.

Vesta, goddess of the hearth, carries a simple flame as a symbol of fire in the home.

Mars (*Aries*), god of war, is identified by his weapons and his helmet.

Venus (*Aphrodite*), goddess of love and goodness, is represented by a dove. Born out of the foam of the sea, she is often represented standing in a shell or surrounded by sea deities such as Neptune (*Poseidon*), god of the sea who is armed with a trident.

Ceres (*Demeter*), protectress of the earth, tillage, corn and fecundity, is represented with a sheaf of corn and a scythe.

apartments were in the left wing; the right housed the banqueting halls, galleries and libraries.

The visit starts in one of the side galleries **(1)**, built in front of Nero's house as a basement to Trajan's Baths, and continues through a series of rather dark rooms, one of which houses remains of the buildings destroyed by the fire of 64 **(2)**. The visitor then arrives at the Nymphaeum of Ulysses and Polyphemus and the Room of the Golden Vault **(3)**, both of which were decorated by Fabullus with brilliantly coloured landscapes and mythological scenes.

The visit continues to the cryptoporticus that links the two wings; signatures of artists who snuck into the ruins are found on the corridor ceiling. Just before the eastern wing, the Room of Achilles **(4)** is decorated with friezes and garlands. The eastern wing houses the Octagonal Room **(5)**, where the skilful architectural design may be fully appreciated. The room is well lit by an opening and blossoms into a *nymphaeum* and four *triclinia*.

The visit ends in the Room of Hector and Andromache **(6)**, where the Laocoön statue perhaps emerged in 1506 (now on display in the Vatican).

Fori Imperiali★★★

Now crowded with souvenir stalls and tourists, the imperial Fora once evoked the power and splendour of ancient Rome. Glimpses are still possible, amid the traffic and hustle of the modern city, in Trajan's Markets and the column celebrating his victory over the Dacians. Further from the vortex of Piazza Venezia, quiet corners unfold into medieval alleys. The once-disreputable Suburra district now gleams with craft shops and student hangouts.

A BIT OF HISTORY

The Roman Forum grew too small to hold the Assemblies of the People, the judicial hearings, the conduct of public affairs and commercial matters. Caesar constructed a new meeting place to the north; the trend continued with Augustus, Vespasian, Nerva and Trajan. These complexes flexed the imperial muscle with porticoes, temples, libraries and basilicas. The old forum was not in any way abandoned. Octavius erected a temple there to the divinity of Caesar; as the Emperor Augustus, he was himself honoured with a commemorative arch in 19 BC, although work on his own forum had been underway over 10 years. A temple to Vespasian stood at the foot of the Capitoline Hill.

Badly quarried and pillaged during the medieval era and the Renaissance, the imperial *fora* disappeared under new buildings. The Fascists cleared the area for military parades. They demolished 16C structures, levelled the Velian Hill and sketchily excavated the imperial level, then paved the **Via dei Fori Imperiali** right through the area.

This wide road passes through the imperial *fora* in a straight line from Piazza Venezia, opening a clear view of the Colosseum, a solid reminder of Roman grandeur. Pedestrians can stroll here on Sundays, when the road is closed to traffic until 6pm, like much of the historic centre and the Appian Way.

- **Michelin Map:** 38 L 12–13 M 12–13.
- **Location:** The imperial *fora* extend roughly from the *Basilica di Massenzio e Costantino* (Maxentius and Constantine) to Piazza Venezia, along Via dei Fori Imperiali and Via Alessandrina. They fill the valley between Capitoline Hill to the southwest and the Quirinal and Viminal Hills to the northeast.
- **Don't Miss:** The markets and column of Trajan.
- **Timing:** Allow at least two hours.
- **Also See:** *COLOSSEO-CELIO; FORO ROMANO–PALATINO; FONTANA DI TREVI–QUIRINALE; PIAZZA VENEZIA; SANTA MARIA MAGGIORE–MONTI–ESQUILINO.*

GETTING THERE

BY METRO: Line B: Colosseo or Cavour (both Metro stations are approximately 400m/440yd from the Foro di Augusto).

MERCATI DI TRAIANO – MUSEI DEI FORI IMPERIALI ★★

Via IV Novembre 94. &🕐*Open daily 9:30am–7:30pm; 24 and 31 Dec 9:30am–2pm.* 🕐*Closed 1 Jan, 1 May, 25 Dec.* 🎫*€11.50 (€15 museum+exhibition).* ☎*06 06 08. www.mercatiditraiano.it.*

About 150 shops occupied the terraces against the Quirinal Hill above the forum. The market was not simply a retail space – like the Forum Boarium and the Forum Holitorium – but a centre for the acquisition, division and redistribution of supplies, administered by the imperial authorities.

First is a magnificent vaulted room where the civil servants may have worked. The buttresses are of interest; no equivalent structure has been found among the monuments of ancient Rome. **Via Biberatica★** serves the upper part of the semi-circle, which forms the façade of the market and is lined with well-preserved shops and houses. The street's name may have derived from the Latin verb *bibere* (to drink), suggesting that it was once home to a number of taverns. The original paving remains, curving from the Torre del Grillo to the Via Quattro Novembre. From Via Biberatica, walk down through the market. The long, vaulted shops on the first floor probably hawked wine and oil; they open on to a vaulted arcade.

Semi-circular Façade

The façade and the tiers demonstrate the genius of architect **Apollodorus of Damascus**, who gave a monumental appearance to this utilitarian complex. The shallow shops on the ground floor opened directly onto the curving street; they may have sold fruit and flowers. The **Museo dei Fori Imperiali** in the old market buildings displays artefacts uncovered in recent digs.

DOMUS ROMANE DI PALAZZO VALENTINI

Via Foro Traiano 85.
🕐*Open daily 9:30am–6:30pm (last departure)* 🕐*Closed Tue, 1 Jan, 1 May, 25 Dec.* € 12 + 1.5€ *pre-sale fee, booking required.* 📞*06 22 76 12 80. www.palazzovalentini.it.*
A pioneering project that has turned archaeological excavations into a museum visit. At Palazzo Valentini, enjoy an astounding visit to the remains of a patrician "domus" from the imperial age, with mosaics, decorated walls, polychrome flooring and other vestiges of the past. A realistic reconstruction of the site is given with 3D animation, films and special effects. The visit also offers the chance to admire the remains of a monumental public building, the shafts of colossal monolithic columns made of Egyptian granite (the largest used in ancient Rome), and the virtual reconstruction of Trajan's Column.

FORO TRAIANO★★★

Trajan's Forum consisted of a covered market with a concave façade and the forum itself: a square, the Basilica Ulpia, Trajan's Column, two libraries and the Temple of Trajan.
The forum was inaugurated by Trajan, the most renowned of the Antonine Emperors, in 113. Its construction had

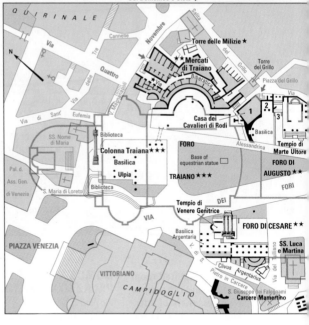

SS. Domenico e Sisto ✐

involved work on a huge scale, including the cutting back and levelling of a spur of the Quirinal, which extended towards the Capitoline. Just as Caesar had financed his forum with booty from the Gauls, so Trajan spent the spoils of war with the Dacians, a redoubtable people who lived in what is now Romania. Even after the emperor's death, the prestige of his forum did not fade. It hosted official demonstrations: here Hadrian publicly burned the records of debts of certain citizens. And Marcus Aurelius (161–80) auctioned his treasures to finance wars against the Marcomanni (German tribe).

Trajan's Forum – extending from Caesar's to beyond the two domed churches of St Mary of Loreto and the Holy Name of Mary – was the largest of the imperial *fora* and certainly the most beautiful. Historian **Ammianus Marcellinus** (c. 330–400) recounts a visit made by **Constantinus II** (356). The eastern emperor was speechless at the Forum, "the sanctuary of the old power... but on arriving in Trajan's Forum... he was stupefied".

Forum

The entrance was set in a slightly curved wall facing southeast. The northeast and southwest walls were relieved by two apses, one of which is still visible, running parallel with the concave façade of the market and marked by two columns (one remains). The wall on the apse's far left is the forum's outer wall: huge blocks of peperine and travertine.

Colonna Traiana★★★

Originally there were rooftop terraces on the libraries, which made it easier to view this extraordinary work. Designed by **Apollodorus of Damascus**, the column stands about 38m/125ft high and consists of 17 marble drums. Battle tales – Trajan versus the Dacians – spiral upward. Laid in a straight line, the sculpture would be 200m/656ft long; no other imperial victories were celebrated with so much genius and effort. The column is also noteworthy technically (the precise seam between drums) and historically, as a record of the Dacian campaigns and of Roman military technique. Learn more about the

FORI IMPERIALI

0   100 m

— Extant parts
— Non-extant parts

Arco dei Pantani
Via Bacina
Via Madonna dei Monti
Argiletum
Cavour
Tor de'
Conti
Torre de' Conti
Via del Colosseo
VISITOR CENTRE
Basilica
4
FORO
IMPERIALI
Tempio di Minerva
Tempio della Pace
FORO
DELLA PACE
DI
Biblioteca
NERVA
SS. Cosma e Damiano
Argiletum
4
FORO ROMANO★★★
Curia★★
Via Sacra★

Basilica Ulpia and Libraries

Named after Trajan's family, this basilica ends in two semi-circles, one below at the corner of Via Magnanapoli. It was opulent with five aisles, a marble floor and two storeys of marble and granite columns *(some standing, some marked by their bases)*. Beyond lay two public libraries *(biblioteca)*: one contained Greek works, the other Latin manuscripts and Trajan's personal records. Between the two was a courtyard; at its centre stood Trajan's Column, a masterpiece of classical art.

Piazza del Foro

At the centre of the forum stood an equestrian statue in gilded bronze of the Emperor Trajan *(statua equestre di Traiano)*, which Constantinus II dreamed of imitating. Historian Marcellinus recounts that a prince in the imperial suite made a subtle suggestion: "Begin, sir, by building a stable in this style… so that the horse you envisage will be as well housed as this one." Porticoes with statues of illustrious men ran down the sides of the forum. *There is a good view of the ruins from Via Alessandrina.*

Foro di Augusto★★

Piazza del Grillo 1.
3D shows with audioguide in different languages (www.viaggioneifori.it).
℘06 06 08.

Augustus' Forum is separated from Trajan's Forum by a building **(1)** constructed by Domitian, which later housed the Knights of Rhodes *(see below)*. The edifice is embellished with a fine 15C loggia. Octavian, who took the name **Augustus** as emperor, wanted to avenge the murder of his dear adopted father Caesar. He finally defeated the murderers, Cassius and Brutus, at Philippi (a town in northern Greece) in 42 BC. He vowed to dedicate a temple to Mars Ultor (the Avenger), sited in a new forum. Building began in 31 BC, after a considerable amount of demolition work. The

carving and examine a replica close-up at the Museo della Civiltà Romana *(See palazzo Valentini, virtual reconstruction of Trajan's Column; see EUR)*.

The shaft's diameter is not uniform; two-thirds of the way up, it bulges slightly to prevent the illusion of concavity. The size of the panels and the figures also increases towards the top of the column, originally brilliantly coloured.

A bronze statue of Trajan stood atop the column (probably installed posthumously). In 1587, Pope Sixtus V replaced it with a statue of St Peter, one of Rome's patrons. Although a pagan monument, Trajan's Column was never maltreated by the Christians, who believed the prayers of St Gregory saved the emperor's soul. A golden urn – containing the ashes of Trajan – resided inside the column, until its theft in the Middle Ages.

Inside, a spiral staircase remains (*closed to the public*), lit by windows in the decorative panels. The design makes them scarcely visible outside.

Trajan's successor, Hadrian, erected a temple to the deified emperor, but the ruins have been erased.

site extended from the old Forum to the edge of the unsavoury Suburra district. A high wall isolated it from the hovels and frequent fires; its irregular line reveals the difficulties the builders had to overcome.

The two sides facing southeast and northwest bowed into two semi-circles, which are still visible. In the recesses stood bronze statues of the most famous citizens "who had brought Rome from insignificance to greatness" (Suetonius): Aeneas, the kings of Alba, the founding fathers of the Julian family, Romulus, Marius, Sulla and other great generals of the Republican era.

Against the centre of the back wall stood the **Temple of Mars Ultor,** which was approached by a majestic flight of steps. A few columns to the front and side remain. This temple played an important role in public life; it served as a reliquary for Caesar's sword. Here the members of the imperial family came for the ceremony of the *toga virilis,* a rite of manhood (at about 17). Here too the magistrates appointed to the provinces were invested with authority *(imperium).* And they also deposited the trophies of their victories here on their return.

The Basilicas

These were formed by two porticoes, one on each side of the temple, in front of the semi-circular recesses. Marble statues stood between the columns. Two have been re-erected in front of a room **(2),** which housed a colossal statue of Mars or Augustus.

Two flights of steps flanked the temple and linked Augustus's Forum with Suburra. Atop the steps, near the three re-erected columns, is a fine arch, known as Arco dei Pantani. (*There is a better view of it from Via Tor de' Conti.*)

Augustus' successors made further embellishments: **Tiberius** (14–37) erected two commemorative arches **(3),** one on each side of the temple, in honour of Drusus and Germanicus, who pacified Germany and Pannonia (western Hungary). The Emperor Claudius

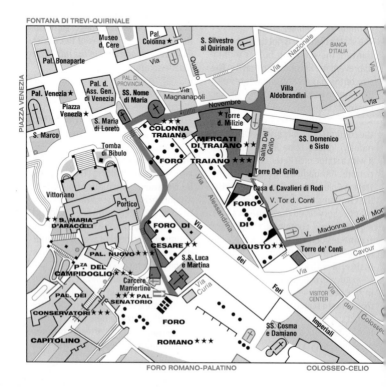

(41–54) continued to dispense justice there. According to Suetonius: "One day, when he was hearing a case in Augustus's Forum, he was attracted by the cooking smells coming from the Temple of Mars next door: leaving his court, he went to join the Salian priests at their table."

FORO DI NERVA

Although begun by Domitian, this forum was completed and inaugurated by Nerva in 98. Very little remains of the long and narrow complex, traversed by the Argiletum, a street linking the old Roman Forum with the Suburra district. For this reason, it was also known as the *Forum Transitorium*. Here stood the Temple of Minerva; its lovely ruins were still visible early in the 17C, until Pope Paul V had them demolished.

The columns and cornices were used in the construction of the Pauline Fountain on the Janiculum. Against the east wall stand two beautiful **columns★ (4)** and

some fragments of a frieze that adorned the wall enclosing the forum.

The junction of Via dei Fori Imperiali and Via Cavour stands more or less at the point where the Fora of Nerva *(west)* and Vespasian *(east)* met. Little remains.

FORO DI VESPASIANO

This forum was built by Vespasian from 71–75. It formed a square adjoining the old Forum and extended approximately from the Basilica of Maxentius and Constantine in the south to the Conti Tower *(Torre dei Conti)* in the north. In the south corner was a library, now occupied by the church of St Cosmas and St Damian. It was also called the "Peace Forum". To commemorate his conquest of the Jews in 71, Vespasian erected a Temple of Peace. It housed treasures that had been looted from the Jewish Temple in Jerusalem: the golden seven-branched candlestick, the tablets of the Law of Moses and the silver trumpets.

FORO DI CESARE★★

3D shows with audioguide in different languages. Info: www.viaggioneifori.it.
℘06 06 08.

For his forum, Caesar chose a central position at the foot of the Capitoline, near the old Roman Forum. In order to clear the site, he had to relocate the Curia Hostilia and the Comitium, and purchase and demolish the elegant houses already *in situ*. This exercise

Foro di Cesare

© alxpin/iStockphoto.com

cost the exorbitant sum of 60 million *sesterzi*, according to Cicero (then consul and a friend of Caesar's). However, Suetonius – the emperor's biographer – puts the figure at 100 million. Negotiations began in 54 BC, when Caesar was rich with the spoils gained in the conquest of Gaul (58–51 BC); work started three years later. This forum was rectangular and extended from the *Curia (east)* to *Via di San Pietro in Carcere (west)*, the long sides running more or less parallel with the Clivus Argentarius. Domitian undertook restoration work (81–96), following the fire that destroyed part of the Capitoline in 80. Trajan completed the work. About two-thirds of Caesar's forum has been uncovered; the rest is beneath Via dei Fori Imperiali.

The Ruins

First to catch the eye are three beautiful standing columns, richly sculpted, which belonged to the **Temple of Venus Genitrix** and date from the time of Domitian and Trajan. Caesar claimed that his family (the *gens Iulia*) descended from Venus through her son, Aeneas, and the Trojan War hero's son, Lulus. He dedicated a temple to her after his victory at Pharsalus against Pompey, who was killed by Ptolemy, Cleopatra's brother.

This temple, to the north of the forum, was a veritable museum: besides the statue of Venus in the *cella*, there was a golden statue of Cleopatra, some Greek paintings and, in front, a statue of Caesar's horse. This extraordinary animal had curiously split hooves, which resembled human feet. Soothsayers claimed this abnormality was a sign of divine intervention and meant that his master would be ruler of the world. The edge of the forum was lined with shops, still visible beneath the Clivus Argentarius. During Trajan's reign (2C), a portico was added down the long side nearest the Clivus Argentarius. Its two long rows of granite columns still remain. It has been identified as the **Basilica Argentaria,** where the money changers *(argentari)* plied their trade.

ADDITIONAL SIGHTS
Santi Luca e Martina
Via della Curia 2. Access from Via dei Fori Imperiali. ⏱Open Sat 8am–8pm. ☎*06 67 98 848 (Accademia Nazionale di S. Luca).*

On the site of the Senate Archive (Secretarium Senatus, an annex of the Curia), a church was built in about the 7C and dedicated to Martina, who had been martyred under Septimius Severus. From 1588, it also honoured St Luke, since in that year Pope Sixtus V gave the church to the members of St Luke's Academy, a guild of painters who recognised the evangelist as its patron saint. According to a 6C legend, he had painted a portrait of the Virgin Mary.

In 1634, a terracotta sarcophagus was found containing the remains of St Martina. Cardinal Francesco Barberini commissioned Pietro da Cortona to build a new shrine above the old one. Da Cortona designed a beautiful **façade★**. Its shallow convex curve is reminiscent of the style of Borromini. So, too, is the interior, designed on the Greek cross plan and decorated with pale stuccoes. **Carcere Mamertino** (🕯*see below*), the old Roman prison, stands opposite.

◗ Follow the Clivus Argentarius and cross Via dei Fori Imperiali. Walk alongside Trajan's Forum as far as Trajan's Column.

Note the symmetry of the domes of **SS. Nome di Maria** and **Santa Maria di Loreto**. In 1507, the latter was begun by Antonio da Sangallo the Younger and was completed in 1577 by Giacomo del Duca, from Sicily.

Torre delle Milizie★
Via IV Novembre.
🔒*Closed temporarily.* 🖉*06 67 90 048.*
The **Militia Tower** is one of the best-preserved of medieval Rome. It was the keep of a castle built by Pope Gregory IX (1227–41), At this time, the papacy often used force to establish faith in the empire. The tower leans slightly because of an earthquake in the 14C; it has lost its top storey and crenellations. It has been known as "Nero's Tower": legends claim the mad emperor, dressed in costume, watched the great fire from here. Rumors insist he sparked the inferno: "charmed by the beauty of the flames", in Suetonius's account, while strumming his lyre.

From Via Quattro Novembre, there is a view of the trees in the public gardens

Via Panisperna 89

From 192–37, this building was home to the group of young Italian physicists known as the "boys of Via Panisperna". Enrico Fermi, a 25-year-old wunderkind was their leader, nicknamed "the Pope".He fled to America in the 1930s to protect his Jewish wife Laura. Four years later, Fermi won the Nobel Prize, after designing the first man-made nuclear reactor and discovering beta decay. The palazzo now houses the offices of the State Police *(Polizia di Stato).*

of the **Villa Aldobrandini** and the Baroque façade of the **church of San Domenico e San Sisto** (completed in 1655).

◗ Turn right into Salita del Grillo.

This quiet, picturesque street takes its name from the Marquess del Grillo, known for his jokes and jibes. Beside the arcade stands the **tower** of his mansion.

Casa dei Cavalieri di Rodi
Piazza del Grillo 1.
🎫*Guided tours only Tue and Thu 10am–1pm.* 🕐*Closed Aug and public holidays. Booking required.* ☞*€4.* 🖉*06 06 08.*
Marco Barbo, was appointed Grand Master of the Order of the Knight Hospitallers of St John by his uncle Pope Paul II (1464–71). He reconstructed this building (House of the Knights of Rhodes), part of a medieval convent on the remains of the Temple of Mars Ultor. Some of the windows show that Venetian craftsmen were employed. The beautiful 15C loggia overlooking Trajan's Forum is supported on Roman columns.

◗ Continue along Via Tor de' Conti.

The Via Tor de' Conti skirts the imposing wall built of large blocks of tufa and travertine, which separated Augustus's Forum from the slummy Suburra dis-

Casa dei Cavalieri di Rodi

trict. Note the fine arch (Arco dei Pentani) that marked the entrance to the Forum.

At the end of the street the imposing mass of the **Torre de' Conti** (1238) can be seen. The tower was inhabited until an earthquake in 1348 reduced it to rubble.

▷ Turn left into Via Madonna dei Monti and left again into Via del Boschetto to reach Via Panisperna.

The peaceful Via Madonna dei Monti leads to what was the **Suburra** district, the most disreputable in ancient Rome. This zone, which harboured thieves and hired assassins, bequeathed its name to a nearby square. The narrow alleys, now lively with craft shops, were once frequented by the scandalous Empress Messalina, who frequented the local brothels in secret.

Via Panisperna crosses the **Viminale**, one of the seven hills of Rome, which probably takes its name from the very large number of willow trees or from the temple dedicated to Jupiter Vimineus that stood there. The tree-lined courtyard of the **Church of San Lorenzo in Panisperna** (St Lawrence in Panisperna) is a tiny oasis from another era, separating this place of worship from the chaos of the city. On 10 August, the feast of St Lawrence, the nuns continue an age-old tradition of offering blessed bread.

Carcere Mamertino (Carcer Tullianum)

Clivo Argentario 1.
⚷ *Temporarily closed at the moment of writing.* ⏱ *8:30am–4:30pm.* 💳 *€10.*
📞 *06 69 92 46 52. www.tullianum.org.*

The **Mamertine Prison** was the Roman State jail; it consists of two rooms, one above the other, hollowed out of the Capitoline Hill beneath the church of San Giuseppe dei Falegnami (St Joseph of the Carpenters). On the right of the entrance is a list of names of well-known people who perished here.

In 104 BC, **Jugurtha** died of starvation, while his conqueror Marius led his victory parade through the forum. **Vercingetorix** was beheaded here in 46 BC, after Caesar's triumph. However, enemy chiefs often escaped death; Jugurtha and Vercingetorix had not been considered worthy of such clemency. It was here, on 5 December 65 BC, that Catiline's fellow conspirators were strangled after Cicero's fourth rabble-rousing speech.

In the Middle Ages, a legend arose that **St Peter** had been imprisoned here; hence the name *San Pietro in Carcere* (St Peter in Prison). On the left of the entrance is a list of Christian martyrs who died here.

The lower chamber *(tullianum)* was built at the end of the 4C BC and was used as a cistern or a tomb. Legend tells how Peter and Paul made water miraculously spout from the earth, so they could baptise their gaolers. The spring and the pillar, to which the prisoners were chained, can still be seen.

Foro Romano–Palatino★★★

The core of ancient Rome, the Forum has decayed into a sea of columns, crumbled walls and monumental arches. Now wildflowers and stray cats rule these ruins, the crucible of western civilisation for 12 centuries. Historian Georgina Masson noted that: "though they revered it as the cradle of their institutions, the Romans continued to alter, add to and rebuild the temples in the Forum. This was partly due to damage by fire and earthquake, but also to their desire to make it worthy of the growing power of Rome". This rich mix is the obvious starting point for a visit to Italy's capital city. Overlooking the Forum is the Palatine Hill, where umbrella pines shade the impressive husks of aristocratic houses. Quiet and gracious, this landscape invites travellers to stroll and daydream antiquity back to life.

FORO ROMANO

Largo della Salara Vecchia 5/6. Combined ticket with the Colosseum and Palatino, valid for 2 days.
Open last Sun of Oct–15Feb 8:30am–4:30pm; 16Feb–15Mar 8:30am–5pm; 16Mar–last Sat 8:30am–5:30pm; last Sun of Mar–Aug 8:30am–7:15pm; Sept 8:30am–7pm; 1 Oct–last Sat Oct 8:30am–6:30pm.
Closed 1 Jan, 1 May and 25 Dec.
€12. 06 39 96 77 00. Admissions 30 min before entry. www.coopculture.it

Bit of History

In about 750 BC, the site was a marshy valley, subject to flooding by the Tiber and by streams from the seven surrounding hills (*See HISTORY: map of Rome during the empire*). Small villages of rough shacks grew up the hillsides. Their inhabitants, the Latins and the Sabines, were farmers who would fight each other, when pressed. The valley, which later became the Forum, was a

- **Michelin Map:** 38 M 12–13, N 12–13.
- **Location:** The Forum unfurls southeast of the Capitoline, flowing up towards Palatine Hill. Enter from the *Largo della Salara Vecchia - ex Largo Romolo e Remo* or *Via di San Gregorio Magno*. One of the city's few public toilets hides by the Temple of Castor and Pollux on the northwestern end of the Forum.
- **Don't Miss:** View the ruins from the Capitoline terrace and the Farnese Gardens on the Palatine Hill.
- **Timing:** Allow a half day to explore properly. A cursory walk-through takes 1hr.
- **Kids:** Gameboard carved on the steps of the Basilica Julia.
- **Also See:** *CAMPIDOGLIO; COLOSSEO–CELIO; FORI IMPERIALI; PIAZZA VENEZIA.*

GETTING THERE

BY METRO: Line B: Colosseo.

burial ground and a meeting place. Here too people traded and worshipped. Two centuries later, the marshy valley had become a real town square, thanks to the **Etruscans**. The origin of this high civilisation remains uncertain, but this north-central people spread down the boot to *Magna Graecia* (southern Italy). In Rome, they built a citadel on the Capitoline, unified the villages and organised the social life of the community. Etruscan kings governed here from 616 to 509 BC. They fortified the city and drained the Forum into the Tiber, through the channel that became the Great Sewer (Cloaca Maxima).

FORI IMPERIALI ★★★

SS. Luca e Martina

Secretarium Senatus
V. d. Curia
S. Giuseppe dei Falegnami
Carcere Mamertino

Via di S. Pietro in Carcere

CAMPIDOGLIO-CAPITOLINO

★★ Curia

Argiletum

S. Lorenzo in Miranda/
★★ Tempio di Antonino e Faustina

Basilica   Emilia

★★ Arco di Settimio Severo

Comitium

Tempio della Concordia

Tabularium

3

2

★★ Tempio di Vespasiano e Tito

5   4

6   Rostra ★

7

Colonna di Foca ★

8

9   10

Via   Sacra ★

1

Tempio del Divo Giulio

11

Regia

Colonne   onorarie

Arco di Augusto

★★★ Tempio

15

Vicus Jugarius

★★★ Tempio di Saturno

★★★ Tempio di Castore e Polluce

V. d. Campidoglio

★ Portico degli Dei Consenti

★★ Basilica   Giulia

12

13

Monte   Tarpeo

Clivus   Capitolinus

Via   della   Consolazione

14

S. Maria Antiqua

N

Tempio di Augusto

Vicus

Horrea Agrippiana

The Republican Era

Romans overthrew the last Etruscan king, Tarquin the Proud, in 509 BC and instituted the consulate. During this Republican era, Rome began to develop into the capital of an empire. The Forum, barely 2ha/5 acres in extent, hosted many pivotal events.

The city state warred with its neighbours, expanding its territory steadily. All victorious generals processed in triumph through the Forum. A slave rode behind them in the chariot, holding a crown above their heads and whispering "look behind" or "you are only mortal". The Roman conquests brought immense riches: the confiscated enemy treasuries, indemnities paid by the conquered nations and the tributes from the provinces. Money-changing, loans and credit were arranged in the Forum. The **Temple of Saturn** dates to 496 BC, the

fabled "Golden Era" and served as the state treasury.

The men who decided the destiny of Rome met in the **Comitium**. Here stood the **Curia**, the seat of the highest level of Republican government. Two hundred senators, appointed for life, decided foreign policy, directed military operations, drew up peace treaties and enacted measures for public safety. Opposite the Curia was the Rostra, where orators held forth. In 185 BC, the **Basilica Porcia**, the first building of this sort in Rome, was erected so citizens to assemble under cover.

For 100 years, the Republican regime tore itself to pieces in civil war. In 52 BC, the tribune Clodius was killed by Milo; and cremated at the Comitium. The fire spread, destroying the Curia and the Basilica Porcia. In 44 BC, Caesar rebuilt the Curia and moved the Rostra.

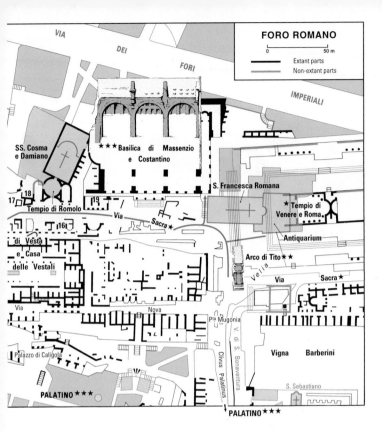

FORO ROMANO

0   50 m

Extant parts
Non-extant parts

VIA
DEI
FORI
IMPERIALI

SS. Cosma
e Damiano

★★★ Basilica di Massenzio
e Costantino

S. Francesca Romana

★ Tempio di
Venere e Roma

18
17
Tempio di Romolo

19

Via
Sacra ★

Antiquarium

Arco di Tito ★★

di Vesta
e Casa
delle Vestali

16

Via
Sacra ★

Via
Nova

Velia
Via

Palazzo di Caligola

Pta Mugonia

V. di S. Bonaventura

Clivus Palatinus

Vigna   Barberini

S. Sebastiano

PALATINO ★★★

PALATINO ★★★

Little remains, as early buildings were made of tufa, peperine or wood. Augustus boasted that he inherited a town built of brick and left a city of marble. Later emperors followed suit, making the site more and more splendid.

The Forum during the Empire

In the Augustan era, the huge popular assemblies and the troop reviews shifted to the Campus Martius. The Forum became the chosen site for monuments: commemorative arches, basilicas and temples dedicated to emperors deified after their death.

The 2C BC satirist Plautus recorded that every sort frequented the crossroads of the empire: "vicious or virtuous, honest or dishonest. If you want to meet a perjurer, go to the Comitium; for a liar and a braggart, try the Temple of Venus Cloacina; for wealthy married wasters, near the Basilica. There, too, you will find well-perfumed prostitutes and men ready to do a deal, while the fish market is frequented by members of the eating clubs. Wealthy and reputable citizens stroll in the lower Forum; the middle Forum near the canal is favoured by the merely showy set…".

In the 3C, building halted: not only for lack of space, but also because of the spread of Christianity. The emperors resisted, but in AD 391, Theodosius finally closed the pagan temples. The Forum's downfall began in 410, when Alaric the Goth descended from the Danube. His savage hordes torched the Curia and the **Basilica Aemilia**. Then followed an earthquake in 442, the depredations of Genseric's Vandals in 455, the armies of Theodoric in 500 and of Belisarius in 537, after which the Forum was dead. Rome's prestige no longer lay

Foro Romano

© Brad Pict/Fotolia.com

in grandiose monuments. Instead, the world celebrated the city as the resting place of St Peter the Apostle.

From the Middle Ages to the Renaissance

Once the Church became organised, the Bishop of Rome – the Pope – was recognised as the head of Christianity. Gradually the imperial buildings were converted into places of Christian worship. Some still survive, a curious juxtaposition of traditions; however, many have disappeared. In the 9C, the buildings began to crumble and earth massed around them, burying the ruins.

The Pope and the Holy Roman Emperor sparked a civil war between the noble Roman families in the 12C. They fortified ancient structures; towers rose between the Temple of Antoninus and Faustina and Caesar's Forum. They also quarried old buildings. Decorations embellished churches and palaces, and the statues and columns were baked in lime kilns to produce chalk.

The deserted Forum became a sewage farm. By the 15C the pillars of the Temple of Vespasian were half underground and the podium of the Temple of the Dioscuri was completely buried; both were surrounded by fields. The Forum had become a cows' field (campo vaccino). Near the Temple of the Dioscuri the marble basin of a fountain was used

as a drinking trough for animals; it is now in the Piazza del Quirinale. When Charles V visited Rome in 1536, Pope Paul III laid out a broad avenue from the Arch of Titus to the Arch of Septimius Severus.

Excavations

Many famous archaeologists, Italians and non-Italians, dug here; Carlo Fea, who began investigations in 1803, Antonio Nibby, Bunsen and Canina, Pietro Rosa, Giuseppe Fiorelli, Rodolfo Lanciani, H Jordan, C Hülsen and Giacomo Boni, who reached the oldest levels. Today Rome Reborn, (www.romereborn. org), reconstruct the city in 3D, via virtual reality.

WALKING TOUR

Certain parts of the ruins may be closed owing to restoration work. The remains of the Basilica Emilia are immediately on your right just inside the Largo della Salara Vecchia entrance. See map pp286-287.

Basilica Emilia (Basilica Aemilia)

Rome's second basilica (179 BC) was frequently restored and reconstructed; a 1C effort remains visible. Like all the ancient basilicas, it served no religious purpose. The huge covered hall sheltered business transactions and judicial hearings, as well as citizens' meetings. Along the south side of the basilica there was a line of shops opening into a portico. Behind these jewellery and perfume boutiques lay the main hall, divided by two rows of coloured marble columns with a finely carved entablature of white marble. In the southeast corner is a Latin **inscription (1)** to Augustus's adopted grandsons, Caius and Lucius, who died before reaching manhood.

Via Sacra★ (Sacred Way)

This street was the most famous street in ancient Rome. The Temple of Vesta and the Regia flanked the Sacred Way, along which victorious generals processed. Dressed like Jupiter and standing in a four-horse chariot, they proceeded to the Capitoline Hill to thank the god for his protection.

Santuario di Venere Cloacina (Sanctuary of Venus Cloacina) **(2)** – A travertine circle marks the site dedicated to the goddess who protected the main sewer *(cloaca)*; traces of its steps are still visible. Here in the 5C BC, the centurion Verginius saved his daughter Virginia from a spurned suitor, Appius Claudius. The government official abused his power and claimed she was a slave. Verginius stabbed his child to preserve her freedom. The people rioted, overthrew the decemvirs and re-established the Roman Republic.

Argiletum – This street, one of the busiest in Rome, separated the Basilica Aemilia from the Curia and led to Suburra, a slum district. Sections of travertine paving remain.

Curia★★

The brick building visible today is not where the **Senate** met in the Republican period. The first Curia was more or less on the site of the chancel and left transept of St Luke's Church, but facing in a different direction. In the 1C BC, Caesar moved and enlarged it; Diocletian remodelled it in the 3C.

The structure was less austere than it is today: the façade, faced with marble and stucco, was surmounted by a tympanum covered in travertine; the bronze door was removed to St John Lateran by Alexander VII in the 17C.

The Curia was a *templum*, a consecrated place, where an augur communicated the wishes of the gods. He would read omens: interpreting the flight of birds, the eating patterns of sacred chickens and unusual events. Every sitting of the Senate began with this ritual.

The senators did not have fixed seats. Once the agenda had been read, each – according to the order fixed by a list – gave his opinion.

The Senate's power waned in imperial times. At the very most, after an emperor's death, they could condemn him and oppose his deification.

The mystery of the Statue of Victory – At the far end of the Curia, there are traces of a pedestal where Victory stood. Octavian contributed this golden statue in 29 BC, after he defeated the armies of Antony and Cleopatra, and became the ruler of the empire. For over three centuries, the emperors worshipped the statue, burning incense on the altar. At their funerals, it led the cortège, which culminated in the deification.

Such pagan capers couldn't last. The statue of Victory became an offence to Christianity. In 382, the Emperor Gratian removed it. The statue has been lost to history since.

Bassorilievi di Traiano★★ (Trajan's Plutei) – The Curia houses two sculpted panels found in the Forum and probably commissioned by Trajan or his successor Hadrian to decorate the Rostra. On the back, the three animals sacrificed during the purification ceremony – a pig, a sheep and a bull – are represented. The sculptor set these scenes against a local background, showing several of the Forum buildings.

Lapis Niger (3)

In 1899, Giacomo Boni, the Forum's lead excavator, discovered black marble slabs *(currently protected by a low fence)*. Beneath these, lay a *stele* with an obscure inscription. The ancients believed this area contained the tomb of Romulus, Faustulus (the shepherd who saw the wolf suckling the twins) or Hostus Hostilius, the father of the third king.

Comitium

(*See The Republican Era, above*).
It extended from the Curia to the Lapis Niger and contained a fountain with a circular base *(remains are still visible)*.

Decennalia Caesarum (4)

In 286, Diocletian decentralised the government; he took charge of the eastern empire and Maximian of the western. Seven years later, they entrusted Gaul and Britain to Constantius, and the Balkan peninsula to Galerius. The first 10 years' reign *(decennalia)* of the two Caesars and the 20 years of the Augusti were celebrated with a column of which only the base remains. The carving shows sacrificial animals and religious ceremonies.

Rostra★

After 338 BC, the **orators' platform** was always called the Rostra. In that year, the Romans attacked Antium (modern Anzio), then notorious for its pirates, and captured the enemies' prows *(rostra)*, which they fixed to the platform. In the Republican period, it stood between the Lapis Niger and the present Curia. The remains seen today are those of the Rostra moved in 44 BC by Julius Caesar. After his assassination, Octavian, **Antony** and Lepidus formed the second triumvirate (late October 43 BC). The period of proscriptions began; **Cicero** was one of the most famous victims. An enemy of Antony, whose illegal acts and imperial ambitions he denounced, the orator was murdered by agents of the triumvirate. His hands and head were exposed on the Rostra.

Arco di Trionfo di Settimio Severo★★

The arch was built in 203 and is surmounted by statues of Septimius Severus, his two sons (Caracalla and Geta) and the figure of Victory. The emperor had just won a series of victories over the Parthians (197–202) and organised a new province, Mesopotamia, in the 3C. Architecture became more complicated:

four detached Corinthian columns form a false portico. Decoration is abundant.

Umbilicus Urbis (5)

This 3C circular temple marked the symbolic centre of the city.

Altare di Vulcano (6)

The **Altar of Vulcan**, a venerable hollow in the tufa, goes back to the time of the kings. Under the Republic, the day of 23 August was devoted to the *Volcanalia* festival: little fishes – or other animals symbolising human lives that people wished to preserve – were offered to the god of fire.

Colonna Miliare d'Oro (7)

The **Golden Milestone** marble column, covered with gilded bronze, was set up by Augustus to mark the point from which mileages were measured. It displayed the distances between the capital and the empire's major cities.
At the Capitoline's foot, splendid monuments flanked the **Clivus Capitolinus**, the road used for religious processions and military triumphs. It led from the Forum to the Temple of Jupiter.

▶ Backtrack to the Temple of Caesar.

Tempio del Divo Giulio

Almost nothing is left of this building, which started the cult of emperor worship. On the evening of the Ides of March 44 BC, the body of Caesar, who had been stabbed to death in the Curia of Pompey, was carried to the Forum and cremated before the Rostra. A column and altar were set up nearby, but were immediately pulled down by Caesar's enemies. They were replaced by a temple consecrated by Octavian in 29 BC to the "god" Julius Caesar.
In a semi-circular recess at ground level stood a round altar *(traces visible)*. In the *cella* was a statue of Caesar, a star on his head. Suetonius explains why he was often represented in this way: "after his apotheosis, during the first days of the games given in his honour by his successor Augustus, a comet appeared at about the eleventh hour and burned for

seven days; it was thought to be Caesar's soul being admitted to heaven...."
When Octavian defeated the fleets of Antony and Cleopatra, he took the prows *(rostra)* of the enemy ships and fixed them to the terrace of Caesar's Temple; the terrace became known as Caesar's Rostra and later emperors often spoke from there.

Arco di Trionfo di Augusto

Two commemorative arches were erected by Augustus between the Temples of Caesar and Castor. The first was built in 29 BC, after his victory at Actium in Greece. Ten years later, as the first became dilapidated, a second celebrated Augustus' recovery of the Roman standards, which had been captured by the Parthians. Only the foundations have been discovered *(the bases of two pillars are visible)*.

Tempio di Castore e Polluce★★★

This early 5C temple honoured Castor and Pollux, known as "the **Dioscuri**": offspring of Leda and the Swan (Jupiter), the twins were brothers to Clytemnestra and Helen of Troy. The chief remains are three columns supporting an architrave fragment: one of the most famous sights of the Roman Forum. The temple's history is surrounded by legends. Early in the 5C BC, Rome attacked its poor, envious neighbours: the conflict came to a head on the shores of Lake Regillus. During the battle, the Romans saw two divine knights fighting on their side: Castor and Pollux. They subsequently announced the victory to the people gathered in the Forum; their thirsty horses drank at Juturna's spring. The son of the dictator Postumius, who had directed the battle against the Latins, erected a temple here.
The three beautiful columns, which were pulled down in 1811, date from a reconstruction undertaken in the Augustan era and belong to the long left-hand side of the sanctuary. The very high podium, the magnitude of the Corinthian capitals and the use of very white marble combine to majestic effect.

The mad Emperor **Caligula** (AD 37–41) built a bridge from the Temple of Castor and Pollux (the antechamber to his palace) to the Temple of Jupiter on the Capitol, so that he could converse with the god, whom he considered his equal, or sometimes even take his place.

Basilica Giulia★★

In 170 BC, the Censor Sempronius Gracchus, father of the tribunes Tiberius and Caius, built a basilica on this site, which was called *Sempronia*.
In 55 BC, Julius Caesar, who was consul, replaced it with another basilica, larger and more elegant, which started the trend for gigantic buildings in the Forum. At 109m/358ft long and 40m/131ft wide, it was paved with precious marble in the centre and white marble in the side aisles.
👤👤 Close observation reveals geometric designs marked out by idlers for their games.
Julius Caesar was murdered before the basilica was finished; it still bears his name, though Augustus completed it.

Colonne Votive/Onorarie

There were seven votive columns, probably erected during Diocletian's reign (AD 284–305) to commemorate army generals. Two have been partly reconstructed.

Lago di Curzio (10)

The **Curtian Lake** refers to a circular paved area, protected by a roof and a railing. During the early Republic, it was a cleft full of water that could not be drained. The Oracle pronounced that the opening would close when Rome threw her dearest treasure into it. A valuable young soldier called **Curtius** rode into it fully armed and the abyss shrivelled to a small pool. The adjacent 1C BC low-relief sculpture illustrating the legend is now housed in the Museo del Palazzo dei Conservatori.

Colonna di Foca★

In AD 608, the eastern Emperor Phocas gave the Pantheon to Pope Boniface IV and it was turned into a church. In gratitude, the donor's statue was set in the Forum. The column had to be taken from an existing building, because no artists were capable of producing such fine sculpture. This monument was the last erected here.

The sacred **fig tree,** symbol of the one that shaded the cradle of Romulus and Remus, the **vine** and the **olive tree (8),** icons of agricultural prosperity, have all been replanted. Here also stood the very popular statue of Marsyas, brought from Greece in the 2C BC. It represented a Silenus – looking, as they all did, like an old satyr, very ugly and often drunk – wearing a skin over his shoulders. He wore a Phrygian cap, symbol of liberty; newly-freed slaves would come and touch the statue.

The **inscription (9),** reconstructed in bronze letters, bears the name of "Naevius" and commemorates the paving carried out by this magistrate in 15 BC.

Tempio di Saturno★★★

From 497 onwards, a temple dedicated to Saturn stood on this site. This god supposedly taught the Romans to cultivate the earth; hence his prestige with this peasant people. Restored several times under the Republic, the temple was then rebuilt in the 4C after a fire. The eight columns of the *pronaos* that remain date from this period; the travertine podium goes back to the 1C BC.

The **Saturnalia** took place here, the wild December festival that overturned the social structure – helping the sun rise again. Distinctions between masters and slaves were suspended; the latter were even entitled to free speech.

The basement housed the **state treasury**. This place may have been chosen because the cult of Saturn was associated with that of Ops, the goddess of abundance. The Senate administered the treasure, assisted by the censors and the quaestors.

Portico degli Dei Consenti★

⊙The best view is from the Capitoline Hill and Via del Foro Romano.
These 12 Corinthian columns were reconstructed in 1858. The portico was built by Domitian in honour of the 12 great gods in the Roman pantheon, who met in council to assist Jupiter. Their statues stood in the portico, two by two: Jupiter and Juno, Neptune and Minerva, Mars and Venus, Apollo and Diana, Vulcan and Vesta, Mercury and Ceres.

It was restored in 367 by the Prefect of Rome, Vettius Agorius Praetextatus, who had been a friend of **Julian the Apostate** and shared his great sympathy for the pagan religions. Certainly, this was the last gesture to paganism in Rome, where 37 Popes had already acceded to the throne of St Peter.

Tabularium

The podium and a few extant pillars form the base of the Senatorial Palace. The Tabularium filled the depression between the Citadel and the Capitol, the two peaks of the Capitoline Hill. Its façade formed the west side of the Forum. It was built in 78 BC to house the state records, including some bronze tablets of the old Roman laws, hence the name. The use of peperine, a very simple building material, and of the Doric order, a plain architectural style, typify the austerity of Republican architecture (⟲ *See Musei Capitolini, CAMPIDOGLIO).*

Tempio di Vespasiano★★

Three very elegant columns, excavated by Valadier in 1811, are still standing; they formed a corner of the earlier part of the temple. Above the architrave is a detailed decorative frieze: a cornice with dentil, ovolo and palm leaf moulding above a band decorated with bucranes and sacrificial instruments. The temple was approached by steps from the Clivus Capitolinus.

Vespasian became emperor in AD 69 following the struggles among the pretenders to Nero's seat. He therefore established a hereditary monarchy founded on primogeniture. He announced to the Senate that "his sons would succeed him or there would be no successor." His elder son Titus assumed the mantle of power and began a temple in honour of his father, who had been deified on his death. In practice, if an emperor ruled well, the Senate would issue a decree raising him to the rank of the gods. All that was needed was a witness who saw an eagle carry off the soul during the cremation.

Titus died before the temple was finished; Domitian, his brother, completed the building and dedicated his two predecessors. Their statues stood on a pedestal in the *cella*.

Tempio della Concordia

The Romans always attributed a divine character to the mysterious forces that influenced events. Thus they worshipped as gods such abstract ideas as concord, justice, liberty and abundance. Most of these divinities were represented by the statue of a female figure: the attributes of Concord were two linked hands and a dove.

The Forum had a Temple of Concord since 367 BC; it commemorated the re-establishment of peace between the patricians and the plebeians, who had been at odds since the beginning of the 5C BC. Some two and a half centuries later – when the assassination of the people's tribune, Caius Gracchus, had restored peace at home – Concord was again honoured and the temple rebuilt. The plan of the building is quite unusual: the *cella* extends laterally beyond the width of the *pronaos*, which was reached by steps from the Clivus Capitolinus.

▶ Retrace your steps and go around the Temple of Castor and Pollux.

Cinta Sacra di Giuturna (12)

Juturna was a nymph who reigned over all the springs in Latium. Lovestruck Jupiter made her immortal. Her shrine contained a spring which played a part in the legend of the Dioscuri. In the basin stands an altar, probably 2C, with low-relief sculptures representing Castor and Pollux and a woman bearing a long torch *(on the front and back)*, and Leda and the swan, and Jupiter *(on the sides)*. The adjacent **aedicule (13)**, partially reconstructed, the round well and the altar were also part of the sacred

precinct. The well is inscribed with the name of Barbatius Pollio, who put up a dedication to Juturna, probably in the reign of Augustus; low-relief figures on the altar.

Santa Maria Antiqua

Opening hours vary.
For additional info: ☎06 399 67 700.
www.coopculture.it
Closed since the 1980s for a complex architectural restoration, the church showcases and extraordinary collection of 6C to 9C artworks on its walls, testifying to the development of not only Roman painting, but the entire Greco-Byzantine world at the time.

Oratorio dei Martiri (14)

The original purpose of the building (Oratory of the Forty Martyrs) is unknown; in the 7C it was decorated with paintings and dedicated to the 40 martyrs of Sebastea in Armenia, who were exposed in chains on a frozen pond.

Tempio e Atrio delle Vestali★★★

In the days when fire was still a precious commodity, the village on the Palatine where Romulus lived must have included a round hut, similar to all the other huts, where the communal fire was kept alight. This process was organised around Vesta, the goddess of fire.

The institution of the cult in Rome goes back to Romulus or Numa Pompilius (715–672 BC). A group of priestesses, known as the Vestal Virgins, at first four in number but later increased to six, officiated in the cult of Vesta.

When the first temple was built, probably late in the 6C BC, it conserved the circular form of the earlier hut. It was destroyed by fire and rebuilt several times, always in circular form, until the time of Septimius Severus. Only the central foundation and a few marble fragments survived to be used in the 1930 reconstruction. It was an enclosed shrine, surrounded by a portico supported on 20 fluted Corinthian columns; the frieze showed the instruments of sacrifice in low relief. The *cella* housed an altar where the fire was kept burning constantly. There was also a secret place, where certain objects that were supposed to have made Rome's fortune were jealously guarded; they included the famous Palladium, a statuette in wood or bone of the goddess Pallas, thought to be able to protect the city that possessed it. It had fallen from the sky on the city of Troy, possibly thrown by Zeus on Olympus. The Romans thought it had come into their possession through Aeneas, who had stolen it from Troy and brought it to Italy.

Next to the temple was the house of the Vestal Virgins: the **Atrium Vestae**. It was a large two-storey building enclosing a courtyard with a portico, containing two pools of water and a garden.

The Vestal Virgins were chosen from the patrician families. They entered into service at the age of 10 and stayed for at least 30 years: 10 as pupils, 10 performing their duties and 10 teaching. Most of the Vestals spent their whole lives in the house. Discipline was strict: a virgin who let the fire go out, a portent of disaster for Rome, was severely punished and one who broke her vow of chastity was buried alive.

From the 3C, statues were erected to the Vestals in recognition of their service. Some of these statues with an inscription on the base have been placed in the courtyard of the house.

Regia

Religious observance in Rome centred on the Regia and the Temple of Vesta. The Regia was held to have been the residence **(16)** of King Numa Pompilius, who succeeded Romulus and organised the state religion. Later it was the residence of the Pontifex Maximus, the head of the college of priests. During the Regal period it was the Pontifex Maximus who kept the religious records. Under the Republic he took charge of the national religion and became so influential that the emperors appointed themselves to the position.

Tempio di Antonino e Faustina★★

The Emperor Antoninus Pius, who succeeded Hadrian in 138 AD, belonged to a rich family originally from Nîmes in France. He was well known for his kindness and reigned for 23 years in peace and moderation. On the death of his wife, Faustina, in AD 141, he raised her to the ranks of the goddesses, in spite of her scandalous behaviour. A huge temple to her was erected in the Forum. When Antoninus himself died, in AD 161, the Senate decided to dedicate the temple to both husband and wife.

The beautiful monolithic columns of the *pronaos* still stand in situ on their high podium. The frieze of griffins and candelabra on the entablature is a masterpiece of fine craftsmanship.

In the 11C the church of San Lorenzo in Miranda was established in the ruins. When Charles V visited Rome in 1536 the façade of the church was set back to reveal the colonnade. In 1602 the church was rebuilt.

Excavations beside the Temple of Antoninus and Faustina have uncovered a cemetery **(17)** dating from the time of Romulus (8C–7C BC).

Tempio di Romolo★

The Romulus to whom the temple is thought to be dedicated was not the founder of Rome, but the son of the Emperor Maxentius. Romulus died in 307. Dating from the early 4C, the construction is circular and flanked by two rooms with apses. In the 6C, when the room behind the temple became the church of St Cosmas and St Damian, the temple itself became a vestibule to the church. The doorway between two porphyry columns set into the concave façade is closed by the 4C **bronze doors★**, whose lock still works.

On the left of the Temple of Romulus are traces of six small rooms, sat either side of a corridor; they may have belonged to a brothel in the Republican era.

The remains of a medieval arcaded building **(19)** high above the Sacred Way indicate how much the ground level in the Forum had risen by the Middle Ages. Higher up the slope, quite in harmony with the ancient monuments below, is the church of Santa Francesca Romana with its Romanesque belfry and three parapet statues.

Basilica di Massenzio e Costantino★★★

This Basilica of Maxentius and Constantine is well known for its summer symphony concerts. Maxentius was proclaimed Emperor by the people after the abdication of joint rulers, Maximian, his father, and Diocletian, in 305. He then constructed a basilica, the last to be erected in Rome.

Built of brick beneath a groined vault, it was different from the other two basilicas, Aemilia and Julia. It was rectangular and divided into three by huge pillars flanked by columns; one long side ran parallel to the Sacred Way and the other followed the line of the present Via dei Fori Imperiali; one of the short sides constituted the main façade *(facing east towards the Colosseum)* and the other projected in an apse.

The Imperial throne, however, was coveted by Constantine, son of the Emperor Constantius, who had reigned jointly with Maximian and Diocletian. He defeated Maxentius at the Battle of the Milvian Bridge in 312 and completed the basilica with modifications. He moved the entrance to the façade overlooking the Sacred Way and graced it with a portico of four porphyry columns *(still visible)*; an apse was eventually added to the opposite façade.

This grandiose building housed some colossal statues; fragments of the statue of Constantine, which stood in the west apse, can still be seen in the courtyard of the Palazzo dei Conservatori. The gilded bronze tiles were used in the 7C to roof St Peter's Basilica.

Antiquarium

The exhibits in this museum, which is housed in a former convent attached to the Church of Santa Francesca Romana, are mostly connected with the Roman Forum: the earliest traces of Ancient Rome taken from tombs dating from 1 000–600 BC or found in the Forum or on the Palatine (hut-shaped urns and hollow tree trunks used as coffins).

Arco di Trionfo di Tito★★

The arch stands on the **Velia**, a spur of the Palatine jutting out towards the Esquiline, and appears in all the views of the Forum.

Titus, the eldest son of Vespasian, succeeded his father as Emperor but his reign was brief: from AD 79–81. In 70 he had captured Jerusalem, thus bringing to a successful conclusion a campaign his father had been pursuing since 66. After his death an arch was erected to commemorate his success. The Fall of Jerusalem was among the most tragic events in Jewish history.

The city was destroyed and the temple, the spiritual bond between Jews of the diaspora, was burned down. In its place Hadrian built a sanctuary to Jupiter and the city was called Aelia Capitolina (Hadrian's family name was Aelius). The single archway of the Arch of Titus was restored by Luigi Valadier in 1821.

At the centre of the panelled vault is a sculpture depicting the apotheosis of Titus: his soul is carried up to heaven by an eagle; this event made him eligible for deification.

The frieze *(above the arch on the side facing the Colosseum)* is indistinct: in a sacrificial procession a recumbent figure represents the Jordan, symbolising the defeat of Palestine.

The two low reliefs under the vault are among the masterpieces of Roman sculpture. On one side, Titus rides in his chariot in triumph, crowned with victory. On the other, the triumphal procession exhibits the booty pillaged from the temple in Jerusalem: the seven-branch candlestick which Moses had made and placed in the Tabernacle as commanded by God on Mount Sinai, the table for the shewbread, which was placed in the temple each week in the name of the 12 tribes of Israel, and the silver trumpets that rang out to announce the festivals.

It was on the Velia that Nero built the vestibule to his Golden House.

Tempio di Giove Statore

On 8 November 63 BC **Cicero** delivered his first Catiline oration here before the Senate. Feelings ran high among his audience, who were impressed by the security measures considered necessary to protect the State.

▶ Bear right up the hill (Clivus Palatinus) to the Palatine.

PALATINO

Via di San Gregorio 30. Combined ticket with the Colosseum and Foro Romano, valid for 2 days.

&⊙*Open last Sun of Oct–15Feb 8:30am–4:30pm; 16Feb–15Mar 8:30am–5pm; 16Mar–last Sat 8:30am–5:30pm; last Sun of Mar–Aug*

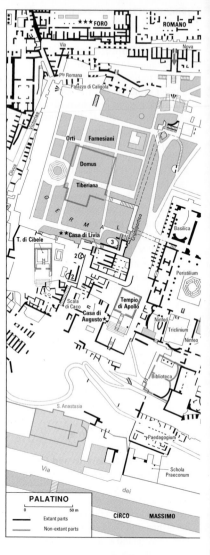

8:30am–7:15pm; Sept 8:30am–7pm; 1 Oct–last Sat Oct 8:30am–6:30pm.
⊙*Closed 1 Jan, 1 May and 25 Dec.*
⊛€*12.* ☏*06 39 96 77 00. Admissions 30 min before entry. www.coopculture.it*

Of the seven hills of Rome, it is the Palatine Hill that captures the visitor's imagination. As the cradle of the Eternal City it is a prime archaeological site. Since the Renaissance it has offered pleasant walks, now among flower beds restored in 2012 and shady plane trees.

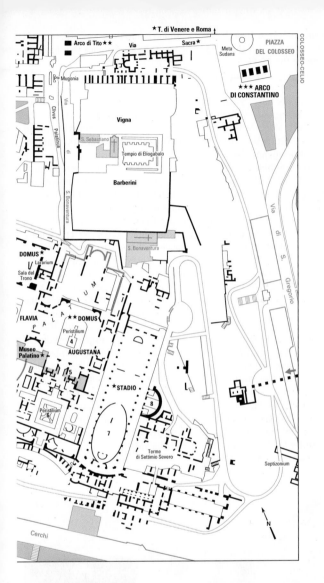

★ T. di Venere e Roma ↑

■ Arco di Tito ★★   Via   Sacra ★   Meta
                                                 Sudans

PIAZZA
DEL COLOSSEO

COLOSSEO-CELIO

★★★ ARCO
DI CONSTANTINO

Via   Pu Mugonia

Clivus   Palatino

Via

di

S. Bonaventura

Vigna

S. Sebastiano

Tempio di Eliogabalo

Barberini

S. Bonaventura

Via

di

S.

Gregorio

DOMUS ★
Lararium
Sala del
Trono

FLAVIA

L
A
V
I
U
M

★★ DOMUS

Peristilium

Museo
Palatino ★

AUGUSTANA

P
A
L
A
T
I
U
M

★ STADIO

8

Peristilium

Terme
di Settimio Severo

Septizonium

N

Cerchi

Byron wrote of the beauty of the
Palatine and its overgrown ruins:

" *Cypress and ivy,*
weed and wallflower grown
Matted and mass'd together,
hillocks heap'd
On what were chambers,
arch crush'd, column strown
In fragments, choked up vaults,
and frescos steep'd
In subterranean damps…"

Origins

It was inconvenient for political reasons that **Romulus** and **Remus** (⟲ *See*
INTRODUCTION), twin sons of the
Vestal Rhea Silvia and the god Mars,
should survive. They were therefore
abandoned on the banks of the Tiber,
but the river was in spate, and their
cradle came to rest on the Palatine.
They survived thanks to a she-wolf
that suckled them in the Lupercal cave.
The shepherd Faustulus, who wit-

nessed this unusual event, took charge of the twins and brought them up. In the middle of the 8C BC Romulus ploughed a deep furrow around the Palatine, lifting his ploughshare in three places. This was the beginning of Rome, a symbolic enclosure with three gateways: the Porta Mugonia, the Porta Romana and the Porta Scalae Caci.

This is obviously a legendary account, but in 1949 traces of huts thought to date from the 8C and 7C BC were excavated on the legendary site of Romulus's house.

During the Republic the Palatine was a quiet residential area. **Cicero** lived on the hill, as did Antony, the Triumvir, and Agrippa – Octavian's friend before becoming his son-in-law. Foreigners came to visit the shepherd's hut and the wolf's cave in the southwest face of the hill.

In 63 BC "on the ninth day before the Kalends of October, a little before daybreak" Octavian was born. When he became the Emperor Augustus, the Palatine began to alter. He enlarged his house and then rebuilt it after it was destroyed by fire in the 3 BC. Tiberius, who succeeded him, Caligula, Claudius and Nero all lived on the Palatine, but it was **Domitian**, the last Flavian Emperor (AD 81–96), who transformed the hill by turning it into the Imperial Palace and gave it the appearance that has now been revealed by archaeologists.

The hollow which divided it into two peaks (Germalus and Palatium) was filled with new buildings, whose ruins now occupy the central section of the plateau: they are the **Domus Flavia** and the **Domus Augustana★**; the **Stadium** also dates from this period. In 191 the buildings on the Palatine were seriously damaged by fire. The Emperor Septimius Severus was not content with simply undertaking repairs. He enlarged the Imperial Palace to the south and built a monumental façade, the Septizonium, parallel with the Old Appian Way, so that travellers arriving in Rome by this route would be immediately impressed by the grandeur of the capital. This section of the palace remained standing until Pope Sixtus V demolished it to provide building materials at the end of the 16C.

The Palatine began to go into decline in the 3C when Diocletian, Galerius, Maximian and Constantius deserted Rome and built new Imperial residences in Nicomedia, Sirmium, Milan and Trier respectively. In 330 **Constantine** moved the Imperial capital to Constantinople, formerly Byzantium, and the Palatine was abandoned.

Domus Augustana, Palatino

©D. Chapuis/Michelin

The Christians generally ignored the Palatine plateau and built only on the slopes: in the 4C a sanctuary was dedicated to St Anastasia on the south side; on the north face the church of St Sebastian was established in what had been a temple to the sun; its builder Emperor Elagabalus dreamed of a religion combining the Oriental cults and appointed himself high priest to the sun god.

In the 11C and 12C Rome became the prize in the struggles between the Pope and the Emperor and was studded with fortresses and towers; hence the description *Roma turrita*. The Frangipani family, which supported the Emperor, fortified the whole of the southeast face of the Palatine. By the time of the Renaissance the buildings on the Palatine (from which the word "palace" is derived) were in ruins. The wealthy Roman families built villas on the site, surrounding them with vineyards and gardens: the Barberini near to St Sebastian; the Farnese on the northwest part of the hill between Tiberius's and Caligula's palaces.

Excavations

Investigative digging began in 1724 at the suggestion of Francis I of Parma, who had inherited the Farnese Villa. The Domus Flavia was the first building to see the light of day. About 50 years later a Frenchman, the Abbé Rancoureuil, excavated the Domus Augustana and the buildings overlooking the Circus Maximus. In 1860, under Napoleon III, archaeologists discovered Tiberius's Palace, Livia's House and the Temple of Apollo, which was first attributed to Jupiter. The identification of the buildings on the Palatine has provoked passionate argument between archaeologists and historians. Many of the constructions have never been discovered but excavations on the Palatine continue, particularly in the area of the Temple of Apollo.

Very little of the ruined buildings remains standing and it requires a great effort of the imagination to evoke the splendour of the ancient palaces on the Palatine.

WALKING TOUR

The Cabins of Romulus were closed for restoration.

Clivus Palatinus

This road approximately follows the hollow between two peaks: the Palatium to the left; the Germalus to the right.

▶ Walk straight up the path (south) leaving on the right the steps that go up to the Farnese Gardens.

The rectangular ditch marks the site of Domitian's Arch. The sections of high brick wall facing down the hill belonged to the portico of the Domus Flavia. The path emerges at the top of the hill in the centre of the artificial plateau, which was created when Domitian filled in the hollow between the Palatium and the Germalus.

Domus Flavia★

This was the centre of official Imperial activity. Although the buildings have been razed to the ground, it is still possible to envisage them. There were three rooms behind the portico:

- ♦ the **Lararium** – the shrine of the household gods, the Lares – was the Emperor's private chapel;
- ♦ the **Throne Room** (Sala del Trono) was enormous (over 30m/98ft wide by 40m/131ft long) with huge statues standing in the recesses in the walls;
- ♦ the **Basilica**, where the Emperor dispensed justice, had an apse at one end and a row of columns down each of the long sides. Outside the west wall are traces of the west portico of the Domus.

Behind these three rooms is a courtyard **(Peristilium)** originally surrounded by a portico (traces of the columns remain). Suetonius wrote that Domitian was so hated by everyone for his injustice and cruelty that he had the walls of the portico faced with phengite (a very shiny stone) so that he could "see by reflection what was going on behind his back". The octagonal basin at the centre of the court,

Interior, Casa di Augusto

©Judy Edelhoff/Michelin

which is now planted with flowers, was probably a fountain.

Beyond the peristyle is the **Triclinium**, the dining room, which was certainly the most beautiful room in the palace; part of the coloured marble floor has been preserved. It was supported on little brick pillars to allow the passage of warm air produced by an underground stove to heat the room.

The *triclinium* was flanked to right and left by two small leisure rooms, known in Latin as the *nymphaea*. The one on the right is well preserved.

The extant building in the far corner of the *nymphaeum* dates from the Farnese era (16C).

The traces of walls, columns and apses on the terrace behind the *triclinium* may mark the site of the libraries of the Imperial Palace.

Sale Sotterranee★ (Underground Rooms) – These rooms are all that remained of houses from the Republican era and of Nero's constructions when they were buried under Domitian's building projects.

- ◆ Beneath the basilica, a rectangular room: the paintings with which it was decorated are conserved in a room east of the Antiquarium; they prob-

ably date from the Augustan era and depict the cult of Isis.

- ◆ Beneath the *lararium*, the **Griffin House** (Casa dei Grifi, ⌒ *Closed to public*), sometimes also erroneously called "Catilina's house": it was built in the 2C BC (walls composed of irregular-sized stones mixed with mortar), altered in the 1C BC (walls composed of regular stone blocks arranged in a diamond pattern) and then altered again by Nero; many of the paintings have been removed to the Antiquarium for safe-keeping; one room contains a stucco relief of two griffins face to face.
- ◆ Beneath the peristyle: a circular chamber containing a well which communicates with another room by a passage. The discovery of this complex early this century caused quite a stir among archaeologists who thought they had found the Mundus. At the time of the founding of Rome the Mundus was a well into which a handful of earth was thrown by each new immigrant who, through this symbolic gesture, became a citizen of the new city. In fact, it is probably only a silo for water or grain.

Museo Palatino

The **Palatine Museum** is housed in a building that once belonged to the Convent of the Visitation, built over the ruins of Domitian's Imperial Palace (structural remains of which can be seen in Rooms **3** and **4**), and contains articles and fragments found on the Palatine. The ground floor is dedicated to the period spanning the foundation of Rome (model of 8–7C BC huts built on the Germalus) and the Republican era; the upper floor contains exhibits relating to the Imperial period. Exhibits include remains of "second style" frescoes from Augustus' House, with architectural cornices and columns and suspended festoons of leaves and flowers between them; a collection of portraits of Emperors and famous characters; and two inlaid-marble panels that demonstrate the fine quality of wall decoration during the Nero period (AD 54–68).

At the end of Room 9, the statue known as the Borghese Hera, a Roman copy of a Greek work from the end of the 5C BC, towers over all the other exhibits.

Casa di Augusto★★

Open by S.U.P.E.R tickets only; 18 €. Mapping projections Mon-Wed-Fri-Sun (Sun closing 2pm). Max. 23 people at a time: highly recommended. ℘ 06 39 96 77 00. www.coopculture.it.

This is not Augusto's own private house but the official Imperial residence. The recently restored rooms are arranged around two peristyles *(peristilium)*; one is very much lower than the other. At the centre of the upper peristyle (4), marked by an umbrella pine, is the base of a construction that was reached by a bridge from the edge of the surrounding basin. Around the sides are various living rooms. The rooms on the south side of the upper peristyle overlook the lower peristyle. The central basin (6), a pattern of compartments, was designed to collect rainwater. The palace itself faces the Circus Maximus from behind a concave façade.

Stadio★

This stadium was one of Domitian's projects. It looks like a gigantic trough (some 145m/159yd long) surrounded by a two-storey portico. Some say it was designed to stage private games and spectacles for the Emperor; others say it was a garden or an athletics ground. The small oval track (7) at the southern end dates from the 6C and is the work of Theodoric, the Ostrogoth, who occupied the Palatine at that period. The huge recess (8) in the centre of the long east side may have been reserved for the emperor.

On the east side of the Stadium are the ruins of a bathhouse attributed to Septimius Severus, but probably built by Maxentius.

▶ Pass the museum and retrace your steps.

Tempio di Apollo

This temple was thought to be dedicated to Jupiter but it is probably the one mentioned by Suetonius: Augustus

built a temple to Apollo "in a corner of his house on the Palatine that had been struck by lightning and which, according to the omens, Apollo was claiming for himself". The temple is fenced off; the podium and a column of the *pronaos* are recognisable.

Casa di Livia★★

See Casa di Augusto.

This house, named after Augustus's wife, was probably where the Emperor himself lived. The diamond pattern on the walls and the style of the decor date the building to the end of the Republic. The wall paintings, which had already deteriorated somewhat, were detached and erected just in front of the walls to which they belonged; this means they can be appreciated in their original setting. The names given to the various rooms do not necessarily correspond to their use. On either side of the centre room (*tablinum* – study) are two narrow rooms (wings) where wax images of the family ancestors were kept or which, in more modest houses, were used as storerooms.

Left wing – The lower part of the wall is decorated to look like marble; above are panels showing people and griffins face to face.

Tablinum – On the right-hand wall: a central panel, surrounded by architectural motifs, shows Io, Argos's daughter; Zeus fell in love with her and turned her into a heifer to protect her from the fury of his wife, Hera, who was nevertheless suspicious and set Argus, who had 100 eyes, to watch over the animal. The painting shows Hermes, who was sent by Zeus to rescue Io. On the left-hand wall: lead pipes engraved with the name IVLIAE AV (Julia Augusta). The archaeologists who discovered this inscription in 1869 thought it referred to Augustus' wife, the Empress, and attributed the house to Livia. The rear wall depicts Galatea fleeing from Polyphemus.

Right wing – The decorations on the left-hand wall, although damaged by the opening of the door, are still fresh: simulated columns flanking garlands of fruit and leaves from which hang baskets, sticks, horned animal heads, lyres and other representations of nature. Above, on a yellow ground, is a frieze of people at work in the open air.

Cisterne (2)
These cisterns date from the 6C BC; one is shaped like a beehive and the other is uncovered.

Scala di Caco
One of the three original approaches to the Palatine, the steps are named after a local villain, **Cacus**, who is linked in legend to Hercules. When Hercules was returning to the Argos with the cattle stolen from Geryon, he halted on the Tiber's banks. Cacus, an evil three-headed monster who breathed fire from his three mouths, stole three animals. He made them walk backwards to avoid detection, but Hercules was not fooled and he killed Cacus.

Capanne del Villaggio di Romolo (Cabins from Romulus's Village) (1)
These huts are some of the earliest traces of the city (8C–7C BC). The modern roof that covers them creates a real reliquary. Three huts have been discovered, oval or rectangular and sunk in the ground. The ring of holes held the posts supporting the walls and the roof. The gap in the south side *(facing the Tiber)* marks the doorway and is flanked by smaller post holes that indicate the possibility of a porch. The ditch was probably to drain off the rainwater from the roof.

Tempio di Cibele
Cybele, the goddess of Phrygia (also called the Mother of the Gods), was the personification of nature's powers. Her cult was introduced into Rome late in the 3C or early in the 2C BC. The temple on the Palatine was inaugurated in 191 and then rebuilt by Augustus after several fires. Today only the base of the *cella* walls remains in the shade of a group of holm oaks.

Domus Tiberiana
The arches facing the Temple of Cybele belonged to the rear façade of Tiberius' Palace. Only a few traces of this huge rectangular building are visible since Cardinal Farnese's gardens cover the greater part of it.

Cryptoporticus
This is a network of passages, partially underground, which probably linked the Imperial buildings that occupied the hill. It dates from Nero's reign, although the arm linking up with Domitian's Domus Flavia must have been added later.

The stuccoes that decorated the vaulting in the section of the passage near Livia's House have been removed to the Antiquarium, replaced by copies. The oval basin **(3)** on the left of the steps leading to Farnese Gardens was a fishtank in the southeast corner of Tiberius's Palace.

Orti Farnesiani★★
The gardens were laid out in the middle of the 16C by Cardinal Alexander Farnese, Paul III's nephew. The entrance, set in a semi-circle at the level of the Forum (which was higher then than now), gave access to a series of terraces rising up the north face of the Palatine. On the flat top of the hill, over the ruins of Tiberius's Palace, stretched the Farnese's magnificent botanical garden, one of the richest in the world at that time. The northwest corner of the gardens gives an excellent **view★★** of the Forum, the Tabularium, the Senatorial Palace, the monument to Victor Emmanuel II, the domes of the church of St Luke and St Martina and of the two churches next to Trajan's Column, the Militia Tower etc. In the northeast corner of the gardens are two buildings (reconstructed) which formed a complex comprising two aviaries above a *nymphaeum*. From the terrace there is a pleasant **view★★**, particularly at sunset, of the basilica of Maxentius, the belfry of Santa Francesca Romana and the upper storeys of the Colosseum.

▶ Leave the Palatine by Clivus Palatinus, turn right into Via Sacra at the Arch of Titus.

Tempio di Venere e Roma★

The temple was built between AD 121–136 by Hadrian, completed by Antoninus Pius and restored by Maxentius, on the site of the vestibule to Nero's Golden House. It was the largest temple in Rome (110m/361ft by 53m/174ft) and designed in the Greek style with steps on all sides (the majority of Roman temples had only one flight of steps leading up to the *pronaos*). It was surrounded by a colonnade and uniquely comprised two *cellae* with apses back to back. One was dedicated to the goddess Rome and faced the Forum; the other was dedicated to Venus and faced the Colosseum.

The plans for the temple were drawn by Hadrian. He also designed two gigantic seated figures to be set in niches that were disproportionately small. The part of the temple facing the Forum has been incorporated into the church of Santa Francesca Romana and the adjoining convent of Olivetan monks. An idea of the temple's appearance is given by a few columns which were re-erected in 1935; the position of the missing parts is marked by bushes of privet, box and oleander.

Santa Francesca Romana

🕐 *Open daily 10am–noon and 3pm–5pm.*

In the 8C an oratory dedicated to St Peter and St Paul was built in the western half of the Temple of Venus and Rome by Pope Paul I. In the following century it replaced the church of Santa Maria Antiqua in the Forum and is also called Santa Maria Nova. The church was placed under the patronage of Santa Francesca Romana (**St Frances of Rome**) when canonised in 1608.

The 12C Romanesque **bell-tower★** is eleganT. The façade by Carlo Lombardi (1615) is characteristic of the Counter-Reformation. The use of a single order of flat pilasters resting on a high portico lends it a certain solemnity. Inside there is a beautiful 17C coffered ceiling. Don't miss the magnificent 12C mosaics portraying the Madonna with child and saints.

▶ Take Via dei Fori Imperiali.

Santi Cosma e Damiano

🕐 *Open 10am–1pm and 3pm–7pm.*
📞 *06 69 90 808.*

The basilica was dedicated in 526 by Pope Felix IV to two saints of Arabian origin, Cosmas and Damian, twin brothers whose help was invoked to cure illness. The church was established in the Temple of Romulus and in an adjacent room which had been the library of Vespasian's Forum; it was the first Christian church to occupy a pagan building in the Roman Forum. When the relics of the two saints were discovered in the 16C the Popes began to alter the original church.

In the 17C Clement VIII reduced the width of the nave by creating side chapels which cut off the outer edges of the mosaic on the chancel arch. The floor was raised, a doorway opened in the west wall and a plaster arcade added in front of the apse.

Ceiling★ – Beautiful 17C coffered ceiling showing the triumph of St Cosmas and St Damian *(centre)* and *(at each end)* the coat of arms with the bees of Cardinal Francesco Barberini, who promoted the greater part of the 17C alterations.

Mosaics★ – Those on the chancel arch date from the late 7C and show the Lamb of God surrounded by seven candelabra and four angels. The angels on the left and right, symbolising the Evangelists, St Luke and St John, have survived the 17C alterations. The lamb and the throne were restored in 1936.

The mosaics in the apse date from the 6C. In the centre is the figure of Christ against a sunset sky. At his sides are the Apostles Peter and Paul presenting St Cosmas and St Damian, dressed in brown. On the left is Pope Felix IV offering a model of his church and on the right St Theodore dressed in a handsome *chlamys* (short mantle), like a Byzantine courtier. Below, partially screened by the Baroque altar (1637), is the Paschal Lamb surrounded by 12 beautiful angels representing the apostles and the Church.

Pantheon ★★★

This square still retains its majesty despite the crowds of tourists, Roma musicians, locals savouring aperitifs and McDonald's fast food wrappers. The Pantheon – remarkably intact and still stunning – dominates the Piazza della Rotonda. Classical and Baroque buildings form a court around this queen of antiquity.

A BIT OF HISTORY

The **Campus Martius** was a marshy plain for census-taking and soldier-drilling. However, in the 2C BC the Romans began to divide the area into lots. In the eastern half, between the Pantheon and the present Corso, Caesar erected the Saepta, an enclosure for the assemblies that elected the tribunes of the people (*comitia tributa*). In about 43 BC, two Egyptian temples – dedicated to Isis and Serapis – were built beside the Saepta (*See HISTORY: map of Rome Empire*).
Each dynasty left its mark here. Augustus' son-in-law, Agrippa, built the original Pantheon, which was rectangular, and, between 25 and 19 BC, the first public baths in Rome (Terme di Agrippa). The structure we see today was built by Hadrian between 118 and 125 BC on the old foundations. Domitian was responsible for a temple to Minerva and a portico

- **Michelin Map:** 38 L 11–12.
- **Location:** The Pantheon stands in the heart of the ancient *Campus Martius*. The Tiber runs to the west and the straight Via del Corso to the east.
- **Timing:** Return after dusk when the square is lively with diners and drinkers.
- **Don't Miss:** Coffee at San Eustachio or Tazzo d'Oro, masterworks in the Galleria Doria Pamphili, Pozzo's frescoes in San Ignazio.
- **Kids:** The elephant obelisk in Piazza della Minerva. The mysterious giant foot at the Via Piè di Marmo.
- **Also See:** *FONTANA DI TREVI–QUIRINALE; ISOLA TIBERINA–GHETTO–TORRE ARGENTINA; MONTECITORIO; PIAZZA NAVONA; PIAZZA VENEZIA.*

to the deified Flavians. The Antonines added a temple to the deified Hadrian. Alexander Severus rebuilt Nero's Baths (Terme di Nerone).
In the 4C, the Christians held sway. They often cannibalized or adapted the ruins of pagan monuments. During the medieval struggle between the Ghibelline

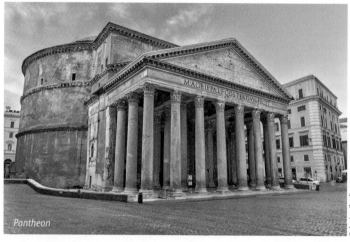

Pantheon

© sborisov/fotolia.com

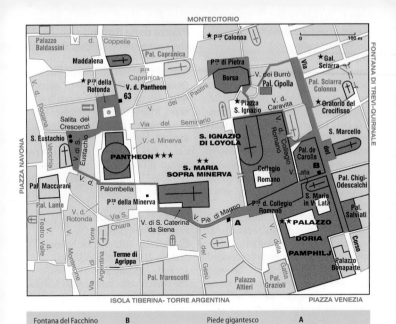

MONTECITORIO

| Fontana del Facchino | B | Piede gigantesco | A |

(empire) and the Guelf (papacy), Rome was peppered with towers.

In the 16C and 17C, the higher clerics and citizens bought hovels and replaced them with unostentatious, but luxurious, palaces.

PANTHEON★★★

Piazza della Rotonda.
Note: The building is a church (Santa Maria ad Martyres) and should be treated as such. ⌖ ⏰ *Open Mon–Sat 8:30am–7:30pm, Sun 9am–6pm.*
⏰ *Closed 1 Jan, 1 May and 25 Dec.*
℘ *06 68 30 02 30.*

Originally the Pantheon was a temple, built by Agrippa, the great town planner, in 27 BC; dedicated to all the gods, it faced south. In AD 80, it was damaged by fire and restored by Domitian. Then Hadrian (117–38) rebuilt it and gave it its present orientation to the north. The first Christian emperors closed the Pantheon, together with all other places of pagan worship. The ruins were sacked by the barbarians in 410, but saved from destruction by Pope Boniface IV, who received it as a gift in 608 from Phocas, the emperor in Byzantium (⏰See FORO ROMANO).

Until 756, when the **Papal States** came into being, Rome was subject to Byzantium. The only eastern emperor to visit the Christian capital was **Constantinus II** in 356, when the Pantheon was despoiled of its bronze tiles for the embellishment of Constantinople. It was restored early in the Renaissance. Then Urban VIII removed the nails and bronze plates that covered the beams of the porch roof and had them made into the magnificent baldaquin now in St Peter's. Pasquino, one of Rome's "talking statues", punned on the pope's family name: *Quod non fecerunt Barbari, fecerunt Barberini* (what the barbarians did not do, the Barberini have done).

Exterior

The Pantheon has a pillared porch, whose pediment bears two inscriptions: the most visible concerns Agrippa's original effort. A mighty bronze door leads into the circular interior, which could contain a 43m (142ft) globe.

Interior★★★

The entrance is under the porch, which is supported on 16 monolithic granite columns, all original except for three

311

(replaced under Urban VIII and Alexander VII due to weakness).

The harmony and grandeur of the interior have an immediate impact. The proportions are striking; the diameter of the building is equal to its overall height. The **antique dome★★★** is an incredibly bold feature; medieval architects lost this technology, which Renaissance artists – like Bramante and Michelangelo – recovered by studying the Pantheon. At the centre of the coffered ceiling is an enormous round opening *(oculus)*, which lights the interior.

A series of superb monolithic columns punctuate round and rectangular recesses. The piers between have shrines with alternating triangular or rounded pediments. The upper stage – between the cornice and the base of the dome – was redesigned in the 18C with the present series of panels and blind windows. A section above the third chapel on the west side has been returned to the original decor.

The recesses have been converted into chapels: in the first to the west of the entrance is an attractive *Annunciation* attributed to Melozzo da Forlì. The next chapel contains the **tomb of Victor Emmanuel II** (1820–78), the first king of unified Italy.

Between the fifth and sixth chapels is the **tomb of Raphael**, composed of a fine antique sarcophagus. He died, aged 37, in 1520. On the upper edge is an inscription by Cardinal Pietro Bembo, poet and humanist (1470–1547), which Alexander Pope translated without acknowledgement for another epitaph:

> "Living, great nature feared
> he might outvie
> Her works; and dying fears
> herself to die."

WALKING TOUR

North of Piazza della Rotonda, Via del Pantheon leads to Piazza della Maddalena.

Piazza della Rotonda★

This square, surrounding the Pantheon, is typically Roman. At the centre is a fountain designed in 1578 by Giacomo Della Porta; in 1711 Clement XI stacked an obelisk on top. Like Piazza della Minerva's, it came from the Temple of Isis.

The **Albergo del Sole** (Hotel of the Sun) at no 63 dates from the 15C. One of the oldest inns in the city, its guests have included Ludovico Ariosto, the poet (1474–1533), and Pietro Mascagni, the musician (1863–1945).

Santa Maria Maddalena

Piazza della Maddalena 53.
🕐*Open Sun–Fri and public holidays 8:30am–11:30am, 5pm–6:30pm; Sat 9am–11:30am.* ✆*06 89 92 81.*

The church, dedicated to Mary Magdalene, stands on the site of a 15C oratory and hospice. These were occupied in 1586 by St Camillus of Lellis, the founder of the Ministers of the Sick, a nursing order. The church was rebuilt in the 17C by Carlo Fontana, who was succeeded by followers of Bernini. The façade was erected in 1735; its contorted lines and abundant decoration are an exaggeration of Borromini's style.

The **interior★** is a rare example of the Rococo in Rome. The elaborate plan, also suggesting Borromini's influence, gives the church a majestic appearance despite its small size. The rich decoration – in stucco, gold and marble – and the frescoes lend the church the charm of an old-fashioned drawing-room.

The relics of St Camillus are venerated at the altar in the south transept beneath the *Glory of St Camillus*, painted by Sebastian Conca. In the passage south of the chancel is a 15C wooden statue of Mary Magdalene. The sumptuous organ dates from the 18C, as do the attractive furnishings in the sacristy.

▶ Return to Piazza della Rotonda.

On the west side of the Pantheon *(Via Salita dei Crescenzi and Via di S. Eustachio)* is the site where the Crescenzi fortress stood in the Middle Ages. Nearby a tower was erected by the Sinibaldi family. Two ancient columns, once part of the baths of Alexander Severus, have been re-erected at the junction of the two streets. 🕭The famous Sant'Eustachio Café is located in Piazza di S. Eustachio. Contrast this with Tazzo d'Oro, another famous nook on Via degli Orfani 8 (⚘ *See Map addresses Pantheon, p317*).

▷ Go southeast along Via della Palombella to Piazza della Minerva.

Piazza della Minerva
👥 **Bernini** suggested this obelisk be supported on an elephant's back. The Egyptian pillar dates from the 6C BC; it was once part of the nearby Temple of Isis. The fantastic marble elephant, affectionately called the "chick of Minerva," was sculpted by one of Bernini's pupils, Ercole Ferrata (1667).

Santa Maria sopra Minerva★★
Piazza della Minerva 42.
🕐*Open Mon–Fri 6:55am–7pm, Sat 10am–12:30pm and 3:30pm–7pm, Sun. 8.10am–12.30pm–3:30–7. ☎06 67 93 926. www.basilicaminerva.it.*
Rome's only Gothic church – all elegant cobalt blue and gilt – contains a censored statue of Christ by **Michelangelo**. Its name translates "Saint Mary over Minerva," a reference to the temple ruins nearby.
In 1280, it was rebuilt, then modified towards the middle of the 15C. The façade was constructed in the 17C; it is rectangular and very plain, with the original 15C doorways. Six plaques *(right)* mark the heights reached by Tiber flood waters. The church has long been the headquarters of the Dominicans, historical rivals of the Jesuits in the defence of Roman Catholic orthodoxy against the Reformation.

Interior
The **works of art★** here rank this as one of Rome's first "museum churches".
South aisle – In the fifth chapel **(1),** the painting by Antoniazzo Romano recalls the beneficence of Cardinal Juan de Torquemada (uncle of the infamous inquisitor), who provided poor girls

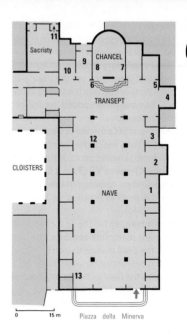

Piazza della Minerva

with dowries. This work, against a gold background, is typical of the style of this late 15C painter. The sixth chapel **(2)** was designed in the late 16C by Giacomo della Porta and Carlo Maderno. A la Counter-Reformation, the marble's extravagance is tempered with a certain severity. The next chapel **(3)** contains one of **Andrea Bregno**'s most famous works *(right)*: the delicate decoration on the tomb of Cardinal Coca (d. 1477).

South transept – The Carafa Chapel **(4)**, which has a finely carved marble altar rail, was built and decorated between 1489 and 1493 with **frescoes★** by **Filippino Lippi**: above the altar, in a typical late Renaissance frame, is an *Annunciation* in which Thomas Aquinas presents Cardinal Oliviero Carafa to the Virgin. The expressive faces, the slender figures and the deeply pleated garments are characteristic of Filippino Lippi's art. The rest of the wall is taken up with an *Assumption* in fine colours. The right-hand wall shows scenes from Thomas Aquinas' life. On the left of the Carafa Chapel is the 13C tomb of Guillaume Durand **(5)**, Bishop of Mende in France (d. 1296), by Giovanni Cosma.

Presbytery – Michelangelo's **Risen Christ★** stands to the left of the high altar **(6)**. The strong, confident pose expressed Christ's voluntary sacrifice. An assistant muddled some bits, yet the muscular, naked statue was much admired in the 16C. Baroque prudes added the discreet bronze loincloth.

The tomb of **St Catherine of Siena**, patron saint of Italy, lies under the main altar. The funeral monuments of the Medici Popes, **Clement VII (7)** and Leo V **(8)**, modelled on commemorative arches, are the work of Antonio da Sangallo (1483–1546).

North transept – The first chapel **(9)** contains many fine **tombs★**; the one with the dead man resting on his elbow *(left)* is by Giacomo della Porta (late 16C). Set into the floor is the resting place of **Fra Angelico**: Giovanni da Fiesole, the Dominican painter who died in 1455. In the next chapel **(10)** is a 15C tomb composed of an antique sarcophagus *(Hercules and the lion)*.

St Catherine of Siena's Chapel (11) – This chapel was built in the 17C using the walls of the room where the saint died (1380) in the neighbouring Dominican convent.

North aisle – Monument to Venerable Sister Maria Raggi **(12)**: flowing garments, an ecstatic expression and lively cherubs exemplify the art of **Bernini** (1643). The Renaissance tomb of Francesco Tornabuoni **(13)** is one of Mino da Fiesole's most successful works because of its fine decorative carving.

▷ Walk west along Via Piè di Marmo.

🚶 The street is named after the enormous stone **foot**, which probably belonged to a Roman statue, although no one knows how it came to be in its present position.

The **Roman College** (Collegio Romano), formerly the **Jesuit College**, was founded in 1583 by Gregory XIII, who strove to re-establish the primacy of Rome after the Council of Trent. At the corner of Via della Gatta, beneath a canopy, is a charming Madonna, so typical of Rome.

Palazzo Doria Pamphilj★
Via del Corso 305.

This palace, one of Rome's largest, was begun in the 15C and gradually enlarged by the succession of noble owners. Inside lies a gallery of the same name, housing a fine collection of paintings and sculpture (🌀*See full entry p316*).

The façade facing the Corso is an imposing 18C construction in the Baroque style, whereas the front onto Via del Plebiscito dates from 1643. The *palazzo* extends the whole length of Via della Gatta behind a 19C façade and round two sides of Piazza del Collegio Romano. Since 1966, it's housed the Anglican Centre in Rome, a tangible outcome of the formal visit paid by Archbishop Michael Ramsey to Pope Paul VI in that year. Students – particularly Roman Catholics curious about the Anglican Communion – can consult the library.

▷ Take Via Lata between Santa Maria in Via Lata and Palazzo del Banco di Roma (Bank of Rome).

Fontana del Facchino
Tucked against the wall *(right)* is an amusing little fountain composed of a porter *(facchino)* holding a barrel with water issuing from the bung hole. According to legend, the sculptor took a drunken Renaissance water-carrier as his model, who is now thus obliged to stay sober for eternity.

▷ Turn right into Via del Corso.

Santa Maria in Via Lata
Via del Corso 306.

🕐*Open Tue–Sun 4pm–7pm /winter 3pm–6pm (Sat also 10am–1pm).* 📞*06 83 39 62 76. www.cryptavialata.it*

The façade is of particular interest. Built between 1658 and 1662 by Pietro Cortona, it marks the transition in Baroque art to the period when detached columns – no longer an integral part of the walls – took on an essential role. Set out along two storeys, the columns seem to support the whole building and create remarkable effects of light and shade.

Underground you'll find the remains of a Roman-era portico 1C AD), later transformed into a warehouse, then into a cult building in the 7C AD. Frescoes portray the stories of Solomon, the Seven Sleepers of Esphesus, and the lives of the saints.

Palazzo Mancini Salviati
Via del Corso 270/272.
It was built in the 17C by the Duke of Nevers, Cardinal Mazarin's nephew, to house the French Academy.

◖ Retrace your steps along Via del Corso.

San Marcello al Corso
Piazza di San Marcello 5.
◖*Open daily 7am–midnight (Sun 9:30 and holidays 9:30am). www.sanmarcello alcorso.eu*
The **church of St Marcellus** was founded in the 4C on the site of a *titulus*, a private house used as a place of Christian worship. It burned in 1519 and was completely rebuilt in the 16C and 17C. In 1683, Carlo Fontana designed the slightly concave Baroque façade. The palms linking the two storeys are typical of the Baroque style, which delighted in the unusual.
The single nave with side chapels, typical of the Renaissance, was designed by **Jacopo Sansovino** (1486–1570) in the 16C. The late 16C coffered ceiling is richly decorated in gold, blue and red.
To the left of the entrance is the tomb of Cardinal Giovanni Michiel, who was poisoned on Alexander VI's orders in 1503. Below it is the tomb of his nephew, Bishop Antonio Orso, who died in 1511. The work was begun in 1520 by **Andrea Sansovino** and finished in 1527 by his pupil **Jacopo Sansovino**.
In the fourth chapel on the right is a fine 15C wooden crucifix. The realistic figure of Christ gave rise to a lugubrious legend: the sculptor craved realism so much he killed a passerby and studied the death throes. When the church burned down in 1519, it is said that the crucifix was recovered intact in the ruins. The frescoes in the vault are by Perin del Vaga, one of Raphael's pupils. In the altar's base is a 3C Roman *stele*, decorated with encrus-

tations of marble in the 12C to serve as a reliquary.
The fourth chapel on the left contains busts of the noble family of the Frangipani; the three on the right were carved by Algardi in 1625.

Palazzo de Carolis
Via del Corso 307.
The palazzo was built between 1714 and 1722 for the in 1722 for the marchese de Carolis and converted into the Banca di Roma in the 20C. In the late 18C, it was the home of the French Ambassador, who held splendid receptions here; guests included the writer Chateaubriand.

◖ Walk north along Via del Corso.

Fondazione Roma Museo
In Palazzo Cipolla, Via del Corso 320 and in Palazzo Sciarra, Via Minghetti 22. www.fondazioneromamuseo.it
Since November 2010, the Museum has extended its schedule and is now able to organise simultaneous exhibitions in two historic *palazzi*.

◖ Go back on your steps and turn right into Via del Caravita to reach Piazza Sant'Ignazio.

Piazza Sant'Ignazio★
The 18C quare mimics a theatre set, in apricot and stone, and has an unusual charm, with curved façades on the street corners.

Sant'Ignazio di Loyola★★
Piazza Sant'Ignazio.
◖*Open Mon–Sat 7:30am–7pm, Sun and public hols 9am–7pm. ℘06 67 94 406. http://santignazio.gesuiti.it/*
The 1626 church is dedicated to the founder of the **Jesuit** Order and of the Roman College, the first free school. Jesuit Orazio Grassi designed the high façade; the two superimposed orders linked by scrolls produce a solemn and austere ensemble.
Central ceiling fresco★★ – For the best view of the stunning central vault fresco and the *trompe-l'œil* cupola, stand on the disc in the nave's centre. The fresco is the

work of **Andrea Pozzo** (1684). A Jesuit, he chose a subject dear to the Counter-Reformation, which exalted the saints in the face of Protestantism. Here St Ignatius is bathed by a divine light, which is reflected on the four corners of the world, shown allegorically. Pozzo used his knowledge of perspective to create the *trompe-l'œil* effect.

The apsidal fresco, also by Pozzo, glorifies the miracles of St Ignatius. The altar at the end of the right transept is dedicated to St Luigi Gonzaga. Above the lapis lazuli urn containing the saint's relics – and between the beautiful green marble columns wreathed in fronds of bronze – is an admirable *Glory to St Luigi Gonzaga*, a carved "marble picture".

▶ Take Via dei Burrò.

Via dei Burrò owes its name to the administrative offices established by Napoleon Bonaparte ("*bureau*" is the French word for "office").

Piazza di Pietra

The south side of this colourful square is occupied by the Stock Exchange. In the 18C, it was the Customs House. Incorporated in the present building are 11 beautiful marble columns of the Corinthian order belonging to an ancient **temple** that honoured **Hadrian**. The ancient columns lend much grandeur.

GALLERIA DORIA PAMPHILJ★★

In Palazzo Doria Pamphilj, entrance at Via del Corso 305. ♿ 🕐*Open daily 9am–7pm.* 🕐*Closed 1 Jan, Easter and 25 Dec.* ♿€12. *Audioguide included in ticket.* ✆*06 67 97 323.* www.doriapamphilj.it/roma/en/
First are the **Sale di Rappresentanza** (Reception Rooms) including the **Sala dei Velluti** (Velvet Room), which retains its original 17C floor. The decorations include an eagle, symbol of the Doria family, of Ligurian origin, and a *fleur-de-lis*. Exhibited in the corner of the **Sala da Ballo** (Ballroom) – reserved for the musicians – is a 17C harp made from ivory and wood. The walls of the Rococo style

Saletta Gialla (Yellow Drawing Room) to the right display tapestry panels depicting Allegories of the Twelve Months, made at the Gobelins factory in Paris during the reign of Louis XV.

The **gallery** itself is quadrilateral in shape. It was once the loggia over the internal 16C courtyard and was closed during the time of Camillo Pamphili (18C) to house the collection of paintings and sculpture. The discovery of a manuscript dating from 1767 has allowed the paintings to be displayed according to their original layout.

First Gallery

This gallery houses paintings by **Annibale Carracci**, including the series of lunettes depicting the Stories of the Virgin Mary. In the **Flight into Egypt ★★**, the religious scene seems to have a marginal role. The gentle, but realistic landscape, takes up almost all the picture, presaging a taste that developed throughout the 17C. In *Erminia Finding Tancred Wounded*, by **Guercino**, the drama is intensified by the contrasts between light and dark. **The Usurers★** by **Quentin Metsys** is an important painting. The characters depicted (especially the two usurers on the left) have exaggerated features.

At the end of the gallery, a small studio houses the **Portrait of Innocent X★★★**, a masterpiece by **Velázquez**, painted in 1650 during his second visit to Rome. The painter produced an official portrait that is realistic and quite lacking in idealisation (note the stern expression). Here, also, is a bust of Innocent X by **Bernini**, an expressive interpretation of the pope's authoritative personality.

Galleria degli Specchi – This "Hall of Mirrors" makes up the gallery's second part. The decor is 18C and the **ceiling** is painted with frescoes by Aurelio Milani, depicting the Labours of Hercules.

Four **small rooms** lead off the gallery, dedicated to the 15C, 16C, 17C and 18C respectively. In the second, the visitor's attention is drawn to the magnificent **Rest after the Flight into Egypt ★★★** by **Caravaggio**. The scene is one of natural beauty: the tired Virgin sleeps with her head gently bent over her child; Joseph seems entranced by the music of the angel, a young man with large dark wings who stands in front of him (unusual). Just visible behind Joseph's shoulder is the donkey, who also seems enchanted by the music. Caravaggio has used the same model for his *Mary Magdalene*, cleverly positioned next to the painting of the Virgin. Even the pose is the same, though Mary Magdalene is depicted as a despairing woman with reference only to earthly pleasures; note the bottle of perfume and jewellery.

St Sebastian by Ludovico Carracci and *Endymion* by Guercino are exhibited in the same room. The main focus in the room dedicated to the 16C is the beautiful **Salome**★★ by **Titian**. In the same room the *Portrait of a Young Man* by Tintoretto, the *Portrait of Two People* by Raphael and a delicate *Winter Landscape* by Peter Bruegel the Elder can also be admired. A masterpiece by Hans Memling, **Mourning the Death of Christ**★★, is exhibited in the 15C room. The dramatic composition is highlighted by the harsh traits and angular position of Christ.

Third Gallery

An unusual painting by Bruegel the Elder, *Battle in the Bay of Naples*, can be seen in this gallery. The **Sala Aldobrandini**, a room to the left at the bottom of the gallery, houses statues from both the archaic and late imperial eras.

Fourth Gallery

At the entrance to this gallery is a **bust of Olimpia Maidalchini Pamphili**★★ by **Algardi**. She is said to have pestered her brother-in-law, Giovanni Battista Pamphili, until he attained the papal throne as Innocent X.

Algardi, who was an accomplished portraitist, knew precisely how to express the energy and ambition of Donna Olimpia, as she was called by the Romans. She is shown in the distinctive headdress, which she alone wore. Paintings in this gallery include a 17C copy of *John the Baptist as a Child* by Caravaggio, which hangs in the Palazzo dei Con-

servatori, and the *Madonna and Child* by **Parmigiano**.

Appartamenti Privati★ (Private Apartments)

These are the rooms inhabited from the 16C to 18C by the families who owned the palace. In the Wintergarden are an 18C sleigh and a fine sedan chair, painted and gilded. The Andrea Doria Room bears the name of the most famous member of the Genoese Doria family; a mercenary *(condottiere)*, he commanded the French fleet for François I before being employed by Charles V.

The frieze in the dining room depicts the various properties belonging to the Doria Pamphili family (19C).

In the Green Drawing Room, one of the many paintings is a graceful *Annunciation* by the Florentine **Filippo Lippi** (1406–69), Botticelli's master. A large 15C Tournai tapestry illustrates the medieval legend of Alexander the Great.

ADDRESSES

TAKING A BREAK

Sant'Eustachio il Caffè – *Piazza S. Eustachio 82. Open 7:30am-1am (Fri 1:30am, Sat 2am). ☎06 68 80 20 48. www.santeustachioilcaffe.it.* This café is famous for its delicious, creamy coffee known as a gran caffè speciale. Pay at the cassa first. Request your espresso amaro (bitter) senza zucchero (without sugar) if you don't want it pre-sweetened.

La Casa del Caffè - Tazza d'Oro – *Via degli Orfani 84. Open 7am-8pm. ☎06 67 89 792. www.tazzadorocoffeeshop.com.* This specialist coffee bar serves strong and aromatic coffee (counter service only). In the summer, don't miss the coffee granita with double helpings of *panna* (whipped cream).

Cremeria Monteforte – *Via della Rotonda 22. Open summer 11am–midnight, rest of the year 10am-11pm. ☎06 68 67 720.* Enjoying the façade of the Pantheon eating ice cream by Monteforte is a unique pleasure. The chocolate mousse is simply the best.

Piramide Cestia–Testaccio★

Ancient Rome's wharf zone contains a hill made of discarded amphorae: it was cheaper to smash the terracotta than ship back empties. Later a slaughterhouse zone, it's now the heartland of the blue-collar-heroes of AS Roma, the football club. Clubs, bars and avant-garde associations now dot this traditional neighbourhood.

Centrale Montemartini, a rare example of industrial architecture, showcases collections from the Capitoline Museums. Perhaps the most moving sight is the Protestant Cemetery, where Keats and Shelley both rest, overlooked by the pyramid of Caius Cestius, a quirky 1C tomb. Celebrate the area's roots with meat dishes such as *la coda alla vaccinara* at Checchino dal 1887.

- **Michelin Map:** 38 R 11–12, S 11–12.
- **Location:** The Testaccio district lies between the Tiber and Piazzale di Porta S. Paolo, the latter a busy intersection of major roads. Centrale Montemartini is on Via Ostiense opposite the General Market.
- **Don't Miss**: The Protestant Cemetery, resting place of Keats and Shelley; Centrale Montemartini, a power-station-turned-museum of ancient sculpture.
- **Timing:** Allow 2 hrs.
- **Also See:** *AVENTINO; SAN PAOLO FUORI LE MURA; TRASTEVERE.*

●●WALKING TOUR

Piramide di Caio Cestio★ (Mausoleum of Caius Cestius)

Caius Cestius, praetor and tribune of the people, (d. 12 BC), devised Rome's most original mausoleum. The marble pyramid testifies to the grandeur of the Augustan era, when a citizen could erect a tomb worthy of a Pharaoh.

Porta San Paolo★

Once part of the 3C **Aurelian Wall** (Mura Aureliane), this gate was originally called the Porta Ostiensis; it opened into Via Ostiense, which led to St Paul's Basilica – hence the medieval name, which stuck. In Aurelian's day, the gate consisted of two arches flanked by two semi-circular towers on the outside. Today is holds a small museum inside (*Museo della Via Ostiense; ○Open Mar–Sun 9am–1:30pm ℘06 57 43 193*).

Via Ostiense

The road dates from the 4C BC; it was one of the most important commercial arteries in antiquity. Use continued in the Christian era, since it led to the site

GETTING THERE
BY METRO: Line B: Piramide Centrale Montemartini – 800m/880yd from station.

of St Paul's martyrdom (Tre Fontane) and to his tomb in St Paul's Basilica.

▶ Take Viale della Piramide Cestia, turn right up the steps in Via Baccio Pontelli and then left into Via Annia Faustina.

The San Saba district occupies one of the peaks of the Aventine. Its elegant mansions – interspersed with open spaces, dating from early this century – have made it a model of town planning.

San Saba★

The church is dedicated to St Sabas, who founded a monastery called the Great Lavra in Palestine in the 5C. Two hundred years later, its monks were dispersed by the Persians and then by the Arabs. Many took refuge in Rome in a building inhabited a century earlier by St Sylvia, the mother of St Gregory the Great. Towards the end of the 10C, the eastern monks constructed the present church on top of their smaller 7C oratory. Over the centuries the building was subject to various alterations, but was restored from 1911.

Façade – The portico is contemporary with the church, but the columns have been replaced with thick pillars. In the 15C, a single storey surmounted by a loggia was built on top of the portico by Cardinal Piccolomini, nephew of Pius II. The main doorframe was decorated in 1205 by one of the **Cosmati**.

Interior – The basilica plan, with a nave and two aisles each ending in an apse, has been conserved. The lack of uniformity between the pillars (bases, shafts and capitals) is typical of medieval buildings, which recycled chunks of ancient sculpture. An unusual feature is the additional aisle on the east side of the church; it probably linked the church to the monastery of the eastern monks. It was the Cluniac monks who rebuilt the convent in a new position in the 13C, thus exposing the additional aisle on the exterior of the church.

The paving was part of the refurbishment carried out by the **Cosmati**.

▷ Via di S. Saba down to Piazza Albania.

In Piazza Albania, at the beginning of Via Sant'Anselmo, are the remains of the 6C BC **Servian Wall** (Mura Serviane). This part was probably rebuilt in the 1C BC.

▷ Take Via M. Gelsomini and Via Galvani as far as Piazza Giustiniani.

Testaccio

This down-to-earth district was abandoned for 1 500 years. In the late 19C it became a working-class neighbourhood, organised according to trendy town-planning principles of the era.

The main attraction is the **Monte Testaccio** (some 35m/115ft high). It takes its name from the ancient *amphorae* reduced to potsherds (*cocci* in Italian) and piled up here. It is, therefore, also called "*Monte dei Cocci*". Excavations have uncovered several "grottoes", some of which revealed what appeared to be ancient restaurants and nightspots. Modern proprietors are following suit in the area – with much success.

Mattatoio

Piazza Orazio Giustiniani 4.
◯*Open Tue–Sun 2pm–8pm during exhibitions.* ◯*Closed 1 Jan, 1 May and 25 Dec.*

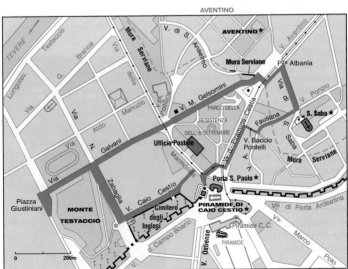

📞 06 39 96 75 00. www.mattatoioroma.it. Installed in the ancient slaughterhouse is this center of contemporary art that hosts many temporary exhibitions. Built between 1888 and 1891 by Gioacchino Ersoch, the building is a wonderful exemple of 19th-century industrial architecture.

▷ Back to previous crossroads; right on Via N. Zabaglia; left on Via Caio Cestio.

Cimitero degli Inglesi

Via Caio Cestio 6. 🕐*Open Mon–Sat 9am–5pm, Sun 9am–1pm.* 🎧*Tours available (prebooking necessary). Donation Welcome.* 📞*06 57 41 900. www.cemeteryrome.it.*

Also known as the **Testaccio Cemetery** and **Cimitero Acattolico**, a better name, since the criterion here was "not Catholic". In the shade of pines and cypresses, many famous people rest: at the eastern end of the gravel path – **John Keats** and his faithful friend Joseph Severn, Axel Munthe, the author of *San Michele*; at the foot of the last tower in the Aurelian Wall – Shelley's tombstone on which Byron had some verses of Shakespeare engraved; halfway down the slope in the main cemetery between two tall cypress trees – a tombstone bearing a bronze medallion marks the grave of **Goethe**'s son. One of the most poignant monuments is the *Angel of Grief* by American sculptor William Story. He concluded this memorial for his wife, then died and was laid beside her.

The cemetery was home to one of Rome's cat colonies, now reduced in numbers.

▷ Continue along Via Caio Cestio; turn left into Via della Marmorata.

On the left is the **Post Office** (Ufficio Postale) of the Aventine district, a good example of Italian rationalist architecture, designed by the architects A Libera and Mario de Renzi, who adhered to the rules of the Modern Movement which formed the debate on architecture between the two World Wars.

CENTRALE MONTEMARTINI★★

Via Ostiense 106 (close to the Pyramid). ♿🕐*Open Tue–Sun 9am–7pm, 24 and 31 Dec 9am–2pm.* 🕐*Closed 1 Jan, 1 May and 25 Dec.* ⊜€11, €12.50 combined ticket with the Musei Capitolini. 📞06 06 08. www.centralemontemartini.org.

This 1912 centre was Italy's first public thermoelectric power station. The steam turbines and diesel engines are still an impressive sight. The power station ran until the 1950s, when technology passed it by. Restoration began in the early 1990s, when the structure, complete with original machinery, became a multimedia centre. Since 1997, the museum has housed sculptures from the Capitoline Museums, which create an interesting contrast between ancient art and industrial archaeology.

Capitoline Museum

The collection is housed in three rooms. The first is the Sala delle Colonne (Reception Room) on the ground floor, displaying the oldest exhibits from the Archaic period to the late Republican era. Among the most interesting artefacts is the group of Heracles and Athena (6C BC), which once adorned the Temple of Fortune and Mater Matuta in the sacred precinct of Sant'Omobono. Also noteworthy are two funerary monuments (1C BC), one decorated with bronze leaf finely inlaid with silver and copper, the

Centrale Montemartini

© Serrano/Sime/Photononstop

other covered with bone. The decoration of both monuments was inspired by the cult of Dionysus. On the walls, a fragment of mosaic depicting fish, thought to be part of the atrium of a house, bears witness to the expressive delicacy and realism achieved in naturalistic reproductions. At the end of the gallery, housing portraits from the late Roman Republic, the **Togato Barberini** and statues of his ancestors are particularly striking (the head is a 17C restoration). The rich drapery of the toga and the transversal folds, showing how the toga would actually have been folded, are good examples of the desire for realism and fine sculpting. On the first floor, the Sala Macchine (Machinery Room) houses a sculpture gallery, with its two powerful diesel engines as a backdrop. Two images of Athena face each other at the ends of the room; one is a huge Roman copy of an original Greek statue dating from the 5C BC, the other was part of the **decoration** of the pediment of the **Temple of Apollo Sosianus**. The sculptures are Greek originals, dating from the second half of the 5C BC. The *cella* of the temple has been partially reconstructed on the back of the pediment. Before entering the third room, note the beautiful basanite **statue of Agrippina praying**: the head is a copy of the original on display in Copenhagen. The Sala Caldaie (Steam Room) houses exhibits from the *horti*, villas and gardens on the outskirts, which were surrounded by greenery and richly decorated with statues, fountains, vases and mosaics. The splendid *Winged Victory*, an original Greek statue (5C BC), comes from the Gardens of Sallust (now in the Ludovisi district). The beautiful **Esquiline Venus★★**, a Roman copy from the Imperial period, was found in an underground room in the Gardens of Lamia (*Giardini di Lamia e Maia*). The gracious **Seated Girl★★** and the two stern magistrates, captured in the act of opening the circus games, come from the Gardens of Licinius (*Giardini di Licinio*).

ADDRESSES

TAKING A BREAK

Città dell'Altra Economia – Caffè Boario – *Largo Dino Frisullo. ✆06 57 58 272. Open 7:30am–midnight. www. cittadellaltraeconomia.org.* Housed in a former slaughterhouse complex, this city-within-a-city includes the Bio space, the Cafè Boario, the restaurant Stazione di Posta (*www.stazionediposta.eu*) and, on Sundays, a market for bio foods.

L'Oasi della Birra – *Piazza Testaccio 40. 8–1:30am, 4:30–1pm. ✆06 57 46 122.* More than 500 beers (mostly draught) are served here, alongside cheeses, soups, *bruschette* and German salami.

Tram Depot – *Via Marmorata 13 (corner Via Manlio Gelsomini) 8:30–2am. ✆06 57 54 406. Open 7:30–2am.* A kiosk in the shade of a garden but not just any one: in retro style two steps from the Piramide Cestia, and with quality street food.

Trapizzino – *Via Giovanni Branca 88. ✆06 43 41 96 24. www.trapizzino.it.* A trapizzino is a triangle of pizza without tomato sauce (in the shape of a tramezzino) and with a variety of Roman toppings.

BARS

Porto Fluviale – *Via del Porto Fluviale 22. ✆06 57 43 199. www.portofluviale.com.* Trattoria, pizzeria, bank, drawing room, street kitchen and cocktail bar. One of the trendiest bars in the city.

♟/EAT

Pizzeria Remo – *Piazza Santa Maria Liberatrice 44. No reserve. ✆06 574 6270.* Thin-based, crunchy pizza like the Romans love it, not like the high, soft pizza from Naples. Tradition at its purest.

Eataly – *Piazzale XII Ottobre 1492. Open daily 9am–midnight. ✆06 90279201. www.eataly.it.* A monument to the best of Italian gastronomy, where you can eat in different theme-based stands or buy top quality gastronomic products.

La Fraschetta di Mastro Giorgio – *Via A. Volta 36. ✆06 57 41 369. www. lafraschettadimastrogiorgio.com.* A trattoria where cold cuts and cheese dishes are prepared directly in the dining room behind a showcase featuring local products. Excellent value for your money.

Piazza San Pietro
© Mariusz Jurgielewicz/age fotostock

VATICAN CITY

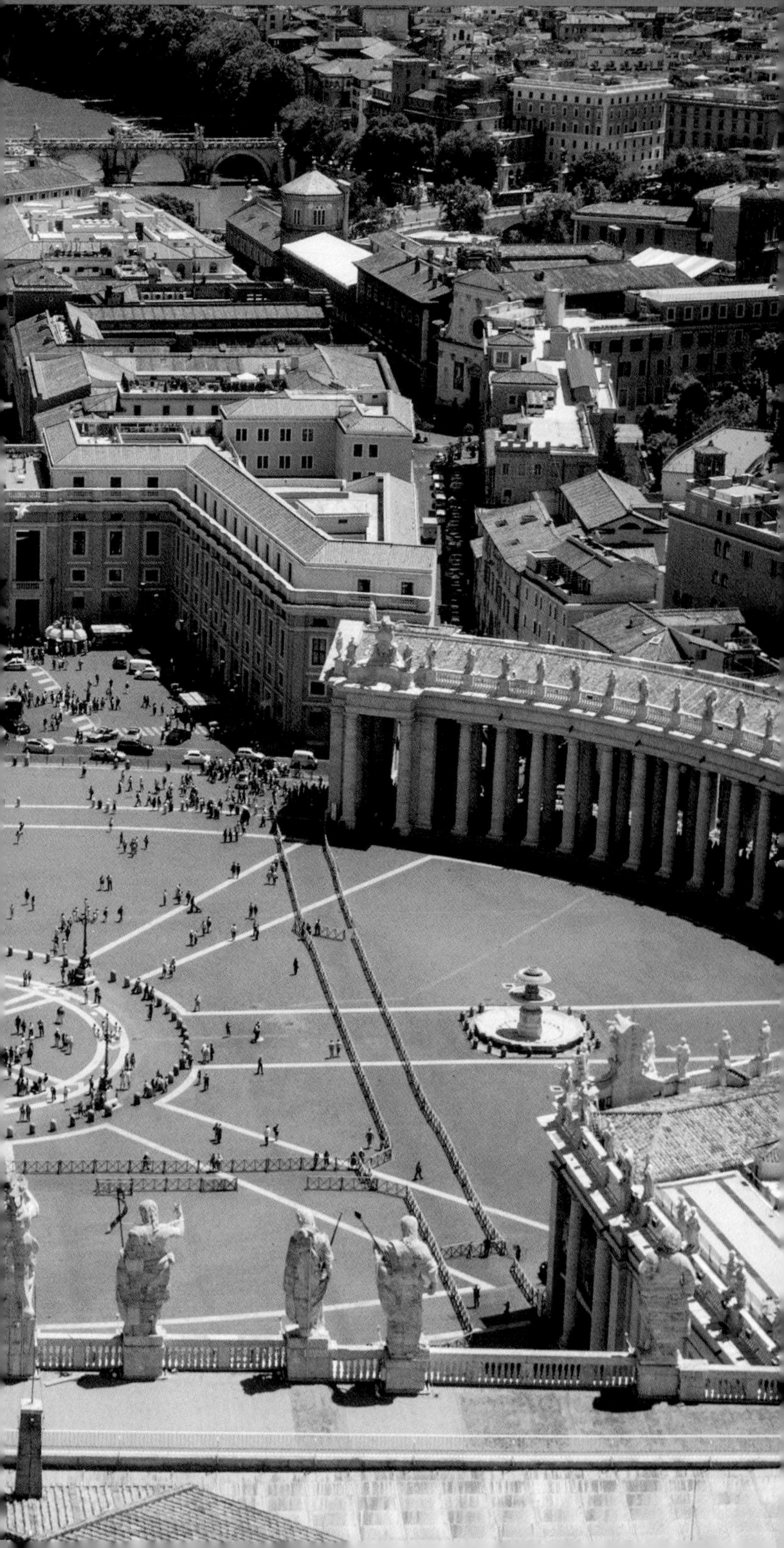

VATICAN CITY

The Vatican City is home to the largest basilica in the world, and a museum containing some of its greatest art treasures. This tiny fortified territory lies inside Italy's capital; it is literally a state within a state. As the heart of the Roman Catholic Church, it extends its influence to all four corners of the globe. Religion aside, the Vatican contains many of Rome's highlights: Bernini's colonnade surrounding St Peter's Square, Michelangelo's frescoes on the ceiling of the Sistine Chapel, and the splendid basilica dome, from which breathtaking views unfurl.

The Vatican State

The wide **Via della Conciliazione** was opened in 1950, a Jubilee Year. The façades of the buildings on the southern end bear the arms of Pius XII *(right)* and of Rome *(left)*. Two rows of street lamps – in the shape of obelisks – line the broad road, which leads directly to St Peter's Basilica *(San Pietro)*.

Once in St Peter's Square, you've left Italy and are in the Vatican State. The Vatican City, north of the Janiculum Hill, is bounded on three sides by the wall overlooking Viale Vaticano and on the east by the curved colonnade in St Peter's Square. It's dominated by the basilica, the Vatican Palaces and the beautiful gardens surrounding the administrative offices of the Papal State. Although the **Ager Vaticanus** lay outside the boundary of ancient Rome, it was nonetheless well known. In the days of the empire, Caligula established a circus here, which was embellished by Nero and hosted the massacre of the first Roman martyrs; their number may have included St Peter. Hadrian built his mausoleum, the present Castel Sant'Angelo, in the gardens belonging to the Domitii. The emperor **Constantine** built over St Peter's tomb, a structure now world famous as the Basilica di San Pietro.

Bishop of Rome – From the first days of Christianity, the bishop was Christ's representative on earth. Rome's bishop

Location

Vatican City anchors the right bank of the Tiber, north of the Janiculum Hill, level with Castel Sant'Angelo, to which it is linked by Via della Conciliazione. The Prati district lies to the north.

maintained that his See had been founded by the apostles, Peter and Paul, and therefore claimed first place in the ecclesiastical hierarchy. The title "pope" derived from the Greek *pápas*, meaning "father". The term initially applied to all patriarchs and bishops, but eventually was reserved for the Bishop of Rome.

Gift of Quiersy-sur-Oise – In 752, the Lombards occupied Ravenna and the imperial territory between the River Po, the Apennines and the Adriatic. In Rome the King of the Lombards, Astolphe, demanded a tribute of one gold piece per head. When the intervention of the emperor in Byzantium, Constantine V (to whom Rome was, in principle, subject), proved useless, Pope Stephen II approached the Carolingian dynasty. In 756, Pepin the Short, king of the Franks, liberated the occupied territory. Power passed, however, to the pope in this "Republic of the Holy Church of God" – and thus the Papal States were born.

"Leonine City" – On 23 August 846, the Saracens invaded Rome, pillaging the basilicas of St Peter and St Paul. In the following year, therefore, Leo IV energetically set to work raising a defensive wall around the Vatican district, known as the Borgo. The wall was restored in the 15C by Nicholas V, reinforced with bastions by Sangallo the Younger under Paul III in the 16C, and extended by Pius IV in 1564 to Porta Santo Spirito.

Lateran Treaty – The unification of Italy (1820–70) would have been incomplete without the Papal States. On 20 September 1870, the troops of King **Victor Emmanuel II** entered Rome and proclaimed the city the capital of the kingdom. On 2 May 1871, the Italian Parliament passed the **Law of the Guarantees** to show that it did not wish to subjugate the papacy. The pope would

GETTING THERE

BY METRO: Line A: Ottaviano–San Pietro (500m/550yd from the entrance to the Vatican Museums and 800m/880yd from Piazza San Pietro) or Cipro–Musei Vaticani (600m/660yd from the entrance to the Vatican Museums)

SAN PIETRO (&see p329)

Basilica – ©*Open 7am–7pm (Oct–Mar 7am–6:30pm).* ©*Closed during Pontifical services.* &*06 69 82.* www.vatican.va. Inappropriately dressed visitors, including children, may be refused access: this applies to those wearing shorts, mini-skirts, sleeveless shirts and those with bare shoulders.

Tesoro (Museo Storico-Artistico) – ©*Open 9am-5:15pm (Oct–Mar 9am-18:15).* ©*Closed Easter and 25 Dec.* &*€6.* &*06 69 88 31 14.*

Grotte Vaticane – ©*Open 7am–6pm (Oct–Mar 7am–4:45pm).* ©*Closed during Pontifical services.* &*06 69 88 31 14.* **Necropoli Vaticana –** *Guided tours only (1hr) 9am–6pm (till 5pm Sat). Closed Sun and Catholic hols. Open Mon–Sat 9am–5pm. Apply well in advance.* &*€13. Children aged 15+ allowed with parents.* &*06 69 88 46 76.* **Ascent to the Dome –** &*€10 (elevator plus 320 steps). Open 8am–6pm (5pm in winter).* &*06 69 88 31 45.*

PAPAL AUDIENCES

When in residence at the Vatican, the Holy Father gives a **public audience** Wed *(10am summer and 10:30am winter)*. Here, also, he celebrates the **Angelus** Sun and public hols at noon. Access is free, but tickets are required for Wed audience. Tickets can usually be picked up without a reservation from the Swiss Guards at the Bronze Doors just past security at St Peter's Basilica. To make a reservation, print out the form (*www.papalaudience.org/tickets*) and fax it 10 days or more in advance. You can pick up tickets the day before the audience 3pm–7pm (–6pm in winter). Or you can pick up tickets on the day of the mass from 7am–3pm.

VATICAN MUSEUMS (&see p338).

Admission times and charges *Viale Vaticano 100.* ©*Open Mon–Sat 9am–6pm (last entrance 4pm) and last Sun/month 9am–2pm (last entrance noon).* ©*Closed, see website.* &*06 69 88 46 76.* www.museivaticani.va. *The Admission Ticket permits the tourist to visit the Vatican Museums and the Sistine Chapel and is valid for the day of issue:* &*€17* & Guided tours are available for the Vatican Museums and Sistine Chapel (2hrs), &*€33 (includes entrance to the Vatican Gardens),* &*€38 (includes Basilica). Book timed admission tickets (&€16) and guided tours online and you can skip the long queues. Audioguides (&€7). Café, currency exchange and cloakroom.* &*06 69 88 31 45.* www.vatican.va. Ticket online. Large handbags and knapsacks must be checked; if you must check your belongings, then you must return to exit via same door.

Loggia di Raffaello – *Open to specialists only by prior request.* The loggia occupies the second floor of the building. This monumental addition to the façade of Palazzo Apostolico, which looked out over Rome, was commissioned by Julius II.

Museo delle Carrozze – *www.musei vaticani.va.* A new layout illustrate the papal means of transport with an unusual collection of saddles, sedan chairs, carriages and automobiles.

MAKING THE MOST OF YOUR VISIT

Allow 1 full day for a visit to all of the galleries. However, the ★★★ **highly recommended** sections take only about 3hrs. A plan detailing is available from the information desk. Some galleries in the Vatican Museums are open in rotation; not all have the same opening times.

VATICAN CITY

retain the Vatican City and receive an annual allowance. Pius IX excommunicated the act's authors and shut himself inside the Vatican, declaring that he was a prisoner. His successors maintained this stance and the Roman Question was not resolved until 1929, when the **Lateran Treaty** was signed on 11 February by Cardinal Gaspari, representing the Holy See, and Mussolini, the head of the Italian government.

The terms recognised the pope as sovereign of the Vatican State: the City itself and a number of properties that enjoy the privilege of extraterritoriality. These include four major basilicas (St John Lateran, St Peter's in the Vatican, St Paul Outside the Walls, Santa Maria Maggiore), the Roman Curia, colleges and seminaries and the villa at Castel Gandolfo; in all 44ha/109 acres and just under 1 000 inhabitants. The treaty also included a financial indemnity and a religious settlement granting the Church a privileged position in Italy in respect of schooling and marriage. The Republican constitution of 1947 established a new relationship between the Roman Church and the Italian State on the basis of the Lateran Treaty. Another agreement modifying the 1929 Lateran Treaty was signed on 18 February 1984 by the President of the Council and the Vatican Secretary of State.

Although the smallest state in physical size, the Vatican spreads the spiritual influence of the Roman Catholic Church throughout the world.

Head of the Roman Church

The pope is also called the Roman Pontiff, the Sovereign Pontiff, the Vicar of Christ, Holy Father and His Holiness. Sometimes he calls himself "*Servus Servorum Dei*", the Servant of the Servants of God. In his mission as Pastor to the Church founded by Jesus Christ, he is assisted by the Sacred College of Cardinals and by the Roman Curia.

College of Cardinals – A cardinal is a high ecclesiastical official. His dress consists of a scarlet cape (a short hooded cloak) worn over a linen *rochet* (a surplice with narrow sleeves). The cardinals

are the pope's closest advisers; they also elect him, assembled in "conclave". In 1586, Sixtus V fixed their number at 70, yet it's risen. Today Benedict XVI has 183; only 120 have electoral power.

Conclave – The cardinals withdraw into a secret meeting to chose the next pope. This method of election was established by **Gregory X** (1271–76), whose own election lasted nearly three years. He imposed very strict regulations, involving confinement and secrecy. For incentive, stalling cardinals would be reduced to one meal after three days, then – if two more passed – bread and water. Now the cardinals meet in conclave in the Sistine Chapel. A vote is held twice a day and after each inconclusive ballot, the papers are burned so as to produce dark smoke. A majority of two-thirds plus one is required; then a plume of clear smoke appears above the Vatican. The senior cardinal appears at the window in the façade of St Peter's and announces the election in the Latin formula: *Annuntio vobis gaudium magnum: habemus papam* (I announce to you with great joy: we have a pope). The newly anointed leader then gives his first blessing.

Roman Curia – The Curia consists of a group of bodies, the dicasteries, which administer the Holy See.

Councils – Within the Roman Church there are two rites (Oriental and Latin); all the constituent churches belong to one or the other and are grouped into dioceses under the direction of **bishops**. The spiritual authority of a bishop is symbolised by a crozier, ring, mitre and his pectoral cross. His dress resembles a cardinal's, but purple. The Episcopal College, consisting of about 4 000 bishops spread throughout the world, is presided over by the pope, who calls them together in an **Ecumenical Council** to discuss the life of the Church.

Papal Audiences – The audiences are held in St Peter's Square in summer. Come winter, they move inside St Peter's Basilica and the huge modern hall designed by Pier Luigi Nervi under Paul VI. During the ceremony, the pope gives his blessing, and preaches

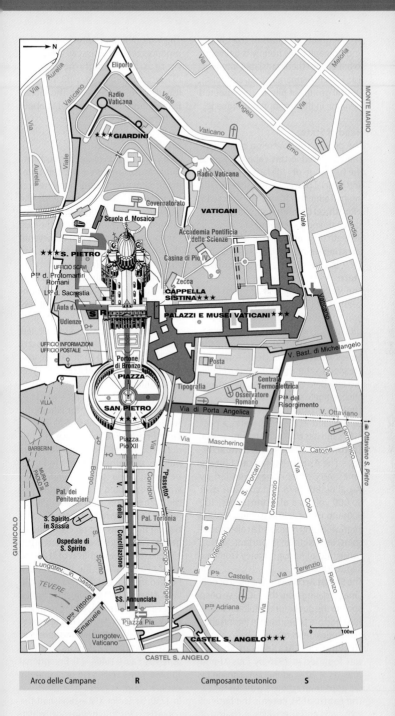

Arco delle Campane	**R**	Camposanto teutonico	**S**

on the great questions of the Church and humanity. His homily is delivered in Italian and then translated into English, French, German, Spanish and Polish. Official groups of pilgrims are greeted by name in the appropriate language.

Head of State

The pope is the Sovereign of the Vatican State and in this capacity wields the full range of legislative, executive and judicial power. He is assisted in the internal administration of the Vatican by a **Pontifical Commission**, composed of cardinals and a lay member.

Beneath the commission is the **Administration** (*Governatorato*), which, since 1969, has been assisted by a **Council of State**.

The Vatican State has a yellow flag, bearing a tiara and crossed keys. Gounod composed its hymn, the *Pontifical March*. The armed regiments were disbanded by Paul VI in 1970; only the **Swiss Guards** have been retained, dressed in their picturesque yellow, red and blue uniforms, supposedly of Michelangelo's design.

The Vatican issues its own stamps, mints coins (valid in Italy), operates a post office and has a railway station.

Cultural, scientific and artistic activity – The **Apostolic Vatican Library** ranks very high; it was founded by Papal Bull in 1475 and contains over 60 000 volumes of manuscripts, 100 000 autographs, 800 000 prints, 100 000 engravings and maps and a collection of coins, including an important section consisting of Roman money from the Republican era.

The **Secret Archives**, composed of documents dating from the 13C, have been open to the public for consultation since 1881 and are of worldwide importance in historical research.

The **Pontifical Academy of Science** was founded in 1936 by Pius XI and consists of 70 Academicians chosen by the pope from scholars worldwide.

The **Fabric of St Peter** is the body of architects and specialists in charge of the conservation of St Peter's Basilica. The mosaic workshop is annexed to it.

The Vatican has a printing works that produces texts in almost all languages; there is also a daily newspaper, *L'Osservatore Romano*, which is published in several languages. The Vatican Radio transmits programmes in about 40 different languages.

Jubilee

Its origins are buried deep in Judaism. When Moses received the Ten Commandments on Mount Sinai, he was also given a set of laws to guide the behaviour of the people of Israel. One insisted: "you shall send abroad the loud trumpet on the tenth day of the seventh month (of the forty-ninth year)… you shall hallow the fiftieth year, and proclaim liberty throughout the land to all its inhabitants; it shall be a jubilee for you." (It is known as the *Yōbēl* in Hebrew, from the name given to the goat-horn instrument.) In the year of the Jubilee, "each man shall return to his property and his family… you shall neither sow, nor reap what grows of itself." The year represented an act of peace and reconciliation with God. This idea was later adopted by Christians, for whom the Jubilee signifies a remission of sins.

Their first Jubilee took place in 1300, during the rule of **Boniface VIII**. A huge number of pilgrims battled to Rome, believing that a full remission of sins would be granted in the centenary of the birth of Christ. This amazing influx led the pope to issue a papal bull, sanctioning the "rules" for receiving indulgences. Each pilgrim was required to pay 15 visits to the two basilicas of St Peter's and St Paul Outside the Walls, which housed the relics of the two saints (30 visits if they were from Rome). Hereafter, Jubilee years were celebrated regularly every 50 years, as decreed by Clement VI (1342–52), with just a few omissions, and subsequently every 25 years, as established by Paul II (1464–71). Exceptional Jubilee years were also occasionally declared, such as 1983.

In 1750, Benedict XIV established the conditions for full indulgence, which included visiting all four major basilicas, confession, communion and prayer.

Ceremonies and visits – The Jubilee year traditionally starts with the special Christmas Eve ceremony: the pope opens the Holy Door, which is closed at all other times. With a gold and silver mallet, he knocks three times on the wall behind which the door is hidden. Workers then knock it down. Until 1983, the doors of Santa Maria Maggiore, St Paul Outside the Walls and St John Lateran were opened by the three cardinals of these churches. However, this tradition was changed for the Jubilee of 2000, when the pope opened all four doors. The door at St Peter's is closed again on 6 January of the following year (5 January for the other three basilicas). The pope blesses the materials used to rebuild the wall and lays the first three bricks.

The pilgrims were known as *Romei*. They came to the city not only to visit the major churches, but also the catacombs, each of which held saints' relics. Their graffiti is still visible: invocations to the saints, prayers, or sometimes simply names carved in the stone.

Accommodation – Suitable shelter had to be found for this huge influx of people, many of whom were destitute. The hospices provided for pilgrims were originally known as *xenodochi*; they often included a hospital, school, and other provisions for the poor. These establishments later came to be known as *scholae peregrinorum*. Many nations built and ran ones for their citizens.

Basilica di San Pietro★★★
(St Peter's Basilica)

The basilica, constructed between 1506 and 1626, was until recently the largest of all Christian places of worship. The grandiose architecture and opulent interior reflects many centuries of Christian history and the spectacle draws pilgrims and tourists alike from all over the world.

A BIT OF HISTORY
The building of St Peter's Basilica is linked to the martyrdom of **Peter** (c. AD 64). When a huge fire destroyed much of Rome, Nero held the Christians responsible and ordered executions. Simon, named "Peter" by Jesus, was probably among the victims.

According to the law, he was simply a Jewish fisherman, a native of Capernaum in Galilee, sentenced therefore to crucifixion in Nero's Circus at the foot of the Vatican Hill. So as to distinguish his own death from Jesus', Peter humbly begged to be crucified upside down.

> **Info:** www.vatican.va.
>
> **Location:** Piazza San Pietro (*For opening times and charges, permissable attire, etc. see the boxed text at the beginning of the chapter*).
>
> **Don't Miss:** Michelangelo's *Pietà*, St Peter's tomb and views from the basilica's dome.
>
> **Timing:** Arrive early to avoid queuing. Allow a minimum of 2hrs. Avoid Papal celebrations, a list of which can be found on the website.

Constantine's basilica – Following his conversion to Christianity, Constantine built a sanctuary in 324 over the tomb of St Peter, Christ's chief apostle. In 326, Pope Sylvester I consecrated the building, which was completed some 25 years later. The basilica had a nave, four aisles and a narrow transept; the apsidal wall stood just behind the present papal altar. The entrance was through an *atrium* graced with a fountain decorated

with the beautiful pine cone *(la Pigna)*, that can now be seen in a courtyard of the Vatican Palace.

The façade gleamed with mosaics. The *confessio* (a crypt containing the tomb of a martyr) was not completely underground; an opening at floor level gave access to the tomb. At the end of the 6C, Pope Gregory the Great raised the chancel; beneath it the confessio took the form of a corridor following the apse's curve and had a chapel called *ad caput*. Barbarians pillaged for more than a century: Alaric in 410 and Totila in 546. In 846, it was raided by the Saracens. Its prestige remained intact. Imperial coronations were held in solemn state. On Christmas Day AD 800, Leo III crowned Charlemagne King of the Romans; 75 years later it was the turn of his grandson, Charles the Bald, during the Pontificate of John VIII, the first soldier pope and the also the first assassinated. Arnoul, the last of the Carolingians, became Pope Formosus in 891. John XII, who lived surrounded by slaves and eunuchs, crowned Otho I the first Emperor of Germany on 2 February 962 and then conspired against him. His intrigues brought the papacy under the Emperor's control for over a century. After 1 000 years, despite frequent restoration and embellishment, St Peter's Basilica needed help.

1452, Nicholas V intervenes – The pope appointed Bernardo Rossellino to restore the basilica. He retained the dimensions of Contantine's building, but proposed a cruciform plan with a dome and a new choir. The pope died in 1455 and the project was abandoned. For the next 50 years his successors were content to shore up the existing building.

1503, Julius II, an energetic pope – His plan for renovation was radical. His architects were **Bramante**, who had arrived in Rome in 1499, and **Giuliano da Sangallo**. The chosen design was Bramante's: a Greek cruciform plan with jutting apses beneath cupolas and over the crossing a central dome similar to the Pantheon's. On 18 April 1506, the first stone was laid at the base of a pillar; a temporary chancel had been provided and a large part of the apse and transept demolished, causing Bramante to be nicknamed the "Destructive Maestro". Sometimes Michelangelo came to watch the work. Julius II had commissioned him to design his tomb, which was to be placed at the heart of the new basilica. The sculptor admired Bramante's plan, but disapproved of his administration. Seen as an intruder, Bramante came to hate him. Believing himself in danger, Michelangelo retreated to Florence, but returned after violently denouncing the

Piazza San Pietro
© fotoVoyager/iStockphoto.com

pope and Rome, where "they turn chalices into swords and helmets".

Julius II died in 1513 and Bramante the next year. For the next 30, the design of the building was the subject of interminable discussion. Raphael and Giuliano da Sangallo argued a return to the Latin cruciform plan. Baldassarre Peruzzi drew designs based on Bramante's. Antonio da Sangallo, Giuliano's nephew, promoted the Greek cross footprint, but suggested a bay in the form of a porch, with two towers flanking the façade, and altering the dome; he died in 1546.

From Michelangelo to Bernini – In 1547 **Paul III** appointed **Michelangelo**, then 72 and chief architect to the Vatican, to end the chaos. "To deviate from Bramante's design is to deviate from the truth", declared the master. He therefore returned to the Greek cruciform plan, simplified to accentuate its circular base – the circle, the sign of infinity, glorifying the Resurrection. The dome was no longer the shallow dome of the Pantheon, but reached high. Michelangelo worked on St Peter's, surrounded by intrigues, refusing any payment, doing all for the glory of God and the honour of St Peter. When he died in 1564, the apse and transepts were complete and the dome had risen as far as the top of the drum. It was completed in 1593

by **Giacomo della Porta**, assisted by Domenico Fontana.

In 1606, **Paul V** (1605–21) finally settled for the Latin cruciform plan; it was more suitable for high ceremony and preaching. The new basilica was to cover all the area occupied by the original church, whereas Michelangelo's plan had not extended as far east. The façade was entrusted to **Carlo Maderno**. The new basilica was consecrated by Urban VIII. The final phase in St Peter's architectural history was directed by **Bernini**, who took over on Maderno's death in 1629. He turned what would have been a fine example of Renaissance architecture into a sumptuous Baroque monument. From Bramante to Bernini, the construction absorbed 120 years, the reigns of 20 popes and the work of 10 architects.

PIAZZA SAN PIETRO★★★ (ST PETER'S SQUARE)

The square, which was intended to isolate the basilica without creating a barrier in front of it, acts, in fact, as a sort of vestibule. The gentle curves of the colonnades, like two arcs of a circle framing the rectangular space, are a gesture of welcome extended to pilgrims. The square was begun by **Bernini** in 1656 under Pope Alexander VII and completed in 1667. By flanking the façade

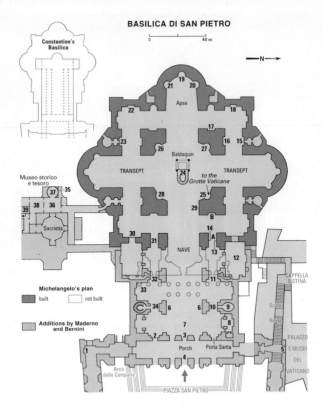

BASILICA DI SAN PIETRO

with a broader and lower colonnade, the architect minimised the width and accentuated the height of the basilica. To create the effect of surprise so dear to Baroque artists, he enclosed the square and masked the façade. The basilica would be hidden from view until visitors entered the gap in the colonnade. Bernini's intention was not fully realised: the triumphal arch intended to link the two arms was not built and Via della Conciliazione gives a distant view of the basilica. Two belfries were planned, but the foundations proved too weak to carry the additional weight. At its widest point, the square measures 196m/643ft across. The **colonnade** is formed by rows of columns, four deep, surmounted by statues and the arms of Alexander VII: a remarkably solemn composition.

At the centre of the square stands an **obelisk**, a granite monolith, carved in the 1C BC in Heliopolis for Caius Cornelius Gallus, the Roman Prefect in Egypt. It was brought to Rome in AD 37 by Caligula, who had it set up in his circus *(left of the basilica)*. **Sixtus V** decided to erect it in St Peter's Square. His official architect was **Domenico Fontana**. The work took four months and gave birth to a legend. The obelisk was to be re-erected on 10 September 1585; 800 men and 75 horses were required to raise the 350t of granite to its full height (25.5m/84ft). After giving his blessing, the pope enjoined absolute silence on pain of death; he set up gallows to underscore the point. The work began, but the ropes chafed on the granite and threatened to give way. Then one of the workers cried out, *"acqua alle funi"* ("water for the ropes"). Even the pope congratulated him for disobeying the order. A relic of the True Cross is preserved at the top of the obelisk.

The two fountains are attributed to Carlo Maderno *(right)* and **Bernini** *(left)*.

Between them and the obelisk are two discs set into the paving to mark the focal points of the two ellipses enclosing the square; from these points the colonnades appear to consist of only one row of columns. This perspective is achieved by increasing the diameter of the columns from the inner to the outer row and placing them an equal distance from one another.

East Front

A majestic flight of steps, designed by Bernini, leads to the east front. On either side stand statues of St Peter and St Paul (19C). The east front, begun by **Carlo Maderno** in 1607 and completed in 1614, was the object of spirited comment; owing to its dimensions (45m/147ft high and 115m/377ft wide), it masks the dome. From the balcony beneath the pediment, the pope gives his blessing *Urbi et Orbi* (to the City and to the world). The horizontal pediment above it is crowned by Christ, John the Baptist and 11 Apostles (minus Peter).

Porch

It was designed by **Carlo Maderno**. On the left behind a grill stands an equestrian statue of Charlemagne (1) (18C). The Door of Death (2), with sober sculptures on its bronze panels, is by **Giacomo Manzù** (1964); low down on the right in the left-hand section is a low-relief figure of John XXIII. The bronze door (3) was sculpted in 1445 by Antonio Averulino, known as **Il Filarete**. The true artistic spirit of the Renaissance is seen in the juxtaposition of religious scenes *(in the six panels)*, episodes from the life of Eugenius IV *(in the spaces below the panels)* and mythological figures, animals and portraits of contemporary personalities *(in the frieze surrounding the panels)*. To the right is the **Holy Door**: only the pope may open and close this to mark the Holy Year.

The "*Navicella*" mosaic (4) by Giotto dates from 1300. Originally from Constantine's Basilica, it was restored and shifted many times since.

At the north end of the porch, in the vestibule of the *Scala Regia (closed to the public)*, stands a statue of Constantine (5), the first Christian Emperor, by Bernini (1670).

Interior

Here everything is so well proportioned that the scale, though large, is not overwhelming. The seemingly life-size angels supporting the holy water stoups (6) are, in fact, enormous. St Peter's Basilica, with its 450 statues, 500 columns and 50 altars, and its reputed capacity to hold 60 000 people, is a record of the history of Christianity and art in Rome.

Nave – The overall length of the church, including the porch, is about 211m/692ft. Comparisons can be made with the length of other world-famous churches by means of marks set in the floor. When **Charlemagne** received the emperor's crown from the pope on Christmas Day AD 800, he knelt on the porphyry disc (7), now let into the pavement of the nave, although originally before the high altar.

Michelangelo's Pietà★★★ – This masterpiece, sculpted in 1499–1500 by Michelangelo at the age of 25, can be seen in the Cappella della Pietà (8). The execution of the profoundly human figures is perfect, revealing an amazing creative power. The piece was commissioned by a French cardinal in 1498 and immediately hailed as genius. Even so, Michelangelo already had enemies, who muttered that the work was not his. He therefore added his signature across the Virgin's sash – his only opus thus marked.

Cappella del Crocifisso o delle Reliquie (Crucifix Chapel or Chapel of Relics) (9) – **Bernini** designed the elliptical chapel, which contains a fine wooden crucifix attributed to Pietro Cavallini (early 14C).

Queen Christina of Sweden's Monument (10) – In 1654 **Queen Christina** abdicated her throne; she was converted to Roman Catholicism and came to live here the following year. She is buried in the "grottoes". Her monument was executed by Jean-Baptiste Theodon from designs by Carlo Fontana (18C).

Pilgrims' Dress and the Rite of Departure

Pilgrims needed to be easily recognisable to obtain hospitality and assistance during their journey – and to distinguish themselves from other travellers. Before leaving home, they made wills and gathered together for Mass and a blessing, where they received a cape, hat, purse and knapsack. Each of these articles had a special name. The cape was dark in colour, usually brown or grey, and was known as the *sanrocchino, schiavina* or *pellegrina*; the broad-brimmed hat was a *petaso*; the knapsack (or bag) was a *capsella* or *pera*; the stave, fitted with a hook and an iron tip, was known as a *bordone, burdo, baculus* or *fustis*. These articles also had symbolic significance: the knapsack represented charity (because it could hold only one day's provisions), the stave could chase off demons and overcome temptation, and the hat was covered with "souvenirs" from the journey – proof of pilgrimage. Objects that the *Romei* would hang from their hats (and sometimes their capes) included crosses, images of St Veronica, keys and portraits of saints and relics.

Countess Mathilda of Tuscany's Monument (11) – She was the first woman to be buried in the basilica. Mathilda received the Emperor Henry IV, when he submitted to Gregory VII at Canossa (1077). This incident is represented in the low-relief carving on the sarcophagus. The monument was designed by Bernini, assisted by pupils (1635).

Cappella del Santissimo Sacramento (Chapel of the Blessed Sacrament) **(12)** – The wrought-iron screen at the entrance is by Borromini. The high altarpiece representing the Trinity is one of the few paintings of St Peter by Pietro da Cortona (most are mosaics). On the altar, the tabernacle, which is similar to the *tempietto* of San Pietro in Montorio, and the kneeling angels are by Bernini (1675); the angel on the right is by a student.

Bernini brings unity to the Basilica – The passage **(A)** marks the line between Maderno's later and Michelangelo's earlier work. Bernini's task was to create a harmonised whole. The first problem was the junction of the nave with the eastern wall of Michelangelo's square plan. As this wall supports the oblique thrust of the weight of the dome, it could not be pierced to create a wide monumental doorway. Bernini erected two columns, like those flanking the doorways in the nave, and filled the space below the arch and the pediment with a shield supported by two angels. The second problem was the pier **(B)**, which

could not be pierced, as it supports the dome. He erected two columns and an arch of identical size to those in the passage. The visitor approaching along the north aisle of the church receives an impression of depth, accentuated by the two narrow arches.

Gregory XIII's Monument★ (13) – The low-relief carving on the white marble sarcophagus (1723) illustrates the 1582 Gregorian reform of the calendar (now adopted worldwide).

Gregory XIV's Monument (14) – According to legend, the monument was despoiled to meet the expense of the pope's illness, which had to be treated with a mixture of gold and precious stones. The plaster sarcophagus was not faced with marble until 1842.

Clement XIII's Monument★★★ (15) – The fine Neoclassical design by Canova dates from 1792. The lack of emotion for which Canova's art is often criticised here contributes to the purity of line. The balance of the whole is, however, upset by the statue on the left, which represents the Triumph of Religion.

Pictures in mosaic – Famous pictures began to be copied in mosaic in the 16C. The Church hoped to make its glories more intelligible to the faithful. This practice was further developed when Benedict XIII founded a mosaic school in 1727. These illustrate the power of St Peter; his walking on the water **(16)** and his raising of Tabitha **(17)**; they celebrate the martyrs, popes, saints and angels challenged by the Reformation.

Cappella di San Michele o di Santa Petronilla (St Michael's or St Petronilla's Chapel) **(18)** – The mosaic illustrates St Petronilla's martyrdom after a painting by Guercino. St Petronilla, whose relics lie beneath the altar, was venerated in St Peter's from 8C. Pepin the Short built a chapel to her, in which Michelangelo's *Pietà* was to have stood.

Apse – The dominant feature is **"St Peter's Chair"**★★★ **(19)**, an extraordinary work designed by **Bernini** to contain the remains of an ancient episcopal chair perhaps used by St Peter. These 4C remains are encased in a throne, decorated with ivory, which was given to John VIII by Charles the Bold at his coronation in 875. Bernini's throne is made of sculpted bronze, apparently supported by the four great Doctors of the Church (measuring between 4.50m/15ft and 5.50m/18ft). Above is a gilded stucco "gloria", veiled in clouds and a host of cherubs. Silhouetted against a sunlike central opening, which lets in the light, is the dove of the Holy Ghost (its wingspan is 1.75m/just under 6ft). This work, completed in 1666 when Bernini was in his 70s, is a crowning example of his astounding art, full of movement and light. **Urban VIII's Monument**★★★ **(20)**, commissioned from **Bernini** in 1628 and finished in 1647, is considered to be the masterpiece of 17C funerary art.

For **Paul III's Monument**★★★ **(21)**, **Guglielmo della Porta** (c. 1500–77), a follower of Michelangelo, conceived a grandiose project: the monument was to be surrounded by eight allegorical statues and placed in the centre of the chancel. Michelangelo objected and asked for the number of statues to be reduced to four. Bernini cut the number to two; the others are in the Farnese Palace.

St Leo the Great's Altar (22) – The **altarpiece**★ is a "picture in marble" by **Algardi** of the pope halting Attila at the gates of Rome. **Alexander VII's Monument**★★ **(23)** – **Bernini** completed this in 1678, two years before his death. He was anxious that he should sculpt the head of the pope, his protector.

The pope kneels among allegorical statues, the work of pupils who have somewhat exaggerated the movement. Even Bernini's own art gives way to excess here (death is represented by a skeleton draped in mottled marble, beckoning the pope).

Baldacchino★★★ – **Bernini**'s canopy, begun in 1624, was unveiled by Urban VIII in 1633. Despite the weight of the bronze and its great height (29m/95ft – the height of the Farnese Palace), it has captured the lightweight effect of a traditional baldaquin, usually of wood and cloth, carried in processions.

Michelangelo's Pietà

© Judy Edelhoff/Michelin

The work attracted much criticism, because the bronze had been taken from the Pantheon and because it was thought to be too theatrical and in bad taste.

The high altar below the baldaquin, where only the pope may celebrate Mass, stands over the *confessio* (24), designed by Maderno, which contains St Peter's tomb.

Piers of the Crossing – Begun by **Bramante** and completed by Michelangelo, they stand at the crossing of the transepts. Their austerity did not please Baroque taste; in 1629 Bernini faced them in marble and created recesses at the base, in which he placed four statues (5m/16ft high).

Each statue represents the relics deposited in the basilica: a fragment of the spear (St Longinus **[25]** by Bernini commemorates the soldier who pierced Jesus' side); the napkin bearing the Holy Image (St Veronica **[26]** wiped Jesus's face on the road to Calvary); a fragment of the True Cross (St Helena **[27]** brought the remains of the Cross to Rome); St Andrew's head (28). The last three are by Bernini's collaborators: Francesco Mochi, Andrea Bolgi and François Duquesnoy.

Dome★★★ – Bramante's design resembled the Pantheon's, but **Michelangelo** made the dome larger and higher. He carried out the work up to the lantern; it was finished in 1593 by **Giacomo della Porta** and **Domenico Fontana**. The whole building seems designed to support the city's largest dome, supposedly a symbol of God's perfection.

The pendentives carry four mosaic medallions (8m/26ft across) of the Evangelists. Above are Christ's words: "Thou art Peter and upon this rock I will build my church; and I will give unto thee the keys of the Kingdom of Heaven".

Statue of St Peter★★ (29) – This 13C bronze by **Arnolfo di Cambio** is greatly venerated. Countless pilgrims have kissed its foot. It is said to have been made out of the bronze statue of Jupiter on the Capitol.

Pius VII's Tomb (30) – Pius VII died in 1823, after bearing the brunt of

the Napoleonic storm. His tomb was designed by **Thorwaldsen**, a Dane.

Leo XI's Monument (31) – **Algardi** was responsible for the white marble monument (1642–44). The low-relief sculpture on the sarcophagus illustrates Henri IV's conversion to Roman Catholicism; the king is being received by the future pope, who was then Clement VIII's legate.

Innocent VIII's Monument★★★ (32) – This is a Renaissance work by Antonio del Pollaiolo (1431–98), one of the few monuments preserved from the earlier church. The tomb is designed in typical 15C style against a wall.

When the monument was re-erected in 162, the two figures were reversed; originally the recumbent figure was above the pope, signifying the supreme power of death. An error has crept into the epitaph, which says that the pope "lived" *(vixit)* rather than "reigned" for eight years, 10 months and 25 days.

John XXIII's Monument (33) – The low-relief sculpture on the right of the chapel of the *Presentation* is by Emilio Greco.

Stuart Monument (34) – **Canova** designed this work (1817–19) to the glory of the last members of the Scottish royal family: James Edward, Charles Edward and Henry Benedict, who are buried in the crypt *(☾See below)*. The monument was commissioned by the Prince Regent and paid for by George III.

The **angels**★ in low relief were much admired by **Stendhal**, who also remarked that "George IV, in keeping with his reputation as the most accomplished gentleman in the three kingdoms, wished to honour the ashes of the unhappy princes, whom he would have sent to the scaffold had they fallen into his hands alive".

Museo Storico e Tesoro★

The Treasury has been pillaged on many occasions – by the Saracens in 846, during the sack of Rome in 1527, by Bonaparte under the Treaty of Tolentino in 1797 – but it has always been rebuilt.

In **Room I (35)** are two mementoes of the 4C basilica: the "Holy Column", which is identical to those reused by Bernini in the balcony chapels, and the gilded metal cockerel (9C), which Leo IV had placed on top of the basilica.

Room II (36) displays a dalmatic, said to have belonged to Charlemagne; it is, in fact, a Byzantine-style liturgical vestment dating from the 10C at the earliest. This room also contains a copy of the wooden and ivory chair contained in Bernini's throne, and a 6C papal cross. The beautiful tabernacle in the **Benefactors' Chapel (37)** is attributed to **Donatello**, the Renaissance master artist from Florence. The plaster mould of the *Pietà* proved valuable when the original was damaged in 1972.

Room III (38) contains the **tomb of Sixtus IV★★★** (1493) by Antonio del Pollaiolo. The accuracy of the portraiture and the delicacy of its execution make it a true masterpiece of bronze sculpture. Several rooms, glittering with gold and silverware and liturgical objects, lead into the **gallery (39)**. Here is the tiara with which St Peter's statue is crowned on ceremonial occasions. Junius **Bassus's sarcophagus★★★** (4C) was found beneath the basilica and is a remarkable example of Christian funerary sculpture, richly decorated with biblical scenes; on the sides are children gathering the harvest, a symbol of the souls saved by the Eucharist.

Grotte Vaticane

Access in the northeast pier supporting the dome.

The grottoes embrace the area beneath the basilica containing the papal tombs and parts of the earlier basilica. They consist of a semi-circular section that follows the line of Constantine's apse, with the Ad Caput Chapel (*See below*) on the eastern side, and three aisles projecting eastwards. Among the tombs in the aisles are those of Pope John Paul II, Christina of Sweden, Benedict XV and Hadrian IV, born Nicholas Breakspear, the only English pope.

Salita alla Cupola★ (Ascent to the Dome)

Access from the exterior to the right of the basilica.

From an internal gallery at the base of the dome, visitors can best appreciate the vast dimensions of the basilica. Two people, opposite one another and facing the wall, can hold a conversation in low voices. An interior stair climbs to a terrace surrounding the lantern at 120m/394ft above St Peter's Square. The **view★★★** is magnificent.

Necropoli Vaticana★★ (Vatican Necropolis)

Constantine filled a pagan necropolis to form a foundation for the original ancient basilica. Two rows of tombs (1C to early 4C) run east to west. One bears an inscription recording the occupant's wish to be buried *"in Vaticano ad circum"*, alluding to Nero's circus, where St Peter may have perished. In another, that of the Julian family, are the oldest known Christian mosaics. These show "Christ as the sun", on a horse-drawn chariot, and Jonah and the fisherman.

▷ Return in the direction of the apse of the present basilica.

Set in the east side of the so-called "Red Wall" (Muro Rosso) is the recess (2C) known as the "Trophy of Gaius" (Trofeo di Gaio); beneath is the **tomb of St Peter**. The emperor enclosed the tomb and trophy – which supposedly marked the grave of an apostle – in marble.

According to the historian Jerome Carcopino, the saint's relics have had a hazardous existence. In 258, fearing desecration during the Valerian persecution, the Christians may have moved them to St Sebastian's Catacombs, which did not then belong to the Church and were therefore unlikely to attract attention from the authorities. Not until 336, when Christians were again entitled to practise their religion, would the relics have been returned to their original resting place in the Vatican.

Cappella Clementina★ (Clementine Chapel) – This is the **Ad Caput Chapel** ("At the Head" Chapel). It stands behind the shrine very close to the apostle's tomb. Some bones, found nearby, could be St Peter's.

Musei Vaticani★★★

(Vatican Museums)

The museums are housed in part of the palaces built by the popes from the 13C onwards. The old entrance hall, opened in 1932, is now solely an exit. A new bronze door, to the left, leads visitors into a spacious, modern area capable of handling 2 000 people at once. From here, a spiral ramp and an escalator lead up to the Cortile delle Corazze (Cuirasses), the Atrio dei Quatt ro Cancelli (Atrium of the Four Gates) and Simonetti's 18C staircases (**A on the plan**).

☺ *The number of masterpieces in the Vatican is so great that a rigorous selection of the outstanding works has had to be made. For a more detailed description of the exhibits, consult the "Guide to the Vatican City" and the "Guide to the Vatican Museums" published by Monumenti, Musei e Gallerie Pontificie.*

▷ **Location:** Entrance in Viale Vaticano; from Piazza Risorgimento take Via Bastioni di Michelangelo and turn left. (*For opening times see the Addresses at the beginning of the chapter*). The official tour starts with the Egyptian and Chiaromonti Museums. The visit of the Pio-Clementino Museum begins from near Bramante's Staircase.

☺ **Don't Miss:** The Raphael Room and the Sistine Chapel.

🕐 **Timing:** Visit the Vatican museums early in the morning, as queues can stretch out endlessly.

Palaces

During the reign of Pope Symmachus (498–514), some buildings probably were erected to the north of St Peter's Basilica. Nicholas III (1277–80) hoped to replace them with a fortress and towers, but his project was only partially realised. When the popes returned from Avignon, they stopped living in the Lateran Palace, destroyed by fire, and settled here.

Nicholas V (1447–55) decided to enlarge the accommodation. Around the Parrot Court *(Cortile del Pappagallo)*, he constructed a palace incorporating the 13C buildings. He kept the fortress-like exterior, but the interior was sumptuously decorated. The chapel by **Fra Angelico** can still be seen. Almost all the popes have altered or enlarged Nicholas V's palace.

Sixtus IV (1471–84) established a library on the ground floor of the north wing (now a conference room) and built the Sistine Chapel to the west. About 300m/984ft north of Nicholas V's palace,

Innocent VIII (1484–92) built a summer residence, the Belvedere Palace. From 1493–94, Alexander VI added the Borgia Tower (Torre Borgia) and created his own apartments above Sixtus IV's library.

Pope Julius II (1503–13) commissioned **Bramante** to link Nicholas V's and Innocent VIII's palaces with two long narrow galleries, thus creating the Belvedere Court (Cortile del Belvedere).

A huge rectangular courtyard, it provided a setting for grandiose spectacles and was later divided into the present Library and Pine Cone Courts (Cortile della Biblioteca e Cortile della Pigna). He lived above Alexander VI's apartments in the rooms painted by Piero **della Francesca**, Benedetto Bonfigli and Andrea del Castagno, and had them redecorated by **Raphael**. The façade was too austere for his taste, so he had another built, consisting of three loggias, one above another. The second floor loggia was decorated by Raphael.

Pius IV (1559–65) commissioned Pirro Ligorio to alter the Belvedere Court. To the north, the architect constructed a large semi-circular niche, in front of which he planted the *pigna*, a huge pine cone (formerly it adorned the fountain in the atrium of Constantine's Basilica). The design is based on classical architecture, particularly Domitian's Stadium on the Palatine Hill. To the south, backing onto Nicholas V's palace, he created a semicircular façade one storey high with a central niche. Later the Belvedere Court was divided by two transverse galleries: between 1587 and 1588, during the reign of Sixtus V, Domenico Fontana built the Papal Library (Sistine Rooms); later, between 1806 and 1823, **Pius VII** built the New Wing (Braccio Nuovo).

The Belvedere Court was thus divided into three separate courts: the Belvedere Court (Cortile del Belvedere), the Library Court (della Biblioteca), the Pine Cone Court (della Pigna).

During the Baroque period, the only addition to the Vatican Palace was the Scala Regia (Royal Stairway – not open), a monumental stairway constructed by **Bernini** between 1633 and 1666. From the Great Bronze Door (Portone di Bronzo), which is the main entrance to the palace a long corridor along the north side of St Peter's Square leads to the Scala Regia.

Papal Court

Sixtus IV (1471–84) created a virtual court like that of a secular prince. He provided his nephews with ecclesiastical titles and benefices, and surrounded himself with rich cardinals, artists and men of letters.

Pope's Apartments

The 16C buildings around Sixtus V's Court (Cortile di Sisto V) contain the present papal apartments. Heads of State, diplomats and other important people enter the Vatican City by the Bell Arch (Arco delle Campane). Papal receptions are held in the pope's private library, a large room between Sixtus V's Court and Majordomo Court (Cortile del Maggiordomo).

In the summer the pope moves to Castel Gandolfo, 120km/75mi SE of Rome.

Museums

Their origins go back to 1503, when Julius II displayed a few classical works of art in the Belvedere Court. His successors continued to collect Greek and Roman, paleo-Christian and Christian antiquities. Clement XIV created a new museum, which was enlarged by Pius VI and is called the Pio-Clementino after the pair. The rooms joining the Belvedere Palace to the West Gallery, now occupied by the Apostolic Library, were constructed by the architect Simonetti. Following the Treaty of Tolentino in 1797, many artworks were sent to Paris. Those that were left were arranged by Canova in a museum called the Chiaramonti Museum (after the pope's family name). Canova had been appointed Inspector General of Fine Arts and Antiquities belonging to the State and the Church by Pope Pius VII. When the lost works were returned in 1816, Pius VII built the New Wing to house them.

In 1837, Gregory XVI opened an Etruscan Museum to house excavated material; an Egyptian Museum opened in 1839; the art gallery *(Pinacoteca)* opened in 1932.

The year 1970 saw the inauguration of a very modern building to house the Antique and Christian Art collections formerly in the Lateran Palace. The Missionary collections were transferred from the Lateran in 1973, the same year as the creation of the History Museum and the Museum of Modern Religious Art. For the interest and diversity of their treasures, the Vatican Museums rank among the best in the world.

FIRST FLOOR
Museo Egizio (Egyptian Museum)

Founded by Pope Gregory XVI, it was laid out in 1839 by Father Ungarelli, an Italian Egyptologist. The collection includes antiquities acquired by the popes in 18C and statues found nearby. These were brought back from Egypt during the empire or are Roman copies of 1C–2C works.

Room I contains inscriptions from the Old Kingdom (c. 2650 BC) to the 6C

MUSEI VATICANI

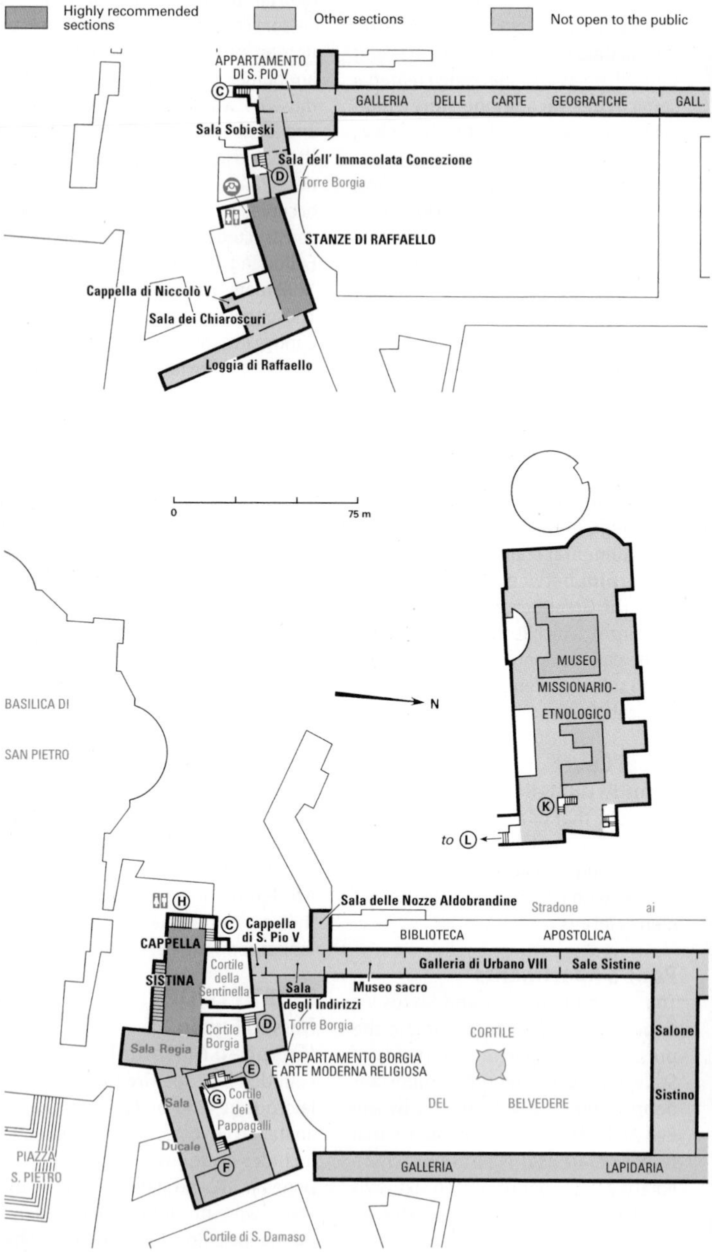

Highly recommended sections

Other sections

Not open to the public

APPARTAMENTO DI S. PIO V

© C

GALLERIA DELLE CARTE GEOGRAFICHE

GALL.

Sala Sobieski

© D

Sala dell' Immacolata Concezione

Torre Borgia

STANZE DI RAFFAELLO

Cappella di Niccolò V

Sala dei Chiaroscuri

Loggia di Raffaello

0   75 m

BASILICA DI

SAN PIETRO

N

MUSEO MISSIONARIO-ETNOLOGICO

© K

to © L

Sala delle Nozze Aldobrandine

© H

© C Cappella di S. Pio V

CAPPELLA

Cortile della Sentinella

SISTINA

Stradone   ai

BIBLIOTECA   APOSTOLICA

Galleria di Urbano VIII   Sale Sistine

Sala

Museo sacro

degli Indirizzi

© D Torre Borgia

Sala Regia

Cortile Borgia

© E

APPARTAMENTO BORGIA E ARTE MODERNA RELIGIOSA

CORTILE

Salone

Sistino

© G Cortile dei Pappagalli

Sala

Ducale

© F

CORTILE   DEL   BELVEDERE

PIAZZA S. PIETRO

Cortile di S. Damaso

GALLERIA   LAPIDARIA

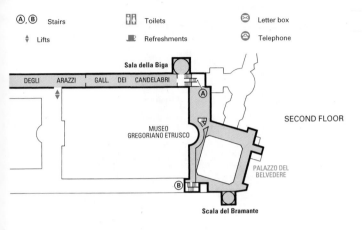

(A), (B) Stairs

Lifts

Toilets

Refreshments

Letter box

Telephone

Sala della Biga

DEGLI   ARAZZI   GALL. DEI CANDELABRI

(A)

MUSEO
GREGORIANO ETRUSCO

SECOND FLOOR

PALAZZO DEL
BELVEDERE

(B)

Scala del Bramante

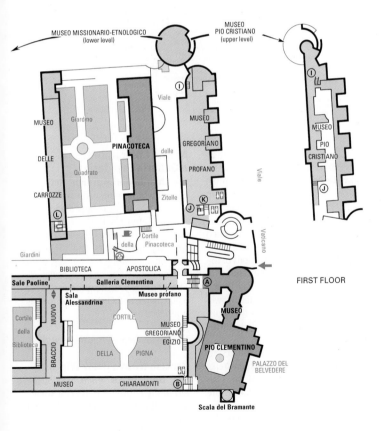

MUSEO MISSIONARIO-ETNOLOGICO
(lower level)

MUSEO
PIO CRISTIANO
(upper level)

Viale

(I)

MUSEO

DELLE

CARROZZE

Giardino

PINACOTECA

Quadrato

delle

Zitelle

MUSEO

GREGORIANO

PROFANO

Viale

MUSEO

PIO

CRISTIANO

(I)

(J)

(L)

(K)

(J)

Cortile
Pinacoteca

della

Giardini

BIBLIOTECA   APOSTOLICA

Viale

Vaticano

FIRST FLOOR

Sale Paoline

Cortile
della
Biblioteca

NUOVO

BRACCIO

Galleria Clementina

Sala
Alessandrina

Museo profano

(A)

CORTILE

DELLA   PIGNA

MUSEO
GREGORIANO
EGIZIO

MUSEO

PIO CLEMENTINO

PALAZZO DEL
BELVEDERE

MUSEO   CHIARAMONTI

(B)

Scala del Bramante

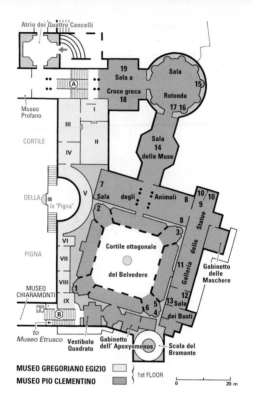

Atrio dei Quattro Cancelli

Museo Profano

CORTILE

DELLA

PIGNA

MUSEO CHIARAMONTI

19
Sala a
Croce greca
18

Sala
Rotonda
15
17 16

Sala
14
delle Muse

7
Sala degli Animali
2

la "Pigna"

VI
VII
VIII
IX

1

Cortile ottagonale
del Belvedere

8
9
10 10

8
3

11

12
13 Sala
dei Busti

6 4 5

Galleria delle Statue

Gabinetto delle Maschere

I
III
II
IV
V

to
Museo Etrusco

Vestibolo Quadrato

Gabinetto dell' Apoxyomenos

Scala del Bramante

MUSEO GREGORIANO EGIZIO
MUSEO PIO CLEMENTINO

1st FLOOR

0   20 m

AD: throne of the statue of Pharaoh Ramses II (19th dynasty; c. 1250 BC).

Room II is devoted to ancient Egyptian funerary art: the mummy of a woman (c. 1000 BC) with henna-dyed hair; sarcophagi in painted wood and stone; canopic vases (organs were mummified separately) and various amulets.

Room III displays reproductions of the sculptures that decorate the Canopus in Hadrian's Villa at Tivoli. The main theme is the reawakening, represented by twin busts on a lotus flower, of Osiris-Apis, also known as Serapis, a deity introduced in the 4C by Ptolemy.

In the **hemicycle (V)** are Egyptian statues discovered in Rome and its environs: the fine Pharaoh's head of the 11th dynasty (c. 2100 BC) exemplifies the art of the Middle Kingdom. The colossal statue of Queen Thuya, Ramses II's mother (c. 1250 BC), is a New Kingdom effort.

Museo Chiaramonti e Galleria Lapidaria

The **Chiaramonti Museum** – set up by Pius VII, whose family name was Chiaramonti – has kept the appearance created by Canova in 1807. It has Roman copies of Greek works, portraits and funerary monuments: one low-relief, bearing a millstone and donkey, commemorates a miller *(on the right, Row X)*. The **Lapidary Gallery** houses over 3 000 pagan and Christian inscriptions *(specialists only)*.

▶ The tour proceeds to the New Wing.

Braccio Nuovo (New Wing)

The **"Doryphoros"** *(third recess on the left of the entrance)* depicts a spearbearer. It is a copy of a bronze original by Polyclitus (440 BC). In all probability the original was the model *(the Kanon)*, that demonstrated Polyclitus' theories about proportions in sculpture.

The **statue of Augustus★★** *(fourth recess on the right)*, known as "from the Prima Porta" because of where it was found, is a fine example of official Roman art. The decoration of the emperor's breastplate is an extraordinarily precise illustration of the King of the Parthians returning the standards lost by Crassus in 53 BC. *The Nile (il Nilo)* is a 1C Roman work inspired perhaps by a Greek original.

The river god is surrounded by 16 children, a symbol of the 16 cubits the river must rise to flood and fertilise the plain. The gilded bronze peacocks may be from Hadrian's Mausoleum. The **statue of Demosthenes** *(recess on the entrance's left)* is a Roman copy of a Greek bronze (3C BC).

◖ Return to Chiaramonti entrance; enter Pio-Clementino Museum (stair B).

Museo Pio-Clementino★★★

The museum is in the Belvedere Palace and Simonetti's 18C extension. **Vestibolo Quadrato** (Square Vestibule) is the atrium of the former Clementino Museum. The sobriety of early Roman art shows in the sarcophagus of **Scipio Barbatus**, carved in peperine (3C BC). Its shape is inspired by the Greek models that the Romans discovered after the capture of Rhegium in 270 BC.

Gabinetto dell'Apoxyomenos – The Apoxyomenos★★★ is the name given to the statue of an athlete scraping his skin with a strigil, post-exercise. It is a 1C AD Roman copy of a Greek original by Lysippus (4C BC). In the weary body, the artist reveals the living human being rather than an idealistic image, as in the classical period.

Scala del Bramante – Bramante's noble spiral stairway, used by men on horseback, was designed in the early 16C, during the alterations ordered by Julius II.

Cortile ottagonale del Belvedere★ (Belvedere Octagonal Court) – The internal courtyard, originally on a square plan and planted with orange trees, acquired its octagonal outline when Simonetti added a portico in the 18C.

The extraordinary **Laocoön★★★ (2)** was unearthed in Nero's Golden House by a group of peasants. This sculpture was the work of a group of artists from Rhodes (1C BC), It represents the death of Laocoön, priest of Apollo, who had incurred the god's anger and, with his two sons, was crushed to death by serpents. Here Hellenistic art attains an intense realism, dubbed "Greek Baroque".

The statue of **Apollo★★★ (1)** was placed in the Belvedere Court by Julius II in 1503. It is probably copied from a 4C BC Greek original by a Roman sculptor. The figure may have held a bow in the left hand and an arrow in the right.

The three **Neoclassical statues** by **Canova** (1757–1822) were bought by Pope Pius VII to make up for the loss of certain works removed under the terms of the Treaty of Tolentino: **Perseus★★ (4)**, who conquered Medusa, and the boxers Kreugas **(5)** and Damozenos **(6)**, who met in fierce combat at Nemea in Argolis.

The **Hermes★★★ (3)** is a 2C AD Roman work, inspired by an original Greek bronze, representing the trickster god. Under the north portico sits the **Ara Casali**, a 3C altar presented to Pope Pius VI. On the front is a scene with Venus and Mars; the back shows Romulus and Remus.

Sala degli Animali (Room of the Animals) – The statue of **Meleager★ (7)** is a 2C Roman copy of a bronze sculpture by Skopas, a Greek artist (4C BC). Beside Meleager is the head of the boar that caused his death, at Diana's behest.

The fine floor mosaics are Roman. A crab made of green porphyry, a rare stone, is displayed in a showcase **(8)**.

The **Sleeping Ariadne★ (9)** is a Roman copy of a Greek original, illustrating the characteristic taste for unusual poses and the elaborate draperies of the Hellenistic period (2C BC). On waking, Ariadne will be married to Dionysius and carried away to Mount Olympus.

The candelabra **(10)** are fine examples of 2C Roman decorative work from Hadrian's Villa at Tivoli.

The statue of **Apollo Sauroktonos★ (11)**, showing the god about to kill a lizard, is a Roman copy of a work by Praxiteles, a Greek artist of the 4C BC. An expert in feminine models, he made the girlish young god very graceful.

In the three rooms of the **Sala dei Busti** (Room of the Busts), divided by fine marble columns, note the austere busts of **Cato and Portia (12)**, a husband and wife group intended for a tomb (1C BC).

Imperial portraits include a particularly expressive bust of Julius Caesar **(13)**.

Gabinetto delle Maschere (Cabinet of the Masks) – This room owes its name to the mosaic of masks (2C) removed from Hadrian's Villa and let into the floor.

The **Venus of Cnidos★★** is a Roman copy of Praxiteles's statue for the sanctuary at Cnidos in Asia Minor (4C BC), which was famous for its artistic merits and for being the first representation of a goddess in the nude. The Greeks – versed in the legend of Actaeon, who was killed for watching a goddess bathing – were shocked.

▶ Return to the Room of the Animals.

Sala delle Muse (Room of the Muses) – Like the statue of the Pugilist *(in the Museo Nazionale Romano)*, the **Belvedere Torso★★★ (14)** is the masterly work of the Athenian Apollonius, Nestor's son, who lived in Rome in the 1C BC. The expressive torso, much admired by Michelangelo and originally thought to represent Hercules, has recently been identified as the Trojan War hero Ajax. According to mythology, he went mad and killed himself when his dead friend Achilles' armour was given to Ulysses. The statue *(of which only the torso remains)* shows him overcome with shame.

Sala Rotonda★ (Round Room) – This fine room by Simonetti (1780) was inspired by the Pantheon. The monolithic porphyry **basin** may have come from Nero's Golden House. The **statue of Hercules (15)** in gilded bronze dates from the late 2C. **Antinoüs (16)**, the young favourite of the Emperor Had-

rian, drowned in the Nile in 130. After his death, the emperor raised him under the name "Osirantinoos" to the ranks of the gods. He bears the attributes of Dionysius and the Egyptian god Osiris (on his head is the *uraeus*, a serpent – part of the headdress of the Pharaohs). The bust of **Jupiter★ (17)** is a 4C BC Roman copy.

Sala a Croce Greca (Greek Cross Room) – Two large porphyry **sarcophagi★** have pride of place. The one belonging to St Helena **(18)**, the Emperor Constantine's mother, dates from the early 4C and is heavily sculptured with conquering Roman cavalry and barbarian prisoners, an inappropriate theme for such a holy woman. This suggests that the sarcophagus was originally intended for her husband or her son. The other is the sarcophagus of Constantia **(19)**, Constantine's daughter, and dates from the middle of the 4C.

▶ Simonetti Stairs **(A)** to second floor.

SECOND FLOOR
Museo Gregoriano Etrusco★
Founded in 1837 by Gregory XVI, this museum houses objects from southern Etruria. The oldest artefacts *(9C–8C BC cinerary urns in the form of a house)* are in **Room I**. Items retrieved from the **Regolini-Galassi tomb,** south of Cerveteri, in **Room II**, are particularly fine; these include a bronze throne and jewellery. The incomparable golden **clasp★★**, decorated with lions and ducks, shows the Etruscan's skill in such work.

The **Bronze Room (III)** houses the **Mars★★** found at Todi, a rare example of a large late 5C BC bronze statue. The style is akin to rigourous classical Greek works. The oval cist *(last case to the right of the Mars)*, a toilette receptacle, is decorated with the Battle of the Amazons; fantastic figures adorn the handle.

In the hemicycle, note the striking large black-figure **amphora★★★** *(second middle glass case to the left of the entrance)*, painted by Exekias; this object is a rare example of his artistry. It illustrates Achilles playing draughts with Ajax.

Halls and Galleries
Sala Della Biga (Biga Room)
Don't miss the 1C Roman **two-horse chariot★★** *(biga)*. It was reconstituted in the 18C, when the body of the chariot was recovered from St Mark's Basilica; it had served as an episcopal throne.

Galleria degli Arazzi (Tapestry Gallery)
The tapestries were hung by Gregory XVI in 1838. Facing the windows: the New School series, commissioned by Leo X in the early 16C, was woven by Pieter van Aelst's workshops in Brussels from cartoons by Raphael's pupils.

Galleria delle Carte Geografiche★
The ceiling is decorated with stuccowork and paintings by a group of 18C Mannerists: 80 scenes from the lives of the saints closely associated with the maps below. The extraordinary maps on the walls were painted from 1580–83 from cartoons by Fr Ignazio Danzi.

Below, the 16C cartography is embellished with inscriptions, ships and turbulent seas.

Sala Sobieski e Sala dell'Immacolata Concezione
In the former hangs a 19C painting by Jan Mateiko of John III Sobieski, King of Poland, repulsing the Turks at the Siege of Vienna (1683). The 19C frescoes in the latter illustrate the dogma of the Immaculate Conception.

Stanze di Raffaello★★★ (Raphael Rooms)
During part of the year, to avoid overcrowding, access from the Room of the Immaculate Conception via an external terrace is one-way. The visit to the Raphael Rooms then starts in the Hall of Constantine. The rest of the year the tour circles through the exhibits in the opposite direction.
These rooms were built during the reign of Nicholas V (1447–55) and decorated

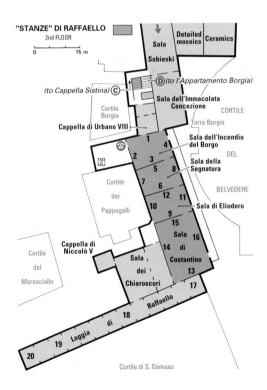

with frescoes by **Piero della Francesca** among others, except the Hall of Constantine, which was part of the 13C wing of the papal palace.

On becoming pope in 1503, Julius II arranged to have the rooms redecorated by Sodoma, Perugino and others. In 1508, on Bramante's recommendation, he sent for a young painter from Urbino. Charmed by Raphael's youthful grace, he entrusted the whole to him; the other painters were dismissed and their work effaced.

The frescoes here are among the masterpieces of the Renaissance. They were damaged by the troops of Charles V, during the sack of Rome in 1527, but have been restored.

Sala dell'Incendio del Borgo (Room of the Borgo Fire) (1514–17)

This room was the last one painted by Raphael. The immediate success of his work and the large number of commissions that followed led him to rush. From 1515, he worked with a group of assistants, including Giulio Romano. In this room he only designed the frescoes and some of the cartoons, completed by his team. The ceiling frescoes are by Perugino.

In the fresco of the *Coronation of Charlemagne* (1) the emperor is portrayed as François I of France and Leo II as Leo X. *The Borgo Fire* (2) shows Leo IV quenching an 847 conflagration with the sign of the cross. Inspired, like all Renaissance artists, by antiquity, Raphael painted the colonnade of the Temple of Mars Ultor on the left; the old man supported by a youth recalls Virgil (Aeneas fleeing Troy). In the *Battle of Ostia* (3), Leo X is again represented in the guise of Leo IV, who defeated the Saracens nearby in 849.

A medieval legend is depicted in the *Oath of Leo III* (4). According to this account, when Leo III sought to clear himself of a libel in St Peter's itself, a voice rang out, declaring "It is for God not men to judge bishops" *(Latin inscription to the right of the window)*. Leo III is portrayed as Leo X.

Sala della Segnatura (Signature Room) (1508–11)

This room was used as a library, a study and for signing papal bulls. It was the first room painted by Raphael. The decorative theme, probably proposed by a court scholar versed in neo-Platonic philosophy, illustrates the three great principles of the human spirit: Truth, Goodness and Beauty.

Part of the ceiling decoration is attributed to Sodoma and the octagonal area to Bramantino (c. 1465–1530). The name *Dispute over the Blessed Sacrament* (5) is wrongly attributed to the fresco illustrating the Glorification of Religion: at the top, surrounding the Trinity, appears the Church victorious with Mary, St John the Baptist, the Apostles, Prophets and Patriarchs, martyrs and angels.

On earth, grouped around the altar, stand the Doctors of the Church, the popes and the faithful, including Dante *(right)*, crowned with laurel, Savonarola, Sixtus IV, Fra Angelico and Gregory the Great, with the features of Julius II. The lines converge on the Host, the incarnation of Christ, linking the Church on earth and the Church in heaven.

The *School of Athens* (6) depicts a crowd of philosophers standing beneath the vaults of a classical building designed by Bramante. In the centre are Plato and Aristotle, representing the two main streams of Classical thought. Plato's raised finger indicates the realm of ideas; Aristotle's open hand indicates that without the material world ideas would have no existence. Raphael has given Plato the face of Leonardo da Vinci. On the left, Socrates, in a tunic, is speaking to his pupil Alcibiades. Euclid, who resembles Bramante, is tracing geometric figures on a slate. In the right-hand corner, Raphael included himself in a black beret beside Sodoma, in a tunic and white beret. In the foreground is the solitary figure of Heraclitus, his head resting in his left hand; he has the features of Michelangelo, who was at that time decorating the Sistine Chapel. Raphael added this figure when the fresco was almost finished, honouring his rival.

The Cardinal and Theological Virtues (7) – Above the window are Strength *(oak branch, emblem of the Della Rovere family to which Julius II belonged)*, Prudence and Temperance, Faith, Hope and Charity *(as cupids)*. On the right Raimond de Pennafort hands Gregory IX (1234) the body of rules which make up canon law (Decretals); on the left Justinian approves the "Pandects", a collection of Roman jurisprudence, comprising civil law. Gregory IX is a portrait of Julius II. Beside him stand Cardinal Giovanni de' Medici (future Leo X) and Alessandro Farnese (future Paul III).

Note the *"Parnassus"* **(8)** on the opposite wall. Around Apollo and the nine Muses are grouped the great poets, starting with Homer, Virgil and Dante.

Sala di Eliodoro (Heliodorus Room) (1512–1514)

This was the suite's private antechamber and was decorated by Raphael after the Signature Room. The theme is the divine protection of the Church.

The biblical subject of the *Expulsion of Heliodorus from the Temple* **(9)**, taken from the Book of Maccabees (Heliodorus, intent on stealing the temple treasure, is expelled by the angels), was probably chosen by Julius II himself, whose own policy was to expel usurpers from papal property. He appears on the left. This excellent portrait reveals the authority of the pope, who fought alongside his own soldiers and one day broke his cane across Michelangelo's back. This fresco is exceptional for Raphael in the vigour and movement of the figures (including a person flattening himself against a pillar).

The *Miracle of the Bolsena Mass* **(10)** commemorates the miracle today celebrated as the feast of Corpus Christi. In 1263, a priest, who doubted the doctrine of the real presence, saw blood on the host at the moment of consecration, while celebrating Mass in Bolsena. Julius II is kneeling before the priest. The pope, his suite and the Swiss guards are among Raphael's masterpieces.

An episode described in the Acts of the Apostles is depicted in *St Peter Delivered from Prison* **(11)**. According to this account, Peter, chained in Rome, dreamt that an angel liberated him and on waking found, lo, that he was free. Note the various light sources: the moon, the guard's torch, the angel. This anticipates the genius of Caravaggio and Rembrandt by more than a century. In *St Leo the Great Repulsing Attila* **(12)**, Raphael shows Leo I meeting the Huns and repelling their advance, aided by the appearance of St Peter and St Paul armed with swords. The artist has moved the event to the gates of Rome, indicated by the Colosseum, a basilica and an aqueduct. A large part of the painting *(right)* was executed by Raphael's pupils.

Sala di Costantino (Hall of Constantine)

In 1520, Raphael died. This room was finished by his followers, led by Giulio Romano and Francesco Penni. Here begins Mannerism; overwhelmed by the legacy of Raphael and Michelangelo, artists began to abandon national idealism in favour of exaggerated form and contorted movement.

The Apparition of the Cross **(13)** and the *Battle of the Milvian Bridge* **(14)** are by Romano. Penni crafted *The Baptism of Constantine* **(15)**. Pope Sylvester, who baptised Constantine, is shown in the Basilica of St John Lateran.

The two artists collaborated on *Constantine's Donation* **(16)**, which is set inside the old St Peter's and shows the emperor Constantine (306–37) giving Rome to the pope, thus founding the temporal power of the papacy.

Loggia di Raffaello★★ (Raphael's Loggia)

🕐*Open to specialists only. Access via the Hall of Constantine. On the second floor of the galleried building.*

At the beginning of the 16C – before the construction of St Damasus' Court (Cortile di San Damaso) and the buildings on its north, south and east sides – the façade of the 13C palace gazed over Rome. Julius II (1503–13) decided to give it a new look. He engaged Bramante to design three superimposed loggias. Work began in 1508; when Bramante died in 1514, only the first tier had been built. Julius II's successor, Leo X, appointed Raphael to take over.

The loggia is divided into 13 bays; the vault of each is decorated with four paintings, representing scenes from the Old Testament, except in the first bay **(17)**, which has scenes from the New Testament. The loggia is sometimes called "Raphael's Bible". These charmingly fresh paintings include *Moses in the Bullrushes* **(18)**; *Building Noah's Ark* **(19)**; and *Creation of the Animals* **(20)**.

Sala dei Chiaroscuri e Cappella di Niccolò V (Chiaroscuro Rooms and Nicholas V's Chapel)

The rooms owe their name to the monochrome paintings of saints and apostles executed from Raphael's cartoons by his followers (1517). The paintings were restored in the late 16C.

Cappella di Niccolò V★★ (Nicholas V's Chapel)

The chapel is one of the oldest parts of the Vatican Palace. It probably formed part of a tower, which was absorbed into the first papal palace in the 13C. Nicholas V converted it to a chapel and had it decorated by **Fra Angelico** (1447–51), a Dominican monk and master of Florentine art. He was assisted by Benozzo Gozzoli, also from Florence.

In the angles are the Doctors of the Church; the Evangelists are on the ceiling. The two-tier wall paintings illustrate the lives of St Stephen and St Lawrence *(upper tier)* and were extensively restored in the 18C and 19C.

The **Life of St Stephen** is depicted in the upper level. On the right are two legendary episodes in the saint's life: being ordained deacon *(left)* by St Peter (whose figure shows great nobility); distributing alms *(right)*. Above the entrance door: preaching in a square in Florence *(left)* and addressing the Council *(right)*. On the left: the stoning of St Stephen.

The **Life of St Lawrence** is represented in the lower level. Sixtus II, resembling

Nicholas V, ordains St Lawrence as deacon. Above the door: St Lawrence receiving the treasure of the Church from Sixtus II and distributing alms to the poor. The portrayal of a blind man *(right)* is exceptional in the idealised art of the Renaissance. Left: the Roman Emperor Decius pointing to the instruments of torture; the saint's martyrdom.

▶ Leave Nicholas V's Chapel, return to the first Raphael Room (Borgo Fire). Pass through Urban VIII's Chapel and turn right to the Borgia Apartment.

Appartamento Borgia★ (Borgia Apartment)

These rooms, which formed the suite of Alexander VI, the Borgia pope from Spain, now house examples of modern art. They are decorated (end of 1492–94) with paintings by **Pinturicchio**, full of pleasant fantasy. The first, known as the **Sybilline Room (I)**, has figures of sybils and prophets. In the **Creed Room (III)** the prophets and apostles carry scrolls bearing the articles of the Creed.

Next is the **Liberal Arts Room (IV)**, probably Alexander VI's study. It is decorated with allegories of the seven subjects taught in medieval universities. The **Saints' Room (V)** was probably painted by Pinturicchio; elsewhere pupils assisted. The legendary lives of the saints are combined with mythology, a common practice in the Renaissance period. Facing the window is one of Pinturicchio's best works, St Catherine of Alexandria arguing with the philosophers, against his usual landscape of delicate trees, rocks and hills. In the centre is the Arch of Constantine. Before the emperor, St Catherine expounds her arguments in defence of the Christian faith. The vault is painted with mythological scenes.

The **Mysteries of the Faith Room (VI)** depicts the principal mysteries in the lives of Jesus and his mother. On the wall framing the entrance: the Resurrection; on the left: a very fine portrait of Alexander VI, in rapt adoration.

The **Pontiffs' Room (VII)** was used for official meetings. The ceiling, which

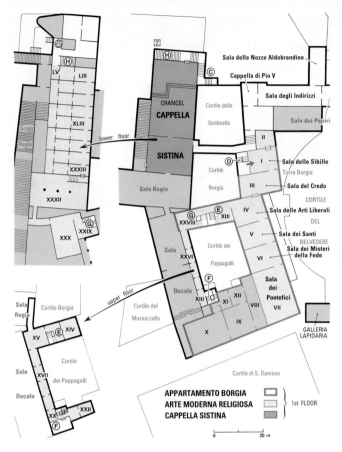

Sala delle Nozze Aldobrandine

Cappella di Pio V

Sala degli Indirizzi

Sala dei Papiri

CHANCEL
CAPPELLA

Cortile della
Sentinella

II

SISTINA

Cortile
Borgia

I — Sala delle Sibille
Torre Borgia

III — Sala del Credo

CORTILE

Sala Regia

IV — Sala delle Arti Liberali
DEL

XXVIII XIII

V — Sala dei Santi
BELVEDERE

VI — Sala dei Misteri
della Fede

Cortile dei
Pappagalli

Sala

XXVI

Sala
dei
Pontefici
VII

Ducale

XIII XI XII

VIII

IX

X

GALLERIA
LAPIDARIA

LV LIII

XLIII

Scala

Regia

XXXIII

XXXII

XXX XXIX

Sala
Regia

Cortile Borgia

lower floor

upper floor

Cortile del
Maresciallo

XV

XIV

Cortile
dei Pappagalli

XVII

Ducale

XXII

Sala

Cortile di S. Damaso

APPARTAMENTO BORGIA
ARTE MODERNA RELIGIOSA — 1st FLOOR
CAPPELLA SISTINA

0   20 m

collapsed in 1500 – narrowly missing Alexander VI – was reconstructed in the reign of Leo X and has stucco ornaments and "grotesques" by Perin del Vaga and Giovanni da Udine. At one time, the room was hung with portraits of the popes, hence its name.

Collezione d'Arte Moderna Religiosa★★

Some of the world's greatest artists mingle here.

On the upper floor, the **Chapel of Peace** by Giacomo Manzù (Room XIV) leads into a room devoted to Rouault (Room XV). Then follows a series of smaller rooms revealing traces of the 13C palace and containing works by **Chagall, Gauguin, Klee, Kandinsky**, Utrillo, Odilon Redon, Braque, Moore, Morandi, De Pisis, etc.

Downstairs in rooms partially beneath the Sistine Chapel gleams stained glass by Fernand Leger, Jacques Villon and George Meistermann.

There are several canvases by Ben Shahn, Jack Levine, Bernard Buffet, Yugoslavian naive paintings, sculptures by Marini, Lipchitz and Mirko, **Picasso** ceramics and Bazaine tapestries.

At the inauguration on 23 June 1973 Paul VI declared: "Even in our arid secu-larised world, there is still a prodigious capacity for expressing beyond the truly human what is religious, divine, Christian."

▶ Return to first floor for the Sistine Chapel (Staircase H).

Ceiling of the Sistine Chapel

© lexan/iStockphoto.com

FIRST FLOOR
Cappella Sistina★★★

Named after Pope Sixtus IV, the chapel was built from 1477–80. As well as being the papal palace chapel, it served a defensive role and boasts external crenellations.

The long chamber is lit by 12 windows. **Sixtus IV** sent for painters from Umbria and Florence to decorate the walls. His nephew **Julius II** (1503–13) commissioned Michelangelo to redecorate the ceiling (originally it depicted a starry sky). Twenty years later, the artist was again engaged by **Clement VII** and **Paul III** to paint the wall behind the altar. The chapel is not only the setting for the most solemn ceremonies of the Holy See, where the cardinals meet in conclave, but also a masterpiece of Renaissance art. Its dimensions – 40.23m/132ft long, 13.41m/44ft wide and 20.70m/68ft high – are exactly the same as those given in the Bible for Solomon's Temple.

Side Walls

Sixtus IV wanted to perpetuate the decorative tradition of the early Christian basilicas. The lowest section represents the curtains that hung between the columns of the old basilicas. Between the windows are portraits of the early popes from St Peter to Marcellus I (308–09). The figures of Christ and the first three popes were obliterated when the Last Judgement bloomed above the altar.

The paintings halfway up the walls depict parallel scenes in the lives of Moses and Jesus, showing human condition before and after the Messiah.

Life of Moses – *(South wall from the Last Judgement). Moses in Egypt* **(I)** by **Perugino** is followed by *Moses' Youth* **(II)** by **Botticelli**; the two female figures of Jethro's daughters show the more lyrical side of the artist's style. These are followed by *Crossing the Red Sea* **(III)** and *The Giving of the Tablets of the Law on Mount Sinai* **(IV)** by **Cosimo Rosselli**. In *The Punishment of Korah, Dathan and Abiram* **(V)**, for denying Moses' and Aaron's authority over the Jewish people, Botticelli set the scene against a background of Roman monuments: the Arch of Constantine and the Palatine Septizonium (*⚓ See FORO ROMANO–PALATINO*). *The Testament and Death of Moses* **(VI)** is by **Luca Signorelli**.

Life of Christ – *(North wall from the Last Judgement)*. The series begins with the *Baptism of Jesus* **(VII)** by **Perugino** and **Pinturicchio**, featuring many members of Sixtus IV's court. The next panel, *The Temptation of Christ* and *The Healing of the Leper* **(VIII)**, directly faces the papal throne; here **Botticelli** has given greater weight to the healing scene in deference to Sixtus IV, who had written a theological treatise on the subject; he also painted the Temple in Jerusalem to look like the Santo Spirito Hospital, which the pope reconstructed. The small scenes at the foot of the painting represent the

Temptation of Christ (left to right). The next is an illustration of *The calling of St Peter and St Andrew* **(IX)** by **Ghirlandaio**. In *The Sermon on the Mount* and *The Healing of the Leper* **(X)**, **Cosimo Rosselli**, assisted by Piero di Cosimo, made one of the first attempts to paint a sunset. *The Delivery of the Keys to St Peter* **(XI)** is a masterpiece by **Perugino**; the Arch of Constantine appears twice flanking the Temple in Jerusalem, as imagined by the artist. The final panel is *The Last Supper* **(XII)** by Rosselli: Judas is face to face with Jesus, apart from the other apostles.

Ceiling

When Julius II abandoned his project for a funerary sculpture, **Michelangelo** returned unhappily to Florence. In 1508, he was recalled to Rome by the pope, who asked him to paint the Twelve Apostles on the ceiling of the Sistine Chapel. The pope gave him a free hand and instead of the blue star-spangled vault (some 520m2/660sq ft), he created a masterpiece filled with powerful movement. The animated figures compose an epic of the creation of the world and the history of the human race. Julius II came regularly to ask Michelangelo when he would finish. From atop the scaffolding came the regular reply, "when I can".

On 14 August 1511, bursting with impatience, the pope insisted on seeing the fresco; he was overwhelmed. About a year later, it was finished.

From the Creation to the Flood –
Starting from the altar.
(1) *God divides the light from the darkness.*
(2) *Creation of the sun, the moon and plant life.*
(3) *God divides the waters from the earth and creates living creatures in the seas.*
(4) *Creation of Adam.*
(5) *Creation of Eve.*
(6) *Original sin and expulsion from the Garden of Eden.*
(7) *Noah's sacrifice*: contrary to biblical chronology, this scene precedes the flood. Michelangelo may have wanted to stress Noah's loyalty to God, thus justifying his ark salvation.

(8) *The Flood*: the first scene painted. Some figures are too small in proportion to their surroundings.
(9) *Noah's Drunkenness*: Noah is scorned by his son. Michelangelo pessimistically reminds us that life on earth began again under a bad omen.

The "Ignudi" (10) – Michelangelo frescoed these figures at each corner of the central panels. They glorify the human body. Modelled on classical sculptures, the *Ignudi* influenced many Renaissance and Mannerist artists.

Prophets and Sibyls – There is great variety in these 12 portraits: *Zacharias* **(11)**, the old man with a beard; *Joel* **(12)**, the critic; the *Erythraean Sibyl* **(13)**, not knowing where to begin her study; *Ezekiel* **(14)**, in earnest debate; the *Persian Sibyl* **(15)**, short-sighted and bowed with old age; *Jeremiah* **(16)** in his melancholy; *Jonah* **(17)**, symbol of Christ's Resurrection, ejected from the whale in a movement recalled by Baroque artists; the *Libyan Sibyl* **(18)**, her study completed, descending from her throne with gracefulness; *Daniel* **(19)**, inspired by a new idea; the *Cumaean sibyl* **(20)**, a muscle-bound giant apparently puz-

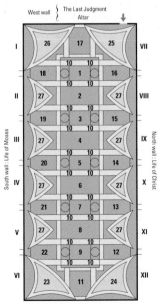

CAPPELLA SISTINA

zled by what she is reading; *Isaiah* **(21)**, troubled by an angel; the young *Delphic Sibyl* **(22)**.

Bible Stories – At the centre of these four scenes are the heroes of the Jewish people – David, Judith, Esther, Moses. Also *Judith and Holophernes* **(23)**, *David and Goliath* **(24)**, *the Punishment of Haman* **(25)** and *the Brazen Serpent* **(26)**.

Jesus' Forefathers (27) – Their names *(above the windows)* correspond to the scenes in the triangular sections. Jewish families wait for deliverance.

The Last Judgement

Twenty years after painting the ceiling, in 1534, **Michelangelo** was sent for by Clement VII to complete the decoration of the chapel. The pope, who had seen Rome sacked by Charles V's troops in 1527, wanted *The Last Judgement* to deliver its message boldly from above the altar as a warning to the unfaithful. Paul III took up his predecessor's idea and work began in 1535. The 15C frescoes were obliterated, as well as two panels in the series depicting Jesus's ancestors. When the fresco was unveiled on 31 October 1541, people were amazed and dumbfounded. Stamped with the mark of violence and anger, this striking work, with its mass of naked bodies writhing in a baleful light, is an expression of misfortune: Rome had been sacked in 1527; Luther's doctrine was dividing the western Church. In the 16C and 18C, the fresco was touched up. The austerity of the Counter-Reformation moved Pius IV to have the naked figures clothed by Daniele da Volterra; in all about 30 figures were clothed.

This fresco introduced a new style in the history of art, which led to the Baroque. The composition follows a strict scheme: the elect are welcomed on high by the angels *(left)* as the damned tumble headlong into hell *(right)*.

At the bottom *(left)* the dead slowly awake; in vain the devils try to restrain them. Above, the elect seem drawn by the movement of Christ's right hand. Beside the terrifying figure of Christ the Judge, the Virgin turns away from the horrific spectacle. Around them are the saints, bearing the instruments of their martyrdoms: St Andrew with his cross beside the Virgin, beneath them St Lawrence and his gridiron, St Bartholomew with his skin *(in its folds appears the distorted face of Michelangelo)*.

In his boat, Charon waits for the damned, whom he throws into the river of hell. Minos, the master of hell, his body wreathed by a snake *(in the corner)*, resembles Biagio da Cesena, the master of ceremonies at the papal court. The fresco as a whole is dominated by angels bearing the Cross, the Crown of Thorns, the Column and the other instruments of the Passion.

Pavement and Choir Screen

The chapel has a 15C Cosmati pavement. The choir screen and the choristers' gallery are by **Mino da Fiesole** (15C).

Biblioteca Apostolica★ (Vatican Library)

Cappella di San Pio V (Pius V's Chapel) – On display are the varied treasures of the Sancta Sanctorum, the private chapel of the popes in the Lateran Palace.

Sala degli Indirizzi (Room of the Addresses) – Secular items from the Roman and early Christian era are exhibited together with religious items from the Middle Ages to the present day.

Sala delle Nozze Aldobrandine (Aldobrandini Marriage Room) – A fresco from the Augustan period depicts wedding preparations *(centre wall)*.

Museo Sacro (Sacred Museum) – Founded in 1756 by Benedict XIV, it contains early Christian antiquities.

Sale Sistine (Sistine Rooms) – Beyond the Gallery of Urban VIII, with its instruments of astronomy and *mappa mundi*, are the Sistine Rooms, created by Sixtus V (1585–90) to hold archives.

Salone Sistino★ (Sistine Salon) – *Used for temporary exhibitions*. The salon was built in 1587 by Sixtus V and was the reading room of the Vatican Library. The Mannerist decoration by Cesare Nebbia shows episodes of Sixtus V's Papacy, the history of books, the Councils of the Church and the inventors of the alphabet *(on the pillars)*. It contains 17C cupboards painted in the 19C.

The Vatican Library is followed by the Pauline Rooms, created by Paul V.

Next come the Alexandrine Room, created by Alexander VIII (1690), and the **Clementine Gallery**, commissioned by Clement XII. Next is the **Profane Museum**, which was founded in 1767 by Clement XIII (Etruscan, Roman and medieval artefacts).

Pinacoteca★★★ (Picture Gallery)

Italian Primitives – *Room I.* The 12C *Last Judgement* **(1)**, painted on wood, exemplifies the Roman School and is very similar to Byzantine art.

Giotto and his School – *Room II.*
The **Stefaneschi Triptych (2)** is named after the cardinal who commissioned it and was executed by **Giotto**, no doubt with the assistance of his pupils, in 1315. It was intended originally for the high altar of Constantine's Basilica.

Florentine School: Fra Angelico and his pupil Benozzo Gozzoli, Filippo Lippi – *Room III.* These artists are among the great 15C painters. Fra Angelico's (1400–55) slightly old-fashioned style, which links him to the Middle Ages, nonetheless expresses his deep religious feeling, as the small painting of the *Virgin and Child with Saints and Angels* **(3)** demonstrates; the two *scenes from the Life of St Nicholas of Bari* **(4)** come from an altarpiece predella. The *Coronation of the Virgin* **(5)** is by **Filippo Lippi** (1406–69) and *St Thomas Receiving the Virgin's Girdle* **(6)** by Benozzo Gozzoli (1420–97).

Melozzo da Forlì (1438–94) – *Room IV.*
The graceful **Musical Angels (7)**, with their bright colours, elegant curls and delicate features, are remarkable. They are fragments of a fresco depicting the *Ascension of Christ* from the basilica of the Holy Apostles *(Santi Apostoli)*. The fresco (transferred to canvas) of *Sixtus IV and Platina the Librarian* **(8)** adorned the pope's library.

Polyptychs – *Room VI. The Virgin and Child* **(9)** is by **Carlo Crivelli** (1430–93), a Venetian. While the Florentines were

Restoring the Chapel

This vast undertaking, carried out by Italian experts and financed by Japanese patrons, took 18 years to complete. Twelve (1980–92) were spent on Michelangelo's frescoes. Most of the restoration work consisted of cleaning the frescoes, darkened by dust and candle smoke, with a mixture of bicarbonate of soda and ammonium. After 500 years, Michelangelo's original colours – ranging from bright orange, clear pink, pale green to brilliant yellow and turquoise – sparkle gloriously.

experimenting with line, the Venetians were taking an interest in colour. In addition, Crivelli had a marked taste for gold decoration *(very beautiful painted fabrics)*.

15C Umbrian School – *Room VII. The Virgin and Child* **(10)** by **Perugino** and the Coronation of the Virgin **(11)** by Pinturicchio illustrate the clear and poetic style of the Umbrian artists.

Room VIII: Raphael★★★ (1483–1520) – The artistic development of the painter of the Stanze is illustrated by three works. The *Coronation of the Virgin* **(12)**, painted in 1503 has a youthful freshness and shows the influence of Perugino. The *Madonna of Foligno* **(13)** was painted in 1511–12 while Raphael was in Rome at the height of his glory; the fine portrait of Sigismondo dei Conti, on his knees, which dominates the picture, the exquisite pose of the Virgin and the luminosity surrounding her are the work of a master. The *Transfiguration* **(14)**, with its dramatic contrasts in chiaroscuro, was intended for Narbonne Cathedral in France and was completed by Raphael shortly before he died in 1520.

Room IX – With his *St Jerome★★* **(15)** **Leonardo da Vinci** (1452–1519) shows his mastery of anatomy, expression and light. The picture was reassembled from two pieces, one found in an antique shop and the other at a shoemaker's.

The **Pietà (16)** by the Venetian **Giovanni Bellini** (1429–c. 1516) combines accurate drawing with fine tonality.

Room X – In his *Madonna of San Nicola dei Frari* **(17)** Titian uses the marvellous Venetian palette. The *Coronation of the Virgin* **(18)**, by Giulio Romano *(upper part)* and Francesco Penni *(lower part),* shows the Mannerist style.

In Veronese's *Sant'Elena* **(19)** the saint is depicted in an unusual position, with her hand supporting her head.

Mannerists – *Room XI.* The works include *Rest on the Flight into Egypt* **(20)** by **Federico Barocci** (1528–1612), as delicate and luminous as a pastel.

Caravaggio and his followers – *Room XII.* The *Descent from the Cross*★★ **(21)** by **Caravaggio** (1573–1610) clearly expresses the painter's reaction to Mannerist sentimentality. His characters, even in the most religious scenes, are drawn from life. The firmness of his line and the way the light falls further

emphasise his realism (note how Nicodemus and St John hold the body of the dead Christ). Mary Magdalen, her head bowed, is a truly remarkable figure. Caravaggio had a great influence on the French painter **Valentin** (1594–1632) – *Martyrdom of St Processus and St Martinian* **(22)**. **Guido Reni** (1575–1642) was also inspired – *Crucifixion of St Peter* **(23)**.

Rooms XIII–XIV – These rooms contain works from the 17C and 18C, particularly by **Pietro da Cortona**, the great Baroque artist. Note the portrait of Clement IX **(24)** by Carlo Maratta (1625–1713).

Musei Gregoriano Profano e Cristiano★

A modern building begun in 1963 houses the **Profane** and **Christian Museums**, opened in 1970. It contains the Museum of Antique Art assembled by Gregory XVI (1831–46) and the Museum of Christian Art founded in 1854 by Pius IX.

Gregorian Profane Museum

It is divided into four sections: Imperial copies, 1–2C Roman statues; sarcophagi and 2–3C Roman sculpture. The modern materials – metal, concrete and wood – provide an ideal setting for the exhibits, which can be viewed from all sides.

Among the major pieces are the **Cancelleria Reliefs★**. One sculpture shows Vespasian's arrival in Rome after his election to the Imperial throne. The other shows his son Domitian's departure on a campaign. When the Senate banned memorials of Domitian, his head was with that of his successor, Nerva.

Mosaics from Baths of Caracalla★ – *Visible from the Christian Museum.* They date from the 3C and show the figures of athletes, gladiators and their trainers.

Christian Museum *(up Staircase I)*

Statue of the Good Shepherd – It is heavily restored and probably dates from the 3C. The Christian artist adapted the pagan image of a shepherd offering his finest animal to the gods.

Sarcophagi – Christian artists decorated the sarcophagi with garlands, baskets and *putti*, using the pagan motifs to

PINACOTECA

Cortile della Pinacoteca

which they added the symbolic themes of sheep – Christ's flock, vine branches – symbol of union with God through the Eucharist, etc.

▶ Take staircase K.

Museo Missionario-Etnologico (Missionary-Ethnological Museum)

Founded in 1927 by Pius XI, it was first housed in the Lateran Palace, but moved into ultra-modern premises in the Vatican during Paul VI's reign. Items include illustrations of the great world religions (Buddhism, Hinduism, Islam) and Christian artefacts designed in ethnic styles from every continent except Europe.

▶ Take staircase L.

Museo delle Carrozze (Carriage Museum)

The museum, opened in 1973 in an underground chamber, displays the first "popemobile".

VATICAN CITY AND GARDENS

The Bell Arch (Arco delle Campane) leads into Piazza dei Protomartiri Romani, which sits more or less in the centre of the Circus of Caligula and Nero, where many early Christians were martyred. A black stone with a white border marks the former site of the obelisk, now in St Peter's Square. On the left is the German and Dutch burial ground, which legend insists has earth brought from Jerusalem. Next, on the left, comes the church dedicated to St Stephen, where Charlemagne spent the night before being crowned in 800. After the **Mosaic School** (Scuola del Mosaico) are buildings where the Vatican State is administered.

The tour finishes with a view of the dome of St Peter's, designed by Michelangelo, rising majestically above the magnificent **gardens★★★**; the fountains and statues are gifts from various countries. Pius IV's "Casina" is a charming 16C building decorated with paintings and stucco-work.

ADDRESSES

TAKING A BREAK

Vatican Museums – Choose one of two caffes at ground level with sidewalk tables: in Corte della Pigna or another by the carriages. Now you can even order a bottle of Italian wine or Champagne with your meal.

Gelateria dei Gracchi – *Via dei Gracchi 272.* ℘*06 32 16 668.* 🄳. This small gelateria serves excellent artisanal ice cream and *granita* using quality ingredients.

Franchi Gastronomia – *Via Cola di Rienzo 200-204. Prati district. 7:30am–9pm. Closed Sun.* ℘*06 68 65 564. www.franchi.it.* One of Rome's best, this fine gourmet shop/*rosticceria* serves delicious hot and cold food to take away. Perfect for a picnic along the Tiber.

🍽/EAT

Giacomelli – *Via Emilio Faà di Bruno 25,* ℘*06 37 25 910.* A famous pizzeria where you can try a number of traditional Italian pies, all served on typical stainless steel platters.

L'Arcangelo – *Via Giuseppe Gioacchino Belli 59.* ℘*06 32 10 992.* Stop in here for superlative supplì (traditional fried Roman antipasti), your introduction to a range of retooled traditional Roman dishes.

Taverna Angelica – *Piazza Amerigo Capponi 6,* ℘*06 68 74 514. www.tavern aangelica.it. Sun also lunch.* An intimate ambience and friendly service add to this restaurant's draw – along with house specials, such as calamari and fillet of sea bass with potato souffle.

BARS

Il Sorpasso – *Via Properzio 31-33.* ℘*06 89 02 45 54.* This casual wine bar offers simple, tasty fare plus a good wine selection. It draws a lively, local clientele.

SHOPPING

Shops selling religious articles are mostly located on Via della Conciliazione, along with general souvenir shops.

Villa Adriana, Tivoli
© AZemdega/iStockphoto.com

Lago di Bracciano★★

39km/24mi northwest of Rome

North of Rome, Lake Bracciano occupies a series of craters in the Sabatini Mountains (Monti Sabatini), not far from Viterbo. The peaceful scenery makes this spot a popular getaway for Romans. A boat service plies the lake, allowing visitors to explore the villages with their charming old houses and narrow alleyways. At nightfall, rustling reeds and lapping water provide a welcome contrast to the noise and traffic of the capital.

Lago di Bracciano is of volcanic origin, like the lakes at Castelli Romani. The eighth largest lake in Italy, it produces a fairly rich variety of fish including pike, eel, carp and *latterino*, a local fish. In AD 109, Trajan built an aqueduct (30km/19mi long) to carry water to Trastevere in Rome.

 DRIVING TOUR

36km/22mi

Anguillara-Sabazia★

The village is set on a rocky promontory (185m/607ft above sea level). Access to this medieval town is through an impressive 16C gate decorated with a clock. Opposite is Via Umberto I, which climbs to the top of the village. Immediately after the gate is a small belvedere *(left)* that has a fountain containing eels. A flight of steps *(left)* leads to the 18C Collegiate Church of the Assumption *(Collegiata dell'Assunta)*: from the small square stretches a magnificent **view** across the lake. Narrow but enchanting streets lead down to the lake.

▷ On leaving the town, turn left after the garden into Via Trevignanese.

- **Michelin Map:** 563, P 18.
- **Location:** By bus (COTRAL): departure from Via Lepanto. By train (FS): departure from Ostiense, Termini or Tiburtina Stations. By car: take S 2 (Via Cassia), direction Viterbo; after crossing the Rome ring road (Grande Raccordo Anulare) and passing through Giustiniana, bear left towards Bracciano–Anguillare; after about 7.5km/5mi bear right in Osteria Nuova into Via Anguillarese to Anguillara-Sabazia.
- **Kids:** The military aerospace museum at Vigna di Valle.

Trevignano Romano

This characteristic village has developed around an outcrop of basalt beside the lake. For an extraordinary view, take a walk along the lakeside at sunset. The medieval town extends along the lake shore like a fishbone and climbs the hill, crowned by the ruins of the Orsini Rock (Rocca degli Orsini). From Via Umberto I *(right)*, the road climbs to the church of the Assumption and its frescoes inspired by the School of Raphael. Beyond the clock tower in Piazza Vittorio Emanuele III is the town hall *(right)* with its 16C door.

▷ Take Via IV Novembre to Bracciano.

Bracciano★

All the main streets converge on Piazza 1 Maggio. On the right is the town hall in Piazzetta IV Novembre. To the left Via Umberto I leads to Piazza Mazzini, where there is a splendid view of the cylindrical towers of the impressive **Orsini-Odescalchi Castle** (*see below*).
Castello Orsini-Odescalchi★★★ – *Piazza Mancini 14.* ⊙*Open Mar–Oct Mon–Fri 10am–6pm, Sat and Sun and holidays 10am–7pm (rest of the*

year Mon–Fri til 5pm, Sat-Sun til 6pm). €8.50, children €6 (ages 6-12); Sat, Sun and holidays guided tours (1hr). For more information, visit the website. 06 99 80 43 48 (museum) or 06 99 80 23 79. www.odescalchi.it.

The castle was originally built around the medieval Rock of the Prefects of Vico, who governed till the 13C. It passed to the Orsini family in 1419.

Six impressive cylindrical – but somewhat irregular towers – mark the outer limits of the castle, which was built almost entirely of lava rock atop volcanic tufa. Two walls surround the monument and the medieval township.

Interior★ – A spiral staircase leads up to the first rooms on the main floor. **Room I** (library): Pope Sixtus V stayed there in 1481, fleeing the plague in Rome. The ceiling fresco is by Taddeo Zuccari. **Room III**: interesting original coffered ceiling. **Room VII**: a bust of *Paolo Giordano II Orsini* by **Bernini** and a bust of *Isabella de' Medici* by one of Bernini's pupils. **Room XVII**: room leading to a loggia with a magnificent view of the old rock.

The **Sentry Walk** (Cammino di Ronda) connects the towers (another glorious panorama here). Steps then lead down to the charming **Central Courtyard★** (Cortile Centrale) with its double doors and external staircase made of lava.

▶ Return to Piazza Mazzini and turn left into Via della Collegiata.

In the square beyond the archway is **St Stephen's Church**, once inside the Rock of the Prefects. Walk through the old town's narrow, picturesque streets.

▶ From Bracciano go to Anguillara-Sabazia. After about 5km, turn to Vigna di Valle.

⚇ Museo Storico dell'Aeronautica

Airport "Luigi Bourlot", Vigna di Valle. Open Tue–Sun 9am–5pm (til 4pm in winter). Closed 1 Jan, Easter and 25 Dec. Free entrance. 06 99 88 75 09/8. www.aeronautica.difesa.it.

The **Aerospace Museum** explores the history of flight via photographs, weapons, uniforms and shining ranks of restored planes.

▶ Take Via Agostino Fausti and then Via Braccianese to return to Rome.

ADDRESSES

⚇STAY

Campeggi – Pleasant, well-equipped lakeside camping sites. Starting from Bracciano and moving clockwise: Camping Porticciolo, Camping Azzurro, Camping Roma Flash, Camping Village Lago di Bracciano, Camping Smeraldo, Parco del Lago Glamping & Lodges, Camping Vigna di Valle. All campsites offer lodgings, chalets, bungalows and mobilehomes.

⚇⚇⚇⚇ **Relais I Due Laghi** – *Via della Marmotta, Le Cerque, 3km/2mi northeast of Anguillara Sabazia.* 06 99 60 70 59. www.iduelaghi.it. 24 rooms. ⌐. This attractive hotel offers country-house style, comfort and luxury in a rustic atmosphere, with a hint of Etruscan influence in its architecture and a swimming pool. The gentle hills and pasture surrounding the hotel provide a bucolic backdrop for horseriding and drag hunting.

⚇/EAT

Acquarella – *Via Acquarella 4, Trevignano Romano.* 06 69 98 53 61. www.ristoranteacquarella.it. Closed Tue. Enjoy traditional dishes. Fresh ingredients, capably prepared: simply a good meal.

La Grotta Azzurra – *Piazza Vittorio Emanuele III 4, Trevignano Romano.* 06 99 99 420. Closed Tue, 25 Dec. This restaurant serves traditional, homemade dishes. In summer, meals are served in the garden, overlooking the lake.

La Posta de Cavalieri – *Via della Marmotta, Le Cerque, Anguillara Sabazia.* 06 99 60 70 59. www.iduelaghi.it. Enjoy imaginative dishes in this elegant country eatery, which also offers attractive outdoor dining in summer. It offers fish from the lake, meat and cheeses that are produced by the restaurant.

Castelli Romani★★

About 35km/ 22mi southeast of Rome

This attractive region of gently rolling hills, old villages and volcanic lakes is a popular weekend destination. The landscape is dotted with fine 17C mansions and graced with magnificent gardens, ponds and fountains, and a Greek-Orthodox abbey. The "Castelli" are in the Alban Hills (Colli Albani), also volcanic in origin. They form a circle whose circumference is the edge of an immense burnt-out crater. Meadows and sweet chestnut trees spread up the hillsides; the lower slopes are covered with shady olive groves and lush vineyards that produce the area's famous wines.

- **Michelin Map:** 563, Q 19–20.
- **Location:** A car is the easiest way to get to – and around – the area, but most villages mentioned are also accessible by train from Termini Station, or by bus (COTRAL) from Anagnina, the last station on Metro line A.
- **Don't Miss:** The strawberries of Nemi, Rocca di Papa, the Palazzo Chigi and roast pork of Aricca, the papal palace at Castel Gandolfo.
- **Timing:** Allow one day.

A BIT OF HISTORY

The history of the Alban Hills is linked to that of Rome. Cicero and the Emperors Tiberius, Nero and Galba had country houses here. Cato the Censor was born near Tuscolo in 234 BC. During the Middle Ages, the region southeast of Rome became known as the *Castelli Romani*, or "Roman Fortresses". While anarchy reigned in Rome, the noble families sought refuge. Thirteen outlying villages were fortified: Frascati, Grottaferrata, Marino, Castel Gandolfo, Albano, Ariccia, Genzano, Nemi, Rocca di Papa, Rocca Priora, Monte Compatri, Monte Porzio Catone and Colonna.

🚗 DRIVING TOUR

122km/76mi. One day.

From Rome take Via Tuscolana S 215 (exit 21 on Michelin map 563). After crossing the GRA (ring road) continue to Frascati.

On the outskirts of Rome, the route passes **Cinecittà**, the Italian equivalent of Hollywood. The studios at Cinecittà are open to the public.

Cinecittà Studios★

Via Tuscolana 1055. Exhibit open daily (except Tue) 9:30am–6:30pm; english guided tours (€15) with visits to the sets included) at 11:30am and 3:15pm. Closed 1 Jan, 24 and 25 Dec. 06 72 29 32 69. www.cinecittasimostra.it.

These studios, set amid 40ha/99 acres of umbrella pines, include 22 stages, 300 dressing rooms, 21 makeup stations and a huge outdoor tank. Fascist-era Deco style buildings prevail. Among the movies filmed here were *Ben-Hur, La Dolce Vita, Fellini's Casanova,* Zeffirelli's *Romeo and Juliet, and* Mel Gibson's *The Passion of Christ.* The exhibit features props and costumes including those worn by Elizabeth Taylor in *Cleopatra* and Cameron Diaz in *Gangs of New York.* The guided tour generally includes a visit to the set of the former BBC series *Rome.*

Frascati★

Antiquity's affluent and insouciant youth loafed here. From the main square, Piazza G. Marconi, sprawls an extensive view downhill as far as Rome.Frascati has gained a reputation for white wine and 16C and 17C villas, especially **Villa Aldobrandini★**, set high above its ter-

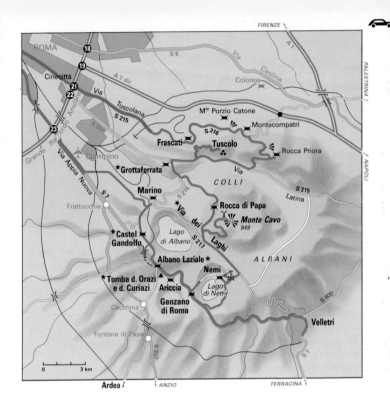

races, clipped avenues, fountains and rockeries *(Via Cardinal Massaia 18. Gardens, nymphaeum and terrace are freely accessible Mon-Fri 9am-5pm: booking required at ☏06 94 22 560; www.aldo-brandini.it).*

▶ From Piazza G. Marconi, drive to Ville Tuscolane and Monte Porzio Catone.

The road offers a good view of **Monte Compatri** and **Monte Porzio Catone** as it climbs up to **Rocca Priora,** which clings to the north rim of the crater.

▶ Continue downhill; turn right into Via Latina; after 4km/2.5mi turn right to Tuscolo (no sign) into a winding road leading to the ruins.

Tuscolo

It was in his villa in Ancient Tusculum that Cicero set his series of philosophical treatises known as the *Tusculanes.*

The city was once the fief of the counts of Tusculum; from 10C-12C this powerful family owned most of the Castelli and extended its power as far as Rome, also providing several Popes. Tusculum was destroyed in 1191 in an engagement with the Romans and never rebuilt. A few traces survive: up the slope to the left near the large cross, now half hidden in the trees on what was once the citadel, are ruins of a small theatre, with the remains of a water cistern at the back.

▶ Return downhill; turn right into Via Latina. In Grottaferrata take Corso del Popolo (main street).

Grottaferrata

In 1004, Greek monks settled in the ruins of a Roman villa, once perhaps owned by Marcus Tullius Cicero.

Abbazia★ – The fortresslike **abbey** rises at the end of the main street. In the castle's courtyard is a bronze statue of St Nilus. The large doorway opens onto

Nemi

a courtyard flanked by the church of St Mary of Grottaferrata (♨ *See below*) and the Sangallo Doorway. The small **museum** is housed in the rooms previously occupied by the commendatory cardinals. On display are Roman and Greek finds and paintings from the Old Testament from the church's central nave. One room is decorated with frescoes by Francesco da Siena in 1547. **Santa Maria di Grottaferrata★** – *Second castle terrace*. In the narthex *(on the left)* is a marble font (10C). The Byzantine-style doorway is carved with animals and leaves. St Nilus' Chapel *(right)* has a 17C coffered ceiling and is adorned with frescoes (1608–10) by Domenichino. In the right aisle is the *cripta ferrata*, the villa room converted for Christian worship (5C).

▶ Turn left into Viale San Nilo; after the lights, turn right into Via Roma.

Rocca di Papa

The village fans out on a picturesque **site★** on the slopes of Monte Cavo, facing the Alban lakes and hills. It lies at the heart of hunting country and known for rabbit dishes *(coniglio alla cacciatora)*.

▶ Before Via dei Laghi, turn left to Monte Cavo, surmounted by TV masts.

Monte Cavo

Alt 949m/3 114ft.
Huge paving stones remain from the ancient Sacred Way leading to the Temple of Jupiter atop Monte Cavo. Here the Latin League met. In the 4C BC, Rome defeated the other cities and set her cap on the peninsula. From the square is a fine **view★**.

▶ Return downhill; turn left and left again into S 217, Via dei Laghi.

Via dei Laghi★

This is a beautiful road winding between oak and sweet chestnut woods.

▶ After 3.5km/5.5mi turn right to Nemi.

Nemi

The village occupies a charming **site★★** in a natural amphitheatre on the steep slopes of a crater now filled by Lake Nemi. One tower of the Ruspoli Castle still stands, the only trace of the medieval *castello*. In June, delicious wild strawberries are served in Nemi.

▶ Drive towards the lake.

Lago di Nemi (Lake Nemi) – The road down passes through fields of daisies, poppies and strawberries. The lake is called "Diana's Mirror" because it reflects the sacred wood next to the Temple of Diana. In 1929 the water level was lowered to recover two ancient boats (AD 37–41).
They were burnt during WWII; a few charred remains are in the **museum** *(Via del Tempio di Diana 13.* ♿ ⏱*Open*

Mon–Sun 9am–7pm; 🕐*closed 1 Jan, 1 May and 25 Dec;* ✆€3; ☎*06 93 98 040).*

▶ Continue on Via dei Laghi to Velletri.

Velletri
The town has been prominently involved in Italian history: it resisted Joachim Murat, was captured by Fra Diavolo, the Calabrian brigand chief, was fought over by the troops of Garibaldi and Naples and damaged by bombardments during the Second World War. It is now a prosperous modern town on the south-facing slope of a crater in the Alban Hills, at the centre of a wine-producing region.
The imposing 14C **Torre del Trivio** rises from the main square, Piazza Cairoli.

▶ From Velletri drive to Ariccia.

Ariccia
The main square, with its two fountains, bears the styling of **Bernini**. The **church of the Assumption** on the left *(south side)* is elegantly flanked by two porticoes *(the circular interior, capped by a dome, is worth a visit)*. However, this town is most famous for its roasted suckling pig *(porchetta)*.

▶ Stop on the outskirts of Ariccia.

Tomba degli Orazi e dei Curiazi★ (Tomb of the Horatii and the Curiatii)
At the entrance to Albano, on the left, over a wall and below the level of the road.
Said to be the tomb of the legendary Horatii and Curiatii brothers, This late Republic monument is made of huge blocks of volcanic peperine.

ALBANO LAZIALE
The town probably derives its name from Domitian's Villa Albana. Monuments to note include the brick church of **Santa Maria della Rotonda★** *(take Via Cavour, turn right into Via A. Saffi, then left into Via della Rotonda)*, a converted *nymphaeum*, with a Romanesque bell-

tower (13C). The town has also preserved part of an old Roman gate, the **Porta Pretoria** *(return to Via Cavour, then turn into Via A. de Gasperi)*. A public garden, **Villa Comunale★** *(Piazza Mazzini)*, cradles vestiges of Pompey's villa.

▶ Continue to Castel Gandolfo.

Castel Gandolfo★
On the edge of a crater, now Lake Albano, stands Castel Gandolfo, famous as the pope's summer residence .
Alba Longa – The oldest town in Latium was founded, according to legend, c. 1150 BC. Its rivalry with Rome led to the famous battle between the Horatii and the Curiatii. *(*🕐*See APPIA ANTICA).*
Papal Villa – ⚬━*Not open to the public.* In 1628, **Urban VIII** commissioned **Maderno** to build on the site of Domitian's earlier villa (81–96 AD), which had extended as far as Albano Laziale. The Vatican Observatory (Specola Vaticana) was established here in Pius XI's reign.

Lake Albano★
A lovely **view★** unfolds from a terrace at the entrance to the village.

▶ Continue north; turn right into S 7, Via Appia Nuova. In Frattochie, detour south (30km/19mi) to Ardea.

Ardea
The town stands on tufa rock. Remains of the city walls, in the form of square blocks of tufa, can still be seen.

▶ The museum is 100m/110yd after the junction with Via Laurentina.

Museo della Raccolta Manzù★★
(Manzù Collection). ♿🕐*Open Tue–Sun 9am–7:30pm and every fourth Sunday of the month.* 🕐*Closed 1 Jan and 25 Dec. Free entrance.* ☎*06 91 35 022. www.polomusealelazio.beniculturali.it.* Most of the work belongs to the artist's mature period (1950–1970), when he reworked some of themes of his earlier years. The 462 items include sculpture, drawings, engravings and jewellery.

▷ Take Via Laurentina, S 148, to return to Rome.

ADDRESSES

☖ EAT

Il Torchio – *Frascati, Via G. Mameli 3.* ✆*06 94 25 520, 347 73 89 289, or 338 92 62 516. Closed Mon–Tue. www.torchioristorante.com.* A special place: fresh local products, respect for biodiversity and ecocompatible consumption are the main points of the philosophy of this restaurant.

Cacciani – *Via Armando Diaz 13, Frascati.* ✆*06 94 01 991 or 06 94 20 378. Closed Mon, Sun diner. www.cacciani.it.* Beautiful view over the Albini hills which you can enjoy from the terrace, where you can eat in summer, a classic establishment in the local area; seasonal local fish dishes.

Il Grottino – *Via Saponara 2, Castel Gandolfo.* ✆*06 93 61 413. www.ristorante ilgrottino.net.* This restaurant is situated in the upper part of town with a panoramic dining room overlooking the lake. It serves generous portions and offers excellent value for money. Fish and seafood specialities.

Ostia Antica★★

24km/15mi southwest of Rome

The best-preserved Roman ruins outside Pompeii, this archaeological site lies near the coast, amid umbrella pines and cypress trees. Wander the ruined streets of Rome's old port, admiring temples, pubs, baths, blocks of flats and the vast main square. The long grey sandy beach at **Ostia Lido**, the nearest to Rome, stretches to the south of the river mouth.

A BIT OF HISTORY

Ostia, where the Tiber once met the sea, takes its name from the Latin *"ostium"* – mouth. According to Virgil, Aeneas disembarked here. Livy says the fourth king of Rome "extended his dominion to the sea, founded Ostia at the mouth of the Tiber and established salt pans all around". Archaeologists however, place its origins in the 4C BC, but also admit that an earlier village of salt extractors may have existed. Ostia was a military port when Rome embarked on her conquest of the Mediterranean and a commercial port when the victorious city established an organised trade.
Nothing medieval remains except the 15C **castle**, built by Cardinal Giuliano della Rovere (Julius II). ◔*Open Sat, Sun and hols 9:30am-6:30pm.*

⌚ **Michelin Map:** 563, Q 18 .
▷ **Location:** Access by car: along Via del Mare; by underground: (Metro Line B), direction Laurentina to Magliana and then by train to Ostia Antica.

EVOLUTION OF A PORT

Roman control of the mouth of the Tiber – set at c. 335 BC – corresponds with her expansion in the Mediterranean. Several years earlier, the Romans had won their first naval victory at Antium. During the war against Pyrrhus (278 BC), the fleet sent by Carthage to assist the Romans docked in Ostia. During the Punic Wars (264–41 BC and 218–01 BC), Ostia served as an arsenal; Scipio's army embarked here for Spain (217 BC) to prevent reinforcements reaching Hannibal, who had already crossed the Alsps and defeated Flaminius at Lake Trasimeno. Two years later, about 30 ships set sail from Ostia for Tarentum, which was planning an alliance with Hannibal. In 211 BC, Publius Cornelius Scipio (known as Scipio Africanus Major) took ship for Spain to avenge the defeat of his ancestors. Barely 25 years old and exceptionally invested with proconsular power, he covered himself with glory.

The commercial port – At first there was simply a castle *(castrum)* to protect the port from pirates, but by the 1C BC Ostia had become a real town. In 79 BC, Sulla built a rampart around three sides, using the Tiber to protect the fourth. The last bend in the river was then further east, so the river flowed in a straight course along the town's north flank. Rome imported food from her numerous overseas provinces. A cargo of wheat from Sardinia was unloaded in Ostia as early as 212 BC. Protection was essential. The efforts of Pompey in 67 BC and of Agrippa from 63–12 BC had rid the sea of pirates. Only the problem of entering port remained: frequent strong winds restricted access to the summer months and the adjacent coastline consisted of dunes, lagoons and shallows. As a result, the merchant ships usually docked in the Neapolitan ports and the goods had to be carried overland to the capital.

Claudian Harbour – In antiquity, the shoreline ran parallel to the west side of the excavated site. They sited the harbour on the right bank of the river *(roughly the site of Leonardo da Vinci Airport)*. It covered about 70ha/173 acres and was protected by two breakwaters with an artificial island between.

Trajan's Harbour – When the Claudian Harbour became too small, Trajan (98–117) built a second one inland. It was hexagonal in shape, covered 30ha/74 acres and was lined with docks and warehouses. It was joined to the Claudian Harbour by a broad channel and to the Tiber by a canal (Fossa Trajana).

DECLINE AND EXCAVATION

Like Rome, Ostia began to decline in the 4C. The harbours silted up and malaria depopulated the town. Ostia suffered the fate of all Roman ruins and was pillaged for materials. Regular excavations have been undertaken since 1909; the western sectors of the town were excavated from 1938–42.

Between the town and the harbour the **necropolis of Trajan's Harbour** was discovered on the Sacred Island (Isola Sacra), which had been created by digging the Fiumicino channel. Since antiquity, the land has advanced several miles towards the sea.

LIFE IN OSTIA

Ostia was a very busy commercial town and under the empire its population rose to 100 000. Its main streets were lined with shops; administrative buildings clustered around the forum; warehouses and industrial premises were concentrated near the Tiber; the residential districts extended towards the seashore.

The cosmopolitan citizens welcomed a variety of overseas religions. Several

Ruins of the Forum and Capitolium, Ostia Antica

© Judy Edelhoff/Michelin

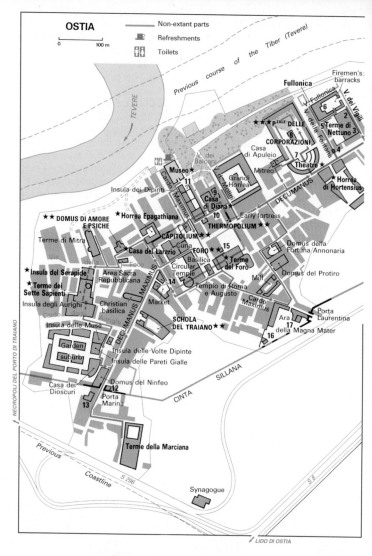

OSTIA

0 —— 100 m

—— Non-extant parts
🍴 Refreshments
🚻 Toilets

Previous course of the Tiber (Tevere)

TEVERE

Previous course of the Tiber (Tevere)

Firemen's barracks

V. dei Vigili

Fullonica / Fullonica

★★ P.ZALE
DELLE
CORPORAZIONI 8

6
5 **Terme di Nettuno** 3
2
4

Casa di Apuleio
Mitreo

V. delle Fontana

7
★ **Theatre**

Casa dei Balconi

V. dei

🚻🚻

★ **Museo**
11

Grandi Horrea

DECUMANUS

★ **Horrea di Hortensius**

Insula dei Dipinti

Cardo Maximus

9
★ **Casa di Diana** ★
10

Early fortress

★★ **DOMUS DI AMORE E PSICHE**

★ **Horrea Epagathiana**

CAPITOLIUM ★★

THERMOPOLIUM ★★

Domus della Fortuna Annonaria

Terme di Mitra

★ **Casa del Larario**

FORO ★★
15
Curia
Basilica
★ **Terme del Foro**

Via dei Molini

★ **Insula del Serapide**

Area Sacra Repubblicana

Circular Temple
14

Tempio di Roma e Augusto

Mill
Domus del Protiro

★ **Terme dei Sette Sapienti**

Insula degli Aurighi

Christian basilica

DECUMANUS MAXIMUS

Market

Cardo Maximus

Porta Laurentina

Ara della Magna Mater
17

SCHOLA DEL TRAIANO ★★

16

NECROPOLI DEL PORTO DI TRAIANO

Insula delle Muse

Garden suburb

Insula delle Volte Dipinte
Insula delle Pareti Gialle

SILLANA

Casa dei Dioscuri

Domus del Ninfeo
12

CINTA

13

Porta Marina

S 296

Previous Coastline

Terme della Marciana

S. 8

Synagogue

LIDO DI OSTIA

places of worship have been discovered: the oriental cults of the Great Mother (Cybele), of Isis and Serapis, of Jupiter Dolichenus and particularly of Mithras. Christianity, too, had its adherents.

Ostia houses – The most common dwelling in this densely populated town was the **insula**, a block of flats to let, several storeys high. Wealthier citizens lived in a **domus**, a detached house with a courtyard and garden.

All the buildings were of brick and probably unrendered. Some have elegant

entrances framed by a triangular pediment resting on two pillars. Here and there, a porch or a balcony adds interest to the street front. Sometimes the brickwork is finished with a decorative effect. **Opus reticulatum** is the technique most frequently used: small squares of dark tufa and lighter limestone are laid on edge to form a net pattern. This technique was practised from the 1C BC to the 2C AD. Later the corners were sometimes reinforced with courses of brick. Another technique used in Ostia,

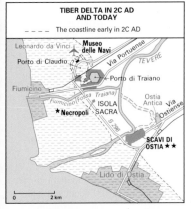

**TIBER DELTA IN 2C AD
AND TODAY**

- - - - The coastline early in 2C AD

Leonardo da Vinci | **Museo delle Navi**
Porto di Claudio
Fiumicino
Fiumicino (Fossa Traiana)
★ Necropoli
ISOLA SACRA
Via Portuense
TEVERE
Porto di Traiano
Ostia Antica
Via Ostiense
SCAVI DI OSTIA ★★
Lido di Ostia

0 ____ 2 km

particularly in the 2C AD, is **opus testa-ceum**: pyramid-shaped bricks laid regularly on their sides – point inwards, flat bottom outwards.

 WALKING TOUR

THE EXCAVATIONS (SCAVI)

Viale dei Romagnoli 717. &*(alternative route for the first half of the visit, ending in the refreshments area).*
◐*Excavations open Tue–Sun*

8:30am–1hr before dusk (Museum open at 9: 30am). ◐Closed 1 Jan and 25 Dec. €10 (exhibitions included). www.ostiaantica.beniculturali.it.

▷ Begin on the left, inside the entrance, but outside the town limits.

Via delle Tombe – Reserved for burials of various types: sarcophagus, *columbarium* or chapel.
Porta Romana (Rome Gate) – This was the main entrance to the town and led into the **Decumanus Maximus**, the east–west axis of all Roman towns. In Ostia, it was paved with large slabs and lined with porticoed buildings and warehouses *(horrea)*. From the outer side of the gate the broad and busy Via Ostiense carried traffic to Rome.
Piazzale della Vittoria – The square took its name from a **statue of Minerva Victoria** (1C) **(1)**, a copy of a Greek work, which probably adorned the town gate.
Terme di Nettuno (Baths of Neptune) – This 2C building has a terrace *(steps up from main street)* with a view of the fine **mosaics★★** depicting the marriage of Neptune and Amphitrite **(3)**.
Via dei Vigili – The construction of this street in the 2C meant the demolition of earlier buildings which contained a **mosaic★(2)** showing the heads of figures symbolising the Winds and four Provinces (Sicily, Egypt, Africa, Spain). At the end of the street stand the **firemen's barracks** *(caserna dei vigili)* built in the 2C; on the far side of the courtyard is the Augusteum (for the cult of the emperor) **(6)**; the mosaic shows a bull sacrifice.

▷ Turn left into Via della Palestra which leads into Via della Fontana.

Via della Fontana – This well-preserved street still contains its fountain **(5)**. On the corner with the Decumanus Maximus stood a tavern; the mosaic orders: *"Dicit Fortunatus: Vinum cratera quot sitis bibe"* (Fortunatus says: Drink wine from the bowl to quench your thirst) **(4)**.
Horrea di Hortensius★ (Hortensius' Warehouses) – These grand 1C ware-

houses *(horrea)*, built around a pillared courtyard and lined with shops, are a striking example of *opus reticulatum*. On the right of the entrance is a small shrine dedicated to Hortensius *(floor mosaic).*

Teatro★(Theatre) – Ostia was probably provided with a theatre under Augustus. It has been much restored. The three fine masks **(7)** come from the stage.

Piazzale delle Corporazioni★★★ – Under the portico in the square were the offices of the 70 trading corporations. Mosaic emblems show what commodity they traded and their country of origin: grain assessors, caulkers, rope-makers, shipbuilders and fitters, from Alexandria, Arles, Narbonne, Carthage etc.

The **temple (8)** in the centre of the square *(only the podium and two columns remain)* is sometimes attributed to Ceres and sometimes to the *Annona Augusta,* the imperial corn supply that was worshipped like a god.

Casa di Apuleio (Apuleius's House) – This house has a pillared atrium and mosaic floors.

Mitreo delle Sette Sfere (Seven Spheres Mithraeum) – This is one of the best preserved of the many temples dedicated to Mithras in Ostia. One can still see the two benches for the initiates and a relief showing the sacrifice of the bull.

▶ Return to the Decumanus Maximus; turn right into Via dei Molini.

Via dei Molini – The street is named after some millstones found in one of the buildings **(9)**. Opposite are the ruins of several warehouses.

▶ Return to the beginning of the street and turn right into Via di Diana.

Piazza dei Lari (10) – In the square *(left)* is an altar dedicated to the Lares. Here also are traces of a primitive fortress *(castrum)* made of huge blocks of tufa.

Casa di Diana★ (Diana's House; ▶*visits possible on Sun at 10.30am on reservation at 06 56 35 80 44)* – Facing onto the square is a striking example of an *insula* (block of flats), with rooms and passages

arranged around an internal courtyard; note the fine corbel in the side street *(Via dei Balconi).*

Thermopolium★★ – This bar's name means "sale of hot drinks". The building had a marble counter, shelving and paintings of the produce on sale.

▶ Turn right into Via dei Dipinti.

Insula dei Dipinti – Block containing several dwellings grouped round a garden; fine mosaics on the wall. At the end of the Via dei Dipinti on the right an oil store **(11)** was found with huge jars half buried in the ground.

Museo★ – **Rooms I** to **IV** are devoted to crafts, illustrated by low reliefs and to the Oriental religious cults, which flourished in Ostia. The Mithras group about to sacrifice the bull (**Room III**) is a clear indication of the strength of this cult, which had some 15 shrines here. **Room VIII** contains a fine 1C BC statue of a Hercules by Cartilius Poplicola as well as a series of **portraits★**, especially of the Antonines; the quality of expression and the fine detail indicate the high standard of 2C Roman portraiture.

Room XI and **XII** contain examples of the rich interior decoration found in Ostia: walls covered with mosaics, paintings and frescoes from the 1C to 4C.

▶ Take the Via del Capitolium which opens into Cardo Maximus.

Cardo Maximus – This important street, at right angles to the Decumanus, kinks left to skirt the temple **Capitolium**.

▶ Enter the Forum.

Capitolium and Forum★★ – The **Capitolium** was the largest temple in Ostia, built in the 2C and dedicated to the Capitoline trio – Jupiter, Juno and Minerva. Although the marble facing is missing from the walls, the brick remains are impressive, as are the steps leading up to the *pronaos*; in front of the steps is a partial reconstruction of the altar.

The **forum** was enlarged in the 2C; the few pillars still standing belonged to the surrounding portico. At the far end stands the **Temple of Rome and Augustus** (1C), a grandiose building once faced with marble, which indicates the loyalty of Ostia, the first Roman colony.

As in all Roman towns, the forum had a **basilica**, a covered building where citizens mingled, and a senate house (**Curia**), where the council met.

▶ Return to Decumanus Maximus.

Tempio Rotondo (Circular Temple) – It was probably dedicated to the cult of the emperors in the 3C.

Casa del Larario★ (House with Lararium) – The building consists of shops ranged around an internal court. The recess, decorated in attractive red and ochre bricks, housed the statues of the Lares.

▶ Continue along the Decumanus Maximus; turn right into Via Epagathiana.

Horrea Epagathiana★ (Epagathus's Warehouses) – This 2C complex has a fine doorway with columns and a pediment. It belonged to two rich freedmen: Epagathus and Epaphroditus.

Casa di Amore e Psiche★★ (House of Cupid and Psyche) – Like most of the buildings facing the shore, this was a private house (4C). It had mosaic and marble floors, and a *nymphaeum* decorated with niches, arcades and columns.

▶ Turn left into Via del Tempio di Ercole, right into Via della Foce and right again into Via delle Terme di Mitra.

Terme di Mitra (Baths of Mithras) – An arcade leads into the 2C building. Inside is a flight of steps descending to the underground *hypocaust* (heating system) and traces of a *frigidarium* (pool and columns with Corinthian capitals).

▶ Return to Via della Foce and walk through the Insula del Serapide.

Insula del Serapide★ (Serapis Flats) – The 2C blocks had porticoes around a courtyard and a bathhouse.

Terme dei Sette Sapienti★ (Baths of the Seven Sages) – There is a mosaic floor in the large circular room and one room is roofed with a dome decorated with mosaics on a white ground.

Insula degli Aurighi (Charioteers' Flats) – Includes a court and portico.

▶ Turn left into Cardo degli Aurighi and right into Via delle Volte Dipinti.

Insula delle Volte Dipinte; Insula delle Muse; Insula delle Pareti Gialle (*⊙Visits possible on Sun at 10.30am on reservation at 06 56 35 80 44*). Houses from the 2C with mosaics and paintings.

Città-Giardino (Garden Suburb) – *Right.* Example of a 2C residential complex with blocks of dwellings surrounded by gardens and fountains *(remains of several fountains, one containing mosaic)*.

Casa dei Dioscuri (Dioscuri House) – It was built in the 4C in one of the garden suburb blocks. The rooms are paved with beautiful multi-coloured mosaics, one of which shows the Dioscuri.

Domus del Ninfeo (House with *Nymphaeum*) – Incorporated in the 4C into a 2C building; one room is screened by three arches supported on slim columns.

▶ Return to Decumanus Maximus; right.

Porta Marina (Marine Gate) – This gate in Sulla's walls gave access to the seashore. A few huge blocks of tufa remain. Inside the gate *(left)* was the tavern of Alexander Helix **(12)** and outside *(right)* a tomb **(13)**.

The Decumanus came to an end outside the gate in a large colonnaded square.

▶ Left on Cartilio Poplicola; walk to end.

Terme della Marciana (Marciana Baths) – Behind the massive pilasters of the *frigidarium* apse, a beautiful **mosaic★** shows athletes in the poses characteristic of the various sports, with trophies and equipment on a table in the centre.

▶ Return to the Porta Marina and walk back along the Decumanus Maximus.

Schola del Traiano★★ – *Right*. This impressive 2–3C building was the headquarters of a guild of merchants. On the left of the entrance is a plaster copy of a statue of Trajan found here, hence the name. Next comes a court with a rectangular central basin surrounded by brick columns. The central room, preceded by two columns, contains a fine mosaic floor. During excavations, a 2C house was discovered on the court's east side, with a *nymphaeum* (paintings and mosaics) and a peristyle.

Basilica Cristiana (Christian Basilica) – *Left*. 4C; a row of columns separates the aisles, which end in apses.

Mercato (Market) – There were two fishmongers' shops **(14)** on either side of an alley, which led to a pillared podium on the west side of the market square. On the third pillar on the left, it says in Latin: "read and know that there is a lot of gossiping in the market."

▷ Right into Via del Pomerio; left into Via del Tempio Rotondo and past the Tempio di Roma e Augusto (left) and Cardo Maximus (right).

Terme del Foro★ (Forum Baths) – The largest baths in Ostia had heating ducts in the walls and a public lavatory **(15)**.

▷ Turn left into Cardo Maximus.

Mulino (Mill) – On the left of the Cardo Maximus are several millstones.

Ara della Magna Mater (Altar of the Great Earth Mother) – This sacred enclosure contains the remains of a temple dedicated to Cybele (the Great Mother – *Magna Mater*) **(16)**. The Sanctuary of Attis **(17)** has a statue of the goddess in the apse and two faun sculptures.

The Cardo Maximus ends at the Laurentina Gate (**Porta Laurentina**) in Sulla's Wall (**Cinta Sillana**).

▷ Turn left into Via Semita dei Cippi.

The **Domus del Protiro** *(right)* is an exception in Ostia for its marble pediment above the door.

Domus della Fortuna Annonaria is a 3C–4C house with a well in the garden and mosaic floors.

▷ Take Via del Mitreo dei Serpenti to return to the Decumanus Maximus.

OUTSKIRTS

Area archeologica del Porto di Traiano

11km/7mi from excavations. Access by car: by SS296 and Via Portuense. ◷*Visit Thu-Sun 9:30am–6pm, only with reservation for groups, also in the afternoon calling ℘337.1175780. www.navigareilterritorio.it.*

It was Trajan (113 AD) who decided to build this port facility, more secure than the hexagonal one built by Claudius with which it communicated. 200 ships could berth here. It was abandoned in the 10-11C AD.

Necropoli del Porto di Traiano★ (Trajan's Port Necropolis)

5km/3mi from excavations. Access by car: by A91 (direction Leonardo da Vinci Airport); than SS 296 (direzione Fiumicino), turn left into Via Monte Cengio; entrance to the necropolis on second on the left, Via Monte Spinoncia 52, Isola Sacra, Fiumicino. ◷*Visit by appointment only Thu-Sat and first and third Sun of month 10am-4pm. ℘06 65 83 888. www.ostiaantica.beniculturali.it.*

Isolated and silent, the necropolis is an impressive place, studded with umbrella pines, cypresses and laurels. The inhabitants of Trajan's Harbour buried their dead here from the 2C–4C.

The simplest tombs are marked by an amphora or a ridge of tiles. Others of brick had one or more chambers for sarcophagi. Sometimes there is a foreourt *columbarium* (with recesses for the cinerary urns), which the owner made available to his household.

The majority of the tombs have a low door beneath a lintel resting directly on the uprights. The inscription gave the name of the dead person, with sometimes a low-relief sculpture depicting their occupation.

Museo delle Navi Romane (Ship Museum) in Fiumicino

Access: Roma Ostiense Station to Leonardo da Vinci Airport and then by train. ↝*Temporarily closed for renovation.* ☎*06 65 29 192.*

The maritime museum is on the site of the Claudian Harbour. It houses the hulls of five Roman **vessels** and smaller articles: pottery, fishing floats, rope, nails, wooden pegs, needles, money. A low-relief sculpture *(copy)* shows the boat that transported Caligula's Obelisk, now in St Peter's Square. The boat was sunk as a foundation for the lighthouse at the harbour mouth. It stood 50m/164ft high and shone 30km/18mi out to sea.

ADDRESSES

🍽/EAT

L'Ostrica Pazza – *Ostia, Lungomare Lutazio Catulo 6a.* ☎*06 97 61 45 35. Closed Mon.* Fish restaurant with welcoming staff, excellent food and dishes presented in an original manner.

Palestrina★

42km/26mi southeast of Rome

According to legend, Ancient Praeneste was founded at the dawn of Roman history by Telegonus, the son of Ulysses and the enchantress Circe. Palestrina, now an attractive small medieval town, still occupies the same position, perched on the slopes of the Prenestini Hills, offering stunning views of the surrounding countryside. Highlights include the ruined temple of the goddess Fortune and the famous Hellenistic Nile mosaic, further examples of the splendour of ancient Rome.

A BIT OF HISTORY

Praeneste rose to its full glory during the early days of its existence, in the 8C and 7C BC; it was besieged subsequently through the centuries because of its strategic position. Under the rule of Rome from the 4C BC, the town became a favourite country retreat in Imperial times for dignitaries and nobles. The cult of Fortune lasted well into the 4C AD, when the temple was abandoned and its site became encroached upon by the medieval city.

- 🕭 **Michelin Map:** 563, Q 20.
- 🛈 **Info:** Palazzo Colonna-Barberini, Via della Cortina. Open Mon–Fri 9am–noon and 3–7pm, Sat 9am–1pm. ☎06 957 3176.
- ▶ **Location:** Palestrina was built on the southern slopes of Monte Ginestro, an outcrop in the chain of Prenestini Hills overlooking the valley. From Rome, drive along Via Prenestina; by bus from Roma Ponte Mammolo (Metro line B).

The superb 8C necropolis, together with the Barberini and Bernardini tombs, in which fabulous funerary ornaments were found *(now displayed at the Museo Nazionale di Villa Giulia in Rome* 🕭*See VILLA GIULIA–VILLA BORGHESE)*, are a lasting testament to Palestrina's illustrious past.

SIGHTS
Museo Archeologico Nazionale di Palestrina

Palazzo Barberini, piazza della Cortina. The entrance to the museum is at the top of the stairs up to the Terrazza degli

Emicicli. &🕐*Open daily 9am–8pm (archaeological area till dusk).* ⊚€5. 📞*06 95 38 100.*
www.comune.palestrina.rm.it.
The palace curves dramatically, embracing the ancient Temple of Fortune. The Palazzo Colonna-Barberini contains one of the largest and finest Hellenic mosaics. The late 2C BC **Nile Mosaic★★** depicts the river in flood: stranded animals, hunters and boaters among the islands and elaborate architecture. Alexandrian artists pieced together this tableau, heavily restored in the 17C *(sliced up and sent to Rome, then reassembled incorrectly)*. It was evacuated in WWII to prevent bomb damage. Conservators used Grand Tour sketches to reassemble it.
The museum also showcases the sculpture, **Il Triade Capitolina★★**. The only known depiction of Rome's three tutelary gods, the Capitoline Triad shows Minerva, Jupiter and Juno squashed onto one throne. Police recovered this statue from the criminal, rather than celestial, underworld after it was stolen in 1992. On leaving the museum, cross the street and descend the terraces.

Tempio della Fortuna Primigenia★

This temple was once a grandiose sanctuary dedicated to the goddess Fortune. Built during the 2C–1C BC, it stands as one of the most important examples of Roman architecture based upon Hellenistic archetypes in Italy.
The complex would have occupied most of the area now covered by the town; it comprised a series of terraces linked by a system of ramps and stairways aligned one above the other. A large basilica-shaped room, two lateral buildings, a natural cave and an apse paved with the famous *Nile Mosaic (⚫See Museo Archeologico Nazionale di Palestrina, p371)* survive from the lower sanctuary that was accommodated on the site of the old forum, on the second level of the temple. The upper was located on the fourth terrace of the temple complex, where Piazza della Cortina now sits. The Palazzo Colonna (11C) – later known as the Palazzo Barberini (1640) – was built on this platform, once graced with steps arranged in semicircles. Here, behind the elegant façade, is the museum.

⚫ Follow the one-way road system into town by means of the Via Anicia.

Town centre

The main square, Piazza Regina Margherita, replaces the old forum. The 11C duomo, flanked by a Romanesque bell-tower, was constructed among the ruins of a Roman temple. It is dedicated to St Agapito, the town's patron. At the centre of the piazza is a statue of **Giovanni Pierluigi da Palestrina** (1524–94), the renowned composer of polyphonic religious music. His house is now a music research center with a 6 000-volume library *(Centro di Studi Palestriniani, Vicolo Pierluigi 3;* 🕐*open Tue–Fri 9am–1pm, Sat and Sun 9:30am-12:30pm, Wed and Thu 9am-1pm and 3–6pm.* ⊚€4; 📞*06 95 38 083).* *www.fondazionepierluigipalestrina.it.*

ADDRESSES

🏠 STAY

Stella – *Piazza Liberazione 3.* 📞*06 95 38 172 or 06 95 38 637. 30 rooms.* 🛏€5. *Restaurant. www.hotelstella.it.* This simple family-run pensione sits in the centre of the old town. A friendly atmosphere and a good restaurant serving regional cuisine.

🍴EAT

Il Piscarello – *Via del Piscarello 2.* 📞*06 95 74 326. www.ristoranteilpiscarello.it. Closed Mon.* This country restaurant is decorated in a pleasant mix of rustic and classical styles and serves a range of traditional meat and fish dishes. In summer, meals can be enjoyed in the garden.

Tivoli★★★

31km/19mi east of Rome

One of the most impressive sites of antiquity lies just outside the town of Tivoli to the east of Rome. The evocative setting and magnificent architecture of Hadrian's Villa has long fascinated visitors, despite its extensive plundering over the centuries. This picturesque little town sits on the lower slopes of the chalky Apennines (Monti Simbruini), where the River Aniene cascades into the Roman plain before joining the Tiber. Famous for its sunset vistas, Tivoli also has two famous and contrasting gardens: the manicured fantasia of Villa d'Este and the shaggy exuberance of Villa Gregoriana.

- **Michelin Map:** 563, Q 20.
- **Info:** Piazzale Nazioni Unite. Open Tue–Sun 10am–1pm and 4–6pm. ℘0774 31 12 49.
- **Location:** Drivers should take the Via Tiburtina or turn off the autostrada 28km from Rome at the Tivoli Exit A24. Access by coach from Rebibbia (last stop on Metro line B).
- **Don't Miss:** Hadrian's Villa, the Villa d'Este, sunset views of Rome.
- **Timing:** Visit Hadrian's Villa in the morning: 2hr 30min. Save the cooler Villa d'Este and Villa Gregoriana – each 1hr 30min – for later in the day.

A BIT OF HISTORY

A Greek seer and a Roman sibyl – Tivoli, Tibur in antiquity, is said to have been founded earlier than Rome by Tiburtus, grandson of the Greek seer Amphiaraos, whom Zeus caused to be swallowed up in the earth outside Thebes. Tibur came under Roman control in the 4C BC and became a holiday resort under the Empire.

Several centuries later, according to a medieval legend, two great prophecies were made by a sibyl. When Augustus asked her whether there would be anyone greater than he, she sent him a vision of the Virgin and Child on the Capitol in Rome and added that on the Child's birthday a spring of oil would bubble up from the ground; this is supposed to have taken place in Trastevere. In 1001 Tivoli rebelled against the German Emperor Otho III, who was in Italy with Pope Sylvester II. The Romans, who had no love for their neighbours in Tivoli, made common cause with the Emperor. The Pope intervened and the Emperor spared the town, but when the Pope and the Emperor returned to Rome, the Romans reproached them for their leniency; both had to flee the mob. Tivoli retained its independence until 1816, when it finally joined the Papal States.

VILLA ADRIANA★★★ (HADRIAN'S VILLA)

Hadrian's Villa is 6km/3.5mi below the main town: about 1.5km/1mi off the highway, turn right onto Via della Rosolina. Tivoli–Rome buses stop on request, just a 15min walk from the site, or take the local CAT #4 from Largo Garibaldi or from Tivoli Station (train starting from Roma Tiburtina). Parking (small fee) at the car park around the ticket booth. Toilets are 300m/330yd from the entrance.
Open 9am–1hr before dusk (last ticket half an hour earlier than that).
Closed 1 Jan, 1 May, 25 Dec. ⊗€10. Audioguide €5. ℘06 39 96 79 00 (info and booking) or 0774 38 27 33. www.coopculture.it.

The perimeter (5km/3mi) enclosed an estate: vast gardens adorned with works of art, an imperial palace, baths, libraries and theatres. Probably the richest building project in antiquity, it was designed largely by the Emperor Hadrian. The complex was a mix of pleasure and politics, private and public spaces, akin to Versailles. When Hadrian died in Baiae in 138, his remains were buried in his huge mausoleum in Rome. The

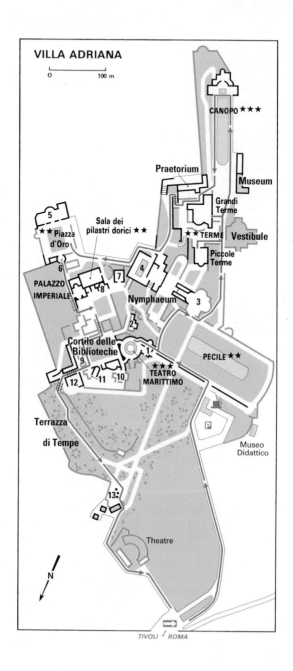

VILLA ADRIANA

0   100 m

CANOPO ★★★

Praetorium

Museum

Grandi
Terme

5

★★ Piazza
d'Oro

Sala dei
pilastri dorici ★★

★★ TERME   Vestibule

Piccole
Terme

6

4

7

PALAZZO
IMPERIALE

8

Nymphaeum

3

2

Cortile delle
Biblioteche

9

1

PECILE ★★

★★★
TEATRO
MARITTIMO

12

7

11

10

Terrazza

di Tempe

P

Museo
Didattico

13

Theatre

N

TIVOLI / ROMA

374

Villa Adriana

© Shimyra/Fotolia.com

emperors who succeeded him probably continued to come to Tivoli. It was here that Zenobia, Queen of Palmyra, ended her days as Aurelian's prisoner.

Then the villa fell into ruin. From the 15C to the 19C, the site was explored; over 300 works were recovered, which now enrich museums and private collections in Rome, London, Berlin, Dresden, Stockholm and St Petersburg.

Since 1870, the site has belonged to the Italian Government, which has organised its excavation. The vegetation has been cleared from the ruins, revealing magnificent vaults, columns, stuccowork and mosaics. The present entrance is probably not the one used in Hadrian's day. The design of the villa is so unusual that archaeologists have not been able to identify the buildings or their uses with any certainty.

Before exploring the site it is advisable to study a model of the villa that is displayed in a room next to the bar.

Pecile★★

The **Poikile** was the name of a portico in Athens, which Hadrian wished to reproduce. Only the north wall remains, through which the visitor enters the excavation site. Notice the lattice-work effect created by small blocks of tufa – *opus reticulatum* – Hadrian's Villa is one of the last examples of this technique,

which fell into disuse in the 2C. The horizontal grooves in the wall were filled with bricks, which disappeared when the villa was plundered for its materials, in particular for the Villa d'Este.

The Poikile was built in the shape of a large rectangle with slightly curved ends and lined with a portico; it was sited so that one side was always in the shade. The apsidal chamber was the **philosophers' room (1)**, possibly for reading.

Teatro Marittimo★★★

This circular construction consists of a portico and a central building. It is surrounded by a canal, spanned by small swing bridges. The theatre was an ideal retreat for the misanthropic Hadrian.

▶ Walk south towards the Ninfeo and climb the steps.

The ruins look down on a *nymphaeum*, which can be reached by part of the **cryptoporticus**, a network of passages. These made it possible to traverse the site underground

▶ Cross the Cryptoporticus (right).

Ninfeo

The *nymphaeum*, the flat area enclosed between sections of high wall, was originally thought to be a stadium. The building *(west)* was composed of three semicircular rooms on a courtyard **(3)**.

Terme★★

The **baths** consist of the Small Baths (Piccole Terme) and the Great Baths (Grandi Terme). They both show the high architectural standards attained in the villa: rectangular rooms with concave walls, octagonal rooms with alternate concave and convex walls, circular rooms with recesses alternating with doors. The most impressive room is in the Great Baths; it has an apse and the remains of some superb vaulting.

The tall building, called the **Praetorium** (Pretorio), was probably a storehouse.

Museo (Museum)

The **museum** contains the results of the most recent excavations: Roman copies of the Amazon by Phidias and Polyclitus; copies of the Caryatids from the Erechtheion on the Acropolis in Athens. These statues adorned the sides of the Canopus.

Canopo★★★ (Canopus)

The route to Canope from Alexandria was a canal lined with temples and gardens. Hadrian had part of his estate landscaped to look like the Egyptian site. He completed the effect with a canal down the centre and a copy of the Temple of Serapis (Tempio di Serapis) at the southern end.

 On leaving the Canopus, bear right between the Grandi Terme and the Pretorio, climb to the upper level and continue towards the Ninfeo before bearing right.

The path goes around a large **fish pond** surrounded by a portico *(Quadriportico con peschiera)* **(4)**.

 Return to the Pretorio and the Grandi Terme and walk as far as the ruins overlooking the Ninfeo and bear right.

Palazzo Imperiale

The **Imperial Palace** complex extended from the Piazza d'Oro to the libraries.

Piazza d'Oro★★ – The rectangular area was surrounded by a double portico; the piazza was an aesthetic caprice.

On the far side are traces of an octagonal chamber **(5)**: each of the eight sides, which are alternately concave and convex, was preceded by a small portico *(one of these has been reconstructed)*. On the opposite side is a chamber **(6)** covered by a dome and flanked by two smaller chambers: the left-hand one contains traces of a black-and-white mosaic.

Sala dei Pilastri Dorici★★ – The **Doric Pillared Hall** takes its name from the surrounding portico, which was composed of pilasters with Doric bases and capitals supporting a Doric architrave *(partial reconstruction in one corner)*. Opposite stood the **firemen's barracks** *(caserma dei vigili)* **(7)**.

Adjoining the **Pillared Hall** *(north side)* is a huge section of curved wall which may have been part of a summer **dining room** *(triclinio estivo)* **(8)**; the oval basins further east mark the site of a **nymphaeum** *(ninfeo di palazzo)*. These buildings overlook a courtyard which is separated by a *cryptoporticus* from the **library court**; the east side of the latter court is composed of a complex of 10 rooms ranged down both sides of a corridor; this was an infirmary **(9)**; each of the rooms held three beds; the **floor★** is paved with fine mosaics. The library courtyard offers a pleasant **view★** over the countryside.

Biblioteche – The ruins of the **library buildings** are on the north side of the courtyard *(Cortile delle Biblioteche)*; according to custom, there was a Greek library **(10)** and a Latin library **(11)**.

Next to the libraries *(east side)* is a group of rooms paved with mosaic, which belonged to a dining room *(triclinio imperiale)* **(12)**.

Terrazza di Tempe

A grove of trees hangs on the slope above a valley, which Hadrian called his **Vale of Tempe**, after the Greek beauty spot in Thessaly. The path runs through the trees past a **circular temple (13)** *(reconstructed)*. It contained a statue of the goddess Venus. Further along *(left)* is the site of a **theatre**.

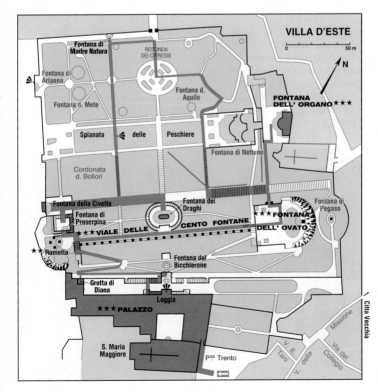 Proceed to Tivoli (town plan in the Michelin Guide Italia).

The **Rocca Pia**, a fortress built by Pius II (1458–64), dominates Piazza Garibaldi.

VILLA D'ESTE★★★

The centre of Tivoli, down the street from Largo Garibaldi. Entrance from the old convent cloisters.
Open Tue–Sun 8:30am–1hr before dusk. Closed 1 Jan, 1 May and 25 Dec. €10. 199 766 166 (0039 04 12 71 90 36 from abroad).
www.villadestetivoli.info.

The fountains are the real draw in this Renaissance pleasure garden. Over 1,200 litres/300 gallons of water per second flowed through its pipes and pumps,

during its prime. Today the spectacle varies – depending on the season, time of day and nearly-completed restoration – but the UNESCO World Heritage Site is always worth a look.

The Cardinal Ippolito II d'Este, squeezed out of Rome after an unsuccessful papal bid, sponsored this extravaganza in 1550. Under his guidance, Neapolitan architect Pirro Ligorio transformed a convent into the ultimate villa, after a careful study of Hadrian's ruins, which he then quarried.

The simple architecture contrasts with the elaborate gardens (3ha/7.5 acres), which descend in a series of terraces on the western slope of the hill. The statues, pools and fountains enhance the natural beauty with all the grace of the Mannerist style. Many distinguished guests visited the villa, including Pius IV and Gregory XII, and after the cardinal's death, Paul IV, Paul V, Pius IX and writers and artists: Benvenuto Cellini, Titian, Tasso and Liszt.

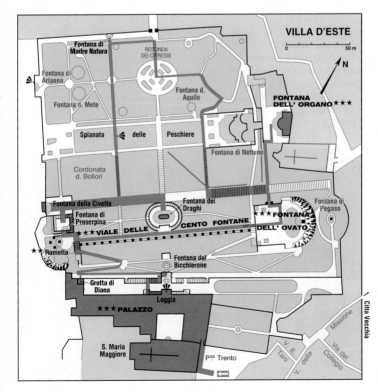

In 1759, when the avenues were overgrown with brambles and the fountains silent, Fragonard and Hubert Robert, who were staying at the French Academy in Rome, came to spend the summer in Tivoli with their patron the Abbé de Saint Non.

There is scarcely a corner of the gardens where they did not set up their easels, nor a perspective that escaped their brushes.

Villa and Gardens★★★

The Old Apartment (*Vecchio Appartamento*) on the first floor of the villa now holds temporary exhibitions.

◐ Descend to the floor below.

Sala grande – The **central Salon** is decorated in the Mannerist style by pupils of Girolamo Muziano and Federico Zuccari. The fountain, a riot of mosaics, faces a wall panel showing the gardens in the 16C. On the ceiling is a fresco of the *Banquet of the Gods*. From the Salon loggia is a lovely **view★**.

Next is a series of four rooms in the west wing. The mythological paintings in the first room are attributed to Muziano and Luigi Karcher: the *Labours of Hercules* surround a fresco of the *Synod of the Gods (ceiling)*. Federico Zuccari and his school painted the allegorical frescoes in the next room, known as

the Philosophers' Hall, and the *Glory of Este* in the third room. In the Hall of the Hunt, Tempesta's efforts show hunting trophies and countryside scenes.

From the balcony is a pleasant view of the gardens and Tivoli itself.

◐ Double flights of steps lead down to the upper garden walk.

Fontana del Bicchierone – The fountain, often attributed to Bernini, consists of a huge moss-covered **beaker**. Water overflows into a shell-shaped basin.

La "Rometta" – This fountain, known as **"mini Rome"** was an attempt by the cardinal to reproduce some of the most famous monuments of classical Rome: a pool bearing a boat (representing Tiber Island) surmounted by an obelisk; higher up next to some artificial ruins an allegorical statue of Rome and the she-wolf.

Viale delle Cento Fontane★★★ – The **Avenue of a Hundred Fountains** is one of the most charming spots here. One side of the walk is lined by fountains of water spouting from small boats, obelisks, animal heads, eagles and lilies, which recall the Este coat of arms.

Fontana dell'Ovato★★★ – The **Oval Fountain** is dominated by the statue of the sibyl, flanked by allegorical figures of rivers. Around the edge of the basin, half covered in moss, are statues of naiads pouring the water of the River

Fontana dell'Ovato

© Pablo Debat/Fotolia.com

Aniene from their water pots. An attractive ceramic decoration adorns the front rim of the oval basin.

Fontana dell'Organo★★★ – The **Organ Fountain** once played music on a hidden water-powered organ. This ingenious mechanism was invented by a Frenchman, Claude Venard, in the 16C. After seeing and hearing the fountain, Montaigne, the French writer and philosopher, wrote in his journal that "the organ music is made by water falling into a cave with such power that the air is forced out through the organ pipes while another stream of water turns a toothed wheel, which operates the keyboard; one can also hear the distorted sound of trumpets".

Spianata delle Peschiere – The three basins were **fishponds** that supplied the cardinal's table on fast days. There is a fine **view★★** of the water spouts and the Organ Fountain.

Fontana della Madre Natura – The **Fountain of Mother Nature** is decorated with a statue of Diana of Ephesus, goddess of fertility.

Fontana dei Draghi – The **Dragon Fountain** was created in honour of Pope Gregory XIII, who visited the villa in 1572, shortly before the cardinal's death; the dragons recall the arms of the pope's Buoncompagni family.

Fontana della Civetta – The **Owl Fountain** is more commonly known as the "Bird Fountain" because of the hydraulic mechanism, originally concealed in a recess, which twittered. Periodically an owl appeared and uttered a mournful screech. Several times restored, the fountain is now silent.

Fontana di Proserpina – (left). The **Fountain of Proserpina** (restored) recalls the mythological girl abducted by Pluto.

⏵ It is possible to walk down to the Villa Gregoriana through the streets of the old town (città vecchia).

The town is agreeably lively and some traces of the past still remain. The **cathedral**, rebuilt in the 17C and flanked by a 12C Romanesque campanile, con-tains a fine group of carved wooden figures depicting the **Deposition★** (13C).

Santa Maria Maggiore

This old abbey church of St Mary Major belongs to the Benedictine convent. It has an attractive Gothic façade and a 17C bell-tower. The interior contains two 15C triptychs (in the chancel). Above the one on the left is a painting of the Virgin by Jacopo Torriti, who also worked in mosaic at the end of the 13C.

VILLA GREGORIANA★

Largo Sant'Angelo.
🕐*Open Tue–Sun 10am–one hour before dusk.* ⊜€7. *℘0774 33 26 50. www.visitfai.it/dimore/ parcovillagregoriana.*

A tangle of paths winds down wooded slopes to where the Aniene plunges through the craggy ravine. Pope Gregory XVI diverted the river to ease flooding in 1831, veiling the cliff in diaphanous spray. Take the path down from the entrance and bear right to the **Great Waterfall★★** (Grande Cascata).

A smaller waterfall, engineered by **Bernini**, flows at the canyon's neck. The path winds past two grottoes, where the torrent spits at visitors in the gloom. The walk is strenuous, but a dramatic payoff awaits: a late Republic **Temple of Vesta**. The hearth goddess's circular shrine later served as a medieval church (Santa Maria della Rotonda). Eighteen Corinthian columns still adorn the hillside, now in the garden of the Ristorante Sibilla (Via della Sibilla 50; ℘0774 33 52 81; www.ristorantesibilla.com).

😷 Solid, non-skid shoes are advisable.

ADDRESSES

🍴EAT

Sibilla – *Via della Sibilla 50, Tivoli. ℘0774 33 52 81. www.ristorantesibilla.com.* This elegant restaurant stands at the foot of the Temple of Vesta. One of the highlights on the menu is grilled meat. Other regional specialities also feature.

Ponte Sant' Angelo over the Tibere and Basilica di San Pietro at sunset

Where to Stay

From modest *pensioni* to luxury hotels, Rome has a wide range of accommodation, although finding value for money can sometimes prove difficult. Visitors should book well in advance as the capital is popular throughout the year. Generally speaking, the low season includes January, the first half of February, the last two weeks of July, the months of August and November and the first two weeks of December. During these periods many hotels offer reasonable rates and special weekend deals or short breaks. Choose a hotel with air-conditioning during the summer, as it is particularly hot during this period. Breakfast may be an additional charge – and even towels in more modest establishments.

SELECTING A DISTRICT

A good selection of *pensioni* and hotels can be found in the **historic centre,** where the atmosphere and high concentration of tourist sights and shops make it particularly popular. However, many of these establishments have limited capacity and are often full. The attractive quarter of **Trastevere,** with its lively nightlife, is also pleasant, although accommodation options here are somewhat limited.
Quieter and cheaper, the **Vatican and Prati** districts are also close to the centre. The choice around **Via Cavour** (near Monti), between Termini Station and the Fori Imperiali, is also good, especially for mid-range hotels.
Many of the cheaper pensioni and smaller hotels are concentrated in the area around **Termini Station**, slightly away from the centre and somewhat lacking in character, but well served by public buses and the Metro system. Most of Rome's luxury hotels are on the **Via Veneto** and around **Villa Borghese**.
Driving in Rome is not advisable as parking can be a major problem (most central hotels do not have private garages or parking). The few private car parks that do exist are extremely expensive and access to the city centre requires a special permit.

TYPES OF ACCOMMODATION
HOTELS AND PENSIONI

Generally, the word *pensione* describes a small, family-run hotel, sometimes within a residential building. It offers simple, basic rooms, often without a private bathroom. The hotels can of course be more lavish, but there are plenty of attractive and convenient *pensioni* on offer. Wherever you choose to stay, it is worth doing some initial research to get the right place for you. Rates vary depending on the time of year and availability of rooms. Given the shortage of rooms in Rome, hoteliers usually request confirmation of booking by email or sometimes even fax, as well as a credit card number. Breakfast is usually included in the price of the room, although this may not be the case in smaller hotels.

HOSTELS AND BUDGET ACCOMMODATION

There is no age limit for Youth Hostel Association membership, which must be renewed annually.
The **Associazione Italiana Alberghi per la Gioventù** (AIG) is situated at Viale Mazzini 88, *06 9 26 14 62. www.aighostels.it.
Those wishing to arrange hostel accommodation in advance from the UK can contact the **Youth Hostels Association**, Trevelyan House, Dimple Road, Matlock, Derbyshire DE4 3YH, *44 (0) 1629 59 27 00, www.yha.org. uk. US visitors can get information on international hostelling through the **Hostelling International USA** *1(240) 650 2100, www.hiusa.org and www.hihostels.com.
Other organisations and properties offer dormitory accommodation or shared rooms at reasonable rates.

© A. Serrano/Sime/Photononstop

BED AND BREAKFAST

The B&B formula has gained in popularity in Italy in recent years, offering visitors the chance to stay in private homes. The house or apartment is also often lived in by the hosts, who let out a few of their rooms (usually between one and three) to guests cheaply. However, guests are usually required to stay for a minimum period and credit cards are rarely accepted. Listings can be found on the website of Bedandbreakfast.it at www.bedandbreakfast.it. Information is also available from **Bed and Breakfast Italia** www.bed-and-breakfast.it (English-speaking helpline) or log on to www.bbitalia.it

SHORT-TERM RENTAL

An apartment *(appartamento)* is often the most atmospheric option. For privacy and authenticity, a short-term rental can't be beaten. Generally cheaper than hotels, apartments also have basic cooking implements and facilities. Good companies include www.realrome.com, www.cross-pollinate.com; www.romesweethome.it and www.flatinrome.com.

HOME SWAP

Increasingly popular, these services allow homeowners to trade places. Find a reputable service, like Home Exchange (*Post Office Box 787, Hermosa Beach, CA, 90254, USA;* ☎*+1 34 76 88 69 25 or 888 609 46 60 toll-free; www.homeexchange.com/en/*) or HomeLink International (*Homelink Italia, Viale P. Frassinetti 62/13 – 31046 Oderzo (TV);* ☎*0422 56 613; www.homelink.org*). Check references carefully.

CONVENTS AND MONASTERIES

As well as providing accommodation for pilgrims, convents and monasteries are also a good option for those on a limited budget. Rooms are reasonably priced, although visitors are usually expected to be in by a specified hour (usually 10:30pm). Occasionally men and women are required to sleep in separate rooms. For more information log on to *www.monasterystays.com* or you can contact the **Peregrinatio ad Petri Sedem**, *Piazza Pio XII 4 (Vaticano–San Pietro district),* ☎*06 69 88 50 38 or* **Centro Italiano Turismo Sociale** (CITS), *Via della Pigna 13a,* ☎*06 48 73 145, www.citsnet.it.*

CAMPSITES

Although Rome's campsites are a fair distance from the centre, they are cheap and in attractive green surroundings. Shade is particularly welcome in the hot summer months, when the downtown humidity becomes almost unbearable. In addition to campsite addresses listed below, a comprehensive list can be found on www.camping.it.

HOTEL

Now that the hotel booking offices in Rome's stations and airports have been permanently closed, reservations are now to be made online.

FOR ALL BUDGETS

The hotels in this guide are grouped according to district and listed according to price (☕ *for coin categories see the Legend on the cover flap)*.

Lodgings marked by the symbol ☺ include campsites, youth hostels and modest but decent hotels and *pensioni* with double rooms. Those on a larger budget will find more charming and comfortable hotels with better quality restaurants marked by the symbols ☺🛏 and ☺🛏🛏.

For those in search of a truly memorable stay, the category highlighted by the symbol ☺🛏🛏🛏 includes luxurious hotels and B&Bs with great atmosphere and a wide range of facilities. The hotels listed have been chosen for their value for money, level of comfort and character. We would be grateful for any comments or suggestions from readers.

DON'T FORGET THE MICHELIN RED GUIDE

For a more exhaustive list of hotels, consult the *Michelin Guide Italia*, the red-cover guide that provides a host of details on many of Rome's hotels and restaurants. It can be found in major bookstores throughout the city.

ACCOMMODATION BY AREA

AVENTINO/PIRAMIDE CESTIA – TESTACCIO

☺🛏 **Hotel Santa Prisca** – *Largo M. Gelsomini 25, Aventino district.* ☎06 57 41 917. www.hotelsantaprisca.it. *48 rooms.*

🍽. *Restaurant.* Flowers, palms and pines wreathe this pleasant hotel on the flanks of the Aventine Hill. The rooms – formerly nuns' cells – are like cameos: small, but finely wrought.

☺🛏🛏 **San Anselmo** – *Piazza San Anselmo 2, Aventino.* ☎06 57 00 57. www.aventinohotels.com. *34 rooms.* 🍽. Swags of marble, faded gilt mirrors and citrus trees lend a Belle Epoque air to this retreat, nestled high on the green-swathed hill. A lovely property.

CATACOMBE DI PRISCILLA

☺🛏 **Hotel Santa Costanza** – *Via XXI Aprile 4, Nomentana.* ☎06 86 00 602. www.hotelsantacostanza.it. ♿ *69 rooms.* 🍽. Comfortable, colourful armchairs fill the lobby of this hotel (completely renovated in 2014), which has good transport connections to the city centre. The breakfast room, with floral designs, has large windows looking out on an internal garden. Well-appointed rooms.

COLOSSEO–CELIO/FORI IMPERIALI/ PIAZZA VENEZIA/RIONE MONTI

☺🛏 **Antica Locanda** – *Via del Boschetto 84, Monti.* ☎06 48 48 94. www.anticalocandaroma.it. *15 rooms.* 🍽. Close to both the Trevi Fountain and Piazza Navona, this intimate hotel couldn't be better placed. All en-suite rooms are air conditioned, with clean, neutral décor that still has some character. The hotel has a great roof terrace for breakfast or drinks.

☺🛏🛏 **Hotel Celio** – *Via dei Santi Quattro 35/c, Colosseo.* ☎06 70 49 53 33. www.hotelcelio.com. *19 rooms.* 🍽. Splendid fragments of frescoes add a touch of originality to the rooms in this elegant family hotel. The hotel also has a suite with a view of the Colosseum. Breakfast is served in the rooms. The Celio has a nice hammam.

☺🛏🛏 **Hotel Solis** – *Via Cavour 311, Fori Imperiali.* ☎06 69 92 33 95. www.hotelsolis.it. *17 rooms.* 🍽. This small, comfortable hotel is family run and is on the first floor of a building a few steps away from the Colosseum. The large rooms are the most modern.

FONTANA DI TREVI–QUIRINALE

⊝⊜⊟⊟ **Hotel Fontana** – *Piazza di Trevi 96, Fontana di Trevi . 📞06 67 86 113. www.hotelfontana-trevi.com. 25 rooms.* 🛏. Admire the Trevi Fountain without having to fight through the crowds. Boasts charming rooms in a romantic old convent.

ISOLA TIBERINA–GHETTO–TORRE ARGENTINA

⊝⊟ **Pensione Barrett** – *Largo Torre Argentina 47, Torre Argentina. 📞06 68 68 481. www.pensionebarrett.com. 20 rooms.* 🛏. Simple, but well looked after and in an excellent location. The rooms have thoughtful and unusual touches, such as a small footbath and tea- and coffee-making facilities. For peace and quiet avoid the rooms overlooking the busy square.

⊝⊟ **B & B Arco del Lauro** – *Via Arco de'Tolomei 29. 📞06 97 84 03 50. www. arcodellauro.it. 6 rooms.* 🛏. Next to Isola Tiberina, in the framework of traditional antique houses of Trastevere, this delightful B&B is managed by a very kind and cheerful host. With white walls and dark parquet, rooms are simple and well decorated, offering all kind of comforts and very nice bathrooms. Perfect for a journey with four people, the family room still has its ancient ceiling.

PANTHEON/MONTECITORIO

⊝⊟ **Hotel Mimosa** – *Via Santa Chiara 61, (2nd floor, no lift), Pantheon. 📞06 68 80 17 53. www.hotelmimosa. net. 11 rooms.* 🛏. The main attraction is its excellent location in a building behind the Pantheon, close to Santa Maria sopra Minerva. The rooms are basic, clean and quiet.

⊝⊟⊟ **Hotel Portoghesi** – *Via dei Portoghesi 1, Montecitorio. 📞06 68 64 231. www.hotelportoghesiroma.it. 27 rooms.* 🛏. Opposite the legendary "*Torre della Scimmia*" (Monkey Tower), this hotel has pleasant rooms decorated with antique furniture. The glass conservatory, used as the breakfast room, and the terrace, with its views over Rome, are delightful. Wi-Fi.

⊝⊟⊟⊟ **Hotel del Sole al Pantheon** – *Piazza della Rotonda 63, Pantheon. 📞06 678 0441. www.hotelsoleal pantheon.com. 25 rooms.* 🛏. One of the world's oldest hotels, this establishment traces its roots to 1467. Elegant and aristocratic, it overlooks the ancient Roman temple and the lively square it anchors. Jean-Paul Sartre and Simone de Beauvoir favoured this hotel.

PIAZZA NAVONA/CAMPO DE' FIORI/ CASTEL SANT'ANGELO

⊝⊟ **Hotel Navona** – *Via dei Sediari 8, (1st floor, with lift, Piazza Navona. 📞06 68 30 12 52. www.hotelnavona.com. 18 rooms.* 🛏€10. This delightful hotel has cool, attractive rooms. The hotel is located in a 16C *palazzo* that was built on top of much older foundations. Breakfast is served at a long table.

⊝⊟⊟ **Hotel Due Torri** – *Vicolo del Leonetto 23, Piazza Navona. 📞06 68 80 69 56. www.hotelduetorriroma.com. 26 rooms.* 🛏. Once the home of cardinals and bishops, this brick-coloured residence stands slightly north of the Piazza Navona. Each room has its own unique décor and is furnished with a parquet floor and high quality furniture, including some genuine antiques. One of our favourite addresses in Rome.

⊝⊟⊟ **Hotel Teatro di Pompeo** – *Largo del Pallaro 8, Campo de' Fiori. 📞06 68 72 812. www.hotelteatrodi pompeo.it. 13 rooms.* 🛏. A boutique hotel now nestles in a medieval *palazzo*, once the Theatre of Pompey – the site of Caesar's assassination in 44BC. The charming hotel rooms are spacious and simply furnished, with coffered ceilings and tiled floors.

⊝⊟⊟⊟ **Hotel Raphaël** – *Largo Febo 2, Piazza Navona. 📞06 68 28 31. www.raphaelhotel.com. 50 rooms.* Easily one of Rome's most romantic hotels, this Relais & Chateaux property offers traditional rooms with antiques or sleekly cool rooms designed by Richard Meier. Don't miss a meal on the terrace near domes that seem close enough to touch and the superb cuisine of Fabrizio Marino in the hotel's restaurant.

PIAZZA DEL POPOLO/ PIAZZA DI SPAGNA

Hotel Panda – *Via della Croce 35, Piazza di Spagna.* ✆*06 67 80 179. www.hotelpanda.it. 28 rooms.* This well-kept pensione in a 19C *palazzo* not far from the Spanish Steps has simply furnished rooms, some with shared bathroom. Although lacking in overall charm, it is recommended for its excellent location and reasonable rates.

Hotel Centrale – *Via Laurina 34, Piazza di Spagna.* ✆*06 87 40 30 890. www.hotelcentraleroma.it. 21 rooms.* This simple hotel is in a side street off the busy Via del Corso – an ideal location for shoppers. Rooms are clean and quiet.

Hotel d'Inghilterra – *Via Bocca di Leone 14, Piazza di Spagna.* ✆*06 69 98 11. www.starhotelscollezione.com. 88 rooms. Restaurant.* Located in the old guest-quarters of Palazzo Torlonia, this hotel has retained the elegance and charm of a 15C residence. Furnishings of the period, valuable paintings and precious carpets recall its prestigious past.

Hotel Parlamento – *Via delle Convertite 5, Piazza di Spagna.* ✆*06 69 92 10 00. www.hotelparlamento.it. 21 rooms.* High ceilings and airy, spacious rooms – 10 renovated – decorated with plants provide this hotel with a pleasant, relaxing atmosphere. In summer, breakfast is served on an attractive terrace facing Piazza San Silvestro.

Hotel de Russie – *Via del Babuino 9, Piazza di Spagna.* ✆*06 32 88 81. www.roccofortehotels.com. 121 rooms. Restaurant.* This A-list hotel is popular with visiting stars and lumineries for its sleek, modern style. Rooms are smaller than you might expect, but full of modern conveniences. Boasts a top-notch health spa.

PORTA PIA–TERMINI

Hotel Marghera – *Via Marghera 29, Termini.* ✆*06 13 89 67 86. 26 rooms.* One of the most charming places in the neighbourhood. A warm ambience characterizes the elegant, English-style rooms. Four-poster beds augment the romantic atmosphere.

The Beehive Hostel – *Via Marghera 8, Termini.* ✆*06 44 70 45 53. www.the-beehive.com. 20 rooms.* This "hotel and art space" is an aesthetic, yet affordable, haven. Contemporary and minimalist in style and uses ecologically friendly products, including handmade soaps. A mix of ensuite rooms, rooms with shared bathroom, and dormitory beds. Reception closes at 11pm.

Hotel Cervia – *Via Palestro 55.* ✆*06 49 10 57. Castro Pretorio. www.hotelcerviaroma.com. 28 rooms.* This comfortable hotel close to Stazione Termini, has been managed by the same family since 1959, and as such has a friendly, homely air. Rooms either share bathrooms or are en-suite.

St Regis Grand Hotel – *Via Vittorio Emanuele Orlando 3. Piazza della Repubblica.* ✆*06 47 091. www.stregisrome.com. 161 rooms. Restaurant.* Plush luxury with a slightly theatrical air about it, thanks to an unapologetic mix of Roman Empire, Regency and Louis XV styles. Rooms are generous in size, and beds are huge. The lobby is a glamorous confection of palms, chandeliers and people-watching.

SANTA MARIA MAGGIORE/ SAN GIOVANNI IN LATERANO

YWCA – *Via Cesare Balbo 4, Santa Maria Maggiore.* ✆*06 48 80 460. www.ywca-ucdg.it. 40 rooms.* Accommodation available to women, couples and groups (not single men) in simple, clean rooms. Many of the rooms, both with and without private bathrooms, are rented out by the year to students. Closed midnight to 7am.

Hotel Piccadilly – *Via Magna Grecia 122, San Giovanni in Laterano.* ✆*06 70 47 48 58. www.hotelpiccadillyroma.it. 55 rooms.* This modern hotel extends over eight floors, with the upper one used as a panoramic breakfast room. The hotel is near the Basilica of St John Lateran and the market at Via Sannio.

Hotel Emona Aquaeductus – *Via Statilia 23, Manzoni.* ✆*06 70 27 827 www.hotelaquaeductus.it.* 🅿 *24 rooms.* In a decentralized and very quiet area, this hotel has an unusual elegance thanks to its room, decorated with unique pieces and offering all kinds of comforts. Beautiful green entranceway.

TRASTEVERE

◒◒ Antico Borgo di Trastevere –
Vicolo del Buco 7. ✆06 588 3774. 12 rooms. ☐. This modest 18C palace has exposed beams, French windows, wooden shutters and balcony flowerpots. All rooms have a private bath, colour television and air conditioning. Expect some late-night noise in this trendy area.

◒◒ Casa di Santa Francesca –
Via dei Vascellari 61. ✆06 58 12 125. www.sfromana.it. 37 rooms. This former medieval nobles' home now offers good value, quiet and peaceful rooms – simply furnished – many with small balconies and views of Trastevere below.

◒◒◒ Guesthouse Arco dei Tolomei –
Via dell'Arco de' Tolomei 27. ✆06 58 32 08 19. www.bbarcodeitolomei. com. 6 rooms. ☐. The owners of this B&B have a lovely sense of colour and design shown in the choice of finely crafted textiles and furnishings. This tranquil oasis in Trastevere has a pleasant internal terrace.

◒◒◒ Ripa Hotel – *Via degli Orti di Trastevere 3. ✆06 58 611. www. worldhotelriparoma.com. 199 rooms. Restaurant.* Self-conscious minimalism rules here. The lobby resembles a contemporary art exhibit with its scarlet and purple pouffes. DJs spin tunes in the downstairs club, dubbed Suite.

VATICANO–SAN PIETRO

◒◒ Colors Hotel – *Via Boezio 31, Prati. ✆06 68 74 030. www.colorshotel.com. 21 rooms.* Polished floors reflect great swathes of bright paint and Italian contemporary flair. A terrace surveys the skyline in this quiet quarter just north of the Vatican. Linen and hot water. Colors is 10–15-minutes from the Metro line A stop Ottaviano-San Pietro.

◒◒◒ Hotel Alimandi Tunisi – *Viale Vaticano, 99, Prati. ✆06 39 74 55 62. www. alimandihotels.com/tunisi. 31 rooms.* The rooms near the Vatican Museums are well appointed and comfortable. The hotel has a terrace on the first floor and

a roof garden for summer barbecues. Free shuttle service to the airport.

◒◒◒ Hotel Atlante Star – *Via G. Vitelleschi 34, Prati. ✆06 68 63 86 . www.atlantehotels.com. 70 rooms.* ☐. *Restaurant ◒◒◒.* This elegant hotel close to St Peter's has a roof garden with a magnificent view of the basilica. The hotel restaurant, Les Étoiles, capitalizes on this splendid location in summer.

VIA VENETO

◒◒◒ Hotel Invictus – *Via Quintino Sella 15. ✆06 42 01 14 33. www. hotelinvictus.com. 22 rooms.* ☐. The rooms in this well-maintained hotel are pleasant and comfortable with good quality furnishings. An ideal location for those wishing to experience the *"Dolce Vita"* ambiance, but with a modern twist.

VILLA BORGHESE–VILLA GIULIA

◒◒◒◒ Aldrovandi Villa Borghese
– *Via Ulisse Aldrovandi 15, Villa Borghese. ✆06 32 23 993. www.aldrovandi.com. 103 rooms. Restaurant ◒◒◒.* ☐. Sitting a few steps from the Villa Borghese, this prestigious hotel has lounges furnished with antiques and magnificent chandeliers. The elegant bedrooms are tastefully decorated. The restaurant Assaje is run by resident chef Claudio Mengoni, working under the supervision of Michelin-starred executive chef Andrea Migliaccio.

◒◒◒◒ Hotel Lord Byron – *Via Giuseppe de Notaris 5, Villa Giulia. ✆06 32 20 404. www.lordbyronhotel.com. 28 rooms.* ☐. *Restaurant ◒◒.* This small, elegant hotel is in a quiet spot, and overlooks the Villa Borghese gardens. Attractive 1920s décor and peaceful atmosphere, away from the bustle of the rest of the city. Rooms are plush, if a little on the small side. The restaurant is well-renowned for fine dining.

CAMPSITES

◒ **Happy Village** – *Via del Prato della Corte 1915, 10km/6mi from the centre. From Termini Station, take Metro line A to Piazzale Flaminio, then the train (linea Roma Nord) to Prima Porta and a shuttle bus (operates 8:30am–noon and 5pm–10:30pm). ✆06 33 62 64 01 or 06 33 61 45 96. www.happycamping.net.*

100 pitches and 80 bungalows. ⌐.
This pleasant campsite in the
northwest of the city has shaded,
terraced clearings on which to pitch
your tent, as well as electrical outlets
for caravans, bathrooms with free
showers, laundry facilities and drinking-
water fountains. A restaurant, bar,
supermarket, children's playground
and swimming pool are on-site.

⌐ **Flaminio Village Camping** –
*Via Flaminia Nuova 821, 8km/5mi
from the centre. From Termini Station,
take Metro line A to Piazzale Flaminio,
then the train (linea Roma Nord) to
Due Ponti (signal to stop the train at
this station). ℘06 33 32 604. www.
campingflaminio.com. 180 pitches and
130 chalets.* ⌐. Shaded by acacia

trees, this campsite has a restaurant,
grocery store, open-air swimming
pool, Internet access and a residential
area for chalets. In high season, staff
organise games and dance lessons.

⌐ **Roma Camping Catelfusano** –
*Via Litoranea 132 (lido di Ostia).
From Termini Station take Metro B to
Magliana, then Metro Roma-Lido to
Colombo then bus 061 (or 07, 070, 062
in summer) and night shuttle no. 2.
Closed Nov-Mar. ℘06 56 23 304.
www.romacampingcastelfusano.it.* ⌐.
A short distance from the beach,
the campsite in Ostia is surrounded
by Mediterranean vegetation
and has bungalows, restaurants
and a small market.

Where to Eat

**The Eternal City ranks among
the world's culinary capitals.
Long a proponent of Slow Food –
local recipes and fresh, indigenous
ingredients – its eateries shine, from
the humblest pizzeria or trattoria to
temples of haute cuisine.**

DINING ETIQUETTE

In Rome, lunch *(pranzo)* runs from
12:30–3pm and dinner *(cena)* from
8–11pm; restaurants generally close
around midnight. Most places shut
one day a week – and for two to three
weeks in August. Here the table is
sold for the evening. Customers are
expected to linger through at least
two or three of the following courses:
antipasto (hors-d'oeuvre), *primo* (pasta
or soup), *secondo* (meat or fish), then
perhaps an *insalata* (salad) or *contorni*
(vegetable), followed by *formaggio*
(cheese) or *dolce* (dessert) and, finally,
caffè (espresso) or liqueur, such as
amaro or grappa.
Avoid tourist menus *(menu turistico)*:
choice is limited and, too often, the
food inferior. Likewise, steer clear of
touts: what decent eatery needs one,

when locals queue hours for prime
tables? Some ritzy establishments,
however, offer a *menu degustazione*
(tasting menu), spotlighting kitchen
prowess and range.

BEVERAGES

Italians wash down meals with *acqua
minerale* (**bottled water**), either flat
(*naturale*) or carbonated (*gassata,
frizzante, con gas*). Ordering tap water
(*l'acqua del rubinetto*) is poor form.
However, Rome's municipal water is
fine to drink, though locals prefer to
fill bottles from the *nasone*, the street
spigots that free-flow from aqueducts.
Carafes of **house wine** (*vino della
casa*) come in litres (*litro*), half-litres
(*mezzo litro*) and sometimes quarters
(*un quartino*), akin to two glasses.
Standard wine bottles hold 750ml; it's
easy to underestimate the 25 percent
extra wallop of a litre. Though Italians
savour *un po' di vino* – a little wine –
they frown on public drunkenness.

WHAT'S IN A NAME?

In general, a **ristorante** offers
elegant cuisine and service, whereas a
trattoria or osteria is more likely to
be family-run and serve homemade

© Lucia Busnello/iStockphoto.com

dishes in a more informal atmosphere. Prices are usually lower in the latter and house wine (of varying quality) is available by the carafe. In typical trattorias, the waiter recounts the day's specials – determine a price before ordering.

WINE BARS

Wine bars *(enoteche)* have become increasingly popular in Italy. Some offer tapas-style snacks.

PIZZERIAS

A pizzeria is a sit-down restaurant, which may serve pasta for lunch and only fire the wood oven at night *(See below, Snacks: "pizza al taglio" below).* Fluffy Neapolitan-style pizza is becoming more and more popular. However, the traditional Roman ones are thin, crispy and drenched in olive oil. Locals rarely share: one pizza apiece is the drill. They generally start with **bruschetta** (toast rubbed with raw garlic, sprinkled with salt, drizzled with olive oil and topped with fresh tomatoes and basil) or **fritto misto alla Romana.** *Fritto misto* comprises different seasonal delicacies, such as zucchini flowers stuffed with mozzarella and anchovies, fillets of salted cod, stuffed giant green Ascoli olives, and potato croquettes dipped in batter and deep fried.

Those not wishing to order pizza may like to try a **crostino** instead: this toasted bread is similar to *bruschetta,* but is covered with melted cheese and Parma ham, or perhaps with *porcini* (cep) mushrooms.

INTERNATIONAL RESTAURANTS

As Italians tend to be very attached to their culinary traditions, ethnic restaurants are rather thin on the ground. Rome has a handful of Asian and Indian eateries, as well as Spanish, Mexican and American ones. Still novelties, these may not satisfy a sophisticated palate.

SNACKS AND CAFFÈ

A *pizza al taglio* shop turns out takeaway slices. Long slabs of **pizza** line the counter. Request the type and amount: the server then bisects the strip, presses the topping-faces together, and wraps the impromptu sandwich in wax paper *(about €3).* Many cafés serve **grilled sandwiches** and pastries, alongside the ubiquitous espresso. Enjoying coffee *al banco* (at the counter) is often much cheaper than *al tavolo* (at the table), especially in tourist hotspots. More informal establishments have customers pay at the *cassa* (register), then present the *scontrino* (receipt) to the server.

Purists drink *caffè* (**espresso**). *Lungo* dilutes the mix with water and *Americano* roughly equates to a regular coffee. *Caffèllatte* means espresso with hot milk, while *cappuccino* adds froth to the cup – expect a sneer if you order either after 4pm, however. Many Italians believe that milk prompts nightmares.

PASTICCERIAS AND GELATERIAS

Pastry shops *(pasticcerie)* offer mouth-watering delicacies. Typical Roman ones include *panpepato*, made from flour mixed with almonds, crystallised fruit, honey, orange rind and spices; *pangiallo*, prepared with maize flour, almonds, walnuts, pine nuts and raisins, *torta di ricotta e visciole* (ricotta and sour cherry tart) of Jewish origin, *zuppa inglese* and *bignè di San Giuseppe*, puff pastry filled with cream. Retreat to a *gelateria* to sample Rome's other confectionary triumphs. Ice creams and sorbets – often made in-house – are served in cones and cups (order at least two flavours). *Grattachecca* is the local version of *granita*, the crushed ice drink. The pieces of ice, scraped off large blocks with a spatula, are covered with sweet, colourful syrups and topped with fresh fruit. Vendors also sell these and water-cooled coconut slices in summer; roasted chestnuts and pumpkin seeds in cooler months. Addresses for snacks, such as pizza slices, ice-cream and pastries are given in the central section of the guide (⟲*See Discovering Rome section*).

FOR ALL BUDGETS

The eateries in this guide have been selected to suit all tastes and budgets, divided by district. Recommendations run from least to most expensive. The price brackets are based on the average cost of a meal per person, excluding drinks.
Restaurants indicated by the symbol ⊖ will charge less than 25€ for a three-course meal (excluding drinks) without sacrificing quality: this is

Italy, after all, where poor quality food is scandalous. This category includes typical trattorias, pizzerias or wine bars. Restaurants in the ⊖⊖ and ⊖⊖⊖ categories will charge between 25€ and 50€, and 50€ and 70€ for a meal. Customers should expect a more refined atmosphere and fine cuisine. The ⊖⊖⊖⊖ category includes some of the best and most elegant restaurants in the city – with prices to match.

BILLS, TIPS, FINE PRINT

Il conto (**the bill**) may include a small charge for *coperto* (cover) or *pane* (bread). These shouldn't impact the modest *resto* (**tip**), usually €2–3. Italians tip about 5 percent in a pizzeria or trattoria. The rate rises in posher places, but rarely tops 10 percent. Some restaurants only note the service charge *(servizio incluso)* in Italian. Stay alert and tip accordingly. More and more small restaurants and family-run trattorias are accepting credit cards now in Rome, but there's no guarantee you'll be able to use your plastic – check before you sit down if in doubt. Large notes (50s, 100s) often cause consternation, especially in cafés. Save coins for small transactions like this.

BOOKING

Book in advance on Fridays and Saturdays, although some small trattorias and pizzerias do not accept reservations. Go ahead and queue – the lively street scene is part of the Roman experience. In the *centro storico*, any establishment worth its salt has patrons waiting; the alternatives probably aren't busy for good reasons. Touts, in particular, are a sign of culinary catastrophe... Run, don't walk, away.

TYPICAL ROMAN CUISINE

Roman cuisine is often referred to as "*cucina povera*" – peasant cooking – because of its simplicity and reliance on fresh produce. A *trattoria* meal may start with an *antipasto* (hors d'oeuvre) of vegetables or mixed cold meats (*affettati*). The *primo* (first) course could be any one of a number of pasta dishes – the famous **fettuccine** egg pasta, **bucatini all'amatriciana** (a sauce made with olive oil, onions and streaky bacon, tomatoes, pecorino cheese), **spaghetti alla gricia** (a type of amatriciana, but without tomato), **tonnarelli con cacio e pepe** (a cheese and pepper sauce), **gnocchi alla Romana** (dumplings made with bran dough) or potato *gnocchi* (traditionally prepared on Thursdays), as well as the well-known **carbonara** dish. The most typical *secondi* – main courses – include **saltimbocca** (veal escalope rolled around a slice of ham and sage), **abbacchio** – suckling lamb cooked in a chasseur sauce (*alla cacciatora*) or grilled on a spit (*alla scottadito* in the Roman dialect), **trippa** (tripe cooked with tomatoes and herbs), **coda alla vaccinara** (oxtail cooked with bacon fat, garlic, green vegetables, salt, pepper, herbs, spices and white wine), **pajata** (lamb offal) and **baccalà** (dried cod), usually fried.

Typical *contorni* (side dishes) include **puntarelle** (greens flavoured with garlic and anchovies), **agretti** (another kind of very delicate salad vegetable served with vinegar), **carciofi alla giudìa** (whole fried artichokes), and **rughetta** (rocket, known as *rucola* in northern Italy). Cheese, especially **pecorino** (accompanied by broad beans in Spring). In the more simple *trattorias* the choice of desserts is usually limited to tiramisù, *panna cotta*, crème caramel or ice cream. Elsewhere, visitors may be able to sample a home-made **torta di ricotta** or **zuppa inglese,** which, despite its name, has Roman origins.
House wines are usually Montepulciano d'Abruzzo (red – *rosso*) and some Castelli Romani blend (white – *bianco*). Orvieto is a reliable and affordable option, as is Montefiascone's Est! Est!! Est!!!. Lazio's most famous vintages are the dry whites – *Vini dei Castelli* (Frascati,

Grottaferrata, Genzano, Marino and Velletri).

RESTAURANTS BY AREA

AVENTINO/PIRAMIDE CESTIA – TESTACCIO

Da Oio a Casa Mia – *Via Galvani 43–5, Testaccio.* 📞*06 57 82 680. Closed Sun.* Brick arches soar over red-checked tables in this neighbourhood trattoria. The menu concentrates on Roman offal like tripe and a scramble of heart, liver, spleen and lung with artichokes or onions. Vegetarians prefer the chickpea soup or *tagliolini cacio e pepe* (broad noodles with sheep's cheese and pepper).

Checchino dal 1887 – *Via Monte Testaccio 30, Testaccio.* 📞*06 57 43 816. www.checchino-dal-1887.com. Closed Sun evenings–Mon, Aug & 25 Dec–31 Dec. Booking recommended.* This restaurant specializes in butchers' off-cuts – oxtail, offal and tripe – as befits it location across from the old slaughterhouse. Specialities include *rigatoni con pajata*, sweetbreads in a white wine sauce and oxtail. Cheaper meals of cheese and vegetables are available at lunchtime.

Estro Bar – *Abitart Hotel, Via Pellegrino Matteucci 20, Ostiense.* 📞*06 57 28 91 41. www.estrobar.it. Closed lunchtime and Sun.* This trendy eatery does triple duty: as a pizzeria, gallery and wine bar in the hip outpost of the Abitart Hotel (*www.abitarthotel.com*), which almost single-handedly is gentrifying Ostiense. The minimalist menu includes nibbles like salami selections and *involtini di melanzana* (aubergine-wrapped cheese).

CATACOMBE DI PRISCILLA (VIA NOMENTANA, VIA SALARIA)

La Mora – *Piazza Crati 13, Catacombe di Priscilla. www.lamora.it.* 📞*06 86 20 66 13. Closed Mon, Tue lunchtime and 15 days in Aug.* This friendly, informal restaurant serves Tuscan cuisine and wood-fired pizzas. Other dishes include focaccia with provola cheese and pork sausage, and, for steak-lovers, a delicious *bistecca alla Fiorentina* from cattle raised in the Chiana Valley.

⊖⊖ **Lanificio Cucina** – *Via di Pietralata 159.* ☎*06 4178 0081. www. lanificio.com. Closed Mon and Sun dinner.* In an old industrial building on the edge of a Tiber tributary, this place has dissimilar furtniture and shared table to enjoy a refreshing Spritz and some creative dishes.

COLOSSEO–CELIO/FORI IMPERIALI/ PIAZZA VENEZIA/RIONE MONTI

⊖ **Enoteca 313** – *Via Cavour 313.* ☎*06 67 85 496. www.cavour313.it. Closed Jul-Aug.* In addition to the excellent wine list, this wineshop with kitchen just a couple of steps from the Imperial Forums offers top-notch sausages and vegetables in oil, sought-after cheeses and revisited traditional dishes.

⊖⊖ **Cuoco & Camicia** – *Via di Monte Polacco 2.* ☎*06 88 92 29 87, www. cuocoecamicia.it. Closed Mon.* Chef Riccardo Loreni cooks with creativity and flavor, well loved by regular customers. For lunch the bistrot-like atmosphere serves the day's special on black tables; for dinner, seasonal menu with candles.

⊖⊖ **Hasekura** – *Via dei Serpenti 27, Monti.* ☎*06 48 36 48. www.hasekura.it. Closed Sun and Aug.* This simply furnished Japanese restaurant is noted for its fresh ingredients and excellent sushi. This trendy address offers better value for money at lunchtime.

EUR

⊖⊖⊟ **Il Fungo**– *Piazza Pakistan 1a, 14th floor.* ☎*06 59 21 980. www. ristoranteilfungo.it. Closed Sat lunchtime and Sun dinnertime.* At the top of a stylized mushroom-shaped building, a panoramic terrace where you can enjoy meat and fish dishes prepared with recognised creativity.

⊖⊖⊟ **Vicolo 88** – *Viale America 18.* ☎*06 8772 8001 or 373 740 2948. www. vicolo88. it. 12:30-3pm and 7:30-11pm.* A new restaurant with a new concept: bistrot for lunchtime and refined cuisine for dinner with a fusion/ Mediterranean style. Do not miss the lounge bar and the beautiful terrace.

FONTANA DI TREVI–QUIRINALE

⊖ **Antica Pizzeria Est! Est!! Est!!! Ricci**– *Via Genova 32, Quirinale.* ☎*06 48 81 107. www.anticapizzeriaricciroma.it. Closed Mon.* One of the oldest pizzerias in Rome (the locale first opened in 1888, and has been run by the same family for four generations), its decor dates from the early 20C. (Look for the small cherub pouring the so-called "mayor's water".) The white wine that gives its name to the restaurant is highly recommended.

⊖⊖ **Il Giardino di Albino** – *Via Zucchelli 29, Trevi.* ☎*06 48 85 202. www.ilgiardinodialbino.com. Closed Mon.* This warm, friendly family offers typical Sardinian cuisine. Both the fish and meat dishes are excellent.

ISOLA TIBERINA–GHETTO–LARGO ARGENTINA

⊖⊖ **Al Pompiere** – *Via S. Maria de' Calderari 38, Torre Argentina.* ☎*06 68 68 377. www.alpompiereroma.com. Closed Sun.* A range of Roman-Jewish traditional dishes served in the spacious rooms of an old *palazzo*. The *crostata di ricotta e visciole* (ricotta and sour cherry tart) is highly recommended.

⊖⊖ **Renato e Luisa Quelli della Taverna** – *Via dei Barbieri 25, Torre Argentina.* ☎*06 68 69 660. www.renato eluisa.it. Dinner only. Closed Mon. Booking recommended.* Run by two friends, this friendly taverna serves drinks and pasta in terracotta crockery, as in days gone by. Try the fabulous focaccia.

⊖⊖ **Sora Lella** – *Via di Ponte Quattro Capi 16, Isola Tiberina.* ☎*06 68 61 601. www.trattoriasoralella.it. Closed Sun. Booking recommended.* This famous restaurant was once run by Lella Fabrizi, the sister of the actor Aldo. It is now managed by her son, who has extended the traditional range of family recipes to include new specialities. Don't miss the ricotta cake with sour cherry jam and the desserts.

⊖⊖⊟ **Piperno** – *Via Monte de' Cenci 9, Ghetto.* ☎*06 68 80 66 29. www.ristorantepiperno.it. Closed Sun dinnertime, Mon and Aug.* This ghetto favourite serves Jewish-Roman fare, including *carciofi alla giudia* (deep-fried artichokes) and *zuppa* *di ceci* (garbanzo-bean soup). The elegant cuisine is matched by the setting, a secluded piazza engulfed by the 15C Palazzo Cenci, where a noble family self-destructed.

MONTE MARIO–FLAMINIO

⊖⊜ **Osteria dell'Angelo** – *Via Giovanni Bettolo 24, Monte Mario. ℘06 37 29 470. Tue –Sun dinner only, Sat. lunch and dinner. Closed Sun and 2 weeks in Aug.* This lively trattoria, decorated with rugby shirts, serves a selection of traditional Roman dishes, including *tonnarelli cacio e pepe, rigatoni con pajata, coda alla vaccinara* and *trippa alla Romana* (*See Typical Roman Cuisine.*) The fixed-price dinner menu is good value for money.

⊖⊜⊜⊜ **La Pergola** – *Via Cadlolo 101, Hotel Cavalieri Hilton, Monte Mario. ℘06 35 09 2152. www.romecavalieri.com. Dinner only. Closed Sun–Mon, a fortnight in Jan and Aug. Booking recommended.* Atop Monte Mario preens this famous restaurant, reputed to be Rome's best. German Chef Heinz Beck intuits Italian fare, turning out dishes like fillet of John Dory with curry, scampi and vegetables or fried zucchini flower with shellfish.

PANTHEON/MONTECITORIO

⊖⊜ **Eau Vive** – *Via Monterone 85, Pantheon. ℘06 68 80 10 95. www.restaurant-eauvive.it. Closed Sun. Booking recommended.* This restaurant is run by missionary nuns of different nationalities and is inside the 16C Palazzo Lante. French specialities can be sampled in the large, frescoed dining room on the first floor.

⊖⊜ **Grano** – *Piazza Rondanini 53, Pantheon. ℘06 68 19 20 96. www.ristorantegrano.it.* Small outdoor tables make a pleasant place to sit and explore the menu of Mediterranean and classic home-cooked Italian food.

⊖⊜ **Osteria dell'Ingegno** – *Piazza di Pietra 45, Montecitorio. ℘06 67 80 662. www.osteriadellingegno.com. Closed 2 weeks in Aug. Booking recommended.* This charming bistro is always crowded at lunchtime. The menu includes elaborate dishes flavoured with herbs and a wide selection of charcuterie and cheeses.

⊖⊜ **Vecchia Locanda** – *Vicolo Sinibaldi 2, Pantheon. ℘06 68 80 28 31. www.vecchialocanda.eu. Closed Sun. Booking recommended.* In a typical narrow street between Largo Argentina and the Pantheon, this small, elegant restaurant is known for its beef and fresh homemade pasta. The atmosphere resembles a Roman inn's, with tables outside in summer.

⊖⊜⊜⊜ **La Rosetta** – *Via della Rosetta 8, Pantheon. ℘06 68 61 002. www.larosetta.com. Booking recommended.* This restaurant is well-known because of its excellent seafood, including *sashimi* (raw fish).

PIAZZA NAVONA/CAMPO DE' FIORI/ CASTEL SAN ANGELO

⊖ **Da Francesco** – *Piazza del Fico 29, Piazza Navona. ℘06 68 64 009. www.dafrancesco.it. Booking recommended.* The attractive *Piazza del Fico* is home to this lively trattoria which serves typical Roman dishes, including pizzas, an excellent focaccia with dry-cured ham and various types of pasta. A cheerful atmosphere.

⊖ **La Montecarlo** – *Vicolo Savelli 13. ℘06 68 61 877. www.lamontecarlo.it.* Just a short walk away from the piazza Alessandria market, this pizzeria offers a rich menu of fresh fish, antipasti and a warm, enthusiastic welcome.

⊖⊜ **Cul de Sac** – *Piazza Pasquino 73, Piazza Navona. ℘06 68 80 10 94. www.enotecaculdesacroma.it.* Winebar and food with French atmosphere: lots of Gallic cheeses plus Italian wines and traditional dishes.

⊖⊜ **Enoteca L'Angolo Divino** – *Via dei Balestrari 12, Campo de' Fiori. ℘06 68 64 413. www.angolodivino.it. Closed Mon lunchtime, Sun and 1 week in Aug.* This old wine and oil store has been converted into a rustic, simply furnished wine bar, lined with bottle-filled shelves. The snacks on offer include tarts and roulades. A selection of over 600 labels of organic and natural wines.

⊖ **Pizzeria Da Baffetto** – *Via del Governo Vecchio 114, Piazza Navona. ℘06 68 61 617. www.pizzeriabaffetto.it. No lunch weekdays. Closed Tue. Second location at Vicolo della Cancelleria 13.* Summer of Love radicals made this place trendy. Now everyone jostles for a seat at the straightforward establishment. The pizzas are crisp, and the service brusque in classic Roman style.

🍷🍷 **Osteria Ar Galletto** – *Piazza Farnese 104, Campo de' Fiori.* 📞*06 68 61 714.* This Piazza Farnese restaurant was founded in 1484 and was once known as the *Osteria dei Borgia*. Ham is still cut by hand in front of customers and there is a wide choice of sauces for pasta.

🍷🍷🍷🍷 **Pierluigi** – *Piazza de' Ricci 144, Campo de' Fiori.* 📞*06 68 68 717. www.pierluigi.it. Booking recommended.* Set in one of the most pleasant squares in Rome, this restaurant, open since 1938, has an intimate ambience and outdoor and indoor tables. The menu focuses on fish. Pasta dishes are delicious and service is impeccable. The lovely piazza adds to the overall experience.

PIAZZA DEL POPOLO/ PIAZZA DI SPAGNA

🍷🍷 **GiNa** – *Via San Sebastianello, 7/A, Piazza di Spagna district.* 📞*06 67 80 251. Closed 1 week in Aug.* This tasteful white-on-white restaurant is perfect for a quick bite or a relaxed meal. Gina also provides hampers for picnickers in the nearby Villa Borghese.

🍷🍷 **La Penna d'Oca** – *Via della Penna 53, Piazza del Popolo.* 📞*06 32 02 898. www.ristorantepennadoca.com. Tue–Fri only dinner, Sat–Sun lunch and dinner. Closed Mon. Booking recommended.* This charming restaurant serves traditional cuisine, innovative fish and seafood dishes (try the conch pie served with red onion) and homemade bread. Summertime veranda.

PIRAMIDE CESTIA–TESTACCIO

Nuovo Mondo – *Via Amerigo Vespucci 15/17.* 📞*06 57 46 004.* This popular locale is renowned for pizza dough so thin it's almost transparent. Relax and enjoy your meal at one of the small tables, sitting elbow-to-elbow with a broad range of different clientele.

🍷🍷 **Bucatino** – *Via Luca della Robbia 84/86. www.dabucatino.it* 📞*06 57 46 886. Closed Mon.* Traditional, generous Italian

cuisine. After appetizing antipasti, you'll be delighted with a selection of meats, fish and offal, all cooked to perfection. Relaxed, warm and welcoming.

🍷🍷 **Felice** – *Via Mastro Giorgio 29, Testaccio.* 📞*06 57 46 800. www.felice atestaccio.it.* Overhauled interior and price list, but fortunately not the culinary tradition, which remains as it was.

PORTA PIA–TERMINI

🍷 **Trimani il Wine Bar** – *Via Cernaia 37/b, Porta Pia.* 📞*06 44 69 630. www. trimani.com. Closed Thu and Sun and a fortnight in Aug.* This bar, run by one of the oldest families in the Roman wine business, offers an impressive selection and fine cuisine. Summer brings outdoor seating.

SAN LORENZO FUORI LE MURA

🍷🍷 **Tram Tram** – *Via dei Reti 44.* 📞*06 49 04 16. www.tramtram.it - 12:30pm-3pm, 7:30-11pm. Closed Mon.* The real Roman *trattoria*, unpretentious and never disappointing. Professors from the nearby university La Sapienza usually meet here.

🍷🍷 **Farinè** – *Via degli Aurunci 6/8, San Lorenzo district.* 📞*06 44 51 162 www. farinelapizza.it.* Three different formats of pizza, top quality ingredients and good choice of real ales and wines.

SANTA MARIA MAGGIORE/ SAN GIOVANNI IN LATERANO

🍷 **Pizzeria La Gallina Bianca** – *Via A. Rosmini 5-12, Santa Maria Maggiore.* 📞*06 47 43 777. www.lagallinabianca roma.it.* This popular, rustic-style pizzeria also serves excellent *fritti* (deep-fried specialities). Indulge in homemade desserts, including a tiramisù with strawberries.

🍷🍷 **Ginza** – *Via Emanuele Filiberto 249/251* 📞*06 700 57 39. 12-3pm, 7pm-12am.* A great choice of sushi and sashimi in a fresh atmosphere thanks to its typical Japanese design.

🍷🍷 **Charly's Saucière** – *Via di San Giovanni in Laterano 270, San Giovanni in Laterano.* 📞*06 70 49 56 66. No lunch. Closed Sun, 2 weeks in Aug and 24–26 in Dec. Booking recommended.* Renowned as one of Rome's genuinely French

© H. hughes/hemis.f

outlets, it has an old-fashioned, welcoming ambiance. Traditional meat and fish dishes predominate, in addition to Swiss specialities, in honour of the chef's country of origin.

TRASTEVERE–GIANICOLO

Pizzeria Panattoni Ai Marmi – *Viale Trastevere 53/59, Trastevere.* ℘*06 58 00 919. No lunch. Closed Wed and 10–26 in Aug.* Huge slab tables earn this classic pizzeria two nicknames: *I Marmi* (the Marbles) and the less-appetizing *l'Obitorio* (the Morgue). That – and the cranky service – still don't scare off customers. Waiters slam down vast, crispy pizzas, chilled Peroni beer and serviceable house red, scowling at celebrities and "nobodies" alike.

Pizzeria Dar Poeta – *Vicolo del Bologna 45/46, Trastevere.* ℘*06 58 80 516. trastevere.darpoeta.com.* The queue is worth the wait here. Expect quirky combinations (like apples and Gran Marnier) and soft, dripping pizzas on slow-risen bases. The bill is scrawled on the tablecloth, but the atmosphere is jovial and the food extraordinary.

Jaipur – *Via San Francisco a Ripa 56, Trastevere.* ℘*06 580 3992. www.ristorantejaipur.it. Closed Mon mornings.* Rome's best Indian restaurant serves North Indian specialities from a clay tandoori oven. Dine outside on this pleasant side street. Spice fans should exaggerate their normal

preferences: Italians prefer ethnic food far more mild than most foreigners.

Thai Inn – *Via Federico Ozanam 94, Gianicolo, Monteverde.* ℘*06 58 20 31 45. Closed Mon in Sept–Jun.* These Thai chefs would stand out in any city – and are worth the bus trip. Christmas lights, blue lanterns, aquariums, bamboo matting, fake flowers and butterflies create a tranquil atmosphere.

Antico Arco – *Piazzale Aurelio 7, Gianicolo, Monteverde.* ℘*06 58 15 274. www.anticoarco.it.* Internationally acclaimed nouvelle cuisine stars here such as lasagna with guinea-fowl or pigeon breast with fruits and mashed potatoes The cellar contains some 1 200 labels. The vine-swathed restaurant sits inside an 18C *palazzo*.

Enoteca Ferrara – *Piazza Trilussa 41, Trastevere.* ℘*06 58 33 39 20. www.enotecaferrara.it. Closed Sun in Aug.* Nibble at the bar – or book a table to seriously imbibe. The international wine list, 850-bottles strong, is the main draw, however the kitchen turns out thoughtful dishes like perch with red cabbage and *involtini di pesce spada* (swordfish fillets rolled around cinnamon-flecked filling).

VATICANO–SAN PIETRO

Taverna Angelica – *Piazza Amerigo Capponi 6,* ℘*06 68 74 514. www.tavernaangelica.it. No lunch Mon–Sat. Closed Aug. Booking* recommended. Rustic fare with a modern twist, delivered with flair in this cosy restaurant, tucked away in the Borgo Pio district near St Peter's Basilica. The menu is primarily seafood and selected meats, and there's a comprehensive Italian wine list to complement every dish.

Venerina – *Borgo Pio 38, Prati. 06 68 64 551. www.ristorantevenerina.it.* Pasta and risotto dishes feature largely on the menu of this restaurant situated just paces away from the Vatican walls. Choose from traditional Roman cooking or international fare, both prepared with local produce in season. Tables on the cobbled streets outside provide entertainment as you watch the world go by.

VIA VENETO

Doney – *Via Vittorio Veneto 125, Via Veneto. 06 47 08 27 83. www. restaurantdoney.com.* Freshly updated décor inside greets diners to this longstanding fixture in the Via Veneto. Patrons savour juniper-flavored grilled veal *tagliata*, a selection of fish or other inventive dishes. The lengthy sidewalk set-up is ideal for alfresco dining or pre-dinner cocktails.

VILLA BORGHESE–VILLA GIULIA

Al Ceppo – *Via Panama 2, Parioli district. 06 85 30 13 70. www.ristorantealceppo.it. Closed Mon mornings. Booking recommended.* In the smart Parioli district, this restaurant has a rustic, yet elegant, feel. Innovative cuisine uses seasonal produce and is based on traditional recipes. Desserts include chestnut ice cream with hot chocolate sauce.

Sapori del Lord Byron – *Via Guiseppe de Notaris 5. 06 32 20 404. www.lordbyronhotel.com. Closed Sun. Booking recommended.* Set in the luxurious Hotel Lord Byron, in the exclusive Parioli district, this Art Deco-style restaurant is synonymous with haute cuisine all the way. A mixture of regional dishes is executed to perfection and presented with flair. The award-winning wine cellar includes famous Italian and international wines, as well as those from small local wine producers – and the sommelier is incredibly knowledgeable and helpful.

Entertainment

THEATRES AND CLASSICAL MUSIC VENUES
TICKETS

Tickets for plays and concerts (and sporting events) can be purchased from some agencies in Rome. The most central include **Orbis** *(Piazza Esquilino 37, Santa Maria Maggiore district, 06 48 27 403, www. boxofficelazio.it* and, above all, the **Box Office di Feltrinelli** *(largo Torre Argentina 11, 199 151 173; Viale Giulio Cesare 88, Prati, Vaticano district, 199 151 173)* offers a comprehensive ticketing service.

Also available are online and automated ticketing systems: **www. ticketone.it** (concerts, museums, shows and sport); **www.vivaticket.it** (events and shows); **www.listicket. com** (for all events); also available electronic ticketing services in many *tabaccherie* and Lotto outlets.

PUBLICATIONS

Information on films, plays, concerts and exhibitions is listed in **oggiroma** *(www.oggiroma.it)*. Cultural events are detailed in **Time Out Rome** *(www. timeout.com)* and **Wanted in Rome** *(www.wantedinrome.com)*.

VENUES

Venues range from traditional theatres, usually in the old centre, to modern venues staging more contemporary and experimental shows, often near the university.

Teatro dell'Opera – *Piazza Beniamino Gigli 7, Santa Maria Maggiore–Monti. 06 48 16 01 or 06 48 17 003. www. operaroma.it.* Tickets can be purchased in advance or up to 1hr prior to shows. Recommended for fans of classical music, opera and ballet, this large theatre provides subtitles for shows in foreign languages. In summer, open-air performances are organised amid the romantic outdoor setting of Caracalla's Baths.

Teatro Olimpico – *Piazza Gentile da Fabriano 17, Flaminio. ☎06 32 65 991. www.teatroolimpico.it. Box office open Mon–Sun 10am–7pm.* This theatre on the banks of the Tiber is the headquarters of the Accademia Filarmonica Romana. Musical shows, ballet and some comic opera are staged here.

Teatro Sistina – *Via Sistina 129, Piazza di Spagna. ☎06 42 00 711 or 392 85 67 896. www.ilsistina.it. Box office open Tue–Sat 10am–7pm.* Renowned for its excellent acoustics, this theatre hosts famous musicals, as well as concerts by acclaimed international performers.

Auditorium Parco della Musica – *Viale Pietro de Coubertin 30, Flaminio. ☎06 80 24 12 81 or 892 101 (fee). www.auditorium.com.* Home to the Accademia Nazionale di Santa Cecilia, this prestigious concert hall is the setting for concerts by some of the best-known orchestras and conductors from across the globe.

Teatro Argentina – *Largo di Torre Argentina 52. ☎06 68 40 00 311. www.teatrodiroma.net. Box office open Tue–Sun 10am–7pm.* Built at the beginning of the 18C, this large theatre staged the first performance of the Barber of Seville in 1816. The theatre enjoys an excellent location opposite the Roman ruins of Largo Argentina, and offers a programme mainly of drama.

Teatro Quirino Vittorio Gassman – *Via delle Vergini 7. Ticket office in Via delle Vergini (corner of via Minghetti), Fontana di Trevi. ☎06 67 94 585. www.teatroquirino.it. Box office open Mon–Sun 10am–7pm.* The theatre is known for its emphasis on traditional drama, although experimental plays are also occasionally performed here.

Teatro Eliseo – *Via Nazionale 183, Quirinale. ☎06 83 51 02 16. www.teatroeliseo.com. Box office open Mon 1–7pm, Tue–Fri 10am–7pm, Sun 10am–4pm and during performances.* In addition to well-known drama, this theatre hosts works by the greatest 20C Italian writers, such as Aldo Palazzeschi and Eduardo de Filippo. Dance performances are also occasionally held here.

Teatro Parioli – *Via Giosuè Borsi 20, Parioli. ☎333 99 51 643. www.teatropariolipeppinodefilippo.it. Box office open Thu–Sat 10am–2pm, 3pm–7pm, Sun 10am–2pm.* Now home to Neopolitan comedies, this venue formerly hosted the recording of the popular Italian TV *Maurizio Costanzo Show*.

Casa dei Teatri – *Villa Doria Pamphilj, Largo 3 Giugno 1849 (corner of Via di San Pancrazio; entry Arco dei Quattro Venti). ☎06 45 46 06 91. Open Tue–Sun 10am–4pm.* An innovative spin on theatre, the recently founded Casa dei Teatri, located in the Villino Corsini in Villa Pamphili, looks at performance from all angles, and combines its productions with research, training courses and workshops.

CINEMA
SCREENS

In addition to arthouses and multiplexes, Rome has small clubs like **Filmstudio** (*Via degli Orti d'Alibert 1/c, Trastevere; ☎334 17 80 632*), which also provide subscription packages, much like social clubs *(centri sociali)*. Cinemas typically screen at 2:30pm, 4:30pm, 6:30pm, 8:30pm and 10:30pm.
Smaller venues close for the summer but outdoor screens take up the slack.

OPEN-AIR CINEMAS

In July and August, open-air "villages" set up for the *Estate Romana* festival offer cinema-lovers the opportunity to see a number of films. Among the long standing venues taking part in this festival, **Cineporto** screens the most successful films of the previous season every year under the pine trees near the Ministero degli Affari Esteri (*www.cineporto.com; Largo Marcello Mastroianni 1; entrance on Piazzale del Brasile; ☎06 86 39 85 60*), while the **Isola del Cinema** (*L'Isola Tiberina between the Ponte Cestio and Ponte Fabricio; ☎06 58 33 31 13; www.isoladelcinema.com; open Jul–Sept*) shows a mix of popular and lesser-known fare.

☺ Night-time Snacks ☺

Some city bakeries open their doors to night owls.
The best known are in **Trastevere** and **Testaccio.**
(🕯 see Discovering section).

At the **Nuovo Sacher**, owned by Italian film legend Nanni Moretti, a projector is outside in summer. English offerings are typically Mon–Tue (Largo Ascianghi 1, Trastevere; ✆06 58 18 116; www.sacherfilm.eu).
For films in original language and historical Italian (and other) films, **Azzurro Scipioni** (Via degli Scipioni 82, Prati district. ✆06 39 73 71 61. www.silvanoagosti.com).

FILM CENTRE AND FESTIVAL

The **Casa del Cinema** celebrates western filmmaking. The elegant building – formerly "home of the roses" – stands in a pastoral stretch of the Village Borghese, just 50m/55yd from the Via Veneto. Visitors can attend screenings, view archival DVDs, browse the bookshop or loiter in the café (Largo Marcello Mastroianni 1, enter from the Piazzale del Brasile, Parcheggio di Villa Borghese; ✆06 06 08; www.casadelcinema.it; the Casa del Cinema opening hours follow that events programme).

Auditorium Parco della Musica

©RoeDeRo/iStock

The **Rome Independent Film Festival** takes place in early April each year (Places of projection vary, ✆06 45 42 50 50; www.riff.it).
The undisputed protagonist of the film season is the **Festival Internazionale del Film di Roma**, held in the Auditorium (Viale Pietro De Coubertin 10; ✆06 40 40 19 00. www.romacinemafest.it).

NIGHTLIFE

🕯 See Discovering Rome for additional bars, pubs or other night spots.

DISTRICTS

Rome after-hours mainly concentrates in five areas, each attracting different patrons. The district between **Piazza Campo de' Fiori** and **Piazza Navona** has a wide choice of pubs and bars, drawing a mix of young students, tourists and theatre-goers (especially to the elegant bars around Piazza Navona). On the streets of **Trastevere,** the bars and restaurants are typically Roman in character and host live music. The majority of the city's most popular nightclubs are concentrated in the **Testaccio** district, particularly in Via di Monte Testaccio, and more recently, in the nearby Via di Libetta, Via dei Magazzini Generali and Porto Fluviale in the Ostiense district. Numerous other locations can be found in the **San Lorenzo** and **Pigneto** university neighbourhoods.
🕯 A list of suggestions for bars, pubs and nightclubs is given below.

ESTATE ROMANA FESTIVAL

In summer, most nightclubs move out to their cooler premises along the exclusive Fregene Beach. Open-air concerts are held in the various "villages" within the capital, where books, records, homemade products and clothes – as well as sandwiches and drinks – can be bought, before dancing the night away or sitting at a table to enjoy the music. The most famous of these include **Testaccio Village,** which welcomes a number of international artists every year;

the **Centrale Live Foro Italico,** where annual cabaret shows are held; **Parco di Villa Celimontana,** for jazz concerts; **Rock in Roma,** (*www.rockinroma.com* in Ippodromo Capannelle); **Parco di Villa Ada Savoia,** for new sounds and for Latin-American music, the **Fiesta** (*Via delle Tre Fontane 24, EUR district; ℘06 87 46 32 96; www.fiesta.it).* Music, stands, festivals and cinema at **Eutropia** in the Città dell'Altra Economia in Testaccio.
For further information, access www.estateromana.comune.roma.it.

VENUES

Akab Club – *Via di Monte Testaccio 69, Testaccio. ℘06 57 25 05 85. Open 11:30pm-5am. Closed Tue–Wed.* A large number of new venues have opened in this district in the last few years. Akab has a cellar and an upper floor, which is used for concerts and theme evenings.

Alexanderplatz – *Via Ostia 9, Prati. ℘06 83 77 56 04. Open 20pm, performances 10pm. Jul–Aug.* Some of the greatest jazz musicians in the world have played here in the past 15 years. Concerts start 10pm.

Goa Club – *Via Libetta 13. ℘06 574 8277. www.goaclub.com. Open Thu-Sat 11pm-3am. .* A huge loft differently decorated each year where the biggest DJs play the best electronic music every weekend.

Planet Roma – *Via del Commercio 36, Piramide Cestia-Testaccio. ℘06 57 47 826 or 331 76 05 752. www.planetroma.com.* Newly refurbished, what used to be the legendary Alpheus is still one of the most important discotheques in the city. 4 rooms and a courtyard for all kinds of events, from dance to cabaret, as well as live music and art.

Big Mama – *Vicolo S. Francesco a Ripa 18, Trastevere. ℘06 58 12 551. Closed summer. www.bigmama.it.* Brick walls and huge names: this club has international jazz and blues appeal.

Ex-Dogana – *Via dello Scalo di San Lorenzo 10. www.exdogana.com. Open 12am-2pm (5pm Fri).* A repurposed industrial space that hosts exhibitions of contemporary art, a club, a bar, a karaoke... It's impossible to get bored here.

Jonathan's Angels – *Via della Fossa 16, Piazza Navona. ℘06 68 93 426.* It's often difficult to find a seat in this popular piano bar, deliberately kitsch and decorated with paintings by the owner, an enigmatic figure who dominates the till. Nip out the back and enjoy the eccentricity of Rome's most famous toilet, complete with statuary.

Radio Londra– *Via di Monte Testaccio 67. Testaccio. ℘06 57 47 904. Closed Tue. www.radiolondradiscobar.com.* For more than 15 years, Radio Londra has been one of the most "underground" clubs in Rome. You dance beneath the vaults of a grotto.

Piper–*Via Tagliamento 9, Catacombe di Priscilla. ℘06 85 55 398. www.piperclub.it. Closed Jun–mid Sept.* Opened in 1965, this famous nightclub now organises theme evenings, including rock, underground and 1970s music.

Gregory's Jazz Club–*Via Gregoriana 54/a, Piazza di Spagna. ℘06 67 96 386 or 327 82 63 770 (from 7pm). Closed Mon. www.gregorysjazz.com.* A cult place for jazz and blues lovers, also for connoisseurs of whisky and lovers of the atmosphere of the clubs of the past.

Monk – *via Giuseppe Mirri 35, Stazione Tiburtina. ℘06 64 85 09 87. www.monkroma.club.* Music and shows to see in a city garden while lounging on deckchairs, but you can also play ping-pong, basketball or billiards. Other activities too by night

Trinity College – *Via del Collegio Romano 6. ℘06 678 6472. www.trinity-rome.com. 12:30pm-3am.* A pub in true Irish style organized on two floors of a wonderful ancient building. British and Irish beers to drink watching a sport match among Italian and foreign people.

Shopping

Unlike other capital cities in Europe, Rome does not have many large department stores, preferring a wide range of small shops and boutiques to suit all tastes and budgets. Visitors will have no difficult in buying antiques, craft products and high-quality food produce throughout the city, especially in the historic centre, as well as an excellent selection of the latest fashions.

The following section gives information on where to shop in Rome, with descriptions of the different areas of the city that specialise in certain products. Each category lists shops, detailed in the *Discovering Rome* section. In general, clothes stores are closed on Monday morning; food shops close on Thursday afternoon. With the exception of the historic centre, where shops tend to stay open all day, shops are open from 10am–1pm and from 4pm–7:30pm (winter) or 5pm–8pm (summer). Credit cards are accepted in most stores, with the exception of small food shops.

FASHION

Many luxury stores are located in **Via Veneto,** and some of the best-known names in the Italian fashion world can be found in the area between **Via del Corso** and **Piazza di Spagna,** especially in Via Frattina, Via Borgognona *(Laura Biagiotti, Fendi etc)* and Via Bocca di Leone *(Versace).* Particularly worthy of mention in this district is **Bulgari,** one of the original goldsmiths in Rome, which is situated at the beginning of **Via dei Condotti.** In the same street, **Raggi** is quite popular with young people for its reasonably priced and striking jewellery. Other famous names in this district include Armani, Gucci, Prada and Valentino. **Via del Corso,** packed with youngsters on a Saturday afternoon, is home to a variety of

shops selling all kinds of goods, as are **Via Nazionale, Via del Tritone** and **Via Cola di Rienzo.**

These shops have been selected for their prices and original goods:

PIAZZA DEL POPOLO

Bomba – *Via dell'Oca 39/41.* 🖉 *06 36 12 881. www.cristinabomba.com. Open Tue –Sat 11am–7:30pm (Mon open 3:30pm).* This boutique specialises in women's clothes: simple, elegant and sought-after designs.

SAN GIOVANNI IN LATERANO

David Saddler – *Via Appia Nuova 47.* 🖉 *06 99 70 67 96. www.davidsaddler.com. Open Mon–Sat 10am–8pm; Sun 10:30am– 1:30pm, 3–8pm.* This shop has a number of outlets in the city for those who like classical styles and sells a range of English-style jackets, trousers, gloves and shirts at reasonable prices.

PIAZZA DEL POPOLO

De Clercq & De Clercq – *Via dei Prefetti 10.* 🖉 *06 68 13 68 26. www. declercqdeclercq.com. Open Tue–Sat 11am–7pm (Mon 3–7pm).* All the exquisite jumpers and tops here are made from natural fibres, including cashmere and silk.

PIAZZA DI SPAGNA

Beauty Camiceria – *Via Francesco Crispi 10.* 🖉 *06 67 95 146. Open Tue–Sat 10:30am-7pm.* Shirts both prêt-à-porter and tailor-made for men and women. A historic shop open since 1946.

Sermoneta Gloves – *Piazza di Spagna 61.* 🖉 *06 67 91 960. www. sermonetagloves.com. Open Mon–Sat 10am–7pm.* A rainbow of colours and a wide variety of styles of leather gloves. Pick your pair in the windows downstairs, then go upstairs for service.

CAMPO DE' FIORI

Franco Borini – *Via dei Pettinari 86/87.* 🖉 *06 68 75 670. Open Tue–Sat 10am–7:30pm (Mon 11–7:30pm).* Extreme footwear stars here: square-toed shoes, extremely high heels, outrageous designs and acid-bright colours abound.

© G. Wyn Williams / age fotostock

FONTANA DI TREVI–QUIRINALE

AS Roma Store–*Piazza Colonna 360. ☎06 69 78 12 32 . www.asromastore.it. Open Mon–Sat 10am–7pm.* The official shop of the AS Roma soccer team, offering everything a "wolves" fan could wish for. Other AS Roma stores: Via del Corso 25-26-27, Via Nazionale 195, Via Arenula 82.

Del Giudice–*Via Stelletta 24. ☎06 68 80 97 24. delgiudiceroma.com. Open Mon –Sat 10:30am–1:30pm, 2:30–7:30pm.* Located on a side street off Via della Scrofa, this handbag haven has been offering original, well-made creations since 1959. A must-see for lovers of all things Made in Italy!

PIAZZA NAVONA

Maga Morgana – *Via del Governo Vecchio 27. ☎06 68 78 095. Open Mon-Sat 9:30am-8pm.* Fashionistas in the know head here for unique knitwear, vintage T-shirts and funky style pieces.

ANTIQUES

Stroll in the Piazza di Spagna district along **Via del Babuino,** home to the city's most prestigious antique dealers, and **Via Margutta,** with its many art galleries and craft shops, which still specialise in the restoration of marble and silver objects.
The most lively area, especially during fairs, is **Via dei Coronari,** not far from Piazza Navona.

Wandering through the narrow alleyways around **Piazza Campo de' Fiori** and **Piazza Farnese,** don't be surprised to see second-hand dealers and craftsmen busy at work in the sunshine. Particularly worthy of note are some of the long-established shops and those with a real flavour of the past, though far from the city's famous streets.

PIRAMIDE CESTIA–TESTACCIO

Le Bambole – *Via Luca della Robbia 11. ☎06 57 56 895. www.lebambole-testaccio.it. Mon 4pm–7:30pm, Tue–Sat 9am–1pm, 4–7:30pm. Closed Mon mornings, Sun and Aug.* Two artists skilfully repair antique dolls in this unusual shop.

CAMPO DE' FIORI

Comics Bazar – *Via dei Banchi Vecchi 127/128. ☎06 68 80 29 23. Open Tue–Sat 9:30am–7:30pm (Mon 3–7:30pm).* Furniture – including items by Thonet – and bric-à-brac jumble together in this curious shop.

PANTHEON

Ditta G. Poggi – *Via del Gesù 74/75. ☎06 67 93 674. www.poggi1825.it. Open Mon–Sat 9am–2pm, 3–7:30pm.* This shop, opened in 1825, provides students of the nearby Fine Arts School with materials.

Libreria Antiquaria C. E. Rappaport – *Via Sistina 23. ☎06 48 38 26. www.rappaport.it. Mon–Fri 10am–1pm, 3–7pm, Sat by appointment.* The perfect bookshop for collectors of old books, prints and old maps, some of which are particularly valuable and can fetch considerable prices.

FONTANA DI TREVI–QUIRINALE

Antica Farmacia Pesci – *Piazza Fontana di Trevi 89. ☎06 67 92 210. www.anticafarmaciapesci.it. Open Mon–Sat 8am–8pm.* Rome's oldest pharmacy, dating to the mid-16C, retains a number of its old features, including jars and the huge structure that once separated the laboratory from the shop.

PIAZZA DI SPAGNA

Hausmann & Co. – *Via del Corso 406. ☎06 68 71 501. www.hausmann-co.com. Mon–Sat 10:30am–7pm. Other locations in Via Condotti 28 and Via del Babuino 63.* This shop, the official watch-maker to the Vatican City, was founded in 1794 and continues to mend and sell magnificent old timepieces, amid sumptuous red velvet décor.

VATICANO–SAN PIETRO

Italia Garipoli – *Borgo Vittorio 91/a. ☎06 68 80 21 96. Closed Tue–Sat 10am–7pm.* As well as producing and selling precious lace and embroidery, this shop also restores valuable clothes and fabrics.

FOOD AND DRINK

FORI IMPERIALI

La Bottega del Cioccolato – *Via Leonina 82. ☎06 48 21 473. www.labottegadelcioccolato.it. Open Mon–Sat 9:30am–7:30pm (Dec always open).* As the name suggests, this shop specialises in items made from chocolate.

CATACOMBE DI PRISCILLA

Gatti e Antonelli – *Via Nemorense 211. ☎06 86 21 80 44. www.gattiantonelli.it. Mon–Sat 8:30–1:30pm, 4:30–7:30pm, Tue 8:30am–1:30pm, Sun 9am–1pm. Closed Tue afternoons and 15 days in Aug.* This shop may make the best pasta in Rome.

PORTA PIA–TERMINI

Latticini Micocci – *Via Collina 14. ☎06 47 41 784. Open Mon–Sat 9am–7:30pm. Closed in Aug 15–30.* Known throughout the city as *"Micocci on Via Collina"*, this friendly shop is paradise for cheese-lovers, with its excellent buffalo mozzarella and a wide selection of French and Piedmontese cheeses. Make sure you sample the sheep's ricotta and the creamy yoghurt.

VATICAN CITY

Castroni – *Via Cola di Rienzo 196, Prati district. ☎06 68 74 383. www.castronicoladirienzoshop.com. Open 8:30am–8pm. Other locations at Via Frattina and Viale Marconi (closed Sun).* Worth a visit for the freshly-roasted espresso coffee beans alone, this delicatessen sells delicious specialities from around the world. Local delights include Italian hams.

Bar Pasticceria Antonini – *Via Sabotino 19/29, Prati district. ☎06 37 24 354. www.antoniniroma.it. Open 7am–9pm.* A real institution for its pastry shop (*millefoglie* and *torte alla fragoline di bosco*), but also ice-cream, hot food, delicious aperitifs and a catering service.

PIRAMIDE CESTIA–TESTACCIO

Il Canestro – *Via Luca della Robbia 12, Testaccio district. ☎06 574 6287. www.ilcanestro.com. Open Mon–Sat 9am–8pm. Other locations at Viale Gorizia 51 (Trieste district) and Via San Francesco a Ripa 106 (Trastevere district).* Health foods and natural cosmetics jostle together in this mellow, earthy store, which has an informal deli attached.

Volpetti – *Via Marmorata 47. Mon–Fri 8:30am–2pm, 4:30–8:15pm; Sat 8:30am–8:15pm. Closed Sun. ☎06 57 42 352. www.volpetti.com.* Umbrian brothers supply Rome's gourmands with wild boar ham, Piemontese cheese with white truffles (*crutin*), Italian caviar (*caviale*) and other offerings in this iconic deli. This new bistro – Taverna Volpetti – lets visitors savour the superior quality of foodstuffs and products sold in the shop.

BOOKSTORES

The most famous bookshops tend to sprawl in spacious premises in the centre of Rome, often on a number of floors. They offer a wide selection of books of all kinds, and also sell DVDs, CDs and gadgets.
Feltrinelli (www.lafeltrinelli.it) has several bookshops at strategic locations throughout the city, such as Piazza Colonna 31-35/Galleria Alberto Sordi, 33, Via del Babuino 39/40, Via V.E. Orlando 78/81 (near Piazza della Repubblica), where the whole shop is dedicated to foreign books, and Largo Argentina 5/A (&199 151 173); **Mondadori** (www.mondadoristore.it) has branches at Via Appia Nuova 51 (San Giovanni in Laterano; &06 70 45 0153) and Via del Pellegrino 94 (Piazza Navona; &06 68 61 279). Other bookshops include **Ibs.it** (listed below). **Borri Books** (Stazione Termini, www.borribooks.com; &06 48 17 940). The smaller bookshops mentioned below either contain interesting and original features or offer visitors a chance to purchase rare literary works.

SAN GIOVANNI IN LATERANO
Italy Comics – Via Tarquinio Prisco 76. &06 78 25 926. www.ecomics.it. Open Tue–Sat 3:30–7:15pm (Sat also 9am–1:30pm). Closed Mon and Sun. This shop specialises in Japanese and American comic books, available in both Italian and the original language, and has a large science fiction section.

CAMPO DE' FIORI
Fahrenheit 451 – Piazza Campo de' Fiori 44. &06 68 75 930. www.libreria fahrenheit451.wordpress.com. Open Mon 4–10pm, Tue–Sat 10am-1:30pm and 4–12pm, Sun 11am–2pm and 4–10pm. Although this bookshop on Campo de' Fiori looks tiny, inside it is a maze of small rooms and nooks and crannies that are perfect for browsing.

Libreria Del Viaggiatore – Via del Pellegrino 165. &06 83 50 34 90. Closed Sun–Mon. 10:30am-7:30pm. As its name suggests, this small shop specialises in travel literature. Shelves are stacked with a mind-boggling

array of maps, guidebooks to all destinations, history, cookery books and travel anthologies, some in English.

CASTEL SAN ANGELO
Letture d'Estate – Giardini di Castel Sant' Angelo. Only in summer. www. invitoallalettura.org. The regular invitation to the world of literature is offered under a new guise. The new edition is still dedicated to books but offers more activities and readings beneath the trees in the Gardens of Castel Sant'Angelo.

FONTANA DI TREVI–QUIRINALE
Ibs + Libraccio – Via Nazionale 254/255. &06 48 85 405. www.ibs.it. Mon–Sat 9am–8pm, Sun 10am–1:30pm, 4–8pm. This bookshop is tastefully decorated in early 20C style and offers a wide selection. There's a pleasant café on the top floor.

PIAZZA DI SPAGNA
Anglo American Book – Via della Vite 102. &06 67 95 222. www.aab.it. Closed Sun and Mon morning. Enjoy your reading with 40,000 English-language titles.

MUSIC SHOPS

Rome has a number of small, independent music and record shops dotted around, mostly located outside the frantic centre of the city.

PORTA PIA – TERMINI
Discoteca laziale – Via Giolitti 263. Termini. &06 44 71 45 00. www. discotecalaziale.com. Mon–Sat 9am–7:30pm. Closed Sun. Disks of all kinds for music of all kinds.

OTHER SHOPS
PANTHEON
Barbiconi – Via di S. Caterina da Siena 58-60 (junction with Via dei Cestari). &06 67 94 985. www.barbiconi.it. Closed Sat afternoon, Sun. This is the most famous of the shops along Via dei Cestari, selling religious garments, vestments and church ornaments.

FONTANA DI TREVI–QUIRINALE
Becker & Musicò – *Via di S. Vincenzo 29.*
☏06 67 85 435. www.gustotabacco.it.
Becker & Musicò specialises in articles
for smokers, and also has a workshop,
which makes wooden pipes from the
white heath tree *(Erica arborea).*

VILLA BORGHESE–VILLA GIULIA
O. Testa – *Piazza Euclide 27/28, Parioli.*
*☏06 80 70 118. www.otesta.it. Closed
Sun.* In the exclusive Parioli district, this
classic Italian chain is a rite of shopping
passage for most Italian men, and full
of well-priced, Italian chic, from suits
and sweaters to shirts – these days the
shops also include a ready-to-wear
casual line for women. *Show Room,
Via Frattina 104, ☏06 67 91 294.*

VATICANO–SAN PIETRO
Savelli Arte & Tradizione – *Via
Paolo VI 27-29 (on the corner of Piazza
del Sant'Uffizio). ☏06 63 11 64. www.
savellireligious.com.* This popular and
large shop, opened in 1898, is known
for its delicate religious mosaics, as well
as all sorts of spiritual articles and gifts.

PIAZZA NAVONA
Al Sogno – *Piazza Navona 53. ☏06 68
64 198. www.alsogno.com. Open 10am–
10pm (–8pm Nov–Mar).* This magical
shop on the corner of Piazza Navona
is devoted to dolls, puppets and teddy
bears of all sizes and descriptions.

DEPARTMENT STORES

The most exclusive department
stores include the **Galleria Alberto
Sordi** (*☾See Addresses p136*), **La
Rinascente** *(Via del Tritone 61 / Via dei
Due Macelli 23, ☏06 87 91 61, Fontana
di Trevi district, and Piazza Fiume, Porta
Pia district, 06 88 41 231),* and **Coin**
*(Piazzale Appio 7, San Giovanni district;
Via Giolitti 10, Stazione Termini district,
☏06 47 82 59 09; and Via Cola di Rienzo
173, Prati district; ☏06 36 00 42 98.
www.coin.it),* whose larger outlets
also have a household articles and
furnishings department.

LATE-NIGHT SHOPPING

Shops in Rome close at around
7:30pm in winter and 8pm in summer,
although some may stay open later.

The Galleria Alberto Sordi shopping
centre *(Via del Corso)* and the
Rinascente stores have recently
extended their opening hours until
9pm and 10pm on some nights.
Newspapers can now be bought late
at night or early in the morning almost
as soon as they are printed from a
number of **newsstands.**
Some of the most centrally located
can be found at Via Veneto, Viale
Trastevere and Piazza Sonnino, Piazza
dei Cinquecento, Piazza Colonna,
Piazza Cola di Rienzo, Viale Manzoni
and Via Magna Grecia.
For those visitors who require more
than just an early morning croissant
after a long night in the capital, the
Carrefour Market *(Piazzale Eugenio
Morelli 52 or Via Casilina 288; carrefour.
it)* offers a wide range of groceries
and other items, and is open 24 hours
a day. Inveterate smokers have been
able to buy cigarettes from automatic
machines for some years now and will
also find a few **tabacchi** (tobacconists)
that stay open late.
To buy **fresh flowers** at any time of
the day or night, head for the flower
stalls at Lungotevere Milvio, Piazzale
degli Eroi and Via Latina on the corner
of Piazza Galeria, Piazzale del Parco
della Rimembranza and Via Portuense
on the corner of Via Rolli.

MARKETS

Fruit and vegetable markets are held
in the different districts of the city.
These offer a panoply of bright colours
and fresh smells, where the lively
conversation of the locals, punctuated
by the cries of the stallholders, provide
a genuine flavour of everyday Rome. It
is also pleasant to wander through the
many antique and flea markets, where
you might just pick up an unusual
souvenir or original item of clothing.

**Il Mercatino del Borghetto
Flaminio** - **Garage Sale Rigattieri
per Hobby** – *Piazza della Marina 32,
Flaminio. Open Sun 10am-7pm. Closed
Aug. €1,60.* Stalls vend clothes and
other items at this market, which
specialises in chic second-hand

goods, antiques and general bric-à-brac to rummage about in.

La Soffitta sotto i Portici – *Piazza Augusto Imperatore, Piazza di Spagna. Open 1st, 2nd and 3rd Sun in the month. Closed Aug.* Frequented by collectors of paintings, prints, frames, small items of furniture, ceramics and lace.

Mercatino Biologico – *Via Cardinale Merry del Val, Trastevere. Open 2nd Sun in the month (closed Jul-Aug).* This market sells environmentally friendly produce, including organic food, recycled paper, plant-based soaps and wooden toys.

Farmer's Market Garbatella – *Via Francesco Passino 22.* Friendly produce, including organic food.

Mercatino dell'Antiquariato di Ponte Milvio – *Via Capoprati, Piazzale di Ponte Milvio. Open Sun 9am-7pm. www. pontemilvioantiquariato.it.* This market under Milvio Bridge sells a panopoly of furniture, craftwork and art.

Mercato dell'Antiquariato di Fontanella Borghese – *Piazza Borghese, Piazza di Spagna. Open Mon–Sat 10am –7pm.* An excellent market for those interested in old books and prints.

Mercato dell'Antiquariato di Piazza Verdi – *Piazza Verdi, Villa Borghese. Open from 9am 4th Sun in the month.* As well as antiques and arts and crafts, this market also sells amphorae, old friezes and coats of arms. Entertainment and a wide selection of books for children.

Mercato di Campo de' Fiori – *Campo de' Fiori. Open Mon–Sat 7am–2pm.* Once the largest in Rome, this now sells vegetables, fish, kitchen gadgets and gorgeous cheap floral bouquets.

Mercato di Piazza S. Cosimato – *Piazza San Cosimato, Trastevere. Open Mon–Sat 6am–1:30pm.* This market is one of the busiest in central Rome, and is divided into two sections: the *fruttaroli*, who buy their produce every morning from the wholesale market, and the *vignaroli*, who sell produce grown in their own garden.

Nuovo Mercato Esquilino –*Via Principe Amedeo 184. Open Mon–Sat 7am–2pm.* Despite transferring to an old rebuilt barracks, it is still called the historic

Campo de' Fiori market

market of Piazza Vittorio and is still one of the cheapest in Rome. Renowned for its reasonable prices, its excellent selection of cheeses and Oriental spices.

Nuovo Mercato di Testaccio – *Via Volta or Via B. Franklin 12e. www. mercatoditestaccio.it. Open Mon–Sat 7am–3:30pm.* Nicknamed *"er core de Roma"*, the heart of Rome, this market has a wide selection of goods. A large number of stalls sell shoes at factory prices. Renovation has brought 2 bars, flowershops, loads of fruit and vegetables, and a special Roman street food outlet, the Mordi e Vai, where you can have delicious panini with allesso di scottona (boiled beef).

Mercato di Via Sannio – *Via Sannio, San Giovanni in Laterano. Open Mon–Sat 8am–2pm.* A wide choice of reasonably priced new and second-hand clothes, as well as shoes sold at factory prices.

Porta Portese – *Via Portuense, Trastevere. mercatidiroma.com. Open Sun 6am–2pm.* This market sells a bit of everything and is often referred to as the flea market. It opened officially during WWII. Articles on sale include general bric-à-brac, new and second-hand clothes, photographic equipment, books and records.

Pulp Fashion – *Via di Monte Testaccio 66. Open Sun 6pm–midnight.* Amazing market specialized in items from the 1970s, such as hippy clothes, vinyl records and punk stuff.

INDEX

INDEX

INDEX

INDEX

INDEX

W

Y

Z

🏠 STAY

🍷 EAT

MAPS AND PLANS

THEMATIC MAPS

MAPS AND PLANS
Rome

Ancient Rome

Vatican City

Excursions from Rome

MAP LEGEND

	Sight	Seaside resort	Winter sports resort	Spa
Highly recommended	★★★	≜≜≜	✻✻✻	⳾⳾⳾
Recommended	★★	≜≜	✻✻	⳾⳾
Interesting	★	≜	✻	⳾

Selected monuments and sights

◉ ⇨	Tour - Departure point
⛪ ✝	Catholic church
⛪ ✝	Protestant church, other temple
✡ ✉ ☪	Synagogue - Mosque
▰	Building
■	Statue, small building
✝	Calvary, wayside cross
◉	Fountain
•━●━•►	Rampart - Tower - Gate
✕	Château, castle, historic house
⁂	Ruins
⌣	Dam
✿	Factory, power plant
☆	Fort
⌒	Cave
▱	Troglodyte dwelling
⯒	Prehistoric site
▼	Viewing table
Ψ	Viewpoint
▲	Other place of interest

Special symbols

ⓐ	Underground line A (Battistini-Anagnina)
ⓐ	Underground line B (Rebibbia-Laurentina)

Additional symbols

🛈	Tourist information
═══ ═══	Motorway or other primary route
❶ ❶	Junction: complete, limited
⊏══⊐ ══	Pedestrian street
⌶⊏⊐⊐⊐⊐⊐	Unsuitable for traffic, street subject to restrictions
⊏⊐⊐⊐ ----	Steps – Footpath
🚂 🚉	Train station – Auto-train station
🚌 🚌SNCF	Coach (bus) station
•━━•━━	Tram
ⓐ	Metro, underground
🅿	Park-and-Ride
♿	Access for the disabled

Sports and recreation

🏇	Racecourse
⛸	Skating rink
≗ 🏊	Outdoor, indoor swimming pool
🎬	Multiplex Cinema
⚓	Marina, sailing centre
⛺	Trail refuge hut
□━■━■━□	Cable cars, gondolas
□━╀━╀━□	Funicular, rack railway
🚂	Tourist train
◆	Recreation area, park
🎠	Theme, amusement park
🦌	Wildlife park, zoo
✿	Gardens, park, arboretum
☺	Bird sanctuary, aviary
🚶	Walking tour, footpath
☺	Of special interest to children

Abbreviations

H	Town hall (Municipio)
J	Law courts (Palazzo di Giustizia)
M	Museum (Museo)
P	Local authority offices (Prefettura)
POL.	Police station (Polizia) (in large towns: Questura)
T	Theatre (Teatro)
U	University (Università)

⊗	Post office
☏	Telephone
⊠	Covered market
⋅✕⋅	Barracks
△	Drawbridge
∪	Quarry
✕	Mine
Ⓑ Ⓕ	Car ferry (river or lake)
🚢	Ferry service: cars and passengers
⇌	Foot passengers only
③	Access route number common to Michelin maps and town plans
Bert (R.)...	Main shopping street
AZ B	Map co-ordinates

COMPANION PUBLICATIONS

travelguide.michelin.com
www.viamichelin.com

MAPS OF ITALY

Michelin Plan of Rome 38
♦ a complete 1:10 000 scale plan of
Rome, including major thoroughfares,
one-way streets, main car parks, post
offices and the most important public
buildings in the city.
♦ an alphabetical street index
♦ practical information

Map of central Italy 563
A 1:400 000 scale map of central Italy
with an index of place names.

Italy Road Atlas
A useful spiral-bound atlas with a
full index of towns and cities.

ROUTE PLANNING

Michelin is pleased to offer a route
planning service at
www.viamichelin.com

Choose the shortest route, a route
without tolls, or the Michelin
recommended route to your destination;
you can also access information
about hotels and restaurants from
The Michelin Guide, and tourist sites
from *The Green Guide*.

YOUR OPINION IS ESSENTIAL TO IMPROVING OUR PRODUCTS

Help us by answering the questionnaire on our website:
satisfaction.michelin.com

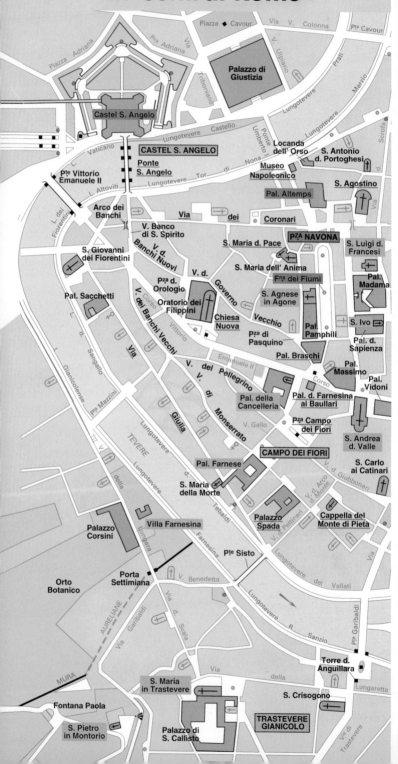

Principal sights in Central Rome

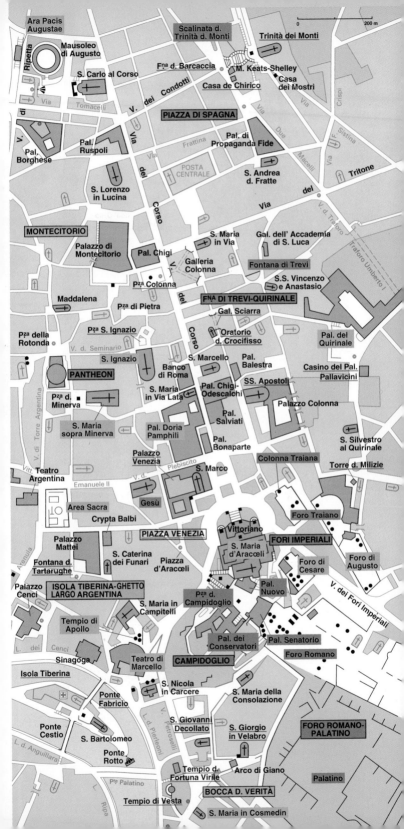

Ara Pacis Augustae
Ripetta
Mausoleo di Augusto
S. Carlo al Corso
V. di
Via   Tomacelli
Pal. Borghese
V. di
Pal. Ruspoli
S. Lorenzo in Lucina
MONTECITORIO
Palazzo di Montecitorio
Pal. Chigi
Pza Colonna
Maddalena
Pza di Pietra
Pza della Rotonda
Pza S. Ignazio
V. d. Seminario
S. Ignazio
PANTHEON
Pza d. Minerva
S. Maria sopra Minerva
V. di Torre Argentina
Teatro Argentina
Vitt.
Area Sacra
Crypta Balbi
Palazzo Mattei
Fontana d. Tartarughe
Palazzo Cenci
ISOLA TIBERINA-GHETTO LARGO ARGENTINA
Tempio di Apollo
Sinagoga
Isola Tiberina
Ponte Cestio
S. Bartolomeo
Ponte Rotto
L. d. Anguillara
Pte Palatino
Ripa

Scalinata d. Trinità d. Monti
Trinità dei Monti
Fna d. Barcaccia
M. Keats-Shelley
Casa de Chirico
Casa dei Mostri
V. dei   Condotti
PIAZZA DI SPAGNA
Via
Via
Frattina
Via
Crispi
POSTA CENTRALE
Pal. di Propaganda Fide
S. Andrea d. Fratte
Macelli
Via
F. Sistina
Tritone
del
Via
S. Maria in Via
Gal. dell' Accademia di S. Luca
V. d. Traforo
Traforo Umberto I
Galleria Colonna
Fontana di Trevi
Corso
S.S. Vincenzo e Anastasio
FNA DI TREVI-QUIRINALE
Gal. Sciarra
Oratorio d. Crocifisso
Gal. Sciarra
Pal. del Quirinale
S. Marcello
Pal. Balestra
Casino del Pal. Pallavicini
Banco di Roma
SS. Apostoli
S. Maria in Via Lata
Pal. Chigi-Odescalchi
Palazzo Colonna
Pal. Doria Pamphili
Pal. Salviati
S. Silvestro al Quirinale
Pal. Bonaparte
Plebiscito
Colonna Traiana
Torre d. Milizie
V. d.
S. Marco
Emanuele II
Gesù
PIAZZA VENEZIA
Vittoriano
S. Maria d'Aracœli
FORI IMPERIALI
Foro Traiano
Foro di Cesare
Foro di Augusto
S. Caterina dei Funari
Piazza d'Aracœli
Pal. Nuovo
V. dei Fori Imperiali
S. Maria in Campitelli
Pza d. Campidoglio
L. dei   Cenci
Teatro di Marcello
CAMPIDOGLIO
Pal. dei Conservatori
Pal. Senatorio
Foro Romano
S. Nicola in Carcere
S. Maria della Consolazione
V. di Pierleoni
S. Giovanni Decollato
S. Giorgio in Velabro
FORO ROMANO-PALATINO
Ponte Fabricio
L. d. Pierleoni
Tempio d. Fortuna Virile
Arco di Giano
Palatino
Ple Palatino
Tempio di Vesta
BOCCA D. VERITÀ
S. Maria in Cosmedin

0   200 m